Advance Praise for *Generative Programming*

"The book develops strong themes around unifying principles that tie the pieces together, most notably domain engineering and metaprogramming. It's crucial to understand that this book is not just some refreshing diversion nor just an exposition of some noteworthy niche techniques. It is a harbinger of a broader enlightenment that opens the door to a new age."

> —from the foreword by JAMES COPLIEN, a Distinguished Member of Technical Staff at Lucent Technologies' Bell Laboratories, Naperville, IL

"*Generative Programming* offers a well-written and comprehensive discussion that integrates object technology and domain engineering. The authors' approach to software systems generation provides very clear insights into practices essential for systematic reuse and software product lines."

> —SHOLOM COHEN, a Senior Member of the Technical Staff of the Software Engineering Institute (SEI), Pittsburgh, PA, and a co-developer of the Feature Oriented Domain Analysis (FODA) method

"If you believe that the systems you develop today will share concepts with the systems you will develop tomorrow, then the practical techniques presented in this book will reduce your time to market, decrease your engineering costs, and improve your software quality. These techniques are essential for both practitioners and researchers concerned with modern system development."

> —JAMES NEIGHBORS, President of Bayfront Technologies, Inc., Newport Beach, CA, and the author of the Draco approach

"The authors present a grand tour of Generative Programming which is bound to become a classic. They properly focus on the generally unappreciated connection between Domain Specific Languages and Generative Programming as a motivation for future development. The wide-ranging and practical methods for Domain Analysis and Domain Engineering describe the first steps that developers can take right now. They are valuable both when existing systems are used or in preparation for emerging new generative technologies."

> —CHARLES SIMONYI, Chief Architect at Microsoft Research, Redmond, WA, and the inventor of Intentional Programming

Generative Programming

Methods, Tools, and Applications

Krzysztof Czarnecki and
Ulrich W. Eisenecker

Addison-Wesley

Boston • San Francisco • New York • Toronto • Montreal
London • Munich • Paris • Madrid
Capetown • Sydney • Tokyo • Singapore • Mexico City

Many of the designations used by manufacturers and sellers to distinguish their products are claimed as trademarks. Where those designations appear in this book, and we were aware of a trademark claim, the designations have been printed with initial capital letters or in all capitals.

The authors and publisher have taken care in the preparation of this book, but make no expressed or implied warranty of any kind and assume no responsibility for errors or omissions. No liability is assumed for incidental or consequential damages in connection with or arising out of the use of the information or programs contained herein.

The publisher offers discounts on this book when ordered in quantity for special sales. For more information, please contact:

Pearson Education Corporate Sales Division
One Lake Street
Upper Saddle River, NJ 07458
(800) 382-3419
Corpsales@pearsontechgroup.com

Visit AW on the Web: www.awl.com/cseng/

Library of Congress Cataloging-in-Publication Data

Czarnecki, Krzysztof.
    Generative programming : methods, tools, and applications / Krzysztof Czarnecki and Ulrich Eisenecker.
        p. cm.
        ISBN 0-210-30977-7
        1. Generative programming (Computer science)
I. Eisenecker, Ulrich. II. Title.
QA76.624.C93 2000
006.3'1—dc21   00-028389

ISBN 0-201-30977-7

Text printed on recycled paper

1 2 3 4 5 6 7 8 9 10—CRS—0403020100

First printing, May 2000

Brief Contents

Contents

Foreword

by James Coplien

The advent of most any new programming book evokes the question: What is, or will be, the place of this book in history? That a book even evokes that question itself says something exciting, something about paradigm shifts or about new ideas or about breaking with old ways. And it is a curiously pertinent question for this book in these times.

Over the past ten years the object-oriented literature has seen a peppering of apparently unrelated ideas ranging from subject-oriented programming to components. What they all had in common is that there was something decidedly *un*object-oriented about each of them, though each of them spent time in the object-oriented limelight. But in the past one or two years many of these fragments have found common ground and have rallied together around common themes: metaobject protocols, reflection, intentionality, an insightful interpretation of components, the cutting of features across structure and, in general, the breakdown of classic models of simple modularity. For me, one of the highlights of 1999 was the First International Symposium on Generative and Component-Based Software Engineering (GCSE '99) in Erfurt, Germany, where many researchers had already linked many of these ideas together and shared a consciousness about their significance. But it is just one forum where these ideas came together; one sees the same things at many conference workshops and in some of the emerging literature.

It's always difficult to assess history from within the events that contribute to it, but it is perhaps no less responsible nor dangerous to do so than to try to interpret it after the fact, distanced from the firsthand events. In that spirit, look around and consider that we might, right now, be at a crucial turning point in computer science, particularly in the area of programming and design technique. The industry has been struggling with how to move beyond the limiting confines of the object paradigm. Patterns were one noble attempt and, though they have done much good to draw attention to the value of experience and of the human element in programming, it is unlikely that computer science will ever achieve anything remotely approaching Alexander's vision or level of systems thinking. It is rare that software achieves a true paradigm shift in the Kuhnian sense. Perhaps we're a conservative bunch. And our fascination with novelty sometimes keeps us even from the simplest learnings; many of the tenets of the vernacular components movement hark back to early principles of object-oriented design that experience suggests should have been dropped after only a few years of experience.

But there are new signs of seeds of change. Perhaps the industry can't easily suffer a revolution, but it can tolerate a move to new techniques that build on the status quo. There is a strong and recurring move to find programming and design expression that go beyond objects and things to concepts and features. That is the essence of intentional programming, for example and, to a large degree, of techniques such as domain engineering. This vein of thought is blossoming in a wide range of forums across the industry. We see it in the vulgar (non-Alexanderian) pattern movement; we see it in aspect-oriented programming; we see it in the resurgence of generic programming and in techniques such as multiparadigm design. And as conferences like OOPSLA focus less and less on the foundations of those things called objects and more and more on conceptual extensions, we start thinking less about parts and more about systems and features. And as OOPSLA shrinks, conferences like GCSE are becoming more numerous and popular. There is a broad-based move in this direction today. And this book finds itself squarely in the middle of this shift. I believe that the reader should neither underestimate the significance of this shift nor of this book's role in both communicating and shaping that shift. We are at the threshold of an evolution, and this book is one of the early normative works of this new genre.

This book perhaps reflects a degree of maturation in computer science that, for the first time, attempts to legitimize an integrative view in its own right rather than extol a technique by differentiating it from its predecessors. As such, the book covers much ground and embraces many disciplines: components, objects, aspects, reflection, intentional programming and generic programming for the technology-focussed, and domain engineering for the systems thinkers. It is a great introduction to both emerging and established techniques for those who are encountering them for the first time. An uninformed glance at this book might take it to be a compendium of existing practice, certainly in the area of domain engineering, but in the broader arena of *things beyond objects* as well.

Yet this book is more than a collection of techniques. The book develops strong themes around unifying principles that tie the pieces together, most notably domain engineering and metaprogramming. The authors treat the reader to a broad survey of domain engineering and guide the reader to appreciate its essence. Perhaps more than any single idea, domain engineering provides a common thread or theme that one could use to "explain" generative programming. But more than that, the authors draw on other schools of programming as building blocks that can be used to delineate *gestalten* that amplify each other in a broad, cogent vision called generative programming. The result is certainly more than the sum of the parts; most of the parts have been around for years, but an understanding of how to bring them together is just now emerging and receiving broad exposure.

It's crucial to understand that this book is not just some refreshing diversion nor just an exposition of some noteworthy niche techniques. It is a harbinger of a broader enlightenment that opens the door to a new age. It is the coming of age of techniques, such as reflection, metaprogramming, and aspects that could augment and even displace objects as the foundations of mainstream programming practice in the years to come.

And even if the historical analysis is wrong, it doesn't diminish the book's value. The ideas are sound and timeless. Though the book builds most heavily on the C++ legacy, the ideas should provoke thought in any partisan linguistic community and indeed in the communities for most programming ideologies.

This book is just a beginning. This book invites others to follow: those who will bring methods and processes to help the designer and programmer better master and apply generative programming, and those who will bring formalisms and unifying models that will carry this work into the next generation of research. To those researchers and practitioners who are willing to go behind the confines of objects, this book raises the bar and challenges them to carry its own ideas further. I am sure nothing would please the authors more than if you took up the challenge. The first joy of publishing a book comes for an author when holding the first copy between one's hands, almost in wonder. But the greater joy comes much later, and only vicariously, as the book visibly leaves its mark on emerging practice. Few books offer this return on the authors' investment. I am both hopeful and confident that this will be one of these books, and that is because I believe the power of these ideas will draw you in as a reader and excite you to adopt these new expressive programming and design constructs. I wish you great pleasure in learning from this book, as I did, and exhort you to seek your own place in history as a pioneer who helps take these ideas forward into our discipline through the artisanship of your own programs.

James Coplien
Naperville, Illinois
February 2000

Acknowledgments

First, we would like to thank our families for their love, encouragement, and patient support, which made this book possible.

During our research that led up to this book, we had the pleasure to supervise two brilliant students, Tobias Neubert and Johannes Knaupp, to whom we owe special thanks. Tobias implemented the more comprehensive version of the generative C++ matrix library presented in Chapter 14 and is also responsible for many improvements of the configuration generator concept. Johannes contributed several improvements of the template metaprogramming techniques, extended the C++ matrix library, and developed a configuration generator for the family of LU matrix factorization algorithms. He also reviewed parts of this book.

Special thanks also goes to Charles Simonyi, Greg Shaw, and the entire Intentional Programming (IP) team at Microsoft Research for providing us with the IP system and for patiently teaching Krzysztof Czarnecki the ways of IP during his research visit in January 1998.

We would also like to thank Gregor Kiczales, Crista Lopes, John Lamping, and other members of the Aspect-Oriented Programming (AOP) team at Xerox PARC for explaining the AOP ideas to us, providing us with an early version of AspectJ, and sharing many stimulating thoughts.

During the Dagstuhl seminar on "Generic Programming" in March 1998, together with Robert Glück, David Vandevoorde, and Todd Veldhuizen, we started an informal working group on Active Libraries. Our numerous discussions at Dagstuhl and later by e-mail significantly influenced the last phase of this work. We would like to thank all of the group members.

During several conferences and workshops, we met many interesting people from the software reuse, object-oriented, and other communities who gave us invaluable feedback in discussions or by reviewing parts of this book and shared with us their ideas. Our thanks go to Mehmet Aksit, Ira Baxter, Don Batory, Ted

Biggerstaff, Kai Böllert, Ulrich Breymann, Greg Butler, Simon Dobson, William Harrison, Mike van Hilst, Sholom Cohen and the participants of the WISR'97 working group on Domain Engineering and Object Technology, Jim Coplien, Serge Demeyer, Stan Jarzabek, Ullrich Köthe, Shriram Krishnamurthi, Karl Lieberherr, Andrew Lumsdaine, Satoshi Matsuoka, Mira Mezini, Pavol Navrat, Oscar Nierstrasz, Harold Ossher, Elke Pulvermüller, David Quinlan, Dirk Riehle, Lutz Röder, Jeremy Siek, Mark Simos, Yannis Smaragdakis, Douglas Smith, Andreas Speck, Christoph Steindl, Patrick Steyart, Allan Stokes, Peri Tarr, Hans Wegener, Bruce Weide, Eric Van Wyk, and many members of the Working Group on Generative and Component-Based Software Engineering (www.prakinf.tu-ilmenau.de/~czarn/generate). We also would like to thank many other researchers including John Favaro, Martin Griss, and Jim Neighbors, whose work played important roles in developing our ideas. Knowing that this list is certainly not exhaustive, we hope that those who we have forgotten to mention will forgive us.

We would like to thank the entire team at Addison-Wesley, especially Marina Lang, Heather Peterson, John Fuller, and Anne Marie Walker for their assistance and support in bringing this book project to a successful end.

Part of this work was developed during the doctoral research of Krzysztof Czarnecki, which was funded by Daimler-Benz AG and the German Federal Ministry of Education, Science, Research and Technology (BMBF) through the OSVA project. Many thanks go to his Ph. D. supervisors at the Technical University of Ilmenau, Dietrich Reschke and Reinhold Schönefeld, his colleagues at DaimlerChrysler Research and Technology in Ulm, especially his managers Wolfgang Hanika and Roland Trauter, his colleagues from the OSVA project team, Bogdan Franczyk, Michael Jungmann, Wolfgang Köpf, and Witold Wendrowski, and last but not least, Udo Gleich.

Material Available Online

You can download the source code of the examples in this book at www.generative-programming.org. This site also contains links to other online resources related to Generative Programming, and we will use it to publish future updates and corrections.

Chapter 1

What Is This Book About?

1.1 From Handcrafting to Automated Assembly Lines

The expectations regarding software engineering are high. They concern mastering high complexity, achieving high productivity and quality, and facilitating effective maintenance and evolution. Unfortunately, current software engineering does not meet these high expectations. It lags more than a century in development behind manufacturing. It is more like a cottage industry handcrafting one-of-a-kind solutions than mature engineering.

Generative Programming is about manufacturing software products out of components in an automated way, that is, the way other industries have been producing mechanical, electronic, and other goods for decades. The transition to automated manufacturing in software requires two steps. First, we need to move our focus from engineering single systems to engineering families of systems—this will allow us to come up with the "right" implementation components. Second, we need to automate the assembly of the implementation components using generators.

Let us explain this idea using a metaphor [CE99a]: Suppose that you are buying a car and instead of getting a ready-made car, you get all the parts necessary to assemble the car yourself. Actually, maybe some of the parts are not a perfect fit, and you have to do some cutting and filing to make them fit (i.e., adapt them). This is the current practice in component-based software engineering. Brad Cox compares this situation to one at the brink of the industrial revolution: It took over 25 years of unsuccessful attempts, such as Eli Whitney's pioneering effort, until John Hall finally succeeded in manufacturing muskets from interchangeable parts in 1826 (see [Cox90, Wil97]). It then took several decades before this groundbreaking idea of mass manufacturing from interchangeable parts spread to other sectors.

Even if you use a library of designed-to-fit, elementary components (such as the C++ Standard Template Library [STL], see

Section 6.10), you still have to assemble them manually and there is a lot of detail to consider. In other words, even if you don't have to do the cutting and filing, you still have to assemble the car your-self—that's the "Lego principle" of component technology.

Surely you'd rather be able to order a ready-made car by describing it in abstract terms, saying only as much as you really need to, for example, "Get me a Mercedes-Benz S-Class with all the extras" or "a C-Class customized for racing with a high-performance V8 engine, four-wheel vented disc brakes, and a roll cage." And that's what Generative Programming means for the application programmer: Programmers state what they want in abstract terms and the generator produces the desired system or component.

This magic works if you *(1)* design the implementation com-ponents to fit a common product-line architecture, *(2)* model the configuration knowledge stating how to translate abstract require-ments into specific constellations of components, and *(3)* imple-ment the configuration knowledge using generators. These steps correspond to what happened in car building: The principle of interchangeable parts was the prerequisite for the introduction of the assembly line by Ransom Olds in 1901, which was further refined and popularized by Henry Ford in 1913, and finally auto-mated using industrial robots in the early 1980s.

NOTE

Some people think that the main purpose of an assembly line is to produce masses of the same good, which in software corresponds to copying CD-ROMs. Nothing could be further from the truth. For example, the Mercedes-Benz assembly line in Sindelfingen, Germany, produces hundreds of thousands of variants of the C-, E-, and S-Class (there are about 8,000 cockpit variants and 10,000 variants of seats alone for the E-Class). There are almost no two cars that are the same rolling off the assembly line on the same day. This means that the right kind of engine or any other component has to be available at the right place and time on the assembly line. Further-more, suppliers have to provide the right parts at the right time (to mini-mize storage costs). The whole process starts when different people order different cars at car dealerships. The fulfillment of customer orders requires an enormous logistic and organizational effort involving a lot of configura-tion knowledge (in fact, they use product configurators based on configura-tion rules). Thus, the analogy between the automobile industry and building customized software solutions using a gallery of standard compo-nents (e.g., SAP's R3 modules) is not that far-fetched after all.

INDUSTRIAL REVOLUTION

The industrial revolution, that is, the transition from cut-to-fit craftsmanship to the automated mass-production of goods from interchangeable parts, took about 200 years. This transition had three major milestones: the introduction of *interchangeable parts*, *assembly lines*, and *automated assembly lines* (see Figure 1–1).

1980s

Automated Assembly Lines
First industrial robot
installed in 1961
at General Motors;
1970's advance of microchips

1901

Assembly Lines
Introduced
by Ransom Olds;
popularized and refined
by Henry Ford in 1913

1826

Interchangeable Parts
Successfully introduced
by John Hall (after 25 years
of unsuccessful attempts!)

Figure 1-1 Major milestones of the industrial revolution

Introduction of Interchangeable Parts

Allan Willey describes the introduction of interchangeable parts in manufacturing as follows (paraphrase from [Wil97]): While we take the concept of interchangeable parts for granted today, at the beginning of the 19th century no manufactured goods were produced that were built from interchangeable parts. The story begins in 1785 when Thomas Jefferson, while Ambassador to France, visited the shop of Honore Blanc, a French mechanic, who was building muskets using hand-crafted parts of such precision that they could be interchanged. Guided by his intuition, Jefferson immediately became convinced of the value of this idea. Later, in 1798, while vice president of the United States, Jefferson played an important role in awarding a government contract to Eli Whitney to manufacture 4,000 muskets by September 30, 1800, using the concept of interchangeable parts. Whitney's plan had three principles: *(1)* the use of water-powered machinery, *(2)* producing uniform or interchangeable parts, and *(3)* run by unskilled but "steady, sober people." Whitney never succeeded with this plan. He delivered the final set of muskets in 1809, nine years behind the schedule. None of the muskets contained interchangeable parts, and the cost to the government exceeded the original contract amount many times. However, he inspired several other contenders with the idea of manufacturing small arms from interchangeable parts. In particular, Roswell Lee and

James Stubblefield, the superintendents of the two government-owned armories in Springfield and Harper's Ferry, maintained constant interchanges of ideas, visits, evaluations of performance, and so on. They both also worked with outside contractors to promote uniformity. The final success was achieved by John Hall, who worked at Harper's Ferry. Hall set up an entirely separate operation in 1822, and over the next four years, first built the manufacturing machinery, then built the rifles. Thus, the first goods to be manufactured with truly interchangeable parts were rifles in 1826, one year after Eli Whitney's death. However, it still took two more decades for this concept to spread throughout the whole small arms industry. In 1834, Simeon North was producing parts that were interchangeable with those produced by Hall. Finally, in 1845, there were several national armories and private contractors manufacturing the Model 1841 muskets and rifles from interchangeable parts.

Introduction of Assembly Lines in the Automobile Industry

Automobiles, in the form that they exist to this day, appeared in the 1880s (see [Mur99]). The first lightweight, high-speed gasoline engine was successfully produced by Gottlieb Daimler, while Karl Benz fitted a gasoline engine to a three-wheeled frame in 1885, creating the first true automobile. However, the manufacturing process of the motorcar remained slow and cumbersome and, generally, automobiles were both unattainable by and unnecessary to the general population. The situation changed in 1901 when Ransom Olds employed an assembly line method to mass-produce vehicles—the same idea that Eli Whitney pioneered for manufacturing muskets a century before. The great success of the assembly line method came when Henry Ford began using it in 1908 to produce the famous Model T. This method allowed him to make cars affordable to the general population: The price of a Model T barely changed since its introduction in 1908— it remained consistent with the average annual earnings in the United States.[1] The number of cars in the United States grew between 1910 and 1920 from 458,000 to 8 million and reached 27 million in 1929, when Ford lost its market lead to General Motors [Pak96]. To meet the growing demand for automobiles of all types, Ford greatly increased production in 1913 by introducing the conveyor belt to an assembly line for manufacturing automobile bodies and motors. This method more than tripled production [Enc98]. Although Ford neither originated nor was the first to employ the assembly line principle, he is regarded to be chiefly responsible for its

---

1. According to [Pak96], the price of a Model T in 1912 was $600 and the average annual earnings in the United States at that time was $592. In 1916, the price was $360 and the average earnings $708, and in 1924 the price was $290 and the average earnings $1,303. In 1996, the starting price of a new Ford Taurus was $21,000, and the average annual earnings was $26,000.

general adoption and for the consequent great expansion of American industry.

Automation of Assembly Lines

Richard Jarrett describes the quest of robots in manufacturing as follows (paraphrase from [Jar90]): The first industrial robot was installed at a General Motors factory in New Jersey by a company called Unimation in 1961. The first robots were quite inflexible and inefficient. They generated piles of press cuttings but no revenue, and Unimation failed to show profit until 1975. The boom for industrial robots occurred in the 1980s. This was mainly due to the introduction of microchips, which became "the brain" of robots. Other factors were the competition between the United States and Japan, wage inflation, and the increasing cost of human workers. By the end of 1984, there were about 100,000 robots installed throughout the world. Today, the challenge to automation is to make robots profitable in small- to mid-volume manufacturing where they still have a hard time competing with traditional job-shop technologies.

1.2 Generative Programming

Definition of Generative Programming

Generative Programming (GP) is a software engineering paradigm based on modeling software system families such that, given a particular requirements specification, a highly customized and optimized intermediate or end-product can be automatically manufactured on demand from elementary, reusable implementation components by means of configuration knowledge.

The elements of a generative domain model

Generative Programming focuses on software system families rather than one-of-a-kind systems. Instead of building single family members from scratch, they can all be generated based on a common *generative domain model* (see Chapter 5), that is, a model of a system family that has three elements: a means of specifying family members, the *implementation components* from which each member can be assembled, and the *configuration knowledge* mapping between a specification of a member and a finished member. You are confronted with a similar setting when you order a car: There is a system for ordering cars, there are the components from which cars are assembled, and there is the configuration knowledge of how to assemble a car corresponding to a given order. The terminology used to specify family members is referred to as the *problem space*, whereas the implementation components with their possible configurations form the *solution space* (see Figure 1–2).

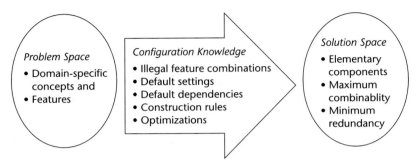

Figure 1-2 *Elements of a generative domain model*

The configuration knowledge specifies

♦ Illegal combinations of system features (e.g., you cannot order a cabriolet with a sunroof)
♦ Default settings (e.g., if you don't specify a sunroof, none is assumed)
♦ Default dependencies (e.g., an electric car with a DC engine requires no gear transmission)
♦ Optimizations (e.g., tuning the engine for maximum performance)
♦ Construction knowledge specifying which configurations of components satisfy which configurations of features

In car manufacturing, a large portion of the necessary configuration knowledge is embodied in an automated assembly line. Similarly, in Generative Programming, we want to capture the configuration knowledge in program form.

The problem with current software engineering is that we usually end up with a concrete software system, but don't know how we got there. Most of the design knowledge is lost, and this makes software maintenance and evolution very difficult and costly to perform. In Generative Programming, we strive to capture as much of the production knowledge in program form as possible. The production knowledge includes not only the configuration knowledge, but also measurement instrumentation, testing strategies and plans, error diagnosis, debugging support, program visualization, and so on. These various aspects are domain specific and are packaged in reusable libraries, which we refer to as *active libraries* [CEG+98].

Active libraries package general and domain-specific reusable abstractions together with code supporting the programmer in their usage. They extend the programming environment with abstraction-specific code for program visualization, debugging, error diagnosis and reporting, optimization, code generation, versioning, and so on. An example of such an *extendible programming environment* based on active libraries is the Intentional Programming system described in Chapter 11. An important idea of Intentional Programming is that active libraries of language abstractions replace *fixed* programming languages. Fixed programming languages (e.g., C++ or Java) force us to use a certain fixed set of language abstractions, whereas active libraries allow us to use a set of abstractions optimally configured for the problem at hand. They enable us to provide truly multiparadigm and domain-specific programming support.

Developing for and with reuse

Frameworks and components are currently considered to be the most effective technologies for achieving software reuse. Unfortunately, none of the popular object-oriented (OO) analysis and design methods support their development. Generative Programming, on the other hand, encompasses two complete development cycles: one for designing and implementing a generative domain model (development *for reuse*), and another for using the generative model to produce concrete systems (development *with reuse*). Both processes are different from a process of developing a one-of-a-kind system, such as the Unified process (see Chapter 3). The scope of development for reuse is a system family, not a single system, and development with reuse has to be carefully designed to take advantage of reusable assets in a systematic way.

Scoping a system family

The most important property of the development cycle for reuse is that it is focused on system families (see Chapter 2). Its first step involves determining the *scope* of the family of interest, that is, deciding which features should be included and which should not. This requires analyzing project stakeholders and their goals, current and potential markets, technology forecasts, and so on. Family or domain scoping is very important in order to avoid ad hoc generalization, where important features and variation points are easily missed and unnecessary ones creep in, causing excessive development and maintenance costs.

Feature modeling

The next step in the development cycle is to determine the common and variable features of the family members and the dependencies between the variable features. The results of this analysis are documented using *feature models* (see Chapter 4), which have several advantages over other modeling notations, such as the Unified Modeling Language (UML). First, feature models represent variation points and dependencies between them in an explicit way. This representation provides the basis for deriving the categories of implementation components for a system family, the means for specifying family members, and the configuration knowledge. Second, feature models distinguish between variability within a family member and between different family members. This way we avoid "fat" components or frameworks ending up in "fat" applications. This problem is common to current framework and component technologies, where mechanisms for implementing intra-application variability (e.g., dynamic polymorphism) are also used for inter-application variability. Finally, feature models provide an implementation-independent means of representing variability, which allows you to keep decisions about variability mechanisms out of the analysis model. This is different in current OO notations, such as the UML: The moment you draw a UML class diagram, you have to decide whether to use inheritance, aggregation, class parameterization, or some other implementation mechanism to represent a given variation point.

Designing and implementing a system family model

Based on the feature models, we design a generative domain model for the family consisting of means of specifying family members, a common architecture including categories of implementation components, and the configuration knowledge mapping between the specification of a member and the assembly of implementation components implementing it. Finally, we implement the model using appropriate component-based and generative technologies.

The concept of implementation components

As stated previously, family members are assembled from elementary implementation components. These components are designed to minimize code duplication and to be combinable in as many ways as possible to maximize reuse. These principles are also central to *generic programming* (see Chapters 6 and 7), a prominent example of which is the Standard Template Library (see Section 6.10). Generative Programming goes beyond generic programming by not only capturing the elementary building blocks of a system family, but also the configuration knowledge, allowing us to automatically generate family members from higher-level specifications. For example, you may specify that you need a matrix type for storing lower-triangular matrices, which is optimized for speed and performs bounds checking. A generator implementing the configuration knowledge for a set of matrix implementation components will automatically assemble the desired matrix type, and you won't need to worry about what containers, adapters, and algorithms the matrix type gets assembled from. In other words, generic programming represents an important approach for organizing the solution space of a generative domain model (see Figure 1–2), but this is only one-third of a generative domain model.

Generic programming

COMPONENTS

The idea of software components is now very popular in the software industry. We define software components simply as building blocks from which different software systems can be composed. As discussed earlier, we want them to be plug-compatible by design and to be combinable in as many ways as possible. We want to minimize code duplication and maximize reuse. These and other properties determine the quality of components, but, in general, are not necessary or sufficient for a component to be a component.

A component is always a part of a well-defined production process. For example, a brick is a component in the process of building houses, not cars. The often cited criteria, such as binary format, interoperability, language independence, and so on are always relative to the production process. For example, if you need containers in C++, STL components, which are source level, are just fine to use. If you need to build graphical user interfaces (GUIs), you need visual components (e.g., JavaBeans). If you need language-independent, distributed components, you may use the Common Object Request Broker Architecture (CORBA) technology.

Trying to come up with a general classical definition for software components is not only futile, but harmful. We have a classical definition for objects. A classical definition means that we can provide a single set of necessary and sufficient properties to define an object: An object has an identity, state, and behavior. [Boo84]

The concept of a "component" has a completely different quality. It is an example of a natural concept, rather than an artificial, constructed concept. According to the theory of concepts (see Appendix A), we can easily construct concepts using a classical definition—"objects" and many mathematical concepts are constructed, classically defined concepts. However, most natural concepts do not have a classical definition, that is, you cannot find a single set of necessary and sufficient properties defining them. As an example, try to define the concept of a "table." Is a "table" a top with four legs? Well, some tables have three, two, or even just one leg. And in Japan, you'll find tables with no legs. Okay then, is it a table top? Well, what is a "table top"? Is it a flat, horizontal working surface? Hmm, not every top has to be flat and horizontal, and not every table is used for working. It is a known phenomenon that you won't be able to find classical definitions for such natural, superordinate concepts (see Appendix A).

Nevertheless, you'll probably find most tables to be very useful. If you are not used to tables without legs, then such tables might not be the best choice for you. The situation is similar to the concept of "components." Depending on the context, you may find components that share some important properties, but you won't be able to come up with the general set of necessary and sufficient properties for all components. This is the situation with components in manufacturing, and if we want to apply this concept with all its advantages to software engineering, we should not try to reduce it to fit a classical definition of some single component model.

Just as it took several decades for the idea of interchangeable parts to be widely used in manufacturing, the transition to interchangeable software components will not happen instantly. In particular, there is a cultural change required on the part of customers, consultants, and vendors to accept solutions based on standard componentry, rather than "artistic" individual solutions. However, given the enormous economical pressure towards standardized solutions, the change will inevitably take place in the long term.

The introduction of interchangeable software components requires product-family architectures to be in place. Only then will it be possible to easily and quickly say whether a component offers what a given system expects or not. Thus, we'll need more architectural standardization in different industries before the idea of software components truly takes off. [CE99a]

Aspect-Oriented Programming

Most current programming methods and notations concentrate on finding and composing functional components, which are usually expressed as objects, modules, and procedures. However, several properties, such as error handling, synchronization, persistency, and security cannot be expressed using current (e.g., OO) notations and languages in a cleanly localized way. Instead, they are expressed by small code fragments scattered throughout several functional components. This problem is being addressed by *Aspect-Oriented Programming* (AOP) (see Chapter 8), where such properties crosscutting several functional components are cleanly captured by modular units called *aspects*. In an AOP system, components and aspects are *woven* together to obtain a system implementation that contains an intertwined mixture of aspects and components. Aspect-oriented composition addresses the fragmentation problem occurring in object-oriented frameworks, where adding new variation points usually results in the proliferation of "little classes and methods" and, thus, in the excessive increase of complexity. AOP complements generic programming with more powerful parameterization techniques for the solution space. Rather than having to map certain features from the problem space to sets of scattered, little components in the solution space, we can map them directly to single, well-localized aspects in the solution space.

*Metaprogram-
ming and
generators*

Checking specifications, performing optimizations and weaving, and assembling implementation components all require some form of metaprogramming. Metaprograms are programs manipulating other programs or themselves. An example of metaprograms are generators (see Chapter 9), which take a high-level specification of a system and produce its implementation. We use generators to implement generative domain models. Generators embody the configuration knowledge and assemble the implementation components according to a system specification.

*Cooperating
generators*

We said that the family members of a generative domain model are assembled from elementary implementation components. This does not mean, however, that one generator has to assemble all the necessary elementary components itself. A generator may call other generators to generate larger components that it needs, which are not elementary themselves. In general, only small software artifacts will be generated by a single generator. Complete systems will require several cooperating generators, probably from different vendors.

*Searching for
versus
generating
components*

Generative Programming produces a paradigm shift when working with components: Rather than having to search for the needed components, they are generated. Instead of selecting a concrete component from a library by name, you can specify its desired properties and have the library generate the desired component for you. There are two important advantages of this approach. First, the needed components are assembled on demand. Millions of concrete components with all possible combinations of properties do not need to be stored. Only their elementary implementation components are stored, which are much smaller in number. This is so because increasing the set of implementation components by one may potentially double the number of concrete components you can build from this set. Second, by specifying the required properties of the needed component rather than choosing a concrete component from a library, you raise the abstraction level of your code. If better algorithms and data structures satisfying the required properties become available, a new version of the library will be able to generate a better component to suit your needs, and you will automatically take advantage of it without having to modify the client code. This approach will not work if you select a specific concrete component because the library cannot know why you selected this component and, thus, cannot safely replace it with a better one.

*Approaches to
building
generators*

There are several different ways to build generators. First, they can be built from scratch, but it is usually quite costly and does not promote interoperability between them. A second approach and better alternative is to use built-in metaprogramming capabilities of programming languages. A practicable approach is *template metaprogramming* (see Chapter 10), which allows you to embed generators in C++ libraries. Such libraries can be thought of as extending the compiler because they perform jobs usually reserved for compilers, such as optimizations and code generation. The third approach is to use extendible programming environments based on active libraries, such as the Intentional Programming system (see Chapter 11). These allow you not only to distribute library code extending the compiler, but also other parts of the programming environment, for example, editor, debugger, and version control. This way, active libraries can not only provide domain-specific notations, optimizations, error checking and reporting, but also domain-specific support for program debugging, visualization, editing, and versioning. Furthermore, the Intentional Programming system has special facilities for debugging metaprograms and for integrating active libraries from different vendors.

A fresh look at programming languages

Extendible programming environments based on active libraries give us a new perspective on programming languages. We express programs in terms of reusable abstractions, and each time we define a new abstraction, we actually extend the language we use. It is similar to a natural language, where each new word makes the language richer. We can extend a language by defining new procedures, classes, control structures, notations, and so on. Different technologies allow you to extend different aspects of a language. Most languages will allow you to define new procedures, functions, and types, but usually won't let you define new compile-time optimizations, extend the syntax, extend compile-time type checking, extend compile-time error reporting, and so on. Thanks to template metaprogramming, C++ lets you implement compile-time optimizations and error checking, but syntax extensions and domain-specific compile-time error reporting are not possible in C++. Extendible programming environments allow not only syntax extensions and domain-specific compile-time error reporting, but also domain-specific program debugging, visualization, editing, and versioning. They relieve us from the current thinking in closed, fixed languages and compilers. They give us a new way of packaging abstractions, so that one can configure the optimal set of abstractions to use for the problem at hand. They allow us to distribute and combine language abstractions as components.

Generative Programming versus Automatic Programming

An idea related to Generative Programming, which has been around for over 30 years is *Automatic Programming* (e.g., see [Bal85]). The difference between Generative Programming and

Automatic Programming is that Generative Programming acknowledges the possibility of different levels of automations, whereas Automatic Programming aims only for the highest level of automation. Automatic Programming usually involves artificial intelligence techniques and requires huge amounts of domain knowledge even for medium-size, practical problems. On the other hand, the idea of Generative Programming is to provide practical leverage from the state-of-the-art practices in software engineering.

The automation assumption

Generative Programming helps to develop "the right" components for a system family and then builds on this foundation to provide automation on top of the components. Generative Programming is a direct consequence of the "automation assumption" [CE99a]:

> *If you can compose components manually, you can also automate this process.*

Generative Programming and the "automation craze"

Automation is not a result of some "automation craze," but a logical step once you have a plug-and-play architecture in place. The level of automation for a given project is a question of the available technology and how much you want to invest in capturing the domain knowledge. In manufacturing, robots used to be economical only for high-volume production; however, with the advance of numerical control and the increasing flexibility of robots, they are starting to be economical for mid-volume production. Extendible programming environments, standardized domain-specific architectures, and a growing component market will all promote greater automation and specialization in software development.

1.3 Benefits and Applicability

Economies of scope

The idea of Generative Programming is to build generative models for families of systems and generate concrete systems from these models. The implementation components and the configuration knowledge are reused for each generated member, leading to reduced development costs per member. Furthermore, there is the potential of reducing the time-to-market for new members because, rather than having to develop a whole new system from scratch, often only a few missing features need to be added to an existing generative model. Generative Programming brings the benefits of *economies of scope* [Wit96] to software engineering, where less time and effort are needed to produce a greater variety of products. Finally, we can also improve software quality by reusing proven components and by learning from previous errors.

Developing components, libraries, and frameworks

If your business is to build components, libraries, or frameworks, then Generative Programming should definitely be of interest to you. First, even if you do not plan to build generators, you should consider the system-family-oriented approach (see Chapters 2, 3, and 4). Only by focusing on system families will you be able to develop reusable software.

Modeling variation points

Developing reusable components requires not only identifying the common parts of family members, but also relevant variation points. Domain scoping and feature modeling provide a systematic way of determining which features and variation points need to be implemented immediately and which need to be planned for in the future. They are very useful to determine and document the variability of components and frameworks and to model the structure of generic libraries.

Capturing configuration knowledge and simplifying library interfaces

Generative Programming allows you not only to come up with the implementation components, but also to capture the configuration knowledge. This way, you can achieve even higher reuse levels. Most importantly, however, generators and active libraries (see Chapters 8 through 11) will allow you to provide more help to users, shielding them from having to know all the different components contained in your library and all the details concerning their configuration in order to achieve certain properties.

Template metaprogramming

Template metaprogramming (see Chapter 10) is a practicable approach to embed generators in C++ libraries and to achieve both a clean and intentional interface as well as the highest runtime performance at the same time. It is of particular interest to you if you are developing C++ libraries in high-performance areas, such as image recognition and processing, numerical computing, graphics,

---

NOTE

It is not possible to predict the future with one hundred percent accuracy. There will always be relevant features and variation points that we will fail to predict, and we will have to constantly revise our models and components. However, it would be foolish not to take advantage of existing domain knowledge and learn from our own errors and those of others. For example, the introduction of the euro and the year 2000 problem suggest that we should treat date and currency as variation points. Domain scoping and feature modeling allow us to take advantage of existing domain knowledge by analyzing, recording, and managing features and variation points in a systematic way. Furthermore, it is easier to evolve family models than many different concrete systems and components at once.

signal processing, or libraries with lots of variability and dependencies to be resolved at compile time, for example, libraries for date and time or currency.

Metaprogramming environments, automatic refactoring, and capturing design knowledge

Special metaprogramming environments offer more comprehensive support for Generative Programming. As of this writing, such environments are just beginning to appear on the market, for example, the Design Maintenance System (DMS) by Semantic Design (see Section 9.7.1), or are in development, such as the Intentional Programming (IP) system by Microsoft (see Chapter 11). These systems support automatic refactoring, that is, even if you miss some features and variation points during feature analysis, these systems help you to perform the necessary changes of the existing code in a partially automated way. Furthermore, they allow you to capture more design knowledge than you could capture when coding in a general-purpose programming language, such as C++ or Java. This allows a higher automation level of refactoring or any other kind of software maintenance or evolution because fewer preceding design decisions have to be surmised for the code.

Protecting investment

Another great advantage of these systems is that they protect your investment in software. Today, most software is expressed in a concrete programming language, meaning that a large portion of its design is lost. Thus, it is not possible to retarget existing applications onto new platforms without significant costs. This is a major problem, especially in a time where a new programming language enters the mainstream every few years (e.g., C++, Smalltalk, and Java). Systems such as DMS or IP allow you to iteratively evolve and improve your software in a sustainable way. You can add more and more design information to the code over time. This makes semi-automatic retargeting of existing software onto new technologies feasible and cost-effective.

The idea of software reuse

Despite all these advantages, you should keep in mind that building reusable components will cost more than building one system. Building a generative model for a family is even more costly. The idea behind any reuse technology is that the investment in reusable software will pay off after you've reused it in many systems. This means that there must be an actual need for several members of a system family.

The "break-even point"

There is no reliable data for determining the break-even point, that is, the number of systems to be built from a given set of reusable assets to amortize the investment into these assets. But it is definitely important to estimate the potential market and take into account the time needed to build the reusable assets. If your goal is to build just one system in a domain, or if you are on a tight schedule to deliver a system, you definitely do not want to build reusable components and generators just to build this one system. However, if a given domain is strategic to your business and you expect to be active in this domain for the long term, you should consider building and maintaining reusable assets in this domain. Furthermore, those that are already in the business of developing and selling libraries, components, and tools are definitely beyond the break-even point. Finally, it is important to note that even those who build one-of-a-kind systems may still benefit from the components and tools available on the market.

Introducing Generative Programming

As with any new technology, if you are considering using Generative Programming, you need to introduce it in an iterative, controlled way. You should start with pilots focused on some useful, but not failure-critical, domains of manageable size. It is also important to realize that you don't have to aim at the highest levels of automation. Generative Programming gives you the option to decide on how much of the approach to apply. You'll find feature modeling and documenting configuration knowledge useful even without developing any generators. You may use template meta-programming to implement domain-specific optimizations, or configuration generators, or both. If you have access to a system such as DMS or IP, their application may provide you with the highest pay-off, but you should expect a large impact on your development process.

Programming in the small and in the large

It is important to note that you can apply Generative Programming at any level of programming. You'll find scoping, feature analysis, and generation useful at the level of procedures and classes as well as at the level of larger components and whole systems. Generative Programming is also orthogonal to programming languages and paradigms. Indeed, it follows the philosophy of multiparadigm design [Cop98] by encouraging the use of the right paradigm for the right task.

Part I

ANALYSIS AND DESIGN METHODS AND TECHNIQUES

Chapter 2

Domain Engineering

Most software development is mostly redevelopment.

—*D.M. Weiss and C.T.R. Lai,*
Software Product-Line Engineering:
A Family-Based Software Development Process,
Addison Wesley, 1999

2.1 Why Is This Chapter Worth Reading?

The aim of Generative Programming is to enable the transition from handcrafting one-of-a-kind solutions towards automated manufacturing of large varieties of software products optimally satisfying customer needs. This transition will reduce the cost and time-to-market of new applications and result in better quality. At last, software production will come to enjoy the benefits of economies of scale and scope.

The first step in this transition is to move our focus from single systems to system families. Domain Engineering and Product-Line Practices help us to accomplish exactly that. They realize software engineering based on system families. They provide us with answers to questions such as "What is the right size for a system family?" and "How do you analyze and represent the commonalities and variabilities among the members of a system family?" They help us to design the reusable components and the common architecture for a system family. Furthermore, they help us to propose a model of configurable user requirements for ordering system family members and indicate the configuration knowledge needed to automate their production.

In this chapter, we will discuss the basic concepts of Domain Engineering and survey existing Domain Engineering methods. Later chapters will provide the necessary extensions needed for automating the production of family members using generators.

> **NOTE**
>
> At this point you may consider reading Appendix A, which contains some background information on conceptual modeling. This information is useful, but not essential, to understand this chapter.

2.2 What Is Domain Engineering?

Most software systems can be classified according to the business area and the kind of tasks they support, for example, airline reservation systems, medical record systems, portfolio management systems, order processing systems, inventory management systems, and so on. We refer to areas organized around classes of systems as *vertical domains*.[1] Similarly, we can also classify *parts* of software systems according to their functionality, for example, database systems, container libraries, workflow systems, GUI libraries, numerical code libraries, and so on. Areas organized around classes of parts of systems are called *horizontal domains*.

Obviously, specific systems or components within a domain share many characteristics because they also share many requirements. Therefore, a company that has built a number of systems or components in a particular domain can take advantage of the acquired knowledge when building subsequent systems or components in the same domain. By capturing this domain knowledge in the form of reusable assets and by reusing them in the development of new products, the organization will be able to deliver the new products in a shorter time, at a lower cost, and with a higher quality. *Domain Engineering* is a systematic approach to achieving this goal.

> *Domain Engineering is the activity of collecting, organizing, and storing past experience in building systems or parts of systems in a particular domain in the form of reusable assets (i.e., reusable work products), as well as providing an adequate means for reusing these assets (i.e., retrieval, qualification, dissemination, adaptation, assembly, and so on) when building new systems.*

Application Engineering   Domain Engineering encompasses *Domain Analysis*, *Domain Design*, and *Domain Implementation*. The results of Domain Engineering are reused during *Application Engineering*, that is, the

---

1. We'll give a precise definition of a domain in Section 2.7.1.

process of producing concrete systems using the reusable assets developed during Domain Engineering. As shown in Figure 2–1, Domain Engineering and Application Engineering are two parallel processes.

Table 2–1 explains the distinction between conventional software engineering and Domain Engineering: Conventional software engineering concentrates on satisfying the requirements for a *single system*, whereas Domain Engineering concentrates on providing *reusable* solutions for a *family of systems*. By putting the qualifier "domain" in front of analysis, design, and implementation, we emphasize the *family orientation* of the Domain Engineering process components.

Single-system engineering

Indeed, if you take a look at the software engineering methods practiced today (including the popular object-oriented analysis and design methods), you will realize that they aim at the development of "this specific system for this specific customer and context." We refer to such methods as *single-system engineering methods*.

Multi-system scope development

Domain Engineering, on the other hand, aims at the development of reusable software, for example, a generic system from which

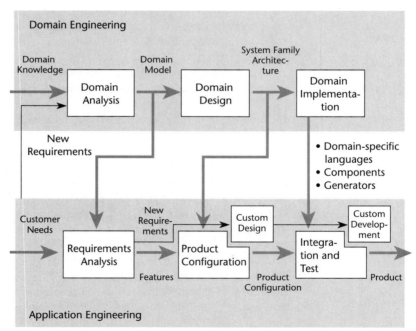

Figure 2-1 *Software development based on Domain Engineering (based on [MBSE97])*

Table 2-1 Three Main Process Components of Domain Engineering	
Domain Engineering Process Component	**Main Purpose**
Domain Analysis	Domain scoping and defining a set of reusable, configurable requirements for the systems in the domain
Domain Design	Developing a common architecture for the systems in the domain and devising a production plan
Domain Implementation	Implementing the reusable assets, for example, reusable components, domain-specific languages, generators, a reuse infrastructure, and a production process

you can instantiate concrete systems and/or components to be reused in different systems. Therefore, Domain Engineering has to take into account different sets of customers (including potential ones) and usage contexts. We say that Domain Engineering addresses *multisystem scope* development.

Domain Engineering can be applied to a variety of problems, such as development of domain-specific frameworks, component libraries, domain-specific languages, and generators. Domain Analysis, which is the first component of Domain Engineering, is more general. You can apply it to nonsoftware domains. For example, it has been used to prepare a survey of Architecture Description Languages (see [Cle96, CK95]). In fact, to mention a completely different application, specialty stores (e.g., music, wine, or liquor stores) could use it to classify and select their merchandise.

At the beginning of this section, we said that there are vertical domains, domains of systems, and horizontal domains, domains of parts of systems. Applying Domain Engineering to a vertical domain results in reusable software, which you can instantiate to yield any concrete system in the domain. For example, you could produce a *system framework* (i.e., reusable system architecture plus components) covering the scope of an entire vertical domain. On the other hand, applying Domain Engineering to a horizontal domain yields components (i.e., reusable system parts). Obviously, you should model vertical domains using several horizontal domains. We will return to the notion of vertical and horizontal domains in Section 2.7.2 and in Chapter 3.

*Components
and other
reusable assets*

In our terminology, a component is a *reusable* piece of software that is used to build more complex software. However, as already indicated, components are not the only work products of Domain Engineering. Other work products include reusable, configurable requirements, analysis and design models, architectures, patterns, domain-specific languages, frameworks, production plans, generators, and so on. In general, we refer to any reusable work product as a *reusable asset*.

2.3   Domain Analysis

The purpose of *Domain Analysis* is to:

♦ Select and define the domain of focus
♦ Collect the relevant domain information and integrate it into a coherent *domain model*

The sources of domain information include existing systems in the domain, domain experts, system handbooks, textbooks, prototyping, experiments, already known requirements on future systems, current or potential customers, standards, market studies, technology forecasts, and so on.

It is important to note that Domain Analysis does not only involve recording the existing domain knowledge. The systematic organization of the existing knowledge enables and encourages us to actually extend it in creative ways. Thus, Domain Analysis is a *creative* activity.

*Domain model:
commonalities,
variabilities, and
dependencies*

A *domain model* is an explicit representation of the *common* and the *variable* properties of the systems in a domain, the semantics of the properties and domain concepts, and the *dependencies* between the variable properties. In general, a domain model consists of the following components.

♦ *Domain definition:* Defines the scope of a domain and characterizes its contents by giving examples of existing systems in the domain, counterexamples (i.e., systems outside the domain), and generic rules of inclusion or exclusion (e.g., "Any system having the capability X belongs to the domain."). It also gives the rationale for including or excluding a given system or capability.
♦ *Domain lexicon:* Defines the domain vocabulary.
♦ *Concept models:* Describe the concepts in a domain in some appropriate modeling formalism (e.g., object diagrams, interaction and state-transition diagrams, or entity-relationship and data-flow diagrams) and informal text.

♦ *Feature models:* Define a set of reusable and configurable requirements for specifying the systems in a domain. Such requirements are generally referred to as *features*. A feature model prescribes which feature combinations are meaningful, which of them are preferred under which conditions and why. Feature models represent the configuration aspect of the concept models previously described and, in the end, the configuration aspect of the whole reusable software. Furthermore, a feature model is the basis for developing the means of ordering concrete systems during Application Engineering. It is like an ordering brochure telling a customer which features are covered by both the available components and the default production process (i.e., additional features require custom development).

Feature models represent an important contribution of Domain Analysis to software engineering and are essential to Generative Programming. We will provide an introduction to feature models later in Section 2.7.4, and then discuss them in great detail in Chapter 4.

In general, Domain Analysis involves the following activities.

♦ *Domain scoping:* Identifies the domain of interest, the stakeholders and their goals, and defines the scope of the domain
♦ *Domain modeling:* Yields the domain model

The process of domain scoping is a crucial part of Domain Engineering because it is aimed at finding a domain scope that is economically viable and promises business success. We'll discuss domain scoping in more detail in Section 2.7.2.

Table 2–2 gives you a more detailed list of Domain Analysis activities. This list was compiled by Arango and is based on the study of eight different Domain Analysis methods (see [Ara94]).

2.4   Domain Design and Domain Implementation

The purpose of *Domain Design* is to develop an architecture for the family of systems in the domain and to devise a production plan. Let us first discuss the concept of software architecture.

Shaw and Garlan define software architecture as follows [SG96].[2]

> Abstractly, software architecture involves the description of elements from which systems are built, interactions among those elements, patterns that guide their composition, and

---

2. This definition was reprinted from [SG96] by permission of Prentice-Hall, Inc., Upper Saddle River, NJ. Copyright © 1996 by Prentice-Hall, Inc.

Table 2-2 Common Domain Analysis Activities (based on [Ara94])	
Major Activities of Domain Analysis	**Detailed Activities**
Domain scoping	*Select domain* Perform business analysis and risk analysis in order to determine which domain meets the business objectives of the organization. Identify stakeholders and their goals.
	Domain description Define the boundary and the contents of the domain.
	Data source identification Identify the sources of domain knowledge.
	Inventory preparation Create inventory of data sources.
Data collection (domain modeling)	*Abstraction recovery* Recover abstractions.
	Knowledge elicitation Elicit knowledge from experts.
	Literature review
	Analysis of context and scenarios
Data analysis (domain modeling)	*Identification of entities, operations, and relationships*
	Modularization Use some appropriate modeling technique, for example, object-oriented analysis or function and data decomposition. Identify design decisions.
	Analysis of similarity Analyze similarities between entities, activities, events, relationships, structures, and so on.
	Analysis of variations Analyze variations between entities, activities, events, relationships, structures, and so on.
	Analysis of combinations Analyze combinations suggesting typical structural or behavioral patterns.

(continued)

Table 2-2 Common Domain Analysis Activities (based on [Ara94]) *(continued)*

Major Activities of Domain Analysis	Detailed Activities
	Trade-off analysis Analyze trade-offs that suggest possible decompositions of modules and architectures to satisfy conflicting sets of requirements found in the domain.
Taxonomic classification (domain modeling)	*Clustering* Cluster descriptions.
	Abstraction Abstract descriptions.
	Classification Classify descriptions.
	Generalization Generalize descriptions.
	Vocabulary construction
Evaluation (domain modeling)	Evaluate the domain model.

constraints on these patterns. In general, a particular system is defined in terms of a collection of components and interactions among these components. Such a system may in turn be used as a (composite) element in a larger system design.

Buschmann et al. offer another definition of software architecture [BMR+96].[3]

A software architecture is a description of the subsystems and components of a software system and the relationships between them. Subsystems and components are typically specified in different views to show the relevant functional and nonfunctional properties of a software system. The software architecture of a system is an artifact. It is the result of the software development activity.

---

3. This definition was reprinted from [BMR+96] by permission of John Wiley & Sons Ltd. Copyright © 1996 by John Wiley & Sons Ltd.

Just as the architecture of a building is usually represented using different views (e.g., static view, dynamic view, specification of materials, and so on), the adequate description of a software architecture also requires multiple views. For example, the "4+1 View Model" of software architecture popularized by the Rational methodologist Philippe Kruchten consists of a logical view (class, sequence, collaboration, activity, and state-transition diagrams), a process view (process diagrams), a physical view (package diagrams), a deployment view (deployment diagrams), plus a use case model, which ties all these views together (see Figure 3–1 in Section 3.6.1).

The elements in a software architecture and their connection patterns are designed to satisfy the requirements on the system (or systems) to be built. When developing a software architecture, we have to consider not only functional requirements, but also non-functional requirements, such as performance, robustness, failure tolerance, throughput, adaptability, extendibility, reusability, and so on. Indeed, one of the purposes of software architecture is to be able to quickly tell how a piece of software satisfies its requirements. Eriksson and Penker [EP98] say that "architecture should serve as a map for the developers, revealing how the system is constructed and where specific functions or concepts are located."

Architectural patterns

Certain recurring arrangements of elements have proven to be particularly useful in many architectural designs. We refer to these arrangements as *architectural patterns*. Each architectural pattern aims to satisfy a different set of requirements and can be documented using the usual pattern form consisting of sections, such as name, context, forces, solution, consequences, and examples. Buschmann et al. have compiled a (partial) list of architectural patterns (see [BMR+96] for a detailed description of these patterns).[4]

- *Layers pattern:* An arrangement into groups of subtasks in which each group of subtasks is at a particular level of abstraction.
- *Pipes and filters pattern:* An arrangement that processes a stream of data, where a number of processing steps are encapsulated in filter components. Data is passed through pipes between adjacent filters, and the filters can be recombined to build related systems or system behavior.
- *Blackboard pattern:* An arrangement where several specialized subsystems assemble their knowledge to build a partial or approximate solution to a problem for which no deterministic solution strategy is known.

---

4. The following list is a paraphrase from [EP98], reprinted by permission of John Wiley & Sons, Inc. Copyright © 1998 by John Wiley & Sons, Inc.

◆ *Broker pattern:* An arrangement where decoupled components interact by remote service invocations. A broker component is responsible for coordinating communication and for transmitting results and exceptions.

◆ *Model-view-controller pattern:* A decomposition of an interactive system into three components: A model containing the core functionality and data, one or more views displaying information to the user, and one or more controllers that handle user input. A change-propagation mechanism ensures consistency between user interface and model.

◆ *Microkernel pattern:* An arrangement that separates a minimal functional core from extended functionality and customer-specific parts. The microkernel also serves as a socket for plugging in these extensions and coordinating their collaboration.

Real architectures are usually based on more than one of these and other patterns at the same time. Different patterns may be applied in different parts, views, and at different levels of an architecture.

The architectural design of a system is a high-level design: Its goal is to come up with a flexible structure that satisfies all important requirements and still leaves a large degree of freedom for the implementation. As a rule, we use the most stable parts to form the "skeleton" and keep the rest flexible and easy to evolve. But even the skeleton has to be modified sometimes. According to [SCK+96], the following list distinguishes between generic and highly flexible architectures, depending on the amount of flexibility an architecture provides.

◆ *Generic architecture:* A generic architecture can be thought of as a fixed frame with a number of sockets where we can plug in some alternative or extension components. The components and the sockets must clearly specify their interfaces, that is, what they expect and what they provide. In other words, a generic architecture has a fixed topology[5] and fixed interfaces.

◆ *Highly flexible architecture:* A highly flexible architecture supports structural variation in its topology; it can be configured to yield a particular generic architecture. In other words, a flexible architecture componentizes even the "skeleton" and allows us to

---

5. By "topology" we mean a set of system and component interfaces together with the dependencies between them. In terms of the concepts introduced later in this book, we can define "topology" more precisely as the interfaces of implementation component categories plus the implementation component configuration language (ICCL).

configure it and to evolve it over time. In particular, it allows us to negotiate and configure interfaces. The notion of a highly flexible architecture is necessary because a generic architecture might not be able to capture the structural variability in a domain of highly diverse systems.

An architecture for a system family has to include an explicit representation of the variability (i.e., configurability) it covers. One way to capture this variability is to provide configuration languages for the configurable parts. You'll see concrete examples of configuration languages in Chapters 12, 13, and 14.

It is important to note that the development of an architecture is often not a "green field effort" because of constraints dictated by existing legacy software, prescribed middleware technology, industry standards that need to be followed, and so on. All these constraining factors have to be taken into account during architectural design.

The second artifact to be developed during Domain Design is the production plan, which describes how concrete systems will be produced from the common architecture and the components. The production plan describes the interface to the customers ordering concrete systems, the process of assembling the components, the process of handling change requests and custom development, and the measuring, tracking, and optimizing of the production processes. We can distinguish between three automation levels of the assembly process [Coh99].

♦ *Manual assembly:* The architecture and the components are accompanied by a developer's guide, and applications have to be assembled from components manually.

♦ *Automated assembly support:* The assembly of components is supported with various tools including component browsing and search tools and generators automating selected aspects of application development. For example, the IBM San Francisco Frameworks [Boh98] can be classified at this level. San Francisco offers a common architecture, a vast base of components and patterns from the financial and accounting domains, a set of browsers and generators, and a roadmap for creating applications.

BIBLIOGRAPHIC NOTE

Software architecture is a relatively young field with very active research. You will find more information on this topic in [SG96, BMR+96, Arch, BCK98].

Domain
Implementation

◆ *Automatic assembly:* This is the most mature level, where a set of tools supports the process of ordering an application by a customer, and the entire application can be generated based on the order record (except for the parts requiring customary development, of course). Generative Programming intends to achieve this level.

Finally, Domain Design is followed by Domain Implementation, which involves implementing the architecture, the components, and the production plan using appropriate technologies.[6] The implementation of the production plan may require writing developer's guides, implementing domain-specific languages and ordering GUIs, generators, and a reuse infrastructure (i.e., an infrastructure supporting component retrieval, qualification, dissemination, and so on), and establishing the application production processes.

2.5 Application Engineering

Application Engineering is the process of building systems based on the results of Domain Engineering (see Figure 2–1). During the requirements analysis for a new concrete application, we take advantage of the existing domain model and describe customer needs using the features (i.e., reusable requirements) from the domain model. This process can be supported by appropriate application ordering tools. Of course, new customer requirements not found in the domain model require custom development. The new requirements should also be fed back to Domain Engineering to refine and extend the reusable assets. Finally, we either manually assemble the application from the existing reusable components and the custom-developed components or use generators to produce it automatically.

2.6 Product-Line Practices

Domain Engineering covers the development of reusable assets and a production plan for producing concrete systems from the assets. Application Engineering is the process of producing the concrete systems. However, in order to successfully introduce and run both processes in an organization, we have to address a wealth of issues that go beyond the scope of current Domain Engineering methods.

---

6. Some authors (e.g., [FPF96, p. 2]) divide Domain Engineering only into two parts, Domain Analysis and Domain Implementation, and regard the development of an architecture merely as an activity within Domain Implementation.

In particular, there are management and organizational issues concerning establishing both processes and the feedback loop between them. There are questions about how to successfully build a business case for a transition to family-oriented development, how to launch and institutionalize it, manage risks, and perform planning and tracking. Furthermore, we need to address issues, such as market analysis and technology forecasting, in order to determine what features are needed now and in the future. We need support for deciding between development, purchase, mining, and outsourcing of assets. We need methods for evaluating and testing architectures, COTS (Commercial Off-The-Shelf) software, generic and generative models, and so on. We need approaches for measuring and optimizing the development processes and their interaction. We need efficient configuration management techniques and tools and appropriate implementation technologies.

The different issues discussed in the previous paragraph are subjects of the *Framework for Product Line Practice*, an initiative of the Software Engineering Institute (SEI). The idea behind this framework is to identify the different issues and practices relevant to establishing and running successful product lines in an organization. The structure of the framework is shown in Figure 2–2. The framework is documented in a "living" guidebook, which addresses the different practice areas and contains references to various approaches, methods, case studies, and other materials. The guidebook is being constantly updated based on a series of workshops run by SEI. It is available at www.sei.cmu.edu/plp/.

NOTE ON TERMINOLOGY

The terms *product line* and *system family* are closely related, but have different meanings. A system family denotes a set of systems sharing enough common properties to be built from a common set of assets. A product line is a set of systems scoped to satisfy a given market. As noted in [CN99], a product line need not be a system family, although that is how its greatest benefits can be achieved. Likewise, a system family need not constitute a product line if the member systems differ too much in terms of market target, that is, a system family could serve as a basis for several product lines. Historically, the term "product line" is a younger term than "system family." A *domain* encapsulates the knowledge needed to build the systems of a system family or a product line. More precisely, system families and product lines constitute two different scoping strategies for domains. We'll discuss this topic in more detail in Section 2.7.2.

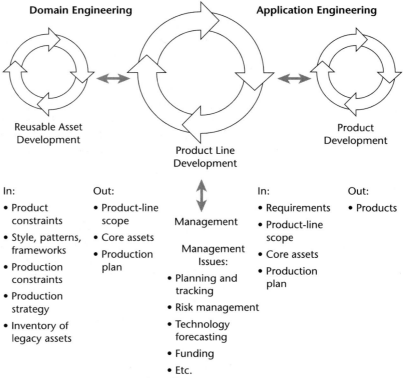

Figure 2-2 *Structure of the SEI Framework for Product Line Practice (based on [CN99])*

2.7 Key Domain Engineering Concepts

Domain Engineering enriches traditional software engineering with a number of novel concepts, such as domain, domain scope, features, and feature models. Because these concepts are used in later parts of this book, let us take a closer look at them now.

2.7.1 Domain

As is often the case, the term "domain" is assigned somewhat different meanings in different disciplines and communities, such as linguistics, cultural research, artificial intelligence (AI), object-oriented technology (OO), and software reuse. Mark Simos et al. distinguish between two general usage categories of this term [SCK+96].

1. Domain as the "real world"
2. Domain as a set of systems

A domain as the "real world" encapsulates the knowledge about a problem area (e.g., a bank accounting domain includes concepts such as accounts, customers, deposits, withdrawals, and so on), but not about the software automating and supporting the processes in the problem area, which is a separate entity. This notion of a domain has been traditionally used in OO, AI, and knowledge-engineering communities. For example, the UML (Unified Modeling Language) glossary gives the following definition [BRJ99].

> Domain: An area of knowledge or activity characterized by a set of concepts and terminology understood by practitioners in that area.

In the software reuse community (and particularly in the field of Domain Engineering), the term "domain" encompasses not only the "real world" knowledge in a given problem area, but also the knowledge about how to build software systems in that area. This corresponds to the "domain as a set of systems" view.

It is essential to realize that a domain is defined by the consensus of its *stakeholders*, that is, people having an interest in a given domain. Examples of stakeholders in the context of software development are managers, marketing people, developers, vendors, contractors, standardization bodies, investors, customers, and end-users. Part of the domain scoping process is identifying the stakeholders of a given domain. Stakeholder identification is not a static process of just documenting who is a stakeholder, but is a dynamic process of getting people "on board." Thus, the definition of a domain is always subject to politics and legacies.

Srinivas makes the key observation that the significance of a domain is *externally* attributed [Sri91].

NOTE

Some earlier works on Domain Engineering even equate a domain to a set of systems, for example, [KCH+90, p. 2]: "Domain: A set of current and future applications that share a set of common capabilities and data," or [Bai92, p. 1]: "Domains are families of similar systems." However, we interpret this "domain as a set of systems" view as the assertion that a domain encompasses the knowledge used to build a family of software systems.

Nothing in the individual parts of a domain either indicates or determines the cohesion of the parts as a domain. The cohesion is external and arbitrary—a collection of entities is a domain only to an extent that it is *perceived* by a community as being useful for modeling some aspect of reality.

Shapere explains this community-based notion of a domain as follows [Sha77] (paraphrase from [Sri91]).

In a given community, items of real-world information come to be associated as bodies of information or *problem domains* having the following characteristics.

♦ Deep or comprehensive relationships among the items of information are suspected or postulated with respect to some class of problems

♦ Problems are perceived to be significant by the members of the community

It is also important to note that knowledge contained in a domain usually includes both formal models, which can often be inconsistent among each other, for example, alternative domain theories, and informal expertise, which is difficult or impossible to formalize, as exemplified by the problems in the area of expert systems (e.g., see [DD87]). Furthermore, any real domain is infinite in the sense that you can always refine it with more details, distinctions, alternatives, and so on. Consequently, attempts to completely formalize any but the most trivial domains are doomed to failure.

At last, let us formulate the definition of the term "domain," which we'll adopt for the rest of this book.

Domain: An area of knowledge
♦ *Scoped to maximize the satisfaction of the requirements of its stakeholders*
♦ *Includes a set of concepts and terminology understood by practitioners in that area*
♦ *Includes the knowledge of how to build software systems (or parts of software systems) in that area*

2.7.2 Domain Scope and Scoping

There are two kinds of domain scope with respect to the software systems in a domain.

♦ *Horizontal scope or system category scope:* Addresses the question: How many different systems are in the domain? For example, the domain of containers (e.g., sets, vectors, lists, maps, and so on) has a larger horizontal scope than the domain of matrices because (presumably) more applications need containers than matrices.

♦ *Vertical scope or per-system scope:* Addresses the question: Which parts of these systems are in the domain? The larger parts of the systems are contained in the domain, the wider its vertical scope. For example, the vertical scope of the domain of containers is smaller than the vertical scope of the domain of portfolio management systems because containers capture only a small slice of the functionality of a portfolio management system (e.g., you use a container to manage a collection of financial instruments in a portfolio).

Based on the per-system scope, we distinguish between the following kinds of domains [SCK+96].

♦ *Vertical* versus *horizontal* domains
♦ *Encapsulated* versus *diffused* domains

Vertical domains contain complete systems (see Figure 2–3). Horizontal domains contain only parts of the systems in the domain scope. Encapsulated domains are horizontal domains where the system parts in the domain are well-localized with respect to their systems. Diffused domains are also horizontal domains, but they contain several different parts of each system in the domain scope.

The scope of a domain can be established using different strategies [SCK+96].

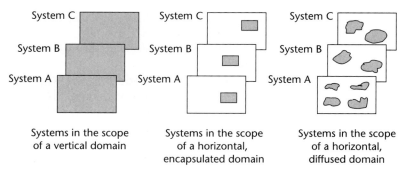

| Systems in the scope of a vertical domain | Systems in the scope of a horizontal, encapsulated domain | Systems in the scope of a horizontal, diffused domain |

Figure 2-3 Vertical, horizontal, encapsulated, and diffused domains. (Each rectangle represents a system. The shaded areas depict system parts belonging to the domain.)

NOTE ON TERMINOLOGY

The usage of the terms "horizontal" and "vertical" is different in Domain Engineering and in the Object Management Architecture (OMA) defined by the Object Management Group (OMG). The OMG uses the term *vertical domain interfaces* to denote component interfaces specific to a specialized market (e.g., manufacturing, finance, telecom, transportation, and so on) and the term *horizontal facilities* (or *common facilities*) to denote generic facilities, such as printing, database facilities, electronic mail facilities, and so on. Thus, the OMG distinguishes between horizontal and vertical components, whereas in Domain Engineering we say that components generally have a horizontal nature because their scope does not cover whole systems but rather parts of systems. However, as previously stated, families of components can have different *horizontal scopes*, for example, containers are used in more applications than matrices.

1. Choose a domain from the existing "native" domains (i.e., a domain that is already recognized in an organization);
2. Define an innovative domain based on:
   • A set of existing software systems sharing some commonalities (i.e., a family of systems)
   and/or
   • Some marketing strategy
   The last two strategies yield a product family or a product line, respectively.[7]

♦ *Product family:* "A product family is a group of products that can be built from a common set of assets." [Wit96] A product family is defined on the basis of similarities between the structure of its member products. Product family members share at least a common generic architecture. That is, product families are scoped primarily based on technical commonalities between the products.

♦ *Product line:* "A product line is a group of products sharing a common managed set of features that satisfy the specific needs of a selected market." [Wit96] Thus, the definition of a product line is based on a marketing strategy rather than technical similarities between its member products. The features defined for a product line might require totally different solutions for different member

---

7. Unfortunately, the terms product family and product line are sometimes used interchangeably in the literature.

products. A product line might be well-served with one product family; however, it might also require more than one product family. On the other hand, a product family could be reused in more than one product line.

Domain scoping   We establish the scope of a domain during the *domain scoping* activity of Domain Analysis. The scope of a domain is influenced by several factors, such as the stability and the maturity of the candidate areas to become parts of the domain, available resources for performing Domain Engineering, and the potential for reusing the Domain Engineering results within and outside an organization. In order to ensure business success, we have to select a domain that strikes a healthy balance among these factors. An organization that does not have any experience with Domain Engineering should choose a small and useful, but not failure-critical, domain, for example, an important aspect of several systems it builds. After succeeding with the first domain, the organization should consider adding more and more domains to cover its product lines.

It is important to note that the scope of a domain not only needs to be established, but also maintained afterwards. This is necessary in order to take advantage of new business opportunities, market and technology trends, new insights, the market position of the organization, and so on.

2.7.3 Relationships between Domains

We distinguish three types of relationships between domains.

- A *is contained in* B: All knowledge in domain A also belongs to domain B, that is, A is a *subdomain* of B.[8] For example, the domain of matrix packages is a subdomain of the domain of matrix computation packages because matrix computations cover both matrices and matrix computation algorithms.
- A *uses* B: Knowledge in A references knowledge in B in a significant way, that is, it is worthwhile to represent aspects of A in terms of B. We say that B is a *support domain* of A. For example, the storage aspect of a matrix package can be implemented using a container package. That is, the domain of container packages is a support domain of the domain of matrix packages.
- A *is analogous to* B [SCK+96]: There is a considerable amount of similarity between A and B; however, it is not necessarily worthwhile to express one domain in terms of the other. We say that A

---

8. In [SCK+96], B is referred to as *generalization* of A and A as *specialization* of B.

is an *analogy domain* of B. For example, the domain of numerical array packages is an analogy domain of the domain of matrix packages. They are both at a similar level of abstraction (in contrast to the more fundamental domain of containers, for example, which could be a support domain of both of them), but have clearly different focuses (see [Cza98]). Yet there is a considerable amount of similarity between them, and studying one domain may provide useful insights into the other one.

2.7.4 Features and Feature Models

As stated previously, features and feature models are used in Domain Analysis to capture the commonalities and variabilities of systems in a domain. Both concepts were originally introduced by the Feature-Oriented Domain Analysis (FODA) method (see Section 2.8.1).

Two definitions
of features

In general there are two definitions of features found in Domain Engineering literature.

1. An end-user-visible characteristic of a system, that is, the FODA definition

or

2. A distinguishable characteristic of a concept (e.g., system, component, and so on) that is relevant to some stakeholder of the concept

FODA subscribes to the first definition, that is, it defines features as the properties of a system which *directly affect* end-users [KCH+90, p. 3 and p. 35].[9]

> Feature: A prominent and user-visible aspect, quality, or characteristic of a software system or systems [Ame85]. [. . .]
>
> For example, when a person buys an automobile, a decision must be made about which transmission feature (e.g., automatic or manual) the car will have.

The second definition is used in the context of two other methods, namely ODM (see Section 2.8.2) and Capture (see Section 2.8.4). We prefer this definition because it is more general.

Elements of a
feature model

The features of a software system are documented in a *feature model.* A FODA feature model consists of the following four key elements.

1. *Feature diagram:* Represents a hierarchical decomposition of features including the indication of whether or not a feature is mandatory, alternative, or optional

---

9. A user may be a human user or another system that typically interacts with the systems from a domain.

NOTE

FODA features can be viewed as features in the sense of Conceptual Modeling (see Appendix A) with the additional requirement of directly affecting the end-user. On the other hand, ODM features do not have this requirement and are fully equivalent to features in Conceptual Modeling.

---

2. *Feature definitions:* Describe all features including the indication of whether a feature is bound at compile time, activation time, or at runtime (or other times)
3. *Composition rules for features:* Indicate which feature combinations are valid and which are not
4. *Rationale for features:* Indicates the reasons for choosing or not choosing a given feature

Let us now take a closer look at each of these elements.

The key part of a feature model is a *feature diagram*. An example of a simple feature diagram representing a car is shown in Figure 2–4. In general, a feature diagram has the form of a tree in which the root represents the concept being described and the remaining nodes denote features. There are three FODA types of features in our sample diagram:

1. *Mandatory features:* Each system in the domain must have certain features, for example, all cars have a *transmission*.

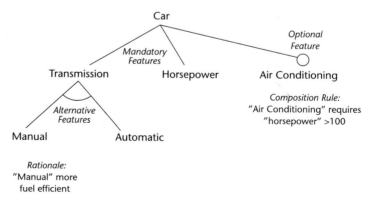

Figure 2-4 *Example showing features of a car (from [KCH+90]). Alternative features are indicated by an arc and optional features by an empty circle.*

NOTE

Strictly speaking, these simple FODA definitions of mandatory, alternative, or optional features need to be refined. First, we have to distinguish between *direct features* (those hanging directly under the root) and *subfeatures* (those having other features as their parents). The original FODA definitions of mandatory, alternative, or optional features hold for the direct features only. In the case of a subfeature, the property of being mandatory, alternative, or optional is relative to only those systems that also possess its parent feature, for example, a mandatory subfeature is one that a system possessing its parent feature must also possess. The optional feature "air conditioning" could have the mandatory subfeature "fan," which would be present in all cars having air conditioning. We'll discuss the ins and outs of feature diagrams in Chapter 4.

---

   2. *Alternative features:* A system can possess only one feature at a time, for example, a *manual* or *automatic* transmission.
   3. *Optional features:* A system may or may not have certain features, for example, *air conditioning*.

Composition rules

Feature interdependencies are captured using *composition rules* (see Figure 2–4). FODA prescribes two types of composition rules.

   1. *Requires rules:* Capture implications between features, for example, "*air conditioning* requires *horsepower* greater than 100" (see Figure 2–4).
   2. *Mutually-exclusive-with rules:* Model constraints on feature combinations. An example of such a rule is "*manual* is_mutually_exclusive_with *automatic*". (In our example, however, this rule is not needed because *manual* and *automatic* are alternative features. In general, mutually-exclusive-with rules allow us to exclude combinations of features where each feature may be seated in quite different locations in the feature hierarchy.)

NOTE

The FODA-style feature diagrams subsume both the featural and the dimensional descriptions from classical conceptual modeling, which we discuss in Appendix A. This is illustrated in Figure 2–5.

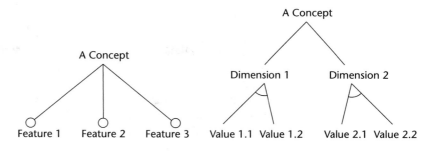

a. *Featural Description*   b. *Dimensional Description*

Figure 2-5 *Representation of featural and dimensional descriptions using FODA feature diagrams*

Both kinds of FODA composition rules are examples of *hard constraints*. However, we can also have *weak constraints*, that is, ones that suggest default feature combinations, but can be overridden if necessary. We'll discuss them in Section 4.4.2.

Rationale

We can also annotate features with *rationales*. A rationale documents the reasons or trade-offs for choosing or not choosing a particular feature. For example, a manual transmission is more *fuel efficient* than an automatic one. Rationales are necessary because, in practice, not all issues pertaining to the feature model can be represented formally as composition rules (due to the complexity involved or limited representation means). For example, *fuel efficient* could be modeled as a feature in Figure 2–4. In this case, the dependency between *manual* and *fuel efficient* could be represented as the following composition rule: *fuel efficient* requires *manual*. However, one quickly recognizes that the dependency between *fuel efficient* and *manual* is far more complex. First, we would need some measure of *fuel efficiency* and, second, *fuel efficiency* is influenced by many more factors than just the type of car transmission. The problem becomes similar to the problem of representing human expertise in expert systems [DD87]. Thus, stating the rationale informally allows us to avoid dealing with this complexity.

Based on the purpose of a feature, FODA distinguishes between *context*, *representation*, and *operational features* [MBSE97].[10]

---

10. The original FODA description in [KCH+90] uses a slightly different categorization: It distinguishes between *functional*, *operational*, and *presentation* features.

NOTE ON TERMINOLOGY

The term "rationale," used in Domain Engineering literature, denotes two different meanings: *(1)* The trade-offs for choosing or not choosing a particular feature, that is, the FODA definition (this notion is similar to the forces section in the description of a design pattern [GHJV95]); and *(2)* The particular reason for choosing a specific feature after considering a number of trade-offs (this would correspond to recording the information about which forces were directly responsible for arriving at the decision made). The latter definition is used in Capture (see Section 2.8.4). This definition is motivated by the work on *design rationale capture* [Shu91, Bai97], the goal of which is to record the reasons for selecting a particular design alternative by a (not necessarily software) designer during the design of a specific system.

♦ *Context features:* "Are those that describe the overall mission or usage patterns of an application. Context features would also represent such issues as performance requirements, accuracy, and time synchronization that would affect the operations."

♦ *Representation features:* "Are those features that describe how information is viewed by a user or produced for another application (i.e., what sort of input and output capabilities are available)."

♦ *Operational features:* "Are those features that describe the active functions carried out (i.e., what the application does)."

Of course, other types of features are also possible. For example, Bailin proposes the following feature types: *operational, interface, functional, performance, development methodology, design,* and *implementation features* [Bai92].

Finally, FODA features are classified according to their binding time into *compile-time, activation-time,* and *runtime features* [KCH+90].

♦ *Compile-time features:* Are "features that result in different packaging of the software and, therefore, should be processed at compile time. Examples of this class of features are those that result in different applications (of the same family) or those that are not expected to change once decided. It is better to process this class of features at compile time for efficiency reasons (time and space)."

♦ *Activation-time features* (or *load-time features*): Are those "features that are selected at the beginning of execution, but remain stable during the execution. [...] Software is generalized (e.g., table-driven software) for these features, and instantiation is done by providing values at the start of each execution."

♦ *Runtime features:* Are those "features that can be changed inter- actively or automatically during execution. Menu-driven soft- ware is an example of implementing runtime features."

Binding time, binding location, and binding site

The FODA classification of features according to binding time can be further refined with other times, for example, preprocessing time, linking time, installation or deployment time, and so on. In general, feature binding time can be classified according to the spe- cific times in the life cycle of a software product. Different prod- ucts could have their product-specific times (e.g., debugging time, customization time, testing time, or, for example, the time when something relevant takes place during the use of the system, e.g., emergency time, maintenance time, idle time, and so on). Also, when a component is used in more than one location in a system, the provided component features could depend on this *location*. Furthermore, feature binding could depend on the usage context or current users of a system. For this reason, Simos et al. intro- duced the more general term *binding site* ([SCK+96]), which cov- ers all of these cases (i.e., binding time and context). We will discuss this concept in more detail in Section 4.4.4.

The feature model plays an important role in Generative Pro- gramming. First, it defines the scope and configurability aspect of a system family. It also serves as a basis for designing the family architecture and implementation components. Furthermore, it provides the configuration knowledge needed to automate the pro- duction of family members. Finally, it allows us to derive a model of configurable user requirements for ordering family members by the customers.

We will return to the topic of feature models in Chapter 4. In particular, we will define an extended feature diagram notation and list additional information that should be captured in a feature model amenable to automation.

2.7.5 Method Tailoring and Specialization

Different kinds of systems require different modeling techniques. For example, most important aspects of interactive systems are cap- tured by use cases and scenarios. On the other hand, large data- centric applications are sometimes more appropriately organized around entity-relationship diagrams or object diagrams. Addi- tional, special properties, such as real-time support, distribution, high availability, and fault tolerance require specialized modeling techniques. Furthermore, different organizations will have different constraints on the development processes. Therefore, several Domain Engineering methods were designed to be specialized and tailored for the specific needs of different categories of domains and organizations. In Chapter 5, we will present DEMRAL (Domain Engineering Method for Reusable Algorithmic Libraries), a specialization of a more general Domain Engineering method for the purpose of developing reusable algorithmic libraries.

2.8   Survey of Domain Analysis and Domain Engineering Methods

A large number of Domain Analysis and Domain Engineering methods exist; however, two of them deserve our special attention because they belong to the most mature and best documented methods currently available. These methods are *Feature-Oriented Domain Analysis* and *Organization Domain Modeling*. We describe them in Sections 2.8.1 and 2.8.2, respectively. For completeness, Sections 2.8.3 through 2.8.8 contain short descriptions of twelve other Domain Engineering methods and approaches. Each has made important contributions to some aspects of Domain Engineering, such as faceted classification, rationale capture, formal modeling, and so on.

Historically, the development of Domain Engineering methods followed the development of Domain Analysis methods. Two surveys of Domain Analysis methods have been published to date, namely [WP92] and the more comprehensive [Ara94]. Compared to these surveys, the chapter you are reading now also reflects the newer development in the field.

2.8.1   Feature-Oriented Domain Analysis (FODA)

FODA is a Domain Analysis method developed at the Software Engineering Institute (SEI). The method is known for the introduction of feature models and feature modeling.

NOTE ON TERMINOLOGY

The original descriptions of the methods surveyed in this chapter refer to analysis, design, and implementation as "phases." As you might have already noticed in the previous sections, we've called these activities "process components" rather than "phases" (the reason is to avoid the waterfall-like implication of the term "phase"). However, in order to be consistent with the original method descriptions, the following survey sections still use the old term "phase."

The original description of FODA is [KCH+90]. Later, FODA became a part of *Model-Based Software Engineering (MBSE)*, a comprehensive, family-oriented approach encompassing both Domain and Application Engineering. FODA constitutes the Domain Analysis component of MBSE. As of this writing, the work on MBSE has been superceded by the SEI Framework for Product Line Practice described in Section 2.6.

2.8.1.1   FODA Process

The FODA process consists of two phases.[11]

1. *Context Analysis:* The purpose of which is to define the boundaries of the domain to be analyzed, that is, domain scoping.
2. *Domain Modeling:* The purpose of which is to produce a domain model.

The FODA Context Analysis defines the scope of a domain that is likely to yield useful domain products. Factors, such as availability of domain expertise and project constraints, are used to limit the scope of the domain. Furthermore, the relationships between the domain of focus and other domains or entities are established.

During the FODA Domain Modeling phase, the main commonalities and variabilities between the applications in the domain are identified and modeled. This phase involves the following steps.

1. *Information Analysis:* Captures domain knowledge in the form of domain entities and the relationships between them. The particular modeling technique used in this phase

---

BIBLIOGRAPHIC NOTES

MBSE is described in [MBSE97] and [Wit94]. A case study of applying FODA to the Army Movement Control Domain can be found in [CSJ+92, PC91]. FODA tool support is outlined in [Kru93]. A number of other military projects using FODA are listed in [CARDS94, p. F.2]. FODA has also been applied in the area of telecommunications systems, for example, [Zal96, VAM+98]. We describe FODA based on its revised and updated definition in [MBSE97].

---

11. Originally, FODA contained a third phase called Architectural Modeling (see [KCH+90]). This phase was converted into the Domain Design phase of the Model-Based Software Engineering (MBSE).

could be object-oriented modeling, entity-relationship modeling, or semantic networks. The result of Information Analysis is the *information model,* which corresponds to the concept model mentioned in Section 2.3.

2. *Feature Analysis:* "Captures a customer's or end-user's understanding of the general capabilities of applications in a domain. For a domain, the commonalities and differences among related systems of interest are designated as *features* and are depicted in the *feature model.*" [MBSE97]

3. *Operational Analysis:* Identifies the commonalities and differences between control and data flows within the application domain. The analysis yields the *operational model* representing how the application works by capturing the behavioral relationships between the objects in the information model and the features in the feature model.

Another important product of this phase is a *domain dictionary,* which defines the terminology used in the domain (including textual definitions of the domain concepts and features).

2.8.2 Organization Domain Modeling (ODM)

ODM is a Domain Engineering method, chiefly developed by Mark Simos of Synquiry Ltd. (formerly Organon Motives, Inc.). The origins of ODM date back to Simos's work on the Reuse Library Framework (RLF), a knowledge-based reuse support environment [Uni88]. During its evolution, ODM assimilated ideas from many other domain engineering approaches as well as work in nonsoftware disciplines, such as organization redesign and workplace ethnography [SCK+96]. The current version 2.0 of ODM is described in [SCK+96], a comprehensive guidebook with almost five hundred pages. (This guidebook replaced the original ODM description in [SC93].) ODM has been applied and refined on a number of projects, most notably the *Software Technology for Adaptable, Reliable Systems* (STARS) project (see Section 2.10). Organizations that used ODM include Hewlett-Packard, Lockheed Martin (formerly Loral Defense Systems-East and Unisys Government Systems Group), Rolls-Royce, and Logicon [SCK+96].

The following are some unique aspects of ODM.

♦ *Focus on stakeholders and settings:* Any domain concepts and features defined during ODM have explicit traceability links to their stakeholders and relevant contexts (i.e., settings). ODM introduces the notion of a *grounded* abstraction, that is, abstraction based on stakeholder analysis and setting analysis, as opposed to the "right" abstraction (a term used in numerous text-books on software design), which is based merely on intuition.

♦ *Types of domains:* ODM distinguishes between horizontal versus vertical, encapsulated versus diffused, and native versus innovative domains (see Sections 2.7.1 and 2.7.2).

♦ *More general notion of feature:* ODM uses a more general notion of feature than FODA (see Section 2.7.4). An ODM feature does not have to be end-user visible, but it has to be relevant to some stakeholder. ODM features directly correspond to the notion of features discussed in Appendix A.

♦ *Binding site:* In FODA, a feature can be bound at compile, start, or runtime (see Section 2.7.4). ODM goes beyond this and introduces the notion of *binding site,* which allows for a broader and finer classification of binding times and contexts depending on domain-specific needs. We discuss this idea in Section 4.4.4.

♦ *Analysis of feature combinations:* ODM includes explicit activities aimed towards improving the quality of features, such as feature clustering (i.e., analyzing the co-occurrence of features), as well as building a closure of feature combinations (i.e., enumerating all valid feature combinations or at least the representative ones). The latter can lead to the discovery of innovative system configurations, which were not considered beforehand.

♦ *Conceptual modeling:* ODM uses a very general modeling terminology similar to that discussed in Appendix A. Therefore, ODM can be specialized for use with any specific system modeling techniques and notations, such as object-oriented analysis and design (OOA/D) methods or structured methods. In Chapter 5, we'll present a specialization of ODM for developing algorithmic libraries.

♦ *Concept starter sets:* ODM does not prescribe any particular concept categories to look for during modeling. Other methods specifically concentrate on some concept categories, such as objects, functions, algorithms, data structures, and so on, whereas ODM proposes the use of *concept starter sets* consisting of different combinations of concept categories to jump-start modeling in different domains.

♦ *Scoping of the asset base:* ODM does not require the implementation of the full domain model. There is an explicit ODM task whose goal is to determine the part of the domain model to be implemented based on project and stakeholder priorities.

♦ *Flexible architecture:* ODM postulates the need for *flexible architectures* because *generic architectures* are not sufficient for domains with a very high degree of variability (see Section 2.4).

♦ *Tailorable process:* ODM does not commit itself to any particular system modeling and engineering method or any market or stakeholder analysis method. For the same reason, the user of ODM has to provide these methods, select appropriate notations and tools (e.g., feature notation, object-oriented modeling, and so on), and also invest the effort of integrating them into ODM.

The following section gives a brief overview of the ODM process.

2.8.2.1 The ODM Process

The ODM process described in [SCK+96] consists of three main phases.

1. *Plan Domain:* Represents the domain scoping and planning phase corresponding to Context Analysis in FODA.
2. *Model Domain:* Produces the *domain model* and corresponds to Domain Modeling in FODA.
3. *Engineer Asset Base:* Produces the architecture for the systems in the domain, the components, and other reusable assets.

Plan Domain and Model Domain clearly correspond to a typical Domain Analysis. Engineer Asset Base encompasses both Domain Design and Implementation.

Each of the three ODM phases consists of three subphases and each subphase is further divided into three tasks. We have summarized the complete ODM process (as defined in [SCK+96]) in Table 2–3.

2.8.3 Draco

Draco is an approach to Domain Engineering as well as an environment based on transformation technology. Draco was developed by James Neighbors in his Ph.D. work [Nei80] to be the first Domain Engineering approach. The main ideas introduced by Draco include *Domain Analysis, domain-specific languages,* and *components as sets of transformations.* This section gives a brief overview of Draco. A more detailed discussion is given in Section 9.8.1.

The principal idea behind Draco is to organize software construction knowledge into a number of related domains. Each Draco domain encapsulates the needs and requirements and different implementations of a collection of similar systems. Specifically, a Draco domain contains the following elements ([Nei84, Nei89]).

Table 2-3 Summary of the ODM Process

ODM Phase	ODM Subphase	Performed Tasks
Plan Domain	Set objectives	• Determine the stakeholders (i.e., any parties related to the project), for example, *end-users, customers, managers, third-party suppliers, domain experts, programmers, subcontractors* • Analyze stakeholders' objectives and project objectives • Select stakeholders and objectives from the candidates
	Scope domain	• Identify and characterize domains of interest • Define selection criteria (based on the stakeholders and objectives) • Select the domain of interest (choosing between *vertical* versus *horizontal*, *encapsulated* versus *diffused*, *native* versus *innovative* domains)
	Define domain	• Define the domain boundary by giving examples of systems in the domain, counterexamples (i.e., systems outside the domain), as well as generic rules defining what is in the domain and what is not • Identify the main features of systems in the domain and the usage settings (e.g., development, maintenance, customization contexts) for the systems • Analyze the relationships between the domain of focus and other domains
Model Domain	Acquire domain information	• Plan the domain information acquisition task • Collect domain information from domain experts, by reverse-engineering existing systems, literature studies, prototyping, and so on • Integrate the collected data, for example, by presorting the key domain terms and identifying the most important system features
	Describe domain	• Develop a lexicon of domain terms • Model the semantics of the key domain concepts • Model the variability of concepts by identifying and representing their features
	Refine domain	• Integrate the models produced so far into an overall consistent model • Model the rationale for variability, that is, the trade-offs for using or not using certain features • Improve the quality of features by clustering and experimenting with innovative feature combinations

(continued)

Table 2-3 Summary of the ODM Process *(continued)*

ODM Phase	ODM Subphase	Performed Tasks
Engineer Asset Base	Scope asset base	• Correlate identified features and customers • Prioritize features and customers • Based on the priorities, select the portion of the modeled functionality for implementation
	Architect asset base	• Determine external architecture constraints (e.g., external interfaces and the allocation of features to the external interfaces) • Determine internal architecture constraints (e.g., internal interfaces and allocation of groups of related features to internal interfaces) • Define asset base architecture based on these constraints
	Implement asset base	• Plan asset base implementation (e.g., selection of tools, languages, and other implementation strategies) • Implement assets • Implement infrastructure (e.g., domain-specific extensions to general infrastructures, asset retrieval mechanisms, asset qualification mechanisms)

♦ *Formal domain language (also referred to as "surface language"):* The domain language is used to describe certain aspects of a system and is implemented by a parser and a pretty printer. The internal form of parsed code is a *parse tree*. (The term *domain language* is equivalent to the more common term *domain-specific language*.)

♦ *Set of optimization transformations:* These transformations represent rules of exchange of equivalent program fragments in the domain language and are useful for performing optimizations on the parse tree.

♦ *Set of transformational components:* Each component consists of one or more *refinement transformations* capable of translating the objects and operations of the source domain language into one or more target domain languages of other, underlying domains. There is one transformational component for each object and operation in the domain. Thus, transformational components implement a source program (written in the source domain language) in terms of the target domains. Draco refers to the underlying target domains as *refinements* of the source domain. As a result, the construction knowledge in Draco is organized into domains connected by *refinement* relationships.

♦ *Domain-specific procedures:* Domain-specific procedures are used whenever a set of transformations can be performed algorithmically. They are usually applied to perform tasks such as generating new code in the source domain language or analyzing programs in the source language.

♦ *Transformation tactics and strategies (also called optimization application scripts):* Tactics are domain-independent and strategies are domain-dependent rules helping to determine when to apply which refinement. Optimizations, refinements, procedures, tactics, and strategies are organized into metaprograms (i.e., programs generating other programs).

It is important to note that, in Draco, a system is represented by many domain languages simultaneously.

The results of applying Draco to the domain of real-time applications and the domain of processing standardized tests are described in [Sun83] and [Gon81], respectively.

2.8.4 Capture

Capture, formerly known as KAPTUR (see [Bai92, Bai93]), is an approach and a commercial tool for capturing, organizing, maintaining, and representing domain knowledge. Capture was developed by Sidney Bailin.

The Capture tool [Bai92] is a hypertext-based tool allowing the user to navigate among assets (e.g., architectures and components). The assets are documented using informal text and various diagrams, such as entity-relationship diagrams. The assets are annotated by their *distinctive features*, which document important design and implementation decisions. Features are themselves annotated with *trade-offs* that were considered before making a decision and a *rationale* for the particular decision that was made.

2.8.5 Domain Analysis and Reuse Environment (DARE)

DARE is both a Domain Analysis method and a tool suite supporting the method [FPF96]. DARE is a commercial product developed by William Frakes (Software Engineering Guild) and Rubén Prieto-Díaz (Reuse, Inc.).

Clusters and facets

The DARE tool suite includes lexical analysis tools for extracting domain vocabulary from system descriptions, program code, and other sources of domain knowledge. One of the most important tools is the *conceptual clustering* tool, which clusters words according to their conceptual similarity. The clusters are manually refined further into *facets*, which are main categories of words and phrases that fall in the domain [FPF96]. The idea of using facets to describe and organize systems and components in a domain has its roots in the application of library science techniques, such as faceted classification, to component retrieval [Pri85, Pri87, PF87, Pri91a, Pri91b, OPB92].

The main work products of DARE include a *facet table*, *feature table*, *system architecture*, and *domain lexicon* and are organized into a *domain book*. The DARE tool suite includes appropriate tools for creating and viewing these work products.

2.8.6 Domain-Specific Software Architecture (DSSA) Approach

The *DSSA* approach to Domain Engineering was developed under the *Advanced Research Project Agency's (ARPA) DSSA Program* (see [Hay94, TTC95]). The DSSA approach emphasizes the central role of the concept of *software architecture* in Domain Engineering. The DSSA process is described in [CT93, TC92]. Its structure is similar to the generic process structure described in Sections 2.3 and 2.4. The main work products of the DSSA process include the following [Tra95].

- ◆ *Domain Model:* A domain model corresponds to the concept model in Section 2.3 (i.e., concept model in ODM or information model in FODA), rather than to a full domain model.
- ◆ *Reference Requirements:* Reference requirements are equivalent to the feature model in Section 2.3. Each *reference requirement* (or *feature* in the terminology of Section 2.3) is either mandatory, optional, or alternative. The DSSA Reference Requirements include both functional and nonfunctional requirements.
- ◆ *Reference Architecture:* A DSSA Reference Architecture is an architecture for a family of systems consisting mainly of an *architecture model*, *configuration decision tree* (which is similar to the FODA feature diagram in Section 2.7.4), *design record* (i.e., description of the components), and *constraints* and *rationale* (the latter two correspond to FODA configuration rules and rationale in Section 2.7.4).

The need to formally represent the components of an architecture and their interrelationships led to the development of *Architecture Description Languages* or *ADLs*. The concept of ADLs is described in [Cle96, Arch, SG96].

The DSSA approach has been applied to the avionics domain under the *Avionics Domain Application Generation Environment (ADAGE)* project involving Loral Federal Systems and other contractors (see [ADAGE]). As a result of this effort, a set of tools and other products supporting the DSSA process have been developed, including the following [HT94].

♦ *DOMAIN:* A hypermedia-based Domain Analysis and requirements capture environment
♦ *MEGEN:* An application generator based on module expressions
♦ *LILEANA:* An ADL based on the ADA annotation language ANNA [LHK87] and the module interconnection language LIL [Gog83]. LILEANA is described in [Tra93, GT96].

Other DSSA program efforts resulted in the development of other Domain Engineering tools and products (see [HT94] for more details), most notably the following ADLs: *ArTek* (developed by Teknowledge [THE+94]), *ControlH* and *MetaH* (developed by Honeywell [BEJV96]), and *Rapide* (developed at Stanford University [LKA+95]).

2.8.7   Algebraic Approach

The *algebraic approach* to Domain Engineering was proposed by Yellamraju Srinivas in [Sri91] (see [Smi96, SJ95] for more recent work). This section gives a brief overview of this approach. A more detailed description follows in Section 9.8.3.

The main idea of this approach is to formalize domain knowledge in the form of a network of related *algebraic specifications* (also referred to as *theories*). An algebraic specification consists of two parts: one part defines a *language* and the other contains *axioms* and *inference rules* constraining the possible meanings of the language. Algebraic specifications can be related using *specification morphisms*. Specification morphisms define translations between specification languages that preserve the *theorems* (i.e., all statements that can be derived from the axioms using the inference rules). Thus, in the algebraic approach, the domain model is represented as a number of formal languages including translations between them. From this description, it is apparent that the algebraic approach and the Draco approach (see Section 2.8.3) are closely related.[12] In fact, the only difference is that the algebraic

---

12. As indicated in [Sri91, p. 91], the work on Draco had a major influence on the algebraic approach to Domain Engineering.

approach is based on the algebraic specification theory (see, e.g., [LEW96]) and the category theory (see, e.g., [BW85]). Similar to Draco, the algebraic approach lends itself to an implementation based on transformations. The inference rules of a specification correspond to the optimization transformations of Draco, and the specification morphisms correspond to the refinement transformations.

First success reports on the practical use of the algebraic approach include the application of the transformation-based system *KIDS* (*Kestrel Interactive Development System*, see [Smi90a]) in the domain of *transportation scheduling* by the Kestrel Institute. According to [SPW95], the scheduler generated from a formal domain model using KIDS is over 20 times faster than the standard, hand-coded system deployed by the customer. This proves the viability of the algebraic approach in narrow, well-defined domains. A successor system to KIDS is SPECWARE [SJ95], which is explicitly based on category theory (i.e., it uses category theory concepts both in its design and user interface).

2.8.8 Other Approaches

Other approaches to Domain Engineering include the following.

- *Family-Oriented Abstraction, Specification, and Translation (FAST):* FAST is a product line approach covering both Domain and Application Engineering and was developed by David Weiss et al. at Lucent Technologies Bell Laboratories. FAST was greatly influenced by the work on SYNTHESIS (Weiss was one of the developers of SYNTHESIS). The FAST approach has been applied in over 25 domains [CHW98], and the experience from its application at Lucent shows decreases in development time and cost for family members of 60% to 70% [WL99]. An extensive FAST guidebook was published as a book, namely [WL99].
- *PuLSE:* PuLSE [BFK+99] is a product line approach covering both Domain and Application Engineering and was developed at Fraunhofer Institute for Experimental Software Engineering (IESE). An important aspect of PuLSE is the principle of streamlining and "gently" extending the notations and approaches already used in a given organization to make them appropriate for product line development rather than introducing new ones.
- *SYNTHESIS:* SYNTHESIS [SPC93] is a Domain Engineering method developed by the Software Productivity Consortium in the early 1990s. The structure of the SYNTHESIS process is principally consistent with the generic process structure described in Sections 2.3 through 2.5 (although it uses a slightly

different terminology). A unique aspect of SYNTHESIS is the tailorability of its process according to the levels of the *Reuse Capability Model* [SPC92]. This tailorability allows an organization to control the impact of the reuse process installation on its own structures and processes.

♦ *Defense Information Systems Agency's Domain Analysis and Design Process (DISA DA/DP):* DISA DA/DP [DISA93] is similar to MBSE (see Section 2.8.1) and ODM (see Section 2.8.2). However, it only includes Domain Analysis and Domain Design. DISA DA/DP uses the object-oriented Coad-Yourdon notation [CY90].

♦ *Joint Integrated Avionics Working Group (JIAWG) Object-Oriented Domain Analysis Method (JODA):* JODA [Hol93] is a Domain Analysis method similar to FODA (however, JODA does not include a feature model) and is based on the object-oriented Coad-Yourdon notation and analysis method [CY90].

♦ *Approach by Gomaa:* [Gom92] describes an early object-oriented Domain Engineering method developed by Hassan Gomaa. An environment supporting the method is set out in [GKS+94].

♦ *Intelligent Design Aid (IDeA):* IDeA is a design environment supporting Domain Analysis and Domain Design [Lub91], which was developed by Mitchell Lubars. The unique aspect of IDeA is its iterative approach to Domain Analysis, whereby specific problems are analyzed one at a time and each analysis potentially leads to an update of the domain model.[13]

♦ *Reusable Ada Products for Information Systems Development (RAPID):* RAPID is a Domain Analysis approach developed by Vitaletti and Guerrieri [VG90] and utilizes a similar process to the aforementioned Domain Engineering methods.

2.9 Domain Engineering and Related Approaches

Domain Engineering addresses the following two aspects.

♦ *Engineering reusable software:* Domain Engineering is used to produce reusable software.

♦ *Knowledge management:* Domain Engineering should not be a one-time activity. Instead, it should be a continuous process

---

13. In [Lub91] the term *domain engineering* is defined as the phase in which reusable assets identified during *domain analysis* are constructed. This terminology is inconsistent with the more common terminology, where Domain Analysis is a part of Domain Engineering.

whose main goal is to maintain and update the knowledge in the domain of interest based on new experience, scope broadening, and new trends and insights (e.g., see [Sim91] and [Ara89]).

Current Domain Engineering methods concentrate on the first aspect and do not address knowledge evolution and management. The latter aspect is addressed more adequately in the work on *Organizational Memory* [Con97, Buc97], *Design Rationale Capture* [MC96], and *Experience Factory* [BCR94]. These three approaches have much in common with Domain Engineering, although they all come from different directions and each of them has a different focus.

- ◆ Domain Engineering concentrates on delivering reusable software assets.
- ◆ Organizational Memory concentrates on providing a common medium and an organized storage for the informal communication among a group of designers.
- ◆ Design Rationale Capture is concerned with developing effective methods and representations for capturing, maintaining, and reusing records of the issues and trade-offs considered by designers during design and the ultimate reasons for the design decisions they make.
- ◆ Experience Factory provides a means for documenting the experience collected during past projects. It primarily concentrates on conducting mostly quantitative measurements and analyzing the results.

As the research in these four areas advances, the overlap between them becomes larger. We expect that future work on Domain Engineering will address the knowledge management aspect to a larger degree (e.g., see [Bai97]).

2.10   Historical Notes

The idea of Domain Engineering can be traced back to the work on program families by Dijkstra [Dij70] and Parnas [Par76]. Parnas defines a "program family" as follows [Par76].

> We consider a set of programs to constitute a family, whenever it is worthwhile to study programs from the set by first studying the common properties of the set and then determining the special properties of the individual family members.

The term "Domain Analysis" was first defined by Neighbors in his Ph.D. work on Draco [Nei80] as the activity of identifying objects and operations of a class of similar systems in a particular problem domain.

Major efforts aimed at developing Domain Analysis methods (including SEI's FODA and the work by Prieto-Díaz et al. at the Software Productivity Consortium) followed in the late 1980s. A comprehensive bibliography of work on and related to Domain Engineering from the period 1983–1990 can be found in [HNC+90].

A large share of the Domain Engineering work was sponsored by the U.S. Department of Defense research programs related to software reuse including *Software Technology for Adaptable, Reliable Systems (STARS)* [STARS94], *Comprehensive Approach to Reusable Defense Software (CARDS)*, and DSSA (see Section 2.8.6).

Domain Engineering methods, such as MBSE, ODM 2.0, and FAST, can be classified as second generation methods. As of this writing, there is a trend in the field to integrate Domain Engineering and OOA/D methods (see Chapter 3). Domain Engineering and related approaches are being integrated into the emerging field of Product-Line Practices (see Section 2.6).

A partial genealogy of Domain Engineering methods is shown in Figure 2–6.

2.11 Summary

Domain Engineering represents a valuable approach to software reuse and multisystem-scope engineering. Table 2–4 compares conventional software engineering and Domain Engineering based on their work products. Domain Engineering moves the focus from

Table 2-4 Comparison between Conventional Software Engineering and Domain Engineering

Software Engineering	Domain Engineering
Requirements Analysis Produces requirements for one system	*Domain Analysis* Produces reusable, configurable requirements for a class of systems
System Design Produces design of one system	*Domain Design* Produces reusable design for a class of systems and a production plan
System Implementation Produces system implementation	*Domain Implementation* Produces reusable components, infrastructure, and production process

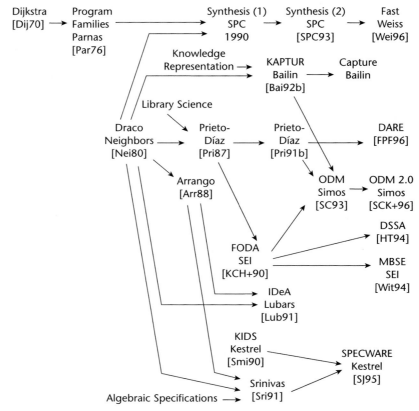

Figure 2-6 *Partial genealogy of Domain Engineering. This is an*
updated version of the genealogy published in [FP96].

code reuse to reuse of analysis and design models. It also provides
us with a useful terminology for talking about reuse-based software engineering. Another important contribution is the split of
software engineering into *engineering for reuse* (Domain Engineering) and *engineering with reuse* (Application Engineering).

Most of the Domain Engineering methods surveyed in this
chapter comprise—apart from differences in terminology and
slightly different groupings—a similar set of activities, which we
described in Sections 2.3 through 2.5. These activities are also well
exemplified by MBSE and ODM (see Sections 2.8.1 and 2.8.2).

However, as the overall process framework remains quite stable, significant variations regarding the concrete modeling techniques and notations, approaches to software architecture, and

component implementation techniques are possible. In particular, questions regarding the relationship between Domain Engineering and object-oriented technology are interesting. How do OOA/D and Domain Engineering fit together? We will address this topic in Chapter 3. Furthermore, we will discuss method extensions and implementation technologies necessary for automating the production of system family members in Chapter 5.

Chapter 3

Domain Engineering and Object-Oriented Analysis and Design

3.1 Why Is This Chapter Worth Reading?

Object-oriented analysis and design methods represent a major advance over structural methods and have been widely embraced in our industry. Unfortunately, they are not designed to support software reuse. For example, they are inappropriate for developing frameworks and components. The integration of Domain Engineering and OO technology provides a solution to this problem. As a result, we get powerful OO modeling techniques embedded in a development framework geared towards system families.

In this chapter, you'll learn about the shortcomings of OO technology with respect to software reuse and how to integrate Domain Engineering and OO methods to address this problem. We will also give you a survey of such integrated methods.

3.2 OO Technology and Reuse

In the early days of OO, there was the belief that objects are reusable by their very nature and that reusable OO software simply "falls out" as a by-product of application development (e.g., see [HC91]). Today, the OO community widely recognizes that nothing could be further from the truth. Reusable OO software has to be carefully engineered, and engineering *for reuse* requires a substantial investment (e.g., see [GR95]).

So how does today's OO technology address reuse? As Cohen and Northrop [CN98] suggest, we should answer this question from two perspectives: the problem space (i.e., analysis methods) and the solution space perspective (i.e., implementation technologies).

3.2.1 Solution Space

Two important areas of OO technology connected to the solution space that address multisystem-scope development are frameworks and design patterns. A framework embodies an abstract design for a *family* of related systems in the form of collaborating classes. Similarly, design patterns provide reusable solutions to recurring design problems across different systems. Patterns, as a documentation form, also prove useful in capturing reusable solutions in other areas, such as analysis [Fow97], architecture [BMR+96], and organizational issues [Cop95].

Unfortunately, two main problem areas still remain.

♦ Only very few OO Analysis and Design (OOA/D) methods provide any support for the development of frameworks. Similarly, there is little systematic support in both finding and applying patterns. Because these issues are related to the analysis of the problem space, we will discuss them in the following section.

♦ A major problem of the current framework technology is the excessive complexity explosion and performance degradation as the generality of a framework increases. For example, by applying the classic design patterns from [GHJV95], we can add new variation points to a framework. However, this usually causes an excessive fragmentation of the design, resulting in "many little methods and classes." Also, framework technology heavily relies on dynamic binding, even for implementing variability between applications, in which case static binding and partial evaluation (see Chapter 10) are more appropriate. This causes unnecessary performance penalties and unused code to remain in the delivered applications. Furthermore, current OO languages do not allow us to adequately separate and capture important aspects, such as synchronization, remote communication, memory management, persistency, and so on. All these problems also apply to component technologies, such as ActiveX or JavaBeans. Addressing them requires a combination of techniques, such as new linguistic constructs, new composition mechanisms, metaprogramming capabilities, and so on. We will discuss these issues in Chapters 8 and 9.

3.2.2 Problem Space

Traditional OOA/D methods, such as OOSE [JCJO92], Booch [Boo94], OMT [RBP91], or even the current version 5.0 of the

Rational Unified Process [JBR99], focus on developing single systems rather than families of systems.[1] Given this goal, the methods are inadequate for developing reusable software, which requires focusing on classes of systems rather than single systems.

In this context, traditional OOA/D methods have the following deficiencies (in terms of process and modeling notation).

♦ *No distinction between engineering for reuse and engineering with reuse:* Taking reuse into account requires splitting the OO software engineering process into engineering *for reuse* (i.e., Domain Engineering) and engineering *with reuse* (i.e., Application Engineering). The scope of engineering for reuse is a system family, which enables the production of *reusable* components. The process of engineering with reuse has to be designed to take advantage of the reusable assets produced during engineering for reuse. Current OOA/D processes lack any of these properties. OOA/D methods come closest to a form of Application Engineering with only opportunistic (rather than systematic) utilization of reusable assets.

♦ *No domain scoping phase:* Because OOA/D methods focus on engineering single systems, they lack a domain scoping phase, where the target class of systems is selected. Also, OOA/D methods are aimed at satisfying "the customer" of a single system rather than analyzing and satisfying *stakeholders* (including potential customers) of a class of systems.

♦ *No differentiation between modeling variability within one application and between several applications:* Current OO notations make no distinction between intra-application variability, for example, variability of objects over time and the use of different variants of an object at different locations in an application, and variability between applications, that is, variability across different applications for different users and usage contexts. Furthermore, OO implementation mechanisms for implementing intra-application variability (e.g., dynamic polymorphism) are also used for inter-application variability. This results in "fat" components or frameworks ending up in "fat" applications.

♦ *No implementation-independent means of variability modeling:* Furthermore, current OO notations do not support variability modeling in an implementation-independent way, for example, the moment you draw a UML class diagram, you have to decide whether to use inheritance, aggregation, class parameterization, or some other implementation mechanism to represent a given variation point.

---

1. See [Fow96] for a survey of OOA/D methods.

*Collaborations
and roles*

In contrast to the traditional OOA/D methods, a few newer methods, such as OOram [Ree96] and Catalysis [DW97], explicitly support modeling frameworks and the application of design patterns. One of the contributions of OOram to framework modeling is the recognition that the fundamental abstractions of object-oriented designs are not classes but *collaborations*. A collaboration consists of a number of *roles* communicating according to a certain pattern. Concrete objects may play more than one role in one or more collaborations. Thus, classes are merely synthesized by composing collaborations. Modeling a framework as a composition of collaborations is more adequate than modeling it as a composition of classes because extending a framework usually requires the coordinated extension of more than one class.

As of this writing, OOram is the only OOA/D method that truly recognizes the need for a specialized engineering process for reuse. The method includes a domain scoping activity based on the analysis of different classes of consumers. It also includes an analysis of existing systems. Unfortunately, it does not include feature modeling. We will discuss OOram in Section 3.6.2.

As stated previously, a general problem of all OOA/D methods is inadequate modeling of variability. Although the various modeling techniques used in OOA/D methods support variability mechanisms (e.g., inheritance and parameterization in object diagrams, composition of collaboration diagrams, and so on), OOA/D methods do not include an abstract and concise model of commonality, variability, and dependencies. There are several reasons for providing such a model.

♦ Because the same variability may be implemented using different variability mechanisms in different models, we need a more abstract representation of variability (see Sections 3.6.3 and 4.5).
♦ The user of reusable software needs an explicit and concise representation of available features and variability.
♦ The developer of reusable software needs to be able to answer the question: Why is a certain feature or variation point included in the reusable software?

The lack of domain scoping and explicit variability modeling may cause two serious problems.

♦ Relevant features and variation points are missin
♦ Many features and variation points are included
  this causes unnecessary complexity and costs (bo
  and maintenance costs).

Covering the right features and variation points requires a careful balance between current and future needs. Thus, we need an explicit model that summarizes the features and the variation points and includes the rationale and the stakeholders for each of them. In Domain Engineering, this role is played by a *feature model* (see Sections 2.7.4 and 4.4). A feature model captures the reusability and configurability aspect of reusable software.

3.3 Relationship between Domain Engineering and Object-Oriented Analysis and Design (OOA/D) Methods

As we discussed in Chapter 2, Domain Engineering focuses on engineering solutions for classes of software systems. On the other hand, current OOA/D methods focus on engineering single systems. Because of this difference in focus, we concluded in the previous section that current OOA/D methods are inappropriate for developing reusable software.

Although Domain Engineering supports a multisystem-scope engineering process and provides adequate variability modeling techniques, OOA/D methods give us very effective system modeling techniques. Thus, Domain Engineering Methods and OOA/D methods are good candidates for integration. Indeed, this integration represents a recent focus of the Domain Engineering community (e.g., see [CN98]).

3.4 Aspects of Integrating Domain Engineering and OOA/D Methods

When integrating development methods, we have to consider a number of specific areas that need to be integrated.

- ◆ *Method goals:* For example, Domain Engineering methods focus on supporting the development of models for classes of systems, whereas OOA/D concentrates on single systems.
- ◆ *Principles:* For example, Domain Analysis, in addition to modeling domain concepts, also investigates alternative implementation strategies (in order to provide the terminology and scope for further phases), whereas OOA avoids dealing with implementation issues.
- ◆ *Processes:* For example, Domain Engineering covers engineering for reuse and Application Engineering covers engineering with reuse, whereas the distinction between engineering *for* and *with* reuse is not present in most OOA/D methods.

♦ *Models and notations:* For example, Domain Engineering introduces new kinds of models, such as feature models, whereas OOA/D provides the necessary system modeling techniques.

Integration of methods is often a very complex task because today's methods are also complex. Additionally, it may also be a long and costly process because the integrated methods can only be tested and improved while being applied on real projects. (The general issues concerning method integration are discussed in [Son97].)

Because OOA/D methods are currently more widely used than Domain Engineering, we first take a look at the required changes to OOA/D methods.

♦ *Process changes:* The required process changes include introducing separate processes for engineering for reuse (Domain Engineering) and engineering with reuse (Application Engineering). The Domain Engineering process may have a complex structure including an Application Family Engineering process and multiple horizontal Domain Engineering processes, as described later in Section 3.5. The Application Engineering process is often quite similar to a conventional OOA/D process with the main difference being that it concentrates on developing solutions in terms of the available reusable assets. The Domain Engineering processes, on the other hand, have to additionally include domain scoping and feature modeling activities.

♦ *Variability and dependency modeling:* Variability and dependency modeling lies at the heart of Domain Engineering. Variability is represented in different models at different stages in the development process. Variability modeling usually starts at the taxonomic level by developing the vocabulary to describe different instances of concepts. For example, usually we first talk about different kinds of bank accounts (e.g., savings account or checking account) before we build the object model of bank accounts. Feature models allow us to capture this taxonomic level and to provide a road map to variability in other models (e.g., object models, use case models, interaction and state-transition models, and so on). They are a necessary extension of the set of models currently used in OO software engineering. Capturing dependencies between features is also essential. It allows us to perform automatic configuration (e.g., constraint-based configuration), which relieves the reuser of some of the manual configuration work.

♦ *Development of a reuse infrastructure:* In addition to developing the reusable assets, we also have to develop and install a reuse infrastructure for packaging, storing, distributing, retrieving, evaluating, and integrating these assets.

As already stated, the integration between Domain Engineering and OOA/D methods represents a recent focus of the Domain Engineering community. We can classify the integration efforts into four categories.

♦ *Upgrading older Domain Engineering methods:* Older Domain Engineering methods, such as FODA (see Section 2.8.1), used techniques of structured analysis and design as their system engineering method. Recent work concentrates on replacing these older techniques with newer OOA/D techniques, for example, work on FODAcom [VAM+98], an OO upgrade of FODA specialized for the telecom domain.

♦ *Specializing customizable Domain Engineering methods:* Newer Domain Engineering methods, such as ODM (see Section 2.8.2), treat system engineering methods as their parameters. Thus, before applying a parameterized Domain Engineering method, it needs to be specialized for some concrete system engineering method. However, such specialization may represent a substantial effort. As noted in [Sim97], ODM has been specialized for use with the OOA/D method Fusion [CAB+94]. Another example of such an effort is Domain Engineering Method for Reusable Algorithmic Libraries (DEMRAL), which is described in Chapter 5.[2]

♦ *Extending existing OOA/D methods:* The third approach is to extend one of the existing OOA/D methods with the concepts of Domain Engineering. An example of such effort is Reuse-driven Software Engineering Business (RSEB) [JGJ97], which is based on the OO modeling notation UML [Rat98c] and the OO Software Engineering (OOSE) method [JCJO92]. As stated earlier, upgrading an OO system engineering method for Domain Engineering requires substantial changes in its process architecture. Additionally, the modeling notations have to be extended for modeling variability (e.g., by adding feature diagrams and variation points).

♦ *Second generation integration:* Finally, FeatuRSEB [GFA98] is an example of an integration of two methods, which already combine Domain Engineering and OOA/D concepts: FODAcom and the RSEB method, which we mentioned in the previous paragraphs. One of the weaknesses in the original description of

---

2. It has to be noted that DEMRAL is more than a simple specialization of ODM because it also integrates novel concepts, such as feature starter sets and configuration DSLs.

RSEB was the lack of variability modeling using feature models. The integration with FODAcom concepts addresses this problem. On the other hand, RSEB has a stronger OO focus than FODAcom. Thus, both methods profit from this integration.

We describe these different integration efforts in Section 3.6.

3.5 Horizontal versus Vertical Methods

In Section 2.7.2, we introduced the notions of vertical and horizontal domains. Horizontal domains encompass only one system part, for example, GUIs, database systems, middleware, matrix computation libraries, container libraries, frameworks of financial objects, and so on. Vertical domains, on the other hand, cover complete systems, for example, flight reservation systems, medical information systems, CAD systems, and so on. Obviously, different kinds of domains require different Domain Engineering methods. Organizations specializing in one or more horizontal domains would use specialized methods for these domains. We refer to such Domain Engineering methods as *horizontal*. An example of a horizontal Domain Engineering method is DEMRAL (see Section 3.6.5). In the case of vertical domains, we have to develop and maintain the overall reusable architecture for the entire system scope and apply the specialized horizontal methods in order to develop reusable models of the subsystems. We refer to a Domain Engineering method covering a vertical domain as a *vertical* Domain Engineering method. An example of a vertical engineering method is RSEB, which we'll discuss in Section 3.6.3. In general, we want to develop modular Domain Engineering methods, so that they can be configured to suit the specific needs of different organizations. One way to achieve this goal is to have a vertical method "call" different specialized horizontal methods for different subsystems.

There may be significant differences between domains and thus between Domain Engineering methods. One of the major methodical differences is the modeling style.

- ♦ *Interaction style:* The main aspect of the interaction style is the interaction between entities, for example, interaction between components, procedure call graphs, message flows, and event flows. Interaction can be modeled using use cases, collaborations, and sequence diagrams.
- ♦ *Algorithmic style:* The main aspect of the algorithmic style is algorithms performing complex computations on abstract data types. Algorithms can be specified using pseudocode or some specialized specification notations.

♦ *Data-centric style:* The main aspect of the data-centric style is the structure of the data, for example, in database modeling. The structure of the data can be modeled using entity-relationship or object diagrams.

♦ *Data-flow style:* The main aspect of the data-flow style is data flow, for example, in pipes-and-filters architectures in signal processing. Data flow can be specified using data-flow diagrams.

Of course, we often need to capture all of these fundamental aspects, namely interaction, algorithms, data structures, and data flow, for a single system part. However, it is also often the case that one of these aspects plays a dominant, unifying role. For example, most business applications have an interactive nature because they usually have an interactive GUI and are organized as interacting components in a distributed and open environment. Furthermore, the interaction aspect is also dominant in large technical systems (e.g., CAD systems). Indeed, the interaction aspect plays an important role in all large systems because the subsystems of large systems are glued by interaction implemented using procedure calls, message passing, event notification, and so on. This is also the reason why most of the modern OOA/D methods are use case and scenario centric; for example, Rational Unified Process (see Section

---

NOTE

Because both interaction and algorithms express behavior, the reader may ask what the difference is between the interaction and the algorithmic styles. These two styles are best exemplified by the two different views in the worlds of Smalltalk and C++. The main metaphor of Smalltalk is to view objects as interacting agents. In C++, on the other hand, methods and functions are viewed more like mathematical operations on abstract data types. Both views are compatible, that is, we can use the interaction metaphor in C++ and the operation metaphor in Smalltalk. However, committing to one view as the primary view shapes many concrete design decisions in both languages in different ways. It is interesting to note that Wegner [Weg97, Weg98] considers interaction as *the* new quality of the OO paradigm. His thesis is that a classic Turing machine, although capable of representing algorithms, cannot adequately capture interactions. The new aspects of interaction are time and openness. As a result of openness, a system may receive nonalgorithmic stimuli from the environment, which leads to nonalgorithmic system behavior (which cannot be encoded by classic Turing machines).

3.6.1) has these properties. Similarly, the vertical Domain Engineering method RSEB (see Section 3.6.3), aimed at developing large systems, is also use case centric. On the other hand, some specialized horizontal Domain Engineering methods may not be use case centric, for example, DEMRAL, which is specialized for algorithmic libraries. As noted previously, a vertical Domain Engineering method calls specialized horizontal Domain Engineering methods. Thus, it is possible that use cases are applied at the system level but not at each subsystem level.

Moreover, each domain may have some special properties requiring special modeling techniques, for example, real-time support, distribution, concurrency, persistency, and so on. Thus, Domain Engineering methods have to support a variety of specialized modeling techniques for these different aspects.

3.6 Selected Methods

We will now survey a number of OOA/D methods, which, except for the first one, namely Rational Unified Process 5.0, incorporate some aspect of Domain Engineering. We discuss the Unified Process as an example of a prominent OO method that is not designed to support software reuse.

3.6.1 Rational Unified Process 5.0

Rational Unified Process 5.0 [JBR99] is a *de facto* standard UML-based OO software system engineering process propagated by Rational Software Corporation. The process originated from the OO Software Engineering method by Jacobson et al. [JCJO92], which later evolved into the Rational Objectory Process [Rat98a, Rat98b]. Unified Process's goal is "to ensure the production of high-quality software, meeting the needs of its end-users, within a predictable schedule and budget." The Unified Process is an *iterative* and *use-case-centric* process, which is a prerequisite for the successful development of large software systems. Use cases are used as the integrating elements of the whole system under construction and across all development phases and models. This view has been propagated in the "4+1 View Model" of software architecture by Kruchten (see Figure 3–1).

The Unified Process is organized along two dimensions (see Figure 3–2).

♦ *Time dimension:* Representing the life-cycle aspect of the process over time

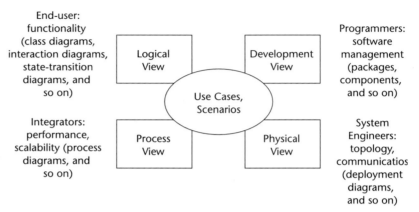

End-user:
functionality
(class diagrams,
interaction diagrams,
state-transition
diagrams, and
so on)

Programmers:
software
management
(packages,
components,
and so on)

Integrators:
performance,
scalability (process
diagrams, and
so on)

System
Engineers:
topology,
communicatios
(deployment
diagrams,
and so on)

Logical
View

Development
View

Use Cases,
Scenarios

Process
View

Physical
View

Figure 3-1 *The "4+1 View Model" of the architecture of a software-intensive system (adapted from [Kru95], © 1995 IEEE)*

♦ *Process components dimension:* Grouping activities logically by nature

The time dimension is organized into cycles, phases, and iterations separated by milestones. A cycle is one complete pass through all phases. Process components are described in terms of activities, workflows organizing the activities, produced artifacts, and workers.

By its definition, the Unified Process focuses on the development of a single system. Thus, it is inadequate for engineering reusable software due to the deficiencies we discussed in previous sections.

♦ No distinction between engineering for reuse and engineering with reuse
♦ No domain scoping and multisystem-scope stakeholder analysis
♦ No feature analysis activities
♦ No feature models

NOTE

A *use case* is a class of scenarios describing a certain usage of a system, for example, scenarios describing *withdrawal* in a banking system. The concept of a use case has been introduced in [JCJO92]. See [JBR99 and EP98] for more information on use cases.

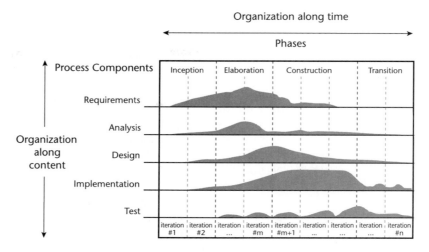

Figure 3-2 *Unified Process phases and components (adapted from [JBR99])*

3.6.2 OOram

OOram [Ree96] is a generic framework for creating a variety of OO methodologies based on role modeling. OOram was developed by Trygve Reenskaug of Norway and its history can be traced back to the 1970s. For example, the early OOram ideas were applied in the Smalltalk Model-View-Controller paradigm, which was developed by Goldberg and Reenskaug at the Xerox Palo Alto Research Center from 1979 to 1980 [Ree96].

The central idea behind OOram is *role modeling*. Role modeling concentrates on *collaborations* of objects and the *roles* those objects play in collaborations rather than the classes of objects. Classes are merely synthesized by composing the roles their instances play in different collaborations. The role model is represented by a number of views, most notably the *collaboration view* showing the relationships between roles and the *scenario view* concentrating on the interactions. Although the original description in [Ree96] introduces its own notation, we can also use the UML notation for representing these views. In particular, collaboration diagrams can be used for the collaboration view and sequence diagrams for the scenario view.

Although other OO methods, such as the Unified Process, also embrace the idea of scenario analysis, they concentrate on deriving concrete object classes from scenarios (e.g., start with use cases, derive collaboration and sequence diagrams, and finally define the classes). In OOram, on the other hand, there is a focus on the *composition* of collaborations. New collaborations can be added to existing compositions as needed and the participating classes are updated accordingly. Thus, in OOram, collaborations are the primary building blocks, not classes.

Frameworks represent one possible target technology for OOram because framework designs are naturally represented as compositions of collaborations. Role modeling also has a strong relationship to design patterns because some collaborations are instances of design patterns. The relationship between role modeling, frameworks, and design patterns is currently an area of active research (e.g., [Rie97]). We will revisit this topic in Section 9.8.2.7.

OOram refrains from prescribing a comprehensive and elaborate process. Because a specific process has to be optimized to a specific combination of products, people, and work environments, OOram provides a framework of guidelines backed with a set of comprehensive case studies. In [Ree96], Reenskaug et al. note: "Many managers dream of the ultimate work process that will ensure satisfactory solutions from every project. We believe that this dream is not only futile: It can even be harmful."

OOram distinguishes between three kinds of processes [Ree96].

1. "The *model creation process* focuses on how to create a model or some other manifestation of thoughts for a certain phenomenon. Examples include creating a role model, performing role model synthesis, and creating object specifications."
2. "The *system development process* covers the typical software life cycle, from specifying users' needs, to the installation and maintenance of the system that meets these needs."
3. "The *reusable assets building process* is the least mature software engineering process, but we expect it will be an essential contributor to future productivity and quality. Our focus is on the continuous production of several closely related systems in which we build on a continuously evolving set of reusable components. Creating a system mainly involves configuring and reusing robust and proven components, and possibly adding a few new components to complete the system."

Thus, the need for a dedicated engineering-for-reuse process is one of the fundamental principles of OOram.

Reenskaug et al. also make the very important observation that the creation of reusable objects shares a lot of properties with product development, whose life cycle can be divided into five phases [Ree96].

1. *Market analysis:* "The developer must understand the needs of the potential users and balance these needs against the costs of alternative solutions. The developer must also understand the potential users' working conditions to make the reusable component practically applicable."
2. *Product development:* "The reusable component must be designed, implemented, and tested in one or more prototype applications."
3. *Product packaging:* "Documentation is an important part of a packaged reusable component. The documentation includes work processes for the application of the component, installation procedures, and technical information."
4. *Marketing:* "The users of the reusable component must be informed and persuaded to apply it."
5. *Application:* "The reusable component must be applied and must help its users to increase the quality of their products and reduce their expenditure of time and money."

One of the four case studies in [Ree96] describes the process of developing an OO framework. The outline of this process is as follows.

- ◆ Step 1: Identify Consumers and Consumer Needs
- ◆ Step 2: Perform a Cost-Benefit Analysis
- ◆ Step 3: Perform Reverse Engineering of Existing Programs
- ◆ Step 4: Specify the New Framework
- ◆ Step 5: Document the Framework as Patterns Describing How to Solve Problems
- ◆ Step 6: Describe the Framework's Design and Implementation
- ◆ Step 7: Inform the Consumer Community

Steps 1–3 represent some form of Domain Analysis with domain scoping, stakeholder analysis, and analysis of existing applications. Unfortunately, OOram does not include feature modeling and feature models. We will discuss the importance of the latter two in Chapter 4. In Step 5, the approach advocates the standard technique of documenting frameworks using patterns (also see [Joh92, MCK97]).

3.6.3 Reuse-driven Software Engineering Business (RSEB)

RSEB [JGJ97] is a reuse- and object-oriented software engineering method based on the UML notation, the OO Software Engineering (OOSE) method by Jacobson et al. [JCJO92], and the OO Business

Process Reengineering [JEJ94]. The method has been developed based on the research at Hewlett-Packard (M. Griss) and Rational Software Corporation (I. Jacobson and P. Jonsson, formerly Objectory AB). It has been designed to facilitate both the development of reusable object-oriented software and software reuse. Similar to the Unified Process, RSEB is an iterative and use-case-centric method.

Let us first introduce some RSEB terminology [JGJ97].

- *Application system:* An application system in RSEB corresponds to the term *software system* as used throughout this text. RSEB authors note that "we use the term application system instead of the looser term application because we want to stress that application systems are software system products and are defined by system models."
- *Component:* "A component is a type, class, or any other work product (e.g., use case, analysis, design, or implementation model element) that has been specifically engineered to be reusable." Thus, the RSEB definition of a component corresponds to the term *reusable asset* as used throughout this text.
- *Component system:* A component system is a system product that offers a set of reusable features. Component systems are more generic, reusable, and specializable than application systems, but on the other hand, require more effort to engineer. Examples of component systems are reusable GUI frameworks, reusable mathematical libraries, or more sophisticated component systems from which complete application systems can be generated. If we analyze a class of application systems and decompose it into generic subsystems, component systems provide reusable solutions for the subsystems.

RSEB has separate processes for engineering for reuse (i.e., Domain Engineering) and engineering with reuse (i.e., Application Engineering). Domain Engineering in RSEB consists of two processes [JGJ97].

- *Application Family Engineering:* A process that develops and maintains the overall layered system architecture.
- *Component System Engineering:* A process that develops component systems for the different parts of the application system with a focus on building and packaging robust, extendible, and flexible components.

In RSEB, Application Engineering (i.e., the process of building concrete systems based on reusable assets) is called *Application System Engineering*.

The split of Domain Engineering into Application Family Engineering and Component System Engineering is based on a clear separation of focuses: engineering the overall architecture versus engineering reusable solutions for the subsystems. The RSEB book describes a generic Component System Engineering process based on the general OOSE process components. This is a good start. However, as we noted in Section 3.5, there will be rather different specialized horizontal Domain Engineering methods because different subsystems may require different modeling styles and modeling techniques. Thus, the Application Family Engineering process may "call" different specialized horizontal Domain Engineering methods, such as DEMRAL (see Section 3.6.5), as its Component System Engineering methods for different subsystems (see Figure 3–3).

Variation points   RSEB explicitly focuses on modeling variability. At the abstract level, the notion of *variation points* is introduced as an extension of the UML notation. A variation point "identifies one or more locations at which the variation will occur." [JGJ97] A variation point is shown as a solid dot on a modeling element, such as a use case or a component (see Figure 3–4). For example, the component `Account` has the variation point {`Account Overdrawn`}, and two variant components, `Deduct Fee` and `Overdraft Not Allowed`, are associated with this point using simple UML associations. Similarly, the use case `Withdraw Money` also has the variation point {`Account Overdrawn`}. Two variant use cases, `Deduct Fee` and `Overdraft Not Allowed`, are associated with this point using the «extends» relationship. Each variant use case describes what should happen if an

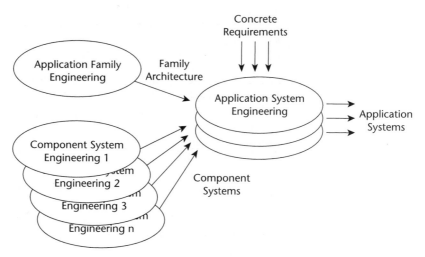

Figure 3-3 *Flow of artifacts in RSEB with specialized Component System Engineering processes*

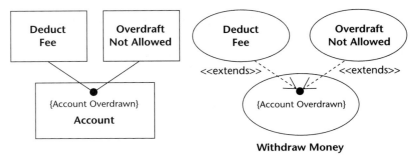

Figure 3-4 *Variation points in components and use cases (adapted from [JGJ97])*

Variability mechanisms

account is overdrawn. We will extend the notion of variation points with different categories of variation in Section 4.4.1.7.

Variation points are implemented in more concrete models using different *variability mechanisms*. Indeed, any model used in the process should support some kind of variability mechanism. Examples of variability mechanisms are summarized in Table 3–1.

An important contribution of RSEB is variability modeling in use cases. The RSEB book lists a number of important reasons for variability in use case models.

♦ Varying user or system interfaces
♦ Different entity types referenced, for example, account in withdrawal may be a checking or a joint account
♦ Alternative and optional functionality
♦ Varying constraints and business rules
♦ Error detection
♦ Performance and scalability differences

The variability mechanisms available in use case modeling include use case templates, macros and parameters, use case delegation (i.e., *uses* relationship), and use case extensions [JGJ97].

A key idea in RSEB is to maintain explicit traceability links connecting representations of variability throughout all models, that is, variability present in use cases can be traced to variability in the analysis, design, and implementation object models. In UML, the traceability links are modeled using the «trace» dependency relationship.

As stated previously, RSEB is based on the OOSE method and thus each of the three processes, Application Family Engineering, Component System Engineering, and Application System Engineering, have the five main OOSE process components.

Table 3-1 Some Variability Mechanisms (adapted from [JGJ97])

Mechanism	Type of Variation Point	Type of Variant	Use Particularly When
Inheritance	Virtual Operation	Subclass or Subtype	Specializing and adding selected operations, while keeping others
Extensions	Extension Point	Extension	Attaching several variants at each variation point at the same time
Uses	Use Point	Use Case	Reusing abstract use case to create a specialized use case
Configuration	Configuration Item Slot	Configuration Item	Choosing alternative functions and implementations
Parameters	Parameter	Bound Parameter	Selecting between alternative features
Template Instantiation	Template Parameter	Template Instance	Doing type adaptation or selecting alternative pieces of code
Generation	Parameter or Language Script	Bound Parameter or Expression	Doing large-scale creation of one or more types or classes from a problem-specific language

- ◆ Requirements capture
- ◆ Robustness analysis
- ◆ Design
- ◆ Implementation
- ◆ Testing

Additionally, Component System Engineering and Application System Engineering have a sixth process component, namely *packaging*, whose purpose is packaging the component system (documenting, archiving for later retrieval, and so on) or packaging the application system (documenting, developing installation scripts, and so on).

Unfortunately, despite the RSEB focus on variability, the process components of Application Family Engineering and Component System Engineering do not include the Domain-Analysis-like activities of domain scoping and feature modeling.

The purpose of domain scoping in Application Family Engineering would be to scope the application family or the product line with respect to classes of current and potential stakeholders. This kind of scoping is referred to as *application family scoping*. We already discussed issues concerning application family scoping in the context of product lines and families in Section 2.7.2.

The kind of scoping required for Component System Engineering is a *component-oriented* one. The issues in this process include the following.

◆ Reusability of the component system across multiple product lines or families within an organization
◆ Marketing opportunities of a component system outside an organization
◆ Technical issues, such as the nature of the domain and the required modeling techniques
◆ Organizational issues, such as staffing and concurrent engineering

Component-oriented scoping corresponds to the decomposition of the applications in an application family into generic subsystems and thus represents an important aspect of the application family architecture development.

Another shortcoming of RSEB is the lack of feature models. In RSEB, variability is expressed at the highest level in the form of variation points (especially in use cases), which are then implemented in other models using various variability mechanisms. However, Griss et al. report in [GFA98] that these modeling techniques turned out to be insufficient in practice. They summarize their experience in applying a purely use-case-driven approach in the telecom domain as follows.

> In the telecom sector, lack of explicit feature representation can be especially problematic, even in the presence of use case modeling. First, use case models do not explicitly reveal many of the implementation or technical features prevalent in telecom systems, such as "switch types." Second, telecom services can require very large numbers of use cases for their descriptions; and when the use cases are parameterized with RSEB variation points describing many extensions, alterna-

tives, and options, the domain engineer can easily lose his way when architecting new systems. Reusers can easily get confused about which features and use cases to use for which application systems.

This experience prompted them to devise FeatuRSEB [GFA98], which addresses all these problems by extending RSEB with explicit domain scoping and feature modeling activities and with feature models. We describe this new method in the following section.

3.6.4   FeatuRSEB

FeatuRSEB [GFA98] is a result of integrating FODAcom [VAM+98], an object-oriented adaptation of FODA for the telecom domain, into RSEB, in a cooperation between Hewlett-Packard and Intecs Sistemi.

FeatuRSEB extends RSEB in two important ways.

◆ Application Family Engineering and Component System Engineering are extended with explicit domain scoping, domain planning, and feature modeling activities.
◆ Feature models are used as the primary representation of commonalities, variabilities, and dependencies.

Both the Unified Process and RSEB subscribe to the "4+1 Model View" of architecture by Kruchten (see Figure 3–1) of developing several models, plus one that ties them all together. The role of this unifying "+1" model in the Unified Process and RSEB is played by the use case model, whereas the "+1" model in FeatuRSEB is the feature model. Griss et al. note that the feature model serves "as a concise synthesis of the variability and commonality represented in the other RSEB models, especially the use case model." [GFA98] In other words, FeatuRSEB is *feature model centric*. They further state that, as a FeatuRSEB principle, "not everything that *could* be a feature *should* be a feature. Feature descriptions need to be robust and expressive. Features are used primarily to discriminate between *choices*, not to describe functionality in great detail; such detail is left to the use case or object models."

Griss et al. also describe the important relationship between use case models and feature models: A use case model captures the system requirements from the user perspective (i.e., "operational requirements"), whereas the feature model organizes requirements from the reuser perspective based on commonality and variability analysis (and, we should add, dependency analysis).

The feature models in FeatuRSEB consist, like their FODA counterparts, of feature diagrams annotated with constraints, binding time, category, rationale, and so on.

The feature modeling steps in FeatuRSEB include the following [GFA98].

1. Merge individual exemplar use case models into a domain use case model (known as the Family Use Case Model in the RSEB). Use variation points to capture and express the differences. Keep track of the originating exemplars using «trace».
2. Create an initial feature model with *functional features* derived from the domain use case model (typically using use case names as a starting point for feature names).
3. Create the RSEB analysis object model, augmenting the feature model with *architectural features*. These features relate to system structure and configuration rather than to specific function.
4. Create the RSEB design model, augmenting the feature model with *implementation features*.

Thus, FeatuRSEB distinguishes between functional, architectural, and implementation features.

Griss et al. also propose an implementation of the feature diagram notation in UML and give some requirements on tool support for feature models. We will discuss both topics later in Section 4.7.

3.6.5 Domain Engineering Method for Reusable Algorithmic Libraries (DEMRAL)

DEMRAL is a Domain Engineering method for developing algorithmic libraries, for example, numerical libraries, container libraries, image processing libraries, image recognition libraries, speech recognition libraries, graph computation libraries, and so on. Thus, it is a horizontal method. The main abstractions in algorithmic domains are abstract data types (ADTs) and algorithms. Excellent performance, effective representation of a myriad of ADT and algorithm variants, achieving high adaptability and reusability, and providing an abstract interface are the main design goals in DEMRAL. The method has been created as a specialization of ODM described in Section 2.8.2.

A fundamental aspect of DEMRAL is feature modeling. Indeed, feature modeling is the driving force in DEMRAL. DEMRAL involves creating a high-level feature model of the domain of focus and feature models of each concept in the domain. DEMRAL also integrates concepts from Aspect-Oriented Programming, such as aspectual decomposition and the application of domain-specific languages (DSLs) for expressing different aspects (see Chapter 8).

An important concept in DEMRAL is *configuration DSLs*. A configuration DSL is used to configure a component. It allows different levels of control, so that clients may specify their needs at the appropriate level of detail. DEMRAL provides an approach for deriving configuration DSLs from feature models.

DEMRAL also gives advice on implementing domain models using OO techniques and metaprogramming (e.g., generators, transformation systems, or built-in metaprogramming capabilities of programming languages).

DEMRAL is described in detail in Chapter 5.

Chapter 4

Feature Modeling

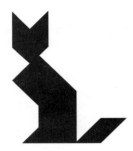

4.1 Why Is This Chapter Worth Reading?

Feature modeling is the greatest contribution of Domain Engineering to software engineering. Feature modeling is a must if you engineer for reuse. This is because reusable software contains inherently more variability than concrete applications and feature modeling is the key technique for identifying and capturing variability. Feature modeling helps you to avoid two serious problems.

♦ Relevant features and variation points are not included in the reusable software.
♦ Many features and variation points are included but never used and thus cause unnecessary complexity and both development and maintenance costs.

Feature models produced during feature modeling provide us with an abstract (because it is implementation independent), concise, and explicit representation of the variability present in the software. And you'll find feature modeling to be useful at any level: You can use it at the system level, at the subsystem level, as well as down to classes and procedures.

In this chapter, you'll learn how to represent feature models and how to perform feature modeling.

4.2 Features Revisited

We discussed the notion of features in the last two chapters. We saw that different methods and approaches used slightly different interpretations of features. Before we move our attention to feature modeling, we first summarize what we have said about features so far.

Following the conceptual modeling perspective (see Appendix A) and the ODM perspective (see Section 2.8.2), a feature is an important property of a concept instance. Features allow us to express the commonalities and differences between concept instances. They are fundamental to formulating concise descriptions of concepts with large degrees of variation among their instances. Organized in feature diagrams (see Section 4.4.1), they express the configurability aspect of concepts.

A feature should have a concise and descriptive name—much as in the case of a design pattern. The name enriches the vocabulary for describing domain concepts. By organizing features into feature diagrams, we actually build taxonomies.

Features are primarily used in order to discriminate between instances (and thus between choices). In this context, the quality of a feature is related to properties, such as its primitiveness, generality, and independency. We discuss these concepts in Section A.3.5.

In the context of Domain Engineering, features represent reusable, configurable requirements and each feature has to make a difference to someone, such as a stakeholder or a client program. For example, when we build an order processing system, one of the features of the pricing component could be *aging pricing strategy*, that is, you pay less for older merchandise. This pricing strategy might be particularly interesting to stores selling perishable goods.

Features may occur at any level, for example, high-level system requirements, architectural level, subsystem and component level, and implementation-construct level (e.g., object or procedure level).

Modeling the semantic content of features usually requires some additional modeling formalism, such as object diagrams, interaction diagrams, state-transition diagrams, synchronization constraints, and so on. Thus, feature models are usually just one of many other kinds of models describing a piece of reusable software.

4.3 Feature Modeling

Feature modeling and feature models

Feature modeling is the activity of modeling the common and the variable properties of concepts and their interdependencies and organizing them into a coherent model referred to as a feature model.

By concepts, we mean any elements and structures in the domain of interest. We discuss the notion of concepts and conceptual modeling in detail in Appendix A. But let us make a few remarks about concepts here.

Many OO enthusiasts do not distinguish between concepts and OO classes. For them, "everything is an object." Of course, this is a quite naive or even profane view of the world.

There is an obvious similarity between OO classes and concepts: OO classes represent a generic description of a set of objects. Similarly, concepts represent a generic description of a set of concept instances. So what is the difference between concepts and OO classes? In order to answer this question, we have to move to the instance level. Objects, that is, the instances of OO classes, have some predefined semantic properties: They have state, exhibit some well-defined behavior, and have a unique identity (see [Boo94]). Instances of concepts, on the other hand, do not have any predefined semantics. They could be anything. This difference is shown in Figure 4–1.

We can think of concepts as "reference points" in the brain for classifying phenomena. A concept represents a class of phenomena. Of course, it is important to give names to relevant concepts, so that we can talk about them without having to list all their properties (which in most cases, as shown in Appendix A, is impossible anyway). Furthermore, as discussed in Section A.3.1, concepts are inherently subjective: Their information content depends not only on the person, but also on time, context, and other factors.

So why do we define feature modeling around concepts and not classes of objects? The reason is that we want to model features of any elements and structures of a domain, not just objects. It should be possible to describe variability of use cases, OO classes, functions, procedures, and so on, not just OO classes. This way, we can use feature modeling together with various other

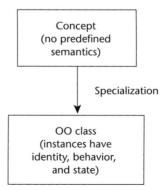

Figure 4-1 *Difference between a concept and an OO class*

modeling techniques, such as use case modeling, class modeling, specifications of functions, procedures, and so on.

Feature modeling may play different roles in different Domain Engineering methods, such as the following.

♦ Producing a feature model representing the configurability aspect of reusable software as in, for example, FeatuRSEB (see Section 3.6.4).
♦ Being the "driving modeling activity," for example, all modeling in DEMRAL (see Chapter 5) starts as feature modeling, and other modeling techniques are "called" from feature modeling.

We refer to the latter as *feature-driven modeling*. Feature-driven modeling is useful whenever variability constitutes the main aspect of the modeled software.

There are three important aspects of feature modeling.

♦ *"Micro-cycle" of feature modeling:* What are the basic steps in feature modeling? How do we identify features? We investigate these questions in Section 4.9.1.
♦ *Integration in the overall software engineering process:* The micro-cycle of feature modeling may be integrated into the overall software engineering process in different ways. For example, in FeatuRSEB, it accompanies all other modeling activities (see feature modeling steps in FeatuRSEB in Section 3.6.4). In DEMRAL, as noted earlier, it constitutes the main modeling activity. Another aspect is the relation between feature models and other models produced during development. As already discussed, we need to maintain traceability links showing the connections between variability representations in different models.
♦ *Content aspect of feature modeling:* Features have some semantic content and feature modeling may focus on different kinds of content at a time, for example, functional aspects, data-flow aspects, interaction aspects, synchronization aspects, and so on. Different model representations are used for different contents. This issue is related to decomposition techniques, which we discuss in Section 4.9.2.

It is important to note that feature modeling is a creative activity. It is much more than just a simple rehash of the features of existing systems and the available domain knowledge. New features and new knowledge are created during feature modeling. For example, one technique used in feature modeling is the analysis of combinations of variable features, which may lead to the discovery of innovative feature combinations and new features. The systematic organization of

NOTE ON TERMINOLOGY

In some Domain Engineering methods, feature modeling is referred to as feature analysis. However, we prefer the term "feature modeling" because it emphasizes the creative aspect of this activity.

existing knowledge allows us to invent new, useful features and feature combinations more easily.

Before we answer the question of how to perform feature modeling in Section 4.9, we first describe the elements of feature models.

4.4　Feature Models

A *feature model* represents the common and the variable features of concept instances and the dependencies between the variable features. Feature models are created during feature modeling.

A feature model represents the *intention* of a concept, whereas the set of instances it describes is referred to as the *extension* of the concept.

A feature model consists of a feature diagram and some additional information, such as short semantic descriptions of each feature, rationales for each feature, stakeholders and client programs interested in each feature, examples of systems with a given feature, constraints, default dependency rules, availability sites (i.e., where, when, and to whom a feature is available), binding sites (i.e., where, when, and who is able to bind a feature), binding modes (e.g., dynamic or static binding), open/closed attributes (i.e., whether new subfeatures are expected), and priorities (i.e., how important a feature is). We discuss all of these items in Section 4.4.2.

From a feature diagram of a concept, we can derive *featural descriptions* of the individual instances of the concept. A featural description of an instance is a *set of features*.[1] Two feature diagrams are *equivalent* if the set of all instance descriptions derivable from the first diagram is equal to the set of all instance descriptions derivable from the other diagram.

---

1. If the feature diagram of a concept is not a tree, but a more general graph, then, in general, featural descriptions of instances cannot be represented by feature sets. In this case, we have to represent them as subgraphs of the feature graph. However, we will only consider feature diagrams that are trees.

We describe feature diagrams in the following sections. All the additional information contained in a feature model is described in Section 4.4.2.

4.4.1 Feature Diagrams

In this section, we introduce a slightly modified and extended version of the FODA feature diagram notation (see Section 2.7.4) as well as some useful vocabulary for talking about feature diagrams.

A feature diagram consists of a set of nodes, a set of directed edges, and a set of edge decorations. The nodes and the edges form a tree. The edge decorations are drawn as arcs connecting subsets or all of the edges originating from the same node (see, e.g., Figure 4–5). Effectively, edge decorations define a partitioning of the subnodes of a node (i.e., they divide the subnodes into a number of disjoint subsets).

The root of a feature diagram represents a concept. We refer to it as the *concept node*.[2] The remaining nodes in a feature diagram represent features and we refer to them as *feature nodes*. Throughout the text, we usually leave out the word "node" and simply say "feature" instead of "feature node" and "concept" instead of "concept node."

The parent node of a feature node is either the concept node or another feature node. Consider Figure 4–2, which shows a feature diagram with the three features f_1, f_2, and f_3 of the concept C,

---

NOTE

In some cases, representing a feature diagram using a more general directed graph would certainly be useful. For example, we might want to allow for multiple references to one subgraph in order to avoid its duplication within the diagram. In the following discussion, however, we assume that the diagram is a tree. A practical approach to avoiding the duplication of feature subtrees in a larger feature diagram is to only include the roots of the subtrees in the larger diagram and to show the duplicated subtree in a separate diagram.

---

2. Sometimes, when we draw a large feature diagram, it is convenient to split it into a number of smaller diagrams. In this case, the roots of the smaller subdiagrams are *features* of the concept represented by the root of the original diagram rather than concepts.

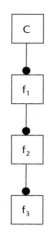

Figure 4-2 *Feature diagram with three features*

where the parent of f_1 is C, the parent of f_2 is f_1, and the parent of f_3 is f_2. Given these relationships, we say that *(i)* f_1 is a *direct feature* of C, *(ii)* f_2 and f_3 are *indirect features* of C, *(iii)* f_2 is a *direct subfeature* of f_1, and *(iv)* f_3 is an *indirect subfeature* of f_1.

As in FODA, we distinguish between *mandatory*, *alternative*, and *optional features*. In addition to these feature types, we also introduce *or-features*. Furthermore, optionality can be combined with alternative features and with or-features resulting in the two additional feature types *optional alternative features* and *optional or-features*. However, as we see later in Section 4.4.1.5, the optional or-feature type is equivalent to the optional feature type and thus it is redundant.

A description of an instance of a concept is a set of nodes that always includes the concept node and some or all of the feature nodes. A valid description of an instance is derived from a feature diagram by adding the concept node to the feature set, by traversing the diagram starting at the root, and depending on the type of the visited node, including it in the set or not. The node types and the criteria for the inclusion of a feature in an instance description are defined in the following sections.

4.4.1.1 Mandatory Features

A *mandatory feature* is included in the description of a concept instance if and only if its parent is included in the description of the instance. Thus, for example, if the parent of a mandatory feature is optional and not included in the instance description, the mandatory feature cannot be part of the description. Please remember that the concept node of a feature diagram is always included in any instance description derived from the diagram.

A mandatory feature node is pointed to by a *simple edge* (as opposed to an *arc-decorated edge*) ending with a filled circle as in Figure 4–3. Features f_1, f_2, f_3, and f_4 are mandatory features of concept C. According to Figure 4–3, every instance of concept C has features f_1 and f_2, and every instance of C that has f_1 also has f_3 and f_4. Thus, effectively, every instance of C has f_3 and f_4. Finally, we conclude that every instance of C can be described by the feature set $\{C, f_1, f_2, f_3, f_4\}$.

4.4.1.2 Optional Features

An *optional feature* may be included in the description of a concept instance if and only if its parent is included in the description. In other words, if the parent is included, the optional feature may be included or not, and if the parent is not included, the optional feature cannot be included.

An optional feature node is pointed to by a simple edge ending with an empty circle as in Figure 4–4. Features f_1, f_2, and f_3 are

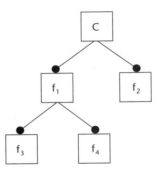

Figure 4-3 *Example of a feature diagram with mandatory features*

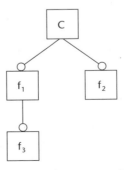

Figure 4-4 *Example of a feature diagram with optional features*

optional features of concept C. According to Figure 4–4, an instance of C might have one of the following descriptions: $\{C\}$, $\{C, f_1\}$, $\{C, f_1, f_3\}$, $\{C, f_2\}$, $\{C, f_1, f_2\}$, or $\{C, f_1, f_3, f_2\}$.

4.4.1.3 Alternative Features

A concept may have one or more sets of direct *alternative features*. Similarly, a feature may have one or more sets of direct *alternative subfeatures*. If the parent of a set of alternative features is included in the description of a concept instance, then exactly one feature from this set of alternative features is included in the description; otherwise none are included.

The nodes of a set of alternative features are pointed to by edges connected by an arc. For example, in Figure 4–5, C has two sets of alternative features: one set with f_1 and f_2 and another set with f_3, f_4, and f_5. From this diagram, we can derive the following instance descriptions: $\{C, f_1, f_3\}$, $\{C, f_1, f_4\}$, $\{C, f_1, f_5\}$, $\{C, f_2, f_3\}$, $\{C, f_2, f_4\}$, or $\{C, f_2, f_5\}$.

A feature (or concept) with a single set of direct alternative subfeatures (or features) and no other direct subfeatures (or features) is referred to as a *dimension* (e.g., f_1 in Figure 4–6). We also found it useful to broaden the notion of dimensions to include features (concepts) with a single set of direct alternative subfeatures (features) and one or more direct mandatory subfeatures (features). According to this broader definition, f_2 in Figure 4–6 is also a dimension, but f_3 is not.[3]

Dimensions can also be alternative, that is, we can have *alternative dimensions* (see Figure 4–7).

Similarly, we can have *optional dimensions* (see Figure 4–8).

An alternative feature can also be optional, as f_1 is in Figure 4–9. However, as we will see in Section 4.4.1.5, during the normal-

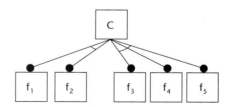

Figure 4-5 *Example of a feature diagram with two sets of alternative features*

---

3. According to the terminology introduced in Section 4.4.1.7, dimensions with direct mandatory subfeatures (or features) are referred to as *inhomogeneous dimensions*.

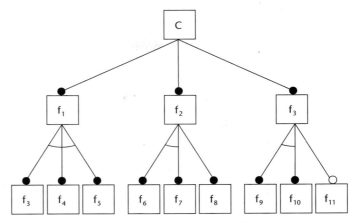

Figure 4-6 *Example of a feature diagram with two dimensions*

ization of a feature diagram, all features of a set of alternative features containing one or more optional alternative features are replaced by optional alternative features (see Figure 4–12).

4.4.1.4 Or-Features

A concept may have one or more sets of direct *or-features*. Similarly, a feature may have one or more sets of direct *or-subfeatures*. If the parent of a set of or-features is included in the description of a concept instance, then any nonempty subset from the set of

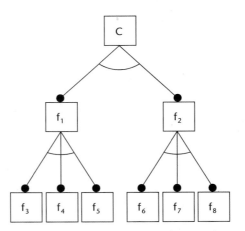

Figure 4-7 *Example of a feature diagram with two alternative dimensions*

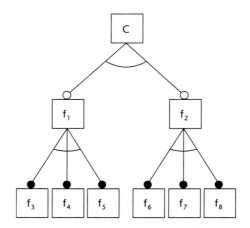

Figure 4-8 *Example of a feature diagram with two optional dimensions*

or-features is included in the description; otherwise, none are included.

The nodes of a set of or-features are pointed to by edges connected by a filled arc. For example, in Figure 4–10, C has two sets of or-features: one set with f_1 and f_2 and another set with f_3, f_4, and f_5. A total of $(2^2-1)\cdot(2^3-1)$ or 21 different instance descriptions may be derived from this diagram.

An or-feature can also be optional, for example, f_1 in Figure 4–11. However, as we will see in Section 4.4.1.5, during the normalization of a feature diagram, all or-features of a set of or-features containing one or more optional or-features are replaced by optional features (see Figure 4–13).

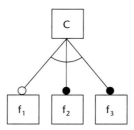

Figure 4-9 *Example of a feature diagram with one optional alternative feature*

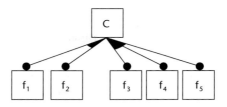

Figure 4-10 *Example of a feature diagram with two sets of or-features*

4.4.1.5 Normalized Feature Diagrams

A node in a feature diagram can have mandatory feature subnodes (e.g., f_1 in Figure 4–3), optional feature subnodes (e.g., f_1 in Figure 4–4), alternative feature subnodes (e.g., f_1 in Figure 4–5), optional alternative feature subnodes (e.g., f_1 in Figure 4–9), or-feature subnodes (e.g., f_1 in Figure 4–10), and optional or-feature subnodes (e.g., f_1 in Figure 4–11). Thus, in addition to the mandatory, alternative, optional, and or-feature nodes, we also have *optional alternative feature nodes* and *optional or-feature nodes*. Now let us take a closer look at the latter two kinds of features.

If one or more of the features in a set of alternative features is optional, it has the same effect as if all the alternative features in this set were optional. This is illustrated in Figure 4–12.

Similarly, if one or more of the features in a set of or-features is optional, it has the same effect as if all the features in this set were optional or-features. Furthermore, all of the optional or-features can be replaced by optional features. Therefore, if one or more features in a set of or-features is optional, we can replace all of these features by optional features. This is illustrated in Figure 4–13. We conclude that the category of optional or-features is redundant because it is equivalent to optional features.

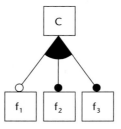

Figure 4-11 *Example of a feature diagram with an optional or-feature*

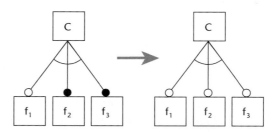

Figure 4-12 *Feature diagram with one (or more) optional alternative feature is normalized into a diagram with all optional alternative features*

Normalized feature diagrams

Any feature diagram can be transformed into a feature diagram that does not have any optional or-features and whose sets of alternative features may contain either only alternative features or only alternative optional features. The transformation can be accomplished as follows. Let O_i be a set of alternative features containing one or more optional alternative features, and let P_j be a set of or-features containing one or more optional or-features. The transformation requires us to replace *(a)* all the nonoptional alternative features in every O_i of a diagram by optional alternative features and *(b)* replace all features in all P_j by optional features. The resulting feature diagram is referred to as a *normalized feature diagram* and is equivalent to the original feature diagram.

Subnode categories: mandatory, optional, alternative, optional alternative, and or-feature nodes

A feature node in a normalized feature diagram can be classified according to its *subnode category* as one of the following: *mandatory*, or *optional*, or *alternative*, or *optional alternative*, or *or-feature node*.

Subnode partitioning

Furthermore, the set of subnodes of any node of a normalized feature diagram can be partitioned into the following disjoint (possibly empty) sets: one set of mandatory feature nodes, one set of

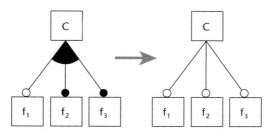

Figure 4-13 *Feature diagram with one (or more) optional or-feature is normalized into a diagram with all optional features*

optional feature nodes, one or more sets of alternative feature nodes, one or more sets of optional alternative feature nodes, and one or more sets of or-feature nodes. This partitioning is referred to as *subnode partitioning* and each of the resulting sets is called a *subnode partition* of the parent node.

4.4.1.6 Expressing Commonality in Feature Diagrams

Feature diagrams allow us to represent concepts in a way that makes the commonalities and variabilities among their instances explicit. We first take a look at representing commonality.

Depending on the focus, there are two types of commonalities. If we focus on the concept node, we might ask the question: What features are common to all instances of the concept? On the other hand, if we focus on a particular feature node, we might ask: What features are common to all instances of the concept that have that particular feature? In order to answer these questions, we introduce the notions of *common features* and *common subfeatures*.

Common features

A *common feature* of a concept is a feature present in all instances of a concept. All mandatory features whose parent is the concept are common features. Also, all mandatory features whose parents are common are themselves common features. Thus, a feature is a common feature of a concept if it is a mandatory feature and either a direct feature of the concept or there is a path of mandatory features connecting the feature and the concept. For example, in Figure 4–3, f_1, f_2, f_3, and f_4 are common features.

Common subfeatures

A *common subfeature* of a feature f is a (direct or indirect) subfeature of f, which is present in all instances of a concept that also have f. Thus, all direct mandatory subfeatures of f are common subfeatures of f. Also, a subfeature of f is common if it is mandatory and there is a path of mandatory features connecting the subfeature and f.

4.4.1.7 Expressing Variability in Feature Diagrams

Variable features

Variability in feature diagrams is expressed using optional, alternative, optional alternative, and or-features. We refer to these features as *variable features*.

Variation points

The nodes to which variable features are attached are referred to as *variation points*.[4] More formally, a variation point is a feature (or concept) that has at least one direct variable subfeature (or feature).

---

4. The term *variation point* was first introduced in RSEB [JGJ97] (see Section 3.6.3). According to [JGJ97], a variation point "identifies one or more locations at which variation will occur."

*Dimensions and
extension points*

Different important types of variation points, such as *dimensions* and *extension points,* are defined in Table 4–1.

*Homogeneous
versus
inhomogeneous
variation points*

Moreover, we distinguish between *homogeneous* versus *inhomogeneous variation points.* A variation point is homogeneous if all its direct subfeatures (or features) belong to the same subnode category (i.e., they are all optional, or all alternative, and so on); otherwise it is inhomogeneous.

*Singular versus
nonsingular
variation points*

We can further categorize variation points according to whether they allow us to include at most one direct variable subfeature (or feature) in the description of an instance or more than one direct variable subfeature (or feature). The first category is referred to as *singular variation points* and it includes dimensions, dimensions with optional features, and extension points with exactly one optional feature. The second category is referred to as *nonsingular variation points* and it includes extension points with more than one optional feature and extension points with or-features.

*Mutually
exclusive
features*

Similar to the way we generalized mandatory features to common features, we can also generalize alternative features to *mutually exclusive features*: Two features in a feature diagram of a concept are mutually exclusive if none of the instances of the concept has both features at the same time. Given a tree-shaped feature diagram, two features are mutually exclusive if they are both in the same set of alternative features, or if the direct parent or any of the indirect parents of the first feature is in the same set of alternative features as the direct parent or any of the indirect parents of the other feature.

*Simultaneous
versus
nonsimultaneous
variation points*

Finally, we also distinguish between simultaneous and nonsimultaneous variation points. Two variation points of a feature diagram are *simultaneous* if and only if they are not mutually exclusive and neither of them is a direct or indirect variable subfeature of the other one. For example, f_1, f_2, and f_3 in Figure 4–6 are simultaneous variation points. Analogously, two variation points are *nonsimultaneous* if and only if they are either mutually exclusive or one of them is a direct or indirect variable subfeature of the other one. Examples of nonsimultaneous variation points are f_1 and f_2 in Figure 4–7.

4.4.2   Other Information Associated with Feature Diagrams in a Feature Model

A complete feature model consists of a feature diagram and other information associated with it, including the following.

♦ *Semantic description:* Each feature should have at least a short description describing its semantics. It may also be useful to

Table 4-1 Types of variation points

Type of variation point	Definition	Example
Dimension	Feature (or concept) of which all direct subfeatures (or features) are alternative features	
Dimension with optional features	Feature (or concept) of which all direct subfeatures (or features) are alternative optional features	
Extension point	Feature (or concept) that has at least one direct optional subfeature (or feature) or at least one set of direct or-subfeatures (or or-features)	
Extension point with optional features	Feature (or concept) of which all direct subfeatures (or features) are optional features	
Extension point with or-features	Feature (or concept) of which all direct subfeatures (or features) are or-features	

attach some models in appropriate formalisms (e.g., an interaction diagram, pseudocode, equations, and so on.). Eventually, there will be traceability links to other models implementing this feature. We may also assign categories to features, for example, categories indicating the aspect a given feature belongs to (e.g., *functional*, *performance*, *interface*, and so on).

♦ *Rationale:* A feature should have a note explaining why the feature is included in the model. Also, each variable feature should be annotated with conditions and recommendations specifying when to select it and when not to.

♦ *Stakeholders and client programs:* Each feature should be annotated with stakeholders (e.g., users, customers, developers, managers, and so on) who are interested in the feature and, in the case of a component, with the client programs (or examples of such) that need this feature.

♦ *Exemplar systems:* If possible, we should annotate features with known systems (i.e., exemplar systems) implementing them.

♦ *Constraints and default dependency rules:* Constraints are hard dependencies between variable features, possibly over multiple feature diagrams. Two important kinds of constraints are *mutual-exclusion constraints* (i.e., constraints describing illegal combinations of variable features) and *requires constraints* (i.e., constraints describing which features require the presence of which other features). *Default dependency rules* suggest default values for unspecified parameters based on other parameters.[5] We distinguish between *horizontal* and *vertical constraints* and default dependency rules. Horizontal constraints and default dependency rules describe dependencies between features of a similar level of abstraction (e.g., constraints within one feature diagram are usually horizontal features), whereas vertical constraints and default dependency rules map high-level specification features onto implementation features. Constraints and default dependency rules allow us to provide automatic (e.g., constraint-based) configuration, which relieves the reuser of much manual configuration work.

♦ *Availability sites, binding sites, and binding mode:* Availability site describes when, where, and to whom a variable feature is available, and binding site describes when, where, and by whom a feature may be bound. Binding mode determines whether a feature is statically, changeably, or dynamically bound. We discuss availability site, binding site, and binding mode in Section 4.4.4.

♦ *Open/closed attribute:* We mark variation points as *open*[6] if new direct variable subfeatures (or features) are expected. For ex-

---

5. In contrast to requires constraints, default dependency rules *suggest* default values, that is, their suggestions can be overridden. In other words, they are a kind of "weak constraints."

6. We indicate openness in a feature diagram by ellipses (e.g., see Figure 14-2) and/or by enclosing a feature name in brackets (see Figure 12-1).

ample, the element type of a matrix could have integer, long, float, double, and complex as alternative subfeatures. We would mark it *open* to indicate that, if needed, other number types may be added. By marking a variation point as *closed*, we indicate that no other direct variable subfeatures (or features) are expected.

♦ *Priorities:* Priorities may be assigned to features in order to record their relevance to the project. We discuss priorities in the following section.

4.4.3 Assigning Priorities to Variable Features

We annotate variable features with priorities in the following situations.

♦ *Domain scoping and definition:* Priorities can be used in order to record the typicality rates of variable features based on the analysis of known exemplar systems and the target application areas. They may also be adjusted according to the goals of the stakeholders to record the relevance of each variable feature for the project. For example, the definition of the *domain of matrix computation libraries* involves the construction of a feature diagram of the concept *matrix computation library* (see Figure 14–1 in Section 14.3.1). The features of a matrix computation library are determined based on the analysis of existing matrix computation libraries and their application areas. The variable features are annotated with priorities stating how important it is for a library to provide them. For example, every matrix computation library has to provide dense matrices or sparse matrices or both; however, dense matrices are more commonly implemented than sparse matrices. This type of concept definition corresponds to the probabilistic view of concepts discussed in Section A.2.3.

♦ *Feature modeling:* The variable features of feature diagrams produced during feature modeling can also be annotated with priorities in order to record their relevance to the project and to help decide which features to implement first. For example, one dimension in the feature diagram of a matrix is its *shape*, such as *rectangular*, *triangular*, or *Toeplitz*. We can assign a lower priority to Toeplitz than to rectangular or triangular because Toeplitz is "more exotic" than the other two, and it can also be represented using the rectangular shape.

♦ *Implementation scoping:* The first phase of domain design is implementation scoping, whose purpose is to determine which features will be implemented first. This decision is based on the priorities assigned to variable features in feature models.

The assigned priorities may change in the course of a project, and we will have to update the feature models accordingly. Furthermore, you may also consider recording different kinds of priorities at the same time, for example, priorities expressing relevance to the stakeholders, typicality rate based on existing systems, potential market size, and so on.

We do not prescribe any specific schema for assigning priorities. However, please note that priorities can potentially conflict with the constraints of a feature model because constraints define dependencies between features. Thus, for example, given the features f_1 and f_2, if there is a constraint requiring the inclusion f_2 whenever f_1 is included, the priority of f_2 has to be at least as high as the priority of f_1.

4.4.4 Availability Sites, Binding Sites, and Binding Modes

Availability site describes when, where, and to whom a variable feature is available. An available variable feature has to be bound before it can be used. Binding site describes when, where, and by whom a feature may be bound (and unbound, if applicable). Binding mode determines whether a feature is statically, changeably, or dynamically bound.

Before describing availability sites, binding sites, and binding modes in more detail, we first introduce the concept of sites.

4.4.4.1 Sites

A *site* defines the when, where, and who for a domain. Each domain may have its own site model, which may be arbitrarily complex. A simple site model might consist of a number of predefined times, usage contexts (e.g., different usage contexts of a system and/or usage locations of a component within a system), and stakeholder models (e.g., users, customers, developers, and so on).

Based on a generic product lifecycle, important times include construction time, compile time, debugging time, load time, runtime, and post runtime. However, sometimes we might want to define sites relative to product-specific workflows, use cases, and so on.

4.4.4.2 Availability Sites

The variability available in a system or a component usually depends on its current site. We can model this by annotating each variable feature with its availability sites, that is, the sites at which the feature is available for selection. For example, using availability site annotations, we can specify which items of a menu will be shown to whom, at what time, and in which context.

Please note that availability sites may potentially conflict with feature constraints. Thus, for example, given the features f_1 and f_2, if there is a constraint requiring the inclusion f_2 whenever f_1 is included, the set of availability sites of f_1 has to be a subset of the availability sites of f_2.

4.4.4.3 Binding Sites and Binding Modes

An available variable feature has to be bound first before it can be used. Binding corresponds to selecting a variable feature—just like selecting an item from a menu of options.

Binding sites   We usually control binding by annotating variation points with binding sites, that is, sites at which the variable subfeatures of a variation point may be bound; however, if more control is needed, we can also annotate the variable features themselves.

Binding mode   In addition to annotating a variation point or a variable feature with binding sites, we can also annotate them with a *binding mode*. We have the following binding modes.

- ◆ *Static binding:* A statically bound feature cannot be rebound. An example of static binding is static binding and inlining of methods in C++.
- ◆ *Changeable binding:* A changeably bound feature remains bound between uses, but you can unbind it if necessary. An example of changeable binding is the dynamic inlining performed by Sun's HotSpot.[7] HotSpot can inline methods at runtime if it discovers that the target of a method call is the same. But if the target changes at some point (e.g., because new code is dynamically loaded), it can actually undo the inlining. You can view changeable binding as an optimized form of dynamic binding.
- ◆ *Dynamic binding:* In this mode, a feature is automatically bound before use and unbound after use. Dynamic binding is useful in cases where we have to switch features at a high frequency. An example of dynamic binding is dynamic binding of methods in C++ or Java. In its usual implementation, the target of a dynamically bound method call is determined on each call (e.g., using a *virtual function table*).

4.4.4.4 Relationship between Optimizations and Availability Sites, Binding Sites, and Binding Modes

The knowledge of binding site may be used to reduce the memory footprint of an application and improve its execution speed. For example, certain features may be needed only for certain application

---

7. See www.javasoft.com/products/hotspot

variants. Obviously, we do not want to link unused features to an application.[8] This can be achieved by applying technologies, such as configuration management, preprocessors, generators, and static configuration using parameterized classes (e.g., C++ templates). If different features are needed at different times during runtime, we may want to use dynamic linking. Binding site modeling is especially relevant for dynamic and distributed architectures supported by the Java technology, where we have to pay special attention to network bandwidths and the widely differing resources available to different users on the network.

Binding mode tells us something about the stability of a configuration, and we can use this knowledge to optimize execution speed. For example, if a feature is bound statically, we know that the feature cannot be rebound, and we can optimize away any dispatching code, indirection levels, and so on. In the case when a feature should be bound statically at compile time, we can use implementation techniques, such as static method binding, parameterized classes, static metaprogramming, partial evaluation at compile time, and so on. In the case of changeable binding, it is useful to collect statistics, such as frequencies of rebounds and average time between rebounds for different features. Based on these statistics, we can decide whether to apply runtime optimizations for certain features. An example of technology using profile-based, runtime optimizations is Sun's HotSpot. Finally, if we need maximum flexibility, we have to use dynamic binding. Implementation techniques for dynamic feature binding include dynamic method binding, flags, dispatch tables, interpreters, and dynamic reflection.

4.5 Relationship between Feature Diagrams and Other Modeling Notations and Implementation Techniques

Feature diagrams allow us to express variability at an abstract level. As stated previously, the variability specified by a feature diagram is implemented in analysis, design, and implementation models using different variability mechanisms. We already discussed several variability mechanisms in Section 3.6.3 (see Table 3–1). For example, variability mechanisms for use cases include parameters, templates, extends relationships, and uses relationships. Variability

---

8. In the current practice, this obvious rule is not always followed. For example, OO frameworks, which provide a common base of features for a family of applications, are usually fully linked to an application, even if the application does not need all features.

mechanisms for class diagrams include inheritance, parameterization, dynamic binding, and cardinality ranges.

The following example illustrates the point that feature diagrams express variability at a more abstract level than class diagrams. Figure 4–14 shows a feature diagram of a simple car. The car consists of a car body, transmission, and an engine. The transmission may be either manual or automatic. Furthermore, the car may have a gasoline engine or an electric engine or both. Finally, the car may pull a trailer.

Figure 4–15 shows one possible implementation of our simple car as a UML class diagram. The car is represented as the parameterized class `Car`, where the `transmission` parameter implements the transmission dimension. `CarBody` is connected to `Car` by a part-of relationship. The optional `Trailer` is connected to `Car` by the association `pulls`. The cardinality range `0..1` expresses optionality. Finally, cars with different engine combinations are implemented using inheritance and aggregation (classes `ElectricCar`, `GasolineCar`, and `ElectricGasolineCar`). If there were additional constraints between features in the feature model, we could have implemented them as UML constraints (e.g., using the UML Object Constraint Language [Rat98d]).

Obviously, the implementation in Figure 4–15 is just one of many possible implementations. For example, we could use dynamic parameterization (see Section 4.5.5) to parameterize transmission instead of static parameterization. Another possibility would be to enlarge the inheritance hierarchy to accommodate different transmission and engine combinations. Thus, we see that

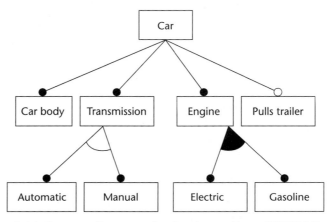

Figure 4-14 *Feature diagram of a simple car (from [CE99b])*

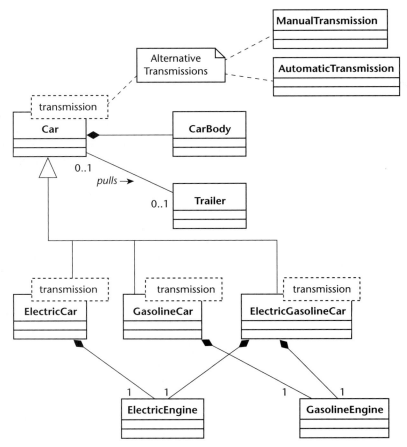

Figure 4-15 *One possible implementation of the simple car from Figure 4–14 using a UML class diagram (from [CE99b])*

the feature diagram in Figure 4–14 represents the variability of our car abstractly, that is, without committing to any particular variability mechanism.

In the following five sections, we investigate a number of important variability mechanisms available in current OO programming languages, namely single inheritance, multiple inheritance, parameterized inheritance, static parameterization, and dynamic parameterization. In Chapter 8, you'll see that these variability mechanisms may cause unnecessary complexity when used for parameterizing certain kinds of features, namely *aspects*. Examples of aspects are synchronizing concurrent execution and

---

NOTE ON TERMINOLOGY

Variability mechanisms are sometimes also referred to as "composition mechanisms." We will use the latter term in Chapter 8.

---

access, exception handling, profiling, security, transaction control, distributed data transfer, domain-specific optimizations, and so on. The main property of aspects is that they "crosscut" several modular components. We'll discuss techniques for implementing aspects without the usual complexity and unwieldiness of the traditional technologies in Chapter 8.

4.5.1   Single Inheritance

Single inheritance may be used as a static, compile time variability mechanism.[9] It is well suited for implementing statically bound, nonsimultaneous, singular variation points. For example, Figure 4–17 shows the implementation of the dimension from Figure 4–16. Each subclass may add some attributes and methods specific to it, for example, ΔEmployee indicates the attributes and methods specific to Employee.

We can also implement a nonsingular variation point using single inheritance; however, we will have to implement some features more than once. For example, Figure 4–19 shows the implementation of an extension point with or-features from Figure 4–18. Please note that ΔShareholder is implemented in three

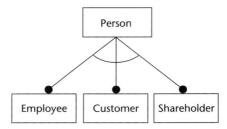

Figure 4-16 *Example of a dimension*

---

9. Some dynamic languages (e.g., Smalltalk or CLOS) allow us to modify the inheritance hierarchy at runtime. However, in most cases, dynamic variability is needed at the instance level and not the class level.

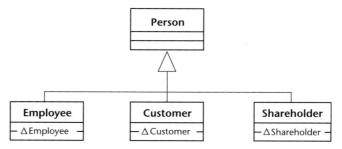

Figure 4-17 *Implementation of a dimension as an inheritance hierarchy*

classes (`Shareholder`, `ShareholderCustomer`, and `ShareholderEmployeeCustomer`) and ΔEmployee in three other classes (`Employee`, `EmployeeCustomer`, and `EmployeeShareholder`).

Similarly, if we were to implement a feature diagram containing two or more simultaneous variation points using single inheritance, the resulting inheritance hierarchy will also contain duplicate feature implementations. This is illustrated in Figure 4–20 and Figure 4–21.

In general, a feature diagram can be implemented as a single inheritance hierarchy without feature duplication if and only if the diagram contains *(1)* no variation points, or *(2)* exactly one variation point that is singular, or *(3)* more than one singular variation point, all of them being nonsimultaneous. A feature diagram cannot be implemented as a single inheritance hierarchy without feature duplication if and only if the diagram contains at least one nonsingular variation point or at least two simultaneous singular variation points.

In cases where the use of single inheritance causes feature duplication, we should consider using other variability mechanisms, such as multiple inheritance, parameterized inheritance, static parameterization, or dynamic parameterization.

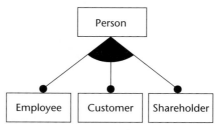

Figure 4-18 *Example of an extension point with or-features*

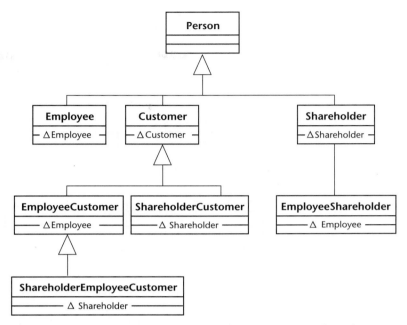

Figure 4-19 *Implementation of an extension point with or-features as a single inheritance hierarchy*

4.5.2 Multiple Inheritance

The extension point with or-features from Figure 4–18 may also be implemented as a multiple inheritance hierarchy. This is shown in Figure 4–22. Please note that we do not have to duplicate features.

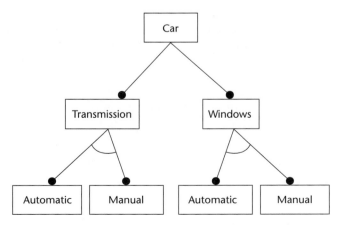

Figure 4-20 *Feature diagram with two simultaneous dimensions*

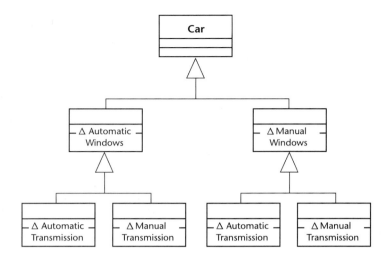

Figure 4-21 Implementation of two simultaneous dimensions as a single inheritance hierarchy (the names of the subclasses are not shown)

The classes ΔEmployee, ΔCustomer, and ΔShareholder are referred to as *mixins*. Unfortunately, the multiple inheritance hierarchy has more complicated relationships than the single inheritance hierarchy in Figure 4–19. A more flexible solution is to use parameterized inheritance, which we discuss in the following section.

4.5.3 Parameterized Inheritance

C++ allows us to turn the superclass of a class into a parameter. We refer to this language feature as *parameterized inheritance*. Parameterized inheritance represents an attractive alternative to multiple inheritance for implementing statically bound extension points. An implementation of the extension point with three or-features from Figure 4–18 using parameterized inheritance is shown in Figure 4–23. The mixin classes take their superclasses as parameters. We can compose them to implement any of the six relevant composite classes. In C++, we can implement the mixin ΔEmployee as follows:

```
template<class superclass>
class Employee : public superclass
{
  //employee members...
};
```

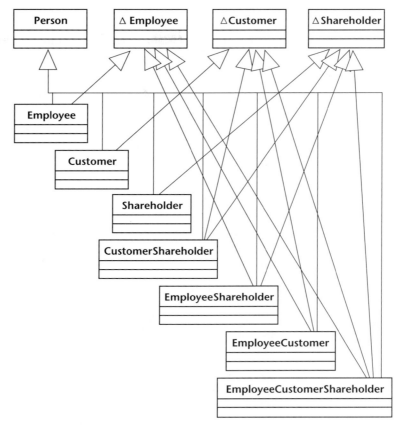

Figure 4-22 *Implementation of an extension point with three or-features as a multiple inheritance hierarchy*

We would then implement the remaining mixins ΔCustomer and ΔShareholder in a similar way. Given these mixins and the class Person, we can define ShareholderCustomerEmployee (shown in Figure 4–23) as follows:

```
Shareholder<Customer<Employee<Person> > >
```

and ShareholderEmployee as:

```
Shareholder<Employee<Person> >
```

There are a few peculiarities of mixin composition based on parameterized inheritance, which we would like to point out. First,

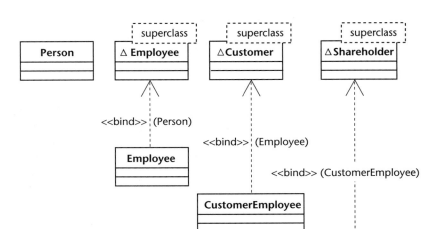

Figure 4-23 *Implementation of an extension point with three or-features using parameterized inheritance (the classes* Customer, *Shareholder,* ShareholderEmployee, *and* ShareholderCustomer *are not shown)*

if the mixins use public inheritance, the composition order has no influence on the interface of the resulting composition, that is, Customer<Employee<Person> > and Employee<Customer<Person> > would have the same interface (although the C++ compiler will still consider them as two different types). In terms of the influence of the composition order on the semantics of the composition, there are three cases.

- ◆ *Several compositions can be invalid:* For example, consider the data structure Container and the mixins Length, which adds the method length(), and BoundsChecker, which checks if the index of an element to be accessed is within bounds. Assuming that BoundsChecker needs Length, the composition BoundsChecker <Length<Container> > is valid, but Length<BoundsChecker <Container> > is not.
- ◆ *Several compositions can be valid, but each of them can have different semantics:* For example, given Container and the two mixins Trace, which logs each element access, and Synchronize, which synchronizes concurrent access to Container, both

`Synchronize<Trace<Container>` > and `Trace<Synchronize` `<Container>` > are semantically valid, but not equivalent. For example, if a given element access is blocked in `Synchronize`, the first composition would log the access after the access is allowed to proceed, and the second composition would log the access before it blocks.

♦ *Several compositions can be both valid and semantically equivalent:* For example, consider `Container` and the two mixins `BoundsChecker`, which checks if the index of an element to be accessed is within bounds, and `ElementChecker`, which checks the validity of the element being inserted relative to the container (e.g., a container of persons in an insurance application could require its elements to be within a certain age range). Because the mixins do not depend on each other, the compositions `Bounds-Checker<ElementChecker<Container>` > and `ElementChecker` `<BoundsChecker<Container>` > are both valid and equivalent.

4.5.4   Static Parameterization

Parameterized classes (e.g., templates in C++) are well suited for implementing statically bound, simultaneous and nonsimultaneous dimensions. Figure 4–24 shows the implementation of two simultaneous dimensions from Figure 4–20 using static parameterization. Because UML does not provide any notation for associating parameters with candidate parameter value classes, we use UML *notes* for this purpose (e.g., `Alternative Transmissions`).

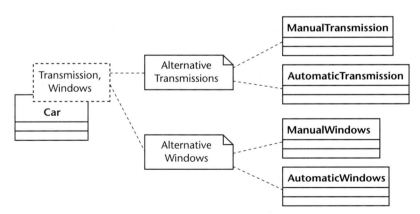

Figure 4-24 *Implementation of two simultaneous dimensions using static parameters*

4.5.5 Dynamic Parameterization

If we use dynamic method binding, a variable can hold objects of different classes at runtime. We refer to this mechanism as *dynamic parameterization*. In C++, the classes of the varying objects must have a common superclass that declares a virtual interface. This is shown in Figure 4–25. The class diagram implements the feature diagram with two simultaneous dimensions from Figure 4–20. In a Smalltalk implementation, the classes `Transmission` and `Windows` are not needed. In a Java implementation, we would implement `Transmission` and `Windows` as interfaces.

Dynamic parameterization should be used only if dynamic binding is required (or if changeable binding is required and no other appropriate technology is available).[10] Otherwise, we should use static parameterization to avoid binding overhead and the inclusion of unused alternative features in the application.

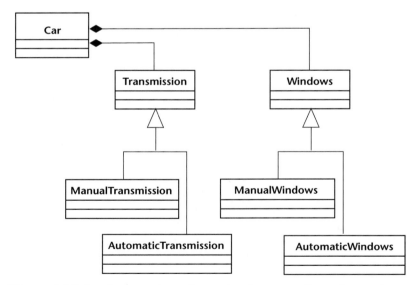

Figure 4-25 *Implementation of two simultaneous dimensions using dynamic parameterization*

---

10. Please note that some implementations of OO languages optimize dynamic dispatch using techniques such as method inline caching (e.g., most Smalltalk implementations) and adaptive compilation (e.g., Self [Höl94]).

4.6 Implementing Constraints

Feature models contain not only mandatory and variable features, but also dependencies between variable features. These dependencies are expressed in the form of constraints and default dependency rules. Constraints specify valid and invalid feature combinations. Default dependency rules suggest default values for unspecified parameters based on other parameters.

Constraints and default dependency rules allow us to implement automatic configuration. For example, in addition to our feature diagram of a car (see Figure 4–14), we could also have an extra feature diagram defining the three high-level alternative features of a car: *limousine*, *standard*, and *economy*. Furthermore, we could have the following vertical default dependency rules relating the three high-level features and the variable detail features from Figure 4–14.

♦ Limousine implies automatic transmission and electric and gasoline engines.
♦ Standard implies automatic transmission and gasoline engine.
♦ Economy implies manual transmission and gasoline engine.

Given these default dependency rules, we can specify a car with all extras as: *limousine and pulls a trailer*.

Just as we need variability mechanisms in order to implement feature diagrams in other models, we also need means of implementing constraints. If we use the UML for analysis and design models, we can express constraints using the UML Object Constraint Language [Rat98d]. For the concrete implementation of constraints, however, we have several possibilities. Configuration constraints at the file level can be managed by a configuration management system. Configuration constraints at the class and object level are best implemented as a part of the reusable software. In the case of dynamic configuration, we would implement them simply by writing runtime configuration code (e.g., *object factory* code configuring the "hot spots" of an OO framework at runtime). In the case of static configuration (e.g., configuring statically parameterized classes), we need static metaprogramming. Static metaprogramming allows us to write metacode that is executed by the compiler. Thus, we write static configuration code as static metacode. This configuration metacode and the parameterized classes to be configured constitute one program. When we give this program to the compiler, the compiler configures the classes by executing the configuration metacode, and then compiles the configured classes, all in one compiler run. We will discuss static metaprogramming in C++ in Chapter 10. If our programming language does not support static metaprogramming, we could still use a preprocessor. However, the problem with this approach is that a preprocessor usually does not have access to the programming language level (e.g., it cannot read the values of static constants, access class metainformation, and so on). Finally, we could also implement a dedicated generator.

Simple constraints can be implemented directly as imperative code. However, if we have to manage a large number of complicated constraints, it may be necessary to use a constraint solver engine.

4.7 Tool Support for Feature Models

As of this writing, feature models are not supported by the commercially available and widely used CASE tools. In order to adequately support feature modeling, a CASE tool should:

♦ Support the feature diagram notation
♦ Help to manage all the additional information required by feature models
♦ Allow us to hyperlink feature models with other models (e.g., linking semantic descriptions of features with other models, providing traceability links to other models, and so on)

An additional useful feature would be a constraint management facility (including consistency checking) for complex feature models. As noted in [GFA98], some kind of integration with configuration management would also be useful.

Given the growing acceptance of the UML in the software industry, it would certainly be desirable to extend UML with the feature diagram notation.

Griss et al. describe in [GFA98] an approach for implementing the feature diagram notation using the predefined UML modeling elements. They implement features as classes with the stereotype «feature». Furthermore, they use an *optionality attribute* to indicate whether a feature is optional or not and introduce the special node type called "variation point," which corresponds to a dimension in our terminology. Features are related using the *composed_of relationship* and, in the case of dimensions, the *alternative relationship*. Finally, they have a *binding time flag* indicating whether a dimension is bound at use time (e.g., runtime) or at reuse time (e.g., compile or construction time).

The approach in [GFA98] does not distinguish between different kinds of variation points (e.g., different kinds of dimensions, extension points, and inhomogeneous variation points; see Section 4.4.1.7). Second, it does not allow inhomogeneous variation points with alternative subfeatures in the diagram (because there is a special dimension node type). It also does not support or-features. Furthermore, it does not distinguish between availability sites, binding sites, and binding mode.

A very nice feature of the approach by Griss et al. is the possibility of expanding and collapsing features in the diagram. A collapsed feature is represented by an icon. In the expanded version, on the other hand, some of the additional information (e.g., feature category, semantic description, and so on) can be directly viewed and edited.

From our experience, we find it useful to be able to draw all kinds of inhomogeneous variation points in a feature diagram because, in some situations, they allow us to create more concise and natural diagrams. One possibility to extend the approach by Griss et al. to handle inhomogeneous variation points would be to use constraints between relationships. In UML, we can draw a dashed line connecting a number of associations and annotate it with a constraint that refers to all these associations. Thus, we could use such dashed lines annotated with OR or with XOR in order to represent edge decorations. Indeed, the OR-annotated dashed line connecting associations is already predefined in UML. Associations connected by such a dashed line are called *or-associations*. Unfortunately, or-associations actually have XOR-semantics.

To our taste, the approach for implementing a feature diagram notation based on stereotyped classes is an instance of "diagram hacking." In UML, stereotypes are used to define new modeling elements based on existing ones such that the properties of the base elements are inherited. However, as we discussed in Section 4.3, concepts and features are not classes (although some of them may be implemented as classes). Although creating a stereotype for concepts and features derived from classes allows us to inherit some useful properties, we also inherit undesired properties, for example, class properties, such as being able to have attributes and methods. We find this approach quite confusing.

A more adequate approach is to extend the UML metamodel with concepts and features. Of course, we can make the UML feature diagrams look exactly as defined in this chapter. Unfortunately, as of this writing, only very few CASE tools support editing their own metamodels.

Due to this inadequate support for feature modeling by current CASE tools, we maintained our feature models for the different applications described in Chapters 12, 13, and 14 in a word processor.

4.8 Frequently Asked Questions about Feature Diagrams

This section provides answers to a number of frequently asked questions concerning feature diagrams.

Q1: What are the semantics of the edges in a feature diagram?

The edges in a feature diagram do not have any complete semantics of their own. They can only be interpreted together with their decorations. Edges and decorations together only state whether a particular feature (i.e., property) can, must, or cannot be asserted of a concept instance when constructing a featural description of a concept instance. In particular, you should not associate any relationship semantics, such as "consists-of" or "is-part-of" or any other relationship kind, with the edges in a feature diagram. The reason is that a feature diagram models the configurability aspect of a concept, and by associating structural relationship semantics with its edges, you actually start to import structural information into it. Next, you would add cardinalities, roles, and so on. Finally, you would end up with a notation similar to entity-relationship or object diagrams and completely miss the real purpose of feature diagrams. The idea of feature diagrams is to explicitly represent the configurability aspect and leave other aspects, such as structural modeling, to other, more appropriate notations, for example, entity-relationship or object diagrams. The very advantage of feature diagrams is that they avoid cluttering the configurability aspect with other aspects.

Q2: If you cannot associate relationship semantics with the edges of a feature diagram, how do you represent the configurability of relationships?

If you need to represent a relationship in a feature diagram because it is variable—for example, optional or alternative—you simply model it as a feature. We have already seen an example of this technique in the car feature diagram in Figure 4–14, where the optional relationship "pulls a trailer" is modeled as an optional feature.

It is important to keep in mind that a feature is a *property* of a concept instance. And a property is an assertion, that is, a sentence

---

NOTE

You'll find cases of attaching relationship labels to the edges of feature diagrams in the literature. For example, the original FODA description [KCH+90] interprets feature diagram edges as "consists-of" relationships.

in the sense of predicate logic. For example, the semantics of the feature `engine` in Figure 4–14 is the sentence, "Engine is a part of a car." Please do not misinterpret this feature as representing the actual car part *engine*. `engine` is merely the name of the feature, and its semantics is the sentence, "Engine is a part of a car" (which relates an instance of a car and an engine with the part-of relationship). So we would actually keep the sentence "Engine is a part of a car" as a semantic description of the feature `engine` in the feature model. It is important to remember that, in general, the semantic definition of a feature could be arbitrarily complex and could utilize different modeling notations. With appropriate tool support, you could directly navigate from a feature to its semantic definition.

Q3: Isn't a feature diagram just a part-of hierarchy?

No. Feature diagrams merely represent a configuration space of properties. As explained in the previous paragraph, you can represent part-of relationships as features, but features can also represent any other kind of semantic contents. Consequently, you can have a feature that can be implemented as a single component, or an aspect, or certain configurations of components and aspects. For example, the abstract feature "optimized for speed" of a system is not implemented by some single "optimized-for-speed component," but rather by a certain configuration of components maximizing the execution speed. We call such features abstract because they are not implemented as concrete components, but translate to different configurations of concrete components in different situations (i.e., they are implemented using configuration knowledge).

Q4: Wouldn't it be useful to have cardinalities in feature diagrams?

No. At first, you might think that because expressing whether a car has 4 or 6 wheels is an important configuration knowledge, it would be nice to annotate edges with cardinalities. However, because the only semantics of an edge (together with its decorations) is whether to assert a feature or not, annotating it with the cardinality 4 would only mean asserting this feature four times. This is of no use because asserting the sentence "a car has a wheel" one or several times makes no difference—it still means "a car has a wheel". This would be different if we could attach the relationship label "part-of" to the edge. However, as stated before, this is not allowed in order to avoid cluttering feature diagrams with structural information.

An obvious solution is to express cardinalities using features. Figure 4–26 shows you three different ways of representing cardinalities in a feature diagram.

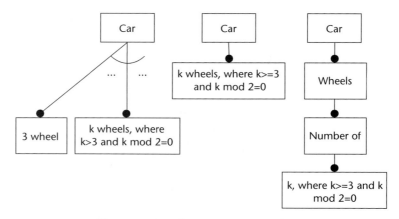

Figure 4-26 *Different ways of representing cardinalities in a feature diagram*

Q5: A feature diagram is a tree. Isn't this a serious limitation?

No. You use the tree structure of a feature diagram to capture the main dependencies between features (using the selection mechanisms *mandatory*, *alternative*, *or*, and *optional*). Dependencies that do not fit into this structure are documented separately as constraints. Using a hierarchical decomposition for the primary structure of a feature configuration space is important for reasons of understandability.

We like to view feature diagrams as follows: Suppose you have a definition of a concept in the form of a database of facts to assert about each particular instance. Each assertion would have to have a precondition stating when it is okay to assert it. Such a database is hard to understand—you don't see its structure. So what you can do is organize it into a tree in a way that nodes represent the assertions, and subnodes can only be asserted if the parent node is asserted. The nice thing about it is that you only have to care about a set of subnodes if their common parent is asserted. Furthermore, you have the selection mechanisms for subnodes (such as alternative, or, optional, and so on). Of course you won't be able to express all preconditions in this tree structure, so you need extra constraints for the remaining dependencies. What is in the tree and what is in the "leftovers" is a matter of taste. But in any case, you should use the tree to convey the primary structure (whatever you believe it to be). A desirable property of the structure is to minimize the number of "leftovers," so that you can view the tree as the first approximation of the database structure. Thus, you see that a feature diagram is a means to represent the structure of a database of assertions! (This also may explain better why we'd like to keep the "base-level" structural information, like relationships and cardinalities, out of feature diagrams.)

4.9 Feature Modeling Process

So far we have discussed how to represent feature models. In the rest of this chapter, we describe how to perform feature modeling.

4.9.1 How to Find Features

In this section, we address the following three important questions.

- What are the sources of features?
- What are the strategies for identifying features?
- What are the general steps in feature modeling?

Sources of features include the following.

- Existing and potential stakeholders
- Domain experts and domain literature
- Existing systems
- Pre-existing models (e.g., use-case models, object models, and so on)
- Models created during development (i.e., you also get new features during design and implementation)

Strategies for identifying features include both top-down and bottom-up strategies.

- Look for important domain terminology that implies variability, for example, checking account versus savings account, diagonal versus lower triangular matrix, thread-safe versus not thread-safe component, and so on. It is important to keep in mind that anything users or client programs might want to control about a concept is a feature. Thus, during feature modeling, we document not only functional features, for example, operations such as matrix addition and multiplication, but also implementation features, such as algorithm variants for implementing the operations, various optimizations, alternative implementation techniques, and so on. In this aspect, Domain Analysis is different from classical software analysis, where the usual rule is to avoid analyzing any implementation issues.
- Examine domain concepts for different sources of variability, for example, different stakeholders, client programs, settings,

Feature starter set

contexts, environments, subjective perspectives, aspects, and so on. In other words, investigate what different sets of requirements these variability sources may postulate for different domain concepts (we discuss these issues in Section 4.9.2).

♦ Use *feature starter sets* to start the analysis. A feature starter set consists of a set of perspectives for modeling concepts. Some combinations of perspectives are more appropriate for a given domain than for another. For example, for abstract data types in algorithmic domains, we use a starter set containing modeling perspectives, such as attributes, operations, synchronization, memory management, optimizations, and so on (see Section 5.8.2.2.1). Other domains and concepts may require investigating other perspectives, such as distribution, security, transactions, historization, and so on. Starter sets may also contain examples of features, sources of features, and so on. Thus, starter sets are reusable resources capturing modeling experience. As stated earlier, there will be different starter sets for different categories of domains. Ideally, feature starter sets are updated during each new project. We discuss feature starter sets in Section 4.9.2.

♦ Look for features at any point in the development. As mentioned before, we have high-level system requirements features, architectural features, subsystem and component features, and implementation features. Thus, we have to maintain and update feature models during the entire development cycle. We may identify all kinds of features by investigating variability in use case, analysis, design, and implementation models.

♦ Identify more features than you initially intend to implement. We found that this useful strategy allows us to "create some room for growth." Although we will not be able to identify all features that may be relevant in the future, it is a big gain if we identify some of them. At some point in domain design, there should be an extra scoping activity where we actually decide which features to implement. Therefore, we should record priorities of variable features when we first document them. By having documented potential features, we will be able to develop more robust client and configuration interfaces, even if not all of the features will be implemented at first. We will see a concrete example of applying this strategy in Chapter 14.

Feature modeling is a continuous, iterative process with the following steps.

1. Record similarities between instances, that is, common features, for example, all accounts have an account number.

2. Record differences between instances, that is, variable features, for example, some accounts are checking accounts and some are savings accounts.

3. Organize features in feature diagrams (see Section 4.4.1), that is, organize features into hierarchies and classify them as mandatory, alternative, optional, or-, and optional alternative features.

4. Analyze feature combinations and interactions. We may find certain combinations to be invalid (*mutual-exclusion constraints*), for example, a collection cannot be *unordered* and *sorted* at the same time. We may discover dependencies allowing us to deduce the presence of some features from the presence of others (*requires constraints*), for example, if a collection is *sorted*, it is also *ordered*. We may also find innovative combinations, which we did not think of previously. Furthermore, when we investigate the relationship of two features, we may discover other features. For example, when we analyze different combinations of matrix shapes (e.g., rectangular, diagonal, triangular, and so on) and matrix element containers (e.g., array, vector, list, and so on), we realize that even for the same combination of shape and container, different layouts for storing the elements in the container are possible (e.g., a rectangular matrix can be stored in a two-dimensional array row- or column-wise). Therefore, we introduce the new feature *storage format*. Similarly, by investigating the relationship between matrix operations and matrix shapes, we will realize that various *optimizations* of the operations due to different shapes are possible. We say that new features may emerge from the *interaction* of other features.

5. Record all the additional information regarding features, such as short semantic descriptions, rationales for each feature, stakeholders and client programs interested in each feature, examples of systems with a given feature, constraints, default dependency rules, availability sites, binding sites, binding modes, open/closed attributes, and priorities. All these concepts are explained in Section 4.4.2.

We refer to these steps as the "micro-cycle" of feature modeling because they are usually executed in small, quick cycles. To give you a concrete example of how to perform feature modeling, we describe how we actually came up with the feature models during the development of the matrix computation library described in Chapter 14.

Start with steps 1 and 2 in the form of a brainstorming session by writing down as many features as you can. Then try to cluster them and organize them into feature hierarchies while identifying the kinds of variability involved (i.e., alternative, optional, and so on). Finally, refine the feature diagrams by checking different combinations of the variable features, adding new features, and writing down additional constraints. Maintain and update the initial feature models during the rest of the development cycle. You may also start new diagrams at any point during the development.

As the feature modeling process progresses, some new features may be recognized as special cases of old ones, and other new features may subsume other old features. For example, we may have already documented the matrix shapes square, diagonal, lower triangular, upper triangular, bidiagonal, and tridiagonal. Later, we recognize that the shape *band* subsumes all these shapes because each of these special shapes can be described as the band shape with certain lower and upper bandwidth. However, this does not imply that we should replace the special shapes by the band shape in the feature model. The feature model rather should include all these shapes as well as the relationships between them. If there is a name for a certain property in the domain vocabulary, it usually indicates the relevance of this property. Obviously, properties that play an important role in the domain (e.g., certain matrix shapes that are more common than others and/or are important for optimizing certain algorithms) should have unique names in the model.

Section 5.9.7 describes an approach for deriving reuser- and implementer-oriented feature diagrams from the analysis feature diagrams. Such an approach is important because the implementers of features have a different focus than the reusers of features. The reusers need features that allow them to specify their needs at the most adequate level of detail (which is different for different reusers or client programs). Implementers, on the other hand, decompose their solution into elementary, reusable pieces, which they can use and reuse within the implementation and across implementations of different product lines. Some of them may be too implementation oriented to be part of the reuser-oriented feature diagrams.

During development, we have to maintain traceability links from the feature diagrams to other models and update the domain dictionary whenever we introduce new features.

A feature diagram and the additional information constitute a feature model. See the discussion of feature models in Section 4.4.

4.9.2 Role of Variability in Modeling

Now that we know how to perform feature modeling, we would like to investigate how feature modeling fits into other modeling activities. However, before we address this question, we first need to introduce the principle of separation of concerns (see Section 4.9.2.1) and two important decomposition techniques based on this principle (see Section 4.9.2.2). Then we discuss the integration of feature modeling and the decomposition techniques in Section 4.9.2.3

4.9.2.1 Separation of Concerns

One of the most important principles of engineering is the *principle of separation of concerns* [Dij76]. The principle acknowledges that we cannot deal with many issues at once, but rather with one at a time. It also states that important issues should be represented in programs intentionally (i.e., explicitly, declaratively, and with little or no "extra noise") and should be well localized. This facilitates understandability, adaptability, reusability, and the many other good qualities of a program because intentionality and localization allow us to easily verify how a program implements our requirements.

Unfortunately, the relevant issues are usually mutually dependent and overlapping because they all concern one common model (i.e., our program being constructed). Thus, if we try to represent all these issues explicitly and locally, we will introduce a lot of redundancies. This causes maintenance problems because we have to make sure that all the redundant representations are consistent. Also, the overall model becomes very complex because we have to maintain all the knowledge relating the different representations.

On the other hand, if we choose a less redundant representation of our solution to a problem, some issues will be well localized and others will not. This is similar to the idea of representing a signal in the time domain and in the frequency domain (see Figure 4–27). In the time domain, we can explicitly see the amplitude of the signal at any time, but we cannot see the component frequencies. In the frequency domain, on the other hand, we can see the component frequencies, but we cannot see the amplitude of the whole signal at a given time. If we keep both representations, we see both properties, but introduce redundancy.

Ideally, we would like to store our solution to a problem in some efficient representation, that is, one with minimal redundancies, and have some supporting machinery that allows us to extract any perspective on the model we might need. It should be possible

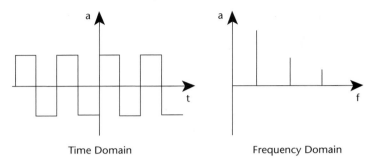

Figure *4-27 Representation of a signal in the time and in the frequency domain (from [Kic98])*

to make changes in the extracted model and have the machinery update the underlying model automatically for us. (Of course, as we make more and more changes, the machinery might need to transform the underlying representation into some other form to reduce the accumulated redundancies.)

Unfortunately, our ideal solution is impractical—at least given today's technology. First, we would have to model an enormous amount of formal knowledge in order to be able to extract any desired perspective on a large system automatically. Second, we would need some very efficient transformation and reasoning machinery (most probably involving AI techniques) to perform the extraction. Nevertheless, transformation systems and other tools, such as some CASE tools, already allow us to compute different perspectives on software models, for example, extracting control and data flow. Furthermore, the Intentional Programming system (see Chaper 11) has the potential to bring us closer to this vision.

We have to look for more practical solutions to address our problems: The purpose of today's modeling techniques is to develop models that meet the requirements (i.e., functional requirements and qualities, such as performance, throughput, availability, failure safety, and so on) and, at the same time, strike a balance between:

♦ Separation of concerns (i.e., having the most important issues as localized as possible)
♦ Complexity of compiler (or view rendering) implementation (i.e., trying to localize certain issues may considerably increase the complexity of the needed transformations; see Section 8.7.2)
♦ Minimal redundancy

♦ Ability to accommodate anticipated change and also unanticipated change to some degree[11]

The result of such a balance is what we might call a "clean" and adaptable code. Different decomposition techniques help us to achieve this balance.

4.9.2.2 Decomposition Techniques

We distinguish between two important kinds of decomposition of a concept.[12]

♦ *Modular decomposition:* Modular decomposition involves decomposing systems into *hierarchical (*i.e., *modular) units* (e.g., modules, components, objects, functions, procedures, and so on). The word "hierarchical" indicates that a unit may contain other units, and so on. The boundaries of such units are drawn in such a way that they encapsulate some cohesive "model neighborhoods." The goal is to achieve high cohesion within the units and minimal coupling between the units.

♦ *Aspectual decomposition:* The main idea behind aspectual decomposition is to organize the description of a concept (e.g., a system, a domain, a component, a function, and so on) into a set of perspectives, where each perspective concerns itself with a different aspect and none of which is itself sufficient to describe the entire concept. An important property of such decomposition is that each perspective yields a model with a different structure, and all of these models refer to the same concept. As a consequence, there are locations in one model that refer to locations in other models (e.g., see Figure 8–7 in Section 8.5.2), which is referred to as *crosscutting*. Examples of aspects include interactions, algorithms, data structures, data flow, synchronization, error handling, memory management, and historization. More

---

11. Accommodating unanticipated change involves strategies, such as avoiding overspecification (i.e., fixing more detail than necessary) and providing mechanisms for noninvasive changes. An example of an approach for avoiding the overspecification of data structures in OO programs is Demeter. We discuss it in Section 8.3.3. Mechanisms for achieving noninvasive changes are discussed in Sections 8.3, 8.5.1.3, and 8.5.7.

12. Please note that, in this context, we view *decomposition* as a constructive activity: In problem reduction by decomposition, we do not decompose any existing structure into its elementary parts, but we actually create the structure and its parts. For example, if we implemented an analysis object using three implementation objects, we had to construct three implementation objects that were not there before.

examples of aspects are given in Chapter 8. Most of the existing modeling techniques apply some form of aspectual decomposition. For example, the UML [Rat98c, BRJ99] deploys different diagrams to describe different aspects of systems (e.g., class diagrams, use cases, interaction diagrams, state-transition diagrams, activity diagrams, and state-transition diagrams). It is important to note that even if we stay within one aspect, we still want to reduce its perceived complexity by dividing it into modular units.

The basic difference between aspects and modular units[13] is shown in Figure 4–28. The drawing on the left shows that modular units are cleanly encapsulated and organized into a hierarchy. The drawing on the right shows that an aspect *crosscuts* a number of modular units.

Thus, the quality of being an aspect is a relative one: A model is an aspect of another model if it crosscuts its structure. The aspect shown in Figure 4–28 is an aspect with respect to the hierarchical structure also shown in this figure. However, at the same time, the aspect could be a modular unit of another hierarchical structure not shown in the figure.

Figure 4–29 shows another view of an aspect: Model A is an aspect of Model C because it refers to many locations in C. For example, C could be a class implementing some abstract data structure and A could be a synchronization specification referring to the methods of the abstract data structure.

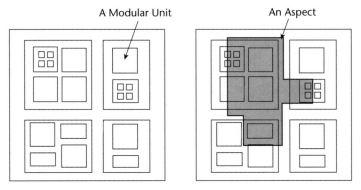

Figure 4-28 Modular versus aspectual decomposition

<hr/>

13. We use the word *modular unit* because, in many languages, *modules* have the predefined meaning of units of compilations.

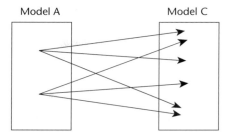

Figure 4-29 *Example of an aspect*

Modular decomposition allows us to do simple refinement by adding structure that never crosses the boundaries of the already established modular units. Whenever we have to add structure that crosses these boundaries, we are actually applying aspectual decomposition.

Aspectual decomposition and modular decomposition complement each other and should be used in combination. They correspond to the natural modeling strategies of humans: We deploy practices of both investigating things from different perspectives and dividing them into hierarchies.

Aspectual decomposition is investigated in the area of Aspect-Oriented Programming (AOP), which we discuss in Chapter 8. As we stated previously, aspectual decomposition is quite common in software development (e.g., the different aspects used in analysis and design methods). However, the AOP research gives aspectual decomposition some new perspectives.

♦ AOP encourages the introduction of new aspects rather than adhering to a small set of general aspects (as in the case of existing OOA/D methods).
♦ It emphasizes the need for specialized aspects and specialized combinations of aspects for different categories of domains.
♦ It postulates the need to support aspects not only in design models, but also in the implementation. In particular, there is the need for new composition mechanisms and aspect languages (ideally, implemented as modular language extensions; see Section 8.7.3).
♦ It concentrates on achieving quality improvements due to aspectual decomposition, such as reduced code tangling, better understandability, maintainability, adaptability, reusability, and so on.

It should be noted that aspects represent perspectives that prove to be useful in constructing past systems, that is, they are based on experience. Thus, different systems of aspects record modeling experience in different categories of domains.

4.9.2.3 Variability in Modeling

In this section, we investigate the question of how variability modeling and the different decomposition techniques fit together.

Variability plays an important role in our modern society, and strategies for coping with variability constitute an essential prerequisite for success. This situation has been accurately characterized by Reenskaug [Ree96].

> It is popular to claim that in our modern society, change is the only constant factor. Enterprises have to be able to adapt to a continuously changing environment.
>
> We believe this to be both true and misleading. It is true in the sense that an enterprise has to keep changing to adapt to changes in its environment. It is also true in the sense that a business has to change the core of its operations to accommodate the transition from manual to computer-based information processing; that it has to move its rule-based operations from people to computer; and that it has to cultivate the creativity, responsibility, and problem-solving capabilities of its human staff.
>
> It is misleading in the sense that you cannot change everything all the time. So the challenge to the evolving enterprise is to identify what can be kept stable and what has to be kept fluid. The stable elements of a business form an infrastructure on which it can build a light and rapidly changing superstructure.

Obviously, software is another point in case. We have to explicitly address variability during modeling. As we have seen so far, this is even more important for reusable software.

If the items that we model contain variability, the variability will emerge in some aspects and modules somehow. In other words, the variability aspect crosscuts modules and other aspects. Indeed, variability is just another aspect of the reusable software.

As stated previously, reusable software usually contains a lot of variability. Therefore, we have to apply variability modeling *in coordination* with other aspectual and modular decomposition techniques. By applying them in a coordinated fashion, we make sure that decomposition decisions are influenced by variability needs. Adding variability "after the fact"—just as adding any other aspect—may cause significant code tangling.

Before we move on, let us first clarify what we specifically mean by variability. In this book, we talk about the variability of *how* computation is done, not about the fact that data gets modified all the time in a running program.[14] We have two kinds of variability sources: *internal variability sources* and *external variability sources*.

The internal source of variability is the evolution of state. For example, if a collection grows beyond a certain limit, we might want to switch to a different sorting algorithm.

External variability sources are more versatile. They include, for example, different stakeholders (including different users, developers, and customers), different client programs, different environments, usage settings, changing requirements, and so on.

In the previous sections, we discussed feature modeling as an effective technique for modeling variability. The question now is how we can integrate feature modeling and the other decomposition techniques.

An example of such an integration is DEMRAL (Domain Engineering Method for Algorithmic Libraries), which we describe in Chapter 5. In DEMRAL, feature modeling and the other decomposition techniques are applied in a coordinated fashion as follows.

- ◆ *Modular decomposition:* The first activity in DEMRAL Domain Modeling is identifying key concepts. DEMRAL specializes in modeling two categories of concepts: abstract data types (ADTs) and algorithms. The key ADTs and algorithm families are later encapsulated in separate packages. New objects and algorithms may also be identified during feature modeling. Other Domain Engineering methods may look for other kinds of concepts, such as workflows, clients, servers, agents, interactions, use cases, and so on.
- ◆ *Aspectual decomposition:* Aspectual decomposition is fundamental to DEMRAL. It is performed in parallel with feature modeling. The idea is to provide so-called feature starter sets, which in the case of DEMRAL are basically sets of aspects suitable for algorithmic domains (see Section 5.8.2.2). The modeling proceeds by modeling each aspect separately in an iterative fashion. Other methods will define their own starter sets appropriate for other kinds of concepts.
- ◆ *Feature modeling:* Feature modeling is performed for each aspect in separation in an iterative fashion. Features relevant for the

---

14. Variability of how computation is done ranges from switching between procedures using flags to program code modification.

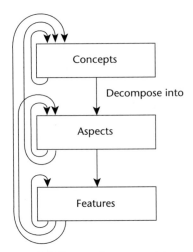

Figure 4-30 *Interaction of different decomposition techniques in DEMRAL*

configurability aspect are organized into feature diagrams. Other features may lead to the development (or reuse) of specialized aspect languages or modular language extensions. Relationships between features of different aspects are also modeled.

♦ *Subjective decomposition:* Subjective decomposition is based on modeling different subjective perspectives of different stakeholders (e.g., users, developers) on a system or a domain. Subjective decomposition has been popularized by the work of Harrison and Ossher on Subject-Oriented Programming (SOP). We discuss SOP in Section 8.3.1. It is important to note that subjects may crosscut many aspects and modules of a system. Subjectivity is accounted for in DEMRAL by considering different stakeholders and annotating features by their stakeholders.

The interaction of the different decomposition techniques is summarized in Figure 4–30.

Chapter 5

The Process of Generative Programming

5.1 Why Is This Chapter Worth Reading?

So far you've learned about Domain Engineering, which you can use to develop and implement a model for a family of systems, that is, a domain model. Being able to develop domain models is the first step towards Generative Programming, however. In Generative Programming, we are not interested in just any kind of domain models, but in *generative* domain models, which allow us to automatically generate a family member based on a specification. In this chapter, you'll learn about the elements of a generative domain model, the steps needed to develop such a model, and domain-specific languages, which are used to specify family members. Finally, we'll give you an example of specializing an existing Domain Engineering method for Generative Programming.

5.2 Generative Domain Models

Generative Programming is about automating the manufacture of intermediate and end-products (i.e., components and applications). This requires modeling product families, designing some means for "ordering" products (i.e., specifying products), providing the implementation components to assemble the products from, specifying the mapping from product specifications to concrete assemblies of implementation components, and implementing this mapping using generators. The "products" that we want to automatically generate range from classes or procedures to whole subsystems or systems.

*Problem space,
solution space,
and
configuration
knowledge*

The key to automating the manufacture of systems is a *generative domain model*, which consists of a *problem space*, a *solution space*, and the *configuration knowledge* mapping between them (see Figure 5–1).

The solution space consists of the implementation components with all their possible combinations. The implementation components are designed to maximize their combinability (i.e., you should be able to combine them in as many ways as possible), minimize redundancy (i.e., minimize code duplication), and maximize reuse. The problem space, on the other hand, consists of the application-oriented concepts and features that application programmers would like to use to express their needs. The configuration knowledge specifies illegal feature combinations (certain combinations of features may be not allowed), default settings (if the application does not specify certain features, some reasonable defaults are assumed), default dependencies (some defaults may be computed based on some other features), construction rules (combinations of certain features translate into certain combinations of implementation components), and optimization rules (certain combinations of implementation components may be more optimal than others).

An important principle in the design of the problem space is that as an application programmer, when you request a component from a generative library, you should be able to specify only as much detail as necessary. You should not be *forced* to specify too much detail: This would make your client code unnecessarily dependent on the implementation of the library. However, if necessary, you should be *able to* specify details or even supply your own implementations for some aspects. Defaults, default dependencies, and hard constraints (i.e., illegal feature combinations) make this kind of flexibility possible. For example, when you use a generative matrix library, you can just request a matrix (if you don't know any special properties at

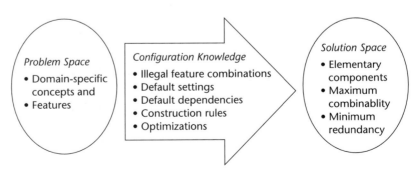

Figure 5-1 *Elements of a generative domain model*

NOTE

The properties of implementation components, that is, maximal combinability, minimal redundancy, and maximum reuse, are also the properties usually required from generic components. Thus, the principles of Generic Programming apply to the solution space. An even higher level of genericity of the implementation components can be achieved using Aspect-Oriented Programming. We'll discuss Generic Programming in Chapter 6 and Aspect-Oriented Programming in Chapter 8.

compile time) and you will get a general, rectangular matrix with dynamically allocated memory. However, if you know that the matrices you'll need at runtime are band matrices of a fixed size, you can request a band matrix with statically allocated memory. Furthermore, some applications may require exotic matrix shapes and formats that are not provided by the library. In this case, you should be able to contribute your own implementation of these aspects.

An important advantage of the separation between the problem and solution space is the possibility to evolve both spaces in a relatively independent way. In particular, you can add new components to the solution space or improve the existing ones and, as long as they can cover the functionality delineated by the problem space, you won't even have to change the existing client code. This is so because the client code orders systems and components by means of the language of the problem space, and the generator takes care of the mapping of the problem specifications onto the configurations of the new components. Thus, adding new components only requires modifying the generator. In fact, during the development of the case studies described in Part III, we were able to modify the layered architecture of the solution space by adding new layers without having to modify the problem space. On the other hand, you can also evolve the existing domain-specific languages of the problem space or even develop alternative ones. The target components need to cover the required functionality, but they do not have to be optimal in terms of combinability and minimal redundancy right from the beginning because you can improve them over time without affecting the problem space.

The problem space will contain different kinds of features including

♦ *Concrete features*: A concrete feature is directly mapped to one (possibly parameterized) component; for example, sorting can be directly implemented by a sorting component.

◆ *Aspect features:* An aspect feature is mapped to an *aspect* in the sense of Aspect-Oriented Programming (see Chapter 8). An *aspect* is a kind of modularity that affects many other components, for example, a declarative description of the synchronization of a number of components. Aspects require code weaving, which involves inserting aspect code into many components.

◆ *Abstract features:* Abstract features do not have any direct implementations whatsoever. They are implemented by appropriate combinations of components and aspects. Examples of abstract features are performance requirements, such as optimizing for speed, or space, or accuracy.

As you can see, Generic Programming and Aspect-Oriented Programming are important implementation techniques for the solution space. We'll discuss them later in Chapters 6, 7, and 8. And the key to abstract features lies in the configuration knowledge, which is implemented using generators. Depending on the complexity of the configuration space, the configuration process may be an algorithmic one (for simple configuration spaces) or search-based (for more complex configuration spaces). We'll discuss different generator implementation technologies in Chapters 9, 10, and 11.

5.3 Main Development Steps in Generative Programming

Generative Programming involves developing and implementing a generative domain model for a family of systems. The following are the main development steps in Generative Programming.

1. Domain scoping
2. Feature modeling and concept modeling
3. Designing a common architecture and identifying the implementation components
4. Specifying domain-specific notations for "ordering" systems
5. Specifying the configuration knowledge
6. Implementing the implementation components
7. Implementing the domain-specific notations
8. Implementing the configuration knowledge using generators

These steps specify what has to be done during analysis, design, and implementation, but not in what order. In our experience, it is best to perform these steps iteratively and incrementally. Typically, you will do some domain analysis, design the target architecture and the implementation components, implement the implementation components, test their assembly manually, design the ordering means and the generator, and finally implement the ordering means and generator. At each step, you may need to go back to modify or extend the existing models and implementations. You would repeat this process to cover more functionality. We would like to emphasize that we found it very useful to practice the manual assembly for a while before trying to build the generator; we do not recommend that you skip this step.

You will see concrete examples of carrying out these steps in Part III of this book. However, before we get there, Part II of this book will discuss the technologies needed in Generative Programming. The first three chapters of Part II focus on technologies for developing the implementation components (i.e., the solution space): Generic Programming (see Chapter 6), Component-Oriented Template-Based C++ Programming Techniques (see Chapter 7), and Aspect-Oriented Programming (see Chapter 8). It is important to note that the principles of Generic and Aspect-Oriented Programming will be also useful in the design of domain-specific notations (i.e., in the problem space). The remaining three chapters of Part II will then discuss technologies for implementing the domain-specific notations and generators: Generators (see Chapter 9), Static Metaprogramming in C++ (see Chapter 10), and Intentional Programming (see Chapter 11), which is a perfect implementation platform for Generative Programming.

Many of the development steps of Generative Programming listed earlier are already familiar to you from the previous chapters. Steps 1–2 correspond to Domain Analysis, steps 3–5 correspond to Domain Design, and finally, steps 6–8 correspond to Domain Implementation. Thus, Domain Engineering provides the necessary foundation for Generative Programming. However, because Generative Programming aims for the highest levels of automation, the Domain Engineering methods suitable for Generative Programming have some special properties, which we'll discuss next.

5.4 Adapting Domain Engineering for Generative Programming

Domain Engineering provides the necessary foundation for Generative Programming: It focuses on system families and helps you to model the problem space, find the implementation components, and model the configuration knowledge.

As you may remember from Section 2.4, the goals of Domain Design are to develop a common architecture for a system family and to devise a production plan for the family members. For the production plan, we presented three different levels of automation: manual assembly, automated assembly support, and automatic assembly. An example of a library with manual assembly is the STL. Automated assembly support is available in IBM's San Francisco Frameworks, where you can use specialized browsers to locate components and wizards and GUI builders to generate partial aspects of applications. In Generative Programming, we aim for the highest level of automation, that is, automatic assembly.

To be suitable for Generative Programming, a Domain Engineering method has to include the following two activities.

♦ Develop an appropriate means for "ordering" concrete family members
♦ Model the configuration knowledge to a level of detail that is amenable to automation

Concrete systems can be "ordered" (i.e., specified) using textual or graphical domain-specific languages. The ordering process can be supported by interactive tools (possibly with graphical interfaces), which help the user to avoid errors or to detect them quickly. The design of system ordering means is part of Domain Design.

A Domain Engineering method for Generative Programming has to support the modeling of configuration knowledge with all its elements including the illegal feature combinations (i.e., hard constraints), default settings, default dependencies (i.e., weak constraints), construction rules, and optimizations. The configuration knowledge has to be specified in a detailed and precise form, so that it can be implemented using generators.

Generating full applications implies that we need generators for the application logic, user interfaces, database integration, network integration, and so on. Furthermore, you might also want to generate documentation for the generated applications (including manuals, tutorials, help systems, maintenance and troubleshooting notes, and so on). This is so because you neither want to write a new manual or tutorial variant for each newly generated member of a product line nor do you want to give the user of one generated member the documentation for the full family. Another category of artifacts to generate are test data, test scripts, and profiling and testing instrumentation code.

We surveyed different Domain Engineering methods in Chapter 2, and, as you may remember, most methods are intended to be specialized in the context of your organization and the target category of domains. Different domain categories involve different kinds of domain concepts, for example, business systems require modeling business processes and data, and automatic control systems involve modeling state machines and timing conditions. When you specialize a general Domain Engineering method, such as ODM, for a particular domain category, you can also add the steps required for Generative Programming, that is, developing system "ordering" facilities and specifying and implementing configuration knowledge. The form of these steps will also depend on the kind and size of artifacts to be generated (e.g., single classes or whole systems).

Next, we will give you a concrete example of specializing ODM for developing generative algorithmic libraries. You can use this example as a blueprint for developing your own specialized methods for other kinds of domains. But before showing the example, we'll first discuss the concept of domain-specific languages, which are central to Generative Programming.

5.5 Domain-Specific Languages

A domain-specific language (DSL) is a specialized, problem-oriented language. Domain-specific languages play an important role in Generative Programming because they are used to "order" concrete members of a system family.

Domain-specific languages can be textual (e.g., SQL) or graphical (e.g., the graphical specification of a GUI in a GUI builder). They can also have different levels of specialization. You can have

---

NOTE

In the context of domain-specific languages, we use the term "language" in a very general sense. The language could be a separate textual language, such as SQL, or it could be some graphical notation. Furthermore, the language could also be implemented as a conventional library interface consisting of procedures and classes in a general-purpose programming language. In this approach, procedures, classes, and methods represent the vocabulary of the domain-specific language. This way of implementing domain-specific languages has certain limitations, such as the inability to express domain-specific optimizations, domain-specific error reporting, or domain-specific syntax. However, some general-purpose languages may provide built-in metaprogramming facilities that allow you to incorporate such features into procedure and class libraries. For example, in C++, you can use template metaprogramming to implement domain-specific code generation and optimization.

more general modeling DSLs, for example, for expressing synchronization constraints or more specialized, application-oriented DSLs, for example, for defining financial products. In general, you will need several different DSLs to specify a complete application. Furthermore, you may even provide several different DSLs designed for different categories of target users to specify one single application aspect, for instance a version for "dummies" and an advanced version.

Depending on the implementation technology, we distinguish between:

♦ *Fixed, separate DSLs:* Examples of such languages are TeX and SQL. These languages are usually implemented by a separate language translator. These are the kinds of DSLs that most people think of when they hear the acronym "DSL." Unfortunately, these are also the most problematic kinds of DSLs. Developing a translator for a whole language from scratch and maintaining it is usually quite costly. Furthermore, such separate DSLs often contribute to the creation of noninteroperable "technology islands."

♦ *Embedded DSLs:* Embedded DSLs are usually embedded in a general-purpose programming language. The simplest way of implementing embedded DSLs is to use classes and procedures. Unfortunately, this approach has some limitations, such as the inability to express domain-specific optimizations, domain-specific error reporting, or domain-specific syntax. However, some general-purpose languages may provide built-in metaprogramming facilities that will allow you to incorporate such features into procedure and class libraries. For example, in C++, you can use template metaprogramming to implement domain-specific code generation and optimization. Embedded SQL is an example of an embedded DSL, but in most implementations, the SQL code will not be checked during the compilation of its host program. In such cases, errors in the SQL code are detected at runtime, when the code is sent to the server.

♦ *Modularly composable DSLs:* The idea of modularly composable DSLs is to view each DSL as a component. We can have larger or smaller DSL components and they can be composed in different configurations. There are two kinds of modular DSLs: encapsulated DSLs and aspectual DSLs. Encapsulated DSLs (e.g., embedded SQL) are easier to compose because they do not influence the semantics of other DSLs in a composition. Unfortunately, they cannot capture all relevant concerns of application development. Aspectual DSLs (e.g., a language for expressing synchronization constraints or error handling) are those that influence the semantics of other languages, and their implementations have to interact in more complicated ways with the implementations of other DSLs they are supposed to work with. Implementing modularly composable DSLs requires a common language implementation platform providing all the necessary infrastructure for implementing "language plug-ins." An example of such a platform is the Intentional Programming system, which promotes the idea of modularly composable languages. We'll discuss it in Chapter 11.

Modularly composable DSLs have great advantages over monolithic DSLs, including

- ◆ *Reusability:* We can break monolithic languages into modular language extensions, allowing us to use the latter in different configurations.
- ◆ *Scalability:* We can develop a small system using a small configuration of necessary language components. When the system grows to encompass new aspects, we can add new language extensions addressing the new aspects to the initial configuration. Modular language extensions avoid the well-known problems of large and monolithic DSLs that are hard to evolve (see e.g., [DK98]).
- ◆ *Fast feature turnover:* Modular language extensions are a faster vehicle for distributing new language features than conventional, closed compilers. Also, they have to survive based only on their merits because they can be loaded and unloaded at any time. This is not the case for language features of fixed languages, in which case it is usually not possible to get rid of questionable features once they are part of a language (because there may be users depending on them).

It is important to note that, from the linguistic viewpoint, conventional libraries of procedures or classes extend a programming language within its syntax because they introduce new vocabulary (i.e., new abstractions) for describing problems at a higher level. Such extensions are adequate as long as we do not require

- ◆ Syntax extensions
- ◆ Semantic extensions or modifications of language constructs
- ◆ Domain-specific optimizations
- ◆ Domain-specific type systems
- ◆ Domain-specific error checking and reporting

Some languages allow us to implement domain-specific optimizations, error checking, and type systems without leaving the syntax of the language, for example, C++ has this capability thanks to static metaprogramming. Other languages allow us to extend their syntax and semantics by extending the libraries defining them, for example, Smalltalk and CLOS (Common Lisp Object System). You'll see examples of both kinds of extensions in Chapters 8 and 10.

In general, technologies for implementing embedded and modular DSLs covering domain-specific optimizations, error checking, type systems, syntactic extensions, and modifications of language constructs include the following.

♦ *Preprocessors:* Preprocessors are popular for extending existing programming languages. They usually expand macros embedded into the target programming language, which is referred to as the

NOTE ON DOMAIN-SPECIFIC OPTIMIZATIONS

Domain-specific optimizations are usually much more effective than the optimizations normally implemented in conventional compilers. This is so because domain-specific optimizations can utilize domain-specific knowledge, whereas conventional compilers can only perform optimizations at the level of the general-purpose language they implement. Domain-specific optimizations are the key to being able to write clean and easy-to-understand code and still have it compiled into a high-performance executable. For example, if we naively implement matrix addition in an OO language using overloaded binary operators, the performance of such implementation will be unacceptable. Given the expression M1+M2+M3, the sum of the matrices M1 and M2 will be computed first and the intermediate result will be passed as the first argument to the second plus operation in the expression. Unfortunately, intermediate results can cause a significant overhead, especially if the matrices are large. Therefore, such an expression is often manually implemented as a pair of nested loops iterating through rows and columns and adding the corresponding elements of all matrices at once, which neither requires any intermediate results nor an extra pair of loops. The manual implementation, despite its better performance, is more difficult to maintain than the original expression M1+M2+M3. This is so because its intentionality is lost. Domain-specific optimizations offer a solution to this dilemma. In our case, we have to extend the compilation process with a matrix expression optimization, which computes the efficient implementation from the abstract expression automatically. As a result, we can write intentional expressions and get maximum performance at the same time. You'll see how to do this in C++ using template metaprogramming in Chapter 14.

NOTE ON DOMAIN-SPECIFIC ERROR CHECKING AND REPORTING

Domain-specific languages should usually provide domain-specific, compile-time error checking and reporting, but these cannot be implemented by traditional libraries. For example, only some inappropriate uses of the STL components will be detected by the C++ type system. But even if an error in the code using the STL is detected, you'll normally get incomprehensible error reports from the compiler. If the library could contribute domain-specific error checking and reporting to the compilation process, many more inappropriate uses could be detected and reported to the programmer in an intelligible way. As a result, the usage of STL would be greatly simplified.

---

host language. The advantage of preprocessors is that they do not have to understand the host language entirely, and thus their development cost can be much smaller than the cost of developing a compiler for the host language. Moreover, they can be simply deployed in front of any favorite compiler for the host language. Unfortunately, this advantage is also a disadvantage. Errors in the target source are reported by the compiler in terms of the preprocessor output and not in terms of the source given to the preprocessor. Also, debuggers for the host language do not understand the extended language. Thus, preprocessors usually do not adequately support the programmer. Furthermore, if a preprocessor does not completely understand the host language, macros cannot utilize the information contained in the source (e.g., host language constants, constant expressions, and so on), and thus many important kinds of domain-specific optimizations cannot be implemented.

♦ *Languages with metaprogramming support*: Some languages have built-in language extension capabilities. Templates in C++ allow us to implement domain-specific optimizations while staying within the C++ syntax and semantics. Reflective languages, such as Smalltalk or CLOS, allow us to implement any kinds of extensions because their definition is accessible to the programmer as a modifiable and extendible library. The disadvantage of this approach is that it makes it easy for the application programmer to incorporate metacode implementing some ad hoc language extensions in the application. The problem is that this will make the application code hard to understand and maintain. We can avoid it by separating application programming from metaprogramming. Application programming is the job of application programmers and metaprogramming is the job of tool and library developers. Another problem of languages with metaprogramming support is that they usually do not support the metaprogramming task in a comprehensive way, for example, they don't provide special debugging support.

♦ *Modularly extendible compilers and modularly extendible programming environments:* An example of a system in this category is the Intentional Programming (IP) environment described in Chapter 11. Language extensions are implemented in IP as extension libraries, which can extend any part of the programming environment including the editor, compiler, debugger, and so on. IP also clearly separates application programming from metaprogramming and provides an adequate, comprehensive support for metaprogramming.

The latter two technologies allow us to develop *active libraries* [CEG+98], that is, libraries which, in addition to the base procedures and classes to be executed at runtime, also contain metacode for configuration, generation, optimization, error reporting, debugging and profiling, editing and visualization of code, code refactoring, versioning, and so on. Active libraries support application programmers in their task in a more comprehensive way than today's class or procedure libraries.

5.6   DEMRAL: Example of a Domain Engineering Method for Generative Programming

DEMRAL[1] is a specialized Domain Engineering method for developing generative algorithmic libraries. Examples of algorithmic libraries are numerical libraries, container libraries, image processing libraries, image recognition libraries, speech recognition libraries, graph computation libraries, and so on. Such libraries have the following characteristics.

BIBLIOGRAPHIC NOTE

In [Cle00], Cleaveland describes how to use the eXtensible Markup Language (XML) technology to develop DSLs. In this approach, different XML viewing technologies are used to view DSL programs, and different Java-based generative technologies are used to generate Java code.

---

1. <u>D</u>omain <u>E</u>ngineering <u>M</u>ethod for <u>R</u>eusable <u>A</u>lgorithmic <u>L</u>ibraries

♦ The main domain concepts are adequately captured as abstract data types (ADTs) and algorithms that operate on the ADTs.

♦ The ADTs often have container-like properties, such as matrices, images, graphs, and so on.

♦ There is usually a well-developed, underlying mathematical theory, for example, linear algebra [GL96], image algebra [RW96], and graph theory [BM76].

♦ The ADTs and the algorithms normally come in large varieties. For example, there are many different kinds of matrices due to different densities (dense or sparse), shapes (e.g., diagonal, square, symmetric, or band), storage formats, and so on. There are also many different versions of matrix algorithms. For example, the general LU algorithm for matrix factorization has the two main specializations LDL^T and Cholesky, and each of them has many versions for different matrix shapes and different pivoting strategies.

DEMRAL supports achieving the following library design goals.

♦ Providing the client with a high-level, intentional library interface.
  • The client code specifies problems in terms of high-level domain concepts.
  • The interface supports large numbers of concept variants in an effective way.
  • The client code is able to specify problems at the most appropriate level of detail (i.e., it can "order" default implementations of concepts or specify as much detail as it needs, but not more or less).

♦ Achieving high efficiency in terms of execution time and memory consumption.
  • The large number of variants should not have any negative effect on the efficiency.
  • Possibilities of optimizations should be analyzed and useful optimizations should be implemented.
  • Unused functionality should be removed and, whenever possible, static binding should be used.

♦ Achieving high quality of library code, which includes achieving
  • High adaptability and extendibility.
  • Minimal code duplication.
  • Minimal code tangling.

DEMRAL was created while applying the ODM method (see Section 2.8.2) in the development of the matrix computation library described in Chapter 14. In addition to being a specialization of ODM, it is a unique method because it combines ideas from several areas including Domain Engineering, Generators and Metaprogramming, Aspect-Oriented Programming, and Object-Oriented Software Development. Since its inception in [Cza98], we have also used DEMRAL to develop a statistics library for postal automation, which is currently a part of a commercial product [OSVA99], and a library of matrix factorization algorithms [Kna98].

5.7 Outline of DEMRAL

The outline of the DEMRAL activities is shown in Figure 5–2. The DEMRAL development process is iterative and incremental (that's why we call the points in the outline *activities* rather than *phases*). The different activities may be scheduled and rescheduled in arbitrary order during development. For example, identification of key concepts (1.2.1 in Figure 5–2) and feature modeling (1.2.2 in Figure 5–2) will generally require many iterations. Also, the definition of the domain often needs to be revised based on insights from Domain Modeling, Design, and Implementation. Similarly, you may need to refine feature models in Domain Design and Imple-

---

1. Domain Analysis
    1.1. Domain Definition
        1.1.1. Goal and Stakeholder Analysis
        1.1.2. Domain Scoping and Context Analysis
            1.1.2.1. Analysis of application areas and existing systems
                (i.e., exemplar systems)
            1.1.2.2. Identification of domain features
            1.1.2.3. Identification of relationships to other domains
    1.2 Domain Modeling
        1.2.1. Identification of key concepts
        1.2.2. Feature modeling of the key concepts (i.e., identification of commonalities, variabilities, feature dependencies, and feature interactions)
2. Domain Design
    2.1. Identification and specification of the overall implementation architecture
    2.2. Identification and specification of domain-specific languages
    2.3. Specification of the configuration knowledge
3. Domain Implementation (implementation of the domain-specific languages, generators, and implementation components)

Figure 5-2 Outline of DEMRAL

mentation. In fact, any activity may need to be revisited because of external changes, for example, changes of the stakeholder goals or the environment. Finally, we encourage you to do prototyping at any time because it will help you to gain a better understanding of the problem domain and to evaluate alternative solutions and new design ideas.

You should view the process outline in Figure 5–2 as just a default sequence of steps. You will probably develop your own preferred sequence over time. Although the actual development process involves many iterations and other activities, such as prototyping, you can use this default process outline to structure your design documentation. In fact, we used it to document the development of the matrix computation library in Chapter 14.

The DEMRAL activities have been derived from the ODM phases and tasks (see Section 2.8.2.1), but there are several differences.

♦ *Different divisions into top-level activities:* DEMRAL follows the widely accepted division of Domain Engineering into Domain Analysis, Design, and Implementation. But you can easily relate these activities to the ODM phases: Domain Analysis corresponds to Plan Domain and Model Domain; Domain Design corresponds to Scope Asset Base and Architect Asset Base; and finally, Domain Implementation corresponds to Implement Asset Base.

BACKGROUND NOTE

The role of a process outline has been accurately characterized by Reenskaug et al. in [Ree96]: "Documentation is by its nature linear and must be strictly structured. Software development processes are by their nature creative and exploratory and cannot be forced into the straightjacket of a fixed sequence of steps. In an insightful article, Parnas et al. state that many have sought a software process that allows a program to be derived systematically from a precise statement of requirements [PC86]. Their paper proposes that although we will not succeed in designing a real product that way, we can produce documentation that makes it appear as if the software was designed by such a process. The sequences of steps we describe in the following sections and in the rest of the book are therefore to be construed as default work processes and suggested documentation structures. We also believe that you will have to develop your own preferred sequence of steps, but you may want to take the steps proposed here as a starting point." This also applies to DEMRAL.

♦ *Stronger focus on technical issues:* A unique feature of ODM is its strong focus on organizational issues. In our description of DEMRAL, however, we will primarily focus on technical issues. Of course, whenever appropriate, you can extend DEMRAL with the organizational tasks and work products of ODM.

♦ *Only a subset of ODM tasks and work products:* As a specialization of a very general Domain Engineering method, DEMRAL covers only a subset of the ODM tasks and work products. Furthermore, the DEMRAL process outline is less detailed than the ODM outline. In a sense, you can view DEMRAL as a "lightweight" specialization of ODM.

As a specialization of ODM, the special features of DEMRAL include the following.

♦ Focus on the two concept categories: ADTs and algorithms
♦ Addition of the concept of feature starter sets and the predefined feature starter sets for ADTs and algorithms
♦ Use of feature diagrams for feature modeling (ODM does not prescribe any particular feature modeling notation)
♦ Focus on developing domain-specific languages (DSLs)

We'll describe the DEMRAL activities in the remaining sections of this chapter. You'll find a concrete example of applying DEMRAL in Chapter 14 and a detailed description of a comprehensive case study in [Cza98].

5.8 Domain Analysis

Domain Analysis involves two main activities: Domain Definition and Domain Modeling. The purpose of Domain Definition is to establish the domain scope based on the analysis of stakeholders, their goals, and existing systems. This is described in Section 5.8.1. The purpose of Domain Modeling is to model the contents of the domain by finding the relevant domain concepts and modeling their features. This is described in Section 5.8.2.

5.8.1 Domain Definition

The first activity of Domain Definition is to identify stakeholders and their goals. The amount of work needed for this activity depends on the size and the context of the project. The results are cross-checked and prioritized lists of goals and stakeholders. It is important to note that stakeholder analysis is a dynamic, social process, which may involve not only identifying the key players for a domain, but also getting some important people or organizations to become stakeholders. In [Cle00], Cleaveland illustrates, in an excellent and entertaining way, the social aspects of Domain Analysis in an imaginary story of a Domain Analysis project at a computer game company.

Domain features

The next activity is to determine the scope and characterize the contents of the domain by defining its *domain features.* You'll find the domain features by analyzing the application areas and markets of the systems in the domain and by analyzing the existing exemplar systems. For example, if our goal is to define the domain of matrix computation libraries, we need to analyze the application areas of matrix computations and the features of existing matrix computation libraries (see Table 14–1 and Table 14–2 in Section 14.3.1). The analysis reveals that the main features of matrix computation libraries are different types of matrices and computations they provide.

Domain feature diagram

Next, we need to summarize the results of our analysis in a *domain feature diagram.* A domain feature diagram is a concise and convenient means of defining a domain. An example of such a diagram for the domain of matrix computation libraries is shown in Figure 14–1 in Section 14.3.1. This diagram describes which features *are* part and which *can be* part of a matrix computation library. For example, band matrices are optional, but at least dense or sparse matrices have to be implemented, or a library may also implement both dense and sparse matrices (sparse and dense matrices are or-features).

We found it very useful to annotate domain features with priorities. There are at least three important factors influencing the priority of a domain feature.

♦ Typicality rate of the domain feature in the analyzed application areas
♦ Typicality rate of the domain feature in the analyzed exemplar systems

---

NOTE

It is interesting to note that features that are alternative in a feature diagram of a domain concept, for example, the features "dense" or "sparse" of the concept "matrix," usually emerge in the domain feature diagram as or-features. This is so because a library may choose to implement only a selection of alternative features.

♦ Importance of the domain feature according to the stakeholder goals

Feature priorities indicate the importance of the various parts of a domain and will help you to decide which parts to implement first. Of course, you'll need to adjust the priorities over time as the stakeholder goals evolve and more knowledge about the domain becomes available.

Analogy and support domains

Another activity of Domain Analysis is to analyze related domains, such as *analogy* and *support domains*. An analogy domain has significant similarities to the domain being analyzed and thus may provide some useful insights about the latter domain. A support domain, on the other hand, may be used to express some aspects of the domain being analyzed. You'll find examples of both types of related domains in Section 2.7.3.

Domain dictionary and domain knowledge sources

At the beginning of a Domain Analysis, you should establish a *domain dictionary* and a *register of domain knowledge sources* and keep them up to date as the analysis progresses. The domain dictionary should include definitions of the domain concepts and features. The register of domain knowledge sources should contain references to the literature, manuals, and domain experts consulted during Domain Analysis.

5.8.2   Domain Modeling

Domain Modeling involves two activities: *identification of key concepts* and *feature modeling of the key concepts*. The key concepts to be identified during DEMRAL are the main ADTs and algorithms of the domain being analyzed. An important issue to consider in this context is where to draw the boundaries between ADTs and algorithms. We discuss this in Section 5.8.2.1. The next step is to model the common and variable features of the key domain concepts and the dependencies between the variable features. We discussed feature modeling in Chapter 4. The special addition of DEMRAL in this context is the feature starter lists for ADTs and algorithms, which help to jump-start the feature modeling. They are described in Section 5.8.2.2.

NOTE

A domain feature diagram represents a kind of concept definition subscribing to the "probabilistic view" of defining concepts, which we discuss in Section A.2.3.

5.8.2.1 Identification of Key Concepts

By definition, DEMRAL focuses on domains whose main concept categories are ADTs and algorithms. Identifying the key ADTs and algorithms for an algorithmic library is usually quite simple, for example, matrix computation libraries contain matrices and vectors and algorithms operating on them, and image processing libraries contain different kinds of images and image processing algorithms.

An ADT defines a whole family of data types. Thus, a matrix ADT defines a family of matrices (e.g., sparse, dense, diagonal, square, symmetric, and so on). Similarly, we usually have whole families of algorithms operating on the ADTs. For example, matrix computation libraries may include factorization algorithms and algorithms for solving eigenvalue problems. Furthermore, each general version of a factorization algorithm may be specialized for matrices of different properties, for example, there are over a dozen important specializations of the general LU factorization (see Section 14.3.2).

Basic ADT operations and algorithm families

In DEMRAL, we make a distinction between *basic ADT operations* and the *algorithm families* that access the ADTs through the basic ADT operations and through accessing operations (i.e., getters and setters). Examples of basic operations in matrix computations are matrix addition, subtraction, and multiplication. We analyze basic operations as a part of the ADTs because together they define a cohesive *core algebra*. We implement the core algebra in one *component package,* which is separate from the packages containing the more complex algorithm families. For example, a matrix component package would include a family of matrices and vectors and their basic operations (see Figure 5–3). Furthermore, we would have a separate component package for each matrix algorithm family, for example, factorizations, solving eigenvalue problems, and so on.

It is important to note that if we model the key concepts using OO classes, we usually do not want to define the basic operations directly in the class interfaces, but rather as free-standing operators or operator templates. (Of course, this is only possible in a programming language supporting free-standing operators, such as C++.) Our philosophy is that class interfaces should include a minimal set of necessary methods, for example, accessing methods for accessing directly stored or abstract (i.e., computed) states. This way, we avoid "fat class interfaces" and improve modularity because we can define families of operators in separate modules (e.g., files, packages, namespaces, and so on). As a result, it is much easier to add new operators because you can do it without having to touch the class interface files.

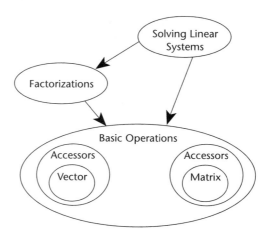

Figure 5-3 *Organization of ADTs and algorithm families in a matrix computation library*

Keeping basic operations out of class interfaces not only leads to better scalability, but also to improved reusability. As a result of such a design, we get many "little" classes and operations, which we can combine in a great number of different ways. We can hide the complexity resulting from a large number of "little" implementation components by implementing configuration generators, which perform the actual configuration work and provide an intentional and easy-to-use interface to the library user. In Chapter 12, we will see how to implement configuration generators in C++ synthesizing classes from little implementation classes and function templates at compile time. Furthermore, expression templates allow us to synthesize optimized configurations out of functional expressions. We'll see that in Section 14.4.2.

Another reason for defining operators outside class definitions is that they often cannot be thought of as a conceptual part of just one class. For example, in the expression M*V, where M is a matrix and V is a vector, the multiplication operation * is equally part of the matrix interface and the vector interface. If dynamic binding is required, the operation * is best implemented as a dynamic multi-method,[2] otherwise we can implement it as a freestanding operator

---

2. By a *dynamic multimethod,* we mean a dynamically bound method where the method lookup selects a method based on both the type of the receiver and the argument types (in fact, the receiver can be seen as yet another argument). Unfortunately, only a few OO languages directly support multimethods (e.g., CLOS [Kee89]). Idioms for simulating multimethods in C++ are described in [Pes98, Cop92].

or as an operator template (possibly specialized). Furthermore, if expression optimizations are required and the implementation language is C++, the operators are most appropriately implemented as *expression templates.* You'll see an example in Section 14.4.2.

Finally, you should consider modeling families of the more complex algorithms (e.g., solving systems of linear equations) as classes rather than procedures or functions (e.g., see [Wal97]). This way, you can organize them into family hierarchies.

5.8.2.2   Feature Modeling

The purpose of feature modeling is to develop feature models of the concepts in the domain. Feature models define the common and variable features of concept instances and the dependencies between the variable features.

We've already discussed how to perform feature modeling in Chapter 4. The only addition of DEMRAL to what we've said there are the concrete feature starter sets for ADTs and algorithms.

5.8.2.2.1   Feature Starter Set for ADTs

A feature starter set defines categories of features to look for during feature modeling. The following list contains the feature starter set for ADTs.

♦ *Attributes:* Attributes are named properties of ADT instances, such as the number of rows in a matrix or the length of a vector. Important features of an attribute are its type, whether it is mutable or not (i.e., whether it's possible to change its value), and whether it is volatile or not (i.e., whether it can be safely cached in a CPU register or whether it can be modified from outside the current execution thread at any time). Other features concern the implementation of an attribute, for example, whether the

---

NOTE

Interestingly, most algebraic specification languages define ADTs using modules consisting of three lists: a list of types, operation signatures, and axioms defining properties of the operations (see Figure 9–32 in Section 9.8.3). This is different from class definitions, where one class definition is supposed to define only one type and a number of operations on that type. Obviously, this OO claim cannot be fully supported because the operations may take arguments of other class types, and thus one class definition often contributes to the definition of other types (after all, the receiver of a method is just another argument). For this reason, we find defining basic operators outside classes to be a conceptually cleaner solution.

attribute is stored directly or computed, whether its value is cached or not, and whether it is *owned* by the ADT or not. If an attribute is owned by the ADT, the ADT is responsible for creating and destroying the values of the attribute. Also, accessing a value owned by an ADT usually involves copying the value (or, in C++, you can also return it as a const reference). We could implement any of these features of a given attribute as a parameter.

♦ *Data structures:* The ADT may be implemented on top of some complex data structures. This is especially the case for container-like ADTs, such as matrices or images. We'll come back to this aspect at the end of this section.

♦ *Operations:* Examples of operations are accessing operations and core algebra operations (i.e., the basic operations used by more complex algorithms). When you model operations, you need to analyze their signatures including operation name, operands and operand types, and different alternative operation implementations. In particular, you should also document any possible optimizations. For example, matrix operations may be optimized with respect to the shape of their operands. Other features of operations include binding mode (e.g., static or dynamic) and binding time (e.g., compile time or runtime). In Sections 7.9 and 8.5.1.2 we'll show you how to parameterize binding mode in C++.

♦ *Error detection, response, and handling:* Error detection is usually performed in the form of pre-, intra-, and post-condition[3] and invariant checking. What is an error and what is not may depend on the usage context of an ADT. Thus, we may want to parameterize error detection (also referred to as *error checking*). In certain contexts, it may also be appropriate to switch off checking for certain error conditions. For example, if the client of a container is guaranteed to access elements using valid indices only, no bounds checking is necessary. Once an error condition has been detected, various responses to it are possible: We can throw an exception, abort the program, or issue an error report [Eis95]. Finally, on the client side, we need to handle exceptions by performing appropriate actions. An important aspect of error response and handling is *exception safety*. We say that an ADT is exception safe if exceptions thrown by the ADT code or the client code do not leave the ADT in an undefined, broken state. Interestingly, this important aspect has only been addressed in the Standard Template Library (STL) in its final standardization phase.

---

3. The programming-by-contract approach propagates the use of pre- and post-conditions. However, we often also want to check for some conditions within a function or method. We refer to such conditions as *intra-conditions*.

◆ *Memory management*: By memory management we mean approaches to allocating and relinquishing memory and various approaches to managing virtual memory. We can allocate memory on the stack or on the heap using standard mechanisms available in most languages. We can also manage memory ourselves by allocating large chunks of memory at once and allocating objects within this customarily managed memory (this is called *memory pool* or *zone management*). We can also use automatic memory management approaches, for example, reference counting or some more sophisticated garbage collection approach (e.g., see [Wil92]). In a multithreaded environment, it may be useful to manage thread-specific memory, that is, per-thread memory, where a thread can allocate its own objects not shared with other threads. Other kinds of memory are memory shared among a number of processes and persistent store. The memory allocation aspect of container elements in the STL is parameterized in the form of *memory allocators* (see [KL98]), which can be passed to a container as a template parameter. Memory management interacts with other features, such as exception safety. One aspect of exception safety is making sure that exceptions do not cause memory leaks. An important aspect of memory management in databases is location control and clustering, that is, where and how the data is stored. Finally, paging and cache behaviors of memory management often need to be tuned to the requirements of an application.

◆ *Synchronization*: If we want to use an ADT in a multithreaded environment, we have to synchronize the access to shared data. This is usually done by providing appropriate synchronization code (you'll see concrete examples in Section 8.5.2 and subsequent sections). The variability of this aspect may include not only different synchronization constraints, but also different implementation strategies. For example, synchronization can be implemented at different levels: the interface level of an ADT or the internal data level. As a rule, the interface-level locking is less complex than the data-level locking. On the other hand, data-level locking allows more concurrency. For this reason, it is usually used in large collections, such as in databases. If we also want to use an ADT in a sequential environment, it should be possible to leave out its synchronization code entirely, or in some cases, to replace it by error checking code. Thus, there is also an interaction between synchronization and error checking. You'll see a concrete example of this interaction in Section 8.5.4.

◆ *Persistency*: Some applications may require the ability to store an ADT on disk (e.g., in a file or in a database). In such cases, we need to provide mechanisms for storing appropriate parts of the state of an ADT and for restoring them. A simple form of persistency is the ability to write an ADT into a stream and read it in back from a stream. Persistency is closely related to memory management.

♦ *Perspectives and subjectivity:* Different stakeholders and different client programs usually have different requirements on an ADT. Thus, we may consider organizing ADTs into a number of subjects corresponding to the different perspectives of stakeholders and/or client programs. We'll discuss subjectivity in Section 8.3.1.

If the ADT has a container-like character (e.g., a matrix or an image), we also should consider the following aspects.

♦ *Element type:* What is the type of the elements managed by the ADT?
♦ *Indexing:* Are the elements to be accessed using an index, for example, integral index, symbolic key, or some other, user-defined key?
♦ *Structure:* How are the elements stored? What data structures are used? For example, the structure of a matrix has a number of subfeatures, such as entry type, shape, format, and representation (see Section 14.3.2).

5.8.2.2.2 Feature Starter Set for Algorithms
The feature starter set for algorithms includes the following feature categories.

♦ *Computational aspect:* This is the main aspect of an algorithm: the abstract, text-book formulation of the algorithm without the more involved implementation issues. We may specify this aspect using pseudocode. Furthermore, we have to investigate the relationships between algorithms, for example, specialization and use, and organize them into families. It may also be useful to classify them into different categories, such as search algorithms, greedy algorithms, divide-and-conquer algorithms, and so on (see Figure 9–36, Section 9.8.3). For example, iterative methods in matrix computations are search algorithms.
♦ *Data access:* Algorithms access ADTs through accessing operations and basic operations. Careful design of the basic operations is crucial in order to achieve both flexibility and good performance. For example, algorithms benefit from optimizations of basic operations. We can use different techniques in order to minimize the coupling between algorithms and data structures, for example, iterators [GHJV95, MS96] and data access templates in C++ [KW97].

◆ *Optimizations:* There are various opportunities for domain-specific optimizations, for example, optimization based on the known structure of the data, caching, in-place computation (i.e., storing result data in the argument data to avoid copying), loop restructuring, algebraic optimizations, and so on.

◆ *Error detection, response, and handling:* This aspect was discussed in Section 5.8.2.2.1.

◆ *Memory management:* Algorithms may also need to make direct calls to memory management services for tuning purposes.

◆ *Parallelization:* Parallelization allows us to increase the execution speed and is particularly relevant in high-performance areas, such as scientific computing. This is an advanced topic (e.g., see [GO93]).

You can also have domain-specific algorithm features, such as pivoting strategies in matrix algorithms (see Section 14.3.2).

5.9   Domain Design

The purpose of Domain Design in DEMRAL is to develop a library architecture, identify implementation components, specify DSLs constituting the application programming interface (API) to the library, and specify the translation of the DSLs into the target architecture (i.e., into configurations of implementation components). Domain Design builds on the results of Domain Modeling, that is, feature models of different aspects of ADTs and algorithm families, and involves the following activities.

◆ Scope domain model for implementation
◆ Identify packages
◆ Develop target architectures and identify the implementation components
◆ Identify user DSLs
◆ Identify interactions between DSLs
◆ Specify DSLs and their translation

5.9.1   Scope Domain Model for Implementation

The DEMRAL process is iterative and evolutionary. This means that we implement the domain model piecemeal, that is, one concept or feature at a time. We conclude each iteration by testing the concept or feature implementation. We select the next concept or feature to be developed based on the priority assigned to it during Domain Analysis. In general, we don't have to develop all features identified during Domain Analysis. However, we can take advantage of knowing the potentially needed features in order to develop a more robust architecture capable of accommodating the new features in the future. That does not mean that we need to put extra, unused functionality into the library in order to support potentially needed features. It only means that given a set of alternative design decisions we can sometimes favor some of them to ease the implementation of anticipated features in the future. Indeed, developers often tend to put too much unused "flexibility" into code, which only unnecessarily complicates it.

5.9.2 Identify Packages

We divide the library to be developed into a number of packages. Each package will contain one algorithm family or ADT family. Packages help us to organize the library at the highest level. This way, we can improve its understandability and maintainability. Furthermore, we can assign each package to a different developer. Finally, library users can selectively import only the packages they need. The library package structure can be modeled using the UML package diagrams. Packages are supported in C++ by the namespace construct and in Java by the package construct.

5.9.3 Develop Target Architectures and Identify the Implementation Components

By looking at the feature models developed during Domain Analysis, you can identify the key areas of functionality. Each of them will require one or more implementation components. The shape of the components will depend on the particular architecture model you select. For example, the case studies presented in Chapters 12, 13, and 14 in Part III use a parameterized, layered architecture model called GenVoca, which we'll discuss in Section 9.8.2 in Part II. The identification of the implementation components usually requires at least some prototyping. An important part of the architecture is the specification of the allowed and preferred configurations of implementation components. We'll demonstrate a concrete architecture development process in Part III.

5.9.4 Identify User DSLs

User DSLs constitute the library API provided to the library users. There are two important kinds of user DSLs in DEMRAL.

♦ *Configuration DSLs:* Used to configure ADTs and algorithms
♦ *Expression DSLs:* Used for writing expressions involving ADTs and operations on them, such as matrix expressions

We'll discuss both kinds of DSLs in Sections 5.9.7 and 5.9.8. Other, more problem-specific DSLs are also possible. For example, we could define a DSL for expressing pivoting in matrix computation algorithms (see [ILG+97]).

5.9.5 Identify Interactions between DSLs

Next, we need to address the following question: What kind of information has to be exchanged between the implementations of the DSLs? For example, the implementation of a matrix expression DSL will need access to different properties of matrices (e.g., element type, shape, format, and so on), which are described by the matrix configuration DSL. This information is necessary in order to implement the operations called in a matrix expression by selecting optimal algorithms for the given matrix arguments. Furthermore, it is used to compute the matrix types for the intermediate results needed during evaluating the expression.

5.9.6 Specify DSLs and Their Translation

Abstract and concrete syntax

We specify a language by specifying its syntax and semantics. At this point, we will only specify the *abstract syntax* of each DSL and leave the *concrete syntax* (also referred to as the *surface syntax*) to Domain Implementation. The difference between abstract and concrete syntax is shown in Figure 5–4. The abstract syntax of a language describes the structure of the abstract syntax trees used to represent programs in the compiler (or another language processor), whereas the concrete syntax describes the structure of programs displayed on the screen. Technologies, such as Intentional Programming, allow us to easily implement many alternative concrete syntaxes for one abstract syntax. We specify syntax using the *Backus-Naur Form* (BNF; e.g., see [Mey90]).

The specification of the semantics of a language is a more complex task. Meyer describes five fundamental approaches to specifying semantics [Mey90].

♦ *Attribute grammars:* Extends the grammar by a set of rules for computing properties of language constructs.
♦ *Translational semantics:* Specifies the semantics by defining a translation scheme to a simpler language.

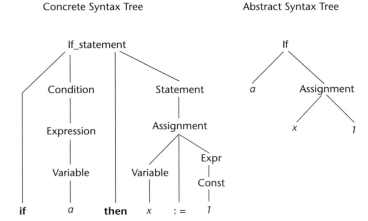

Figure 5-4 *Concrete and abstract syntax tree for the statement* `if a then x:=1` *(adapted from [WM95])*

♦ *Operational semantics:* Specifies the semantics by providing an abstract interpreter.
♦ *Denotational semantics:* Associates with every programming construct a set of mathematical functions defining its meaning.
♦ *Axiomatic semantics:* Defines a mathematical theory for proving properties of programs written in a given programming language.

Each of these approaches has its advantages and disadvantages. In any case, however, formal specification of the semantics of a language is an extremely laborious enterprise.

In the examples in Part III of this book, we will define the semantics of a configuration DSL by specifying how to translate it into valid configurations of implementation components. In the case of an expression DSL, we will specify its translation into code fragments and patterns in the target language (or pseudocode). In effect, we will use a form of translational (but not necessarily formal) semantics.

5.9.7 Configuration DSLs

A configuration DSL allows you to specify a concrete instance of a concept, for example, data structure, algorithm, object, and so on. Thus, it defines a family of artifacts, just as a feature model does. Indeed, a configuration DSL can be represented as a feature model, and we derive it from the Domain Analysis feature model of a concept by tuning it to the needs of the reuser.

Implementation components configuration language (ICCL)

A concept specification written in a configuration DSL is translated into a concrete configuration of the implementation components. Because the implementation components can only be connected in certain ways, we can describe their valid configurations using a language, which we will call the *implementation components configuration language* (ICCL). The configuration DSL is the language of the problem space, and the ICCL is the language of the solution space. The translation between these two languages can be done using a generator executed at compile time or some "factory code" [GHJV95] executed at runtime (see Figure 5–5).

Why do we need both configuration DSLs and ICCLs? The reason is that both kinds of languages have different focuses. The focus of a configuration DSL is to allow the user (or the client program) of a component to specify her needs at a level of detail that suits her best. On the other hand, the focus of an ICCL is to allow maximum flexibility and reusability of the implementation components.

Direct or computed defaults

As stated previously, the configuration DSL should allow the user of a component to specify her needs at a level of detail that suits her best. She should not be forced to specify any implementation-dependent details if she needs not to. This way, we make sure that a client program does not introduce any unnecessary dependencies on the implementation details of the server component. For example, a client might just request a matrix from a generative matrix component. The matrix component should produce a matrix with some reasonable defaults, for example, rectangular

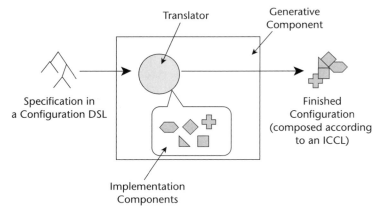

Figure 5-5 *Generative component implementing a configuration DSL*

shape, real element values, dynamic row and column numbers, and so on. In general, the client should be able to leave out a feature in a specification, in which case the feature should be determined by the generative component as a *direct default* or a *computed default* (i.e., a default based on some other specified features and other feature defaults). The client could be more specific and specify features stating some usage profile, for example, need dense or sparse matrix or need space- or speed-optimized matrix. The next possibility would be to provide more precise specifications, for example, the matrix density is 5 percent nonzero elements. Furthermore, the client should be able to specify some implementation features directly, for example, what available storage format the matrix should use. Finally, it should be possible for the client to contribute its own implementation of some features, such as its own storage format. The different levels of detail for specifying a configuration are summarized in Figure 5–6.

The focus of an ICCL is on the reusability and flexibility of the implementation components. This requirement may sometimes conflict with the requirements on a configuration DSL: We strive for small, atomic components that can be combined in as many ways as possible. We want to avoid any code duplication by factoring out similar code sections into small (parameterized) components. This code duplication avoidance and the opportunities for reuse may lead to implementation components that do not align well with the feature boundaries that users want to use in their specifications. An example of a library that only provides an ICCL is the C++ Standard Template Library (see Section 6.10). Users of the STL have to configure the STL implementation components manually (i.e., they have to hardcode ICCL statements in the client code).

The use of a configuration DSL and an ICCL separates the problem space and the solution space. This separation allows a

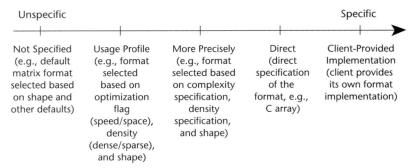

Figure 5-6 Different levels of detail for specifying variable features

NOTE

The idea of the different levels of detail was inspired by the Open Implementation approach to design [KLL+97, MLMK97]. In this approach, the configuration interface of a component is referred to as its *metainterface*.

more independent evolution of the client code, which uses a configuration DSL as the configuration interface to a component, and the component implementation code, which implements the ICCL.

The configuration DSL of a concept can be directly derived from the feature model of the concept. The approach for this derivation involves answering the following questions.

◆ *Which features are relevant for the DSL?* Obviously, a configuration DSL will consist of variation points and variable features only. Other features of a feature model are not relevant for the configuration DSL.

◆ *Are any additional, more abstract features needed?* For example, during Domain Design of the matrix computation library described in Chapter 14, we added the *optimization flag* with the alternative subfeatures *speed* and *space* to the original matrix feature model created during feature modeling. The optimization flag allows us to decide which matrix storage format to use based on the matrix shape and density features (e.g., a dense triangular matrix is faster in access when we store its elements in an array rather than in a vector because we do not have to convert the subscripts on each element access; however, using a vector requires half the storage of an array because only the nonzero half of the matrix needs to be stored in the vector).

◆ *Is the nesting of features optimal for the user?* It may be useful to rearrange the feature diagrams of a feature model according to the needs of the users (which may be different). Also, the target implementation technology may impose some constraints on the DSL. For example, the matrix configuration DSL described in Section 14.4.1.2 uses dimensions as the only kind of variation points. This way we can easily implement it using C++ class templates.

◆ *Which features should have direct defaults and what are these defaults?* Some features should be selected by default if not specified. For example, the *shape* of a matrix is a dimension and should have the default value *rectangular*. Other matrix dimensions with direct defaults include element type, index type, optimization flag, and error checking flag (see Table 14–3 in Section 14.4.1.3.2).

♦ *For which features can defaults be computed and how do you compute them?* Features for which no direct defaults were defined should be computable from the specified features and the direct defaults. For example, the storage format of a matrix can be determined based on its shape, density, and optimization flag. The computed defaults can be specified using dependency tables (e.g., see Table 14–4 in Section 14.4.1.3.2).[4]

Designing new configuration DSLs—and new DSLs in general—is a science in itself. There are both usability and technical criteria you should keep in mind. In terms of usability, you want a DSL to be easy to understand, learn, and use. It should be efficient, that is, you should be able to "order" many systems using only a few language elements. This also implies that there should be reasonable defaults for unspecified properties. Furthermore, you want it to be safe to use, that is, you want to minimize the probability of ordering invalid systems. You will often need to balance safety and simplicity of a DSL. For example, if there are many invalid value combinations for two parameters, you can replace the two parameters with one that takes values representing the valid combinations. This way, you eliminate the opportunity to specify an invalid combination, but possibly make the language more complicated to learn because the new parameter may have a large number of values. Thus, if there are only a few invalid value combinations for two parameters compared to the total number of possible combinations, it is more "efficient" to use two parameters. On the other hand, if there are many more invalid combinations than valid ones, you will probably want to increase the safety by replacing the two parameters with just one. It is interesting to note that the idea of bundling features in consistent and useful ways is similar to the idea of introducing standard products (e.g., standard financial products offered by a given bank, or the different car models offered by a car maker), which helps customers select useful products in large configuration spaces more easily. In terms of technical criteria, you want a DSL to be extensible, modular, and easy to analyze.

You will see a concrete application of this approach in Part III.

5.9.8   Expression DSLs

An important class of DSLs in algorithmic domains are expression DSLs. An expression DSL allows us to write algebraic expressions

---

4. There are also examples of features for which no reasonable defaults exist (neither direct nor computed), for example, the static number of rows of a matrix. Such features have to be specified explicitly, otherwise we have an error.

involving ADTs and operations on ADTs. An example of algebraic expressions is matrix expressions, for example, $M1+M2*M3+M4-M5$, where $+$, $*$, and $-$ are matrix addition, multiplication, and matrix subtraction, and $M1$ through $M5$ are matrices. Another example is image algebra expressions, such as

$$\left(\left(a \oplus s \right)^2 + \left(a \oplus s \right)^2 \right)^{\frac{1}{2}}$$

where a is an image, s is a template (i.e., an image whose values are images), and $\oplus$ is the right linear product operator. This expression is used in the image algebraic formulation of the Roberts edge detector (see [RW96]).

The analysis leading to an expression DSL starts by listing the operations and the ADTs they operate on. For example, matrix computations involve vector and matrix operations (e.g., matrix addition, subtraction, and multiplication). BLAS [BLAS97, LHKK79] is a standard set of basic matrix operations, and Image Algebra [RW96] defines several dozens of basic operations for image processing.

Next, we need to analyze the systematic relationships between the operations and the properties of their operands. For example, adding two lower-triangular matrices results in another lower-triangular matrix, adding a lower-triangular matrix and an upper-triangular matrix results in a general square matrix, adding two dense matrices results in a dense matrix (in general), and so on. If we know that a certain property of a matrix does not change during the entire runtime, we can encode this property in its static type. We can then use the static properties of the arguments to derive the static properties of operation results. This corresponds to domain-specific type inference. Incompatible combinations of argument properties and operations should be reported at compile time. This is called domain-specific compile-time error reporting. We specify the inference rules and illegal property combinations using *dependency tables* (see Section 14.4.2.8). You can implement domain-specific compile-time error checking and reporting in C++ using *expression templates* (see Section 14.4.2.2).

Finally, we need to investigate opportunities for optimizations. We distinguish between the following two types of optimizations.

♦ *Optimizations of single operations:* This kind of optimization is performed by selecting specialized algorithms based on properties of the participating ADTs. For example, we use different addition and multiplication algorithms depending on the shape of the argument matrices. The specification of such optimizations involves specifying the different algorithms and the criteria for selecting them (e.g., see Section 14.4.2.7).

♦ *Optimizations of whole expressions:* This kind of optimization involves the structural analysis of the entire expression and generating customized code based on this analysis. Examples of such optimizations are elimination of temporaries and loop fusing. The optimizations may be performed at several levels of refinement. Sophisticated optimization techniques for expression DSLs are described in [Big98a, Big98b]. We can implement expression optimizations in C++ using expression templates (see Section 14.4.2.2)

5.10   Domain Implementation

Different parts of an algorithmic library require different implementation techniques.

♦ ADTs, operations, and algorithms can be adequately implemented using parameterized functions, parameterized classes, and mixin layers (e.g., the GenVoca model discussed in Section 9.8.2). All of these abstraction mechanisms are available in C++.

♦ The implementation of configuration generators and expression optimizations require static metaprogramming capabilities. Here we can use built-in language capabilities, such as template metaprogramming in C++ (see Chapter 10), custom-developed preprocessors or compilers, or specialized metaprogramming environments and tools, such as Intentional Programming (see Chapter 11) or Open C++ [Chi95].

♦ Domain-specific syntax extensions require preprocessors, custom compilers, or extendible compilers (e.g., Intentional Programming). However, the C++ vector library Blitz++ (see Section 8.7.4) demonstrates that a rich language, such as C++, allows us to simulate a great deal of mathematical notations without the need of syntax extensions.

We will demonstrate the following two implementation approaches in Part III:

♦ An implementation in C++ including a GenVoca architecture using C++ class templates, a configuration generator using template metaprogramming, an expression DSL using expression templates (see Chapters 12, 13, and 14)

♦ An implementation using the Intentional Programming System (see Section 14.4.3).

Part II

IMPLEMENTATION TECHNOLOGIES

Chapter 6

Generic Programming

6.1 Why Is This Chapter Worth Reading?

Generic programming, greatly popularized by the C++ Standard Template Library (STL) of container data structures and algorithms, is about representing domains as collections of highly general and abstract components, which can be combined in vast numbers of ways to yield very efficient, concrete programs. In the context of Generative Programming, generic programming represents an important technique to organize the solution space of a generative domain model, that is, the implementation components from which concrete systems can be built. We want the implementation components to be highly orthogonal, reusable, and nonredundant (see Section 5.2), and generic programming can help us to achieve this goal.

In this chapter, you'll learn about the principles and techniques of generic programming including type parameterization, different kinds of polymorphism, the concept of parameterized components, and principles of generic analysis and design. All these ideas will be demonstrated using C++ and Java code examples.

6.2 What Is Generic Programming?

Throughout literature, the term *generic programming* has been used in at least four different but related meanings.

1. Programming with *generic parameters*
2. Programming by abstracting from concrete types
3. Programming with parameterized components
4. Programming method based in finding the most abstract representation of efficient algorithms

The first meaning is probably the most commonly used. Generic parameters are type or value parameters of types. They allow us to avoid unnecessary code duplication in statically typed languages (e.g., C++ or Ada). For example, if we want a sorting routine to work with different element types, we would declare element type as a generic parameter of the routine. This way, we avoid writing almost the same sorting code for different types. Programming languages may provide generic parameters not only for procedures or functions, but also for classes, modules, packages, and so on. For example, the C++ template mechanism allows us to define generic parameters for freestanding functions, classes, and member functions.

Genericity and polymorphism

The sorting routine previously mentioned uses a generic parameter so that it can be used with different element types. We say that the routine is *generic*. The ability of code to work with different types is also referred to as *polymorphism* and can be accomplished not only through generic parameters but also through *subtyping* in connection with dynamic binding. For example, the routine for sorting a set of elements of a certain type requires that the type includes an operation for comparing two elements. There are potentially an infinite number of such types and a sorting routine that is capable of working with all of them is polymorphic. As stated earlier, one approach to achieving this polymorphism is to declare element type as a parameter of the routine. This is referred to as *parametric polymorphism*. An alternative solution is to use an abstract type (e.g., an interface in Java or an abstract class in C++) in place of the element type in the routine. The abstract type is defined to include the comparison operation and its use in the routine implies that the routine works for all subtypes of the abstract type. This technique is referred to as *subtype polymorphism*. We see that, in the context of making code work with different types, genericity and polymorphism are very closely related. They both support "programming by abstracting from concrete types."

Parametric and subtype polymorphism

Parameterized programming

Because the concept of types in modern programming languages goes beyond elementary types, such as character or integer, to include interfaces as sets of operation signatures, generic parameters are also useful whenever we want to parameterize components by other components. For example, in addition to element type, we could also parameterize the comparison strategy of a sorting routine or the memory allocation part of a container. The use of parameters as a component composition mechanism has been the focus of *parameterized programming* [Gog96].

Both ideas of making code work with many types and parameterizing components by other components have been elevated to a new level in the work by Stepanov, Musser, and colleagues on the

STL [MS96], a C++ library of container data structures and algorithms. This development has been driven by the goal of "finding the most abstract representations of efficient algorithms." [Rus98] An important point here is that the abstraction process should not force us to compromise efficiency, that is, the abstract algorithm can be instantiated back for a concrete case, and the result is as efficient as the original algorithm we abstracted from. The implementation techniques deployed for this purpose in the STL include but are not limited to type parameterization. Examples of the other techniques are *iterators*, *adapters*, *function objects*, and *traits* (see Sections 6.10.1, 6.9.2, 6.8, and 10.10). The STL view of generic programming is reflected in the following definition [JLMS98].

> *Generic programming is a subdiscipline of computer science that deals with finding abstract representations of efficient algorithms, data structures, and other software concepts, and with their systematic organization. The goal of generic programming is to express algorithms and data structures in a broadly adaptable, interoperable form that allows their direct use in software construction. Key ideas include*
>
> ◆ *Expressing algorithms with minimal assumptions about data abstractions and vice versa, thus making them as interoperable as possible.*
> ◆ *Lifting of a concrete algorithm to as general a level as possible without losing efficiency; that is, the most abstract form such that when specialized back to the concrete case the result is just as efficient as the original algorithm.*
> ◆ *When the result of lifting is not general enough to cover all uses of an algorithm, additionally providing a more general form, but ensuring that the most efficient specialized form is automatically chosen when applicable.*
> ◆ *Providing more than one generic algorithm for the same purpose and at the same level of abstraction, when none dominates the others in efficiency for all inputs. This introduces the necessity to provide sufficiently precise characterizations of the domain for which each algorithm is the most efficient.*

The work on the STL actually goes beyond mere programming to include methodological aspects. Indeed, the approach for developing generic libraries outlined in [MS93] utilizes a form of domain analysis (see Section 6.11).

6.3 Generic versus Generative Programming

The American Heritage Dictionary of the English Language defines the terms *generic* and *generative* as follows.[1]

♦ *generic*: [. . .] Relating to or descriptive of an entire group or class [. . .]

♦ *generative*: [. . .] Having the ability to originate, produce, or procreate [. . .]

These definitions bring the difference between generic and generative programming to the following point.

> *Generic programming focuses on representing families of domain concepts, whereas generative programming also includes the process of creating concrete instances of concepts.*

Although generic programming exploits commonalities and variabilities within a family and seeks to represent them as concisely as possible, generative programming additionally exploits the dependencies between the variabilities, introduces the separation between problem space and solution space, and utilizes configuration knowledge to map between these spaces.

In generative programming, the principles of generic programming are applied to the solution space, where we try to come up with as generic a set of implementation components as possible, that is, components that maximize the number of their possible combinations and minimize redundancy while preserving maximal efficiency in terms of execution time and resource consumption. However, in the problem space, generative programming encourages specialized, domain-specific representations, which could oppose the spirit of generic programming, but are user friendly by definition.

In terms of technology, generic programming has a particular focus on parameterization, whereas generative programming additionally deploys metaprogramming (see Chapters 9, 10, and 11). Metaprogramming is instrumental in implementing the mapping between problem space and solution space, for example, through automatic configuration. Furthermore, it enables more advanced forms of parameterization involving so-called *aspects*, that is, parameterization of properties that are normally implemented by

---

1. Copyright © 1996 by Houghton Mifflin Company. Reproduced by permission from *The American Heritage Dictionary of the English Language, Third Edition.*

code intertwined with the code of several different components (see Chapter 8).

Finally, much of the work on generic programming focuses on static parameterization, whereas generative programming treats binding time as a parameter of an abstraction.

6.4 Generic Parameters

The primary purpose of generic parameters is to avoid code duplication in statically typed languages. We illustrate this point using a simple example. Suppose we want to write a function for squaring a number. The pseudocode for this function could look like this:

```
sqr(x)
  return x * x
```

In a dynamically typed language, such as Smalltalk, this pseudocode can be typed in almost "as is":[2]

```
sqr: x
  ^x * x
```

However, if we want to implement it in a statically typed language, we have to declare the type of x and the return type, for example, in C++:

```
int sqr(int x)
{ return x * x; }
```

This implementation works only for x of type int, that is, it is more special than the pseudocode or the Smalltalk code, which work for any object that understands the message "*", or, in other words, for any type including the operation "*". In C++, we could provide a set of squaring functions for different number types, for example:

```
int sqrInt(int x)
{ return x * x; }
```

---

2. For demonstration purposes, we implemented sqr: as a class method of some math utility class. Alternatively, we could have implemented it as a method of Number, that is:

```
sqr
  ^self*self
```

```
double sqrDouble(double x)
{ return x * x; }
```

```
//...
```

Overloading   We can improve this solution by using *overloading*, that is, all versions have the same name but different argument types:

```
int sqr(int x)
{ return x * x; }
```

```
double sqr(double x)
{ return x * x; }
```

```
//...
```

This solution is still tedious, error prone, and hard to maintain because of massive code duplication. Type parameters provide an elegant solution to this problem. In C++, generic parameters are supported in the form of function templates and class templates. We can implement our squaring function as a function template:

```
template <class T>
T sqr(T x)
{ return x * x; }
```

The idea is that the compiler will automatically generate an appropriate concrete function for each parameter type the function is called with, for example:

```
int a = 3;
double b = 5.0;
int aa = sqr(a); // compiler generates sqr() for T = int
double bb = sqr(b); // compiler generates sqr() for T = double
```

It is interesting to note that our sqr() template will work not only for all number types, but also for any type providing the operation "*", just as the Smalltalk implementation of sqr(). There is, however, a difference between these implementations: The sqr() template is statically type-checked and no runtime errors of the form "operation '*' not found" are possible, whereas the Smalltalk version is dynamically type-checked and a runtime error is possible if an object that does not provide "*" is passed to sqr:. On the other hand, the Smalltalk version is more flexible because the type of x is not fixed at compile time and objects of different types can be passed at runtime to sqr:.

Type parameters allow us to ensure proper typing at compile time. For example, we can implement a procedure swap() for swapping the value of two variables and make sure that both variables have the same type (see Figure 6–1).

6.5   Parametric versus Subtype Polymorphism

As we discussed in Section 6.2, abstracting from concrete types can also be achieved using subtype polymorphism. The idea is to list the operations called on a given variable in the code we want to abstract and to use an abstract type including these operations as the type of the variable. For example, the swap routine from the previous section invokes the following operations on its arguments.

- "assign", which in C++ is denoted by "=" as in a=b;
- "copy", which in C++ is automatically called when initializing a variable as in int c=a;

Next, we define the abstract type Swappable, which includes "assign" and "copy" as its operations. In other words, we factor out the commonality among all the different types that can work with the swap routine into the separate type Swappable. Finally, we rewrite the swap routine to use Swappable as the type of its arguments.

Unfortunately, this is not as straightforward as simply replacing the type parameter in the template version from Figure 6–1 by Swappable. The problem is that the declaration Swappable c = a; would attempt to create an instance of Swappable. This, of course, cannot succeed because Swappable is an abstract type. The solution is to provide Swappable with a virtual copy function and to rewrite

```
template <class T>
void swap (T& a, T& b)
{ const T c = a; a = b; b = c;
}
//...
int a = 5, b = 9;
swap(a,b); //OK
double c = 9.0;
swap(a,c); //error! call to swap ambiguous since a and c
           //have different types
```

Figure 6-1 swap() *implementation using type parameters*

the swap code to call this function. A subtype of Swappable has to specialize this function to return a copy of itself with the correct type. The copy function is an example of a *factory method* and the object being copied acts as a *prototype* (see [GHJV95]). At this point, the swap code will work for all concrete subtypes of Swappable. For all other types that are not subtypes of Swappable, such as int and double, we need to write an *adapter* [GHJV95]. The full code of this example is shown in Figure 6–2.

After applying all these design patterns, the entire swap code gets rather complicated. The C++ compiler will principally generate an overloaded assignment operator in the form classname& operator = (const classname& rhs) if it is not provided by the programmer. Thus, it is futile to define a virtual assignment operator in the base class because it will never be called from a derived class. The solution is to provide a virtual assign() function that performs the assignment correctly and an overloaded assignment operator that calls the assign() function using late binding. In addition to this complexity, the implementation in Figure 6–2 has two other problems.

♦ Writing adapter classes for new types requires quite an effort.
♦ Static type checking is compromised because an attempt to swap the value of two variables of different types is not detected at compile time. Our implementation will still prevent such a swap using the C++ runtime type information mechanism (see dynamic casts in both assign() member functions in Figure 6–2), but only at runtime.

```
class Swappable
{ public:
    virtual Swappable& assign(const Swappable& rhs) = 0;
    Swappable& operator=(const Swappable& rhs)
    { return assign(rhs);
    }
    virtual Swappable* copy() const = 0;
    virtual void print(ostream& os) const = 0;
    virtual ~Swappable() {};
};

ostream& operator<<(ostream& os,const Swappable& rhs)
{ rhs.print(os);
  return os;
}
```

(continued)

Figure 6-2 swap() *implementation using subtype polymorphism*

```
class Int: public Swappable
{ public:
    Int(int n):value(n) {}
    Int& operator=(const Int& rhs)
    { return assign(rhs);
    }
    Int& assign(const Swappable& rhs)
    { if (this != &rhs)
      value = dynamic_cast<const Int&>(rhs).value;
      return *this;
    }
    Swappable* copy() const
    { return new Int(value);
    }
    void print(ostream& os) const
    { os << value;
    }
  private:
    int value;
};

class Double: public Swappable
{ public:
    Double(double n):value(n) {}
    Double& operator=(const Double& rhs)
    { return assign(rhs);
    }
    Double& assign(const Double& rhs)
    { if (this != rhs)
      value = dynamic_cast<const Double&>(rhs).value;
      return *this;
    }
    Swappable* copy() const
    { return new Double(value);
    }
    void print(ostream& os) const
    { os << value;
    }
  private:
    double value;
};
```

(continued)

Figure 6-2 swap() *implementation using subtype polymorphism (continued)*

```
void swap (Swappable& a,Swappable& b)
{ Swappable* c = a.copy();
  a = b;
  b = *c;
  delete c;
}

// ...

Int a = 5, b = -1;
swap(a,b);
Double c = 5.5, d = -1.1;
swap(c,d);
```

Figure 6-2 swap() *implementation using subtype polymorphism (continued)*

Another example where static typing is compromised is when you use subtype polymorphism to develop container data structures, such as vectors and lists. We discuss this case in Section 6.5.1 in the context of Java.

So our conclusion is that, in a statically typed language, subtype polymorphism is not always a suitable alternative to parametric polymorphism (also see [Mey88]). On the other hand, it is the only alternative if the argument types vary at runtime because subtype polymorphism is based on dynamic binding and parametric polymorphism is based on static binding. For this reason, we find it useful to distinguish between *dynamic* and *static parameterization* during modeling. We will revisit this topic in Section 7.6.

6.5.1 Genericity in Java

As of this writing, Java does not support parametric polymorphism. Thus, in cases where parametric polymorphism would be useful, we have to use subtype polymorphism instead. As an example, consider a generic class Pair with two instance variables and the method max(), which compares the contents of both variables and returns the greater one. The generic class works properly with any type providing the comparison operation "greater". A possible implementation of Pair in C++ as a class template is shown in Figure 6–7.

The corresponding Java code in Figure 6–8 has to use subtype polymorphism, which is analogous to the C++ implementation of swap() in Figure 6–2. The required interface for classes that should work with Pair is defined as the Java interface Greater (this is

POLYMORPHISM

The word *polymorphism* is derived from the Greek language and means "the ability to have many forms." In computer science, it refers to the idea of being able to write code against an abstract interface and plug in different concrete implementations behind the abstract interface. Programming languages support polymorphism with many different mechanisms. We list some of them in the following paragraphs. The original definition of polymorphism by Strachey from 1967 distinguishes between *parametric* and *ad hoc polymorphism* [Str67].

> Parametric polymorphism is obtained when a function works uniformly on a range of types; these types normally exhibit some common structure. Ad hoc polymorphism is obtained when a function works, or appears to work, on several different types (which may not exhibit a common structure) and may behave in unrelated ways for each type.

Cardelli and Wegner refined this definition in [CW85] as shown in Figure 6–3. Parametric polymorphism is obtained using generic parameters. *Inclusion polymorphism* corresponds to subtype polymorphism in OO languages, that is, variables of a given type can also hold objects of its subtypes. *Coercion* refers to the automatic application of built-in or user-defined type promotions and conversions, for example, when adding an integral and a floating-point number, the integral operand is converted into a floating-point number. *Overloading* means providing different implementations of functions for the same function name, but different operand types. Overloading and coercion may conflict, for example, if both an overloaded function and an appropriate conversion are equally applicable.

All the previously discussed variants of polymorphism are available in C++ [Eis99]. Templates correspond to parametric polymorphism (Figure 6–4), virtual functions to subtype polymorphism (Figure 6–5), function overloading to overloading, and built-in or user-defined conversion operators or

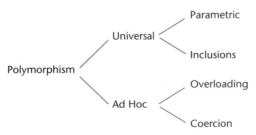

Figure 6-3 Classification of polymorphism by Cardelli and Wegner (from [CW85], © 1985 Association for Computing Machinery)

constructors to coercion. The only kind of polymorphism allowing runtime variability in C++ is subtype polymorphism (thanks to dynamic binding). The remaining forms are completely resolved at compile time. All kinds of polymorphism in C++ rely on a static type system.

Java provides only a limited variety of polymorphism mechanisms. It supports subtype polymorphism, but not parametric polymorphism. The latter is quite problematic for a statically typed language (see Section 6.5.1). Automatic promotions and type conversions are available for built-in types, but not for user-defined types. Functions can be overloaded as in C++, but operators cannot be overloaded by the user. Subtype polymorphism occurs in Java in its pure form. Java provides so-called *interfaces* to represent types. Interfaces correspond to C++ abstract classes containing declarations of pure virtual methods, but no method implementations. An interface can be used to declare the type of a variable that can point to any object of any class implementing this interface. The introduction of interfaces relieves classes of their double role of being types and implementation repositories at the same time and lets them concentrate on the latter. Because this is not the case in C++, we sometimes say that C++ supports *subclass polymorphism* rather than subtype polymorphism. However, this is not as bad as sometimes argued. Interfaces can be implemented in C++ as abstract classes with no method implementations. Furthermore, we can use private inheritance as pure implementation inheritance and public inheritance as interface inheritance.

The situation is very different in dynamically typed languages, such as Smalltalk ([Eis99]). Because dynamically typed languages lack a static type system, parametric polymorphism makes no sense in such languages. The form of subtype polymorphism found in Java or C++ is not possible because variables have no statically declared type. If a message is sent to a Smalltalk object, Smalltalk first checks whether the object understands the message or not. If it does, the corresponding method is executed, otherwise it reports a "message-not-understood" error. Unlike C++ or Java, Smalltalk does not require that the different implementations of a polymorphic message are defined in classes derived from a common superclass or interface that originally defines or declares the polymorphic message. This idea is illustrated in Figure 6–6. The Smalltalk variant of polymorphism does not rely on compile-time type information (which is absent in Smalltalk), but is resolved at runtime. This kind of polymorphism is referred to as *unbounded polymorphism* [GR95] because it does not depend on the existence of a method prototype in a common superclass or interface. Overloading makes no sense in the absence of statically declared types of variables. Type conversions are implemented as explicit methods (e.g., asString). Type promotions (e.g., in arithmetic expressions) can be implemented using so-called *double dispatching* (see [Bec97]).

Other forms of polymorphism found in programming languages are *bounded parametric polymorphism* (or *constrained genericity*) and *F-bounded polymorphism*. They are discussed in Section 6.6.

---

analogous to the abstract class `Swappable` in Figure 6–2). Primitive types and existing classes not implementing `Greater` require adapters before we can pass their values or instances to `Pair`. Figure 6–8 includes `GreaterInteger`, an adapter for `Integer`.[3]

Because both instance variables in the template-based solution in Figure 6–7 are bound to the same type, for example, `int` or `double`, we explicitly check for type equality in the Java solution in Figure 6–8. However, both solutions still have different semantics.

```
class A
{ public:
    void hello() const
    { cout << "Instance of A" << endl;
    }
};
class B
{ public:
    void hello() const
    { cout << "Instance of B" << endl;
    }
};

template <class T>
void test(const T& v)
{ v.hello();
};
// ...
A a;
B b;
test(a); //prints "Instance of A"
test(b); //prints "Instance of B"
```

Figure 6-4 *Parametric polymorphism in C++*

---

3. Because the Java wrapper classes for basic types, such as `Int`, are declared as `final`, we cannot simply extend them and are forced to use adapters.

```
class ClassWithHello
{ public:
    virtual void hello() const = 0;
};

class A: public ClassWithHello
{ public:
    void hello() const
    { cout << "Instance of A" << endl;
    }
};

class B: public ClassWithHello
{ public:
    void hello() const
    { cout << "Instance of B" << endl;
    }
};

void test(const ClassWithHello& v)
{ v.hello();
};
//...
A a;
B b;
test(a); //prints "Instance of A"
test(b); //prints "Instance of B"
```

Figure 6-5 *Subtype polymorphism in C++*

◆ The Java version uses runtime type identification (RTTI) to check type equality at runtime, whereas the C++ solution is type-checked at compile time.
◆ The Java solution makes sure that both objects referenced by the instance variables have the same type. The situation in the C++ solution is somewhat more complicated. If T is a pointer or reference type, for example, B* or B&, each of the referenced objects can be of type B or a subtype of B. If B is a primitive type, type equality is guaranteed. If T is not a pointer or reference type, the values of both instance variables have the same type T.

Another problem of the Java solution is that the return type of max() is Greater. If we use Pair with GreaterInteger and need to perform computations on the result of max(), we have to cast the

```
instance method for class A:
hello
  "A inherits from Object
  Object does not understand 'hello'"
  Transcript show: 'Instance of A'; cr.

instance method for class B:
hello
  "B inherits from Object"
  Transcript show: 'Instance of B'; cr.

Execute the following code:
| v |
v := A new.
v hello. "prints 'Instance of A' in the Transcript"
v := B new.
v hello. "prints 'Instance of B' in the Transcript"
```

Figure 6-6 *Unbounded polymorphism in Smalltalk*

result back to GreaterInteger. This is demonstrated in the last line of Figure 6–8, where we call intValue() on the result of max(). This problem is particularly annoying in the case of container classes, such as lists, vectors, sets, and so on. Container classes are fundamental constructs in a programming language and have to work with different element types. The usual solution in Java is to use Object as an element type. We can put elements of different types in such containers. Unfortunately, when we take them out of

```
template <class T>
class Pair
{ public:
    Pair(T p1, T p2): p_1(p1),p_2(p2)
    {}
    T max() const
    {  return (p_1 > p_2) ? p_1 : p_2;
    }
  private:
    T p_1, p_2;
}
```

Figure 6-7 C++ *implementation of* Pair *as a class template*

```
interface Greater {
  public boolean greater(Object operand) throws
    IllegalArgumentException;
}

public class Pair {
  public Pair(Greater p1,Greater p2) throws
    IllegalArgumentException {
    if (p1.getClass() != p2.getClass())
       throw new IllegalArgumentException (
          "Components must be of the same type.");
    p_1 = p1;
    p_2 = p2;
  }
  public Greater max() throws IllegalArgumentException {
    return p_1.greater(p_2) ? p_1 : p_2;
  }
  private Greater p_1,p_2;
}

class GreaterInteger implements Greater {
  public GreaterInteger(Integer n) {
    i = n;
  }
  public boolean greater(Object j) throws
    IllegalArgumentException {
    if (this.getClass() != j.getClass())
       throw new IllegalArgumentException (
          "Operands must be of the same type.");
    return i.intValue() > ((GreaterInteger)j).intValue();
  }
  public int intValue() {
    return i.intValue();
  }
  private Integer i;
}

// ...
GreaterInteger i1 = new GreaterInteger(new Integer(2));
GreaterInteger i2 = new GreaterInteger(new Integer(3));
Pair p = new Pair(i1,i2);
System.out.println(((GreaterInteger)p2.max()).intValue());
// ...
```

Figure 6-8 Implementation of generic Pair *in Java using an interface*

the container, we have to manually cast them back to their original types, which is tedious and error prone. In effect, we are unnecessarily postponing type checking until runtime. Using `Object` as the element type of collections is referred to as the "Java generic idiom." This idiom is applied in Sun's Java Developer's Kit 1.2 (JDK 1.2) collection classes [Sun] and in other collection libraries, for example, the Java Generic Collection Library (JGL) [OS] and the Container and Algorithm Library (CAL) [X3M].

Because of the problems with subtype polymorphism previously outlined, several proposals for extending Java with genericity were published. We take a brief look at some of them.

Constrained genericity

One of the most popular generic extensions to Java is GJ [BOSW98] (which is a successor of Pizza [OW97]). GJ extends Java with generic parameters for classes and methods. GJ supports so-called *constrained genericity*, meaning that we can specify some constraints on type parameters (we discuss constrained genericity in Section 6.6). In GJ, we can annotate a type parameter with the interface that any actual parameter has to conform to. For example, we could define our `Pair` class as follows:

```
class Pair<T implements Greater<T> > {
//...
}
```

It is interesting to note that the interface `Greater<>` also takes `T` as a parameter. This form of parametric polymorphism, where the constraint on a parameter is parameterized itself, is referred to as *F-bounded polymorphism* (see [CCH+89]).

Homogeneous versus inhomogeneous translation

In general, parameterized classes as in GJ can be translated into ordinary Java classes using either *homogeneous* or *heterogeneous translation* [OW97]. The homogeneous translation involves generating one concrete class for a parameterized class. The concrete class uses the constraining type (or `Object` if no parameter constraint is specified) in place of the type parameter. The translation also automatically inserts the necessary casts into the client code. In other words, the homogeneous translation uses the same idiom as the one used by programmers to implement containers in Java. In the heterogeneous translation, on the other hand, a concrete class is generated for each instantiation of a generic class for a different type, for example, `PairForInteger`, `PairForDouble`, and so on. This is similar to how templates are instantiated in C++. Thus, the heterogeneous translation tends to generate a larger Java program than the homogeneous one—an effect often referred to as *code bloat*. On the other hand, the heterogeneous code may run faster because no extra casts

Code bloat

have to be inserted into the client code. An important advantage of the homogeneous translation is the ability to compile generic code to use the original Java collections from JDK 1.2 [Sun], for example, `LinkedList<String>` will simply compile to `LinkedList`. Because of these and other advantages, GJ uses homogeneous translation. An implementation of GJ is available at [GJ].

The proposal for extending Java with genericity in [MBL97] introduces generic parameters for classes, but not for methods. An interesting difference to GJ is that the parameter constraints can be specified by listing the required operations rather than referring to a separately defined interface. Using this approach, our generic `Pair` class could be defined as follows:

```
class Pair[T] where T { boolean greater(T t); } {
//...
}
```

Unfortunately, as suggested in [MBL97], an efficient implementation of this approach requires some small changes to the Java Virtual Machine (JVM).

As of this writing, it is unclear whether any of these proposals will be allowed into the Java standard or not.

6.6 Bounded versus Unbounded Polymorphism

Some languages, such as Eiffel and Ada, allow you to explicitly specify the properties a type must have in order to be used in place of a type parameter. We have already seen examples of this feature in the previous section:

```
class Pair<T implements Greater<T> > {
//...
}
```

and

```
class Pair[T] where T { boolean greater(T t); } {
//...
}
```

NOTE

Other genericity extensions for Java based on generic parameters are [AFM97, BD98]. An interesting approach proposed in [Tho97] is to use so-called *virtual types*, which are a kind of "virtual typedefs".

Constrained genericity

This feature is referred to as *bounded parametric polymorphism* [AC96], or *constrained genericity* [Mey88]. The previous examples demonstrate two different approaches to specifying the constraints on type parameters: The first approach is to use an interface defined elsewhere, for example, Greater<>. The other approach is to list all the required operations in place. For example, if our Pair<> from the previous section should implement an operation for checking the equality of its members in addition to the operation max(), T will have to provide not only greater(), but also isEqual():

```
class Pair[T] where T {
    boolean greater(T t);
    boolean isEqual(T t);} {
//...
}
```

F-bounded polymorphism

As far as the explicit specification of the required interface is concerned, bounded parametric polymorphism is similar to subtype polymorphism: In both cases, the interface a parameter[4] has to conform to is explicitly specified (i.e., the type of the parameter has to be a subtype of the specified type). The only difference is that with parametric polymorphism the type of the parameter is fixed at compile time and with subtype polymorphism the type may vary at runtime. Please note that the constraining interface can itself take generic parameters. As already stated, this is referred to as *F-bounded polymorphism*.

Unconstrained genericity

In C++, there is no way to explicitly specify constraints on template parameters. This is referred to as *unbounded parametric polymorphism* or *unconstrained genericity*. Because template instantiation is done during compile or link time, the compiler or the linker can detect if an undefined operation is called on an actual parameter before runtime.[5] Unbounded parametric polymorphism

---

4. Here we use "parameter" to mean an object or a value a piece of code needs, but not a type parameter.

5. The decision about which template instantiations are necessary can only be made when the complete program is available, that is, at link time. Different C++ implementations use different template instantiation strategies. In some implementations (e.g., Borland C++), the compiler produces all instantiations, and the linker gets rid of the unnecessary ones. In other implementations (e.g., AT&T cfront or compilers based on the EDG frontend), the compiler does not instantiate any templates during compile time, and the linker (or prelinker) calls the compiler to generate the necessary instantiations during link time.

corresponds to unbounded polymorphism, as in Smalltalk. The main difference is that the type of parameters in Smalltalk may vary at runtime, and the runtime system checks whether an actual parameter provides the requested operation or not.

Both bounded and unbounded forms of polymorphism have their advantages and disadvantages. Explicitly specifying the interfaces required from parameters facilitates static type checking: It makes static type checking in the case of subtype polymorphism possible, and it allows separate compilation of generic modules in the case of parametric polymorphism. Furthermore, parameter constraints describe the import interface of a piece of code. Such specifications are certainly useful for reusers, who can immediately see what is required of other components to plug them into the code. They are also useful to modeling and configuration tools.

On the other hand, unbounded forms of polymorphism have a lightweight nature: You have less to type in and you don't have to duplicate the interface information, which is implicitly present in the implementation code anyway. Furthermore, they involve "lazy" type checking. In the case of C++ templates (i.e., unbounded parametric polymorphism), type checking is done during template instantiation, that is, when the template is *used* for instantiation. In the case of unbounded polymorphism, for example, in Smalltalk, type checking is done when an operation is called on a parameter at runtime. This "laziness" guarantees full flexibility of the polymorphic code. Bounded polymorphism allows specifying *more* constraints than actually required in the code (i.e., we have the possibility for overspecification), whereas unbounded polymorphism and unbounded parametric polymorphism check what is really needed from a parameter at runtime or compile/link time.

6.7 A Fresh Look at Polymorphism

The different forms of polymorphism we have discussed so far (see the Polymorphism sidebar on pp. 177), came from different languages and directions. This may explain the proliferation of different names in the context of polymorphism found in literature, which is sometimes quite confusing. Our discussion has already pointed out many connections between the different forms of polymorphism. Let us now round up this discussion with a classification that makes these connections explicit.

*Universal versus
ad hoc
polymorphism*

Cardelli and Wegner made the distinction between *universal* and *ad hoc polymorphism* (see Figure 6–3). Universal polymorphism allows writing code that works with different types, and ad hoc polymorphism is responsible for selecting the right server code to be executed. For example, we use type parameters to make code work with different types, and overloading to automatically select the appropriate implementation. The idea is that you can call an operation on a type parameter and, thanks to overloading, be sure the appropriate implementation gets called depending on the actual type of the parameter, for example:

```
template<class T>
T sqr(T x)
{   return x * x; //* is overloaded for different types, e.g.
                  //int or double
}
```

Without overloading, the type parameter in the previous code would be quite useless because the operation would work for just one type, for example:

```
template<class T> //T is useless since multiplyInt() requires
                  //it to be int
T sqrInt(T x)
{    return multiplyInt(x, x); //call to
                               //int multiplyInt(int,int)
}
```

Overriding

Similarly, subtype polymorphism is used together with *overriding*, which refers to providing different implementations of one virtual method in different classes. For example, the polymorphic swap function in Figure 6–2 works for all subtypes of Swappable, such as Int and Double, which implement the assignment operator and the virtual functions assign(), copy(), and print().

The different forms of universal polymorphism we have discussed so far can be easily classified according to two criteria.

♦ Whether the interface required from a parameter is specified explicitly or not
♦ Whether the type of parameters is bound statically or dynamically

Uniform terminology of polymorphism

This classification is shown in Table 6–1. These two criteria also define a more uniform terminology, for example, unbounded polymorphism should be more appropriately referred to as *unbounded dynamic polymorphism* and subtype polymorphism as *bounded dynamic polymorphism*.

As noted earlier, the different kinds of universal polymorphism require some kind of ad hoc polymorphism, such as overloading or

Table 6–1 Classification of Universal Polymorphism

Names Found in the Literature	Bounded or Not (i.e., interface required from a parameter specified explicitly or not)	Binding Mode of the Type of Parameters	Available in Languages
Unbounded polymorphism	Unbounded	Dynamic	Smalltalk
Unbounded parametric polymorphism (or unconstrained genericity)	Unbounded	Static	C++
Subtype polymorphism	Bounded	Dynamic	C++, Java, Eiffel
Bounded parametric polymorphism (or constrained genericity)	Bounded	Static	Eiffel, Ada

overriding, to work with. Abstractly, both overloading and overriding represent a kind of name overloading, that is, the function or method name has an overloaded meaning—it refers to different implementation codes for different argument types. The main difference is that overloading involves static binding, whereas overriding is based on dynamic binding (also called *dynamic dispatch*). This difference is shown in Table 6–2, which also indicates that different languages may use a different number of argument types for distinguishing between overloaded names.

Overloading is provided by many statically typed languages (e.g., C++ and Java; however, C and Pascal do not support overloading). Please note that overloading uses all argument types to distinguish between different overloaded implementations, but not the return type. Overloading (and also overriding) on the return type is usually not supported because a function can be called "just for its side effects," for example:

```
foo();
```

instead of:

```
ResultType temp = foo();
```

Table 6-2 Classification of Name Overloading Mechanisms

Names Found in the Literature	Binding Mode (when is the appropriate implementation code selected?)	Number of Arguments Used to Distinguish between Overloaded Names	Available in Languages
Overloading	Static	All	C++, Java
Partial specialization	Static	Some	C++
Overriding with single dispatch	Dynamic	Only the first (i.e., the "receiver")	C++, Java, Smalltalk
Overriding with multiple dispatch (i.e., multimethods)	Dynamic	All	CLOS

In the former call, the compiler (or the runtime system) would have no idea which of the different implementations provided for different result types to select.

Partial specialization is a kind of overloading where an implementation is selected based on the type of some arguments, while the type of the remaining arguments is parameterized. This feature is available in C++ both for class and function templates (see Section 7.4.4).

Partial specialization

Overriding using *single dispatch* is the most popular kind of overriding in OO languages. Single dispatch corresponds to the Smalltalk idea of sending a message to an object, where the appropriate method (i.e., message implementation) is selected based on the type of the receiver. We can also view a message send as a function call whose first argument is the receiver, that is, self in Smalltalk or this in C++. Single dispatch introduces asymmetry with respect to the arguments because the first argument is treated specially. As we will discuss in Section 6.10.2, this asymmetry turns out to be problematic for modeling some domains.

Single dispatch

A dispatch mechanism that uniformly uses all argument types for selecting the method is referred to as *multiple dispatch*, or *multimethods*. Only a few languages provide multimethods, for example, CLOS [Kee89] and Cecil [Cha97]. In other languages, such as Smalltalk or C++, we have to use appropriate idioms to simulate this feature (e.g., see [Bec97] for a Smalltalk implementation and [Pes98, Cop92] for C++ implementations).

Multiple dispatch and multimethods

Please note that dynamic forms of universal polymorphism from Table 6–1 work with the dynamic forms of ad hoc polymorphism from Table 6–2. Similarly the static forms from Table 6–1 work with the static forms from Table 6–2.

6.8 Parameterized Components

Function objects

We started our discussion of generic parameters by showing how they help us to write code that works with different types—as in the case of the procedure swap() or containers. But generic parameters are also useful whenever we want to parameterize a part of an algorithm, for example, the comparison strategy in a sorting routine. One way of parameterizing the comparison strategy is to encapsulate it as an object and to pass it to the sorting routine as an extra parameter (see Figure 6–9). Such an object is referred to as a *function object*. In C++, the actual functionality of a function object is usually implemented by the operator (), so that it can be invoked similarly to a function. Function objects are particularly interesting if we want to accumulate or preserve state between function calls and/or organize the function objects into hierarchies to capture design commonalities and variabilities.

If the type of a function object passed to some code is unknown at compile time, that is, it can vary at runtime, we can implement the operator () as virtual. However, in the case of our sorting routine, the comparison strategy does not vary at runtime, and we do not have to preserve any state between calls. In such a case, it is more efficient to implement the comparison as an inline static function of a struct (see Figure 6–10). This implementation does not involve any function object, but the strategy is passed as a type parameter and then inlined directly in the sorting procedure by the compiler (if the appropriate compiler switches are enabled). The result is equivalent to directly using > or < in bubblesort() instead of C::compare(). Please note that we use a struct rather than a class because we only need one public member function. This way it saves us from typing the access control modifier public:; that is because members of a struct are public by default.

The previous example represents the application of the *strategy pattern* [GHJV95]. Indeed, nearly every design pattern listed in [GHJV95] is about making some part of a design variable; for example, *bridge* lets you vary the implementation of an object; *state* allows you to vary behavior depending on the state; and *template method* provides a way to vary computation steps while keeping the algorithm structure constant. Most of the standard implementations of these patterns utilize dynamic parameterization allowing parameters to vary at runtime (more specifically, the dynamic forms of polymorphism from Table 6–1). However, reusable models are also full of static variation points, that is, ones

```
template <class T>
void swap (T& a,T& b)
{ const T c = a; a = b; b = c;
}

template <class T>
class greater
{ public:
    bool operator()(const T& a,const T& b) const
    { return a > b;
    }
};

template <class T>
class less
{ public:
    bool operator()(const T& a,const T& b) const
    { return a < b;
    }
};

template <class T,class C>
void bubblesort (T a[],unsigned int size,const C& comp)
{ for (unsigned int i = 0;i < size; ++i)
  for (unsigned int j = i+1;j < size; ++j)
  if (comp(a[i],a[j])) //call the parameterized function object
  swap(a[i],a[j]);
};

// ...

int x[] = {-1,-2,-3,-4,-5};
bubblesort(x,sizeof(x)/sizeof(x[0]),greater<int>());
bubblesort(x,sizeof(x)/sizeof(x[0]),less<int>());
```

Figure 6-9 *Bubblesort with parameterized sorting order using a function object*

that vary from application to application rather than within one application at runtime. Such variation points are better implemented using static parameterization—as we've demonstrated for the previous strategy pattern. We discuss template-based implementations of other design patterns in Chapter 7.

```
template <class T>
void swap (T& a,T& b)
{ const T c = a; a = b; b = c;
}

struct greater
{
  template<class T>
  static bool compare(const T& a,const T& b)
  { return a > b;
  }
};

struct less
{
  template<class T>
  static bool compare(const T& a,const T& b)
  { return a < b;
  }
};

template <class C,class T>
void bubblesort (T a[],unsigned int size)
{ for (unsigned int i = 0;i < size; ++i)
  for (unsigned int j = i+1;j < size; ++j)
  if (C::compare(a[i],a[j])) //directly replaced by
                              //a[i]<a[j] or a[i]>a[j]
  swap(a[i],a[j]);
};

//...
int x[] = {-1,-3,-2,-4,1};
bubblesort<greater>(x,sizeof(x)/sizeof(x[0]));
bubblesort<less>(x,sizeof(x)/sizeof(x[0]));
```

Figure 6-10 *Bubblesort with parameterized sorting order using a static strategy*

6.9 Parameterized Programming

Generic programming gained much attention during the standardization of Ada [ANSI83], which provides parameterized modules referred to as *generics*. At that time, Joseph Goguen applied ideas from his earlier work on the programming and specification language OBJ [Gog79] to develop a theoretical basis for specifying and building libraries of generic modules in Ada [Gog84, Gog85, Gog96]. This work is known as *parameterized programming* and it can be seen as an approach to developing libraries of parameterized components in general. An instance of parameterized programming is the C++ Standard Template Library, which we discuss in Section 6.10.

Module expressions

The idea of parameterized programming is to represent reusable software as a library of parameterized components, which can be combined in a vast number of ways. The components can be composed by means of *module expressions* (also called *type expressions*), for example, A[B[C,D]], which correspond to template instantiation expressions in C++, for example, A<B<C,D> >.

6.9.1   Types, Interfaces, and Specifications

Export and import interfaces

An important idea of parameterized programming is to explicitly specify the interface provided and used by a component. Provided or *export interfaces* can be represented in Java by having classes *implement* interfaces (as in Figure 6–8) or in C++ by deriving implementation classes from purely abstract classes (as in Figure 6–5). Used or *import interfaces* correspond to type parameter constraints or supertypes, that is, interfaces constraining the type of a parameter as discussed in Section 6.6. Unfortunately, constraints are not available for C++ template parameters.

In general, an *interface* is the part of a component that is visible to other components as a contract. This includes both the syntax of the visible part, for example, signatures of the operations, and the semantics, for example, the behavior of the operations. In this sense, to us, the terms *interface* and *type* are synonymous. In practice, however, programming systems only support specifying the syntactic part of an interface, but not the semantic part. This is due to the enormous effort involved in formally specifying and proving even simple real-world systems. Semantic specification is a subject studied in the area of "formal methods." In practice, only small kernels of safety-critical systems (such as control software for nuclear power plants or rockets) are formally specified and proved.

NOTE

The terminology used by Goguen in [Gog96] is somewhat different: He refers to interfaces provided by components as *specifications* and to import interfaces as *theories*.

*Abstract
datatypes*

*Algebraic
specifications*

However, it is useful to take a look at a simple formal specification of an *abstract data type* (ADT) because this will give us important practical insight for structuring interfaces of ADTs (see Section 6.10.2). Currently, type theorists consider ADTs to be *classes of algebras*, where an algebra consists of a number of value sets and operations on these sets (see [LEW96] and also Section 9.8.3). Thus, ADTs can be specified using so-called *algebraic specifications*. An algebraic specification consists of:

♦A *signature* containing both a list of types, which are symbols representing the value sets, and a list of operation signatures on the types.
♦A list of *axioms*, which are properties constraining the meaning of the operations.

Figure 6–11 gives you a partial specification of the ADT LIST.

As an example of a generic ADT specification, we could rewrite the LIST specification to take ELEM as its type parameter. Furthermore, we could add the operation asString to LIST, which returns a STRING describing a LIST. This will require ELEM to provide asString, too. We can express this by constraining the ELEM parameter by the interface STRINGABLE (see Figure 6–12).

Of course, there may be many different concrete implementations of a specification. In a library of generic components, we

```
specification LIST:
    signature:
        types = {LIST, ELEM, INTEGER} //list of types
        operations = {
            . : ELEM, LIST → LIST,    //list constructor
            head : LIST → ELEM,       //operation for accessing the head
            tail : LIST → LIST,       //operation for accessing the tail
            length : LIST → INTEGER   //operation returning the list length
        }
    axioms:
        variables = {l : LIST, e : ELEM}
        head(e.l) = e
        tail(e.l) = l
        length(e.l) = length(l) + 1
        //...
```

Figure 6-11 Partial specification of the ADT LIST

```
specification STRINGABLE:
    signature:
        types = {STRINGABLE, STRING}
        operations = {
            asString : STRINGABLE → STRING
        }
    axioms:
        //no axioms

specification LIST [ELEM : STRINGABLE] :   //ELEM is a type parameter
    signature:
        types = {LIST, STRING, INTEGER} //list of types
        operations = {
            //operations as in Figure 6-11
            //...
            asString : LIST → STRING
        }
    axioms:
        variables = {l : LIST, e : ELEM}
        //axioms as in Figure 6-11
        //...
        asString(e.l) = asString(l) + asString(e)
        //...
```

Figure 6-12 *Partial specification of a generic* LIST

would have specifications representing interfaces provided by components, their concrete implementations, and specifications of
interfaces required from parameters. A component can be used as
a parameter of another component if its interface is a subtype of
the required parameter interface. In general, this means that the
subtype has to provide at least the operations of the supertype
(syntactic conformance), and also supertype axioms have to be
derivable from the subtype axioms (semantic conformance).

As already stated, in practice, we only specify the signature, that
is, the syntactic part of an interface, and compilers would only check
the syntactic type conformance. Therefore, in literature, the synonymous terms *interface* and *type* usually mean a *specification signature*.

6.9.2 Adapters

If a component does not completely fit into the parameter of another
component, we can adapt it using an *adapter* (see design pattern
"adapter" in [GHJV95]). In the simplest case, an adapter can do

THE EVOLUTION OF TYPES

The notion of types has evolved over time. Srinivas describes this evolution as follows [Sri91].

> The history of type evolution shows that types have evolved in a demand-driven way, responding to changing needs. As types become more expressive, we can tackle more complex problems, thus producing positive feedback in the form of more complex needs. Thus, the chain of more expressive types producing more complex needs and more complex needs motivating more expressive types continues.
>
> To illustrate this, we observe that initially, in assembly languages, there was only one type: addressable storage unit. To control the complexity of assembly language code, Fortran had a rudimentary notion of types: integers, reals, characters, booleans, arrays. This, and more powerful control structures, enabled us to produce complex programs, which needed a better notion of typing to impose some structure on them. Structured types in Algol and Pascal, and classes in Simula responded to this need. Around this time it was perceived that types are not just sets of values, but collections of sets and operations [Mor73]. This led to the notion of abstract data types, which was incorporated into languages like CLU [LAB+81] and Ada.
>
> Two other trends then joined this evolution: first, Simula's classes evolved into objects, message passing, and very late binding (e.g., Smalltalk, C++); second, functional programmers discovered that they could simultaneously have the convenience of untyped languages and the discipline of strong typing by using polymorphism and letting the compiler infer the types of expressions (e.g., ML [MTH90], Miranda [Tur85]). All these developments have renewed the interest in the theory of types, with "genericity" and reuse perceived as attractive programming techniques.

As stated in Section 6.9.1, the current theoretical model of types are algebras, that is, collections of sets and operations on these sets, and abstract data types are considered to be classes of algebras with certain structural properties.

Due to practical considerations, however, types in current programming languages are actually signatures, that is, syntactic parts of algebraic specifications.

---

syntactic mapping, for example, map operation names. However, it can also adjust the functionality of the adapted component.

An example of a simple generic adapter is shown in Figure

NOTE

In [Gog96], Goguen refers to adapters as *views*. It is important to note that the term "adapter" is not always used to mean an adapter in the sense of [GHJV95], but it sometimes also refers to a bridge or a decorator. We explain the differences in Table 7–1 in Section 7.6.

6–13. Money is a class that has no public assignment operator, but the method `assign()` instead, which has the same functionality. In order to be able to use Money in the generic procedure `swap()` from Figure 6–1, we need to provide an adapter that maps the assignment operator required by this procedure onto Money's `assign()`. Please note that the two type conversion operators in MoneyAdapter allow us to use an instance of MoneyAdapter wherever an instance of Money is expected.

6.9.3 Vertical and Horizontal Parameters

Layered architectures represent an important architectural style. The idea is that a layer uses the lower-level services from the layer

```
class Money
{ public:
    Money(unsigned u):amount(u) {}
    Money& assign(const Money& rhs)
    { if (this != &rhs)
      amount = rhs.amount;
      return *this;
    }
  private:
    Money& operator=(const Money& rhs)
    { return *this;
    }
    unsigned amount;
};

template <class T>
class MoneyAdapter
{ public:
    MoneyAdapter(T& m):moneyref(m), moneycpy(0)
```
(continued)

Figure 6-13 Generic adapter for Money

```
      {}
      MoneyAdapter(const MoneyAdapter& ma)
        :moneyref(ma.moneyref), moneycpy(0)
      { moneycpy = new T(ma.money());
      }
      MoneyAdapter& operator=(const MoneyAdapter& ma)
      { money().assign(ma.money());
        return *this;
      }
      ~MoneyAdapter()
      { delete moneycpy;
      }
      operator T&()
      { return money();
      }
      operator const T&() const
      { return money();
      }
  private:
      const T& money() const
      { return moneycpy ? *moneycpy : moneyref;
      }
      T& money()
      { return moneycpy ? *moneycpy : moneyref;
      }
      T& moneyref;
      T* moneycpy;
};

// ...
Money a(5),b(99);
MoneyAdapter<Money> c = b;
MoneyAdapter<Money> e = a;
Money d(3);
d.assign(c);
swap(c,e);
```

Figure 6-13 *Generic adapter for* Money *(continued)*

below it and provides higher-level services to the layer above it. In
a sense, a layer represents a virtual machine mapping a higher-level
interface onto a lower-level interface.

    Figure 6–14 shows several parameterized components orga-
nized into two layers. We refer to the relationships between com-

ponents of different layers as *vertical* and to those between components of one layer as *horizontal*. This also applies to parameters: We have *vertical parameters*, that is, parameters expecting components from lower layers, and *horizontal parameters*, that is, parameters expecting components from the same layer, or global or primitive types that do not contribute to the vertical structure.

For example, a stack container can be implemented as a wrapper on an ordered container, such as a vector or a list:

```
template<class ElementType, class OrderedContainer>
class Stack
{
    //...
};
```

According to the previous definition, `ElementType` is a horizontal parameter and `OrderedContainer` is a vertical parameter. In [Gog96], Goguen uses a notation that differentiates between vertical and horizontal parameters: the vertical parameter list is enclosed in (), and the horizontal parameter list is enclosed in []. In C++, there is no syntactic difference between horizontal and vertical parameters. However, you can use traits classes in order to implicitly pass horizontal parameters, so that template instantiation expressions directly represent the vertical structure of a composition. This is described in Section 9.8.2.4.

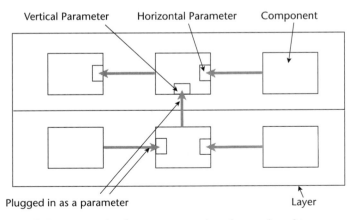

Figure 6-14 *Parameterized components in a layered architecture. Horizontal parameters express configuration within one layer, whereas vertical parameters represent refinement.*

NOTE

The distinction between vertical and horizontal parameters was introduced by Goguen and Burstall in [GB80].

6.9.4 Module Expressions

As we mentioned at the beginning of Section 6.9, *module expressions* (also called *type expressions*) define concrete compositions of parameterized components. For example, in C++, given the templates Stack<> and Vector<>:

```
template<class ElementType, class OrderedContainer>
class Stack
{
    //...
};

template<class ElementType>
class Vector
{
    //...
};
```

we can define a stack of integers using a vector as follows:

```
Stack<int, Vector<int> >
```

We come back to the topic of parameterized programming when we discuss the GenVoca model in Section 9.8.2. GenVoca is a particular kind of parameterized programming, where the parameterized components are layers containing one or more classes. GenVoca provides a nice notation for specifying structures of parameterized components. Suppose that we have three components, A, B, and C, which all export the same interface S (i.e., they are of type S), where A takes a parameter of type T, and B takes a parameter of type S. We could write this information as follows:

```
S : A[x:T], B[x:S], C
```

Similarly, we could also have the components D and E implementing type T:

NOTE

In [Gog96], Goguen gives a more elaborate model of module expressions including mechanisms for hiding and renaming module features (e.g., module operations).

```
T : D[x: S], E
```

Given these components, examples of valid module expressions are A[D[C]], B[A[E]], or C. A compact notation for representing the parameter structure of a set of parameterized components is a GenVoca grammar discussed later in Section 9.8.2.2. The GenVoca grammar for our example is as follows:

```
S : A[T] | B[S] | C
T : D[S] | E
```

The vertical bars separate alternatives, and parameters are enclosed in brackets.

6.10 C++ Standard Template Library

The *Standard Template Library* (STL) is a C++ library of reusable containers, such as list, vector, and set, and algorithms working on the containers, for example, searching and sorting. The STL probably represents the most advanced instance of generic programming that is widely available to C++ programmers. Furthermore, the development of the STL itself shaped the field of generic programming in important ways. Examples of other generic C++ libraries that follow the STL design are the matrix computation library *Matrix Template Library* (MTL) [SL98a] and the image processing library *VIGRA* [Köt98, VIGRA].

The STL origins go back to the work of David Musser and Alex Stepanov on an Ada library of generic algorithms [MS89a, MS89b]. The original STL implementation was achieved at Hewlett-Packard Laboratories by Alex Stepanov, Meng Lee, and their colleagues. The original STL reference document [SL95] has been incorporated in a modified form into the ISO C++ Standard, and the STL currently represents an important part of the C++ Standard Library.

The main development goal for the STL was to represent algorithms in as general a form as possible without compromising their efficiency. The STL makes extensive use of C++ templates to make code more general. It exclusively uses static binding and often inlining also in order to preserve maximal efficiency. A key design aspect of the STL is the use of *iterators* to decouple algorithms from containers. Iterators are an abstraction of pointers. They are used to navigate and access elements of a container and provide standardized interfaces for this purpose. This way, it is possible to write algorithms that work on a variety of containers with different storage formats. We explain this idea in more detail in Section 6.10.1.

The STL consists of different kinds of components, some of which are

◆ Containers
◆ Algorithms
◆ Iterators
◆ Function objects (see Section 6.8)
◆ Allocators (used for allocating memory)

The containers are implemented as class templates and the algorithms as function templates. We discuss this kind of library organization in Section 6.10.2.

Because the STL is such a complex library, we cannot discuss all of its details here. However, there are several excellent books describing various aspects of the STL, for example, [MS96, Bre98, Aus98]. Worth mentioning is the online STL documentation by SGI, which is available on the Internet [SGI].

6.10.1 Iterators

Iterators function like pointers: They point to elements and provide a dereferencing operator and navigation operations for repositioning them. For example, in C++, * is the dereferencing operator, and ++ advances an iterator to point to the next element in a container. The role of a pointer can be played by a simple C pointer or by an object that overloads these and other related operators.

Iterators help to minimize the dependencies between algorithms and the containers they operate on. They provide an abstract view on the containers: They abstract from the storage specifics of the container. For example, the operator ++ of an iterator for a vector may simply involve incrementing a pointer, whereas the same operation of a tree iterator has to perform a tree walk.

*Forward and
random access
iterators*

There are different categories of iterators (e.g., see [SGI]). For example, there are *forward iterators* and *random access iterators*. Forward iterators are used by algorithms that need to simply iterate through the elements of a container. They provide the operation ++, which gets you to the next element. In contrast to a forward iterator, a random access iterator allows you to position it at any element of a container at once using the operator [].

Iterators make it possible to write a single version of an efficient algorithm, which works on many different data structures. For example, we can use iterators to write efficient algorithms that work both on sparse and dense matrices. A sparse matrix uses a storage format that stores only its nonzero elements. On the other hand, a dense matrix is usually stored directly in a two-dimensional array (e.g., a vector of vectors). Due to these differences in storage, dense matrices provide faster random access (e.g., using the operator []) than sparse matrices because the latter have to map matrix element indices to the indices of the internal storage format. Now consider the usual implementation of matrix-vector multiplication for dense matrices, which uses the random access operator [] to access matrix elements. This implementation would be slow for sparse matrices because random access is slow in this case. However, iterating through all matrix elements (without requiring any particular order) is equally fast for dense and sparse formats. We can use this property to implement a general and efficient matrix-vector multiplication. All we need to do is to reformulate the matrix-vector multiplication such that it only involves iterating through all matrix elements and combining them appropriately with the vector elements. As a result, we get only one implementation of matrix-vector multiplication based on a forward iterator, which efficiently works on sparse and dense matrices (see [SL98a] for sample code). The key observation here is that the matrix-vector multiplication does not require random access but instead only a forward iterator, which is more general.

6.10.2   Freestanding Functions versus Member Functions

In OO languages, ADTs are specified using interfaces (e.g., Java) or purely abstract classes (e.g., C++) and implemented using classes. Operations on ADTs are usually implemented as methods, or in C++ terminology, member functions. The term "member functions" suggests that they are considered parts of the classes they are defined in. The idea that a method is part of a class is related both to the idea of a class being an encapsulation of data and operations and to the Smalltalk metaphor of sending messages to objects.

This view of an operation as a part of one type is often unnatural because many operations are defined on more than just one type. For example, if you consider the multiplication of a matrix and a vector, should the operation be part of the matrix or the vector? Either of these choices is unnatural. The operation is defined on both types, and thus it is an equal part of both types.

How can we properly model ADTs in an OO language? In C++, the answer is simple: You define most operations as freestanding functions rather than methods. Classes representing ADTs should include a minimal set of necessary methods, mainly constructors, destructors, accessing methods for stored or computed attributes, and means of accessing and navigating their data (e.g., the operator [] or iterators). This way we can avoid "fat interfaces," which cause scalability problems.

Designs organized into classes with narrow interfaces and freestanding functions are more flexible and scalable. Families of algorithms can be implemented by separate modules containing sets of functions. For example, consider the class Image representing 2-D images. Good candidates for methods in Image are accessing methods for the number of rows and columns, the pixel accessing operator [], or methods returning pixel iterators. Operations, such as drawLine(), drawRectangle(), drawCross(), drawCircle(), and so on are better implemented as freestanding functions. First, over time there is a good chance that you will add more and more of such operations. If they were implemented as methods, you would have to modify the interface part of Image and this would require recompiling all modules depending on the class Image. In an image processing library, where almost anything depends on Image, you will have to recompile a lot of code, resulting in long compilation times. Furthermore, not every function is needed by everyone. By defining operations as freestanding functions, you can group them into separate modules. Users will be able to include only those

NOTE

Interestingly, in most algebraic specification languages, ADTs are specified by modules consisting of a *list of types*, a list of operation signatures, and a list of axioms (see Figure 6–11). This is different from classes because a class is supposed to define only *one type* and a number of operations on that type. Obviously, this claim cannot be fully supported because the operations may take arguments of other classes and thus contribute to the definition of other types.

modules they are interested in. In the end, you will avoid the nightmare of maintaining class interfaces with hundreds of methods or very deep class hierarchies.

What if you need different implementations for different combinations of type arguments? If static binding is sufficient, you can use function overloading (this is the case in the STL). You can also use full and partial template specialization to avoid code duplication. For example, you can provide the default implementation as a template parameterized on all argument types and provide full and partial specializations of the template for special cases. You can also use the idiom described in Section 7.5 to prohibit the instantiation of the templates for certain combinations of argument types.

If dynamic binding is required, multimethods would be an ideal solution, that is, virtual methods that use all arguments for dispatch (see Section 6.7). Unfortunately, they are not supported in C++. In this case, you have to use idioms simulating multimethods (see [Bec97, Pes98, Cop92]).

There are situations where it is useful to implement algorithms on ADTs as separate objects or classes rather than functions. We discuss the criteria for when to implement an algorithm as a function or an object or a class in Sections 5.8.2.1, 6.8, and 7.6.

Although defining most operations outside an ADT class represents a conceptually cleaner solution, this is not possible or not practicable in all OO languages. For example, in Smalltalk, you have no other reasonable choice than to implement operations as methods. Smalltalk is based on the message-sending style, which is the only natural style in Smalltalk.

6.11 Generic Methodology

There are no widely used "generic A/D methods" as there are OOA/D methods. However, Musser and Stepanov retrospectively summarized the approach they used to develop the STL in four steps [MS93].

1. The first step involves selecting the most efficient algorithms and data structures, identifying container access operations on which the algorithms depend, and generalizing these operations with respect to the algorithms. This step concentrates on efficiency and commonality.
2. The second step is to implement variants of access operations using different container representations, different memory allocation strategies, different ways of error handling, and so on. This step focuses on variability.

3. Step three is to practice software reuse in the library itself by factoring out small algorithmic building blocks into separate routines that can be reused in larger algorithms. This step again addresses commonality.
4. Step four is to prepare the documentation that includes comparisons between the various algorithms, descriptions of their properties, the appropriate contexts for using them, and so on.

These steps are reminiscent of Domain Engineering (see Chapter 2). Indeed Domain Engineering supports generic programming well because it focuses on system families. In particular, feature diagrams (see Section 4.4.1) represent a very useful modeling notation for generic programming. Feature diagrams allow us to represent the parameterization space of concepts. Whenever we model a family of concepts, we should start with a feature diagram rather than an inheritance diagram. As an example, consider a list of elements. A list can hold references to original elements or their copies. Furthermore, a list may hold elements of different types or elements of the same type. The former is referred to as an *inhomogeneous* (or polymorphic) list and the latter as a *homogeneous* (or monomorphic) list. The inheritance diagram for the different kinds of lists is shown in Figure 6–15 and the corresponding feature diagram in Figure 6–16. The feature diagram is easier to extend with new variable features than the inheritance diagram. Furthermore, it does not imply any particular variation mechanism, such as inheritance, dynamic parameterization, or static parameterization (see Section 4.5).

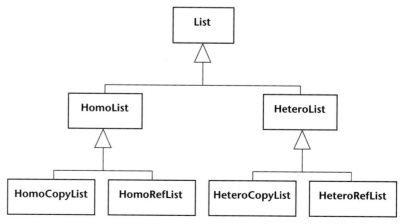

Figure 6-15 Inheritance diagram of a sample list

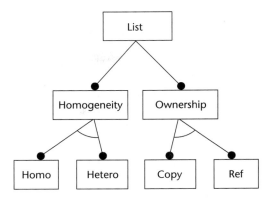

Figure 6-16 *Feature diagram of a sample list*

Because generic libraries utilize static parameterization extensively, it is interesting to take a look at how the UML supports it. UML has a way of expressing generic parameters of classes, which is shown in Figure 6–17. Generic parameters are enclosed in a dashed rectangle. In addition to type parameters, value parameters are possible, for example, integer parameters, as indicated in Figure 6–17. The notation does not support constrained type parameters. In other words, the UML parameterized classes directly correspond to C++ class templates.

The same parameterization notation used for classes can be also used for other UML modeling elements, such as collaborations and packages.

Figure 6–18 shows a sample UML model of a parameterized stack. The stack takes `ElementType` and `OrderedContainer` as its parameters (the latter is a container for storing stack elements). `Vector` and `Deque`[6] are containers that can be alternatively used in place

Figure 6-17 *Notation for a parameterized class in UML v1.1.* `T` *is a type parameter and* `i` *an integral parameter*

---

6. "Deque" stands for "double-ended queue," that is, a list that can be accessed at both ends.

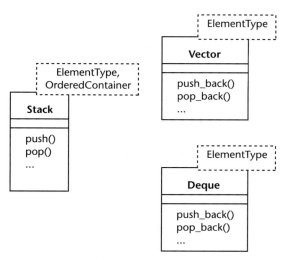

Figure 6-18 *Generic Stack and two alternative containers for storing its elements*

of `OrderedContainer` of `Stack`. The stack method `push()` is implemented in terms of `push_back()` of the parameter `OrderedContainer`, which adds an element to the back end of the latter. Similarly, `pop()` is implemented in terms of `pop_back()`.

The UML parameterization notation has several problems.

♦ It does not indicate which classes and data types can be used in place of a type parameter in a generic library.
♦ A type parameter can be used for different purposes, for example, as type of an owned part object, as type of an associated object, as type of a method argument, or as type of the superclass. These different uses are difficult, if not impossible, to represent explicitly in the previous notation.
♦ The notation does not show which operations are required from actual type parameters.

These problems render this notation virtually useless for documenting generic libraries.

As discussed in Section 6.10.2, freestanding functions are very important in generic libraries, but you will not find a modeling element for representing freestanding functions in UML v1.1.

In general, generic programming is poorly supported by OO modeling and programming tools. For example, most browsing facilities in OO integrated development environments are based on inheritance hierarchies and provide little help in organizing generic libraries.

6.12 Historical Notes

Generic parameters were originally introduced in the functional programming language ML [Mil84]. ML types can contain "type identifiers," which can be bound to different types in different contexts. ML relies on type inference to support the programmer as much as possible. For example, it allows the programmer to omit type declarations in places where the type can be inferred from the context. Constrained type parameters were implemented in CLU [LAB+81]. CLU also has iterators as a built-in language construct.

A visionary statement was made by James Neighbors in [Nei80], where he classifies parametric program generation as a powerful technique for automatic program customization.

> Parametric program generation trims and customizes a large model of a class of systems for a specific application. The parameters to the parametric program generation process remove unnecessary options of the general model and fill in some application-specific detail.

Generic programming gained much attention during the standardization of Ada [ANSI83]. At that time, Joseph Goguen published a paper on parameterized programming [Gog84] presenting the ideas we described in Section 6.9. In that paper, he characterized parameterized programming as follows.

> The basic idea of parameterized programming is to maximize program reuse by storing programs in as general a form as possible. One can then construct a new program module from an old one just by instantiating one or more parameters.

In [CW85], Cardelli and Wegner gave their classification of polymorphism, where they considered type parameterization and subtype polymorphism as related techniques (see Section 6.5)

With Scheme and Ada as their background, Musser and Stepanov defined generic programming in [MS89a] as follows.

> By generic programming, we mean the definition of algorithms and data structures at an abstract or generic level, thereby accomplishing many related programming tasks simultaneously. The central notion is that of generic algorithms, which are parameterized procedural schemata that are completely independent of the underlying data representation and are derived from concrete, efficient algorithms.

Finally, the work on the STL [MS93, SL95] represents the most advanced and widely-available instance of generic programming, where the focus is on finding the most abstract representations of efficient algorithms. Stepanov characterized the relationship between generic programming and the STL as follows [Rus97].

> Generic programming is a programming method that is based on finding the most abstract representations of efficient algorithms. That is, you start with an algorithm and find the most general set of requirements that allows it to perform and to perform efficiently. The amazing thing is that many different algorithms need the same set of requirements, and there are multiple implementations of these requirements. The analogous fact in mathematics is that many different theorems depend on the same set of axioms, and there are many different models of the same axioms. Abstraction works! Generic programming assumes that there are some fundamental laws that govern the behavior of software components and that it is possible to design interoperable modules based on these laws. It is also possible to use the laws to guide our software design. STL is an example of generic programming. C++ is a language in which I was able to produce a convincing example.

Chapter 7

Component-Oriented Template-Based C++ Programming Techniques

7.1 Why Is This Chapter Worth Reading?

Components are designed to be used for building applications by composition. A component has a well-defined interface comprising the services both provided to other components and used from other components. Today, component-oriented principles (see the Components sidebar in Chapter 1 on page 9) are most notably implemented in component technologies, such as JavaBeans [Sun97a] or Component Object Model (COM) [Ses97]. However, we can also apply component-oriented thinking at the class and source level, of which the Standard Template Library (see Section 6.10) provides a convincing example. Indeed, we can apply component-oriented principles at different levels and in different contexts in software development.

This chapter focuses on how to apply component-oriented principles in C++ programming. Although dynamically configurable designs are extensively discussed in [GHJV95], we will complement that work with programming techniques and idioms for static configuration. In particular, we present template-based versions of the design patterns bridge, wrapper, adapter, strategy, and template method (see Sections 7.6, 7.7, and 7.8). We will show how to switch between static and dynamic configuration by parameterizing method binding mode (see Section 7.9). We will also demonstrate how to model static properties of components (see Section 7.11.1) and how to encapsulate configuration knowledge in configuration repositories (see Section 7.11.2). Section 7.11.5 will provide you with the first idea of how to combine all these different techniques with automatic configuration. We will continue this theme in Chapters 10 and 12 by eventually showing you how to write system generators using template metaprogramming.

7.2 Types of System Configuration

The structure of a configurable system is determined by the configuration of its components. The configuration of a *static* system remains constant during runtime, whereas the configuration of a *dynamic* system varies over time. Furthermore, there is the question of whether all components and configurations of a system are designed before runtime and if the dynamic reconfiguration can only take place within the statically predefined configuration space, or whether new components and configurations can be produced during runtime. The different possibilities are depicted in Figure 7-1. Reflective systems offer maximum flexibility—they can evolve and adapt in ways that were not (completely) determined at design time. Post-runtime optimizations are less flexible: New components and configurations may be produced at runtime, but the system (or a part of the system) has to be shut down and recompiled in order to apply them (e.g., profile-based compilation fits into this category).

C++ provides language features supporting systems with statically defined components and configurations, that is, the lower

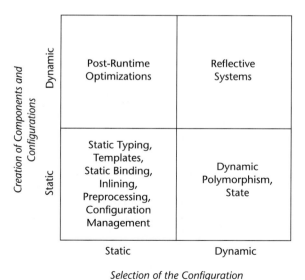

Figure 7-1 Types of system configuration

two quadrants of Figure 7-1. Reflective systems are best implemented using dynamic languages, such as Smalltalk or CLOS.

7.3 C++ Support for Dynamic Configuration

C++ supports dynamic configuration primarily through dynamic polymorphism, that is, virtual methods. When a piece of code calls a virtual method (rather than a nonvirtual one), the target component implementing the method may vary at runtime. However, all components and their possible configurations are defined before runtime. Dynamic creation and selection of new components and configurations requires language features for modifying program code at runtime. Such features are available in Smalltalk or CLOS (see Section 8.5.7 for examples), but not in C++.

OO frameworks are primarily based on dynamic configuration, and the use of virtual methods for dynamic configuration is the subject of many design patterns in [GHJV95].

Another C++ feature useful for dynamic configuration is the *runtime type information (RTTI)*. This feature allows us to discover the type of an object at runtime.

7.4 C++ Support for Static Configuration

Dynamic configuration is widely applied in OO frameworks, whereas static configuration is less known. This is probably due to the fact that dynamic configuration is more general because it can also be used in cases where static configuration would be sufficient. For this reason, in some languages, such as Smalltalk and Java, methods are always bound dynamically. C++, on the other hand, gives more control to programmers by allowing them to choose between features supporting dynamic configuration (e.g., virtual methods) or features supporting static configuration (e.g., static binding, inlining, and templates).

Static configuration offers the following advantages over dynamic configuration.

♦ Better efficiency because it avoids the cost of virtual function calls or even function calls altogether (thanks to inlining) and allows for many compile-time optimizations
♦ Smaller executables because only the needed code ends up in the executable rather than the whole framework

C++ supports static configuration with the following features.

♦ Static typing
♦ Static binding

- ◆ Inlining
- ◆ Templates
- ◆ Parameterized inheritance
- ◆ typedefs
- ◆ Member types
- ◆ Nested classes

We discuss each of these in the following subsections.

7.4.1   Static Typing

Static typing provides the basis for static configuration. Components and configurations can be represented as types and type expressions (e.g., template instantiation expressions) and manipulated by the compiler at compile time.

7.4.2   Static Binding

In C++, a method is statically bound by default. If we want a method to be bound dynamically, we have to explicitly declare it as *virtual* in a superclass.

Static configuration is well served by static binding. Static binding not only avoids the cost of virtual member function calls, but also enables the compiler to apply more optimizations because the targets of nonvirtual member function calls are known at compile time.

7.4.3   Inlining

In C++, we can declare a function to be `inline`, for example, [Str97]:

```
inline int fac(int n) { return (n<2) ? 1 : n*fac(n-1); }
```

The `inline` specifier is a *hint* to the compiler that it should consider generating code for a call to `fac()` inline rather than generating a function call to a separately generated function implementation. Conceptually, inlining involves replacing the function call directly by the function body. Whether a compiler actually inlines a function or not and to what degree, depends on the compiler. A sophisticated compiler may replace the call to `fac(7)` by the constant `5040`. Another compiler may replace it by `7*fac(6)`, and yet another compiler may abstain from inlining recursive functions altogether.

A member function defined directly within a function definition is considered to be `inline`; for example, the following code:

WHAT IS THE COST OF VIRTUAL MEMBER FUNCTION CALLS?

The simple answer is "a virtual member function call costs about twice as much as a nonvirtual member function call or about as much as three simple assignment statements. This suggests that virtual functions can be used freely whenever the body of the function is larger than perhaps 5 to 10 lines of code since the additional overhead will be insignificant." [EGK97]

In "number crunching" areas, such as image processing or numeric codes, the inner code of an algorithm loop is usually relatively small (e.g., few additions), but is repeated for many pixels or matrix elements. Therefore, the inner processing step of an algorithm should almost never be implemented using virtual functions!

Except for the aforementioned performance critical code sections, the cost of virtual calls is quite acceptable. Measurements on a number of benchmark programs (which included systems such as compilers and typesetting programs) showed that these programs spend about 4 percent of their time in virtual dispatch code [DH96]. This number increased to about 13 percent when all functions in these programs were made virtual.

How Does the Cost of Virtual Calls Come About?

The standard implementation of virtual dispatch in C++ uses so-called *virtual function tables* (*VFTs*; also *vtbls*), which are basically tables of function pointers. An object instance has a pointer to the appropriate VFT. In a typical implementation, a virtual call involves

- ♦ Two indirections to get the function pointer from the VFT (i.e., get the VFT address and then the function address from the VFT)
- ♦ One extra indirection to get the pointer casting offset from the VFT (the offset is needed for multiple inheritance to work correctly)
- ♦ Offset addition (i.e., object address plus the pointer casting offset)
- ♦ Function call

All of this is done in five instructions, which, if you assume one cycle per instruction, costs five cycles (see [DH96] for details).

The exact cost of virtual function calls is actually difficult to predict. The previous numbers represent a simplified model of the *direct cost* of virtual calls. Modern processors (e.g., Pentium) can minimize this cost even further by executing the five dispatch instructions in parallel. Furthermore, the direct cost is not the only one. There is also the *indirect cost* of virtual calls: Virtual calls may prevent the compiler from applying various optimizations because the targets of such calls are unknown at compile time.

```
class Foo
{public:
  void bar() { /*...*/ }
  //...
};
```

is equivalent to:

```
class Foo
{public:
  void bar();
  //...
};
inline void Foo::bar() { /*...*/ }
```

In order to enable inlining, the definition of a function has to be in the same compilation module as the client code making the call. This can be achieved by placing the function definition (not just the declaration) into a header that is included in the client code. Furthermore, most compilers provide switches controlling the level of inlining. Because inlining impairs debugging, it is useful to switch off inlining for compiling a debugging version of a program. This is usually the default setting.

Recompiling an application with the inlining option switched on usually produces a faster executable (however, the compilation time may increase). In order to verify whether a particular function call was actually inlined or not, we have to take a look at the generated code. Compilers usually provide switches for generating assembly code commented with the original source code, so it is easy to find the actual generated code for a given line of source code.[1]

Inlining may potentially lead to much larger executables because each inlined call to a function duplicates the corresponding function body. For this reason, inlining should be limited to small functions only. In fact, there is also another reason: The cost of a function call is usually insignificant for longer functions (e.g., longer than five lines or so), which makes inlining such functions pointless.

Surprisingly, inlining can even be used to eliminate unnecessary code, which is the opposite of code bloat. In particular, we use inlining to eliminate calls to empty functions. Figure 7-2 illustrates a case where this is very useful. The method at() of Vector<> is

---

1. Consult the manual of your C++ compiler about the appropriate optimization and assembler generation options.

used to access a vector element. The first line of this method is a call to checkBounds(), whose purpose is to check whether the index supplied to at() is valid or not. checkBounds() is expected to be a static method of the actual type used in place of the parameter Bounds-Checker. Figure 7-2 contains two alternative bounds checking components: SimpleBoundsChecker and EmptyBoundsChecker. Please note that EmptyBoundsChecker implements checkBounds() as an empty method. If we instantiate Vector<> for EmptyBoundsChecker and compile the code using an inlining compiler, the call to checkBounds() in at() of the resulting type will be eliminated altogether.

```
struct SimpleBoundsChecker; //forward declaration
template<class ElementType,
         class BoundsChecker=SimpleBoundsChecker>
class Vector
{
public:
  //...
  ElementType& at(const int& i)
  { BoundsChecker::checkBounds(i, length);
    //...
  }
  //...
};

struct OutOfBounds {};

struct SimpleBoundsChecker
{ static void checkBounds(const int& i, const int& length)
  { if(i<0 || i>=length) throw OutOfBounds(); }
};

struct EmptyBoundsChecker
{ static void checkBounds(const int& i, const int& length)
  {}
};

//...
Vector<int> v1; //v1 uses SimpleBoundsChecker
Vector<int, EmptyBoundsChecker> v2; //v2 uses
                                    //EmptyBoundsChecker
```

Figure 7-2 Vector *with parameterized bounds checking*

Inlining is also useful for optimizing accessing methods. For example, the sample class `Complex` in Figure 7-3 defines the accessing methods for its real and imaginary part inline. Furthermore, the arguments and return values are passed as constant references. This avoids unnecessary copying of the arguments and return values. Returning a constant reference rather than a reference avoids the accidental modification of `r_` outside of `Complex`. Thanks to inlining, a call to `real()` can be directly replaced by `r_` and a call to `real(2.0)` by `r_ = 2.0`.

7.4.4 Templates

We have already discussed the use of templates for generic programming in Chapter 6. We also identified templates as a mechanism for static parameterization (see Sections 7.2 and 7.6). Here we will only briefly review the main features of C++ templates.

Type parameters   C++ templates allow us to define *type parameters*, for example, as in the generic function for swapping two values:

```
template<class T>
void swap(T& a,T& b)
{ T c = a;
  a = b;
  b = c;
}
```

```
template<class Number=double>
class Complex
{
public:
  Complex(const Number& r, const Number& i) : r_(r), i_(i)
  {}
  const Number& real() const { return r_; }
  void real(const Number& r) { r_ = r; }
  const Number& imag() const { return i_; }
  void imag(const Number& i) { i_ = i; }
  //...
private:
  Number r_, i_;
};
```

Figure 7-3 *Sample class* `Complex` *demonstrating inline accessing methods*

In addition to function templates, we can also define class templates, for example:

```
template<class T>
class Vector
{
  T *data;
  //...
};
```

Nontype parameters

Furthermore, we can define *nontype parameters*, whose type can be an integral type (e.g., int, short, or char) or an enumeration type, but not a floating-point type or a class type, for example:

```
template<class T, int size>
class Vector
{
  T data[size];
  //...
};
```

In addition to types and integral constants, templates can also take templates, pointers, or functions as parameters. We'll see these advanced features in Sections 7.6 (see Figure 7-7) and Section 10.9 (see Figure 10-11).

Member function templates

Finally, we can define *member function templates*, for example:

```
class SomeClass
{public:
  template<class T>
  void method(T x) { /*...*/ }
};
```

Member class templates

and *member class templates*, for example:

```
class SomeClass
{public:
  template<class T>
  class MemberClassTemplate
  { /* ... */ };
};
```

Template specialization

Templates can be specialized for particular parameter values. For example, the implementation of swap<>() given previously is very inefficient for vectors because it would swap vectors by copying all their elements. A better implementation for vectors would be to swap their internal representations that store the elements. We can specialize the general swap<>(), so that the special implementation for swapping vectors will be selected automatically. Assuming that Vector provides the method swap() for swapping the representations, the specialization can be implemented like this:

```
template<class T> void swap(Vector<T>& a, Vector<T>& b)
{ a.swap(b);
}
```

Similarly, it is also possible to specialize class templates, for example:

```
template<class T1, class T2>
class Foo
{ //general implementation for Foo<>
  //...
};
```

```
template<>
class Foo<int,double>
{ //special implementation for Foo<int,double>
  //...
};
```

Full versus partial specialization

In the previous example, we provided a special implementation of Foo<> for the case where T1=int and T2=double. This kind of specialization is referred to as *full specialization* because we provided a concrete value for each parameter. However, we can also define a specialization for the case where only some parameters have a certain value, which is referred to as *partial specialization*, for example:[2]

```
template<class T2>
class Foo<double,T2>
{ //special implementation for Foo<double,T2>
  //...
};
```

---

2. As of this writing, only a few C++ compilers support partial template specialization.

Template specialization and member types (which we discuss in Section 7.4.7) represent mechanisms for automatically selecting an efficient implementation at compile time. Furthermore, together with recursive templates, they provide the basis for template metaprogramming, that is, writing programs to be executed by the compiler. We discuss template metaprogramming in Chapter 10.

7.4.5 Parameterized Inheritance

A very useful feature in C++ is the possibility to turn the superclass of a class into a parameter:

```
template<class Superclass>
class SomeClass : public Superclass
{ //...
};
```

This feature is referred to as *parameterized inheritance*. We can use it to implement a static wrapper (see Section 7.7) or an efficient version of a template method (see Section 7.8). We can also use it as an alternative to multiple inheritance for implementing mixin-based designs (see Section 4.5.3).

7.4.6 typedefs

typedefs are used to introduce a new name for a type, for example:

```
typedef int MyNumberType;
```

They are particularly useful for defining short names for template instantiation expressions, for example:

```
typedef Vector<Vector<double, 10>, 10> MyMatrix;
```

In this context, they can be viewed as a kind of "assignment statement" for type expressions, where the name on the right is bound to the type on the left.

7.4.7 Member Types

typedefs can also be used to define a type to be a member of another type, for example:

```
class SomeClass
{public:
  typedef int MyNumberType;
```

```
//...
};
```

We can access `MyNumberType` as follows:

```
SomeClass::MyNumberType i;
```

which is equivalent to:

```
int i;
```

Member types can be overridden in derived classes, for example:

```
class DerivedClass : public SomeClass
{public:
  typedef MyNumberType short;
  //...
};
```

We will use member types to propagate information between components at compile time (see Section 7.11.1) and to implement configuration repositories (see Section 7.11.2).

7.4.8 Nested Classes

C++ allows us to nest classes, for example:

```
class Outer
{ class Inner
  { class MostInner
    { /*...*/ };
    //...
  };
  //...
};
```

Nested classes can be used to uniformly parameterize a number of classes (see Section 7.10) and to organize configuration information into structured configuration repositories with separate name scopes (see Section 7.11.3).

7.5 Prohibiting Certain Template Instantiations

Just as we are able to provide specialized template implementations for certain combinations of parameter values, we want to be able to prohibit the instantiation of a template for certain parameter combinations. As an example, we show how to prohibit swapping pointers to characters using the swap template from Section 7.4.4. For this purpose, we add an appropriate check in swap():

```
template <class T>
void swap (T& a,T& b)
{ TemplateInstantiation<T> check;
  const T c = a; a = b; b = c;
}
```

TemplateInstantiation<> is defined as an empty template:

```
template <class T>
class TemplateInstantiation
{};
```

We can now provide a specialization of TemplateInstantiation<> for char* defining a private constructor:[3]

```
template <>
class TemplateInstantiation<char*>
{private:
  TemplateInstantiation()
  {}
};
```

Now, if we try to swap two C strings, we will get a compile-time error:

```
char *c = "Jack", *d = "Jill";
swap(c,d); //compile-time error!

double x=1.1,y=2.2;
swap(x,y); //OK
```

A slightly different but related technique does not involve object creation, but is based on accessing member types. The idea is to define a checking template, whose base implementation contains some member type:

```
template<class T>
struct CheckParameter
```

---

3. This idiom was suggested by Ulrich Breymann.

```
{ typedef int check;
};
```

The checking template can be used as follows:

```
template<class Parameter>
class ComponentA
{ typedef CheckParameter<Parameter>::check check;
  //...
};
```

Assume that we have two more components:

```
class ComponentB
{ //...
};
```

```
class ComponentC
{ //...
};
```

We can prohibit the use of `ComponentB` as an argument of `ComponentA<>` by providing an empty specialization of `CheckParameter<>` for `ComponentB`:

```
//prohibit ComponentB as an argument of ComponentA
template<>
struct CheckParameter<ComponentB> {};
```

When we try to use `ComponentB` as an argument of `ComponentA<>`, that is, `ComponentA<ComponentB>`, the compiler will report an error stating that `check` is not a member of `CheckParameter<ComponentB>`. Unfortunately, there is no way in C++ to issue a customized compile-time error report next to the erroneous component instantiation.

7.6 Static versus Dynamic Parameterization

Suppose that we are designing a container library. The library should contain different containers, such as deque, vector, and set. It should also provide a stack. We can implement the latter as an adapter on an ordered container, for example, vector or deque. Indeed, this is the way a stack is implemented in the STL. The C++ code is shown in Figure 7-4. The adapter `Stack<>` maps the stack methods empty(), size(), top(), push(), and pop() onto the corresponding methods empty(), size(), back(), push_back(), and pop_back() of the parameter OrderedContainer. Figure 7-4 also shows that Vector<> and Deque<> implement the latter set of methods and thus can be used in place of the parameter OrderedContainer of Stack<>.

We've already shown the corresponding UML class diagram in Figure 6-18 in Section 6.11, where we also identified the following three problems with the standard UML notation.

```
template<class ElementType, class OrderedContainer>
class Stack
{
  typedef OrderedContainer C;
protected:
  C container;
public:
  Stack() : container()         {}
  bool empty() const            { return container.empty(); }
  int size() const              { return container.size(); }
  ElementType& top()            { return container.back(); }
  void push(const ElementType& e) { container.push_back(e); }
  void pop()                    { container.pop_back(); }
};


//implementation of methods of Vector<> not shown
template<class ElementType>
class Vector
{
public:
  Vector();
  bool empty() const;
  int size() const;
  ElementType& back();
  void push_back(const ElementType& e);
  void pop_back();
  //...
};
```

(continued)

Figure 7-4 C++ *stack implementation using static parameterization*

```
//implementation of methods of Deque<> not shown
template<class ElementType>
class Deque
{
public:
  Deque();
  bool empty() const;
  int size() const;
  ElementType& back();
  void push_back(const ElementType& e);
  void pop_back();
  //...
};

void main()
{
  Stack<char, Vector<char> > s1;
  Stack<char, Deque<char> > s2;

  s1.push(1);
  s2.push(2);
}
```

Figure 7-4 C++ *stack implementation using static parameterization* (continued)

♦ The notation does not indicate which classes and data types can be used in place of a type parameter in a generic library.
♦ A type parameter can be used for different purposes, for example, as type of an owned part object, type of an associated object, type of a method argument, or type of the superclass. These different uses are difficult or impossible to represent explicitly in the standard UML notation.
♦ The notation does not show which operations are required from actual type parameters.

It is interesting to compare the previous stack implementation based on static parameterization with the corresponding implementation utilizing dynamic parameterization. The C++ code of the latter is shown in Figure 7-5. The purely abstract class template OrderedContainer<> explicitly captures the interface required by Stack<> and provided by Vector<> and Deque<>. The method

```
template<class ElementType>
class OrderedContainer
{
public:
  virtual bool empty() const                 = 0;
  virtual int size() const                    = 0;
  virtual ElementType& back()                 = 0;
  virtual void push_back(const ElementType& e) = 0;
  virtual void pop_back()                     = 0;
};

template<class ElementType>
class Stack
{
  typedef OrderedContainer<ElementType> C;
protected:
  C& container;
public:
  explicit Stack(C& c) : container(c) {}
  void setContainer(C& c)          { container = c; }
  bool empty() const               { return container.empty();}
  int size() const                 { return container.size(); }
  ElementType& top()               { return container.back(); }
  void push(const ElementType& e)  { container.push_back(e); }
  void pop()                       { container.pop_back(); }
};

//implementation of methods of Vector<> not shown
template<class ElementType>
class Vector : public OrderedContainer<ElementType>
{
public:
  Vector();
  bool empty() const;
  int size() const;
  ElementType& back();
  void push_back(const ElementType& e);
  void pop_back();
  //...
};
```

(continued)

Figure 7-5 *C++ stack implementation using dynamic parameterization*

```
//implementation of methods of Deque<> not shown
template<class ElementType>
class Deque : public OrderedContainer<ElementType>
{
public:
  Deque();
  bool empty() const;
  int size() const;
  ElementType& back();
  void push_back(const ElementType& e);
  void pop_back()
  //...
};

void main()
{
  Vector<char> v;
  Deque<char> d;
  Stack<char> s1(v), s2(d);

  s1.push(1);
  s2.push(2);
}
```

Figure 7-5 *C++ stack implementation using dynamic parameterization (continued)*

setContainer() of Stack<> allows us to replace its ordered container at any time during runtime.

The parameterization structures we have discussed in the context of Stack<> so far are useful in many different situations. Indeed, all design patterns listed in Table 7-1 have a similar structure to the Stack<> example. The differences between the patterns are explained in Figure 7-6.

Whether to use static or dynamic parameterization for a given variation point depends on whether we need dynamic or static configuration. If static configuration is sufficient, we can use static parameterization and this way avoid the overhead of virtual function calls.

In the case of the strategy pattern, we can implement static parameterization in several ways.

Table 7-1   Design Patterns Primarily Based on Parameterization

Design Pattern	Purpose and Example
Bridge	Separates interface from implementation. The implementation is a parameter of the interface. The interface and the implementation can provide different operations. Our stack example in Figure 7-4 is an instance of a bridge. The example has just one component interface Stack<>, but in general we can have a whole hierarchy of component interfaces.
Decorator (wrapper)	Adds functionality to a component. The component is a parameter of a wrapper. In contrast to a bridge, a wrapper exports the same interface as the component. An example of a wrapper is the tracing wrapper in Figure 7-29.
Adapter	Adapts an existing component to a new application context. Thus, similar to a bridge, an adapter may provide different operations than the ones provided by the component being adapted. In contrast to a bridge, an adapter is not designed together with the component, but later, just before the component is used in a new context. An example of an adapter was given in Figure 6-13, Section 6.9.2. Please note that in the STL, the term "adapter" actually refers to a bridge, for example, the STL adapter Stack<> is a bridge.
Strategy	Allows parameterizing algorithms used by a component. The parameter is an algorithm, or more generally, a smaller component. We can say that bridge, decorator, and adapter are about parameterizing "the skin," whereas strategy lets you parameterize "the guts." We have seen an example of a strategy in Section 6.8.

♦ *As an object:* This is similar to the bridge implementation in Figure 7-4. The strategy object provides its functionality through a number of methods and accumulates or preserves some state between calls.

♦ *As a function object:* We have demonstrated this case in Figure 6-9, Section 6.8. The strategy object provides its functionality through the operator ( ) and accumulates or preserves some state between calls.

♦ *As a class (or a struct):* We have demonstrated this case in Figure 6-10, Section 6.8. The strategy class provides its functionality through one or more static methods. No state is preserved between calls.

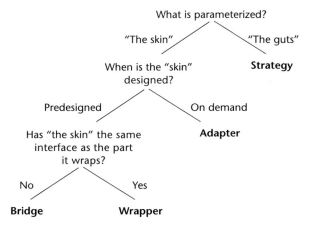

***Figure* 7-6** *Classification of design patterns based on parameterization*

♦ *As a function template parameter:* We can also pass a function as a template parameter. This is shown in Figure 7-7. `integrate()` computes the integral of a function, which is passed as a template parameter. This code is very efficient because `function1()` is inlined in the for-loop.

```
inline double function1(double x)
{ return 1.0/(1.0+x); }

template<double T_function(double)>
double integrate(double a, double b, int numSamplePoints)
{ double delta = (b-a) / (numSamplePoints -1);
  double sum = 0.0;

  for (int i=0; i<numSamplePoints-1; ++i)
    sum += T_function(a + i*delta);

  return sum * (b-a) / numSamplePoints;
}
//...
{ cout << integrate<function1>(1.0, 2.0, 100) << endl;
```

***Figure* 7-7** `integrate()` *takes a function as a template parameter (example from [Vel98c])*

7.7 Wrappers Based on Parameterized Inheritance

We can use parameterized inheritance to implement statically configured wrappers. As we explained in Table 7-1, a wrapper is used to extend the functionality of a component, and it exports the same interface as the component. One way to implement a static wrapper is to use aggregation:

```
template<class Component>
class Wrapper
{
  Component c;
  //...
};
```

We can also implement a static wrapper using parameterized inheritance:

```
template<class Component>
class Wrapper : public Component
{ //...
};

//...
Wrapper<ConcreteComponent> c;
//...
```

This implementation is particularly useful if we want to override only a few methods and inherit the rest.

We can also use parameterized aggregation or inheritance to implement adapters and bridges. The implementation would be similar to a wrapper implementation.

Parameterized inheritance represents an attractive alternative to multiple inheritance for implementing mixin-based designs (see Section 4.5.3). Another application of parameterized inheritance is discussed in the following section.

7.8 Template Method Based on Parameterized Inheritance

The design pattern *template method* [GHJV95] represents one of the fundamental structures used in object-oriented frameworks. The class diagram in Figure 7-8 explains this structure. `algorithm()` is a

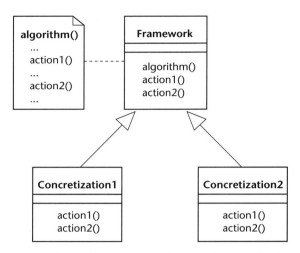

Figure 7-8 *Usual implementation of a template method using inheritance*

method calling a number of abstract methods, for example, `action1()` and `action2()`. Concrete implementations of the abstract methods are provided in subclasses of `Framework`. The usual arrangement is that the base class `Framework` is a part of a framework, and an application defines a concrete subclass. The method `algorithm()` is referred to as a *template method* because it defines the overall algorithm structure, but it lets you vary some of its steps. The corresponding sample C++ code is given in Figure 7-9.

Parameterized inheritance allows us to rewrite the original template method design to avoid the cost of virtual member function calls without compromising its flexibility. The new structure is illustrated in Figure 7-10. Please note that `Framework` expects to inherit `action1()` and `action2()` from its parameter `Concretization`. Because you can explicitly pass `Concretization1` or `Concretization2` to `Framework` as an actual parameter, `action1()` and `action2()` do not need to be virtual. It is interesting to note that, in this design, the framework class inherits from the concretization class and not the other way around.

```
class Framework
{public:
  virtual void action1() = 0;
  virtual void action2() = 0;

  void algorithm()
  {
    //...
    action1();
    //...
    action2();
    //...
  }
};

class Concretization1 : public Framework
{public:
  void action1()
  { cout << "Conretization1::action1()" << endl; }

  void action2()
  { cout << "Conretization1::action1()" << endl; }
};

class Concretization2 : public Framework
{public:
  void action1()
  { cout << "Conretization2::action1()" << endl; }

  void action2()
  { cout << "Conretization2::action2()" << endl; }
};

void main()
{
  Concretization1().algorithm();
  Concretization2().algorithm();
}
```

Figure 7-9 Template method using inheritance

```
template<class Concretization>
class Framework : public Concretization
{public:
  void algorithm()
  { typedef Framework<Concretization> This;
    //...
    This::action1();
    //...
    This::action2();
    //...
  }
};

class Concretization1
{public:
  void action1()
  { cout << "Conretization1::action1()" << endl; }

  void action2()
  { cout << "Conretization1::action2()" << endl; }
};

class Concretization2
{public:
  void action1()
  { cout << "Conretization2::action1()" << endl; }

  void action2()
  { cout << "Conretization2::action2()" << endl; }
};

void main()
{
  Framework<Concretization1>().algorithm();
  Framework<Concretization2>().algorithm();
}
```

Figure 7-10 Template method using parameterized inheritance

7.9 Parameterizing Binding Mode

Parameterized inheritance allows us to parameterize the binding mode of methods, that is, turn the decision—whether a method is statically or dynamically bound—into a parameter. This is illus-

```
template<class BindingMode>
class Component : public BindingMode
{public:
  void method1()
  {//...
  }
  void method2()
  {//...
  }
};

//binding modes
class Static {};

class Mixed
{public:
  virtual ~Mixed() {}
  virtual void method1() = 0;
};

class Dynamic
{public:
  virtual ~Dynamic() {}
  virtual void method1() = 0;
  virtual void method2() = 0;
};

//usage:
//...
Component<Static>  c1; //method1() and method2() are statically
                       //bound
Component<Mixed>   c1; //method1() is virtual and method2() is
                       //statically bound
Component<Dynamic> c1; //method1() and method2() are virtual
//...
```

Figure 7-11 *Parameterizing binding mode*

trated in Figure 7-11. The idea is to let a class inherit from its parameter and provide alternative base classes declaring none, some, or all methods to be virtual.

7.10 Consistent Parameterization of Multiple Components

Sometimes we want to consistently parameterize a number of components. For example, we would like to parameterize a matrix component and a vector component with the same element type, so that their instances can be used consistently in algebraic expressions. Such uniform parameterization of a number of components can be achieved by nesting them into a domain component that takes the common parameters. Figure 7-12 illustrates this approach. Figure 7-13 provides the corresponding C++ code. `Matrix` and `Vector` are implemented as member classes of the class template `MatrixDomain<>`, which takes the common element type as its parameter, that is, `ElementType`. The parameter `ElementType` is then used in `Matrix` and `Vector`. `Scalar` is defined as a member type of `MatrixDomain<>` using `typedef`.

Figure 7-14 shows how to define and use concrete scalars, vectors, and matrices given the matrix domain from Figure 7-13. Please note that we can easily change the scalar type of the entire domain just by modifying the second line in Figure 7-14.

7.11 Static Interactions between Components

Components are composed to build larger components and, eventually, whole applications. It is important to realize that, while we are adding components to a composition, the properties of both the whole composition and the individual components are evolving. From the perspective of a component, we have the following three kinds of interactions.

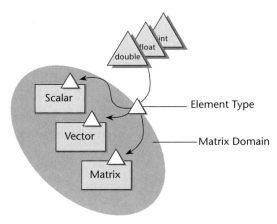

Figure 7-12 Consistent parameterization of a matrix domain

```
template <class ElementType>
class MatrixDomain
{public:
  typedef ElementType Scalar; //provide Scalar as a member
                              //type
  class Matrix
  {public:
    Matrix product(const Matrix& m) const;
    const Scalar& element(const int& r, const int& c) const;
    void element(const int& r, const int& c, const Scalar& e);
    // ...
  };
  class Vector
  {public:
    Scalar vectorProduct(const Vector& v) const;
    Matrix matrixProduct(const Vector& v) const;
    // ...
  };
};
```

Figure 7-13 *Consistent parameterization of a matrix domain*

♦ *The component influences the properties of the whole composition:* For example, piston displacement of the engine of a car is one of the factors determining the overall fuel consumption of the car.

♦ *The whole composition influences some properties of the component:* For example, the color of the dashboard of a car may determine the color of the front panel of the radio built into the dashboard.

```
// make changes as local as possible:
typedef MatrixDomain<double> Domain;
typedef Domain::Scalar Scalar;
typedef Domain::Vector Vector;
typedef Domain::Matrix Matrix;
Vector v;
// initializing elements of v
//...
Scalar s = v.vectorProduct(v);
Matrix m = v.matrixProduct(v);
```

Figure 7-14 *Sample code using the matrix domain*

♦ *The component influences the properties of another component:* For example, installing air conditioning in a car will require a stronger battery.

In the case of dynamic configuration, these three kinds of influence are easily modeled as interacting objects. But how do you implement influences in the context of static configuration? We will address this question in the following sections.

7.11.1 Components with Influence

In order to model the case where a component determines some properties of the whole static composition, we need a way for a component to advertise its properties at compile time. This can be achieved using member types and member constants. For example, consider an array component advertising its ElementType as a member constant. The sample C++ code is shown in Figure 7-15.

Next, we could have a matrix component that delegates storing its elements to a representation parameter, which could be filled in by Array10x10. The matrix component can retrieve the element type from its parameter by accessing the member type ElementType (see Figure 7-16). Please note that the keyword typename is required in ISO/ANSI C++ to tell the compiler that the member of a template parameter (i.e., ElementType) is a type.

```
template <class ElementType_>
class Array10x10
{
public:
  typedef ElementType_ ElementType; //export ElementType
  Array10x10(const int& r, const int& c):r_(r),c_(c) {}
  //inline and const reference
  const unsigned& rows() const { return r_; }
  // ...
  const ElementType& element(const int& r, const int& c) const
  { return elements_[r][c]; }
private:
  int r_,c_;
  ElementType elements_[10][10];
};
```

Figure 7-15 *Simple two-dimensional array exporting its element type as a member type*

```
template <class Rep>
class Matrix
{
public:
  //get ElementType from Rep
  typedef typename Rep::ElementType ElementType;
  Matrix(const int& r, const int& c):rep(r,c) {}
                      //forwarding to rep
  const int& rows() const { return rep.rows(); }
  // ...
  const ElementType& element(const int& r, const int& c) const
  { return rep_.element(r,c); }
private:
  Rep rep_;
};

//...
Matrix<Array10x10<double> > m(3,2), n(2,2);
//...
```

Figure 7-16 Matrix component retrieving element type from its representation

The overall arrangement is illustrated in Figure 7-17.

A component can also advertise its properties using member constants. For example, we could have a vector component with a static size, which advertises the size as a member constant (see Figure 7-18).

Many compilers still do not support the member constant syntax in Figure 7-18. As an alternative, we can define an enumeration

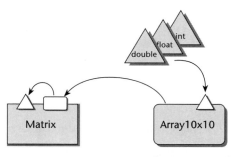

Figure 7-17 Matrix component retrieving element type from its representation parameter

```
template<class ElementType_, int size_>
class Vector
{
public:
  typedef ElementType_ ElementType;
  static const int size = size_;
  //...
private:
  ElementType elements_[size];
};

//still need to define the constant outside of the class
//declaration
template<class ElementType_, int size_>
const int Vector<ElementType_,size_>::size;

//...
typedef Vector<double, 12> MyVector;

cout << "The size of MyVector is " << MyVector::size << endl;
```

Figure 7-18 Vector component advertising its element type and size

type as a member of Vector<> and initialize a member of the enumeration type with the desired value. This is shown in Figure 7-19. Indeed, we prefer to use an enumerator over a static member constant in general. This is so because the syntax is more convenient and static member constants are possible for integral types only and not for any elementary type, as you might expect. If you use an enumerator instead, you won't be tempted to use floating-point numbers or other objects. Furthermore, you won't have to define the constant outside the class declaration to use it in a program (which, according to the C++ standard, is necessary for a static member constant). In fact, for these reasons, Stroustrup considers static member constants as a misfeature (see [Str97, p. 249]).

7.11.2 Components under Influence

Sometimes a property of a component is determined by its environment. Thus, we need a way for a component to retrieve some properties from its environment. This is exactly the opposite situa-

```
template<class ElementType_, int size_>
class Vector
{
public:
  typedef ElementType_ ElementType;
  enum { size = size_ };
  //...
private:
  ElementType elements_[size];
};

//...
typedef Vector<double, 12> MyVector;

cout << "The size of MyVector is " << MyVector::size << endl;
```

Figure 7-19 Exporting size as a member of a member enumeration type

tion to the one we discussed in the previous section, where the environment was able to access some properties of a component.

As an example, consider the matrix domain from Figure 7-12, which contains `Matrix`, `Vector`, and `Scalar`. Suppose that we want to independently parameterize the representation of `Matrix` and `Vector`, but still want all components to use the same `ElementType`. This is shown in Figure 7-20. The representation components `Array10x10` and `DynamicVector` will become parts of `Matrix` and `Vector`, respectively, but need to retrieve `ElementType` from the matrix domain.

Configuration repositories

This complex arrangement from Figure 7-20 can be simplified by encapsulating the configuration knowledge into a separate component: the *configuration repository*. The configuration repository can be thought of as a registry, where all the information about component parameterization is stored. The idea is to pass the repository as a parameter to the components, so that the components can retrieve the actual parameters they need from the repository. This is illustrated in Figure 7-21.

The C++ implementation of the matrix domain is shown in Figure 7-22. Please note that the only parameter of the domain is `Config`, which is the configuration repository. The lines where `Scalar`, `MatrixRep`, and `VectorRep` are retrieved from the repository are highlighted.

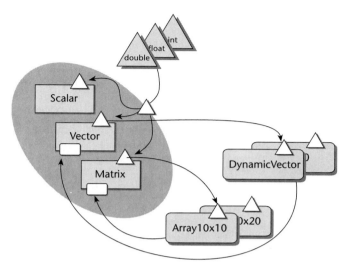

Figure 7-20 *Parameterizing the representations of vector and matrix in a matrix domain*

The implementation of the representation components Array10x10 and DynamicVector is given in Figure 7-23. Similarly, as in the case of the matrix domain, the only parameter of both components is Config.

Finally, Figure 7-24 shows the configuration repository, which contains all the configuration knowledge for our example. Please

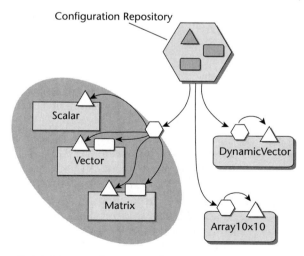

Figure 7-21 *Encapsulating configuration knowledge in a configuration repository*

```
template <class Config>
class MatrixDomain
{
public:
  typedef typename Config::Scalar Scalar;

  class Matrix
  {
  public:
    // ...
    void element(const int& r, const int& c, const Scalar& e)
    { rep_.element(r,c,e); }
  private:
    typedef typename Config::MatrixRep Rep;
    Rep rep_;
  };

  class Vector
  {
  public:
    // ...
    void element(const int& i, Scalar& e)
    { rep_.element(i,e); }
  private:
    typedef typename Config::VectorRep Rep;
    Rep rep_;
  };
};
```

Figure 7-22 *Matrix domain parameterized with the configuration repository*

Traits classes

note that the repository exports all the types required by the components as its member types. This kind of classes bundling different types as their members is known as *traits classes* [Mye95]. Figure 7-25 demonstrates how to use the configuration.

7.11.3 Structured Configurations

If one configuration repository is used as a parameter of more than one component, name conflicts between repository entries for different components are inevitable. For example, both the vector component and the matrix component from Figure 7-22 need a

```cpp
template <class Config>
class Array10x10
{
public:
  typedef typename Config::ElementType ElementType;
  //...
  void element(const int& i, const int& j, const ElementType& e)
  { elements_[i][j] = e;}
private:
  ElementType elements_[10][10];
};

template <class Config>
class DynamicVector
{
public:
  typedef typename Config::ElementType ElementType;
  //...
  void element(const int& i, const ElementType& e)
  { elements_[i] = e;}
private:
  ElementType* elements_;
};
```

Figure 7-23 Representation components parameterized with the configuration repository

```cpp
struct Configuration
{
  typedef double Scalar;
  typedef Scalar ElementType;
  typedef DynamicVector<Configuration> VectorRep;
  typedef Array10x10<Configuration> MatrixRep;
  typedef MatrixDomain<Configuration> Domain;
  typedef Domain::Matrix Matrix;
  typedef Domain::Vector Vector;
};
```

Figure 7-24 Configuration repository for our matrix components

```
// ...
typedef Configuration::Domain Domain;
typedef Domain::Scalar Scalar;
typedef Domain::Vector Vector;
typedef Domain::Matrix Matrix;
Vector v(5);
Scalar s = v.vectorProduct(v);
Matrix m = v.matrixProduct(v);
```

Figure 7-25 *Code demonstrating the use of the configuration repository*

representation component. For this purpose, we provided the differently named entries VectorRep and MatrixRep in the repository (see Figure 7-24). Another solution is to reserve a separate name scope for each component in the repository. This way, we could have the entry Rep for both vector and matrix. Such separate name scopes can be implemented using nested classes (or structs). This approach is illustrated in Figure 7-26.

7.11.4 Recursive Components

Consider a simple list class List, which has two members: head_ and tail_ (see Figure 7-27). Obviously, the type of tail_ is List itself. We say that List is a recursive class.

Next, suppose that we would like to implement a tracing component for List, which logs every call to setHead() and setTail(). The simplest way to do this is to define the tracing component as a static wrapper using parameterized inheritance (see Section 7.7). The problem we are facing at this point is that, if we want to extend List for tracing, we also have to use the extended list type for the member tail_. In other words, we have a situation where deriving a class from a superclass requires changes in the superclass. The solution to this problem is to pass the appropriate tail type to List through a configuration repository (see Figure 7-28). The line where List retrieves FinalList from the repository is highlighted.

The implementation of the tracing wrapper is shown in Figure 7-29. The tracing wrapper takes BaseList as a parameter and retrieves Config from BaseList.[4] In general, we could also have

---

4. The reason we are passing BaseList as a parameter rather than Config is to make the component structure more explicit. We discuss the rationale behind this decision in Section 9.8.2.4.

```
template <class Config> class Array10x10
{public:
  typedef typename Config::ForContainer::ElementType ElementType;
  // ...
};


template <class Config> class DynamicArray
// ...


template <class Config> class MatrixDomain
{public:
  typedef typename Config::Scalar Scalar;
  class Matrix
  { // ...
  private:
    typedef typename Config::ForMatrix::Rep Rep;
    Rep rep_;  };
  class Vector
  { // ...
  private:
    typedef typename Config::ForVector::Rep Rep;
    Rep rep_; };
};


struct Config
{ typedef double Scalar;
  struct ForContainer
  { typedef Scalar ElementType;
  };
  struct ForVector
  { typedef DynamicVector<Config> Rep;
  };
  struct ForMatrix
  { typedef Array10x10<Config> Rep;
  };
  typedef MatrixDomain<Config> Domain;
  typedef Domain::Matrix Matrix;
  typedef Domain::Vector Vector;
};
```

Figure 7-26 Matrix domain with a structured configuration repository

```
template<class ElementType>
class List
{
public:
  List(const ElementType& h, FinalList *t = 0) :
    head_(h), tail_(t) {}
  void setHead(const ElementType& h) { head_ = h; }
  const ElementType& head() const { return head_; }
  void setTail(List *t) { tail_ = t; }
  List *tail() const { return tail_; }
private:
  ElementType head_;
  List *tail_;
}
```

Figure 7-27 Simple list container

```
template<class Config_>
class List
{
public:
  typedef Config_ Config; //export Config
private:
  typedef typename Config::ElementType ElementType; //retrieve the element type
  typedef typename Config::FinalList FinalList; //retrieve the final list type
public:
  List(const ElementType& h, FinalList *t = 0) : head_(h), tail_(t) {}
  void setHead(const ElementType& h) { head_ = h; }
  const ElementType& head() const { return head_; }
  void setTail(FinalList *t) { tail_ = t; }
  FinalList *tail() const { return tail_; }
private:
  ElementType head_;
  FinalList *tail_;
};
```

Figure 7-28 List container parameterized with a configuration repository

```
template<class BaseList>
class TracedList : public BaseList
{
public:
  typedef typename BaseList::Config Config;
private:
  typedef typename Config::ElementType ElementType;
  typedef typename Config::FinalList FinalList;
public:
  TracedList(const ElementType& h, FinalList *t = 0) :
    BaseList(h,t)        {}
  void setHead(const ElementType& h)
  { cout << "setHead(" << h << ")"<< endl;
    BaseList::setHead(h);
  }
  void setTail(FinalList *t)
  { cout << "setTail(t)"<< endl;
    BaseList::setTail(t);
  }
};
```

Figure 7-29 *Tracing list wrapper*

other list wrappers, for example, one defining synchronized access to the list. By using parameterized inheritance rather than a fixed inheritance hierarchy, we can wrap the basic list component with different wrappers in different orders. We will see a larger list example in Section 12.5.

Figure 7-30 shows a configuration defining a traced list of integers. The arrows in the listing visualize the flow of types. Element-Type and FinalList are members of TracedIntListConfig, which is passed to List. Finally, TracedList retrieves TracedIntListConfig from List.

Writing configuration repositories manually can be a tedious exercise. Therefore, we will let the compiler generate configuration repositories automatically from more abstract specifications. This will be demonstrated in Section 12.8.

7.11.5 Intelligent Configuration

Sometimes one parameter of a component is influenced by some other parameters, that is, we need to model dependencies between

```
struct TracedIntListConfig
{
  typedef int ElementType;
  //wrap List into TracedList
  typedef
    TracedList<
      PtrList<TracedIntListConfig> > > Final List;
};
//define a short name for our list
typedef TracedIntListConfig::Final List MyList;
```

Figure 7-30 *Configuration repository for a traced list of integers*

parameters at compile time. For example, a matrix should provide
the operation `determinant()` for computing the matrix determi-
nant only if it is square. Consider a matrix with a statically defined
number of rows and columns. One way of injecting the method
`determinant()` into the matrix is by turning its superclass into a
parameter. This is illustrated in Figure 7-31. `Matrix` retrieves the
appropriate base class from its configuration repository `Config`.
We have two alternative base classes: `Square` and `NotSquare`, where
only the former one defines `determinant()`.

Next, we need a configuration repository that selects the
appropriate base class automatically, depending on whether the
number of rows is equal to the number of columns or not. The
configuration repository is shown in Figure 7-32.

The template `SelectSquareIfTrue<>` uses template specialization in order to provide the appropriate type in its `Base` member.
The implementation is given in Figure 7-33.

```
template <class Config>
class Matrix: public typename Config::Base
{ //...
};

class Square
{public:
 double determinant() const
 // ...
};

class NotSquare {};
```

Figure 7-31 *Matrix with a parameterized base class*

```
template <int r, int c>
struct Configuration
{ typedef SelectSquareIfTrue<r==c>::Base Base;
  //...
};
```

Figure 7-32 *Configuration repository automatically selecting the appropriate base class for matrix*

```
//SelectSquareIfTrue selects Square if cond is true and
//NotSquare otherwise
template <bool cond>
struct SelectSquareIfTrue
{ typedef NotSquare Base;
};
template<>
struct SelectSquareIfTrue<true> //specialization for true
{ typedef Square Base;
};
```

Figure 7-33 *Template for selecting the base class*

Sample code using the configuration is given in Figure 7-34.

This example demonstrates a very simple case of automatic configuration at compile time. Armed with template metaprogramming discussed in Chapter 10, we will show you how to write complex configuration scripts to be executed by the compiler in Chapter 12.

```
// ...

Matrix<Configuration<3,3> > m;
m.determinant();  //OK
Matrix<Configuration<3,4> > n;
n.determinant(); //compiler reports an error
```

Figure 7-34 *Sample code using the automatic configuration*

Chapter 8

Aspect-Oriented Programming

Shotgun surgery:

*You whiff this when every time you make a kind of
change, you have to make a lot of little changes to a lot of
different classes.*

—*Kent Beck and Martin Fowler [FBB+99] describing one
of the "bad smells" often found in OO code*

8.1 Why Is This Chapter Worth Reading?

One of the main principles of good programming is to encode
important issues concerning the system being developed in a
cleanly localized way. Localizing important issues in a single code
section has many advantages. First of all, you can more easily
understand how this issue is addressed in the code because you do
not have to look for it in different places and discern it from other
issues. Moreover, you can easily analyze such code, modify it,
extend it, debug it, reuse it, maintain it, and so on. For example, in
a banking application, there will be well-localized, modular units
(e.g., objects) representing important domain concepts, such as
accounts, customers, currency, and so on. Object-oriented, generic,
and component-oriented programming all allow us to express such
concepts in a cleanly localized way.

Unfortunately, there are also issues that are difficult or impossible to express in a cleanly localized way using traditional modularization constructs, such as components, objects, or procedures.
Maybe you have experienced this problem before. You started
with a nice, clean system design, where all the important domain
concepts were carefully represented as objects or components.
Then, your boss decided that the system should be distributed on
the network. At that point, you had to add support for several new
issues including security control, transaction control, distributed

data transfer, and synchronizing concurrent access and execution. And this turned out to be quite a hassle. Implementing each of these issues required inserting many little code fragments in most of the existing components and objects. You even had to modify the whole component structure to get a reasonable performance. Making all of these changes basically destroyed the original, nice, clean design of the system. We call these issues that are hard to localize using traditional modularization constructs *aspects,* and we say that they "crosscut" modular structures.

In this chapter, you will learn about:

♦ Situations where aspects arise and why they arise
♦ Ways to cleanly localize different kinds of aspects
♦ Technologies that support encapsulating aspects
♦ The role of aspects in the decomposition of problems

8.2 What Is Aspect-Oriented Programming?

Principle of separation of concerns

The need of dealing with one important issue at a time was named by Dijkstra as the *principle of separation of concerns* [Dij76]. Unfortunately, although the principle expresses an important quality of both code and a development process, it does not tell us how to achieve it.

Generalized procedures

Separation of concerns is a fundamental engineering principle applied in analysis, design, and implementation. Most analysis and design notations and programming languages provide constructs for organizing system descriptions as hierarchical compositions of smaller, modular units. However, as Kiczales et al. note in [KLM+97], they concentrate on finding and composing *functional* units, which are usually expressed as objects, modules, procedures, and so on. They also refer to such units as *generalized procedures* because they are called from the client code. But there are also other important issues, which are not well localized in such functional designs, for example, system properties involving more than one functional component, such as synchronization, component interaction, persistency, security control, and so on. They are usually expressed by small code fragments scattered throughout several functional components.

Aspect-Oriented Programming

The latter observation lies at the heart of *Aspect-Oriented Programming* (AOP), a new direction in programming proposed by researchers from Xerox Palo Alto Research Center (Xerox PARC) [AOP, KLM+97, AOP97, AOP98]. The goal of AOP is to provide methods and techniques for decomposing problems into a number of *functional components* as well as a number of *aspects* that crosscut functional components, and then compose these components and aspects to obtain system implementations.

Once we've subscribed to the idea of separating aspects, we need concrete methods and techniques to achieve this separation. In particular, there are three main questions we have to address.

♦ *What are the important issues that need to be separated?* We already mentioned some examples, such as synchronization or component interaction. What we are looking for are reusable sets of concerns to be used in the decomposition of problems. Some of these concerns will be more application-specific, for example, defining financial products or configuring network services. Other concerns will be more general, for example, synchronization or workflow. And some of all the application-specific and general concerns will be aspects. As we discussed in Section 4.9.2.1, by selecting an appropriate set of concerns for a problem, we achieve a "healthy" balance between the localization of relevant issues, complexity, and redundancy. Of course, different domains will require different sets of concerns. Throughout this chapter, we'll give you more examples of important concerns.

♦ *What composition mechanisms other than calling generalized procedures can we use?* If aspects cannot be cleanly separated using method and procedure calls, we need other composition mechanisms to achieve this separation. The hallmark of such mechanisms is achieving loose and declarative coupling between partial descriptions. We would also like the mechanisms to support a broad spectrum of binding times and modes and also non-invasive adaptability (i.e., adaptability by automatic composition and/or transformation rather than manual change).

♦ *How do we capture the aspects themselves?* We express aspects using some appropriate linguistic means: In the simplest cases, we can use conventional class libraries. In other cases, we might want to use specialized languages or language extensions. Each approach has its advantages and disadvantages, and we will discuss them at the end of this chapter.

AOP, while still in its definition phase, already begins to provide benefits by focusing and stimulating existing and new work, addressing these three questions. We will discuss some answers to these questions in this chapter. In most cases, we will concentrate on OO methods and languages, but the AOP idea is not limited to OO.

The message of this chapter is that current programming methods and languages (including OO) do not allow us to cleanly encapsulate certain important design decisions. In this chapter, you will find examples of such shortcomings as well as approaches to overcome them.

8.3 Aspect-Oriented Decomposition Approaches

There are a number of existing approaches that concentrate on encapsulating various system properties including aspects that crosscut modular units of functionality. The following three sections describe three of such approaches. These approaches extend the OO programming model to allow the encapsulation of aspects that in conventional OO programs are usually implemented by slices of several objects (i.e., they crosscut object structures). These approaches also propose concrete composition mechanisms; however, we will postpone discussing them until Section 8.5. Finally, we will explain how Domain Engineering relates to aspect-oriented decomposition.

8.3.1 Subject-Oriented Programming

Subject-Oriented Programming (SOP)[1] was proposed by Harrison and Ossher of the IBM Thomas J. Watson Research Center as an extension of the object-oriented paradigm to address the problem of handling different *subjective perspectives* on the objects to be modeled. For example, the object representing a *book* for the marketing department of a publisher would include attributes such as *subject area* or *short abstract*, whereas the manufacturing department would be interested in rather different attributes such as *kind of paper*, *kind of binding*, and so on. The usage context of an object is not the only reason why different perspectives arise. The approach also seeks to address the problem of integrating systems developed with a large degree of independence, for example, two applications developed for the two different departments of a publisher. In this case, we have to deal with perspectives of different *development teams* on the same objects (e.g., the book object), which may use different names to mean the same thing or the same name to mean different things. Furthermore, the goal is to be able to add previously unforeseen extensions to an existing system in a noninvasive way.

Subjects and mixins   Each perspective gives rise to a so-called *subject*. A subject is a collection of classes and/or class fragments (i.e., *mixins*) related by inheritance and other relationships (e.g., aggregation, association,

---

1. See [SOP, HO93, OKH+95, OKK+96].

> **NOTE**
>
> A *mixin* is a fragment of a class in the sense that it is intended to be composed with other classes or mixins. The term mixin was originally introduced in Flavors [Moo86], the predecessor of CLOS [DG87, Kee89]. The difference between a regular, stand-alone class such as `Person` and a mixin is that a mixin models some small functionality slice, for example, *printing* or *displaying*, and is not intended to be used "stand-alone," but rather to be composed with some other class needing this functionality (e.g., `Person`). One possibility to model mixins in OO languages is to use classes and multiple inheritance. In this model, a mixin is represented as a class, which is then referred to as a *mixin class*, and we derive a composed class from a number of mixin classes using multiple inheritance. Another possibility is to use parameterized inheritance. In this case, we can represent a mixin as a class template derived from its parameter (we will see an application of this technique in Section 8.5.2). Indeed, some authors (e.g., [BC90]) define mixins as "abstract subclasses" (i.e., subclasses without a concrete superclass). SOP provides yet another composition mechanism for composing mixins (however, one that is not based on inheritance).

Composition rules

and so on). Thus, a subject is simply a partial or a complete object model.

Subjects can be composed using *composition rules*. There are three kinds of composition rules.

- ♦ *Correspondence rules:* Allow you to specify the correspondence between the classes, methods, and attributes belonging to the different subjects to be composed (if there is any correspondence)
- ♦ *Combination rules:* Allow you to specify how the corresponding and noncorresponding classes, methods, and attributes coming from the different subjects to be composed contribute to the resulting composite subject
- ♦ *Correspondence-and-combination rules:* Provide a shorthand for specifying correspondence and combination at once

Correspondence rules specify the correspondence (if any) between classes, methods, and attributes of objects belonging to different subjects. For example, we could use a correspondence rule to express that the book in the marketing department application is the same as the book in the manufacturing department application (even if the corresponding classes had different names). We could have further correspondence rules stating the correspondence between methods and attributes of these classes. For example, we could state that the attribute *title* in the first class is the same as the attribute *book_title* in the second class. It is also possible to use a special correspondence rule that will establish both the correspondence of two classes and all of their members having equal names. Of course, we can override this automatic correspondence for some members by defining additional member correspondence rules.

After establishing the correspondence between the two book classes, we can use combination rules to specify how they should be combined. The resulting class will include the independent methods and attributes, and the corresponding methods and attributes will be combined according to the combination rules. For example, a method coming from one class could override the corresponding method coming from the other class, or both corresponding methods could be executed in some specified order. When composing two or more independently developed subjects, we would usually develop an additional, so-called *glue* subject, which would include the code necessary to combine the other subjects.

For convenience, there are also the correspondence-and-combination rules, which provide a shorthand for specifying correspondence and combination at the same time. You can find out about the details of the SOP composition rules in [SOP, OKH+95, OKK+96]. We will also show you an example of a subject-oriented program with simple composition rules in Section 8.5.5.

As of this writing, a prototype support for subjects exists as an extension of IBM's VisualAge for C++ and Smalltalk, and an implementation for VisualAge for Java is under development (see [SOP]). A useful feature of the Java prototype is the possibility to specify correspondence and combination visually using a graphical user interface.

8.3.2 Composition Filters

Inheritance anomalies

The *Composition Filters* (CF)[2] approach by Aksit et al. is motivated by the difficulties of expressing any kind of message coordination in the conventional object model. For example, expressing synchronization at the interface level of an object requires some way of—in effect—injecting synchronization code into all of its methods that need to be synchronized. The straightforward solution of manually inserting this code into the methods (as in Figure 8-9 in Section 8.5.3) results in mixing functionality and synchronization code in a way that limits reusability. For example, when

---

2. See [CF, AT88, Aks89, Ber94, ATB96].

you extend a class by subclassing and define new methods in the subclass, it is usually necessary to update the whole synchronization schema for the subclass, and therefore override most of the inherited methods even if their core functionality remains the same. The reason is that you need to update the synchronization code that is scattered across many methods. This and other related problems are referred to as *inheritance anomalies* [MWY90, MY93].[3] All in all, we can state that one of the problems of the conventional object model is the lack of proper mechanisms to separate functionality from the message coordination code.

Message filters

The CF approach extends the conventional object model with a number of different *message filters* that messages sent between objects have to pass through. Figure 8-1 shows an object in the CF model. The object consists of an *interface layer* and a *kernel object*. The kernel object can be thought of as a regular object defined in a

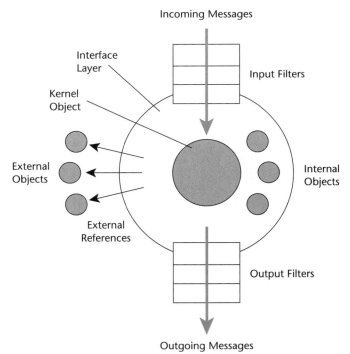

Figure 8-1 *Elements of an object in the CF model (adapted from [Ber94])*

---

3. A practically oriented discussion of inheritance anomalies can be found in [Lea97].

conventional OO programming language, such as Java or C++. The interface layer contains an arbitrary number of *input* and *output message filters*. Incoming messages pass through the input filters and the outgoing messages through the output filters. The filters can modify the messages, for example, by changing the message name or the target object. In effect, they can be used to redirect messages to other objects, for example, the *internal objects*, which are encapsulated in the interface layer or some *external objects* referenced from the interface layer, and used to translate messages (by modifying their names). They can also discard or buffer messages or throw exceptions. Whatever action is taken depends on the type of the filter. There are a number of predefined filter types, for example, *delegation filters* (for delegating messages), *wait filters* (for buffering messages), *error filters* (for throwing exceptions), and new filter types can be added. Whether a filter modifies a message or not may depend on the message and also on some *state conditions* defined over the state of the kernel object.

Message filtering is a very powerful technique, which allows us to implement synchronization constraints [Ber94], real-time constraints [ABSB94], atomic transactions [ABV92], precondition-style error checking [Ber94], and other aspects in a well-localized way. Indeed, any aspect that lends itself to the implementation by intercepting message sends or "wrapping" methods in *before* and *after actions* (i.e., actions executed before or after executing a method) can be adequately represented in the CF model.

Delegation   The message redirecting capability can also be used to implement *delegation* and *dynamic inheritance*. In a nutshell, delegation involves redirecting some messages received by a *delegating object* to another object, called the *delegate object*, which the delegating object holds a reference to. Furthermore, we also have to make sure that when the delegate object uses the keyword *self*, it actually refers to the delegating object and not to itself. This way, the methods of the delegate objects are written as if they were methods of the delegating objects, and the delegate objects can be regarded as true extensions of the delegating objects. This is similar to the relationship between a class and its superclass (to which a class often "delegates work").

In the CF model, delegation means redirecting messages to the external objects and making sure that *self* always refers to the original receiver (see Figure 8-2). Inheritance, on the other hand, means redirecting messages to the internal objects and making sure that *self* always refers to the original receiver. This relationship between inheritance and delegation was originally discussed in [Lie86b, Ste87].

NOTE ON DELEGATION VERSUS FORWARDING

This special interpretation of *self* in the case of delegation is precisely the difference between *delegation* and the more common *forwarding*. Forwarding involves just a simple message call on another object, whereas delegation makes sure that subsequent calls on *self* refer back to the delegating object.

Dynamic inheritance

A filter can also delegate a given message to *different* internal objects based on some state conditions. Consequently, this means that the superclass of an object can change depending on its state, which is referred to as *dynamic inheritance*.

The details of the CF model can be found in [Ber94]. The model has been implemented as an extension of several existing OO languages, such as C++ [Gla95] and Smalltalk [MD95]. Message filters can be implemented as metaobjects, so that they are present at runtime and thus can also be modified at runtime. Some filters, if necessary, can also be compiled away for performance reasons.

8.3.3 Demeter / Adaptive Programming

The original idea behind *Demeter / Adaptive Programming*[4] was to provide a better separation between behavior and object structure

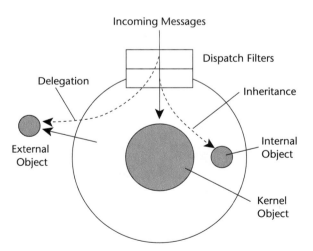

Figure 8-2 Delegation and inheritance in the CF model

---

4. See [Lie92, Lie96, Dem].

NOTE

It is interesting to compare the message filtering idea of the CF model with Enterprise Java Beans (EJB) [Mon99], a component model for the server side. An EJB server automatically manages distributed communication, transaction control, access security, concurrency, and persistency of business components. An important idea in this model is that the business logic of an EJB component and the specification of these aspects are separated. The business logic is implemented in a *bean class* and the aspects are specified in an declarative way in *deployment descriptors*. Based on these descriptors, an EJB server generates appropriate wrappers for the bean objects. These wrappers function like message filters, which together with other parts of an EJB server implement the different aspects of EJB components at runtime.

---

in OO programs. This was motivated by the observation that OO programs tend to contain a lot of small methods that do no or very little computation and call other methods passing information from one part of the object diagram[5] they operate on to other methods operating on other parts of the diagram. Trying to understand the computation in such programs involves an "endless chase" through such small methods and wondering where the "real" computation gets done. In addition to this understandability problem, the more serious flaw with such designs is that a simple change in the computation algorithm may require revisiting a large number of methods.

Law of Demeter   The large number of the small "information-passing" methods in classical OO designs is a consequence of the application of the *Law of Demeter* [LHR88]. Law of Demeter is an OO design principle stating that a method should only contain message sends to the following objects: *self*, local instance variables, and/or method arguments.[6] In particular, we should avoid long sequences of accessing methods (e.g., `object.part1().part2().part3().part4()`), which perform some "deep" access into the object structure because such sequences hardwire large object structures into methods. By following the Law of Demeter, we trade the "structure-hardwiring-in-large-methods" problem for the problem of

---

5. By an object diagram, we mean objects and the relationships between them.

6. Objects created by the method, or by functions or methods that the method calls, and objects in global variables are considered as arguments of the method.

having a large number of small information-passing methods. Given these two alternatives only, the latter is usually the better choice. Unfortunately, even if we follow the Law of Demeter and use many small methods to avoid the "structure-hardwiring problem," a change in the part of the object structure that is not directly involved in the computation, but needs to be traversed by the small information-passing methods, requires manual addition or modification of these methods.

In either case, with or without following the Law of Demeter, we have a tight coupling between the OO code implementing the algorithms and the object structure: The algorithm code contains hard-coded names of classes that are not needed for the computation. For example, in order to compute the total salary paid by a company, we need to visit the `Salary` object of every employee in the company. Let us assume that the company consists of a number of divisions and each division contains a number of employees. One possible solution would be to implement a total-salary-computing method in the `Company` class, which calls a helper method on each `Department` object of the company, which calls a helper method on each `Employee` object of a department. The latter two methods would accumulate the total salary for the departments and return it to the top-level method. Finally, the top-level method would return the total salary for the whole company. The problem with this implementation is that when we want to change the class structure, for example, by inserting *divisions* between the company and the departments, we need to implement a similar helper method in the new `Division` class, even if this method does not really contribute to the computation. Even if we implement the total-salary computation using the *visitor pattern* (see [GHJV95]), we still have to provide the *accept* method in *all* traversed classes as well as specialized methods (one per visited class) in the visitors. The latter need to be extended whenever new classes are added to the traversed portion of the class diagram.

Traversal strategies

A solution to this problem proposed by Karl Lieberherr [Lie96] involves writing behavior code against partial specifications of a class diagram instead of the whole concrete class diagram. The partial specifications mention only those classes that are really needed for the given computation. These partial specifications are referred to as *traversal strategies* [LP97].[7] An example of a very simple traversal strategy for the total salary example is

```
from Company to Salary
```

---

7. In [Lie96], they are called *propagation directives*.

This strategy specifies the traversal of a given concrete class diagram of a company from the Company class to the Salary class. The abstract method computing the total salary would state its job in terms of this abstract traversal specification. The idea is to only state actions to be performed while traversing an object of a given class without saying how this traversal is done (which is up to the traversal strategy). The method code for computing the total salary would state the following actions.

1. Initialize an accumulator variable total when traversing a Company object, and then pass the variable down the company class diagram during traversal.
2. Whenever a Salary object is visited, add its value to the accumulator.
3. Finally, when the traversal is back in Company, return the total.

Structure-shy behavior

Please note that this behavior specification for computing the total salary does not mention any other classes than the ones referenced in the traversal strategy (i.e., Company and Salary, but not Department or Employee). Given this so-called *structure-shy behavior specification* (i.e., the algorithm code written against the traversal strategy) and a concrete class diagram, all the other necessary little "information-passing" methods in Department and Employee can be generated automatically. Moreover, when we extend the class graph with the new class Division, no changes to the structure-shy behavior specification are needed, and we can simply regenerate our concrete program.

The ideas of Demeter have been integrated into OO languages such as C++ (Demeter/C++ [SHS94, Lie96]) and Java (Demeter/Java [LO97]).[8] For example, the Demeter/Java tool processes behavior specifications (wherein the algorithmic parts are expressed in Java) and class diagrams and produces Java programs. Additionally, it also provides a high-level means for instantiating complex object structures using sentences of grammars derived from class diagrams.

8.3.4 Aspect-Oriented Decomposition and Domain Engineering

Aspect languages

The relationship between Domain Engineering and aspect-oriented decomposition can be best explained using the Draco approach to Domain Engineering (see Section 9.8.1). The idea of Draco is to

---

8. Demeter/C++ and Demeter/Java are available at [Dem].

BACKGROUND NOTE

The term Adaptive Programming was introduced around 1991, and it covered the class structure aspect and the structure-shy behavior aspect described previously [Lie98]. Later, it was extended with the synchronization aspect [LL94] and the remote invocation aspect [Lop95] (also see [Lop98]). Indeed, the work on Adaptive Programming and on the synchronization and the remote invocation aspects is one of the important roots of Aspect-Oriented Programming [Lie98]. According to a more recent definition "Adaptive Programming (AP) is the special case of Aspect-Oriented Programming (AOP) where some of the building blocks are expressible in terms of graphs and where the other building blocks refer to the graphs using traversal strategies. A traversal strategy may be viewed as a partial specification of a graph pointing out a few cornerstone nodes and edges. A traversal strategy crosscuts the graphs it is intended for, mentioning only a few isolated nodes and edges. Traversal strategies may be viewed as regular expressions specifying a traversal through a graph. (Formally, a traversal strategy for a graph G is a subgraph of the transitive closure of G with some bypassing information added.) In summary: AP = AOP with graphs and traversal strategies. As an application of the earlier distinction, we can say that AP is a special case of AOP where some of the crosscutting is expressed adaptively using strategies to embed small graphs into large graphs. A key feature of this embedding is that it is specified by hiding the details of the large graphs that makes the graph embeddings 'adaptive' in that they work for a large family of large graphs." [Lie98] More recent work on Demeter [Lie97, ML98] is aimed at extending it with a fragment-based composition mechanism (see Section 8.5.5).

organize domain knowledge into a network of related domains, where each domain provides a *domain language*. In this model, an application is defined in terms of a number of high-level application and modeling domains, whereby each domain is used to describe a certain aspect of the application. Similarly, the domains themselves are defined in terms of other domains. The decomposition based on domains does not necessarily adhere to functional structures. Those domain languages explicitly aimed at capturing crosscutting aspects are *aspect languages* in the AOP sense.

Weaving and aspect weavers

The transformational implementation inherent to the Draco approach is also closely related to the AOP idea. Compiling aspect-oriented programs involves processing a number of separate aspect representations (e.g., a number of aspect programs written in different languages or a number of different constructs within one language) in order to produce the resulting representation of the one common concept described by the crosscutting aspects. This compilation process is referred to as *weaving* [KLM+97] and may involve merging components, modifying them, optimizing, and so on. The goal of weaving is the same as the goal of generators: to compute an efficient implementation for a high-level specification. (We discuss generators in Chapter 9.) However, it is important to note that weaving does not have to be implemented as a static generation process. It can also be realized by runtime interpretation of the aspect programs or runtime generation. Therefore, Kiczales et al. introduced the term *aspect weaver* [KLM+97], which refers to a language processor (e.g., generator or interpreter) for aspect-oriented programs. We will see a concrete example of dynamic weaving in Section 8.6.2.

Finally, aspects influence the way we decompose problems and need to be taken into account during Domain Analysis. We already discussed this topic in Sections 4.9.1 and 4.9.2, where we introduced the idea of *feature starter sets*. Feature starter sets help us to jump-start feature modeling of the key concepts in a domain. For example, the feature starter set for abstract data types, which are common to algorithmic domains, could include concerns, such as operations, attributes, structure, synchronization, error handling, and so on. Some concerns in a feature starter set will be aspects in the AOP sense. It is important to note that as more modeling experience in different kinds of domains is collected, starter sets will develop into "systems of concerns" suggesting canonical ways of decomposing problems in different kinds of domains. Aspects will play an important role in such systems of concerns.

8.4 How Aspects Arise

Examples of aspects

Synchronization, real-time constraints, error checking, and structure-shy behavior are examples of aspects, which the approaches we discussed in the previous sections help us to separate. There are many other examples of aspects, such as object interaction [AWB+93, BDF98], memory management [AT96], persistence, historization, security, caching policies, profiling, monitoring, testing, structure and representation of data, and domain-specific optimizations (e.g., see Sections 5.8.2.2.1 and 5.8.2.2.2). Many aspects arise together in certain kinds of systems. For example, some of the aspects of distributed systems include component interaction, synchronization, remote invocation, parameter transfer strategies, load balancing, replication, failure handling, quality of service, and distributed transactions (e.g., see [Lop97, BG98]).

But how do aspects in the AOP sense arise? Some aspects follow structures that naturally crosscut generalized procedures, such as control flow or data flow. For example, synchronization, real-time constraints, and object interaction follow control flow; and parameter-transfer strategies in distributed systems [Lop97] and caching strategies follow data flow. Furthermore, subjective perspectives modeled in SOP and variability modeled in Domain Analysis are often expressed in terms of incremental deltas that crosscut objects.

Code tangling

Domain-specific optimizations represent another category of aspects. Optimizations involve interleaving and delocalization, that is, some of the high-level concepts of the specification to be optimized are interleaved (i.e., merged) and some of them are distributed among other lower-level concepts. These two effects lie at the heart of the so-called *code tangling* [KLM+97], which is found in the optimized version, that is, the optimized code is hard to understand and maintain. In fact, code tangling occurs whenever we try to implement aspects using generalized procedures only. In the case of optimizations, instead of writing the optimized, tangled code by hand, we should rather represent our program using the high-level, unoptimized code and a set of domain-specific optimizations (i.e., transformations). The optimized code can then be obtained by applying the optimizations to the unoptimized code using a generator. Examples of such optimizations are loop fusing and elimination of temporaries in matrix computation code. We will see an implementation of this aspect of matrix code in Section 14.4.2.

Crosscutting

Crosscutting lies at the heart of aspects. Recalling our discussion from Section 4.9.2.2, modular units of decomposition are organized into clear hierarchies, whereas aspects crosscut such hierarchies. This is illustrated in Figure 8-3. We also stated in Section 4.9.2.2 that the quality of being an aspect is a relative one: *A model is an* aspect *of another model if it crosscuts its structure.* The aspect shown in Figure 8-3 is an aspect with respect to the hierarchical structure also shown in this figure. However, at the same time, the aspect could be a modular unit of another hierarchical structure not shown in the figure.

What is an aspect?

Because an aspect is relative to some model, it might be possible to refactor the model so that the aspect ceases to be an aspect of the model. For example, interaction patterns between a number of components are an aspect of the component structure because they crosscut it. One way to deal with this problem is to introduce a mediator component that encapsulates these interaction patterns (see *mediator pattern* in [GHJV95]). Thus, we can refactor our

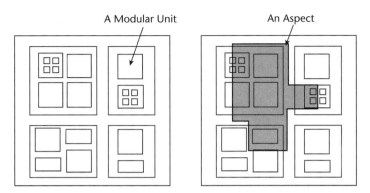

Figure 8-3 *Modular versus aspectual decomposition*

design and turn an aspect into a component. This pattern-based solution is not always an ideal one, however: In addition to simply moving the problem into a new component, it introduces extra complexity and possibly performance penalties. But, nonetheless, it is a solution. In general, it would be foolish to think that we can "get rid" of all aspects simply by refactoring our models. Localizing some issues will always cause some other issues to become aspects (just as in our example with the signal diagrams in Figure 4-27, Section 4.9.2.1). Real systems will always have some "inherent crosscutting" that refactoring will not be able to get rid of. Rather than trying to sweep the problem under the rug, we have to provide adequate technology to deal with the crosscutting.

It is worth noting that the code tangling problem due to crosscutting tends to occur in later phases of the conventional development process. We usually start with a clean, hierarchical functional design, then manually add various aspects (e.g., code optimizations, distribution, synchronization—indeed, all of the aspects listed at the beginning of this section are aspects with respect to functional decompositions), and the code becomes tangled.

Separating aspects from functional code allows us to avoid code tangling. Once we have identified the relevant aspects, we still need to find:

♦ Efficient mechanisms for composing aspects
♦ Appropriate linguistic means of expressing the aspects themselves

Generalized procedures (e.g., objects, procedures, functions, and so on) are appropriate for implementing the modular units of functionality. But we still need mechanisms for dealing with cross-cutting. Appropriate composition mechanisms provide a solution to this problem. We will discuss them in the following section. Applying specialized linguistic means to capture aspects themselves allows us to further reduce complexity. We will discuss this idea in Section 8.6.

8.5 Composition Mechanisms

Function calls, static and dynamic parameterization, and inheritance are all examples of important composition mechanisms supported by conventional languages. However, as we stated in the previous sections, not all relevant aspects found in practice can be adequately composed using these mechanisms and thus we need new ones. Subject composition rules in SOP, message filters in CF, and traversal strategies in Demeter are some examples we have already discussed in Section 8.3 (see [NT95, CIOO96] for more examples).

We'll start our discussion of composition mechanisms by stating some requirements. Next, we'll use a simple example of synchronizing a stack to show how these requirements can be achieved. We will walk through various stages of separation starting with a tangled version of the stack that mixes synchronization with the functionality code, then moving toward a somewhat better version using inheritance, and ending with a cleanly separated version using the composition mechanisms of SOP. In Section 8.6, we will revisit this example and show how to represent the synchronization aspect itself in a more intentional way.

8.5.1 Requirements of Composition Mechanisms

Ideally, we would like the aspect composition mechanisms to allow:

♦ *Minimal coupling* between aspects and components
♦ Different *binding times and modes* between aspects and components
♦ *Noninvasive addition of aspects* to existing code (and thus *noninvasive adaptability* of existing code)

We explain each of these requirements in the following sections.

8.5.1.1 Minimal Coupling

We require minimal coupling between aspects (and aspects and components) rather than complete separation between them because complete separation is possible only in a few trivial cases, and the majority of aspects cannot be completely separated. The reason for the latter is that aspects describe different perspectives on some single models. Even the term *orthogonal perspectives* does not imply complete separation. We can back this observation with a simple example. The drawing to the far left in Figure 8-4 shows three orthogonal perspectives of a 3-D object. In our example, the perspectives are a trapezoid and a triangle on the side planes and a circle on the bottom plane. Next, we might use our three orthogonal planes as a kind of generator, that is, we put some 2-D figures on the planes and interpret them as perspectives of some 3-D object to be built. Even if our perspectives are orthogonal (in terms of angles), the 2-D figure cannot be chosen independently. The middle drawing in Figure 8-4 shows us a set of 2-D figures that are inconsistent in our model, that is, we cannot construct a 3-D object with these figures as its orthogonal perspectives. A consistent set of 2-D figures is shown at the far right of the drawing in Figure 8-4.

Demeter provides an excellent example of composition with minimal coupling. Conventional OO behavior code hardwires the object structure it works on by explicitly mentioning more classes and relationships than it really needs. Classes and relationships required for computation need to be mentioned, but classes and relationships used just for navigation need not. The traversal strategies in Demeter (i.e., the partial class diagram specifications) allow for a declarative, loose coupling between class structure and structure-shy behavior and also between class structure and remote communication (see [Lop98]). They can be viewed as the *aspect composition mechanism* between the class structure aspect and the behavior aspect and the remote communication aspect in Demeter.

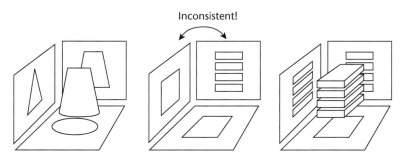

Figure 8-4 *Examples of consistent and inconsistent orthogonal perspectives of 3-D objects*

Join points   The example of traversal strategies as a composition mechanism also illustrates the concept of *join points* [KLM+97]. Traversal strategies are part of the behavior aspect and they mention some of the classes and relationships from the class structure aspect. We say that these classes and relationships represent the join points between the behavior aspect and the class structure aspect. In the case of SOP (see Section 8.3.1), the join points between the subjects and the subject composition rules are class, method, and attribute names. In general, we can distinguish between the following three types of join points between aspects.

- Simple "by name" references to a definition of a language construct (e.g., definitions of classes, methods, attributes, and so on). For example, an aspect could refer to the definition of a method and state that all calls to this method should be logged to a file. Thus, by referring to the definition, we affect all calls to the method.
- References to the uses of a given construct. For example, we could be interested in logging calls to a given method, but only those made within some other specific method.
- References to patterns.[9] Traversal strategies are an example of pattern-based coupling. A structure-shy behavior specification refers to certain regions in a class graph using traversal strategies, that is, patterns.

The essence of separating aspects is illustrated in Figure 8-5. The top box displays some code whose different lines implement two different aspects. Lines implementing one of the aspects are highlighted. (But don't try to read this code—we made it so small so that you would not be tempted to!). By separating these aspects, we get two pieces of code, each implementing one aspect. These

NOTE

It is interesting to note a striking similarity between code transformations discussed in Chapter 9 and aspects: Both aspects and transformations may look for some specific code patterns in order to influence their semantics. For this reason, transformations represent a suitable implementation technology for aspects or aspect languages.

---

9. Here we use the term *pattern* not in the sense of design patterns, but in the sense of pattern matching.

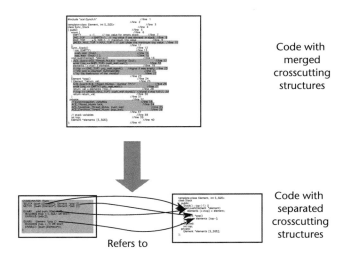

Figure 8-5 *Separating crosscutting structures*

pieces still refer to each other (or, in this particular case, one of them refers to the other one only). The points of reference are the join points. It is important to point out that in the separated case an aspect says something about the model it crosscuts declaratively rather than having the model make calls to the aspect. For example, in Section 8.6, you will see a synchronization aspect that makes statements about a stack, such as "you should not push and pop elements at the same time." Thus, an aspect extends or modifies the semantics of the model it refers to.

Message join points

An important category of join points in OO are *message join points* (or *operation join points*; see [OT98]), that is, points where operations are defined or called. As demonstrated in the CF approach (see Section 8.3.2), they can be used to couple functional designs with aspects, such as concurrency, real-time constraints, atomic transactions, precondition-like error handling, and security. Other aspects amenable to coupling through message join points are profiling, monitoring, testing, caching, and historization. They can all be implemented by intercepting message sends.

8.5.1.2 Different Binding Times and Modes

As stated earlier, there is an important relationship between features and aspects: Some features are aspects in the AOP sense. Features found during Domain Analysis are documented using feature diagrams (see Section 4.4.1), which are annotated with binding times, for example, showing whether they are bound before run-time or during runtime. Indeed, we stated later in Section 4.4.4 that many different, even product-specific, binding times are possible (the generalized concept is referred to as *binding site*). Thus, it is important that a composition mechanism supports different binding times.

We also would like to support both static and dynamic binding (i.e., different *binding modes*). Static binding means optimized and "frozen" binding, such as inlining, in which case rebinding is more difficult and time-consuming because we might possibly need to do some code regeneration. Please note that static binding does not have to happen at compile time because code regeneration or code modification can also be performed at runtime.[10] Dynamic binding, on the other hand, leaves some indirection code between the entities to be bound. This extra code may compute the binding lazily (as in the case of dynamic method binding in OO languages using a virtual function table) or allow a quick rebind (as in the case of a method cache). We should use dynamic binding whenever rebinds are frequent and static binding otherwise. It might also be useful to be able to switch between static and dynamic binding at runtime.

There are several important issues concerning binding time and binding mode. First, the composition mechanism for gluing the concrete feature implementations together needs to support different binding times and modes. In C++, for example, you can use several static composition mechanisms (e.g., templates, C++ static binding, inlining) and virtual methods as a dynamic composition mechanism. Interestingly, you can also parameterize the binding mode using the idiom we discussed in Section 7.9. Thanks to this idiom, you actually get a more general composition mechanism supporting both static and dynamic binding mode.

Second, there is also the configuration code, which computes configurations of concrete features based on abstract and other concrete features, and it should be possible to execute this code at different times. For example, object-oriented frameworks are usually configured using object factory code creating and installing appropriate policy objects. This factory code is usually executed at runtime. If we are using C++ and want to configure the variation

---

10. For example, Sun's HotSpot technology can perform changeable and static binding at runtime. HotSpot locates performance critical methods at runtime through profiling, and if the same code is called many times, HotSpot will inline it. However, if the code needs to be rebound at some point (e.g., when new code overriding this method gets loaded dynamically), it can reverse the inlining. See www.javasoft.com/products/hotspot.

points at compile time, we can use template metaprogramming, which we'll discuss in Chapter 10.

Finally, we want to be able to reuse as much code across different binding times as possible. In other words, we do not want to have different implementation versions of concrete features for different binding times but only one per feature (i.e., binding time should be a parameter of the composition mechanism). As already stated, in C++, we can use the idiom for parameterizing the binding mode to achieve this goal. For example, you can implement a variation point using the strategy pattern with parameterized binding mode shown in Figure 8-6. Context takes a strategy as its parameter. Furthermore, we have two alternative strategies, StrategyA and StrategyB, which take binding mode as their parameters. Dynamic binding mode is represented by DynamicStrategy, which declares doAlgorithm() as virtual, whereas static binding mode is represented by the empty class StaticStrategy (i.e., we use the idiom from Figure 7-11). In order to statically bind Context to a strategy, let's say StrategyA, you pass StaticStrategy as an actual type parameter to StrategyA, and then pass the resulting type to Context. If you need dynamic binding, you pass DynamicStrategy to Context and initialize a context object with the appropriate dynamic strategy through the constructor or later using setStrategy(). In order to use StrategyA or StrategyB as dynamic strategies, you need to parameterize them with DynamicStrategy. As a further optimization, you could declare Context::strategy to be of the type StrategyType instead of StrategyType*. In this arrangement, you would parameterize Context with DynamicStrategy* for the dynamic case and with StrategyA <StaticStrategy> or StrategyB<StaticStrategy> for the static case.

Similarly, as in the case of features, we do not want different versions of configuration code for different binding times. This requirement is impossible to satisfy in C++. You write dynamic configuration code as regular, dynamic C++ code, whereas static configuration code has to use template metaprogramming. As a result, you may find yourself duplicating some of the configuration logic in the static and dynamic code. More advanced languages and tools will hopefully provide a solution to this problem in future.

8.5.1.3 Noninvasive Adaptability

By *noninvasive adaptability*, we mean the ability to adapt a component or an aspect without manually modifying it. This is trivial if the component or aspect provides a parameter (or any other type

```
#include <iostream>
using namespace std;

//context using a strategy
template<class StrategyType>
class Context
{ public:
    Context(StrategyType *s) : strategy(s) {}
    void doWork()
    { strategy->doAlgorithm(); }
    void setStrategy(StrategyType *newStrategy)
    { strategy = newStrategy;  }
  private:
    StrategyType *strategy;
};

//two alternative strategies
template<class BindingMode>
class StrategyA : public BindingMode
{ public:
    void doAlgorithm()
    { cout << "Strategy A: doAlgorithm()" << endl; }
};

template<class BindingMode>
class StrategyB : public BindingMode
{ public:
    void doAlgorithm()
    { cout << "Strategy B: doAlgorithm()" << endl; }
};

//dynamic and static binding mode
class DynamicStrategy
{ public:
    virtual void doAlgorithm() = 0;
};

class StaticStrategy  {};

//...

//statically-bound StrategyA
StrategyA<StaticStrategy> statStrategyA;
```

(continued)

Figure 8-6 *Strategy pattern with parameterized binding mode*

```
//context statically bound with StrategyA
Context<StrategyA<StaticStrategy> >
contextWithStaticStrategy(&statStrategyA);
contextWithStaticStrategy.doWork();

//dynamically-bound strategies
StrategyA<DynamicStrategy> dynStrategyA;
StrategyB<DynamicStrategy> dynStrategyB;

//context dynamically bound with StrategyA
Context<DynamicStrategy>
contextWithDynamicStrategy(&dynStrategyB);
contextWithDynamicStrategy.doWork();

//context dynamically bound with StrategyB
contextWithDynamicStrategy.setStrategy(&dynStrategyA);
contextWithDynamicStrategy.doWork();
```

Figure 8-6 Strategy pattern with parameterized binding mode (continued)

of variation point) for the kind of change we would like to make. However, we would also like to be able, as far as possible, to make unplanned noninvasive adaptations for which no special hooks were foreseen in the component or aspect.

Ideally, we want to express any change as an additive operation: We use some composition operator to add the change to the existing code. The code we want to modify is not really physically modified, but the composition expression itself states that the original code has a modified semantics now. An example of such a composition operator is inheritance: We can define a new class by difference. Unfortunately, inheritance is noninvasive with respect to the superclass only. The client code has to be changed at some location(s) in order to create objects of the new derived class instead of the superclass (unless we combine inheritance with other techniques—see Figure 8-13). Of course, we prefer composition mechanisms that are noninvasive with respect to both the component and the client code, that is, we can modify the meaning of a component without changing its code or the client code.

An example of a composition mechanism supporting this kind of noninvasive adaptability is the composition mechanism of SOP. In SOP, we can write a composition rule that composes a class and an extension to this class and publishes the new class under the same name as the original one, so that no changes in the client code are necessary. We will see an example of such a composition rule in Section 8.5.5. We will also discuss other examples of noninvasive composition mechanisms in Sections 8.5.7 and 8.6.

Noninvasive adaptability is not possible in all cases. The prerequisite is that we have some appropriate "handle" in the code of the component to be adapted. This handle does not have to be an explicit "hook" foreseen during the design. For example, using SOP, we can noninvasively override any method of a component. If a component does not have the appropriate method that we can override to achieve the desired modification, SOP won't help. Thus, the method join points are limited. If our composition mechanism supports pattern join points, we can cover more complicated cases, where the locations to be modified in the component can be identified using a pattern. We could then use a transformation system (see Chapter 9) to generate the modified code. Finally, if the only way to identify some location in the component is by stating "the spot between lines 48 and 49," we need to redesign the component.

Loose coupling is also related to the issue of adaptability. When we change one aspect, it might be necessary to change another one that is intended to be composed with it. If the coupling between the aspects is minimal, then there is less chance that the change of one aspect requires the change of the other one. For example, if we change the class structure of a conventional OO program, we often have to change a large number of methods. On the other hand, when we apply the Demeter approach, we can make more kinds of changes to the class structure without having to change the behavior aspect than we can in the conventional program: Changes to the parts of the class structure that are not mentioned in the traversal strategies usually have no effect on the structure-shy behavior specification.[11] Thus, avoiding overspecification increases adaptability.

8.5.2   Example: Synchronizing a Bounded Buffer

Let us now illustrate the previous points using a concrete example. Imagine that you have a bounded buffer component, for example, a stack or a queue with a limited size, and you want to synchronize access to it in a multithreaded environment. In other words, there

---

11. There are cases where such changes to the class structure could introduce undesired traversals. In such cases, it is necessary to refine the traversal strategies.

will be clients that run in different threads and access the buffer to put elements in and take elements out. Because the buffer is a shared resource, the access of the different clients to it has to be synchronized.

Ideally, we would like to implement the buffer in one piece of code, for example, as a class, and express the synchronization aspect in a separate piece of code. This is shown in Figure 8-7. The synchronization aspect would state some synchronization constraints, such as you should not put and take elements at the same time, you should wait with a put if the buffer is full, you should wait with a take if the buffer is empty, and so on. This is an example of the classical "bounded buffer synchronization," which we'll discuss in Section 8.5.3 in detail.

At this point, we can make two important observations: One observation is that the aspect "says something *about*" the buffer. In order to be able to say something about the buffer, it has to refer to some parts of the buffer. In our case, the synchronization aspect mentions the buffer methods put, take, is_empty, and is_full.

Primary structure

Another important observation is that, although the buffer can be used "stand-alone" (e.g., in a single threaded program), the synchronization aspect cannot. The synchronization aspect doesn't do anything useful on its own. In order to do something useful, it needs to be used with some concrete buffer. This example indicates the kind of asymmetry between components and their aspects that is common in practice (we often refer to the components as the *primary structure*). Nonetheless, a bounded-buffer-synchronization aspect is a reusable piece of code because you can reuse it on a queue, a stack, or some other kind of buffer.

Now, let us take a look at what the composition requirements discussed in the previous sections mean in our context.

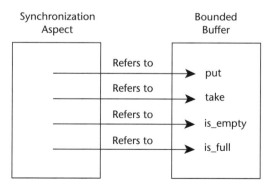

Figure 8-7 Bounded buffer and its synchronization aspect

♦ *Minimal coupling:* We want the aspect to mention as few details as possible about the component. In our case, the aspect refers to the methods put, take, is_empty, and is_full, which is necessary to formulate the synchronization constraints. Thus, we use operation join points to connect the synchronization aspect to the component.

♦ *Different binding times and modes:* In general, we want to be able to plug and unplug an aspect at any time. In the case of synchronization, this will be of particular interest if we have to coordinate a number of components. For example, if the components are dynamically reconfigurable, we also should be able to plug and unplug synchronization aspects dynamically (you'll see an example in Section 8.6.2.1).

♦ *Noninvasive adaptability:* We should be able to add the synchronization aspect to a component without having to modify the component or the client code manually (see Figure 8-8). The composition is taken care of by weaving (static or dynamic). Weaving effectively "injects" aspect code into the component at appropriate places. We will discuss ways of implementing weaving in Section 8.7.2.

In the following sections, we will gradually come to the ideal solution outlined previously. In our discussion, we will use a simple stack component as an example of a bounded buffer. We first start with a "tangled" version of the stack, that is, one that hardwires synchronization directly into the functional code. We then show how to separate the synchronization aspect using design patterns and the SOP composition mechanism. Finally, we give you the ideal solution in Java/AspectJ and in Smalltalk.

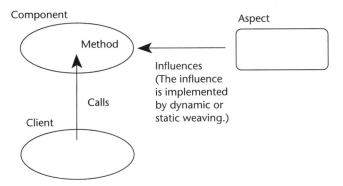

Figure 8-8 *Noninvasive addition of an aspect to a component*

NOTE ON TERMINOLOGY

To be precise, *coordination* is a more general term than *synchronization*. We usually say that we *coordinate* a number of interacting components, but *synchronize* the access to a shared resource. However, we often use these words interchangeably throughout this text.

8.5.3 "Tangled" Synchronized Stack

We start with a simple C++ implementation of a synchronized stack in which the synchronization code is not separated from the functionality code at all. The C++ code is shown in Figure 8-9 (the equivalent Java code is given in Figure 8-22). The stack has a push() and a pop() method (lines 16 and 24), and the code responsible for synchronization has been highlighted. The synchronization code involves five synchronization variables: lock, push_wait, pop_wait (lines 34–36), monitor in push() (line 17), and monitor in pop() (line 26). lock is the most important synchronization variable on which all synchronization locking is performed. The remaining synchronization variables are just wrappers on lock allowing for different styles of locking. The implementation in Figure 8-9 uses the publicly available and portable Adaptive Communications Environment (ACE) library [Sch94], which provides a number of synchronization classes, such as ACE_Thread_Mutex, ACE_Condition_Thread_Mutex, and ACE_Guard. These classes wrap the low-level synchronization variables provided by operating systems (see [Sch95] for a detailed discussion of synchronization wrappers).

Let us first state the synchronization constraints that this synchronization code implements

1. push() is self exclusive, that is, no two different threads can execute push() at the same time.
2. pop() is self exclusive.
3. push() and pop() are mutually exclusive, that is, no two different threads can be executing push() and pop() at the same time.
4. push() can only proceed if the stack is not full.
5. pop() can only proceed if the stack is not empty.

Thus, push() and pop() are both *mutually exclusive* and *self exclusive*. This is achieved by locking the shared lock variable on entering push() and pop() and releasing it on leaving push() and pop(), respectively. This locking is automated using the class template ACE_Guard. We wrap lock into ACE_Guard by declaring the temporary variable monitor at the beginning of push() and pop() (lines 17 and 26). The effect of this wrapping is that lock is locked in the constructor of monitor at the beginning of each of the two synchronized methods and released automatically in the destructor of monitor at the end of each method (as indicated by the comment in lines 21–22). Thus, the programmer does not have to manually release lock at the end of the method, which has been a common source of errors. The declaration of monitor at the beginning of a method amounts to declaring the method as *synchronized* in Java (compare Figure 8-22).

In addition to making push() and pop() mutual and self exclusive, we also need to suspend any thread that tries to push an element on a full stack or pop an element from an empty stack (i.e., constraints 4 and 5). The implementation of these constraints involves the conditional synchronization variables push_wait and pop_wait (lines 35–36 and 14–15). The stack conditions of being full or empty are checked at the beginning of each method (lines 18 and 27) and, if necessary, the current thread is put to sleep by calling wait() on push_wait or on pop_wait. At the end of each method, signal() is called on pop_wait or on push_wait if the state of the stack transitions from empty to not empty or from full to not full. For example, when a thread waits to pop an element from an empty stack and some other thread pushes some element on the stack and executes signal() on pop_wait, the waiting thread wakes up, evaluates its condition (which is false), and pops the element. The synchronization of push() and pop() is an example of the classic *bounded buffer synchronization schema,* which is used for synchronizing concurrent access to data buffers (e.g., see [Lea97]).

The problem with the implementation in Figure 8-9 is that it mixes the synchronization code with the functionality code. This has a number of disadvantages, such as:

♦ *Hard-coded synchronization:* Because synchronization is not parameterized, it cannot be changed without manually modifying the stack class. A reusable component has to work in different contexts and different synchronization strategies might be required in different contexts. In the simplest case, we would also like to use the stack in a single-threaded environment, but the synchronization code introduces unnecessary overhead and, even worse, will cause a deadlock when trying to push an element on a full stack or pop an element from an empty stack in a single-threaded environment.

```
#include "ace\Synch.h"                                              //line  1
                                                                    //line  2
template<class Element, int S_SIZE>                                 //line  3
class Sync_Stack                                                    //line  4
{ public:                                                           //line  5
    enum {                                                          //line  6
      EMPTY        = -1,        // top value for empty stack        //line  7
      ONE_TOP      = EMPTY+1,   // top value if one element in stack //line  8
      MAX_TOP      = S_SIZE-1, // maximum top value                 //line  9
      UNDER_MAX_TOP = MAX_TOP-1 // just under the maximum top value //line 10
    };                                                              //line 11
    Sync_Stack()                                                    //line 12
      : top (EMPTY),                                                //line 13
        push_wait (lock),                                           //line 14
        pop_wait  (lock) { };                                       //line 15
    void push(Element *element)                                     //line 16
    { ACE_Guard<ACE_Thread_Mutex> monitor (lock);                   //line 17
      while (top == MAX_TOP) push_wait.wait();                      //line 18
      elements [++top] = element;                                   //line 19
      if (top == ONE_TOP) pop_wait.signal();     //signal if was empty //line 20
      // the lock is unlocked automatically                        //line 21
      // by the destructor of the monitor                          //line 22
    }                                                               //line 23
    Element *pop()                                                  //line 24
    { Element *return_val;                                          //line 25
      ACE_Guard<ACE_Thread_Mutex> monitor (lock);                  //line 26
      while (top == EMPTY) pop_wait.wait();                        //line 27
      return_val = elements [top--];                               //line 28
      if (top == UNDER_MAX_TOP) push_wait.signal(); //signal if was full//l. 29
      return return_val;                                           //line 30
    }                                                               //line 31
  private:                                                         //line 32
    // synchronization variables                                   //line 33
    ACE_Thread_Mutex lock;                                         //line 34
    ACE_Condition_Thread_Mutex push_wait;                          //line 35
    ACE_Condition_Thread_Mutex pop_wait;                           //line 36
                                                                    //line 37
    // stack variables                                             //line 38
    int top;                                                       //line 39
    Element *elements [S_SIZE];                                    //line 40
};                                                                 //line 41
```

Figure 8-9 *"Tangled" implementation of a synchronized stack in C++*

♦ *Tangled synchronization and functionality aspects:* The functionality code is mixed with the synchronization code, which makes it more difficult to reason about each of these aspects in separation. This causes maintenance problems and impairs adaptability and reusability. More complex components might also require some extra state variables to be used in the synchronization conditions. Such variables are referred to as the *synchronization state*. Thus, our naive, tangled solution also mixes the synchronization state with the logical state of the component. In the stack example, we saw that the synchronization aspect crosscuts the methods of the stack. In general, the situation may be much worse because we often need to coordinate a number of objects and the synchronization code may crosscut all or some of them in different ways. We discuss different kinds of crosscutting found in OO programs in Section 8.5.8.

♦ *Nonintentional representation of the synchronization aspect:* The synchronization constraints are not represented explicitly in the code. For example, instead of the code involving lock and mutex, all we would have to do is annotate the push and pop methods as mutually and self exclusive.[12] Also, the implementation of the conditional synchronization is too implicit and exposes too much detail. We will see a better solution in Section 8.6.1.

8.5.4 Separating Synchronization Using Design Patterns

A standard way of separating synchronization code from the functionality code is to use inheritance (see [Lea97]). The usual implementation involves putting the synchronization into a subclass. The subclass wraps the methods of the superclass that have to be synchronized with appropriate synchronization code. In C++, we can additionally turn the superclass into a parameter, so that the resulting synchronization class template can be reused on a number of related functionality classes. The implementation of the synchronization class uses the *inheritance-based static wrapper idiom* we discussed in Section 7.7. The implementation of the stack and the stack synchronizer is shown in Figure 8-10.

---

12. The keyword synchronized in Java represents a declarative construct for marking methods as self and mutually exclusive at the same time. Unfortunately, this is not always sufficient because methods with read-only access usually need not be self-exclusive, but only mutually exclusive with the writing methods. On the other hand, the latter need to be mutually and self-exclusive. Expressing such synchronization constraints in Java requires quite complex synchronization code (e.g., see [LK97]).

Stack in Figure 8-10 does error checking that is needed if we also want to use it in a single-threaded environment. Trying to push an element on a full stack or pop an element from an empty stack in a single-threaded application is clearly an error. Stack checks for these conditions and throws an exception if necessary. In order to use it in a multithreaded application, we can wrap it in the synchronization wrapper Sync_Stack_Wrapper<Stack<...> >. This will make it thread safe. One of the advantages of the wrapper solution is that we can reuse the synchronization wrapper for different stack implementations, for example, stacks using different data structures for storing their elements.

The stack implementation in Figure 8-10 has one deficiency: If we wrap the stack in the synchronization wrapper for use in a multithreaded environment, the base stack implementation still checks for errors, although the checking is not needed in this case. A solution to this problem is to separate the error checking aspect from the base implementation of the stack using another inheritance-based static wrapper, just as we did with the synchronization aspect. This is shown in Figure 8-11.

Given the code in Figure 8-11, Balking_Stack_Wrapper <Stack<...> > has the same meaning as Stack<...> in Figure 8-10. Now, we can use Balking_Stack_Wrapper<Stack<...> > in a single-threaded application and Sync_Stack_Wrapper<Stack<...> > in a multithreaded application (in both cases, we use Stack from Figure 8-11). Of course, we could further parameterize the synchronization and the error checking wrappers to provide different synchronization, error-checking, and error-response policies.

The stack example also illustrates an important point: There are interdependencies between aspects. Trying to push an element on a full stack or to pop an element from an empty stack concerns both synchronization and error checking and response. In fact, in a multithreaded environment, we treat the following different policies uniformly (i.e., without distinguishing between synchronization and error checking and response) [Lea97].

♦ *Inaction:* Ignoring an action if it cannot be performed
♦ *Balking:* Throwing an exception if an action cannot be performed (e.g., Balking_Stack_Wrapper)

NOTE

In general, we distinguish between *error checking* (i.e., error detection), *response to error* (e.g., throwing an exception or aborting; this is still done on the server side), and *error handling* (e.g., the particular action taken to handle the error; this is usually done in the client code).

```
template<class Element_, int S_SIZE>
class Stack
{  public:
      // export element type and empty and maximum top value
      typedef Element_ Element;
      enum { EMPTY    = -1,
             MAX_TOP = S_SIZE-1};

      // classes used as exceptions
      class Underflow {};
      class Overflow  {};

      Stack() : top (EMPTY) {}
      void push(Element *element)
      {   if (top == MAX_TOP) throw Overflow(); //stack full!
          elements [++top] = element;
      }
      Element *pop()
      {   if (top == EMPTY) throw Underflow(); //stack empty!
          return elements [top--];
      }
   protected:
      int top;
   private:
      Element *elements [S_SIZE];
};
template<class UnsyncStack>
class Sync_Stack_Wrapper : public UnsyncStack
{  public:
      // get the element type and empty and maximum top value
      typedef typename UnsyncStack::Element Element;
      enum { EMPTY    = UnsyncStack::EMPTY,
             MAX_TOP = UnsyncStack::MAX_TOP};
      // declare ONE_TOP and UNDER_MAX_TOP
      enum { ONE_TOP        = EMPTY+1,
             UNDER_MAX_TOP = MAX_TOP-1};

      Sync_Stack_Wrapper()
            : UnsyncStack (),
              push_wait (lock),
              pop_wait (lock) { }
      void push(Element *element)
```

(continued)

Figure 8-10 *Implementation of a stack and a synchronizing stack wrapper using parameterized inheritance*

```
    {      ACE_Guard<ACE_Thread_Mutex> monitor(lock);
           while (top == MAX_TOP) push_wait.wait();
           UnsyncStack::push(element);
           // signal if was empty
           if (top == ONE_TOP) pop_wait.signal();
    }
    Element *pop()
    {    Element *return_val;
         ACE_Guard<ACE_Thread_Mutex> monitor (lock);
         while (top == EMPTY) pop_wait.wait();
         return_val = UnsyncStack::pop();
         if (top == UNDER_MAX_TOP) push_wait.signal();
         // signal if was full
         return return_val;
    }
  private:
    // synchronization variables
    ACE_Thread_Mutex lock;
    ACE_Condition_Thread_Mutex push_wait;
    ACE_Condition_Thread_Mutex pop_wait;
};
```

Figure 8-10 *Implementation of a stack and a synchronizing stack wrapper using parameterized inheritance (continued)*

- ◆ *Guarded suspension:* Suspending a thread until the precondition becomes true (e.g., `Sync_Stack_Wrapper`)
- ◆ *Provisional action:* Pretending to perform an action, but not committing to its effects until success is assured
- ◆ *Rollback/Recovery:* Trying to proceed, but upon failure, undoing any effects of partially completed actions
- ◆ *Retry:* Repeatedly attempting failed actions after recovering from previous attempts

Adding synchronization or error checking by method wrapping (as in `Sync_Stack_Wrapper` or `Balking_Stack_Wrapper`) is not always possible. Sometimes we need to make a call to a synchronizer or an error checker somewhere in the middle of a method. In

---

NOTE

The applicability of these policies is discussed in [Lea97] in detail.

```
template<class Element_, int S_SIZE>
class Stack
{  public:
       // export element type and empty and maximum top value
       typedef Element_ Element;
       enum { EMPTY   = -1,
              MAX_TOP = S_SIZE-1};

       Stack() : top (EMPTY) {}
       void push(Element *element)
       {   elements [++top] = element;
       }
       Element *pop()
       {   return elements [top--];
       }
    protected:
       int top;
    private:
       Element *elements [S_SIZE];
};

template<class UnsafeStack>
class Balking_Stack_Wrapper : public UnsafeStack
{  public:
       // import element type and empty and maximum top value
       typedef typename UnsafeStack::Element Element;
       enum { EMPTY   = UnsafeStack::EMPTY,
              MAX_TOP = UnsafeStack::MAX_TOP};

       // classes used as exceptions
       class Underflow {};
       class Overflow  {};

       Balking_Stack_Wrapper()
            : UnsafeStack () {}
       void push(Element *element)
       {   if (top == MAX_TOP) throw Overflow(); //stack full!
           UnsafeStack::push(element);
       }
       Element *pop()
       {   if (top == EMPTY) throw Underflow(); //stack empty!
           return UnsafeStack::pop();
       }
};
```

Figure 8-11 *Implementation of a stack without error checking and a balking stack wrapper using parameterized inheritance*

this case, we can parameterize the method with the synchronizer or the error checker using the *strategy pattern* (see [GHJV95]]). If static binding is sufficient, we can use a static version of the strategy pattern based on a template parameter. The pattern is illustrated in Figure 8-12. The listing shows three different strategies. Please note that the strategy method someAction() is declared as static in each strategy. If in a certain context no action is necessary, we can use EmptyStrategy, which implements someAction() as an empty method. If we use inlining, someAction() will not incur any overhead. If necessary, we can also pass this as a parameter to the strategy method. Defining the strategy method as static minimizes any overhead; however, if the strategy algorithm needs to retain some state between calls, we would define the strategy method as an *instance* method and add a strategy instance variable to the component (we discuss these and other alternative ways to implement strategy at the end of Section 7.6). If we want to allow for both static and dynamic binding, we need to use the idiom presented in Figure 8-6.

Unfortunately, calling hook methods, such as someAction(), pollutes the code implementing the basic functionality. Sometimes we can solve this problem by splitting methods and classes in a way that the wrapper pattern can be used (e.g., the section of the code that needs to be synchronized could be turned into a separate method). But this increases the "fragmentation" of the design. In order to solve this problem adequately, we need new composition mechanisms that handle the different kinds of crosscutting that appear in OO designs. We discuss them later.

If we decide to use the static wrapper solution presented in this section, we still need to somehow modify the client code in order to create instances of Sync_Stack_Wrapper<Stack<...> > instead of Stack<...>. This can actually be done without modifying any of the existing source files, but requires moving the file implementing Stack into a different directory. Let's assume that Stack is declared in the file stack.h and Sync_Stack_Wrapper is declared in sync_stack_wrapper.h. Furthermore, some client client.cpp includes stack.h and uses Stack. In order to make client.cpp use the wrapped stack instead of Stack, we need to move stack.h into some other directory, for example, original, and create a new stack.h at the same place where the original stack.h resided. The content of the new stack.h is shown in Figure 8-13.

```
class StrategyA
{   public:
        static void someAction()
        {    // do some work
        }
};

class StrategyB
{   public:
        static void someAction()
        {    // do some other work
        }
};

class EmptyStrategy
{   public:
        static void someAction()
        {} // empty action
};

template <class Strategy>
class Component
{   public:
        //...
        void method()
        {   // some method-specific work
            Strategy::someAction();
            // some other method-specific work
        }
        //...
};
```

Figure 8-12 Strategy pattern based on a template parameter

8.5.5 Separating Synchronization Using SOP

Using the SOP approach, we can nicely separate functionality code from the synchronization code by encapsulating them in two separate subjects. In the C++ version of SOP, a subject is modeled simply as a C++ namespace (see [SOP]).

Let us assume that Stack has been defined in the namespace original. The implementation is shown in Figure 8-14.

```
//stack.h
namespace original {
  #include "original\stack.h"
}
namespace extension {
  #include "sync_stack_wrapper.h"
}
// wrap original::Stack into extension::Sync_Stack_Wrapper
// and publish it as Stack
template<class Element, int S_SIZE>
class Stack :
  public extension::Sync_Stack_Wrapper<original::Stack<Element, S_SIZE> >
{public:
  Stack() : extension::Sync_Stack_Wrapper<original::Stack<Element, S_SIZE> >()
  {}
};
```

Figure 8-13 *Content of the new* `stack.h`

Unfortunately, as of this writing, the implementation of SOP/C++ does not support the composition of class templates. Therefore, we implement Stack as a C++ class. The constants Element and S_SIZE are then defined using the preprocessor directive #define in a separate include file (see Figure 8-15).

Next, we define the new namespace sync, which contains the stack synchronization class Stack. We will later compose original::Stack with sync::Stack in order to synchronize it. The code for sync::Stack is shown in Figure 8-16.

sync::Stack is a "vanilla" C++ class, which is very similar to Sync_Stack_Wrapper in Figure 8-10. The differences between sync::Stack and Sync_Stack_Wrapper include the following.

♦ sync::Stack has no superclass.
♦ sync::Stack has the two additional method declarations inner_push() (line 27) and inner_pop() (line 28); the implementations for these methods will be provided upon composition.
♦ push() of sync::Stack calls inner_push() (line 14) and pop() calls inner_pop() (line 21).

Composition in SOP is achieved by writing composition rules that specify the correspondence of the subjects (i.e., namespaces), classes, and members to be composed and how to combine them

```
// stack.h
#include "constants.h"

namespace original {
class Stack
{  public:
      Stack() : top (-1) {}
      void push(Element *element)
      {   elements [++top] = element;
      }
      Element *pop()
      {   return elements [top--];
      }
   private:
      int top;
      Element *elements [S_SIZE];
};
} //namespace original
```

Figure 8-14 Implementation of the class Stack

(see Section 8.3.1). Before we show the subject composition rules for composing the namespaces original and sync, let us first describe the composition requirements in plain English.

1. original and sync should be composed into the new namespace composed by merging their members, for example, classes, operations, attributes, and so on and making sure that if two members have the same name, they correspond. In particular, original::Stack and

```
//constants.h
#ifndef CONSTANTS_H
#define CONSTANTS_H

#define Element int
#define S_SIZE 10

#endif
```

Figure 8-15 Content of constants.h

```
// sync_stack_extension.h                                    // line  1
#include "ace\Synch.h"                                       // line  2
#include "constants.h"                                       // line  3
                                                             // line  4
namespace sync {                                             // line  5
class Stack                                                  // line  6
{ public:                                                    // line  7
    Stack ()                                                 // line  8
    : push_wait (lock),                                      // line  9
      pop_wait (lock) { }                                    // line 10
    void push(Element *element)                              // line 11
    { ACE_Guard<ACE_Thread_Mutex> monitor (lock);            // line 12
      while (top == S_SIZE-1) push_wait.wait();              // line 13
      inner_push(element);          // <--- call inner_push  // line 14
      if (top == 0) pop_wait.signal();  // signal if was empty // line 15
    }                                                        // line 16
    Element *pop()                                           // line 17
    { Element *return_val;                                   // line 18
      ACE_Guard<ACE_Thread_Mutex> monitor (lock);            // line 19
      while (top == -1) pop_wait.wait();                     // line 20
      return_val = inner_pop();     // <--- call inner_pop   // line 21
      if (top == S_SIZE-2) push_wait.signal(); // signal if was full  //l.22
      return return_val;                                     // line 23
    }                                                        // line 24
  private:                                                   // line 25
    //inner methods declarations (bodies provided on composition)  // line 26
    void inner_push(Element *element);                       // line 27
    Element *inner_pop();                                    // line 28
                                                             // line 29
    int top;                                                 // line 30
                                                             // line 31
    // synchronization variables                             // line 32
    ACE_Thread_Mutex lock;                                   // line 33
    ACE_Condition_Thread_Mutex push_wait;                    // line 34
    ACE_Condition_Thread_Mutex pop_wait;                     // line 35
};                                                           // line 36
} // namespace sync                                          // line 37
```

Figure 8-16 Implementation of sync::Stack

sync::Stack correspond and should be merged into composed::Stack. Furthermore, when merging corresponding attributes, for example, original::Stack::top and sync::Stack::top, only one copy should be included in the composite class, that is, com-posed::Stack::top.

2. The "by name" correspondence implied by the previous requirement should be overridden for original::Stack::push() and sync::Stack::push() and for original::Stack::pop() and sync::Stack::pop(): We want sync::Stack::inner_push() and original::Stack::push() to correspond and be combined into combined::Stack::inner_push(). The combined operation should use the implementation of original::Stack::push(). We want the same to happen for sync::Stack::inner_pop() and original::Stack::pop(). Effectively, the push() and pop() of the synchronizer class will call push() and pop() of the original Stack class as their inner methods (see next requirement). This has the effect of wrapping the original push() and pop() into synchron-ization code.

3. If a method is called on *self* inside one of the classes to be composed, we want *self* in the resulting composite class to refer to the composite class. In particular, the call to inner_push in sync::Stack::push, once promoted to com-posed::Stack::push, should call the new inner method, that is, composed::Stack::inner_push. The same applies to the call to inner_pop in sync::Stack::pop.

4. The constructors of both classes to be composed should also be composed. This requirement is taken care of auto-matically by the SOP system.

These composition requirements are encoded by the composi-tion rules shown in Figure 8-17.

The *"ByNameMerge" rule* in Figure 8-17 is a correspondence-and-combination rule, which implements the previous require-ments 1, 3, and 4. It implies "by name" correspondence and "merge" combination of the subjects original and sync. It also specifies that the name of the resulting subject is composed. Please note that the first parameter of this rule indicates the resulting name and the second parameter lists the names to be composed (lists are enclosed in parentheses). The next two "equate" rules are correspondence rules. They implement requirement 2. Because the scope of these two rules is single methods and such scope is smaller than the scope of the merge rule (which was defined over subjects), the equate rules have precedence over the "ByNameMerge" rule.

It is important to note that once we compile some_client.cpp, stack.h, sync_stack_extension.h, and stack.rul, the client code

```
// stack.rul

// requirements #1, #3, #4
ByNameMerge(composed, (original, sync))

// requirement #2
Equate(operation composed.inner_push, (sync.inner_push, original.push))
Equate(operation composed.inner_pop, (sync.inner_pop, original.pop))
```

Figure 8-17 Rules for composing the original *and* extension *namespaces*[13]

in `some_client.cpp` will automatically reference `composed::Stack` at any place it explicitly references `original::Stack`. Thus the SOP composition is noninvasive with respect to both `Stack` and the client code.

8.5.6 Some Problems with Design Patterns and Some Solutions

Design patterns described in [GHJV95], but also in [Cop92, Pre95, BMR+96], represent a tremendous advance towards more flexible and reusable software. When we consider the design patterns collected in [GHJV95], we need at least to distinguish between two important contributions.

♦ Design patterns as a form of documenting recurring problems and solutions in OO designs
♦ Concrete solutions proposed by specific design patterns

In our discussion, we will focus on the concrete structures proposed in [GHJV95].

Design patterns collected in [GHJV95] help us to decouple and encapsulate various aspects of a software system using concrete implementation idioms based on the two object-oriented composition mechanisms: *inheritance* and *object composition* (by object composition, we mean composition by referencing or containing

---

13. This code was designed based on the specifications available from [SOP] in March 1998 and comments from H. Ossher, W. Harrison and P. Tarr of IBM Research. We did not have access to the SOP/C++ prototype environment in order to test this code.

NOTE

Figure 8.17 shows only two kinds of composition rules available in SOP. There are more rules allowing a fine-grained control over the composition of subjects (see [SOP, OKH+95, OKK+96]).

The SOP composition rules work on *labels* of subjects rather than their sources. A label contains all the symbolic information about a subject, such as the names of the classes, methods, and attributes contained in the subject. As a consequence, we can actually compose compiled subjects (in SOP, each subject can be compiled separately). In other words, SOP supports the composition of binary components.

Variability-Oriented Programming (VOP) [Mez97a, Mez97b] is another noninvasive composition approach, which we could use to implement our synchronization example. The major difference between VOP and SOP is that VOP supports both static and dynamic composition of classes and class fragments.[14] Using dynamic fragment composition, we can simplify the implementation of many of the design patterns described in [GHJV95]. For example, the implementation of the visitor pattern given in [Mez97a] requires only a small fraction of the methods in the original implementation in [GHJV95]. We will discuss the advantages of fragment composition over the conventional design-pattern-based solutions in Section 8.5.6.

objects, i.e., association and aggregation). Table 8-1 lists the aspects that some of the design patterns allow us to encapsulate and vary.

Unfortunately, implementation idioms based exclusively on inheritance and object composition introduce more complexity than necessary. For example, in order to be able to vary some algorithm, we can apply the strategy pattern that involves factoring out the algorithm and encapsulating it in an extra strategy object. But often the algorithm is really part of the original object and by encapsulating it into the separate strategy object, we add the extra complexity of:

♦ Handling an additional strategy object
♦ Having to live with a level of indirection between the original object and the strategy object

---

14. According to H. Ossher, one way to achieve dynamic composition in SOP is to use dynamic loading of subjects. This solution is feasible in principle, although not supported by the current prototypes.

Table 8-1 Design Aspects That Design Patterns Let You Vary (excerpt from Table 1.2 in [GHJV95])	
Design Pattern	**Aspect(s) That Can Vary**
Adapter	Interface to an object
Bridge	Implementation of an object
Mediator	How and which objects interact with each other
State	States of an object
Strategy	An algorithm

Similarly, when we decorate an object, we really just want to add or override some of its members. But when we apply the decorator pattern based on object composition, we also end up with two objects and an extra indirection level. A similar observation applies to adapter, state, bridge, and other patterns.

Several researchers identified a number of problems with the implementation of design patterns in conventional OO languages (e.g., see [Sou95, SPL96, Mez97a, Bos98, SOPD]). We group these problems into three major problem categories: object schizophrenia, the preplanning problem, and the traceability problem.

8.5.6.1 Object Schizophrenia

The problem of splitting what is intentionally supposed to be a single object is referred to as *object schizophrenia* [SOPD].

Broken delegation (i.e., the self problem)

One subproblem of object schizophrenia is *broken delegation* [SOPD] (also referred to as the *self problem* [Lie86a]; see Section 8.3.2). For example, if an algorithm is a part of an object and it needs to send a message to the object it is part of, it simply sends this message to *self*. However, if we factor out the algorithm as a strategy object, we need to send the message to the original object. We can no longer think of the algorithm simply as being a part of the original object. Instead, we have the complexity of indirection, for example, any data needed by the algorithm from the original object has to be passed as an extra parameter.

Another problem results from the fact that we have to manage two object identities instead of one. This also causes extra complexity and increases the chance of programming errors, for example, when the component "escapes" its wrapper (i.e., when we accidentally give away a reference to the wrapped object).

Fragment-based composition, as supported by SOP or VOP, allows us to avoid these problems by modeling extensions, such as strategies and wrappers, as true class fragments of the extended class.[15] In other words, we do not have to deal with two object identities and an indirection level, and we can code the fragments as if they were simply parts of the resulting composite objects.

8.5.6.2 Preplanning Problem

Another problem of design patterns is that they allow for adaptability, but only if the need for certain adaptability was anticipated and the appropriate design patterns were applied in the design phase. This is referred to as the *preplanning problem* [SOPD].

As we have seen in previous sections, there are many situations where the fragment-based composition of SOP allows us to noninvasively adapt a component, even if the adaptation has not been anticipated at the design time of the component. We will also show an implementation of another noninvasive composition mechanism in Smalltalk in Section 8.5.7.

8.5.6.3 Traceability Problem

Yet another problem with many design patterns and idioms[16] is their *indirect* representation in the source code. We refer to this problem as the *traceability problem* [Bos98] (also *indirection problem* in [SOPD]). Given a concrete program code, it is usually unclear which design patterns were applied in its design. The code implementing a given pattern is intertwined with the code implementing the functionality and other design patterns and is scattered over a number of components. As a consequence, it is difficult, if not impossible, to distinguish which parts of the resulting program were contributed by which design pattern. Additionally, design patterns increase the fragmentation of the design by introducing many extra little methods and classes. This indirect representation of design patterns causes severe problems for maintenance, reuse, and evolution because the design information is lost.

New language features and composition mechanisms can allow a more direct representation of design patterns. For exam-

---

15. Because SOP supports static composition only, we cannot use it to model dynamic variability. VOP, on the other hand, supports both static and dynamic composition.

16. By idioms, we mean some (often unusual) combination of abstractions specific to some programming language, which are used for implementing some other abstraction that is not a part of this language. Many idioms can be characterized as "elegant tricks."

ple, the Demeter approach replaces the conventional OO implementation idiom of the visitor pattern given in [GHJV95] with a
more direct representation, which, as we discussed in Section
8.3.3, avoids some of its problems. You'll find proposals of other
language constructs for directly representing design patterns in
[SPL96, Mez98a, Bos98].

We can say that patterns and idioms represent just one phase
in the evolution of abstractions, which eventually may become language features. Once some design patterns and idioms become features of programming languages, they lose much of their substance
as patterns. We no longer think of them as design patterns or
idioms in the conventional sense, just as we do not regard inheritance as a design pattern. On the other hand, the documentation
format of design patterns can still be useful for documenting the
applicability of language features for solving specific problems.

8.5.7   Implementing Noninvasive, Dynamic Composition in Smalltalk

Noninvasive, dynamic composition based on intercepting messages can be easily implemented using the reflection mechanisms of
a reflective language, such as Smalltalk [GR83]. By reflective facilities, we mean explicit representations of features of a language, for
example, metaobjects representing classes, methods, and method
execution contexts, which can be accessed and manipulated from
within the language in order to affect its own semantics. In
Smalltalk, such metaobjects exist at the runtime of an application.
As an example of a noninvasive, dynamic composition mechanism,
we will show a Smalltalk implementation of an extremely simplified version of the CF model from Section 8.3.2. Later, in Section
8.6.2, we will use this mechanism to compose synchronization
objects and functionality objects at runtime.

8.5.7.1   Model of the Composition

Listener objects

The model of the composition mechanism is shown in Figure 8-18.
The idea is to be able to attach *listener objects* to a *base object* at
runtime. Both listeners and base objects are simply instances of some
arbitrary classes. We say that a listener is attached to a base object *at*
a certain message *messageA*, meaning that when we send *messageA*
to the base object, the message is redirected to the listener.

By drawing the interface layer in Figure 8-18 around the base
object, we indicate that the dispatch filters, which forward some
messages to the listeners, and the references to the listeners are
added after the base object has been created. However, the interface layer should be transparent with respect to both the environ-

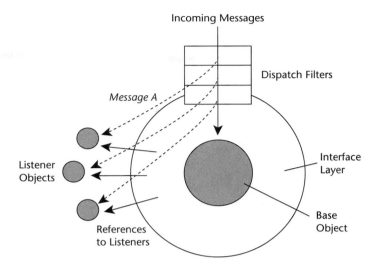

Figure 8-18 *Model of a simple composition mechanism based on message interception*

ment and the base object. In fact, we regard the interface layer as a true part of the base object. Thus, it is not appropriate to implement it as a wrapper based on object composition.

In order to implement this model, all we need is to be able to:

♦ Dynamically override methods on a per-instance basis, that is, in a single instance rather than the whole class; given this ability, we can implement each dispatch filter as a method that forwards to the appropriate listener.
♦ Dynamically add instance variables on a per-instance basis; this ability allows us to add references pointing to new listeners.

In summary, we can attach an object *B* to another object *A* at the message *messageA* by:

♦ Adding an instance variable to object *A* pointing to *B*
♦ Overriding the method *messageA* in object *A*, so that *messageA* is forwarded to *B*

8.5.7.2 Composition API[17]

Given two arbitrary objects referenced by the variables `object2` and `object1`, you can attach `object2` to `object1` at message `messageA` as follows:

---

17. Application Programming Interface

```
object1 attach: object2 at: #messageA.
```

Once you've attached an object, we can also detach it:

```
object1 detachAt: #messageA.
```

You can access the base object (i.e., object1) in the attached object (e.g., object2) like this:

```
self baseObject.
```

After a message has been rerouted to the attached object, you can still call the original method of the base object from within the new method of the attached object (this code remains the same even if the original message has some parameters):

```
self baseCall.
```

Here is an example. If you want to wrap the messageA of object1 in some before and after actions, you need to implement the following messageA in object2:

```
messageA
    self someBeforeAction.
    self baseCall. "calls the original method"
    self someAfterAction.
```

and attach object2 to object1 at messageA:

```
object1 attach: object2 at: #messageA.
```

The complete code implementing the composition mechanism is shown in Appendix C.

It is important to note that we can compose any objects without having to modify the code of any of their classes or clients. Also, we don't have to provide any special "hooks" in any of the objects being composed. Thus, the composition is noninvasive and it avoids the preplanning problem.

8.5.7.3 Instance-Specific Extension Protocol

As stated earlier, the implementation of the composition mechanism utilizes the reflective facilities of Smalltalk including meta-objects representing classes, methods, and method execution contexts and the Smalltalk compiler itself. We also use two important methods providing access to the implementation of Smalltalk, namely `class:` and `become:`. The method `class:` allows us to modify the class of an instance, and `become:` replaces every reference to the receiver by the reference to the argument of this message.

Metaobject protocols

Metaobjects provide representations for the features of a language. The interface defined by the metaobjects of a given language is referred to as a *metaobject protocol* (MOP) [KRB91]. By allowing a write access to metaobjects, as in Smalltalk, we can modify the default semantics of the language. Indeed, in [KRB91], this has been recognized as one fundamental approach to language design. Instead of designing a fixed language, we can design a default language and a MOP, which allows users to customize the default language according to their needs. A reflective language, such as Smalltalk, provides a substantial part of its own implementation as a library of metaobjects to be extended and/or modified by the programmer.

Our implementation of the composition mechanism utilizes a very simple protocol implemented on top of the Smalltalk MOP. The protocol consists of two methods: one for adding/overriding methods to/in instances and another one for adding instance variables to instances. We call this simple protocol the *instance-specific extension protocol*. We will describe its implementation in the following two sections. You'll find the full implementation code in Smalltalk\VisualWorks in Appendix B.[18]

8.5.7.3.1 Defining Methods in Instances

Instance-specific behavior

Our implementation uses the Smalltalk idiom *instance-specific behavior* by Kent Beck (see [Bec93a]). This idiom allows you to

---

NOTE

The precise semantics of `become:` varies in different Smalltalk implementations. For example, in VisualWorks, the references to the receiver and the argument of `become:` are simply swapped. On the other hand, in Smalltalk/V, the references to the receiver are modified to point to the argument object and the references to the argument object remain unchanged.

---

18. VisualWorks is a product of Cincom, Inc. A free noncommercial version can be downloaded at www.cincom.com/visualworks/downloads.html. As of this writing, you can also obtain it from ObjectShare, Inc. at www.objectshare.com/VWNC/.

define a method in one instance without affecting the code of its class. The following sample code demonstrates the use of the idiom:

```
anObjectA
    specialize:
        'whoAreYou
            ^self printString'
```

Executing the previous code will define the method whoAreYou in anObjectA. But how does this work?

The method specialize: inserts a new class between anObjectA and its class, that is, ObjectA, as shown in Figure 8-19. This is possible because we can use the method class: to modify the class of an instance. The new class is an instance of Behavior, which is a metaclass defining some properties for all classes. For example, Behavior defines the variable methodDict containing a method dictionary (see Figure 8-20). A method dictionary is a table that stores the methods of a class. The methodDict variable is present in all Smalltalk classes because they are instances of metaclasses, and the latter are subclasses of Behavior. We use an instance of Behavior instead of Class because Behavior incurs much less overhead. For example, aBehavior does not even have a name. Of course, we set the superclass of aBehavior to ObjectA.

Once we've made aBehavior the class of anObjectA, the string provided as a parameter to specialize: is treated as the source

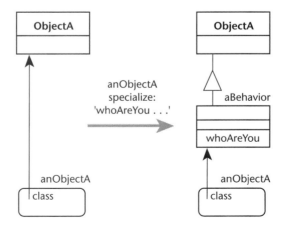

Figure 8-19 Adding a method to an instance

```
Object ()
    Behavior ('superclass' 'methodDict' 'format' 'subclasses')
        ClassDescription ('instanceVariables' 'organization')
            Class ('name' 'classPool' 'sharedPools')
                ... all the Metaclasses ...
            Metaclass ('thisClass')
```

Figure 8-20 *Metaclass hierarchy in Smalltalk/VisualWorks. Subclasses are indented. Instance variables defined by the corresponding class are shown in parentheses.*

code of a new method. The string is compiled and the resulting method is inserted in the method dictionary of aBehavior. If the original class ObjectA already has an implementation of whoAreYou, it will be overridden, that is, you can still access it through super.

Finally, the standard method class is overridden in anObjectA to return its original class ObjectA. This way the new class aBehavior is not visible to the environment. We can say that the new class is a private class of anObjectA.

The implementation of instance-specific behavior makes use of the following reflective facilities in Smalltalk.

♦ Using class Behavior and inserting a method into its method dictionary
♦ Changing the class of an instance using class:
♦ Compiling a method from a string using Compiler and the explicit handling of methods as instances of CompiledMethod

8.5.7.3.2 Adding Instance Variables to Instances
The idiom *adding instance variables to instances* was originally described in [Cza96]. The following sample code demonstrates the use of this idiom:

```
"declare a temporary variable"
| anObjectA |
"initialize the variable with an instance of ObjectA"
anObjectA := ObjectA new.
"add the new instance variable someNewInstVar to anObject"
anObjectA addInstanceVariable: 'someNewInstVar'.
```

NOTES

Also see [Bec95] for the correction of an error in the initial implementation of "instance-specific behavior" in [Bec93a]. The implementation of this idiom depends on the Smalltalk implementation you use. You'll find an implementation in Smalltalk/V in [Bec93b]. The code described in this chapter and given in Appendix B works with Smalltalk\VisualWorks. It requires the compiler to be loaded at runtime because we pass the method code to be installed as a string, which has to be compiled at runtime. However, instead of compiling the string on the fly, we could also insert precompiled methods (this requires some bytecode adaptation of the precompiled method at runtime). The latter solution does not need the compiler at runtime. You'll find the code for this solution at [DCOOL]. Different techniques for implementing method wrappers in Smalltalk are compared in [BFJR98].

```
"set the value of someNewInstVar to 1"
anObjectA someNewInstVar: 1.
"return the value of someNewInstVar"
^anObjectA someNewInstVar
```

The method `addInstanceVariable:` adds an instance variable to an instance in four steps:

1. It inserts aBehavior between the receiver and its class (just as we did for adding a method; see Figure 8-19).
2. It modifies the object format in aBehavior. The object format stored in a class encodes, among other things, the number of instance variables for its instances (see the instance variable `format` in Figure 8-20). The object format in aBehavior is modified in such a way that the number of instance variables it encodes is increased by one.
3. It mutates the receiver, so that it contains the number of instance variables encoded in `format`. This is achieved by creating a new instance of aBehavior, copying the contents of the receiver into the new instance, and replacing the receiver with the new instance using `become:`.
4. It inserts the accessing methods for the new instance variable into the method dictionary of aBehavior.

Here is the implementation of `addInstanceVariable:` (implemented in `Object`):

```
addInstanceVariable: aString
    "Add an instance variable and accessing
```

```
methods based on the name aString"
self specialize.
self incrementNumberOfInstVarsInMyClassFormat.
self mutateSelfToReflectNewClassFormat.
self addAccessingMethodsForLastInstVarUsing: aString.
```

You'll find the full implementation code in Appendix B.

In order to implement adding instance variables to instances, we have used the following reflective facilities of Smalltalk.

♦ Modifying the object format in `Behavior`
♦ Modifying the identity of an object using `become:`
♦ Using all the reflective facilities we've used for instance-specific behavior

8.5.8 Kinds of Crosscutting

The stack example in Figure 8-9 demonstrated the crosscutting of synchronization code and methods of one class. We also saw that method wrapping (i.e., before and after methods) allows us to separate the synchronization aspect from the stack. But what other kinds of crosscutting are common in object-oriented programs?

Class level versus instance level crosscutting

First, we distinguish between crosscutting at the class level and crosscutting at the instance level. If some aspect code crosscuts classes, this means that crosscutting the instances of the class is controlled at the class level. For example, the synchronization code crosscuts the stack at the class level and, in our case, it crosscuts all stack instances in the same way. Class level crosscutting requires composition mechanisms, allowing us to associate aspect code with classes. Furthermore, at the class level, we also distinguish between aspect state shared among all instances and per-instance aspect state.

Shared and per-instance aspect state

Instance-level crosscutting means that we can associate aspect code with individual instances. For example, different instances of a data structure could be associated with different aspect codes implementing different synchronization strategies. We saw an example of instance-level composition mechanism in the previous section.

Different kinds of crosscutting with respect to classes and instances are summarized in Figure 8-21. Each combination of one item on the left and one item on the right indicates a different kind of crosscutting.

Kinds of message join points

Message join points are quite common in OO programming. Examples of aspects amenable to message join points are concurrency, real-time constraints, atomic transactions, precondition-like error checking, security, profiling, monitoring, testing, caching, and historization. These kinds of aspects can usually be implemented as

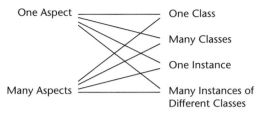

Figure 8-21 *Different kinds of crosscutting with respect to classes and instances*[19]

objects and coupled to the primary structure objects using some kind of message coupling mechanism, such as method wrapping or message interception. Indeed, we also have different possibilities at the method level: We can add a before action, an after action, or both to a method implementation or to a particular method call. The latter actually allows us to add actions *inside* a method implementation by instrumenting calls to other methods inside it. In general, we can distinguish between instrumenting the definition and the use of some language feature, for example, instrumenting method definition versus method calls. In addition to methods, we can also instrument attributes of objects. This is useful if we want to monitor read or write access to attributes. Future versions of AspectJ, which we discuss in Section 8.6.1, will augment Java with composition mechanisms for addressing the different kinds of crosscutting common in OO programs.

Domain-specific optimizations

There are also cases of more complex crosscutting in practice. For example, domain-specific optimizations in vector and matrix code involve crosscutting at the statement level. The usual example for vector code is loop fusing and temporary variable elimination. In this case, the optimizations crosscut vector expression and state-

---

NOTE

Hinkle and Johnson describe how to noninvasively instrument variables in Smalltalk using the Smalltalk reflective facilities in [HJ96]. Instrumented variables are also called "active variables" [MB85].

---

19. Please note that in the case of one aspect and one class or object, the crosscutting still occurs at the method level.

ment structures. We will see examples of such optimizations in Section 14.4.2.1. An even more complex kind of crosscutting is common to cache-based optimizations in matrix code. This kind of optimization requires very complex transformations. Indeed, due to the complexity of such transformations, the quality of the code generated by such optimizers is far beyond the quality of manually optimized code. In general, domain-specific optimizations in scientific computing require complex transformations on parse trees or other program representations.

8.6   How to Express Aspects in Programming Languages

In the previous sections, we have seen that appropriate composition mechanisms (e.g., fragment-based composition in SOP or traversal strategies in Demeter) allow us to reduce the complexity of conventional OO programs. But reducing complexity by untangling aspects and relating them by an appropriate composition mechanism is just the first step. We can further reduce complexity by representing the aspects themselves using appropriate linguistic means.

Whatever solution we find, our goal is to enable a one-to-one encoding of requirements in the language we use. For example, the synchronization of a stack involves four synchronization constraints (see Section 8.5.3). Ideally, we want to be able to express these constraints in the programming language with four corresponding statements.

What different options do we have for capturing aspects? There are three possibilities.

♦ Encode the aspect support as a conventional library (e.g., class or procedure library). We will see an example of this strategy in Section 8.6.2. That section discusses the implementation of a very high-level synchronization library that developers writing a synchronization aspect program can use. The library uses our dynamic composition mechanism for attaching objects from Section 8.5.7 in order to address crosscutting.

♦ Design a separate language for the aspect. We will see an example of a separate synchronization language in Section 8.6.1.

♦ Design a language extension for the aspect. We will discuss this option in Section 8.7.1.

We'll discuss the implementation technologies and the pros and cons for each of them in Section 8.7. We will first demonstrate the separate language approach in Section 8.6.1 and later the class library approach to aspects in Section 8.6.2.

8.6.1 Separating Synchronization Using AspectJ Cool

Cool

As you recall, Section 8.5.5 showed how to separate the synchronization aspect of a stack using SOP. Although the separation was quite satisfying (e.g., it allowed a noninvasive addition or replacement of the synchronization aspect with respect to both the stack implementation and client code), the representation of the synchronization aspect in Figure 8-16 was far from being intentional. In this section, we show a more intentional solution written in *Cool*, an aspect language for expressing synchronization in concurrent OO programs.

AspectJ

Cool was originally designed by Lopes in her dissertation [Lop97] and implemented as a part of the AspectJ[20] environment developed at the Xerox Palo Alto Research Center [AJ, XER98a, XER98b]. AspectJ is an extension to Java that supports aspect-oriented programming. AspectJ version 0.2.0 includes general-purpose crosscutting mechanisms that can be used to capture a range of crosscutting modularities (see Section 8.5.8) including but not limited to synchronization and distribution control. The support for specific aspects is implemented in the form of class libraries, similar to the style we will see in Section 8.6.2.

Ridl

At the time of preparing the examples for this chapter, the strategy of AspectJ (version 0.1.0) was to provide a separate aspect language for each aspect it addressed. The provided languages were Cool (i.e., the synchronization language) and Ridl. Ridl is an aspect language for expressing remote invocation and controlling the depth of parameter transfer (see [Lop97]). Both languages were implemented by a preprocessor that took Java source files and the aspect source files written in these languages and generated pure Java.

The example in this section is implemented using this older version 0.1.0 of AspectJ rather than the more general AspectJ 0.2.0. The older version allows us to demonstrate the use of specialized aspect languages for expressing aspects. The other approach involving class libraries and message-join-point composition mechanisms (which is also used in AspectJ 0.2.0) is demonstrated in Section 8.6.2 using an example from Smalltalk.

Before we show you the more intentional encoding of the stack synchronization aspect using AspectJ Cool, let us first restate the synchronization constraints on the stack we proposed in Section 8.5.3

1. push is self exclusive.
2. pop is self exclusive.

---

20. AspectJ is a trademark of Xerox Corporation.

Coordinators

On-exit and on-entry blocks

3. push and pop are mutually exclusive.
4. push can only proceed if the stack is not full.
5. pop can only proceed if the stack is not empty.

All these statements can be represented directly in Cool as a *coordinator* (i.e., a synchronizing agent). Figure 8-23 shows the Java implementation of the stack and the Cool implementation of the stack coordinator (for completeness, we also include the equivalent "tangled" implementation of the synchronized stack in pure Java in Figure 8-22). We numbered the lines of the stack coordinator, so that we can describe how the previously listed synchronization requirements are reflected in the coordinator code.

The name of the coordinator appearing on line 2 in Figure 8-23 is the same as the name of the Java class it synchronizes, that is, Stack. Line 3 states that push and pop are self exclusive (i.e., requirement 1 and 2).[21] Line 4 states that push and pop are mutually exclusive (i.e., requirement 3). The full and empty states of the stack are modeled by the condition variables full and empty declared on line 5. Lines 7 and 8 say that push can only proceed if the stack is not full (i.e., requirement 4). Line 9 starts the definition of the so-called *on-exit block* of code that is to be executed just after the execution of push of the class Stack.[22] The on-exit block of push (lines 9–12) and the on-exit block of pop (lines 15–18) define the semantics of the states full and empty. Please note that these blocks access the stack variables top, empty_top, and max_top. In general, a read-only access of the variables of the coordinated object is possible, but we are not allowed to modify them. Finally, line 14 states that pop can only proceed if the stack is not empty (i.e., requirement 5).

This simple stack example demonstrates that the stack synchronization constraints can be directly translated into Cool. Thus, the Cool representation of the synchronization aspect is clearly more intentional than the subclass version in Figure 8-10 or the SOP version in Figure 8-16.

---

21. In Cool, methods declared as self-exclusive are re-entrant, that is, the same method can be executed more than once at the same time by the same thread, so that recursive, self-exclusive methods do not deadlock. On the other hand, if one thread is executing a self-exclusive method, any other thread calling this method will be suspended.

22. Of course, in Cool, we can also define *on-entry blocks,* which are executed before the body of the synchronized method is executed. However, we do not need this feature in the stack synchronization example.

```
public class Stack
{    private int empty_top;
     private int one_top;
     private int max_top;
     private int under_max_top;

     public Stack(int size)
     {    elements = new Object[size];
          empty_top = -1;
          top = empty_top;
          one_top = empty_top+1;
          max_top = size-1;
          under_max_top = max_top-1;
     }
     public synchronized void push(Object element)
     {    while (top == max_top)
          {    try
               {    wait();
               }
               catch (InterruptedException e) {};
          }
          elements[++top] = element;
          if (top == one_top) notifyAll();        // signal if was empty
     }
     public synchronized Object pop()
     {    while (top == empty_top)
          {    try
               {    wait();
               }
               catch (InterruptedException e) {};
          }
          Object return_val = elements[top--];
          if (top == under_max_top) notifyAll(); // signal if was full
          return return_val;
     }

     private int top;
     private Object [] elements;
}
```

Figure 8-22 *"Tangled" implementation of a synchronized stack in Java*

```
//in a separate JCore file Stack.jcore23
public class Stack
{    private int empty_top;
     private int max_top;

     public Stack(int size)
     {    elements = new Object[size];
          empty_top = -1;
          top = empty_top;
          max_top = size-1;
     }
     public void push(Object element)
     {    elements[++top] = element;
     }
     public Object pop()
     {    return elements[top--];
     }

     private int top;
     private Object [] elements;
}
```

```
//in a separate Cool file Stacksync.cool        // line  1
coordinator Stack                               // line  2
{    selfex push, pop;                          // line  3
     mutex {push, pop};                         // line  4
     condition full=false, empty=true;          // line  5
                                                // line  6
     guard push:                                // line  7
         requires !full;                        // line  8
         onexit                                 // line  9
         {    if (empty) empty=false;           // line 10
              if (top==max_top) full=true;      // line 11
         }                                      // line 12
     guard pop:                                 // line 13
         requires !empty;                       // line 14
         onexit                                 // line 15
         {    if (full) full=false;             // line 16
              if (top==empty_top) empty=true;   // line 17
         }                                      // line 18
}                                               // line 19
```

Figure 8-23 *Java implementation of a stack and Cool implementation of a stack coordinator*[24]

---

23. JCore is a functional subset of Java, that is, Java without synchronization features (e.g., `synchronize`, `notifyAll()`) and without remote invocation (i.e., RMI [RMI97]). Thus, `Stack` is a valid Java class.

24. This example has been tested using AspectJ version 0.1.0.

The stack coordinator in Figure 8-23 is an example of a per-instance coordinator, that is, each instance of `Stack` will have its own coordinator instance. In addition to the per-instance coordinators, Cool supports per-class coordinators, which can also be shared among a number of classes. The details of the Cool language are given in [XER98b, Lop97].

8.6.2 Implementing Dynamic Cool in Smalltalk

We can also implement Cool-like synchronization using a conventional class library and the dynamic composition mechanism described in Section 8.5.7. Thus, composition based on reflective facilities represents an alternative to static composition using a preprocessor (or a compiler). In contrast to a preprocessor, dynamic composition allows us to connect and reconnect coordinators to individual objects at runtime. A prototype implementation of a dynamic version of Cool in Smalltalk is available at [DCOOL]. We will describe the overall architecture of this implementation in Section 8.6.2.2. But first, we demonstrate its application with an example.

8.6.2.1 Example: Synchronizing an Assembly System

The example involves the synchronization of an assembly system simulating the production of candies (the example was adapted from [XER97]). An assembly system consists of a number of workers, where each worker works independently in a separate thread and consumes and produces some materials (see [Lea97]).

Our sample assembly system is shown in Figure 8-24. There are two candy makers (instances of `CandyMaker`), which make candies and pass them to the packer (an instance of `Packer`) by sending it the message `newCandy:` with a new candy as a parameter. The packer collects a certain number of candies, packages them into a pack, and passes the new pack to a finalizer (an instance of `Finalizer`) by sending it the message `newPack:`. The finalizer also receives labels from a label maker (an instance of `LabelMaker`). Once the finalizer has a pack and a label, it glues the label onto the pack and ships the finished pack.

As stated before, each of the workers works independently in a separate thread. However, the workers have to synchronize their work at certain points. We have the following synchronization constraints.

1. The method `newCandy:` of `Packer` has to be self exclusive because we have more than one candy maker calling this method concurrently.

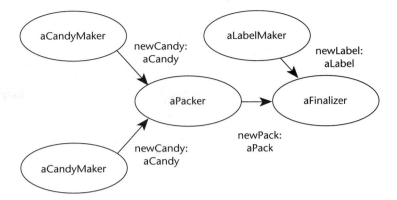

Figure 8-24 *Concurrent assembly system simulating the production of candy*

2. The method newCandy: can only be executed if the pack in the packer is not full, otherwise the thread sending newCandy: is suspended. The packer needs to start a new pack before the thread can be resumed.
3. The packer has to close a full pack by sending itself the message processPack. Thus, processPack requires that the current pack is full.
4. newPack: is sent to the finalizer after finishing the execution of processPack. However, newPack: can only be executed if the finalizer does not currently have a pack, otherwise the thread sending newPack: is suspended. When newPack: exits, the packer starts with a new, empty pack.
5. newLabel: can only be executed when the finalizer does not currently have a label, otherwise the thread sending newLabel: is suspended.
6. The finalizer glues a label to a pack by sending glueLabelToPack to itself. However, glueLabelToPack can only be executed if the finalizer has one pack and one label.
7. Finalizer ships a new candy pack by sending itself shipNewCandyPack. This message is sent right after finishing the execution of glueLabelToPack. When shipNewCandyPack exits, the finalizer has neither a pack nor a label.

Coordinator ports

We will implement these constraints in a coordinator (i.e., a coordination object), which will be connected to some of the workers. Indeed, as we will see later, we only need to attach the coordinator to the packer and the finalizer. In our implementation of *Dynamic Cool* (i.e., a version of Cool that supports dynamic reconfiguration), we connect an object to be synchronized to a *port* of a coordinator. A coordinator has one port for each object it synchronizes. This is illustrated in Figure 8-25.

Starting with the configuration in Figure 8-24, we arrive at the configuration in Figure 8-25 as follows. First, we define the new class `AssemblyCoordinator` as a subclass of `Coordinator`, which is a class provided by the implementation of Dynamic Cool. Then we have to redefine the method `defineCoordination` in `AssemblyCoordinator`. This method defines the synchronization constraints. We will show the contents of this method in a moment. `AssemblyCoordinator` has two ports: the port `#packer` for synchronizing the packer and the port `#finalizer` for synchronizing the finalizer. Given `anAssemblyCoordinator` (i.e., an instance of `AssemblyCoordinator`), the following code connects `aPacker` to the `#packer` port and `aFinalizer` to the `#finalizer` port of `anAssemblyCoordinator`:

```
anAssemblyCoordinator
  register: aPacker at: #packer;
  register: aFinalizer at: #finalizer.
```

The method `defineCoordination` in `AssemblyCoordinator` implements the synchronization constraints. The content of this method is shown in Figure 8-26.

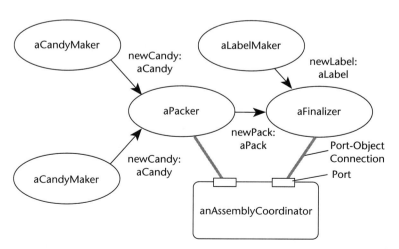

Figure 8-25 Candy assembly system synchronized using a coordinator

```
defineCoordination

  "initialize condition variables"                          "line 1"
   packFull := false. "packer has no full pack"             "line 2"
   gotPack  := false. "finalizer has no pack"               "line 3"
   gotLabel := false. "finalizer has no label"              "line 4"
                                                            "line 5"
   self                                                     "line 6"
                                                            "line 7"
        "define the two ports: packer and finalizer"        "line 8"
        addPorts: #( packer finalizer );                    "line 9"
                                                            "line 10"
        "requirement #1"                                    "line 11"
        selfex:   #( 'packer.newCandy:' );                  "line 12"
                                                            "line 13"
        "requirement #2"                                    "line 14"
        guardOn: 'packer.newCandy:'                         "line 15"
                requires: [ :packer | packFull not ]        "line 16"
                onExit:   [ :packer |                       "line 17"
                            packer candyPack candyCount =    "line 18"
                            packer maxCandyCount             "line 19"
                                ifTrue: [ packFull := true ]];   "line 20"
                                                            "line 21"
        "requirement #3"                                    "line 22"
        guardOn: 'packer.processPack'                       "line 23"
                requires: [ :packer | packFull ];           "line 24"
                                                            "line 25"
        "requirement #4"                                    "line 26"
        guardOn: 'finalizer.newPack:'                       "line 27"
                requires: [ :finalizer | gotPack not ]      "line 28"
                onEntry: [ :finalizer | gotPack := true ]   "line 29"
                onExit:  [ :finalizer | packFull := false ];    "line 30"
                                                            "line 31"
        "requirement #5"                                    "line 32"
        guardOn: 'finalizer.newLabel:'                      "line 33"
                requires: [ :finalizer | gotLabel not ]     "line 34"
                onEntry: [ :finalizer | gotLabel := true ]; "line 35"
                                                            "line 36"
        "requirement #6"                                    "line 37"
        guardOn: 'finalizer.glueLabelToPack'                "line 38"
```

(continued)

Figure 8-26 *Implementation of the synchronization constraints using Dynamic Cool*

```
        requires: [ :finalizer | gotPack & gotLabel ];      "line 39"
                                                             "line 40"
   "requirement #7"                                          "line 41"
   guardOn: 'finalizer.shipNewCandyPack'                     "line 42"
        onExit:    [ :finalizer |                            "line 43"
                gotPack := false. gotLabel := false ].       "line 44"
```

Figure 8-26 Implementation of the synchronization constraints using Dynamic Cool (continued)

There is a close correspondence between the code in Figure 8-26 and the synchronization constraints listed earlier. We indicated which sections of the code implement which constraint in the comments (in Smalltalk, comments are enclosed in double quotation marks). Our goal was to make sure that the notation looked as close as possible to the Cool notation (see Figure 8-23), while its syntax remained valid Smalltalk syntax.

Requires-condition, on-entry blocks, and on-exit blocks

The three condition variables initialized in lines 2–4 are declared as instance variables of AssemblyCoordinator. packFull indicates whether the current pack in the packer is full or not. got-Pack is true if the finalizer has a pack and otherwise false. gotLabel indicates whether the finalizer currently has a label or not. The two ports #packer and #finalizer are defined on line 9 by sending addPorts: to self (i.e., anAssemblyCoordinator). Line 12 declares the set of self-exclusive methods. In our case, we only declare new-Candy: of the object connected to the port #packer as self exclusive. We refer to this method as follows: 'packer.newCandy:'. This *qualified method name* is an element of an array that is passed as an argument to the message selfex:, which is sent to self.[25] The remaining code defines six guards on six different methods. For example, the guard on 'packer.newCandy:' on line 15 is defined by sending guardOn:requires:onExit: to self. The first argument is the qualified method name, the second argument defines the *requires-condition block*, which is implemented as a Smalltalk block returning true or false, and the third argument defines the

---

25. Please note that selfex: is also sent to self because it is separated from the previous message addPorts: by a semicolon, which in Smalltalk indicates that the following message is sent to the same object to which the first message was sent. The sequence of messages separated by semicolons is referred to as a *message cascade*.

on-exit block, which is also defined as a Smalltalk block. Both blocks receive the object connected to the port on which the guard is being defined, that is, in our case, the object connected to #packer.[26] The on-exit block sets packFull to true if the current pack in the packer contains the maximum count of candy. The remaining guards are defined by sending either guardOn:requires:, guardOn:requires:onEntry:, or guardOn:requires:onEntrys: onExit: to self.

The order of sending the messages except for addPorts: is not relevant. addPorts: has to be sent first. Of course, we can also send any of these messages later in order to modify the synchronization constraints at some point in time.

Some of the more interesting features of Dynamic Cool for Smalltalk include the following.

♦ The synchronization constraints in a coordinator can be modified at any time.
♦ The coordinators can be connected and reconnected to objects at any time.
♦ One object can be connected to more than one port of different coordinators (this is shown in Figure 8-27) and/or of the same coordinator. Also, one coordinator may be used to coordinate a number of instances of different classes at the same time.
♦ The same method of one object can be synchronized by more than one coordinator (this is shown in Figure 8-28).
♦ One coordinator can be reused for coordinating instances of different classes.
♦ A number of objects can be synchronized by a group of cooperating coordinators.

Applications of these features include the dynamic adaptation of the synchronization aspect (e.g., due to dynamic load balancing) and the dynamic configuration of components, where each component contributes its own coordinator, which has to be composed with other coordinators.

8.6.2.2   Architecture of the Smalltalk Implementation of Dynamic Cool

The main concepts of the Smalltalk implementation of Dynamic Cool are illustrated in Figure 8-28. This figure shows two coordinators and one object connected to them.

---

26. In Smalltalk, block parameters are declared at the beginning of the block and the declaration part is separated from the body of the block by a vertical bar.

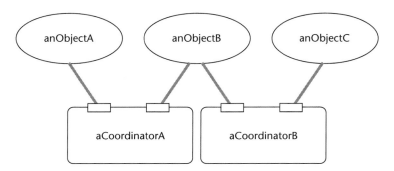

Figure 8-27 *Example of a configuration containing an object connected to two coordinators*

Message coordinators

As stated before, a coordinator has one or more named ports.[27] Each port contains a number of *message coordinators*. There is one message coordinator for each message coordinated at a port. A message coordinator contains all the information required to coordinate one method. In particular, it contains the waiting-condition blocks (including the negated requires-condition block contributed by a guard and the condition blocks computed according to the selex and mutex specifications) and the on-entry and on-exit blocks.

Synchronization listeners

One message coordinator is connected to one *synchronization listener*. A synchronization listener is a special kind of a listener in the sense of Section 8.5.7. It is connected to the synchronized object at the message it synchronizes using the mechanism described in Section 8.5.7. It wraps the corresponding method of the synchronized object into appropriate synchronization code. Specifically, in the before action of this synchronization code, the listener checks all the waiting-condition blocks of all the message coordinators it is connected to. If any of these blocks returns true, the current thread is suspended. Otherwise, the on-entry blocks of the connected message coordinators are executed. Next, the original method of the synchronized object is executed. Finally, in the after action, the on-exit blocks of the connected message coordinators are executed, and the waiting threads are signaled to reevaluate their waiting-condition blocks.

---

27. In the Smalltalk implementation, a coordinator contains an instance of `IdentityDictionary`, which manages its ports. The keys of the dictionary are the port names and the values are the objects representing ports.

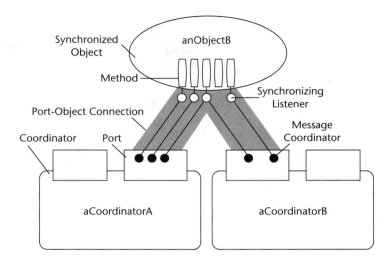

Figure 8-28 *Main concepts of the Dynamic Cool implementation*

As shown in Figure 8-28, one synchronization listener can be connected to more than one message coordinator (however, the message coordinators have to belong to different ports).

In order for this model to support several aspects at the same time, we would need to extend it with mechanisms for ordering aspects and checking their compositions (e.g., see [Böl99]).

8.7 Implementation Technologies for Aspect-Oriented Programming

Providing support for an aspect involves the following two items.

♦ Implementing abstractions for expressing the aspect
♦ Implementing weaving for composing the aspect code with the primary code and/or the code of other aspects

We address each of these points in the remainder of this chapter.

8.7.1 Technologies for Implementing Aspect-Specific Abstractions

As stated earlier, we have three main approaches to implementing the abstractions for expressing an aspect.

♦ *Encode the aspect support as a conventional library (e.g., class or procedure library):* If we use this approach, we still need to provide an appropriate composition mechanism that addresses the kind of crosscutting the aspect involves. An example of this approach is Dynamic Cool discussed in Section 8.6.2.

♦ *Design a separate language for the aspect:* The language can be implemented by a preprocessor, compiler, or an interpreter. Pre-processors, which are often a simple and economical solution, have a number of problems caused by the lack of communication between different language levels. We discussed these problems in Section 5.5. An example of this approach is the original AspectJ Cool discussed in Section 8.6.1.

♦ *Design a language extension for the aspect:* By a language extension, we mean a modular language extension that we can plug into whatever language (or, more appropriately, configuration of language extensions) we currently use. This solution differs from the previous one in technology rather than at the language level. The main question here is whether the programming platform we use supports pluggable, modular language extensions or does it confine us to the use of one fixed language or a fixed set of separate languages. An example of a platform supporting modular language extensions is the Intentional Programming system discussed in Chapter 11.

Using a separate language or a language extension specialized to the problem at hand has a number of advantages over using the conventional library approach. They are summarized in Table 8-2. These advantages are usually cited in the context of domain-specific languages (see Section 5.5).

The conventional library approach does not only have disadvantages. It also has one important advantage: Given the currently available technologies, it is often the only choice. This should change when tools, such as the Intentional Programming system, become widely available.

Advantages of modular language extensions

Modular language extensions have a number of advantages over a fixed set of separate languages.

♦ Language extensions are more scalable. We can plug and unplug extensions as we go. This is particularly useful, when, during the development of a system, we have to address more and more aspects. We can start with a small set of aspects and add new ones as our application grows (just as we add libraries).

♦ Language extensions allow the reuse of compiler infrastructure and language implementation. We do not have to write a new compiler for each new aspect language. Also, one extension can work with many others. Except for some glue code, most of the implementation of a larger language extension can be reused for different configurations.

Table 8-2 Advantages of Specialized Languages over Conventional Libraries	
Properties of Specialized Languages or Language Extensions	**Properties of Conventional Libraries**
Declarative representation	Less direct representation
Requirements can be directly translated into the language, for example, synchronization constraints in Cool. Specialized languages can use whatever domain-specific notation is appropriate, for example, specialized mathematical symbols for matrix code.	Implementing requirements in a general programming language often involves obscure idioms and low-level language details.
Simpler analysis and reasoning	Analysis often not practicable
The language constructs capture the intentions of the programmer directly in the most appropriate form. No complex programming pattern or cliché analysis is needed to recognize domain abstractions because each of them has a separate language construct.	General-purpose constructs can be combined in a myriad of ways. The intention of why they were combined in a given piece of code in this and not some other way is usually lost or, at best, represented as a comment. We also discussed the related traceability problem of design patterns in Section 8.5.6.3. The analysis problem is being addressed in the automatic program analysis community with relatively small or no success. The whole area of program reengineering is also wrestling with this problem.
Forces you to capture all of the important design information.	Design information gets lost.
What otherwise makes a useful comment in a program is actually a part of the language.	See comments in the previous table cell.
Allows domain-level error checking.	Domain-level errors cannot be found statically.
Because you provide all the domain knowledge in a form that the compiler can make use of, the compiler can do more powerful error checking based on this knowledge.	
Allows domain-level optimizations.	Domain-level optimizations are difficult to achieve (only limited to impossible).
Domain-knowledge allows us to provide more powerful optimizations than what is possible at the level of a general-purpose language. We demonstrate this fact in Section 9.8.1.	Most of the languages currently used in the industry do not provide any support for static metaprogramming. Template metaprogramming in C++ allows us to implement only relatively simple domain-specific optimizations.

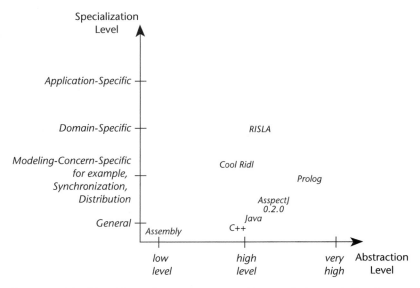

Figure 8-29 *Classifying languages according to their specialization and abstraction levels*[28]

Specialization and abstraction level

We often say that a language is higher level if it allows us to solve problems with less effort. But it is not widely recognized that the "level" of a language has at least two dimensions: *specialization level* and *abstraction level* (see Figure 8-29).

The horizontal axis indicates the abstraction level of a language. If a language has a higher abstraction level, it means that it does more work for you. In other words, you write less program code, but the code does more.[29] On the language implementation side, higher level implies that the implementation does much more code expansion, the runtime libraries are larger, and so on. An assembly language is an example of a very low-level language.

The vertical axis in Figure 8-29 represents the specialization level of a language. More specialized languages are applicable to smaller classes of problems. We listed the advantages of applying

---

28. This figure was suggested by Gregor Kiczales.
29. We stated in Section A.3.6 that abstracting involves forgetting some details (thus, effectively, information loss). When we say that a language is more abstract, we actually mean that the programs we write in this language are more abstract, that is, we do not have to specify all the details needed to do things because this knowledge is contained in the language implementation.

specialized languages in Table 8-2. Examples of modeling-concern-specific languages are Cool and Ridl (Section 8.6.1). An example of a domain-specific language is RISLA [DK98], which is a language for defining financial products.

8.7.2   Technologies for Implementing Weaving

Crosscutting level

In addition to the specialization and the abstraction level, aspect languages address a third dimension, which is the *level of crosscutting* (see Figure 8-30). As we will see later in this section, the process of weaving separated, crosscutting code modules involves merging them in a coordinated way. If you use a compiler for the weaving, the crosscutting level tells you how much transformation work the compiler does for you.

Conceptually, composing separated aspects involves code transformation. This is illustrated in Figure 8-31. Instead of writing the

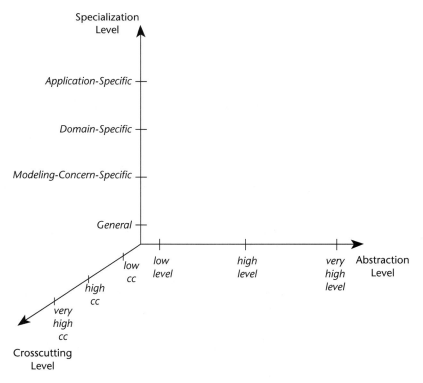

Figure 8-30 *Crosscutting level as the third dimension of languages*[30]

---

30. This figure was suggested by Gregor Kiczales.

low-level tangled code (on the right), we write code with well-separated aspects (on the left) and use a transformation in order to obtain the lower-level tangled code (also referred to as the "woven" code). We can use at least two different technologies for implementing such transformations.

♦ Source-to-implementation transformation
♦ Dynamic reflection

Meta-programming

Both technologies are examples of *metaprogramming*. Metaprogramming involves a domain shift: The metacode is *about* the base code (just as an aspect is about some component[s]; see Figure 8-7). A more implementation-oriented definition of metaprogramming often found in literature characterizes it as "manipulating programs as data."

Source-to-implementation transformation can be implemented in a compiler, a preprocessor, or a transformation system. Compilers and preprocessors usually provide only a low-level interface for writing transformations consisting of parse tree node creation and editing operations (we assume that you have access to the implementation of the compiler or the preprocessor). Transformation systems, on the other hand, give you a more convenient interface including pattern matching facilities, Lisp-like quoting facilities, program analysis facilities (e.g., data and control flow analysis), and so on. We discuss transformation systems in Chapter 9.

If the woven code does not need to be rearranged at runtime, we can do the program transformation before runtime and generate efficient, statically bound code.[31] For example, the AspectJ version described in Section 8.6.1 weaves the code before runtime using a transforming preprocessor. Alternatively, we could also provide some generating capability at runtime (e.g., by including some transforming component or the compiler in the runtime version), so that we can optimize the code if certain aspect constellations are repeatedly needed.

Dynamic reflection

The other technique for weaving aspects is to use dynamic reflection. Dynamic reflection involves having explicit representations of some elements of the programming language being used at runtime (see [KRB91] for a stimulating discussion of this topic). As stated before, examples of such representations are metaobjects representing classes, methods, message sends, method-execution contexts, and so on. Using such metarepresentations, we can mod-

---

31. By statically bound code, we mean that the control transfer from one aspect to another aspect does not involve any special lookup.

ify the meaning of some language elements at runtime and, this way, arrange for a transparent transfer of control between aspects.[32] We have seen a concrete example of applying these techniques in the implementation of the noninvasive composition mechanism and Dynamic Cool in Sections 8.5.7 and 8.6.2.

Interpreting aspects

Now the question is: How do we achieve the transformation of the separated code into the tangled code shown in Figure 8-31 using dynamic reflection? Instead of explicitly transforming the high-level code with separated aspects into the tangled code, the high-level code is interpreted at runtime and the control is transferred between the aspects as often as necessary, so that this execution is effectively equivalent to executing the tangled code. Thus, we achieve the desired effect through *interpretation* of the aspect rather than explicitly generating the tangled code. However, this approach has both its advantages and disadvantages.

The positive side to dynamic reflection is the ability to dynamically reconfigure the code. For example, the Smalltalk implementation of Dynamic Cool allows us to reattach coordinators at runtime. The running system could even produce a new configuration and components that were not preplanned before runtime. On the other hand, the dynamic transfer of control between aspects incurs certain runtime overhead, for example, dynamic method calls, dynamic reification (e.g., requesting the object representing the execution context of a method in Smalltalk[33]), and so on. If the performance is critical and static configuration is sufficient, static code transformation is certainly the better choice.

Separating relevant aspects may often require quite complicated transformations to get back to the lower-level, tangled version. David Vandevoorde [Van98] proposed an illuminating model for visually representing some of this complexity. His idea shows the traceability relationships between the locations in the high-level source and the locations in the low-level code in a two-dimensional Cartesian coordinate system (see Figure 8-32). The horizontal axis of this coordinate system represents the code locations (e.g., line numbers) in the high-level source and the vertical axis represents the code locations in the lower-level, tangled code. Next, we plot the points that represent the correspondence

---

32. Please note that not all languages having metarepresentations allow us to modify them. For example, in contrast to Smalltalk, the metalevel available in Java is read only, that is, we cannot modify it.

33. The implementation of the dynamic composition mechanism in Section 8.5.7 uses this feature in order to find out the parameters of the original method call when `self baseCall` is invoked (see Appendix B).

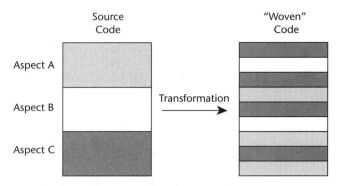

Figure 8-31 *Composing separated aspects involves transformation*

between the locations in the source and the tangled code. For example, the left diagram in Figure 8-32 shows a linear transformation between the location in the source and the transformed code. The semantics of this diagram are as follows: Given the loca-

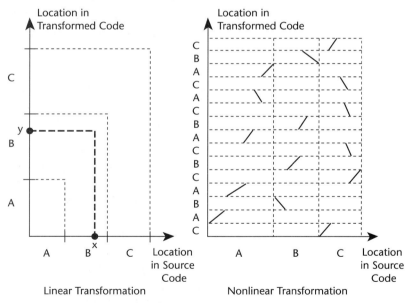

Figure 8-32 *Diagrams illustrating traceability relationships between locations in source and transformed code*[34]

---

34. This illustrative concept was proposed by Dr. David Vandevoorde in private communication.

tion x in the source, the corresponding location y indicates the portion of the transformed code that was derived from the source code at x. Next, we indicate the portions of the source code implementing some aspects, for example, A, B, or C. Given the transformation of locations, we can tell which part of the transformed code implements which aspect. Of course, the whole idea of AOP is that the location transformation is nonlinear. For example, the transformation might look like the one on the right in Figure 8-32.

The traceability relationship between the code locations in the source and the tangled code is often a many-to-many one (see Figure 8-33). Of course, the diagram shows the relationship just for one particular source. A slightly different source might result in a radically different transformation.

The amount of transformation work we have to do depends on the level of crosscutting we are addressing. In Section 8.5.8, we gave a whole set of important aspects of OO programs that can be addressed by the relatively simple message-join-point composition

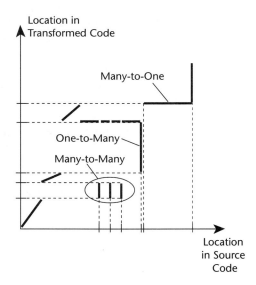

Figure 8-33 *Traceability relationship with one-to-many, many-to-one, and many-to-many regions*[35]

---

35. The transformation shown in Figure 8-33 is actually closer to the kind of transformations done by the AspectJ weaver than the arbitrary one shown on the right in Figure 8-32.

mechanisms, which do not involve complex transformation work. Thus, by adding a few reflective constructs, such as the different kinds of before and after methods to a language, we can already cover a large number of aspects. However, there are also other aspects, such as domain-specific optimizations in numerical computing, which may involve extremely complex, multilevel transformations. But even in this case, at the different individual levels, we often deal with crosscutting that follows some well-structured patterns, such as data or control flow, geometry of the problem, and so on. The kind of programming abstractions needed for capturing the different kinds of crosscutting represents an exciting area for future research.

The code location traceability model we discussed previously allows us to make a number of important points [Van98].

♦ *Verification problem:* The more nonlinear the transformation is, the more difficult it is to compute it and thus more difficult to implement it. In particular, given an implementation, for example, that uses a transformation system, verifying the correctness of the generated code is extremely difficult. This problem is basically the compiler verification problem. The verification is more difficult the higher the abstraction and crosscutting level the source code has. Thus, adequate debugging support for the transformation code is crucial.

♦ *Debugging problem:* In order to be able to find errors in the transforms, we have to be able, as in Intentional Programming (see Chapter 11), to debug the generated code at various levels (i.e., source level, intermediate transformation levels, and the lower level). The debugging support is further complicated by the fact that the transformation may implement a many-to-many relationship between the higher-level concepts and the lower-level concepts. As we'll discuss in Section 11.3.3.1, we also need domain-specific debugging code that allows us to compute the values of some higher-level variables, which are not directly represented in the executable. Finally, domain-specific debugging models are required for the application programmers using the high-level languages because the traditional stepping through the source code is not adequate for all high-level aspects. For example, the mutual exclusion aspect in synchronization code requires special debugging support, such as tools for monitoring waiting threads, deadlock detection, and so on. Another useful feature for the domain-specific level is to be able to navigate from any statement to the aspect modules that affect its semantics. For example, you could click on a method and get a menu of the coordinators that mention this method.[36]

♦ *Transformations allowing separation of some aspects only:* Suppose that we had a set of exemplar programs and, after the programs were written, we came up with a number of aspects that were tangled in these programs and we wanted to separate them. Thus, we would be looking for a transformation that can transform the equivalent versions of the programs with separated aspects into their tangled versions and, of course, one that we can also use for weaving new aspect programs (i.e., it has to be reusable). In other words, we will succeed in separating these aspects in all of these programs, only if we find the transformation for weaving them. Unfortunately, the higher abstraction and crosscutting level the aspects have, the higher the chance that the transformation we are looking for is extremely difficult to compute. Thus, in some cases, it may turn out that a less complicated transformation is more economical, even if it does not separate all of the aspects as well as we would wish.

The challenge of high-level programming is obvious: As we increase the abstraction and the crosscutting levels of a set of aspect languages (while increasing their generality level or keeping it constant), the complexity of the required weaving transformations usually grows rapidly. In this context, it is interesting to realize the impact of this level increase on our industry: The software industry employs hordes of programmers who work as "aspect weavers" by transforming high-level requirements into low-level code. By increasing the abstraction and crosscutting levels of programming languages, we eliminate some of the manual, algorithmic work performed by the programmers. As a consequence, the advances in programming language design and implementation compete with masses of programmers possessing a huge spectrum of highly specialized skills, and thus the automatic transformations required for any progress inevitably get more and more complex. On the other hand, by moving some of the manual work into the aspect weavers, we allow the programmers to concentrate on the more creative parts of software development and enable the construction of even more complex systems.

---

36. As of this writing, this capability is being experimented with in the current AspectJ version.

8.7.3   AOP and Specialized Language Extensions

Each aspect needs some appropriate linguistic support, that is, concern-specific abstractions and composition mechanisms addressing crosscutting. In Section 8.7.1, we discussed the advantages of specialized languages over conventional libraries, and the conclusion of Section 8.7.2 was that a fixed set of composition mechanisms cannot support all kinds of crosscutting. Thus, the model of modular language extensions, as exemplified by the Intentional Programming system, seems to be very appropriate for AOP. It allows a fast dissemination of new composition mechanisms and domain-specific language features or feature frameworks supporting various aspects. More importantly, these extensions can be used in different constellations, each one tuned towards some domain or domain category. Given this language extension model, the discussion whether to support a number of aspects with one separate language per aspect or with one comprehensive language or with some other number of languages becomes pointless.

8.7.4   AOP and Active Libraries

If we subscribe to the idea that the language extension model is well suited for AOP, IP-like extension libraries (see Section 11.4.3) become an attractive vehicle for packaging and distributing such extensions. Indeed, we are already observing a trend towards shifting some of the responsibilities of compilers to libraries. An example of this shift is the Blitz++ library developed by Veldhuizen [Vel96, Vel98b, Bli] and the Generative Matrix Computation Library discussed in Chapter 14.

Blitz++ is a C++ array library for numeric computing. The two most important design goals of Blitz++ are to support a high-level mathematical notation for array expressions and, at the same time, to achieve high efficiency in terms of execution speed and memory consumption. The library is quite successful in satisfying these design goals. For example, instead of writing

```
Array<float,1> A(12);
for (int i=0; i<12; ++i)
    A(i) = sin(2*M_PI / 12*i);
```

we can simply write

```
A = sin(2*M_PI / 12*i);
```

where i is a special placeholder variable. Blitz++ achieves an excellent performance (see benchmark results in [VJ97, Vel97, Vel98a]) by applying optimizations, such as loop fusing and elimination of temporary variables. An important property of these optimizations is that they need some knowledge of the abstractions they are applied to, for example, the array components. Thus, they are most appropriately packaged in the library that contains these components rather being implemented in the compiler.

According to Veldhuizen [Vel98a], there are also strong economical reasons for putting the domain-specific optimizations into a library rather than the compiler. First, specialized domains, such as scientific computing, still represent a small market segment, and major compiler vendors focus on providing greatest support for the average case rather than specialized niches. Supporting a niche is also quite expensive because the cost of compiler development is very high (according to [Vel98a] $80 and more per line of code). Finally, compiler releases represent an extremely slow channel for distributing new domain-specific features. Thus, putting domain-specific optimizations into libraries is certainly the better solution.

However, it is important to note that putting domain-specific optimizations into a library requires some compile-time metaprogramming capabilities of the language used to program the library. In the case of C++, this only became possible after all the C++ language features enabling template metaprogramming became part of its definition during the C++ standardization process (see Chapter 10).

Generative libraries

Both Blitz++ and the Generative Matrix Computation Library described in Chapter 14 are examples of libraries that contain code that extends the compiler. We refer to such libraries as *generative libraries*. The benefit of generative libraries is that we can write high-level code as opposed to tangled code and still achieve excellent performance. Unfortunately, there are severe limitations to template metaprogramming, such as the lack of user-defined error reporting and inadequate debugging support. The situation does not improve substantially if we use preprocessors. Although they allow error reporting at the level of the preprocessed code, they require more development effort for implementing the processing infrastructure and also introduce a split between the preprocessor level and the compiler level. This split makes debugging and reporting of compiler-level errors even more difficult.

Programming environment extension libraries

As we will see in Chapter 11, in addition to domain-specific optimizations, we would also like to package other responsibilities in libraries, such as domain-specific editing and displaying capabilities (including aspect-specific views on the code), domain-specific debugging support, domain-specific type systems, code analysis and refactoring capabilities, and so on. Given an extendible programming environment, such as Intentional Programming, the packaging of all these capabilities becomes more economical because we do not have to reinvent the compiler and programming infrastructure every time we need some new language extension. Also, the problems of template metaprogramming and preprocessors disappear. We refer to libraries extending the whole programming environment as *programming environment extension libraries*.

Active libraries

In general, we use the term *active libraries* [CEG+99] to refer to libraries, which, in addition to the base code implementing domain concepts to be linked to the executable of an application, also contain metacode that can be executed at different times and in different contexts in order to compile, optimize, adapt, debug, analyze, visualize, and edit the base concepts. Furthermore, they can describe themselves to tools (such as compilers, profilers, code analyzers, debuggers, and so on) in an intelligible way.

Active libraries may contain more than one generation metalevel, for example, there could be code that generates compilation code based on the deployment context of the active library (e.g., they could query the hardware and the operating system about their architecture). Furthermore, the same metarepresentations may be used at different times and in different contexts, for example, based on the compile-time knowledge of some context properties that remain stable during runtime, some metarepresentations may be used to perform optimizations at compile time, and other metarepresentations may be injected into the application in order to allow optimization and reconfiguration at runtime.[37] Which metarepresentations are evaluated at which time will depend on the target application.

Compiler middleware, programming environment middleware

The perspective outlined in this section forces us to redefine the conventional interaction between compilers, libraries, and applications. In a sense, active libraries can be viewed as a kind of knowledgeable agents, which interact with each other in order to produce more specialized agents, that is, applications, which allow the user to solve specific problems. All the agents need some infrastructure supporting communication between them, generation, transformation, interaction with programmers, versioning, and so

---

37. This feature marks the difference between the concept of a programming environment extension library and the more general concept of an active library.

on. We refer to such an infrastructure as *compiler middleware*, or even more generally as *programming environment middleware.*

8.8   Final Remarks

The initial contribution of AOP is to focus our attention on the important deficiency of current component technologies: The inability to capture many important aspects of software systems in a cleanly localized way using generalized procedures only.

However, as we have seen in this chapter, AOP also has a profound impact on analysis and design by introducing a new style of decomposition (we will characterize this style as a multiparadigm decomposition style later in this section). It also motivates the development of new kinds of composition mechanisms and new concern- and domain-specific languages. As we go along, we will be able to componentize more kinds of aspects.

Multiparadigm view

Our feeling is that, as we come up with more and more systems of aspects, they will become qualities on their own. From the modeling perspective, we can view systems of aspects as reusable frameworks of system decomposition. Thus, the impact of AOP on modeling methods will be fundamental. In order to understand this impact, we have to realize that most of the current analysis, design, and implementation methods are centered around single paradigms, for example, OO methods around objects and structured methods around procedures and data structures. The insight of AOP is that we need different paradigms for different aspects of a system we want to build. This kind of thinking is referred to as the *multiparadigm view* (see [Cop98, Bud94]).

We certainly do not have to start from scratch. There are whole research communities who have been working on paradigms for different aspects (e.g., synchronization, distribution, error handling, and so on) for decades. By committing to the multiparadigm view in language design and in the development of modeling methods, we will be able to transfer more of the research results of these communities into practice. Thus, although the recognition of the limitations of generalized procedures will be a true "eye-opener" for our industry, this is just the beginning.

Chapter 9

Generators

*I would rather write programs to help me write programs
than write programs.*

—Dick Sites,
  Proving that Computer Programs Terminate Cleanly,
  Ph.D. thesis, Stanford University, 1974, p. 65

9.1 Why Is This Chapter Worth Reading?

Great flexibility, intentional and easy to understand encoding, and
excellent performance are difficult or impossible to achieve simultaneously using our current general-purpose programming languages. For example, if you want to improve the performance of
your code, you can manually optimize it, but this will almost certainly destroy its nice and easy-to-understand structure. Similarly,
if you add aspects, such as error handling or synchronization, it
will have the same effect on your code. Flexibility also suffers
because you cannot easily replace one aspect with an alternative
implementation.

   We can avoid these problems by delegating these "nasty" jobs,
such as optimization and weaving, to generators. Their responsibility is to compute an efficient implementation for a nice and
easy-to-understand specification.

   In this chapter, you'll learn that generators do their work primarily by performing transformations. You'll learn the different
kinds of transformations needed to implement and to evolve a system specification. You will also learn the basic concepts of environments for building powerful generators, that is, transformation
systems. Finally, we'll discuss concrete generative approaches, such
as Draco and GenVoca.

9.2   What Are Generators?

A *generator* is a program that takes a higher-level specification of a piece of software and produces its implementation. The piece of software could be a large software system, a component, a class, a procedure, and so on. (In the following descriptions, we will simply call it a "system.")

Generators address three important issues.

♦ *Raising the intentionality of system descriptions:* Intentional descriptions state directly and explicitly what is needed and avoid any extra clutter or unnecessary implementation details. They possess all the good code properties, such as being easy to understand, analyze, modify, maintain, and so on. We achieve intentionality through domain-specific notations, and we implement such notations using generators.

♦ *Computing an efficient implementation:* Generators bridge the wide gap between the high-level, intentional system specification and the executable implementation. In particular, the implementation has to meet certain performance requirements (e.g., execution speed, response time, memory consumption, utilization of resources, and so on). The challenge is that the structure of the specification is usually very different from the structure of the implementation: There is no simple one-to-one correspondence between the concepts in the specification and the concepts in the implementation. Furthermore, even a slight change in the specification might require a radically different implementation. Generators may need to perform quite complex computations in order to achieve this nontrivial mapping, but they relieve the application programmer from performing this mapping manually.

♦ *Avoiding the library scaling problem* [Big94]: The library scaling problem concerns the horizontal scaling of conventional libraries of components. If a library implements each useful combination of features as a concrete component, adding support for a new feature can potentially double the number of concrete components in the library. Factoring libraries into components corresponding to features and composing them using function or method calls avoids the exponential growth of the library size, but usually results in poor performance. Generators allow us to achieve both effective factoring and excellent performance. They eliminate the calling overhead between components and can often perform various domain-specific optimizations. As a result, we achieve both linear library scaling and very good performance.

The term "generator" is very general and covers many different technologies including compilers, preprocessors, metafunctions that generate classes and procedures, code generators (e.g., as in CASE tools), transformational components, and more. For example, a compiler takes a program written in a higher-level programming language (e.g., C or C++) and generates its implementation in, for example, machine code or bytecodes. Most CASE tools contain generators that produce implementations of (often graphically rendered) models in some programming language. Component-based environments and GUI builders generate implementations of graphically specified configurations of components. There are also generators that produce implementations of programs written in (textual or graphical) domain-specific notations. Finally, you can have relatively small metafunctions (as in C++ template metaprogramming), which generate single classes and procedures.

In general, a generator performs the following tasks (see Figure 9-1).

♦ Checks the validity of the input specification and reports warnings and errors if necessary
♦ Completes the specification using default settings if necessary
♦ Performs optimizations
♦ Generates the implementation

In the simplest cases, these tasks can be implemented as four consecutive and separate phases. However, in many cases it is not possible to perform them in separation, but some or all of them need to be done in parallel and/or iteratively.

Generators expecting a system specification in text form additionally have to perform parsing in order to transform the text into some appropriate internal representation (e.g., an abstract syntax tree). All conventional compilers do parsing. However, in some cases, the programmer can enter the internal data structure directly using some appropriate editing tool, in which case parsing is not necessary. Many CASE tools and the Intentional Programming sys-

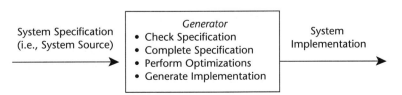

Figure 9-1 Main tasks performed by a generator

tem discussed in Chapter 11 are examples of generating environments that support direct entry and do not require parsing.

The aforementioned generator tasks can be seen as steps of an automatic configuration process. This is so because you can view the generated implementation as a concrete configuration of some implementation abstractions, that is, implementation components ranging from simple assembler codes and control structures to more complex components, such as classes or whole subsystems. In this sense, a generator implements the configuration knowledge of a domain model, and developing a domain model provides the necessary basis for implementing generators (see Section 5.2).

Finally, generators that implement complex specification notations will be quite complex themselves, and we should modularize their internal design. In other words, we will implement larger generators as sets of smaller, cooperating generators. There are many different ways to distribute responsibilities among different generators. The smaller generators can be called from the larger generators to generate some specific implementation component, perform some optimizations, implement some part of the input notation, or implement some intermediate representations produced by other generators.

9.3 Transformational Model of Software Development

Software development can be seen as creating and modifying specifications of systems and their implementations. We view the activity of (creating and) evolving specifications and the activity of implementing specifications as two orthogonal activities. This is shown in Figure 9-2: The horizontal arrows represent system evolution and the vertical arrows represent system implementation.

Both activities can be thought of as series of transformations performed on various representations of the system. Of course, we

---

BIBLIOGRAPHIC NOTES

Generators have been studied in various research communities, most notably in the knowledge-based software engineering or program synthesis community (e.g., [Bal85, RW90, Smi90a, Pai94, SG96, AKR+97]), in the software reuse community (as a means of implementing domain models, e.g., [Nei80, BO92, ADK+98]), and in the formal specification community (as a means of implementing formal specifications, e.g., [BEH+87, HK93, SJ95]). It is worth noting that the reuse community has traditionally had a strong focus on practical applications of generators (e.g., [SSGRG, BT, IPH]; also see [Cle00]). See [Big97] for a survey on generative reuse.

Figure 9-2 Transformational model of software development

would like to automate as much of these activities as possible. Let us first take a look at automating the implementation process. We can have three different levels of automation, which are shown in Figure 9-3. The first level is implementing a system in a general purpose language, such as Java or C++ (Figure 9-3 on the left). The only automatic part here is the compilation of the system source written in the general-purpose language. The application programmers still have to perform a considerable amount of translation work, for example, they must introduce new domain-specific abstractions, manually perform domain-specific optimizations and aspect weaving, and so on in order to bridge the large gap between the requirements and the source. The situation improves if we use domain-specific abstractions provided by libraries and generators. The latter are required in order to automate domain-specific optimizations and weaving and to provide domain-specific notations. This is shown in the middle of Figure 9-3. Finally, we could also reach an even higher level of automation using an interactive transformation system, which allows you to start with a high-level, machine-processable encoding of the functional and nonfunctional requirements and add more and more design and implementation decisions by applying transformations stored in a domain-specific library (Figure 9-3 on the right). The implementation of high-level, declarative functional and nonfunctional specifications can often be *only partially* automated for two reasons.

♦ Many design decisions are open in the specification, which creates an enormous design search space, that is, the programmer has to help to select some transformations.
♦ Not all necessary high-level design decisions are available as transformations in the library (due to their high development

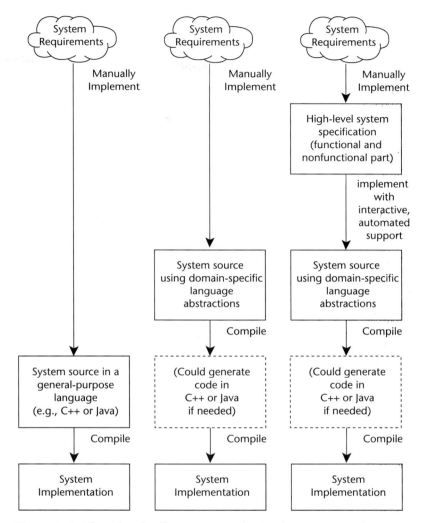

Figure 9-3 Three levels of automating the implementation of a system

System source, compiler transformations, and source-to-source transformations

cost and, possibly, low reusability); that is, the programmer has to perform some (very specialized) translation jobs manually.

The machine-processable system representation manipulated by the programmer is referred to as *system source*. Transformations performed automatically during compilation are called *compiler transformations*, and those performed interactively by the application programmer on the system source are called *source-to-source transformation*.

Now, let us take a look at automating the process of software evolution (see Figure 9-2). Today, automated support for the software evolution activity is very rare and limited. The reason is that evolution is usually specified as changes of the high-level system properties, which are not explicitly (if at all) represented in a system source written in a general-purpose programming language. Furthermore, being able to revise design decisions in an efficient way requires all the design decisions to be present in the source. Unfortunately, they are usually missing in conventional programs written in general-purpose programming languages. Thus, automated support for evolution becomes possible only when we represent systems using high-level, domain-specific notations, which allow us both to explicitly express key system properties and to capture all the design decisions made during development (i.e., the complete design history with rationale; see Figure 9-8). The more higher-level design information contained in the system source, the more automated support becomes possible.

Automated support for software evolution can be provided by transformation systems, which allow you to apply source-to-source transformations.

NOTE

It is important to note that higher levels of automation require implementing generators and transformation systems performing domain-specific transformations. As always, the idea of automation is to move the complexity burden from application programmers to tool and library vendors. The higher the level of automation, the higher the development cost of the generators and domain-specific transformations. Vendors need to balance factors such as development cost and the size of the target market, which limits the level of automation they can provide.

NOTE

It is important to note that the intentionality of the source of a system can be improved in an evolutionary way over time as better abstractions become available. With improving intentionality, more and more kinds of source changes can be automated. This means that transformational development allows us to iteratively improve a given system in a sustainable way.

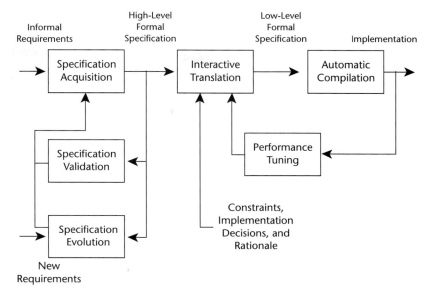

Figure 9-4 *Transformational Life Cycle Model (adapted from [Bal85], © 1985 by IEEE)*

Figure 9-4 shows a model of the complete transformational life cycle.

9.4   Technologies for Building Generators

There are three main ways to build generators.

♦ *Developing generators as stand-alone programs from scratch:* This is the most effort-intensive way of building generators. You have to design and implement the internal source representation as well as the code performing analysis, optimization, and generation from scratch. In case the generator expects input in text form, you will need to build a lexer and a parser for converting the source text into the internal representation. The lexer and the parser can be generated using tools, such as *lex* and *yacc* [LMB95]. But this is the only piece of reusable infrastructure that is available in this approach (and you only need it for generators expecting text). In addition to a large effort needed to build a generator from scratch, this approach also impairs the integration of different notations and development tools. This is because each generator uses its own internal source representation and does not provide any interfacing facilities. As a result, we get a language landscape consisting of islands of noninteroperable domain-specific languages.

♦ *Developing generators using the built-in metaprogramming capabilities of a programming language:* Some languages provide built-in facilities for manipulating language representations at compile time and/or runtime. For example, template metaprogramming lets you write generators in C++, which are executed at compile time and generate code by composing functions and class templates. The great advantage of such generators is that they can be distributed as parts of the conventional procedure and class libraries written in the language. Furthermore, the built-in metaprogramming facilities are optimized for the given language and are much easier to use than manipulating general-purpose internal source representations, such as abstract syntax trees. As a result, it is much easier to write generators using built-in metaprogramming facilities than to write them from scratch. Unfortunately, there are also several disadvantages to this approach. First, the kind of specification notations we can implement this way is limited by the host language. Many languages with built-in metaprogramming don't even allow you to extend the syntax. As a result, the generators you build are inherently bound to a given host language. Furthermore, languages with static metaprogramming facilities do not provide adequate support for debugging the metacode. Finally, such languages make it easy for application programmers to include metacode implementing some ad hoc language extensions directly in the application code, which makes it difficult to understand and maintain and reduces its robustness (metaprogramming should be left to library and tool developers!).

♦ *Developing generators using a generator infrastructure:* The most adequate approach to developing generators is to use a common infrastructure providing all the basic facilities for building generators. This includes a common format for the internal source representation and standard sets of operations for encoding transformations on the representation. Ideally, the generator facilities should support developing any kind of transformations (including optimizations and source-to-source transformations), as provided by transformation systems discussed in Section 9.7. Furthermore, the infrastructure should support building appropriate input and output facilities (e.g., parsers and unparsers or direct editing facilities) and debugging facilities for the notations implemented by the generators. Finally, the infrastructure should also adequately support the activity of developing generators themselves, for example, by providing metacode debugging facilities. An example of such an infrastructure is the Intentional Programming system, which we'll discuss in Chapter 11.

As of this writing, the second approach provides a practicable solution to building generators in C++. We'll demonstrate it in Chapters 12, 13, and 14. The third approach will certainly prevail in the future. We'll also demonstrate an example of using Intentional Programming in Section 14.4.3.

ompositional versus Transformational Generators

ny generators, such as those usually found in CASE environ-
nts or GUI builders, perform only a certain, limited kind of
sformations, which are referred to as *forward refinements* (or
ical transformations). The idea of a forward refinement is illus-
d in Figure 9-5. A forward refinement involves transforming a
er-level representation into a lower-level one, such that the
larity of the higher-level representation is preserved. Each
rd refinement implements a higher-level module in terms of
r more lower-level modules, but within the module bound-
established in the higher-level representation. In effect, for-
refinements implement hierarchical decomposition. We call
tors based on forward refinement *compositional generators*.

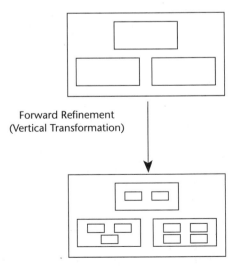

Figure 9-5 *Forward refinement*

This is so because they effectively implement the process of building systems by successively composing smaller components into larger components in a hierarchical way. For example, when you specify a composition of high-level components in a component composition environment, the environment will generate an implementation by gluing the implementations of the high-level components (which themselves are composed from smaller components down to basic abstraction, such as control structures and variable assignments) together.

Horizontal transformations, oblique transformations, and optimizing refinements

Compositional generators do not perform transformations that would redefine the modular structure of a higher-level representation. Examples of transformations that do redefine the modular structure are shown in Figure 9-6. A *horizontal transformation* modifies the modular structure of a representation at the same level, for example, by deleting or merging existing modules or adding new ones. Furthermore, we can have an *oblique transformation*, which has both a vertical and a horizontal component, that is, it refines a higher-level representation into a lower-level one, but also modifies the modular structure of the higher-level representation. A "horizontal component" of a transformation is responsible for modifying the modular structure and is necessary in order to implement *optimizations* and *weaving*. An example of

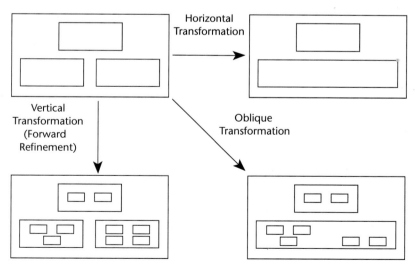

Figure 9-6 Vertical, oblique, and horizontal transformations

an oblique transformation is an *optimizing refinement*, which both refines a higher-level representation into a lower-level one and optimizes the result at the same time.

Generators performing not only forward refinements but also transformations with a horizontal component (i.e., horizontal and oblique transformations) are referred to as *transformational generators*. They are more powerful than compositional generators because they may perform weaving and optimizations, which are crucial for achieving good separation of concerns in the application source and good performance of the generated implementation. Building transformational generators is supported by *transformation systems*, which provide all the necessary infrastructure. An example of a transformation system is the Intentional Programming system described in Chapter 11. We will also discuss transformation systems in Section 9.7.

Vertical, horizontal, and oblique transformations

Transformational generators and transformation systems

NOTE ON TERMINOLOGY

As you can see, this section classifies transformations relative to a system with a vertical and a horizontal axis. The vertical component of a transformation is responsible for moving from a higher-level representation to a lower-level one, and the horizontal component is responsible for restructuring. In general, we distinguish between *vertical transformations*, *horizontal transformations*, and *oblique transformations*. Furthermore, any transformations with a vertical component (i.e., vertical and oblique transformations) are referred to as *refinements*—a term often found in the literature. Consequently, a vertical transformation (i.e., one without any horizontal component) is also called *forward refinement*, and an oblique transformation (i.e., one with both a vertical and horizontal component) is also called an *oblique refinement*.

NOTE

Compositional generators may also perform transformations with some limited horizontal component, for example, inlining. However, the important property of a compositional generator is that it is *mainly* based on forward refinements. The term "compositional generators" was proposed by Batory [Bat96].

9.6 Kinds of Transformations

As discussed earlier, we have compiler transformations applied automatically during compilation and source-to-source transformations applied interactively by the programmer. Let us first discuss compiler transformations.

9.6.1 Compiler Transformations

Refinements, optimizations, and jittering transformations

Compiler transformations may have both a vertical and a horizontal component. As stated previously, transformations with a vertical component are called *refinements*. Refinements are responsible for translating a higher-level representation into a lower-level one (e.g., implementing a C++ class in terms of C abstractions). As already discussed, we can have forward refinements, which perform strictly hierarchical decomposition, and oblique transformations, which additionally change the modular structure (e.g., weaving and optimizing refinements). Furthermore, we have two kinds of horizontal transformations: *optimizations* and *jittering transformations*. Both kinds of transformations operate at one level of abstraction. The purpose of optimizations is to improve some characteristic of the program representation being optimized, such as execution speed or memory consumption. The purpose of jittering transformations is to modify a program representation in order to make other transformations applicable [MB97]. We'll discuss refinements and optimizations in the following two sections.

9.6.1.1 Refinements

A *refinement* adds implementation detail. It usually involves implementing concepts of one abstraction level in terms of concepts of a lower abstraction level. This is the main type of transformation used for implementing a specification. The following are some examples of refinements.

DEFINITION

A *transformation* is an automated, semantically correct (as opposed to arbitrary) modification of a program representation.

BIBLIOGRAPHIC NOTE

Different kinds of transformations are also discussed in [Par90] and [BM97].

♦ *Decomposition:* Concepts of a higher level are decomposed into concepts of a lower level, for example, an abstract data type is implemented in terms of a number of other abstract data types. The decomposition results in a new structural organization of the lower level. In the case of a forward refinement (i.e., hierarchical decomposition), the new structure preserves the modular structure of the higher level. In the case of an oblique transformation, the original modular structure gets modified. For example, we could have an optimizing refinement, which not only maps higher-level constructs onto lower-level ones, but also performs some optimization at the same time. This may result in a many-to-many traceability relationship between the higher-level constructs and the lower-level constructs.

♦ *Choice of representation:* As implementation details are added, we often need to choose an appropriate lower-level representation for the higher-level concepts, for example, a matrix data type can be represented using an array, a vector, or a hash table. The choice of a particular representation depends on the desired performance characteristics and other properties of the higher-level concept (e.g., the shape of the matrix).

♦ *Choice of algorithm:* Operations can be implemented using different algorithms. The choice depends on the required operation properties (e.g., performance characteristics) and the properties of other concepts involved. For example, the choice of the matrix multiplication algorithm depends on the shapes of the operand matrices (see Section 14.4.2.2).

♦ *Specialization:* Abstractions specialized for a certain context of use are often obtained by specializing more general abstractions, that is, ones designed for more than one context. For example, a parameterized module can be specialized by supplying concrete parameters. Another general specialization technique is *partial evaluation.* We will discuss this technique in the following section because it is often used for optimization purposes.

♦ *Concretization:* Concretization involves implementation by adding more detail to abstract concepts. For example, concrete classes add implementation details to abstract classes. Because concepts are often abstract and general at the same time, specialization and concretization may be combined.

9.6.1.2 Optimizations

Optimizations improve some of the performance characteristics of a program (e.g., execution speed, response time, memory consumption, consumption of other resources, and so on). Optimizations involve structural changes of the code. The following are two important types of such changes [BM97].

♦ *Interleaving:* Two or more higher-level concepts are realized in one section of the lower-level code (e.g., one module or class).

♦ *Delocalization:* A higher-level concept is spread throughout the whole lower-level code, that is, it introduces details to many lower-level concepts.

Both types of structural changes make the lower-level code harder to understand and to reason about. For this reason, we want to put optimizations into generators rather than apply them manually, so that we can write an easy to understand source and have a generator produce an optimized implementation.

The following are some examples of optimizations [ASU86, BM97].

♦ *Inlining:* Inlining involves the replacement of a symbol by its definition. For example, a procedure call can be replaced by the body of the procedure to avoid the calling overhead.

♦ *Constant folding:* Constant folding is the evaluation of expressions with known operands at compile time. It is a special case of partial evaluation.

♦ *Data caching:* Instead of computing the same data on each use, the data can be cached, that is, memorized after computing it the first time. This avoids its unnecessary recomputation [BM97].

♦ *Loop fusion:* If two loops have the same (or similar) structure and the computation in both loops can be done in parallel, then the loops can be replaced by one loop doing both computations, that is, the loops are fused. For example, elementwise matrix operations, such as matrix addition involving several operands (e.g., A+B+C+D), can be performed using the same set of loops required for just two operands (e.g., A+B).

♦ *Loop unrolling:* If the number of iterations for a loop is a small constant n known at compile time, the loop can be replaced by n copies of its body expanded inline.

♦ *Code motion:* Code motion is another loop optimization involving recognizing invariant code sections inside a loop and moving them outside the loop.

BIBLIOGRAPHIC NOTE

You'll find the analysis of the effects of delocalization on program comprehension in [LS86] and [WBM98].

- *Common subexpression elimination:* This optimization involves recognizing and factoring out common subexpressions to reuse already computed results.
- *Dead-code elimination:* Unreachable code or unused variables can be eliminated.
- *Partial evaluation:* Partial evaluation is a technique for the specialization of a more general program for a specific context of use. In most cases, programs are specialized at compile time to be used in a specific context at runtime, but specialization at runtime is also possible. The specialization is based on the knowledge of the specific context (i.e., certain parameters are fixed). In abstract terms, partial evaluation can be thought of as partially evaluating a function based on the knowledge of some of its parameters to be constant in the special context. The evaluation involves propagating these constants throughout the implementation of the function and simplifying and optimizing the code (e.g., eliminating unnecessary code, folding constants, unrolling loops, and so on). Partial evaluation is not only an important optimization technique, but also a reuse paradigm, allowing us to automatically specialize a general, reusable piece of software for use in a specific context. In particular, it has been used to specialize scientific code (see [BW90, BF96]). An extensive treatment of partial evaluation can be found in [JGS93]. We'll discuss partial evaluation in Chapter 10.
- *Finite differencing:* Finite differencing is an optimization technique involving the replacement of repeated costly computations by their less expensive differential counterparts (see [PK82]). For example, if the value of some variable x in a loop grows in each iteration by some constant delta, such as by 2, and some other variable y in the loop is computed by multiplying x by a constant factor, such as 3, we can optimize this multiplication by realizing that y also grows by a constant delta, in our example 6. Thus, instead of computing y by multiplying x by the constant factor in each iteration, we obtain the new value of y by adding the constant y-delta to the old y value, in our example 6:

```
int x=0                        int x=0
int y=0                        int y=0
for (int i=0; i<10;i++)        for (int i=0;i<10;i++)
{ x=x+2;             ───────►  { x=x+2;
  y=x*3;                         y=y+6;
  print (x,y);                   print (x,y);
}                              }
```

Most of these optimizations (except for the general forms of partial evaluation and finite differencing) are performed by good optimizing compilers. Unfortunately, compilers can apply them only at a very low abstraction level, that is, the level of the general-purpose programming language they implement (e.g., C or C++). On the other hand, optimizations are most effective at higher levels. For example, given the function EXP(x,y) for raising x to the power of y and implemented using the binary-shift or Taylor expansion method in a general-purpose programming language, it would be extremely difficult or impossible for the compiler to realize that EXP(EXP(x,2), 0.5) is equivalent to x. However, part of the domain knowledge about EXP() is that EXP(EXP(x,2),0.5) == x. If EXP() was a built-in abstraction of the programming language implemented by the compiler, we could implement this EXP()-specific optimization in the compiler. (We'll return to this example in Section 9.8.1). Such optimizations performed based on higher-level domain knowledge are referred to as *domain-specific optimizations*.

Another example of optimizations that conventional compilers usually do not perform are *global optimizations*. Global optimizations involve gathering information from remote parts of a program in order to decide how to change it at a given location. For example, the use of a certain algorithm at one location in a program could influence the selection of a different algorithm at a different location.

The use of domain-specific and global optimizations is one of the important differences between generators based on domain-specific models and conventional compilers.

9.6.2   Source-to-Source Transformations

As the name suggests, source-to-source transformations operate on the source level. The most common kind of source-to-source transformations are those performing restructuring, but you can also support interactive translation with source-to-source refinements and optimizations.

We have two kinds of restructuring transformations.

♦ *Editing transformations:* The purpose of editing transformations is to mechanize some simple editing operations (mainly syntactic ones, i.e., requiring relatively little semantic analysis), such as stylistic improvements (e.g., replacing a prefix increment operator with a postfix one in a for loop), applying De Morgan's laws to logical expressions, automatically converting a code section into a procedure, and so on.

♦ *Refactorings:* In contrast to editing transformations, refactoring transformations reorganize code at the design level. Some refactorings change the horizontal structure of one abstraction layer and others move code between different abstraction layers of the system source. Refactorings are particularly useful for evolutionary development and maintenance.

Examples of refactorings include the following.

♦ *Abstraction and generalization:* Abstraction is the process of recognizing and extracting the common parts in a set of concepts. Generalization involves building a general model for a set of concepts. Abstraction and generalization usually occur together (see Section A.3.6). We typically create a model of a number of concepts by recognizing their common and variable parts and creating parameterized abstractions for the common parts and parameters for the varying parts. For example, we can abstract a number of classes by factoring out common code into one parameterized class and converting the portions varying among them into parameters. Alternatively, we can organize them into a inheritance hierarchy by moving common parts up the hierarchy and representing the varying parts as subclasses.

♦ *Introducing new variation points:* In order to increase the horizontal scope of a model (i.e., its generality), we might want to introduce new variation points, such as new parameters. The variation points can be implemented using different mechanisms.

♦ *Simplification:* Simplifications reduce the representation size of a program (i.e., they make programs shorter, but not necessarily faster). They often improve the understandability of a program.

These and other general classes of refactorings involve many smaller transformations, which usually depend on the modeling paradigm and technology used. Examples of refactorings in the context of object-oriented programs are converting inheritance relationships into aggregation and moving a method up the inheritance hierarchy. A detailed discussion of refactorings for object-oriented code can be found in [FBB+99, Obd92].

BACKGROUND NOTE

The term "refactoring" was originally introduced in the OO community (e.g., [Obd92]).

9.7 Transformation Systems

Whether a generator is primarily based on composition (i.e., forward refinements) or on general transformations has a profound impact on its architecture. Implementing compositional generators is relatively simple because the translation of a higher-level representation can be performed during a simple traversal of the higher-level representation: Whenever a higher-level construct is visited, its implementation is generated. In particular, we do not have to coordinate the generation of implementations for different higher-level constructs at the same time, which is the case in transformational generators.

Most generators currently found in practice have a predominantly compositional character, for example, GUI builders, visual programming environments, and so on. They usually have some kind of graphical interface, where components can be connected through lines, and they do some composition consistency checking. Composition is well suited for very large components, where the time spent for the communication between the components is much smaller than the time spent for computation within the components. The compositional model also allows us to wrap legacy software and use it in compositions with new components (e.g., see [SMCB96, MS97]).

Building transformational generators is inherently more complicated because we need to coordinate the application of different transformations across large, overlapping portions of a program. Building transformational generators is supported by *transformation systems*.

Transformation systems consist of the following elements.

♦ *A common format for the internal program representation:* In many cases, the internal program representation has the form of an abstract syntax tree. Other examples of representations are data and control flow graphs.
♦ *Code analysis facilities:* Transformation systems often provide code analysis facilities, such as data and control flow analysis. They are needed to check the structure of the input program and also to guide the selection of appropriate transformations.

NOTE ON TERMINOLOGY

Not only environments for building transformational generators but also transformational generators are often referred to as transformation systems.

♦ *A transformation engine (also called a rewrite engine):* A transformation engine applies user-provided transformations to the internal program representation. One of the responsibilities of a transformation engine is scheduling transformations, that is, determining the order of applying transformations.

♦ *Input and output facilities for the internal representation:* If the source is given in the form of text, we need a parser to transform it into the internal representation. We can also use various unparsers to transform the internal representation back into a textual representation. One class of output facilities are code-generation backends, which generate the machine code for a given target platform. Another class of input/output facilities are editors, which allow us to directly edit the internal representation and to render it in different ways. The latter are provided by the Intentional Programming system discussed in Chapter 11.

Rewrite rules

Transformations are either specified declaratively as *rewrite rules* or encoded by a piece of procedural code operating on the internal representation. A rewrite rule consists of a left-hand-side pattern, which specifies a pattern to look for, and a right-hand-side pattern, which is the one to replace the left-hand-side pattern in the source. An example of a rewrite rule is the replacement of the division of two equal expressions by 1:

```
x/x → 1 if x ≠ 0
```

This rewrite rule replaces the occurrences of x/x by 1 whenever x ≠ 0.

Metavariables

Let us take a look at how the previous rewrite rule can be used in a transformation system. For the purpose of this example, we assume that the internal program representation is an abstract syntax tree and the source is being imported and exported as text using a parser and an unparser. The application of the rewrite rule to a simple source is shown in Figure 9-7. The transformation engine finds out through pattern matching that the left-hand-side pattern of our rewrite rule matches the expression (y+1/y+1). As a

NOTE ON TERMINOLOGY

Rewrite rules and procedures implementing transformations are sometimes referred to as *transforms* [Bax96]. In such cases, a *transformation* denotes the application of a given transform at a given location in the source.

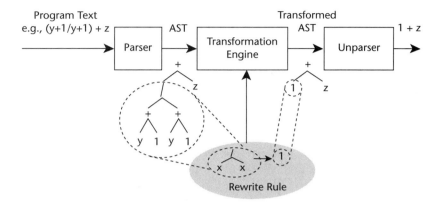

Figure 9-7 *An application of a rewrite rule within a transformation system*

result, the variable x in the rule is bound to y+1, and the expression (y+1/y+1) is replaced by 1. We call x a *metavariable* because it matches against pieces of source.

9.7.1 Scheduling Transformations

One of the main responsibilities of a transformation engine is scheduling transformations, that is, deciding which transformation to apply at which source location in which order. The main challenge is that some transformations have to be applied in a particular order to produce usable results. In some cases, the programmer

---

NOTE

It is worth mentioning that the structure shown in Figure 9-7 resembles the structure of a conventional compiler, which also has a parser and implements optimizations as transformations. The main difference is, however, that a transformation system is an environment for building transformational generators, whereas a compiler is a concrete transformational generator. In the case of a transformation system, users can specify their own transformations and parsers and unparsers. For this reason, transformation systems are sometimes referred to as *open compilers*. More comprehensive transformation systems covering debugging, refactoring, and versioning facilities (such as the Intentional Programming system discussed in Chapter 11) are actually more appropriately called *extendible programming environments*.

---

may schedule a number of transformations procedurally, that is, by implementing a piece of imperative code applying the transformations. However, in order to support extensibility, we also want to be able to specify the (partial) order of applying transformations declaratively based on some declarative configuration knowledge. In the latter case, the transformation engine has to provide appropriate search algorithms for computing a valid transformation schedule.

Derivation tree model

The implementation of a specification using transformations is best illustrated using the *derivation tree model* shown in Figure 9-8 [Bax90, Bax92, BP97]. We start with some functional specification f_0 (at the top), for example, the specification of a sorting problem, and some performance specification G_0 (on the left), for example, the required time complexity and implementation language. Based on the domain model of sorting and some inference, the transformation system determines that, in order to satisfy the performance goal G_0, it must satisfy the goals G_1 and G_2. Then, the system decomposes the goals G_1 and G_2 into further subgoals. The goal decomposition is carried out until a concrete transformation T_1 is applied to the initial functional specification f_0. The following transformations are determined in an analogous way until we arrive at the implementation f_n, which is an implementation of the functional specification f_0 satisfying the performance specification G_0.

The goal decomposition can be done procedurally, that is, by procedural metaprograms (e.g., [Wil83]), or based on inference, that is, planning-style metaprograms (e.g., [McC87, Bax90]), or by some mixture of both (e.g., [Nei80, MB97]). For example, G_0 can be a procedure calling G_1 and G_2, and G_1 can be decomposed into some G_3, G_4, and G_5 goals by inference. Also, the transformations can be applied by procedures or scheduled by inference. The goal decomposition can be viewed as a process of making implementation decisions and asserting new properties of the program under refinement, and then making new implementation decisions based on these properties, and so on. In this sense, the inference is based on the fact that each decision has some pre- and post-conditions.

NOTE

In general, programs manipulating program representations, that is, also procedural or declarative programs scheduling transformations, are called *metaprograms*, and the activity of writing metaprograms is referred to as *metaprogramming*. Metaprogramming is usually the job of library and tool developers, not application developers.

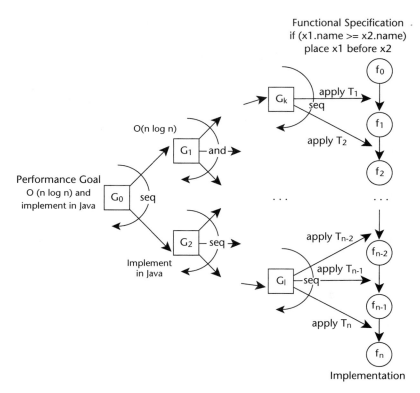

Figure 9-8 *Derivation tree representing the transformational imple-mentation of a functional specification (adapted from [Bax96]). The middle part of the tree is not shown. A goal can be decomposed into a conjunction of subgoals (denoted by "and"), where the order of the subgoal satisfaction is arbitrary, into a sequence (denoted by "seq"), where the subgoals have to be satisfied in the specified order, or into a disjunction of subgoals (denoted by "or"), where only one subgoal needs to be satisfied.*

An important property of the derivation history model is that each step in the derivation tree can be explained, that is, each sub-goal helps to achieve its parent goal. Also, any changes to the functional specification being transformed are well defined in the form of transformations (rather than being some arbitrary manual changes). In [Bax90, Bax92, BP97, BM97, MB97], Baxter et al. describe an approach that allows us to propagate specification changes through an existing derivation tree in a way that only the affected parts of the tree need to be recomputed (this technology is being commercialized by Semantic Designs, Inc. [SD]). The derivation tree model clearly demonstrates the advantages of transformation systems for software maintenance and evolution. Unfortunately, its application requires a comprehensive and detailed domain model, whose development may not be feasible or cost-effective in all cases.

We'll return to the issue of scheduling transformations in Section 11.5.5.

9.7.2 Existing Transformation Systems and Their Applications

Three existing transformation systems deserve our special attention.

♦ *Intentional Programming* [IPH]: A comprehensive transformation-based programming environment.
♦ *Reasoning5* [RM]: Currently the only commercially available general-purpose extendable transformation system with a particular focus on reengineering.
♦ *SciNapse* [AKR+97]: A commercial domain-specific transformation system (i.e., a specific transformational generator) synthesizing high-performance code for solving partial differential equations.

Intentional Programming (IP) is a general-purpose transformation technology under development at Microsoft. IP is organized as an efficient, general-purpose extendible programming environment with remarkable properties. We'll discuss it in Chapter 11 in great detail.

Reasoning5, formerly known as Refine [KM90], was developed by Reasoning Systems, Inc., based on more than 15 years of experience in transformation technology. Reasoning5 represents programs in three forms: syntax trees, data-flow graphs, and control-flow graphs. These representations can be analyzed and manipulated by transformations expressed in the declarative language CQML (*code query and manipulation language*), which also includes high-level concepts, such as sets and relations. Reasoning5 has been primarily used in the area of reengineering and

---

NOTE

A derivation tree of a system represents its *complete design* (i.e., each implementation step plus design rationale). Such information is usually absent from conventional programs written in general-purpose languages, which explains why they are difficult to evolve and maintain.

maintenance, where legacy code, for example, in COBOL, Fortran, or C, is imported using parsers into the internal representations. Transformations can be packaged into problem specific plug-ins (possibly binary plug-ins by third-party vendors). For example, there is a special plug-in for correcting year 2000 problems in COBOL code. Reasoning Systems' technology has also been used as a platform for forward engineering tools, such as the program synthesis environments KIDS and SPECWARE, which are discussed in Section 9.8.3. Reasoning5 is written in Lisp.

A remarkable example of a commercially available domain-specific transformation system is SciNapse (formerly known as Sinapse [Kan93]) by SciComp, Inc. [SC]. The system synthesizes high-performance code for solving partial differential equations and has been successfully applied in various domains, for example, wave propagation [Kan93], fluid dynamics, and financial modeling [RK97]. It accepts specifications in a high-level domain-specific mathematical notation. The refinement process in SciNapse involves performing domain-specific mathematical transformations, selecting an appropriate discretization method based on the analysis of the input equations, selecting appropriate algorithms and data structures, generating the solution in pseudocode, optimizing at the pseudocode level, and, finally, generating C or Fortran code from the pseudocode. At each major refinement stage, SciNapse generates so-called *level summaries*, which inform the user about the current state of the refinement and the intermediate results. The system is built on top of a planning expert system written in Mathematica. The concepts of the problem domain are represented as objects in a knowledge base, and transformations are triggered by rules.

Transformation systems are being applied in various areas including the following.

♦ Implementing specifications (i.e., program synthesis) and meta-programming, such as IP (Chapter 11), Draco (Section 9.8.1), SciNapse, KIDS and SPECWARE (Section 9.8.3), TAMPR [BM84, BHW97], Medusa [McC88], TXL [CS92], Prospectra [HK93], Polya [Efr94], APTS [Pai94], and CIP [BEH+87]
♦ Evolutionary development through refactoring and reengineering legacy systems, such as IP, Reasoning5, DMS [BP97, BM97, MB97], SFAC [BF96], and Refactory [RBJ98]
♦ Symbolic mathematical computations, such as Mathematica [Wol91]
♦ Language prototyping (i.e., generating compilers, debuggers, and syntax-oriented editors from a specification of a language), such as Cornell Generator Synthesizer [RT89], CENTAUR [BCD+89], Popart [Wil91], and ASF+SDF [DHK96].

BIBLIOGRAPHIC NOTE

See [Fea86] for a survey of transformation systems.

9.8   Selected Approaches to Generation

In the following three sections, we will describe three generative
approaches, which we've selected to give you an overview of the
area. The approaches we'll be discussing are

- *Draco:* A prominent example of transformation technology. We
  will demonstrate the advantages of domain-specific notations
  and optimizations using examples from Draco.
- *GenVoca:* A mainly compositional approach with some recent
  transformational extensions. This approach is particularly useful
  for generating object-oriented models. We will use GenVoca in
  our case studies in Part III.
- *An algebraic approach:* A formal approach to generation based
  on algebraic specifications. We'll give you a high-level overview
  of this approach and some application examples.

In Chapters 10 and 11, we'll present two further approaches
to generation, which include

- Implementing configuration generators using template metaprogramming in C++ (see Chapter 10)
- Using the Intentional Programming system, which is a transformational, extensible programming and metaprogramming environment (see Chapter 11)

We'll demonstrate the practical application of these two
approaches in Part III.

9.8.1   Draco

Draco is an approach to Domain Engineering based on domain-
specific languages and transformation technology. The Draco
approach and a prototype of a development environment, also
called Draco, were developed by James Neighbors in his Ph.D.
work [Nei80]. It was the first Domain Engineering approach. Since
then, the original Draco ideas have been translated into commercial products, for example, the Computer-Aided Protocol Engineering (CAPE) environment for prototyping and developing
communication protocols (see [Bey98]). In addition to domain

engineering, the new ideas introduced by Draco include domain-specific languages and components as sets of transformations.

The main idea of Draco is to organize software construction knowledge into a number of related domains. Each Draco domain encapsulates the knowledge for solving a certain class of problems. There are several types of domains in Draco [Nei89, Bax99].

- ♦ *Application domains:* Application domains encapsulate knowledge for building specific applications, for example, avionics, banking, manufacturing, video games, and so on.
- ♦ *Modeling domains:* A modeling domain is the encapsulation of the knowledge needed to produce a part of a complete application. It can be reused in the construction of applications from many different application domains. We can further subdivide this category into *generic application domains*, such as navigation, accounting, numerical control, and so on, and *computing technology domains*, such as multitasking, transactions, communications, graphics, databases, user interfaces, and so on. Some modeling domains can be as abstract as date and time, currency, or synchronization.
- ♦ *Execution domains:* Application domains are eventually refined into execution domains. At a higher-level, the implementation knowledge is organized into *abstract programming paradigm domains*, such as procedural, OO, functional, logic, and so on, which are then concretized by *concrete target language domains*, such as C, C++, or Java.

Application domains are typically expressed in terms of several modeling domains and the latter in terms of execution domains. The lower-level domains are also referred to as refinements of the higher-level domains. An example of a number of interrelated Draco domains is shown in Figure 9-9. It is important to note that Draco domains need not be organized in a strict hierarchy, that is, cycles involving one or more domains are possible (e.g., a part of an operating system could be implemented using a web browser, and a web browser uses an operating system).

A Draco domain contains the following elements ([Nei84, Nei89]).

- ♦ *Formal domain language[1] (also referred to as "surface" language):* The domain language is used to describe certain aspects of an application. It is implemented by a parser and a pretty printer, and the internal form of parsed code is an abstract syntax tree.

---

1. The term *domain language* is equivalent to the term *domain-specific language*.

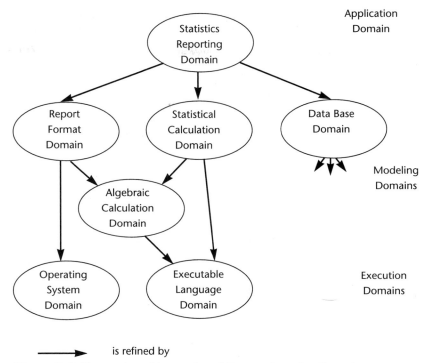

Figure 9-9 *Examples of interrelated Draco domains (based on [Nei84], © 1984 by IEEE)*

- *Optimization transformations:* These transformations represent rules of exchange of equivalent program fragments in the *same* domain language and are used for performing optimizations.
- *Transformational components:* Each component consists of one or more *refinement transformations* capable of translating the objects and operations of the source domain language into one or more target domain languages of other, underlying domains. There is one component for each object and operation in the domain. Thus, transformational components implement a program in the source domain language in terms of the underlying domains.
- *Domain-specific procedures:* Domain-specific procedures are used whenever a set of transformations can be performed (i.e., scheduled) algorithmically. They are usually applied to perform tasks, such as generating new code or analyzing programs in the source language. For example, we could write a procedure implementing a parser from a grammar specification.
- *Transformation tactics and strategies:* Tactics are domain-independent and strategies are domain-dependent rules, which help

to determine when to apply which refinement. Optimizations, refinements, procedures, tactics, and strategies are effectively organized into metaprograms.

Now we illustrate each of these elements using simple examples.

Domain-specific languages are designed to allow writing intentional and easy to analyze specifications. For example, a communication protocol can be nicely defined using a finite state automaton. This idea is used in CAPE, a Draco-based environment for prototyping and development of protocols by Bayfront Technologies [BT]. In CAPE, protocols are specified using the domain-specific language PDL (*protocol definition language*). The style of PDL specifications is illustrated in Figure 9-10.

Draco optimization transformations operate within the same language. The following are examples of simple optimization transformations in the *algebraic calculation domain* (see Figure 9-9).

♦ *Eliminate the addition of zeros:*

```
ADDx0:  X+0  →  X
```

♦ *Replace* EXP(X,2) *by* X*X, *where* EXP(A,B) *raises* A *to the power of* B:

```
EXPx2:  EXP(X,2)  →  X*X
```

The exponentiation function EXP(A,B) can be implemented using the transformational component shown in Figure 9-11. This component defines two alternative refinements of EXP(A,B): one using the binary shift method and one using the Taylor expansion. Each of these refinements has a CONDITIONS section defining when the corresponding refinement is applicable. If a refinement is

```
example1 { InitialState = State1;
          state State1::
                  Event1 -> Action1, Action2 >> State2;
                  Event2 -> Action3;
          state State2::
                  Event1 -> Action4;
                  Event2 -> Action5, Action6 >> State1;
}
```

Figure 9-10 Sample specification in PDL (from [BT])

```
COMPONENT: EXP(A,B)
      PURPOSE:  exponentiation, raise A to the Bth power
      IOSPEC:   A a number, B a number / a number
      DECISION: The binary shift method is O(ln2(B)) while the Taylor
                expansion is an adjustable number of terms. Note the
                different conditions for each method.
      REFINEMENT: binary shift method
            CONDITIONS: B an integer greater than 0
            BACKGROUND: see Knuth's Art of Computer Programming,
                        Vol. 2, pg. 399, Algorithm A
            INSTANTIATION: FUNCTION,INLINE
            ASSERTIONS: complexity = O(ln2(B))
            CODE: SIMAL.BLOCK
              [[ POWER:=B ; NUMBER:=A ; ANSWER:=1 ;
                  WHILE POWER>0 DO
                    [[ IF ODD(POWER) THEN ANSWER:=ANSWER*NUMBER;
                        POWER:=POWER//2 ;
                        NUMBER:=NUMBER*NUMBER ]] ;
                    RETURN ANSWER ]]
      END REFINEMENT


      REFINEMENT: Taylor expansion
            CONDITIONS: A greater than 0
            BACKGROUND: see VNR Math Encyclopedia, pg. 490
            INSTANTIATION: FUNCTION,INLINE
            ASSERTIONS: error = (B*ln(A))^TERMS/TERMS!
            ADJUSTMENTS: TERMS[20] - number of terms, error is
                         approximately - (B*ln(A))^TERMS/TERMS!
            CODE: SIMAL.BLOCK
              [[ SUM:=1 ; TOP:=B*LN(A) ; TERM:=1 ;
                  FOR I:=1 TO TERMS DO
                    [[ TERM:=(TOP/I)*TERM ;
                        SUM:=SUM+TERM ]] ;
                    RETURN SUM ]]
      END REFINEMENT
END COMPONENT
```

Figure 9-11 *Example of a transformational component implementing EXP(A,B) (adapted from [Nei80])*

selected, EXP(A,B) is replaced by its CODE section. The application of a refinement to a specification produces a new specification with new properties, which can be stated in the ASSERTIONS section, for example, the complexity of the implementation. These assertions are attached to the resulting code as annotations.

At any point during the refinement process of a system specification, more than one refinement or optimization transformation might be applicable. This is illustrated in Figure 9-12 showing three alternative paths of refining EXP(X,2) into C programs. EXP(X,2) can either be directly refined using the binary-shift method refinement or the Taylor expansion refinement, or it can first be transformed into X*X using our optimization EXPx2. Thus, the question is: How are the appropriate transformations selected? The transformations are scheduled partly by procedures, tactics, and strategies and partly by the user.

Our example of refining EXP(X,2) illustrates an important point: Optimizations are most effective when applied at the appropriate level of abstraction. EXPx2 simplifies EXP(X,2) into X*X. No such simple optimization can achieve the same result at a lower level. The code produced by the binary-shift method refinement requires an extremely complicated series of transformations in order to be reduced to X*X. For the Taylor expansion code, no such transformations exist because the Taylor expansion is only an approximation of EXP(A,B). Thus, an example of a simple tactic is

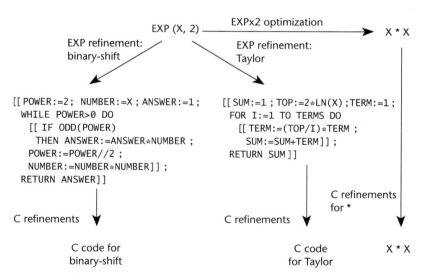

Figure 9-12   Three alternative ways of refining EXP(X,2) into a C program (adapted from [Nei80]). The C code for the binary-shift method and the Taylor expansion implementation are not shown.

to try optimization transformations first before applying any refinements.

Given a comprehensive domain model and a problem specification, we are basically searching for one derivation that leads to an acceptable implementation of the specification. However, the set of possible derivations represents an enormous search space. Construction procedures, tactics, and strategies and component standards help us to considerably limit this search space. Furthermore, in the future, AI planning and configuration techniques could also be used to organize the search more efficiently.

9.8.2 GenVoca

GenVoca is an approach to building software system generators based on composing object-oriented layers of abstraction, whereby layers are stacked. Each layer contains a number of object classes and the layer "above" refines the layer "below" it by adding new classes, adding new methods to existing classes, and so on. This model roughly corresponds to the refinement occurring in OO frameworks. Let us compare the structure of a framework with a GenVoca model by performing the steps needed to transform a framework into a GenVoca model.

The first step is to identify layers of abstraction in a framework (see diagram 1 in Figure 9-13). In our example, we have three layers. The top layer is the most abstract and contains the classes C11 and C13. The middle layer refines the top layer by subclassing C11 with C21 and introduces the new class C22. Finally, the bottom layer refines the classes C21, C22, and C13. C21 and C13 are refined through subclassing and C22 through aggregation. The bottom layer is the most refined.

The second step is to turn the layer hierarchy upside down (see diagram 2 in Figure 9-13). GenVoca follows the traditional layered architecture model, where the more specialized layers sit on top of the more general ones.

The third step is to view each layer as a parameterized component, where "the layer below" becomes a parameter to "the layer above it" (see diagram 3 in Figure 9-13). As you see, a given layer can access the classes contained in its parameter, that is, the layer below it.

Finally, the fourth step is to provide families of alternative, parameterized layers, so that we can use them to compose different frameworks (see diagram 4 in Figure 9-13). This last diagram represents a full GenVoca model. There are a number of additional issues, such as how to specify compositions of layers and which

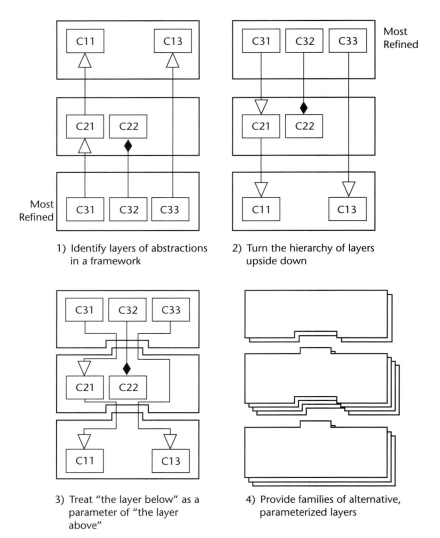

1) Identify layers of abstractions
   in a framework

2) Turn the hierarchy of layers
   upside down

3) Treat "the layer below" as a
   parameter of "the layer
   above"

4) Provide families of alternative,
   parameterized layers

Figure 9-13 From a framework to a GenVoca model

layers can be composed together and which cannot, but we'll discuss them in the following sections.

9.8.2.1 Example: Applying GenVoca to the Domain of Data Containers

As an example of applying GenVoca to a practical problem, we'll discuss the organization of a library of data containers according

BIBLIOGRAPHIC AND HISTORICAL NOTES

The GenVoca model originated in the work of Don Batory on Genesis [BBG+88], a database management system generator, and the work of O'Malley et al. on Avoca/x-kernel [HPOA89, OP92], a generator in the domain of network protocols. These two independently conceived systems shared many similarities, which lead to the formulation of the GenVoca (a name compiled from the names Genesis and Avoca) model in [BO92]. Since then, Batory and colleagues have been working on refining and extending this original model and building new GenVoca generators. P1 [BSS92, SBS93] and P2 [BGT94] were extensions of the C programming languages for defining GenVoca generators; in particular, they were used to develop Predator [SBS93], a data container generator. Work on P++ [SB93, Sin96] involved equivalent extensions of C++. A mechanism for composition validation in GenVoca models was proposed in [BG96, BG97], and more recently, the originally compositional GenVoca model has been extended with transformational techniques [BCRW98]. A Java precompiler for implementing domain-specific language extensions and GenVoca domain models is described in [BLS98]. An interpretation of GenVoca models as configurable framework layers was proposed in [SB98a, SB98b]. Other systems based on GenVoca include the distributed file system *Ficus* [HP94], the *ADAGE* generators in the domain of avionics navigation systems [BCGS95], the generator of query optimizers *Prairie* [DB95], and the implementation of the data container generator in the IP system (see Chapter 11) *DiSTiL* [SB97].

to this model and the advantages of such organization. Data containers (or collections) belong to the most fundamental building blocks in programming, and any general-purpose, industrial-strength programming language has to offer such a library. Examples of data container libraries for C++ include libg++ [Lea88], the Booch C++ Components [Boo87], and the Standard Template Library (STL, see Section 6.10).

Data containers are good examples of concepts that exhibit wide feature variations. For example, the Booch C++ Components

BIBLIOGRAPHIC NOTE

The application of GenVoca to data containers is described in [BSS92, SBS93, Sin96, SB97].

offer various data structures (*bag, deque, queue, list, ring list, set, map, stack, string,* and *tree*), various memory management strategies (*bounded, unbounded, managed, controlled*), various synchronization schemas (*sequential, guarded, concurrent, multiple*), and *balking* and *priority* implementations for queues (see Table 9-1 for explanations). A concrete component can be described through a valid combination of these features, and there are more than 200 valid combinations for the Booch C++ Components.

Implementing all feature combinations as concrete classes is clearly inefficient in terms of development and maintenance costs and scaling, that is, adding a new feature can potentially double the number of concrete classes. The Booch C++ Components library addresses this problem through a careful design avoiding code duplication by means of inheritance and templates, which reduces the number of concrete classes to about 100. On the other hand, a container library of an equivalent scope designed using the GenVoca model requires only about 30 parameterized components (i.e., GenVoca layers) and exhibits even a much lower level of code duplication [Sin96]. This is achieved through consequent interface unification and standardization and aggressive parameterization. At the same time, the library has excellent performance in terms of execution speed.

9.8.2.2 GenVoca Model

In the GenVoca model, each abstract data type or feature is represented as a separate layer, and concrete components (or systems) are defined by type expressions describing layer compositions. For example, the following type expression defines a *concurrent, unbounded, managed bag,* which allocates the memory for its elements from the *heap* and counts the number of elements it contains:

```
bag[concurrent[size_of[unbounded[managed[heap]]]]]
```

Figure 9-14 shows the layered structure equivalent to this type expression. Each layer contributes classes, attributes, and methods implementing the corresponding features to the entire composition. `heap` implements memory allocation from the heap, `managed` manages the allocated memory on a free list, `unbounded` provides a resizable data structure based on `managed`, `size_of` adds a counter attribute and a read-size method, `concurrent` wraps the accessing methods in a semaphore-based serialization code (we'll show the implementation of `size_of` and `concurrent` in Section 9.8.2.3), and, finally, `bag` implements the necessary element management and bag operations.

Table 9-1   A Glossary of the Booch Data Structure Terminology (from [Sin96])

Data Structure Families in the Booch Library

Bag	Unordered collection of objects, which may contain duplicates
Deque	Ordered sequence of objects, where objects may be inserted or removed at either end
Queue	Ordered sequence of objects with "first-in first-out" semantics
List	A linked list of objects, which are automatically garbage collected
Ring List	Ordered sequence of objects, organized in a loop
Set	Unordered collection of objects, which contains no duplicates
Map	A tabular data structure that associates instances of one kind of object with instances of some other kind of object
Stack	Ordered sequence of objects with "last-in first-out" semantics
String	Ordered sequence of objects, where any object may be accessed directly
Tree	A binary tree of objects, which are automatically garbage collected

Data Structure Features That Are Available to Every Family

Bounded	Static memory allocation (upper bound on total number of objects)
Unbounded	Dynamic memory allocation algorithm (no upper bound on total number of objects)
Managed	Free objects are stored on a list for subsequent reuse
Controlled	A version of managed, which operates correctly in a multithreaded environment
Sequential	Assumes a single-threaded environment
Guarded	Assumes a multithreaded environment, where mutual exclusion is explicitly performed by the user
Concurrent	Assumes a multithreaded environment, where the object ensures that all read and write accesses are serialized
Multiple	Assumes a multi-threaded environment, where the object permits multiple simultaneous read access, but it serializes write access

Data Structure Features That Are Available to Deques and Queues Only

Balking	Objects may be removed from the middle of a sequence
Priority	Objects are sorted based on some priority function

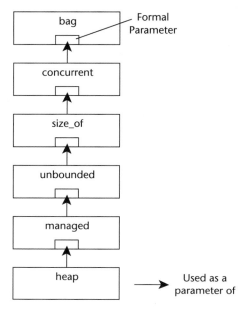

Figure 9-14 Example of GenVoca layering

Each of these layers except heap represents a parameterized component. For example, size_of takes a data structure as its parameter. We denote this as follows: size_of[DataStructure]. In general, a GenVoca layer may have more than one parameter. Thus, GenVoca expressions may represent a tree structure, for example, A[B[D, E], C[F, G]] (see Figure 9-15).

Realms

Each GenVoca layer exports a certain interface and expects its parameters (if any) to export certain interfaces. These contracts

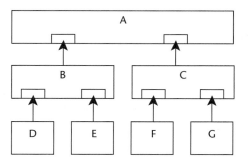

Figure 9-15 Example of a treelike GenVoca layering

can be expressed explicitly by defining layer interfaces at a separate location, and then using them in layer declarations. In Gen-Voca terminology, a standardized layer interface is referred to as a *realm*. A realm can be thought of as a collection of class and method signature declarations (we will see a concrete example of a realm in Section 9.8.2.3). We also say that certain layers or layer compositions "belong to a realm" if they export all the classes and methods declared in the realm (but they are allowed to export other classes and methods at the same time, too). For example, given the realms R and S, and given the layers A, B, C, D, and E, we could write

```
R = {A, B[x:R]}
S = {C[x:R], D[x:S], E[x:R, y:S]}
```

This notation states that:

♦ A and B export the interface R.
♦ C, D, and E export the interface S.
♦ B, C, and E import the interface R.
♦ D and E import the interface S.

Alternatively, GenVoca domain models can be represented more concisely as GenVoca grammars. For our realms R and S and the layers A, B, C, D, and E, we have the following grammar:

```
R : A | B[R]
S : C[R] | D[S] | E[R, S]
```

NOTE

In some cases, we found it useful to have differently named realms, but declare the same interface. We can use such realms to differentiate between layers exporting the same operations in terms of signatures, but of different semantics. For example, the concurrent layer exports the same operations it imports, and the only difference is that the exported operations are serialized. If some other layers require synchronized data structures (which is an example of a configuration constraint), we might want to define the realms SynchronizedDataStructure and DataStructure, even if they declare the same operations. Alternatively, we might just define the DataStructure realm and document the configuration constraint separately (see Section 9.8.2.5). Whichever method works best has to be decided in a specific context.

Symmetric layers

where the vertical bar indicates an "or". Please note that the layer B imports and exports the same realm R. We refer to such layers as *symmetric*. Another example of a symmetric layer is D, which imports and exports S. Symmetric layers are important because they usually strongly increase the number of possible configurations. For example, Unix utilities are symmetric and we can combine them in many different ways using pipes.

*Stacking
GenVoca models*

An important class of GenVoca domain models are so-called *stacking models* [Cza98]. In a stacking model, each layer is limited to one layer parameter and therefore, we can only have simple stacks of layers rather than general treelike layer hierarchies. Stacking models can be represented using an intuitive graphical notation shown in Figure 9-16. In this notation, each box represents a *layer category* containing a set of alternative GenVoca layers. All the layers of one layer category belong to the same realm (i.e., they export the same interface), and each one, except for the layers of the bottom category, takes exactly one parameter whose realm is the one exported by the layers from the category below. The idea is that we can obtain a concrete instance of this model by selecting exactly one layer per layer category. For example, according to Figure 9-16, B[D[F[J]]] is a valid type expression.

We can further extend this model by allowing a layer category to contain layers that export and import the same realm (as A[R1] in R1 in Figure 9-17). And finally, we can also have *optional* layer categories from which exactly one layer or no layer can be selected when constructing a concrete instance.[2] Optional layer categories are marked by a dashed inner box, such as R3 in Figure 9-17.

*Vertical versus
horizontal
parameters*

In addition to layer parameters (i.e., the realm-typed parameters), such as x in B[x:R], layers can also have value parameters (e.g., the maximum number of elements in bounded) and simple

R1:	A,B,C
R2:	D
R3:	F,G
R4:	I,J

R1: A[R2] | B[R2] | C[R2]

R2: D[R3]

R3: F[R4] | G[R4]

R4: I | J

Figure 9-16 Example of a stacking model in a graphical notation and the corresponding grammar

---

2. In other words, the layers contained in an optional layer category are "optional alternative layers."

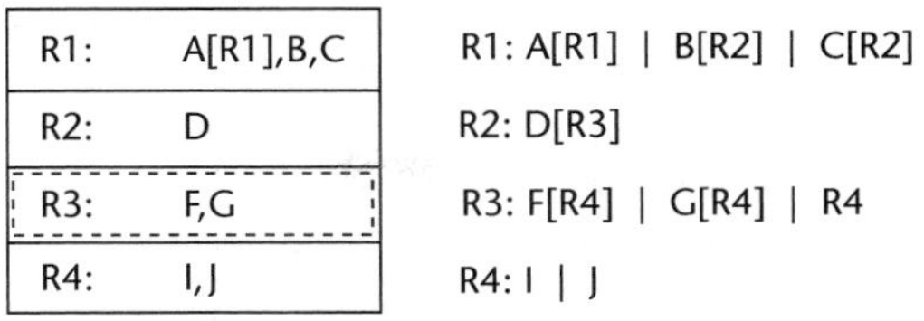

R1:	A[R1],B,C
R2:	D
R3:	F,G
R4:	I,J

R1: A[R1] | B[R2] | C[R2]

R2: D[R3]

R3: F[R4] | G[R4] | R4

R4: I | J

Figure 9-17 *Example of a stacking GenVoca model with an optional layer category (i.e., R3)*

type parameters[3] (e.g., each of the data container layers requires the type parameter *element type*). Value and simple type parameters are referred to as *horizontal parameters* because they do not shape the hierarchy of layers, but only provide some variability within the layers themselves. Layer parameters, on the other hand, are referred to as *vertical parameters* because they shape the layer hierarchy (as in Figure 9-14), and a layer hierarchy represents a hierarchy of refinements (each layer is a refinement). In terms of notation, we enclose horizontal parameters into round braces, and vertical parameters, as usual, into rectangular brackets. For example, the layer B[x:R](y:type, z:int) has one vertical parameter x of type R and two horizontal parameters, namely the type parameter y and the integer constant z. (We discussed horizontal and vertical parameters in Section 6.9.3.)

NOTE

In the GenVoca literature, for example, [SB93], layer parameters are referred to as *realm parameters*. In order to avoid confusion, we do not use this term. Just as a type parameter expects types as its values, a layer parameter expects layers (but not realms) as its values. Realms are types of layer parameters, that is, they constrain layer parameters. The distinction between vertical and horizontal parameters was introduced by Goguen and Burstall [GB80]. We enclose layer parameters, that is, vertical parameters, in rectangular brackets because this is the usual notation of GenVoca. However, in the notation used by Goguen in [Gog96], vertical parameters are enclosed in round parenthesis (i.e., "()") and horizontal parameters are enclosed in rectangular brackets (i.e., "[]").

---

3. By simple types, we mean classes and basic types (e.g., integer) as opposed to layers.

The GenVoca implementation of the Booch Components described in [Sin96] requires 18 realms and 30 layers. The main advantage of expressing the Booch Components in terms of realms and layers instead of inheritance hierarchies and parameterized classes is that layers allow us to refine multiple classes in a coordinated manner (i.e., each layer is a "large-scale refinement"), so that the structure of the library is captured by layers more adequately. For example, a data container layer contains not only the data container class, but also a cursor class (i.e., the iterator) and an element class. All these classes are incrementally refined by each layer in a coordinated fashion as the layers are stacked up.

Next, we will take a look at some concrete examples of realm and layer definitions.

9.8.2.3 Defining Realms and Layers in P++

Before we discuss how to encode GenVoca models in C++, we'll take a look at P++ [SB93, Sin96], an extension of C++ specially designed for implementing GenVoca models. The main difference between P++ and C++ is that P++ allows you to express layer interfaces, that is, realms.

Figure 9-18 shows two realm declarations. Realm DS defines the interface of the data structures used in the data container library described in the previous sections. DS is exported by unbounded and imported by size_of (i.e., we have size_of[x:DS]; see Figure 9-14). size_of augments the DS realm by adding the method read_size() to its container class. Thus, the realm exported by size_of is DS_size. concurrent also exports DS_size, and bag and concurrent import DS_size (i.e., we have bag[x:DS_size] and concurrent[x:DS_size]). Please note that DS_size is declared as a subrealm of DS, that is, it inherits all its classes and methods. Multiple inheritance between realms is also allowed. Realm inheritance is an example of pure interface inheritance as opposed to implementation inheritance.

The implementations of the layers size_of and concurrent are shown in Figure 9-19. The syntax resembles C++ class templates

---

NOTE ON TERMINOLOGY

As already stated, we also refer to "GenVoca layers" as *parameterized components* or simply as *GenVoca components* because they are the elementary blocks for building concrete systems in the GenVoca model. Consequently, in Part III, we will often use the terms *equivalence category of GenVoca components* or *interface of an equivalence category of GenVoca components* rather than "realm."

```
template <class e>
realm DS
{
    class container
    {
        container();
        bool is_full();
        ... // other operations
    };

    class cursor
    {
        cursor (container *c);
        void advance();
        void insert(e *obj);
        void remove();
        ... // other operations
    };
};

template <class e>
realm DS_size : DS<e>
{
    class container { int read_size(); };
};
```

Figure 9-18 *Realm and subrealm declarations (from [BG97], ©*
1997 by IEEE)

with member classes. `size_of` has one horizontal type parameter `e`
(i.e., the element type) and one layer parameter `x` expecting a layer
of the realm `DS<e>`. Furthermore, it exports the realm `DS_size<e>`.[4]
P++ requires you to specify the type of the layer parameters, that
is, layer parameters are an example of *constrained* generic parameters (see Section 6.6). `size_of` implements the method `read_size()`
of `container` and refines the `cursor` methods `insert()` and
`remove()` from the lower layer by adding statements that increment
or decrement the `count` variable. All other `container` and `cursor`
methods declared in the `DS_size` realm but not explicitly implemented in the `size_of` layer are implicitly defined by the *bypass*

---

4. The realm exported by a layer is specified after the name of the layer—this
is not to be confused with the C++ superclass specification.

```
template <class e, DS<e> x>              template <class e, DS_size <e> x>
component size_of :DS_size<e>            component concurrent :DS_size <e>
{                                        {
  class container                          class container
  { friend class cursor;                   { friend class cursor;
    x::container lower;                        x::container lower;
    int count;                               semaphore sem;

    container() { count = 0; };            container() { };
    int read_size()
    { return count; };                     bypass_type bypass(bypass_args)
                                           { bypass_type tmp;
    bypass_type bypass(bypass_args)          sem.wait();
    { return lower.bypass(bypass_args);      tmp = lower.bypass(bypass_args);
    };                                       sem.signal();
  };                                         return tmp;
                                           };
  class cursor                           };
  { x::cursor *lower;
    container *c;                         class cursor
                                         { x::cursor *lower;
    cursor (container *k)                    container *c:
    { c = k;
      lower = new x::cursor(&(c->lower)); cursor (container *k)
    };                                      { c = k;
                                             lower = new x::cursor(&(c->lower));
    e* insert (e *element)                 };
    { c->count++;
    return lower->insert(element);         bypass_type bypass(bypass_args)
    };                                     { bypass_type temp;
                                             sem.wait ();
    void remove()                            tmp = lower->bypass(bypass_args);
    { c->count--;                            sem.signal();
      lower->remove();                       return tmp;
    };                                     };
                                         };
    bypass_type bypass (bypass_args)    };
    { return lower->bypass(bypass_args);
    };
  };
};
```

Figure 9-19 Implementation of the layers size_of *and* concurrent *(from [BG97], © 1997 by IEEE)*

construct, which represents a kind of automatic forwarding mechanism. bypass corresponds to the name of any method declared in DS_size, but not defined in size_of. bypass_type corresponds to the return type of such a method and bypass_args corresponds to the argument list. A slightly different usage of this construct is found in the concurrent layer. The concurrent layer uses the bypass construct to wrap all the container and cursor methods from the lower layer in semaphore-wait and -signal statements.

An important aspect of GenVoca is the ability to propagate types up and down the layer hierarchy. The upward type propagation is achieved through accessing member types of the layer parameter, for example, x::container in size_of, that is, size_of accesses the container class of the layer beneath it. The downward type propagation occurs by means of type parameters of realms, for example, the type parameter e of DS<e> (i.e., the type parameter e of the realm of the parameter x of size_of, huh . . .). Given the layer bounded (see Figure 9-20), which implements a bounded data structure with the type parameter e (i.e., the element type), and the integral constant parameter size (maximum capacity of the data structure), we can write the following type expression:

```
typedef size_of <int, bounded <100> > integer_ds;
```

According to this type expression, integer_ds exports the DS_size interface. It is interesting to note that we provided bounded only with the size parameter, although bounded also expects another parameter, which is e. How does bounded obtain the value for e? The value for this parameter is derived from the realm type of the parameter x of size_of, that is, from DS<e>, and, in our case, it is clearly int (see Figure 9-21). This type inference constitutes an example of downward type propagation. P++ also has a construct for passing types defined within one layer to the layer beneath it. This is accomplished by annotating the newly defined type with the forward keyword and passing it as a parameter to the realm type of a layer parameter, just as we passed e to DS<e> in size_of (see [Sin96] for details).

The overall flow of information in a GenVoca hierarchy of layers is summarized in Figure 9-22.

9.8.2.4 Implementing GenVoca Layers in C++

GenVoca layers can be implemented in C++ as class templates containing member classes. Unfortunately, there is no adequate idiom in C++ to implement realms because C++ templates do not support constrained type parameters, that is, there is no way to specify the

```
template <class e, int size>
component bounded : DS<e>
{

    class container
    {
        e objs[size];
        ... // other methods and attributes
    };

    class cursor
    {
        int index;
        ... // other methods and attributes
    };
};
```

Figure 9-20 *Implementation of the layer* bounded *(adapted from [Sin96])*

realm of a layer parameter. But even without realms, implementations of GenVoca domain models in C++ are, as we will see in Part III, very useful.

Figure 9-23 illustrates the general idea of how to implement a GenVoca layer in C++. ClassA and ClassB are defined as member classes of LayerA, a class template with the parameter LowerLayer. ClassA of LowerLayer is accessed using the scope operator :: and lower is declared to be of this type. The implementation of operationA() in LayerA::ClassA refines operationA() from LowerLayer::ClassA, and the implementation of operationB()

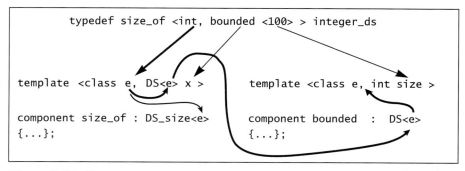

Figure 9-21 *Parameter propagation in a component composition (adapted from [Sin96])*

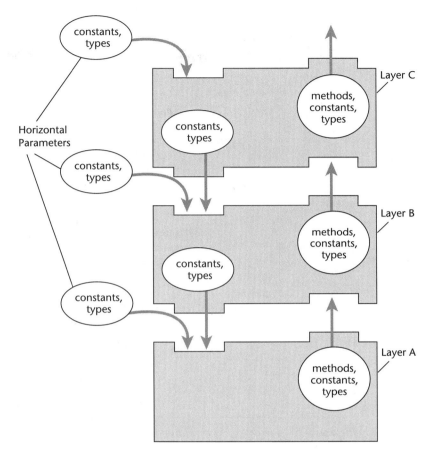

Figure 9-22 *Propagation of types, constants, and methods in a Gen-Voca hierarchy of layers (adapted from [Sin96])*

forwards operationB() to LowerLayer. Because the operations in GenVoca models are usually defined inline, calling operationA() on lower in operationA() of LayerA::ClassA does not incur any extra dispatching overhead. This way, we achieve clearly separated layers of abstraction and, at the same time, do not have to pay any performance penalties.

The implementation in Figure 9-23 is based on aggregation, that is, LayerA holds references to class instances from the layer beneath it (e.g., lower). Some of the operations from the lower layer may be exported unchanged to the upper layer using method forwarding, for example, operationB(); some may be refined, for

```
template <class LowerLayer>
class LayerA
{   public:
        class ClassA
        {   public:
                // refine operationA()
                void operationA()
                {   ... // LayerA-specific work
                    lower.operationA();
                    ... // LayerA-specific work
                };

                //forward operationB()
                void operationB()
                {   lower.operationB(); };

            private:
                typedef typename LowerLayer::ClassA LowerLayerClassA;
                LowerLayerClassA lower;
        };

        class ClassB
        { ... };
};
```

Figure 9-23 Forwarding implementation of GenVoca layer in C++

*Forwarding
static wrapper*
example, operationA(); and yet others may simply be used as supporting methods to implement some new methods of the upper layer. This kind of layer implementation corresponds to a *forwarding static wrapper* shown in Figure 9-24.

Forwarding-based implementation of a layer is adequate only if few or no operations exported by the lower layer are propagated unchanged up to the interface exported by the upper layer. Otherwise, we would have to write many forwarding methods, which is not only tedious, but also impairs adaptability and maintainability because any changes to the interface of the lower level ultimately require changes to the forwarding methods of the upper layers. In P++, this problem is addressed by the bypass construct. But what can we do in C++?

```
template <class Component>
class Wrapper
{   public:
        // refine operationA()
        void operationA()
        {   ... // wrapper-specific work
            component.operationA();
            ... // wrapper-specific work
        };

        //forward operationB()
        void operationB()
        {   component.operationB(); };

    private:
        Component component;
};
```

Figure 9-24 *Example of a forwarding static wrapper*

Inheritance-based static wrapper

In C++, the propagation of operations can be achieved using inheritance. Figure 9-25 shows an *inheritance-based static wrapper*. Please note that we no longer need an instance variable to hold an instance of the component, and the original operation can be called using the C++ scope operator. Based on this idea, we can now rewrite the forwarding layer from Figure 9-23 as an inheritance-based layer as shown in Figure 9-26. Of course, a layer can use forwarding for some of its classes and inheritance for other classes.

NOTE

Wrapper, also referred to as a *decorator*, is a design pattern described in [GHJV95]. We refer to the previous idiom as a *static wrapper*, as opposed to a *dynamic wrapper*, because the association between the component and the wrapper is achieved through the template parameter Component at compile time. A dynamic wrapper, on the other hand, would declare its component variable with the type being an abstract class of a component family and would call virtual methods on the component variable. Thus, the components could be exchanged at runtime. We discussed dynamic and static wrappers in Section 7.6.

```
template <class Component>
class Wrapper : public Component
{   public:
        // refine operationA()
        void operationA()
        {   ... // wrapper-specific work
            Component::operationA();
            ... // wrapper-specific work
        };
};
```

Figure 9-25 *Example of an inheritance-based static wrapper*

In all the C++ examples we have seen so far, types were propagated upwards using the C++ scope operator (e.g., LowerLayer::ClassA). In general, we can use this operator to access any member types, that is, types also defined using the typedef statement. For example, given the class BottomLayer

```
template <class LowerLayer>
class LayerA
{   private:
        typedef typename LowerLayer::ClassA LowerLayerClassA;
        typedef typename LowerLayer::ClassB LowerLayerClassB;
    public:
        class ClassA : public LowerLayerClassA
        {   public:
                // refine operationA()
                void operationA()
                {   ... // LayerA-specific work
                    LowerLayerClassA::operationA();
                    ... // LayerA-specific work
                };

        };

        class ClassB : public LowerLayerClassB
        { ... };
};
```

Figure 9-26 *Inheritance-based implementation of GenVoca layer in C++*

```
class BottomLayer
{ public:
    typedef int ElementType;
};
```

the member type ElementType can be accessed as follows:

BottomLayer::ElementType

We can also use the same accessing syntax for integral constants. The required idiom is as follows:

```
class BottomLayer
{ public:
    enum { number_of_elements = 100 };
};
```

The integral constant number_of_elements is accessed as follows:

BottomLayer::number_of_elements

The idea of how to propagate types and constants upwards over multiple layers is illustrated in Figure 9-27. Using this idiom, we can reach any number of layers down the hierarchy, and then access the members of some layer we are interested in. Please note that we modeled layers as structs instead of classes. We do this in cases where all the members of a layer are public. This saves us from having to write the keyword public:.

We use upward type propagation to supply layers with horizontal parameters rather than defining them as regular template parameters. This way, we avoid mixing vertical parameters (i.e., layer parameters) and horizontal parameters in parameter declarations of a template implementing a layer. Specifying horizontal parameters explicitly would basically obscure the vertical layer structure in type expressions that define concrete instances of a GenVoca model. Furthermore, there are also horizontal parameters that are needed in more than one layer (e.g., element type is required by all layers in the data container example), and by supplying those parameters by propagation, we avoid having to specify the same parameter in a type expression several times.

Configuration repository

However, we still need to solve one problem. The propagation style shown in Figure 9-27 has the disadvantage that a layer *explicitly* asks the layer beneath it for all the types it needs or another

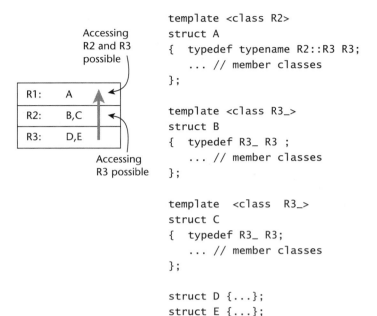

Figure 9-27 Upward type propagation in a GenVoca model

layer above it might need. Thus, layers might have to explicitly pass types they are not interested in themselves. This fact impairs adaptability because the need to propagate a new type might require changes to many layers. This problem can be avoided by passing a standard "envelope" containing all the layers, types, and constants to be propagated rather than passing these elements themselves (see the struct Config in Figure 9-28). We refer to such an envelope as a *configuration repository* because it contains configuration information. (We discussed configuration repositories in Section 7.11.2.) We pass the configuration repository (i.e., Config) to each leaf layer of a GenVoca domain model, that is, to layers that do not have any layer parameters. And this repository is explicitly propagated upwards by all other layers. As a result, Config is the only type explicitly passed between layers, and all other communication between layers goes through this "envelope."

We usually define global types (e.g., Global1 in Figure 9-28) or constants (e.g., Global2) as direct members of Config. On the other hand, all horizontal parameters of a certain layer (e.g., HorizA of A) are preferably wrapped in an extra configuration class specifically defined for that layer (e.g., ConfigA for A). This idiom, called *structured configuration*, prevents name clashes if two layers

```
template <class R2>
struct A
{   // expose Config to upper layers
    typedef typename R2::Config Config;

    // retrieve types and constants from Config
    typedef typename Config::Global1 Global1;
    enum { Global2 = Config::Global2 };
    typedef typename Config::ConfigA::HorizA HorizA;

    ... // Global1, Global2, and HorizA
    ... // are used here
};
```

```
template <class Config_>
struct B
{   // expose Config to upper layers
    // typedef Config_ Config;

    // retrieve types and constants from Config
    typedef typename Config::Global1 Global1;
    enum { global2 = Config::Global2 };
    typedef typename Config::ConfigB::HorizB HorizB;

    ... // Global1, Global2, and HorizB
    ... // are used here
};
```

```
template <class Config_>
struct C {...};
```

```
struct Config
{   typedef int Global1;
    enum { Global2 = 100 };
    struct ConfigA
    { typedef char HorizA; };
    struct ConfigB
    { typedef float HorizB; };
    ...
};
```

R1:	A
R2:	B,C
Config	
export:	
Global1, Global2,	
ConfigA::HorizA,	
ConfigB::HorizB	

Figure 9-28 *Upward propagation of global and horizontal parameters*

need two different horizontal parameters having the same name. We discussed this in Section 7.11.3.

So far we have seen a number of examples of upward type and constant propagation. But how do you propagate types and constants downwards?

The downward propagation of types and constants can be accomplished in an indirect way. The main idea is to put the type expressions assembling the layers into the configuration repository (see Figure 9-29). In other words, we wrap the whole layer hierarchy in our Config class and propagate this class up the very same

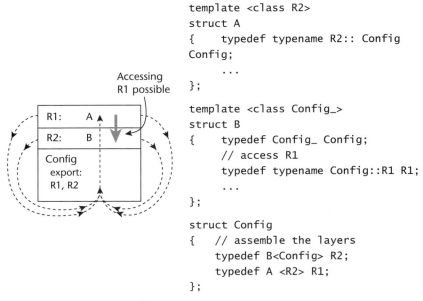

```
template <class R2>
struct A
{    typedef typename R2:: Config
Config;
     ...
};

template <class Config_>
struct B
{    typedef Config_ Config;
     // access R1
     typedef typename Config::R1 R1;
     ...
};

struct Config
{    // assemble the layers
     typedef B<Config> R2;
     typedef A <R2> R1;
};
```

Figure 9-29 Downward type propagation

hierarchy (this is an inherently recursive idiom!). This way, we can access any layer exported in the Config class in any other layer, for example, R1 in R2. In fact, this way we accomplish layer propagation in any direction.

Unfortunately, there is a limitation to the downward propagation: Types propagated downwards can be only referenced in lower layers but not *used* in the C++ sense at compile time. In other words, downwards-propagated types can be used as types in variable and function parameter declarations (i.e., we can reference them), but we cannot access their member types (i.e., their structure is not defined at the time of access). This is so because the hierarchy is built up in C++ in the bottom-up direction (i.e., functionally; the arguments of a template are built before the template is built) and types propagated down to a lower layer are actually not yet defined at the time they are referenced in the lower level. However, even with this limitation, downward type propagation is still useful, for example, to compose recursive types. We will see an example in Section 12.6.

The C++ programming techniques presented in this section cover each of the kinds of parameters and information flows shown in Figure 9-22: vertical and horizontal parameters, upward propagation of operations, types and constants, and downward propagation of types and constants.

9.8.2.5 Composition Validation

A relatively small number of GenVoca layers can usually be composed in a vast number of combinations. Whether two layers can be connected or not depends on the compatibility of their interfaces. Layer A can be used as a parameter of layer B if layer A exports the same realm as B imports or a subrealm of the latter. However, the realm compatibility takes into account only the compatibility of the exported and the imported signatures and not the semantic compatibility of the corresponding operations. Thus, even if a type expression is syntactically correct according to a GenVoca grammar, the system defined by this expression may still be semantically incorrect. For example, the layers implementing the concurrency features (see Table 9-1) in the GenVoca implementation of the Booch Components import and export the same realm, namely DS (see Figure 9-18). Assume that the GenVoca grammar describing the Booch Components contains the following productions:

```
DS_size : guarded[DS_size] | concurrent[DS_size] |
          multiple[ DS_size] |
          size_of[DS] | ...
DS      : bounded | unbounded[Memory] | ...
```

Given these productions, we can define the following container:

```
guarded[guarded[multiple[concurrent[guarded[concurrent[size_of
[bounded]]]]]]]
```

This type expression is syntactically correct, but semantically complete nonsense. Each of the layers guarded, concurrent, and multiple are intended to be used as alternatives, and only one or none is allowed in one expression defining a container. We clearly need a way to express such configuration rules.

In general, the configuration rules can be quite complicated and they can span multiple layers. For example, we can have a higher-level layer that requires that all the data containers used by this layer are synchronized, that is, the expressions defining them have to contain the concurrent layer, but there can be several intermediate layers between the data container and the higher-level layer. In other words, we need to verify the effect of using a layer at a "distance." Furthermore, a layer can affect the use of other layers not only below it, but also above it.

Conditions and
restrictions

A model for defining such configuration constraints for Gen-Voca layers is presented in [BG96, BG97]. The model is based on the upward and downward propagation of attributes that represent constraints on layers or properties of layers. There are two main types of constraints: *conditions* and *restrictions*. Conditions are constraints propagated downwards, and restrictions are constraints propagated upwards (see Figure 9-30). A given layer can be used at a certain position in a type expression if it satisfies all conditions propagated by upper layers down to a specified layer and all the restrictions propagated by lower layers up to a specified layer. We refer to such conditions as *preconditions* and to such restrictions as *prerestrictions* (see Figure 9-30) The use of a layer in a type expression modifies the conditions and restrictions "flowing" through the layer: The conditions leaving a layer in the downward direction are referred to as *postconditions*, and the restrictions leaving a layer in the upward direction are referred to as *postrestrictions*. By modifying the postrestrictions, a layer can express some requirements on the layers above it. Similarly, by modifying the postconditions, a layer can express some requirements on the layers below it.

There are many ways of implementing conditions and restrictions. In the most simple case, layers can propagate their properties, represented as attributes, and check for required or undesired properties. The details of a slightly more elaborate implementation are described in [BG96].

The validation checking mechanism based on constraint propagation also allows the generation of detailed warnings and error reports, which actually give specific hints of how to repair an erroneous type expression [BG96].

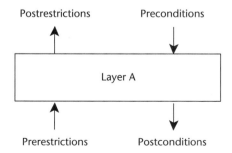

Figure 9-30 *Flow of conditions and restrictions through a GenVoca layer*

NOTE

In [BG96, BG97], composition validation in GenVoca models is referred to as *design rule checking.*

9.8.2.6 Transformations and GenVoca

The GenVoca model, as we've described it so far, represents a classic example of the compositional approach to generation. Each layer represents a *forward refinement*, which results in composing the layers below it. Each layer may refine several classes at once. In other words, you can view a type expression as a specification for applying a series of forward refinements. For example, the type expression:

```
concurrent[size_of[unbounded[managed[heap]]]]
```

when interpreted in a top-down order, denotes the application of the concurrent refinement, then that of size_of, and so on. We can illustrate this refinement using the operation read_size() as an example (see Figure 9-31). The refinement starts with the empty read_size() operation declared in the realm DS_size. concurrent refines read_size() by inlining the highlighted code. size_of finishes the refinement by inlining direct access to counter.

Beyond this transformational interpretation of GenVoca layers as forward refinements, there is also an opportunity to make a truly transformational extension to GenVoca: transformations on type expressions [BCRW98]. Let us take a look at this extension.

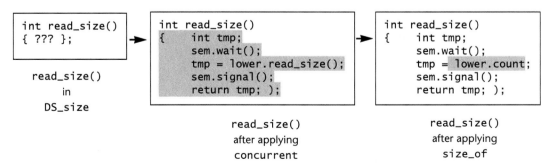

Figure 9-31 Refinement of read_size() *by successive inlining*

Type expressions, such as:

```
bag[concurrent[size_of[unbounded[managed[heap]]]]]
```

are still quite close to the implementation level because each layer represents a single concrete refinement. The layers correspond to features that are determined by factoring out commonalities and variabilities of concrete code of different systems or subsystems. The main goal of this factorization is to minimize code duplication and to be able to compose these features in as many ways as possible. All the features are concrete because each of them is directly implemented as a layer. The writer of type expressions has to know the order of the layers, the design rules, and also the layers that can be regarded as implementation details. However, users can often provide a more abstract specification of the system or component they need. For example, they can specify some usage profile for a data container by stating abstract features, such as the calling frequency of insert, update, remove, and other operations. This information can then be used to synthesize an appropriate type expression. The synthesis is complicated by the fact that different layers have different influence on the performance parameters and that there are a vast number of different type expressions for a given GenVoca domain model. Thus, exhaustive search for a solution is usually not practical, and we have to use heuristic search methods. This search problem is usually addressed in transformation systems by means of inference-based scheduling of transformations deploying rules, procedures, tactics, and strategies. We discussed these components in the context of Draco (see Section 9.8.1). In [BCRW98], Batory et al. describe a prototype of a design wizard that is based on the cost model of various operations on data structures and applies transformations to type expressions that insert, delete, or replace layers in order to improve the performance characteristics of expressions that define data containers. As already stated, in general, the kind of knowledge needed for code synthesis includes not only constraints on component combinations, but also constraints, procedures, and heuristics mapping from higher-level specifications to lower-level specifications.

9.8.2.7 Frameworks and GenVoca

Object-oriented frameworks implement reusable designs for classes of applications. They usually consist of sets of cooperating classes, which application programmers can customize by providing their own specialized classes and integrating them into the framework using subclassing and object composition. The user-defined classes are usually called by the framework and not the other way around. Examples of successful frameworks are ControlWORKS [CW] and Apple's MacApp [Ros95].

GenVoca allows us to organize object-oriented frameworks as a family of configurable layers. This not only helps us to clearly communicate the structure of a framework, but also improves its extensibility and adaptability. But how does this work?

As already stated, OO frameworks are sets of cooperating classes. In fact, not all classes of a framework communicate with all other classes, but rather they are involved in smaller, well defined *collaborations*. Each class participating in a collaboration plays a certain role, and this role usually involves only some of its methods. A collaboration is then defined by a set of roles and a communication protocol between the objects participating in the collaboration. One object can play different roles in different collaborations at the same time. This view of the world is the cornerstone of the analysis and design methods called *role modeling* [Ree96, KO96] and *collaboration-based design* [VHN96, Rie97, VH97]. According to these methods, concrete classes are obtained by composing the roles they play in different collaborations. Such designs are then implemented as frameworks. Unfortunately, when using the conventional framework implementation techniques (e.g., [GHJV95]), the boundaries between collaborations are lost in the implementation. However, we can use the GenVoca model to encapsulate each collaboration as a single layer. This way, we not only preserve the design structure in the implementation, but we can also conveniently configure frameworks in terms of collaborations using type expressions and easily extend the whole model with new (e.g., alternative) layers (see Figure 9-13).

9.8.3 Approaches Based on Algebraic Specifications

There is at least one theory that provides a theoretical foundation for many of the concepts presented in the previous sections, namely the theory of *algebraic specifications*. Algebraic specifications were primarily developed for specifying *abstract data types*. However, it turns out that they are also appropriate for formally

---

BIBLIOGRAPHIC NOTE

Implementing role-based models using GenVoca is discussed in [SB98a, SB98b].

specifying whole domains (see [Sri91]). Furthermore, because they also encourage the transformational implementation style (as we explain later in this section), a number of formal transformation systems are based on them, for example, CIP [BEH+87], SPECWARE [SJ95], and ASF+SDF [DHK96].

First, we will introduce some basic concepts of algebraic specifications. We will then explain how they can be used to specify domains, and finally, we will explain how these specifications are used to generate software systems.

An algebraic specification defines an abstract data type (ADT), that is, a class of concrete data types. It consists of two parts: one part defines the syntax of a language for talking about the instances of an ADT, and the other part defines the semantics of the language. We explain this idea using a simple specification of a list (see Figure 9-32).

Signature and axioms

The sample specification in Figure 9-32 consists of a *signature* and a set of *axioms*. The signature defines a simple language for defining and manipulating lists. It consists of a set of *types* (also referred to as *sorts*) and a set of *operations*. These types and operations are pure symbols. They take on meaning if we assign one set of values to each type and one function defined on these sets to each operation. Such assignment is referred to as an *algebra* and represents a concrete data type (i.e., data types are described as sets of values and relationships between them).

Not every assignment of sets and functions to the signature satisfies the specification. The assignments have to satisfy all the *axioms* of the specification. The axioms are the properties of all algebras described by the specification. In other words, an algebraic specification defines a set of algebras, that is, an ADT.[5] Because axioms are statements in some appropriate logic, we can use inference to derive further properties from these axioms. Any property derivable from the axioms is referred to as a *theorem* (e.g., head(1).tail(1)=1 is a theorem of LIST). The axioms can

BIBLIOGRAPHIC NOTE

You'll find a comprehensive introduction to algebraic specifications in [LEW96].

---

5. It is interesting to note that a class of structurally equivalent (i.e., isomorphic) algebras is referred to as a monomorphic ADT; otherwise the class represents a polymorphic ADT.

```
specification LIST:
    signature:
        types = {LIST, ELEM}
        operations = {
                . : ELEM, LIST → LIST,
            head : LIST → ELEM,
            tail : LIST → LIST
        }
    axioms:
        variables = {l : LIST, e : ELEM}
        head(e.l) = e
        tail(e.l) = l
        ...
```

Figure 9-32 *Algebraic Specification of a list (adapted from [Gog86])*

also be viewed as rewrite rules, which can be applied to the expressions of the language defined by the signature. These expressions are also called *term expressions*. This view explains why algebraic specifications have been used as a formal basis for numerous transformation systems (e.g., [BEH+87, SJ95, DHK96]).

Practical algebraic specifications are usually organized into networks of related smaller algebraic specifications (see [Sri91] for examples). If we consider that each of the smaller specifications defines its own language and that the relationships represent refinement, inclusion, parameterization, and so on, the similarity of this model to the model of Draco is striking. This is why Srinivas proposed in [Sri91] to use algebraic specifications to specify domain models (see Section 2.8.7). In fact, you can view the algebraic theory as a formal theory for a Draco-like transformational model of software development.

Specification and signature morphism

The mechanisms for organizing and composing algebraic specifications lie at the heart of automatic generation of programs from specifications. One of the basic relationships between algebraic specifications is *specification morphism*, which represents a structural relationship between two specifications. A specification morphism between a source and a target specification is defined as a *signature morphism*, that is, a mapping between the sorts and operations of the source and target signatures, which, if used to translate theorems, ensures that the translated theorems of the source specification are also theorems of the target specification. Intuitively, given the source specification A and the target specification B, a morphism from A to B tells us that the ADT specified by A can be obtained from the ADT specified by B by "forgetting" some of the structure of the latter ADT.

Many specification composition mechanisms can be represented as specification morphisms, for example, parameterization, inclusion, derivation, views, and so on.

An example of using algebraic specifications and morphisms to define domain models and to generate systems on this basis is found in the work of Douglas Smith et al. at the Kestrel Institute [KI, SKW85, Smi90a, SJ95, SJ96]. An interesting facet of this work is the development of a formal theory of algorithm design called *classification approach to design* [Smi96], which can be deployed by algorithm synthesizers (e.g., [Smi90a]). The theory is based on algebraic specifications and mainly two organizing structural relationships: *interpretations* and *refinements*. Interpretations define the structural correspondence between a reusable problem specification and the specification of a problem at hand. Constructing an interpretation between the reusable problem specification and the given problem specification is also referred to as *classification* because we classify the given problem as an instance of the known general problem. An interpretation from the specification A to B has the following structure: A → A–B ← B, where the arrows represent specification morphisms and A–B is a specification called the *mediator*. In contrast to a simple morphism, an interpretation can define a mapping not only between types and operations, but also between types and type expressions and vice versa. Effectively, interpretation can be seen as a form of "semantic adapters."

A refinement is a morphism between two specifications, where the refined specification contains more implementation details. Effectively, a refinement defines the relationship between a reusable problem specification and its reusable solution. The reusable problem specification defines the "interface vocabulary" for the solution specification—it basically represents a vertical parameter of the solution specification. Thus, refinements are

BIBLIOGRAPHIC NOTE

The mechanisms for organizing and composing algebraic specifications have been studied in the literature very extensively (see [BG77, Wir83, Gog86, ST88a, ST88b, GB92, LEW96]).

vertical relationships, whereas interpretations are horizontal relationships.[6]

As an example, we consider the problem of sorting a list of numbers. Assume that we specified this problem as the algebraic specification `SortingProblemSpec` (see Figure 9-33). The problem can be solved by applying the *divide and conquer* problem solution strategy. Suppose that the general problem specification `GeneralProblemSpec` and its corresponding divide and conquer solution `DivideAndConquerSolution` are stored in a library (the general problem specification defines some interface symbols, such as the input and the output set for the `DivideAndConquerSolution`). Both specifications are also referred to as *design theories*. We can reuse this problem-solution pair by identifying the correspondence between the symbols in `SortingProblemSpec` and `GeneralProblemSpec`. This step defines the interpretation relationship `I`. Finding this correspondence is often not a trivial task, which, in general, cannot be automated. Different interpretations will finally lead to the derivation of different sorting algorithms, for example, mergesort, insertion sort, or quicksort. Next, the specification `SortingProblemSolution`, which structurally satisfies both `SortingProblemSpec` and `DivideAndConquerSolution`, is determined, whereby various mathematical procedures are used. This process of interpretation and refinement is

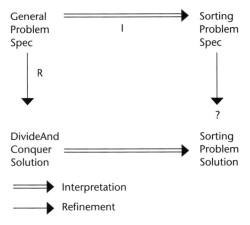

Figure 9-33 *Relationships between the specifications of the sorting example*

---

6. As you may remember, horizontal relationships organize designs within one layer of abstraction, whereas vertical relationships connect different layers of abstraction.

carried on until an executable specification $Spec_n$ is constructed (see Figure 9-34). The details of this sorting example can be found in [Smi96].

Depending on the concrete interpretations and refinements used, we can derive different sorting algorithms. The various sorting algorithms span a design space as shown in Figure 9-35. Also the reusable problem-solving strategies used in algorithm design are organized into a refinement hierarchy (see Figure 9-36). Such design spaces are usually augmented with performance characteristics and design rationale to guide the selection of the appropriate design theory based on a given context.

The domain of sorting is well understood today and can be formally described easily using the previously presented concepts. Such formal description provides a basis for the automatic synthesis of algorithms from specifications. A prominent example of a system capable of such synthesis is *KIDS* (*Kestrel Interactive Development System*) [Smi90a], which has been part of Kestrel Institute's research efforts for over 10 years. Of course, synthesizing sorting algorithms, although interesting from the theoretical viewpoint, provides little leverage for practical software development. However, the work on the transportation scheduling domain at Kestrel demonstrates that there are also practical domains that

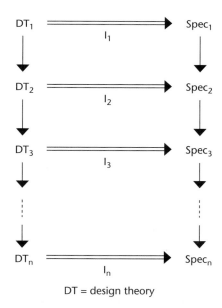

DT = design theory

Figure 9-34 *Ladder construction (from [Smi96])*

are understood well enough and stable enough to be formalized. According to [SPW95, SG96], a transportation scheduler (for planning logistic operations) generated from a formal domain model using KIDS is over 20 times faster than the standard, hand-coded system originally deployed by the customer.

Based on the extensive experience with KIDS, a new system has been built, namely SPECWARE [SJ95, SM96], which is more systematically based on the concepts previously presented than KIDS. In particular, the system is explicitly based on category theory [Gol79], which provides a theoretical foundation for working with specification morphism diagrams (such as Figure 9-34). The

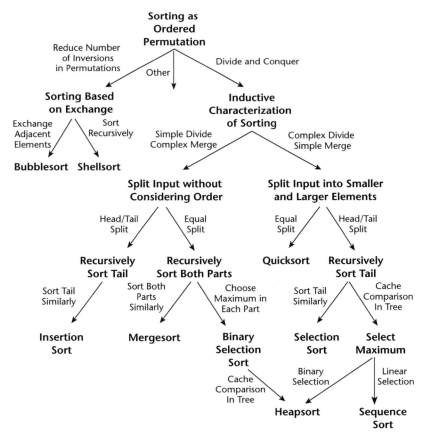

Figure 9-35 *Design space of implementations of sorting (adapted from [Sri91, Bro83], © 1991 by IEEE)*

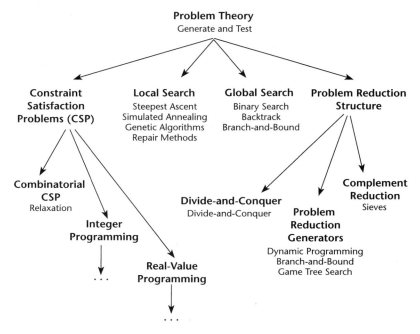

Figure 9-36 *Refinement hierarchy of algorithm design theories (adapted from [Smi96])*

main category underlining SPECWARE is the category of specifications, that is, a category whose objects are algebraic specifications and whose morphisms are specification morphisms. The system supports the user in the construction of interpretation and refinement relationships through various mathematical procedures, for example, constraints propagation, unskolemization, computing colimits (a fundamental operation for composing specifications) and pushouts, and so on. An industrial case study of using SPECWARE in the domain of electrical and mechanical engineering performed at the Boeing company is described in [WHB00].

Chapter 10

Static Metaprogramming in C++

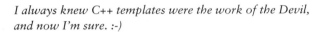

I always knew C++ templates were the work of the Devil, and now I'm sure. :-)

—*Cliff Click cited by Todd Veldhuizen in [Vel98c]*

10.1 Why Is This Chapter Worth Reading?

Metaprogramming is the key technology for developing adaptable and adaptive systems[1] as well as automating the assembly of components in the system families approach. Metaprogramming is about representing and manipulating components that implement the basic functionality of a system. This chapter starts by explaining the concept of metaprogramming and by providing an overview of specific areas of metaprogramming, such as reflection, metalevel architectures, and partial evaluation. This will give you the big picture of the field. We will then move to our main topic, which is template metaprogramming. Template metaprogramming is a form of metaprogramming limited to compile time. The rich C++ template mechanism allows us to write code, which is executed by the C++ compiler during the compilation of a target program. In effect, a C++ program might consist of two kinds of code: static code, which is executed at compile time, and dynamic code, which is compiled and then executed at runtime. The static code can be used to manipulate the dynamic code. This allows for amazing applications including optimizations, code generation,

---

1. Please note the difference between adaptability and adaptivity: *Adaptable* systems can be adapted to a particular deployment environment, whereas *adaptive* systems adapt themselves to a deployment environment.

398 Chapter 10 Static Metaprogramming in C++

automatic configuration of components, writing extremely generic code, and improving program portability. We will present a set of C++ idioms for template metaprogramming and application examples. Among other details, you will learn how to compute the constant data of your program at compile time and how to compute the result type of generic functions, unroll loops, and implement domain-specific languages in C++.

10.2 What Is Metaprogramming?

There is an increasing demand for systems that can be easily configured for a specific deployment environment or can even adjust themselves dynamically to a changing environment at runtime. We want to be able to modify different aspects of components, configure and assemble components using automatic processes, and analyze the operation of the resulting systems. In addition to automating the production of individually configured systems, the produced systems often need to be able to dynamically adjust themselves to a changing environment, for example, by modifying their scheduling and caching policies depending on the current workload or by generating necessary adapters and wrappers before connecting to a new environment. We call such systems *adaptive*. Interestingly, adaptivity is not limited to runtime. We can also have libraries that automatically adapt the code they contribute to a system being compiled. For example, they can adjust their components by selecting algorithms and data representations appropriate for a target deployment platform.

Metaprogram-ming and metaprograms

Automatic configuration and assembly, parameterizing aspects, dynamic and static adaptability and adaptivity require technologies for advertising the functionality of components and manipulating their parameters and/or implementation. This is exactly what *metaprogramming* is about: writing programs that represent and manipulate other programs or themselves (the latter case is called reflection—we'll discuss it in the following section). Programs representing and manipulating other programs or themselves are called *metaprograms*.

The prefix "meta" denotes the property of "being about," that is, metaprograms are programs about programs. Unfortunately, "meta" also tends to convey a flavor of being esoteric and abstruse, implying that anything with "meta" in its name makes a good Ph.D. topic (see our Going "meta" sidebar on the origins of "meta"). Fortunately, metaprogramming has nothing to do with metaphysics, and there is a good chance that you have already engaged in metaprogramming without even knowing about it.

There are plenty of examples of metaprogramming in practice. Program generators, compilers, and interpreters are metaprograms because they represent and manipulate programs in the language they implement. If you have ever written macros to help you avoid writing similar code multiple times, you did metaprogramming. This is so because macros generate code. Some languages provide special support for metaprogramming. For example, Smalltalk and CLOS expose parts of the language (e.g., methods, classes, execution stacks) to programmers, who can access, extend, and modify these parts. Other examples of metaprograms are programs for instrumenting other programs for testing and profiling purposes, aspect programs influencing the semantics of components (see Aspect-Oriented Programming in Chapter 8), code for discovering methods of objects (e.g., in browser or component composition tools), optimizers, tools for automatic refactoring, and much more.

10.3 A Quick Tour of Metaprogramming

In this section, we introduce a number of concepts from metaprogramming, such as reflection, metaobjects, metalevel architectures, and partial evaluation.

Reflection

As stated previously, metaprogramming involves programs operating on other programs or themselves. Compilers and preprocessors are examples of metaprograms operating on other programs. The other case, that is, the case where a program operates on itself, is referred to as *reflection*. More precisely, Smith defines reflection as follows [Smi90b]:

GOING "META"

The word "meta" is borrowed from the Greek word meaning "after" or "beyond" and is used to denote a shift in level. For example, metaphysics deals with concepts beyond the limits of physics and metapsychology goes beyond the limits of psychology. In linguistics, the term "meta" does not imply anything speculative or mysterious, it simply implies the relationship of "being about" something, for example, a metalanguage is a language to describe another language. English grammar is a metalanguage with respect to some text written in English because it explains its structure. The usage of "meta" in linguistics corresponds to its usage in computer science, where metaprograms are programs *about* some base-level programs.

> Reflection: An entity's integral ability to represent, operate on, and otherwise deal with its self in the same way that it represents, operates on, and deals with its primary subject matter.

Reflection is a fundamental concept of self-adaptive systems. A reflective system has to incorporate a model of itself and be able to "re-think" its operation based on the state of the environment and its own representation. Having a model of itself and a model of the environment allows a system to predict the effect of its action and to make more accurate decisions. It is interesting to note in this context that humans are not born with a model of themselves, but learn and develop it while growing up. For example, it is a widely known phenomenon that small children under the age of 15 months are unable to recognize themselves in a mirror (see [Ams72, LB79]).

Gabriel et al. [GBW93] refine the concept of reflection for computer programs as follows:

Introspection, intercession, and reification

> Reflection is the ability of a program to manipulate as data something representing the state of the program during its own execution. There are two aspects of such manipulation: introspection and intercession. Introspection is the ability of a program to observe and therefore reason about its own state. Intercession is the ability of a program to modify its own execution state or alter its own interpretation or meaning. Both aspects require a mechanism for encoding execution state as data; providing such an encoding is called reification.

Metaobjects

Dynamic languages, such as Smalltalk and CLOS provide a high level of support for reflection. The main idea in these languages is to provide as much of their definition as possible in the form of libraries, which are part of the language itself. For example, in Smalltalk, classes are represented by objects, which can be manipulated at runtime and the class objects themselves are instances of metaclasses, which are also modifiable objects. By modifying the metaclasses, you can actually modify the object model of the language. Furthermore, there are objects that represent methods, execution stacks, the processor, and nearly all elements of the language and its execution environment. We refer to such objects as *metaobjects*. Most importantly, regular Smalltalk code can access and modify these metaobjects. We already saw a concrete example of metaprogramming in Smalltalk in Section 8.5.7, where we demonstrated how to add methods to an object at runtime by manipulating its method dictionary and how to use this technique to implement method wrapping.

*Metalevel
architectures*

We can apply reflection as a general principle for architecting flexible systems. The main idea is to split a system into two parts: a metalevel and a base level. As Buschmann et al. describe in [BMR+96], "a metalevel provides information about selected system properties and makes the software self-aware. A base level includes the application logic." This kind of architecture is referred to as a *metalevel architecture*. The design of metalevel architectures is described in [BMR+96] as an architectural pattern. It is important to note that building reflective systems does not require a reflective programming language, but a reflective language greatly simplifies the task. You'll find other patterns based on reflection in [FY95].

*Metaobject
protocols, open
systems, and
metainterfaces*

An important issue in the design of object-oriented metalevel architectures is the design of interfaces to metaobjects, that is, the design of so-called *metaobject protocols* (MOPs). Kiczales et al. discuss this issue in the context of language design in [KRB91]. The main idea here is that the metaclasses that come with an implementation of a language define its default semantics, but users can tailor it according to their needs by deriving new metaclasses from the predefined ones. This idea is useful not only for implementing programming languages, but also any other systems. We also refer to this idea as the "*open systems*" principle, where the designer of a component can improve its reusability by providing users with a well-defined customization interface to the component, the so-called *metainterface*.

Different languages provide different levels of reflection. For example, Java provides a much lower level of reflection than Smalltalk. The Java reflection API, which was introduced in JDK1.1 [Sun97b], allows you to discover methods and attributes in classes at runtime (which is crucial for implementing debuggers, browsers, and GUI builders). Furthermore, you can create objects of classes whose names are not known until runtime. Similarly, you can also call methods and access attributes whose names are not known until runtime (because, e.g., you discover them with the help of reflective facilities, or you compute their names at runtime). Thus, Java's reflexive facilities primarily support introspection (which is required by the JavaBeans component model and the Remote Method Invocation mechanism). In contrast to Smalltalk, Java does not allow you to directly modify classes or methods by modifying their metaobjects at runtime, that is, it does not support intercession the way Smalltalk does. Achieving higher levels of reflection in Java requires modifying the Java virtual machine (e.g., see [GK97]).

C++ provides even less support for reflection than Java: It has only a few rudimentary built-in reflective features limited to the introspection level, the most important being *runtime type-identification* (RTTI). The RTTI mechanism allows you to discover the type of objects at runtime. RTTI provides several layers of facilities. Stroustrup strongly advises in [Str94] to primarily rely on compile-time type checking and limit the use of RTTI to the absolutely necessary cases. If static type checking is not sufficient, you should check the applicability of dynamic casts. The next level is to compare `typeids` of objects, where the name of at least one of the involved types is unknown. Operations on `typeids` for obtaining more detailed information should only be applied for implementing debuggers, database systems, class browsers, and so on. Sophisticated reflective extensions to C++ and reflective facilities built into the IBM System Object Model (SOM) are discussed in [FD98].

Metaprograms can be executed in different contexts and at different times. The typical phases in a lifecycle of an application include compile time, link time, load time, runtime, and post-runtime, all of which constitute a continuum shown in Figure 10-1. Adaptation of a system may be required at any of these times, depending on what information is needed. For example, certain optimizations may be possible at compile time, but others may require information that is not available until runtime. Another possibility is to gather execution statistics at runtime and apply optimizations at post-runtime, so that the next execution of a system is more efficient (i.e., *post-runtime optimizations*). In general, it is useful to be able to execute optimization, configuration, and other metaprograms at different times. This also corresponds to the idea that the binding site of configuration knowledge should be parameterized, that is, we should be able to use it in any context

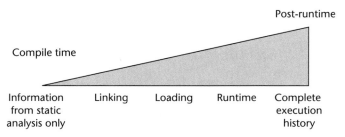

Figure 10-1 *Typical lifecycle of an application (from [ABE+97], © 1997 by IEEE). As the program progresses from compile time to post-runtime, more information, which can be used for optimization becomes available.*

(see Section 8.5.1.2). This is so because different customers may require different levels of flexibility. Some variation points of a product may be fixed at production time for one customer and kept variable for another. Therefore, the code configuring the variation points could be called at production time or later at runtime. In the latter case, it would have to be part of the product.

Partial evaluation

The idea of being able to optimize systems at different times is closely related to *partial evaluation* [JGS93], which we discussed in Section 9.6.1.2. Suppose that you need to run some code multiple times on sets of input data in which one part is varying and another part is constant. In this case, it is useful to pre-evaluate the code with respect to the constant part of the data, that is, partially evaluate it. This way, each time you need to run the code on one set of input data, you only have to do the necessary computation for the variable part, which may save time and other resources.

Binding time analysis

A metaprogram performing partial evaluation is referred to as a *program specializer* (or *partial evaluator*). You give both a program and partial input data to a program specializer, and the program specializer produces a specialized version of the program (also known as a *residual* program). A common technique used by program specializers for determining which parts of a program can be evaluated given the partial input data is *binding time analysis* [JGS93]. It involves labeling program constructs as static or dynamic. For example, Figure 10-2 shows a fragment of scientific computing code, where the parts determined as static by binding time analysis are underlined.

A program specializer, such as C-Mix [And94], would evaluate the static parts and produce a specialized version of the program shown in Figure 10-3.

NOTE

It is important to note that the application phases depend on the application programming model used. For example, consider a large distributed system of high availability. Such a system is "at runtime" most of the time. However, the phases from Figure 10-1 can be relevant for the components that are being replaced in the system. In a typical C++ application, Coplien distinguishes between source time, preprocessing time, compile time, link time, load time, and runtime [Cop98]. Examples of metaprograms applied at source time are automatic source refactoring transformations. If you generate components, you can also distinguish between component generation time and component assembly time. As you see, the relevant times are context dependent!

```
float volumeOfCube(float length)
{ return power(length, 3); }

float power(float x, int n)
{ float r = 1;
  for (int i=0; i < n; ++i) r *= x;
  return r;
}
```

Figure 10-2 Sample code with marked static parts (from [Vel99])

Online and offline specialization

Determining which parts of a program to evaluate is not a trivial problem because we usually do not want to evaluate all the parts that could potentially be evaluated given the input data. For example, the whole input to a scientific program could be known at compile time, but we certainly do not want a program specializer to fully specialize the scientific program, which would amount to "running" the program on the specializer. This would be very inefficient compared to just running the unspecialized program. There are two solutions to this problem. The first solution is to have a human expert annotate the scientific program to tell the specializer which parts should be evaluated and which should not. This is referred to as *offline specialization*. Another solution is to have the specializer use built-in heuristics to decide which parts to evaluate and which not. This is referred to as *online specialization*.

Partial evaluation has been applied in a number of areas including scientific computing (e.g., specializing a Fortran FFT program with respect to a function and a number of points

```
float volumeOfCube(float length)
{ return power3(length); }

float power3(float x)
{ float r = 1;
  r *= x;
  r *= x;
  r *= x;
  return r;
}
```

Figure 10-3 Partially evaluated code (from [Vel99])

[GNZ95]), programming language implementation (e.g., generating a compiler from an interpreter [JGS93]), operating systems (e.g., specializing components of an operating system with respect to states that are likely to occur [PAB+95]), and computer graphics (e.g., specializing ray tracers with respect to a given scene [And93]).

In most cases, partial evaluation is done before runtime. However, it also represents a useful runtime optimization technique (e.g., see [NHCL96]). A running system can use partial evaluation to produce optimized versions of components for dealing with *repeating* tasks and data on a dynamic basis.

10.4 Static Metaprogramming

Static metaprograms

Metaprograms can run in different contexts and at different times. In this chapter, however, we only focus on *static metaprograms*. These metaprograms run before the load time of the code they manipulate.

The most common examples of systems involving static metaprogramming are compilers and preprocessors. These systems manipulate representations of input programs (e.g., abstract syntax trees) in order to transform them into programs in another language (e.g., assembler) or the same language as the input language, but with a modified program structure. In the usual case, the only people writing metaprograms for these systems are compiler developers who have full access to their sources.

Open compilers

The idea of an *open compiler* is to make metaprogramming more accessible to a broader audience by providing well-defined, high-level interfaces for manipulating various internal program representations (see e.g., [LKRR92]). A transformation system is an example of an open compiler, which provides an interface for writing transformations on abstract syntax trees (ASTs). We discussed transformation systems in Section 9.7. Examples of systems supporting static metaprogramming by opening some parts of the compilation process are Open C++ [Chi95], MPC++ [IHS+96], Magik [Eng97], and Xroma [CEG+98]. An open compiler may also provide access to its parser, code generator, or any other of its parts. The Intentional Programming (IP) System, which we'll discuss in Chapter 11, is a good example of a widely open *programming environment*. IP provides APIs not only for extending the compilation system, but also for extending the debugger and the syntax-tree-based source editor.

Two-level languages

An important concept from partial evaluation, which is relevant to static metaprogramming, is that of *two-level* (or more generally, *multilevel*) *languages* [GJ97]. Two-level languages contain static code, which is evaluated at compile time, and dynamic code, which is compiled and later executed at runtime. Multilevel languages simplify the task of writing program generators. For example, the Catacomb system [SG97] uses static code to compose fragments of dynamic code. Indeed, the rest of this chapter is about using C++ as a two-level language for, among other purposes, writing program generators.

10.5 C++ As a Two-Level Language

ISO/ANSI C++ contains an elaborate template mechanism for defining parameterized classes and functions. As we discussed in Section 7.4.4, this includes—among other features—type and integral template parameters and partial and full template specialization. Surprisingly, templates together with a number of other C++ features constitute a Turing-complete, compile-time sublanguage of C++. This makes C++ a two-level language: A C++ program may contain both static code, which is evaluated at compile time, and dynamic code, which is compiled and later executed at runtime. As stated earlier, the static sublanguage is Turing complete, that is, it contains both a conditional and a looping construct and therefore can be used to encode arbitrary algorithms, which are interpreted by the compiler at compile time. The main compile-time conditional construct is template specialization: The compiler has to select a matching template out of several alternatives. The compile-time looping construct is template recursion, for example, a member of class templates used in its own definition. The compiler has to expand such templates recursively. Furthermore, C++ has exact rules about which parts of a program will be evaluated at compile time and which at runtime. For example, an integral expression used to initialize some static part of C++, such as an integral template parameter or a member of an enumeration type, will be evaluated at compile time. All these ingredients make C++ a two-level language.

As a first example, we'll take a look at the static code (i.e., code executed at compile time) for computing the factorial of a natural number. As you may remember, the factorial of n is $1 \cdot 2 \cdot \ldots \cdot (n-1) \cdot n$, and the factorial of 0 is 1. Thus, for example, the factorial of 4 is $1 \cdot 2 \cdot 3 \cdot 4$, that is, 24. First, let's take a look at a conventional C++ factorial function (see Figure 10-4). This is regular dynamic code. (For demonstration purposes, we have chosen a recursive implementation rather than one using a loop, and we test for n==0 rather than n<2.)

The corresponding static code for computing the factorial at compile time is given in Figure 10-5.

TURING-COMPLETENESS

A *Turing-complete* language is a language with at least a conditional and a looping construct. Böhm and Jacopini observed in [BJ66] that a language with a conditional and a looping construct can be used to implement a Turing machine. According to the generally recognized conjecture by the famous mathematician Alonzo Church, any computation for which there exists an effective procedure can be realized by a Turing machine. Under Church's conjecture, any language in which a Turing machine can be simulated is powerful enough to perform any realizable algorithm. In other words, if you can write a given algorithm in C, it is also possible to write it in Smalltalk or assembler. In terms of computing power, all Turing-complete languages are equally powerful, that is, they are equivalent to a Turing machine. If you are interested in reading more about Turing machines and computability, see the standard textbook by Hopcroft and Ullman [HU97].

Because the static C++ level is Turing complete, there are no theoretical limits to what you can implement at that level. In practice, however, there are technical limitations, such as compilation times, compiler limits, and debugging and maintenance problems. Nevertheless, we'll see many useful applications of static programs in the remainder of this chapter.

Before describing how `Factorial<>` works, let us first explain its effect. The idea is that when the compiler instantiates `Factorial<7>`, it computes its member enumerator RET at compile time. Thus, the code generated by the C++ compiler for the whole Figure 10-5 is the same as the code generated for the following line:

```
cout << "factorial(7)= " << 5040 << endl;
```

dynamic_
factorial.cpp

```
int factorial(int n)
{ return (n==0) ? 1 : n*factorial(n-1); }

//...
cout << "factorial(7)= " << factorial(7) << endl;
```

Figure 10-4 Recursive factorial function

static_
factorial.cpp

```
template<int n>
struct Factorial
{ enum { RET = Factorial<n-1>::RET * n };
};

//the following template specialization terminates the
//recursion
template<>
struct Factorial<0>
{ enum { RET = 1 };
};

//...
cout << "factorial(7)= " << Factorial<7>::RET << endl;
```

Figure 10-5 Static code for computing the factorial at compile time

In other words, factorial of 7 is computed before even running the generated executable, and the executable contains none of the Factorial<> code!

But how does Factorial<> work? When the compiler sees Factorial<7>::RET, it instantiates the structure template Factorial<> for n=7. This involves initializing the enumerator RET with Factorial<6>::RET*7 (see Figure 10-5). At this point, the compiler also has to instantiate Factorial<6>::RET. The latter, of course, will require instantiating Factorial<n>::RET for n=5, n=4, n=3, n=2, n=1, and n=0. The last instantiation, that is, Factorial<0>, matches the template specialization for n=0, wherein RET is directly initialized to 1. This template specialization terminates the recursion, just as the conditional operator ?: terminates the recursion in the dynamic implementation in Figure 10-4. Next, the compiler will unroll its internal scope stack (the scope of each template instance being generated was pushed on this stack) and determine the value of RET in Factorial<1>, Factorial<2>,..., and Factorial<6>, and finally, in Factorial<7>, which is 5040.

We can regard Factorial<> as a *function*, which is evaluated at compile time. This particular function takes one number as an argument and returns another in its RET member. However, the arguments and return values of such functions can also be types. For example, the "function" in Figure 10-6 takes a Boolean and two types and returns a type.

NOTE

We could have defined Factorial<> as a class template rather than a structure template. In that case, however, we would have to declare the enumeration type to be a public part of the class. By using a structure template instead, it saves us from typing the access modifier public: because structure members are public by default.

NOTE

RET is an abbreviation for RETURN; we use this name to mimic the return statement of a conventional function.

As you've probably recognized, this function corresponds to an if-statement: It has a condition parameter condition, a "then" parameter Then, and an "else" parameter Else. If condition is true, it returns Then in RET. This is encoded in the base definition of the template. If condition is false, it returns Else in RET, which is encoded in the template specialization. Please note that IF<> uses *partial template specialization* (see Section 7.4.4) because we only need to specialize on the condition for condition==false, while Then and Else remain variable in the

static_if.cpp

```
template<bool condition, class Then, class Else>
struct IF
{ typedef Then RET;
};

//specialization for condition==false
template<class Then, class Else>
struct IF<false, Then, Else>
{ typedef Else RET;
};

//...
IF<(1+2>4), short, int>::RET i; //the type of i is int!
```

Figure 10-6 Implementation of IF<>

template specialization.[2] As you'll see later, IF<> is an extremely useful template. It can be viewed as a conditional control statement at the static level. We will discuss IF<> and other control statements in Section 10.11.1.1.

10.6 Functional Flavor of the Static Level

As you saw in the previous section, static C++ code is very different from dynamic C++ code. The dynamic code is imperative and object-oriented or procedural, whereas the static code is functional. In other words, writing static C++ code is similar to programming in a functional programming language, such as Lisp or ML. Finkel describes functional programming languages as follows [Fin96]:

> . . . functional programming languages have no variables, no assignment statements, and no iterative constructs. This design is based on the concept of mathematical functions, which are often defined by separation into various cases, each of which is separately defined by appealing (possibly recursively) to function applications.

The following sections summarize the programming mechanisms available in C++ at the static level.

10.6.1 Class Templates As Functions

Class templates can be used as compile-time functions: They take types and/or integers as arguments and return types or integers. We saw examples of such usage in the previous section: Factorial<> was a function operating on integers, whereas IF<> operated on types. Indeed, any class template can be viewed as a function because it takes a number of arguments and, once instantiated, yields a new type. However, when writing static code, we separate the return from the template itself. You saw this both in Factorial<> and IF<>, where the return value or type was contained in the RET member (as stated previously, RET is an abbreviation for RETURN). So, a call to a function at the compile-time level looks like this: Factorial<4>::RET.

---

2. As of this writing, only a few C++ compilers support partial specialization. Fortunately, as shown in Section 10.11.1.1, you can also implement IF<> using other techniques.

10.6.2 Integers and Types As Data

Static code operates on integers and types as data. For example, Factorial<> operates on integers and IF<> on types. In Section 10.10.5, you will learn how to represent complex data structures, such as lists or trees, as nested class templates at compile time.

10.6.3 Symbolic Names Instead of Variables

The "variables" of static C++ code are typedef-names and integral constants. They are initialized with a type or value, respectively, only once, and you cannot assign a new type or value to them later. If you need a new type or value, you simply create a new typedef-name or constant (as shown in the next section). Thus, just as in functional programming, static C++ code uses symbolic names rather than true variables.

10.6.4 Constant Initialization and typedef-Statements Instead of Assignment

The role of assignment at the compile-time level is played by integral constant initialization and typedef-statements. If you need an integer value at the static level, use an enumerator, for example:

```
//within some class template declaration
enum { IntermediateResult = Factorial<i>::RET };
```

The constant initializer will be evaluated at compile time. Alternatively, you could use a static member constant and initialize it using a constant expression, for example:

```
//within some class template declaration Foo<>
static const int IntermediateResult = Factorial<i>::RET;
```

However, Stroustrup considers this a misfeature (see [Str97, p. 249]). The direct initialization of a static member constant is only possible for integral types. If you use an enumerator instead, you won't be tempted to use floating-point numbers or other objects. Furthermore, it is still necessary to define the constant outside the class declaration to use it in a program, for example:

```
//outside of the declaration of Foo<>
template<class T>
const int Foo<T>::IntermediateResult;
```

Therefore, we use enumerators to define integer values at the compile-time level rather than static member constants.

Member types are introduced using `typedef`-statements, for example:

```
//within some class template declaration
typedef typename IF<cond,A,B>::RET IntermediateResult;
```

Please note that the keyword `typename` is required in ISO/ANSI C++ to tell the compiler that `RET` is a type.

Because a value or type can be bound at the compile-time level to a symbolic name only once, this name binding corresponds to the way functional programming works rather than to an imperative assignment. As stated previously, if you need another value, you simply introduce a new name.

10.6.5 Template Recursion Instead of Loops

As in functional programming, static C++ code is equipped with recursion rather than with loop statements, such as for- or while-loops. We have already seen an example of template recursion in Figure 10-5, where `Factorial<n-1>::RET` was used to initialize `Factorial<n>::RET`. This template recursion involved a member of a class template, but we will also see template recursion involving function templates in Section 10.12.4 (Figure 10-65). As we'll show in Section 10.11.3, it is also possible to define class templates that mimic loop statements, such as while-, do-, and for-loops. These templates basically hide recursion in their implementation and allow you to express control flow more explicitly.

Number of pending instantiations or recursive template instantiation nesting depth

There is one important detail to know about template recursion, which is the possibility of a runaway (i.e., infinite) recursion and how the compiler handles such a situation. An example of an infinitely-recursive template would be `Factorial<>` in Figure 10-5 after removing the specialization for `n==0`. The compiler catches runaway recursion by keeping track of the number of templates being instantiated at a given time. For example, when the compiler instantiates `Factorial<0>` while computing `Factorial<4>::RET`, all the following instances are said to be *pending* (i.e., their instantiation has been started, but not yet complete): `Factorial<4>`, `Factorial<3>`, `Factorial<2>`, `Factorial<1>`, and `Factorial<0>`. After the number of pending instantiations exceeds some maximum value, the compiler will stop and report an error. The maximum number of pending instantiations (which is also referred to as the maximum *recursive template instantiation nesting depth*) is compiler dependent. The ISO/ANSI C++ Standard recommends an implementation to at least support a maximum of 17. Fortunately, most compilers define a much higher maximum or even allow you to specify the maximum as a compiler option (e.g., *gcc 2.91*).

10.6.6 Conditional Operator and Template Specialization As Conditional Constructs

The conditional operator ?: and template specialization are the conditional constructs of static C++ code. We use the conditional operator whenever we need to return one of two numbers, for example:

```
template<int n1, int n2>
struct Max
{ enum { RET = (n1 > n2) ? n1 : n2 };
};
```

Template specialization is useful whenever we want to select one type out of two or more types. Similarly, as in the case of recursion, we can define class templates that mimic conventional constructs, such as if- and switch-statements. They hide the use of template specialization and make the control flow more explicit. You've already seen IF<> in Figure 10-6, a template for selecting one of two types. We'll show you the static equivalent to the switch-statement, namely SWITCH<>, in Section 10.11.1.2.

10.7 Template Metaprogramming

The mere ability to perform computations at compile time is not very exciting. After all, a C++ compiler is only a very inefficient interpreter of the static code. However, when you consider the possibility of static code to manipulate dynamic code, things get more interesting. This is actually a form of static metaprogramming, which is referred to as *template metaprogramming* (because of its dependence on C++ templates). As you will see in the remainder of this chapter, you can use template metaprogramming for a number of amazing applications including generating and optimizing code, configuring components, increasing code portability, computing constant data of programs, and more.

Template metaprogramming can be divided into several areas (see Figure 10-7) including

♦ Representing metainformation using member traits, traits classes, traits templates, and nested templates

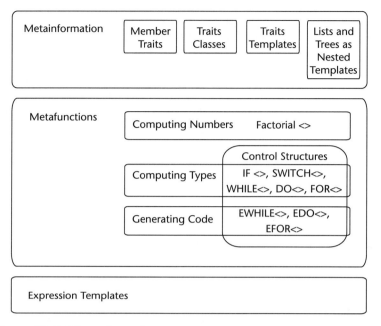

Figure 10-7 Map of template metaprogramming

♦ Writing metafunctions for computing types and numbers
♦ Using static control structures
♦ Using metafunctions to generate code
♦ Developing embedded domain-specific languages using expression templates

The following sections treat each of these areas. We will start with template metafunctions and then move to representing metainformation.

10.8 Template Metafunctions

We refer to class templates, such as Factorial<> (Figure 10-5) or IF<> (Figure 10-6), as *template metafunctions*. They are metafunctions because they operate on elements of dynamic code, that is, they are at the metalevel of the dynamic code. Factorial<> computes constant data of a program that has not yet been generated. Similarly, IF<> selects a type for a program that is yet to be generated by the compiler.

Just as you define functions that call other functions, it is natural to define metafunctions that call other metafunctions. For example, consider *k*-combinations out of *n* elements. The corresponding metaphor is taking *k* balls out of a jar containing *n* unique balls. The number of different possible combinations of *k* balls we can get in this experiment is a function of *k* and *n*. This function is referred to as the *combinatorial coefficient* or *C(k,n)*. We defined it in Figure 10-8. As you can see, *C(k,n)* uses the factorial function (denoted by the operator !), which we defined in Section 10.5.

$$C(k,n) = \frac{n!}{k! \cdot (n-k)!}$$

Figure 10-8 *Definition of C(k,n) where 0 <= k <= n must hold*

We can easily implement *C(k,n)* as a template metafunction calling `Factorial<>`. The code is shown in Figure 10-9.

Sometimes we want to use several statements before returning the value of a metafunction. To illustrate this idea, we can rewrite the metafunction from Figure 10-9 to compute the numerator and the denominator in two separate statements and perform the division in a third statement. The code is shown in Figure 10-10. This time, we define `Combinations<>` as a class template rather than a structure template. That way, the first two statements are private to `Combinations<>`. Finally, we declare and initialize `RET` in the public part.

`combinations. cpp`

```
template<int k, int n>
struct Combinations
{ enum { RET = Factorial<n>::RET /
             (Factorial<k>::RET * Factorial<n-k>::RET) };
};

// ...
cout << "C(2,4) = " << Combinations<2,4>::RET << endl;
```

Figure 10-9 *Template metafunction implementing C(k,n)*

combinations2
.cpp

```
template<int k, int n>
class Combinations
{ enum { num = Factorial<n>::RET,              //statement 1
         denom = Factorial<k>::RET *            //statement 2
                 Factorial<n-k>::RET
       };

  public:
    enum { RET = num / denom };                 //statement 3
};
```

Figure 10-10 Template metafunctions with several statements

Numeric metafunctions can directly operate only on integral numbers because floating-point numbers cannot be used as template parameters or compile-time constant initializers. In cases where you really need floating-point arithmetic, you can implement it on top of integral arithmetic. For example, you can statically represent floating-point numbers using the following template:

```
template<int mantissa_, int exponent_=0>
struct Float
{ enum {
    mantissa = mantissa_,
    exponent = exponent_
  };
  operator const float() const
  { return mantissa_ * pow(10, exponent_); }
};
```

Assuming that you have implemented the metafunction Sqrt<> for computing square root on Float<> (which we leave to you as an exercise!), you can call it for 2.5 as follows:

```
typedef Float<25,-1> F2p5;
typedef Sqrt<F2p5>::RET Result;
cout << Result();
```

10.9 Metafunctions As Arguments and Return Values of Other Metafunctions

Sometimes it is useful to pass a function as an argument to another function, for example, a comparison function to a sorting function. In C++, you can achieve this by passing a function pointer or a function object (or see Section 7.6 for other techniques). A similar facility is also available for template metafunctions. As an example, consider the function *accumulate*, which takes two parameters, namely a natural number *n* and a function *f* defined on natural numbers, and accumulates the return value of $f(i)$ for $i = 0..n$, that is, $accumulate(n, f) = f(0) + f(1) +...+ f(n)$. The implementation of *accumulate* as a metafunction is given in Figure 10-11. It uses the C++ feature of passing a class template as a template parameter. In this example, we pass the metafunction Square<> to Accumulate<> and compute the value of $0^2+1^2+2^2+3^2$.

An alternative technique for passing a metafunction as a parameter is to wrap it into a class, that is, use a member class template. This technique is demonstrated in Figure 10-12. It is particularly useful if your compiler does not support class templates as template parameters. Please note that the functionality of Square is now provided in a member template Apply<>. Because Square is a concrete type, you can simply pass it as an argument to another metafunction. The only difference is that you call Square by accessing Apply<>, that is, Square::template Apply<n>::RET. The template wrapping idiom is not only useful to simulate templates as template parameters; it is actually the only way to *return* a metafunction as a result of another metafunction, for example,

accumulate_ with_ template_as_ template_ argument.cpp

```
template<int n, template<int> class F>
struct Accumulate
{ enum { RET = Accumulate<n-1,F>::RET + F<n>::RET };
};


template<template<int> class F>
struct Accumulate<0,F>
{ enum { RET = F<0>::RET };
};


template<int n>
struct Square
{ enum { RET = n*n };
};


//...
cout << Accumulate<3,Square>::RET << endl;
```

Figure 10-11 *Passing a metafunction as an argument to another metafunction*

```
struct Square
{ template<int n>
  struct Apply
  {  enum { RET = n*n };
  };
};


template<int n, class F>
struct Accumulate
{  enum { RET = Accumulate<n-1,F>::RET + F::template
Apply<n>::RET };
};


template<class F>
struct Accumulate<0,F>
{  enum { RET = F::template Apply<0>::RET };
};


//...
cout << Accumulate<3,Square>::RET << endl;
```

*accumulate_*
*with_*
*template_*
wrapping.cpp

Figure 10-12 *An alternative way to pass metafunctions as arguments*

typedef Square RET;. We will actually use this idiom for the latter purpose in an alternative implementation of IF<> in Section 10.11.1.1.

10.10 Representing Metainformation

In template metaprograms, static code operates on dynamic code. However, in order to manipulate elements of the dynamic code, such as types of runtime objects, you need to know something about them. For example, some static code in a numeric application can be responsible for selecting the types for intermediate variables depending on the type of the input variables (you'll see a concrete example of this in Section 10.10.4). This task requires the knowledge of some characteristics of the numeric types that can be used for the variables. The relevant characteristics may include the value range covered by a numeric type and its precision. Another example where you need to represent the properties of types for static metacode is the static metacode generating algorithms that operate on matrix types. The static code will be interested in matrix characteristics, such as matrix shape and density.

Type characteristics are also referred to as *traits*. The first question about traits is how to encode them. If you want to use traits in static code, there are only two alternatives: You encode them as integral constants or types. The second question is how to associate traits with the type they describe. There are three ways to do this.

♦ *Member traits:* Define each trait as a member type or constant of the type it describes
♦ *Traits classes:* Encapsulate several traits in a separate class
♦ *Traits templates:* Define a class template to hold the traits of a family of types

We'll explain each of these techniques in the following three subsections. After that, we'll show you how to represent more complex metadata, such as lists and trees, using nested templates.

10.10.1 Member Traits

The simplest way to associate a trait with a type is to define it as a member of the type. For example, a statically allocated vector may use this method to advertise its size and element type:

```
template<class ElementType_, int size_>
class Vector
{
public:
  typedef ElementType_ ElementType;
  enum { size = size_ };
  //...
private:
  ElementType elems_[size];
  //...
};
```

We often use member traits to define type identifiers. Type identifiers are necessary whenever static code has to distinguish between several types. The following C++ code demonstrates this idea. FooBase defines type identifiers for the types Foo1, Foo2, and Foo3:

```
struct FooBase
{ enum { fooBase, foo1, foo2, foo3 };
  enum { id = fooBase };
```

```
};
struct Foo1 : FooBase
{ enum { id = foo1 };
  //...
};
struct Foo2 : FooBase
{ enum { id = foo2 };
  //...
};
struct Foo3 : FooBase
{ enum { id = foo3 };
  //...
};
```

Given a typedef-name SomeFoo, which refers to one of the "foo"-types, we can test whether it refers to Foo2 as follows: SomeFoo::id == SomeFoo::foo2. We'll use this technique in Section 14.4.1.2 to implement domain-specific configuration descriptors.

10.10.2   Traits Classes

In most cases, a type has many traits, and we find it convenient to tie them together into one bundle. This can be done by defining the traits as members of an extra class, which we refer to as a *traits class* [Mye95]. The big advantage of a traits class is that it lets you handle a set of traits as a single piece of metainformation. For example, you can easily pass it as an argument to a template metafunction or to a component type rather than having to pass each trait separately. We have already seen the use of traits classes to represent configuration repositories in Section 7.11.2, that is, traits classes containing the configuration knowledge of a component. The following C++ code gives an example of a traits class that describes the properties of a diagonal, 10-by-10 matrix of doubles. The traits class Config is defined as a member class of the matrix type:

```
enum MatrixShapes {rectangular, square, diagonal,
                   lower_triang, upper_triang};
```

NOTE

You'll find an alternative technique to test whether two typenames refer to the same type at compile time in a note in Section 14.4.1.2.

```
class Diagonal10x10MatrixOfDoubles
{
public:
  // traits class
  struct Config
  { typedef double ElementType;
    enum {
      rows = 10,
      cols = 10,
      shape = diagonal };
  };
  // operations and data members
  double at(int i, int j)
  //...
};
```

Of course, traits classes can also be defined outside the types they describe. In Section 12.8, we'll show you how to generate components and their configuration repositories using template metafunctions.

10.10.3 Traits Templates

Another technique to associate traits with types is to use class templates. The idea is to specialize a class template for different types and have each specialization contain the traits of one type. Such a class template is referred to as a *traits template* [BN94, p. 574 and Mye95]. As an example, we take a look at the traits template numeric_limits<>, which is defined in ISO/ANSI C++ in the header <limits> of the Language Support Library. This traits template defines the characteristics of numeric types, such as floating-point and integer types and bool. It defines a large number of characteristics including an indicator, which specifies whether a type is integral or not (is_integer), the maximum number of decimal digits the type can represent (digits10), the maximum finite value the type can represent (max()), the minimum finite value (min()), the numeric precision (epsilon()), and more.

A traits template works like a lookup table. You use the type whose traits you are interested in as a lookup key. For example, to find out the maximum number of decimal digits that can be represented by a float, you pass float as an argument to numeric_limits<> and access the trait digits10:

```
cout << numeric_limits<float>::digits10;
```

How is a traits template, such as `numeric_limits<>`, implemented? The idea is to specialize it for each type you want to define traits for. You define the traits of a type as members of the traits template specialization for that type. In order for both static and generic code to work properly on a traits template, the base template and its specializations have to define the same set of traits. The base definition of `numeric_limits<>` in `<limits>` may look like this:

```cpp
template<class T>
class numeric_limits
{
public:
  static const bool has_denorm = false;
  static const bool has_denorm_loss = false;
  static const bool has_infinity = false;
  static const bool has_quiet_NaN = false;
  static const bool has_signaling_NaN = false;
  static const bool is_bounded = false;
  static const bool is_exact = false;
  static const bool is_iec559 = false;
  static const bool is_integer = false;
  static const bool is_modulo = false;
  static const bool is_signed = false;
  static const bool is_specialized = false;
  static const bool tinyness_before = false;
  static const bool traps = false;
  static const float_round_style round_style = round_toward_zero;
  static const int digits = 0;
  static const int digits10 = 0;
  static const int max_exponent = 0;
  static const int max_exponent10 = 0;
  static const int min_exponent = 0;
  static const int min_exponent10 = 0;
  static const int radix = 0;
  static T denorm_min() throw();
  static T epsilon() throw();
  static T infinity() throw();
  static T max() throw();
  static T min() throw();
  static T quiet_NaN() throw();
  static T round_error() throw();
  static T signaling_NaN() throw();
};
```

Next, we have to provide a specialization of the base template for each numeric type. The specializations for built-in types, such as int or float, are defined in <limits>. Each specialization provides the appropriate implementation of each trait. For example, a specialization for float may look like this (not all members are shown):

```
template<>
class numeric_limits<float>
{
public:
  //...
  static const bool is_specialized = true;  // yes, we have
                                             // metainformation
                                             // about float
  //...
  static const int digits = 24;
  static const int digits10 = 6;
  //...
  static const int max_exponent10 = 38;
  //...
  static float min() throw()      { return 1.17549435E-38F; }
  //...
};
```

The member is_specialized being true indicates that numeric_limits<> is specialized for float. The value of is_specialized in the base template was false. If is_specialized is false, the remaining traits have no meaning. Similarly, there are other traits that indicate the validity of some other traits. For example, max_exponent10 is only meaningful for floating-point numbers, that is, it is not meaningful for numbers where is_integer is true. Please note that some traits are defined as integral static member constants and some as static member functions. The former, for example, digits10 or max_exponent10, can be used by both static and dynamic code. Static member functions are required for noninteger values, and they can only be utilized by dynamic code.

One of the great properties of traits templates is the possibility to extend them to cover new types without having to touch the existing code. For example, you can easily add your own specialization of numeric_traits<> for a new user-defined number type. Adding new traits to a traits template is not that easy because it requires access to the entire source code. But the task can often be simplified if you derive the traits template specializations from common base classes. For example, some traits in `numeric_traits<>` are equal for all integral types, so it makes sense to provide a common base class for all the template specializations for integral types:

```
class IntNumBase
{
public:
  static const bool is_bounded = true;
  static const bool is_exact = true;
  static const bool is_integer = true;
  static const bool is_modulo = true;    .
  static const bool is_specialized = true;
  static const int radix = 2;
};
```

This base class can be used to define specializations of `numeric_traits<>` for integral types, for example:

```
template<>
class numeric_limits<short> : public IntNumBase
{
public:
  // several traits are inherited from IntNumBase
  // define remaining traits here
  // ...
};
```

Similarly, you can define an appropriate base class for the template specializations for floating-point types. Because traits can be overridden in a subclass, you can also use the base class to define some reasonable defaults for a family of types and still have several template specializations provide their own implementations.

Traits templates are particularly useful if we want to associate traits with built-in types (such as `int` or `float`) or types whose sources cannot be modified. In these cases, we cannot use member traits because we cannot add new members to these types. Traits templates do not have this problem.

Traits help us to improve code portability because the application code can use them to find out about the specifics of a particular platform. For example, `numeric_traits<>` allows us to determine the properties of numeric types on a particular platform.

10.10.4 Example: Using Template Metafunctions and Traits Templates to Implement Type Promotions

Traits are the key ingredient that allow static code to usefully manipulate types implementing runtime objects. We will now illustrate this point using an example of a template metafunction, which performs *type promotions*. Type promotions are used in mix-mode arithmetic to avoid loss of precision. For example, in C++, integral and floating-point types can be mixed freely in assignments and arithmetic expressions. Whenever possible, values are converted so as not to loose information. In general, integral operands will be converted to floating-point types whenever any of the other operands is floating-point. Furthermore, short types, such as char or float, will automatically be *promoted* to natural sizes for doing arithmetic, for example, char and short are promoted to int, and float is promoted to double. Type promotions for number arithmetic are done automatically by the compiler. However, when implementing numeric libraries, such as a matrix library or a numeric vectors library, these automatic promotions are not sufficient. In particular, we often need to automatically select appropriate types for intermediate results depending on the types of input variables. For example, the element type of the product of two matrices depends on the element types of the argument matrices. In this particular example, the resulting element type is the conceptually larger one of both argument element types, for example, multiplying a matrix of ints and a matrix of doubles results in a matrix of doubles. Thus, we need a type promotion metafunction that takes two number types and returns the conceptually larger one.

One way to implement a type promotion metafunction is to define a general class template implementing some standard promotion and specialize it for each nonstandard case (see Figure 10-13). Promote<> takes two types as arguments and always returns the second argument. This is correct for some pairs of types, such as int and double. However, it is not correct for double and int. In the latter case, we have to specialize the general template to return the first parameter rather than the second one. We have to provide such specialization for all cases that deviate from the standard case, which is quite a long list.

Fortunately, our IF<> from Figure 10-6 allows a much more concise implementation of Promote<>. The idea is to compare the characteristics of the argument types and return the larger type based on the comparisons. The C++ Standard Library provides characteristics of built-in numeric types in the traits template numeric_limits<>, which we discussed in the previous section.

```
template <class A ,class B>
struct Promote
{ typedef B RET;
};


template<>
struct Promote<double,int>
{ typedef double RET;
};


// And many more specializations...
```

*tedious_*
promote.h

Figure 10-13 *The laborious way to implement* Promote<>

Given the information in numeric_limits<>, Promote<> can do its job as follows: First, we compare the exponents (i.e., max_exponent10) of the two argument types. A type is considered to be smaller if its exponent is smaller (please note that the exponent of integral types is always 0). If the exponents of both types are equal, the type with the smaller number of digits (i.e., digits) is the smaller one. The latter comparison will never happen between an integral and a nonintegral type because this case has already been

promote.h

```
template<class A, class B>
class Promote
{
  enum {
    max_exp_A = numeric_limits<A>::max_exponent10,
    max_exp_B = numeric_limits::max_exponent10,
    digits_A  = numeric_limits<A>::digits,
    digits_B  = numeric_limits::digits
  };
public:
  typedef IF<
    max_exp_A < max_exp_B || ( max_exp_A == max_exp_B &&
                               digits_A < digits_B ),
    B,
    A>::RET RET;
};
```

Figure 10-14 *A concise implementation of* Promote<>

covered by the first comparison. All we need to do is put these comparisons in the condition of an IF<>. This is shown in Figure 10-14.

10.10.5   Compile-Time Lists and Trees As Nested Templates

As stated previously, template metaprograms operate on integers and types as their data. When talking about data, we also have to talk about data structures. We have already seen a basic data structuring mechanism in the context of traits, which is aggregating constants and types as members of other types. This is a kind of struct at the compile-time level. However, there are cases in template metaprogramming where we need more complex data structures, such as lists or trees. For example, the metafunction SWITCH<>, which is the switch-statement of the compile-time level, will take a list of case-statements as an argument. Thus, we need a compile-time list representation to implement SWITCH<> (see Section 10.11.1.2). Furthermore, in Section 14.4.2, we'll discuss implementing domain-specific languages embedded into library APIs. The implementation uses so-called expression templates to generate parse trees of expressions at compile time. These parse trees are manipulated by template metafunctions. Thus, we also need a way to represent trees at the compile-time level.

It turns out that complex compile-time data structures can be easily represented using nested templates. The purpose of this section is to demonstrate this idea by showing you how to implement compile-time singly linked lists and metafunctions operating on such lists. Abstractly, a singly linked list can be viewed as a chain of head-and-tail pairs. This is illustrated in Figure 10-15. The head of each pair in this chain contains an actual list element, and the tail points to the rest of the list. The tail of the last pair points to an element representing an empty list, that is, nil.

Lists of this kind are both simple and powerful. Indeed, they are the only data structure available in Lisp, and this does not impose any limitation on the expressiveness of this programming language. In Lisp, you can create a list by calling the list constructor cons,

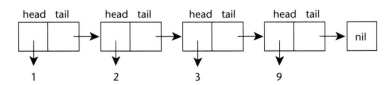

Figure 10-15 *Example of a singly linked list with four elements*

which takes an element and another list, several times. For example, the following Lisp code:

```
(cons 1 (cons 2 (cons 3 (cons 9 nil))))
```

creates this list:

```
(1 2 3 9)
```

(where `nil` represents the empty list). We can rewrite this code in the functional notation as follows:

```
cons(1, cons(2, cons(3, cons(9, nil))))
```

This code can be easily simulated at the compile-time level in C++ using nested templates:

```
Cons<1, Cons<2, Cons<3, Cons<9, End> > > >
```

The idea is to nest templates taking two arguments, namely a head and a tail. The exception is `End`, which represents the empty list. The implementation of `End` and `Cons<>` is given in Figure 10-16. `Cons<>` takes `head_` and `Tail_` as arguments and publishes them as `head` and `Tail`. `End` also defines `head` and `Tail` members, although the reason might not be so obvious to you at this point.

static_lists.cpp

```
// tag marking the end of a list
const int endValue = ~(~0u >> 1); //initialize with the
                                  //smallest int

struct End
{ enum    { head = endValue };
  typedef End Tail;
};

template<int head_, class Tail_ = End>
struct Cons
{ enum    { head = head_ };
  typedef Tail_ Tail;
};
```

Figure 10-16 *C++ implementation of a singly linked compile-time list*

In Section 10.11.1.3, you'll see that metafunctions operating on lists require that End defines the same members as Cons<>. This represents a more general design principle, which we'll discuss.

Template metafunctions can process lists recursively. For example, the metafunction Length<> counts the number of elements in a list (see Figure 10-17).

Examples of two other useful metafunctions are IsEmpty<> and Last<>. IsEmpty<> tests whether a list is empty or not (see Figure 10-18). Last<> returns the last element of a list (see Figure 10-19).

static_lists.cpp

```cpp
template<class List>
struct Length
{ // make a recursive call to Length and pass Tail of the
  // list as the argument
  enum { RET = Length<typename List::Tail>::RET+1 };
};


// stop the recursion if we've got to End
template<>
struct Length<End>
{ enum { RET = 0 };
};


//...
typedef Cons<1,Cons<2,Cons<3> > > list1;
cout << Length<list1>::RET << endl; // prints 3
```

Figure 10-17 Length<> *returns the length of a list*

static_lists.cpp

```cpp
template<class List>
struct IsEmpty
{ enum { RET = false };
};


template<>
struct IsEmpty<End>
{ enum { RET = true };
};
```

Figure 10-18 IsEmpty<>

static_lists.cpp

```
template<class List>
struct Last
{ enum {
    RET = IsEmpty<typename List::Tail>::RET
          ? List::head
          : Last<typename List::Tail>::RET
  };
};


template<>
struct Last<End>
{ enum { RET = endValue };
};
```

Figure 10-19 `Last<>`

Append1<> is an example of a metafunction for manipulating lists (see Figure 10-20). It takes a list and a number and returns a new list computed by appending the number to the end of the original list. The recursion in `Append1<>` is terminated using partial specialization for `List` equal to `End` (n remains variable).

Figure 10-21 shows a general `Append<>` for appending a list to another list.

Figure 10-22 demonstrates the use of our list metafunctions.

Other list metafunctions, such as `Reverse<List>`, `CopyUpTo<X, List>`, `RestPast<X,List>`, `Replace<X,Y,List>`, and so on can be

static_lists.cpp

```
template<class List, int n>
struct Append1
{ typedef
    Cons<List::head,
         typename Append1<typename List::Tail, n>::RET
    > RET;
};


template<int n>
struct Append1<End, n>
{ typedef Cons<n> RET;
};
```

Figure 10-20 `Append1<>`

static_lists.cpp

```
template<class List1, class List2>
struct Append
{ typedef Cons<List1::head,
            typename Append<typename List1::Tail, List2>::RET
        > RET;
};


template<class List2>
struct Append<End, List2>
{ typedef List2 RET;
};
```

Figure 10-21 Append<>

implemented in a similar way as Append<> (we leave it to you as an exercise).

We can make our compile-time list more general by declaring the first parameter of Cons<> to be a type rather than an int and by providing a type wrapper for numbers (see Figure 10-23).

static_lists.cpp

```
void main()
{ typedef Cons<1,Cons<2,Cons<3> > > list1;

  cout << Length<list1>::RET << endl;   // prints 3
  cout << Last<list1>::RET << endl;     // prints 3

  typedef Append1<list1, 9>::RET list2;

  cout << Length<list2>::RET << endl;   // prints 4
  cout << Last<list2>::RET << endl;     // prints 9

  typedef Append<list1, list2>::RET list3;

  cout << Length<list3>::RET << endl;   // prints 7
  cout << Last<list3>::RET << endl;     // prints 9
}
```

Figure 10-22 main() *demonstrating the use of the list metafunctions*

```
template <int n>
struct Int
{ enum { value = n };
};

struct End
{ typedef Int<endValue> head;
  typedef End Tail;
};

template<class head_, class Tail_ = End>
struct Cons
{ typedef head_ head;
  typedef Tail_ Tail;
};
```

Figure 10-23 *More general list*

Such a list can contain both numbers and types as elements.
More importantly, you can have a list with lists as elements, for
example:

```
Cons<Int<1>, Cons<Cons<Int<21>, Cons<Int<31> > >, Cons<Int<22>
> > >
```

This list actually represents a tree shown in Figure 10-24.
Interestingly, this technique allows us to implement a simple Lisp
as a template metaprogram (see [CE98, Cza98]).

Of course, you can also provide more explicit templates for
representing trees. For example, binary trees can be represented
using the templates in Figure 10-25.

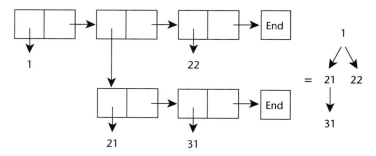

Figure 10-24 *Representing trees as nested lists*

```
struct BTEnd
{ enum { val = endValue };
  typedef BTEnd Left;
  typedef BTEnd Right;
};


template<int val_, class Left_=BTEnd, Right_=BTEnd>
struct BinTreeNode
{ enum { val = val_ };
  typedef Left_ Left;
  typedef Right_ Right;
};
//...
typedef BinTreeNode<1, BinTreeNode<Int<2> >, BinTreeNode<Int<2> > > aTree;
```

Figure 10-25 *Templates for representing binary trees*

10.11   Compile-Time Control Structures

As discussed in Section 10.6, the control flow in template metaprograms is defined using recursion (recursive templates), selective matching (template specializations), and the conditional operator ?:. In contrast to the latter, recursive templates and template specializations do not express control flow explicitly, that is, the way you are used to doing it in dynamic C++ code using the imperative control structures if, switch, while, do, and for. Fortunately, the selection statements if and switch can be conveniently simulated using metafunctions, which is demonstrated in the following subsection. This is also possible for looping statements, although, as you'll see in Section 10.11.2, the result is slightly less satisfying than in the case of selection statements. Nevertheless, looping metafunctions allow you to easily translate algorithms expressed using imperative looping constructs into static code. We'll also make a surprising observation in the context of looping: Concise recursive formulations often lead to efficient static code although as you may know, the opposite is true for dynamic code!

10.11.1   Explicit Selection Constructs (?:, IF<>, and SWITCH<>)

As stated earlier, the condition operator ?: can be used in static code to explicitly select one of two integral constants. You have already seen an analogous construct for selecting one of two types, which was the metafunction IF<> in Figure 10-6. Both constructs represent control flow explicitly and correspond to the selection constructs ?: and if found in C++ at the runtime level.

10.11.1.1 Implementing IF<> without Partial Template Specialization

Let us take a look again at the familiar implementation of IF<> in Figure 10-26. As you can see, this implementation uses partial template specialization. The base template returns Then, whereas the partial template specialization for condition==false returns Else. Unfortunately, many C++ compilers still do not support partial template specialization. The good news is, however, that you can implement IF<> using full template specialization and member templates. Let us take a look at how this works.

The main idea behind IF<> is to have two template implementations, one returning Then and the other returning Else, and to select the appropriate template based on condition. Instead of implementing the templates as a base template and its specialization (as in Figure 10-26), we can also define them as two separate templates SelectThen and SelectElse. Well, to be more precise, we implement them as structs containing templates as members (see Figure 10-27). This is an application of the template wrapping idiom from Section 10.9, so that we can return them as results

if.cpp

```
template<bool condition, class Then, class Else>
struct IF
{ typedef Then RET;
};

//specialization for condition==false
template<class Then, class Else>
struct IF<false, Then, Else>
{ typedef Else RET;
};

//...
IF<(1+2>4), short, int>::RET i; //the type of i is int!
```

Figure 10-26 IF<> implementation using partial template specialization. (For convenience, we have shown the implementation from Figure 10-6 here again.)

```
namespace intimate
{ //selector template selecting ThenType
  struct SelectThen
  { template<class ThenType, class ElseType>
    struct Result
    { typedef ThenType RET; };
  };

  //selector template selecting ElseType
  struct SelectElse
  { template<class ThenType, class ElseType>
    struct Result
    { typedef ElseType RET; };
  };

  //choose selector template depending on condition
  template<bool condition>
  struct ChooseSelector
  { typedef SelectThen RET; };

  template<>
  struct ChooseSelector<false>
  { typedef SelectElse RET; };

}; //end of namespace intimate

//IF<>
template<bool condition, class ThenType, class ElseType>
class IF
{ typedef typename
    intimate::ChooseSelector<condition>::RET Selector;
public:
  typedef typename
    Selector::template Result<ThenType,ElseType>::RET RET;
};
```

*if_without_*
*partial_*
specialization.
cpp

Figure 10-27 IF<> *implementation using full template specialization and member templates*

of another metafunction. We then need the metafunction
ChooseSelector<>, which returns SelectThen or SelectElse
depending on the condition. This template uses full template specialization to do its job. Finally, we call ChooseSelector<> in IF<>

to choose the appropriate selector template and use the chosen selector template to return the appropriate type. The keyword `template` after the scope operator tells the compiler that `Code` is a member template (otherwise the character following `Code` would be interpreted as a less-than-operator).

10.11.1.2   Switch Construct (`SWITCH<>`)

`IF<>` allows us to select one of two types. But sometimes we need to select one type out of more than two types. Obviously, we can use template specialization to do that, for example:

```
template<int tag>
class Type
{ // default implementation...
};

template<>
class Type<1>
{ // implementation A ...
};

template<>
class Type<2>
{ // implementation B ...
};

template<>
class Type<3>
{ // implementation C ...
};

//...
typedef Type<1+1> ResultType; // implementation B is selected
```

However, this code does not make the control flow explicit because the list of alternative type choices is not displayed at the instantiation point. Furthermore, the requirement could be to select one of several existing types, which are not necessarily implemented as a family of template specializations. What we need is an explicit switch construct similar to the switch-statement found at the runtime level. As you know, a switch-statement takes an integral expression and a list of case statements. Each case statement is tagged with an integral constant. The execution of a switch-statement involves evaluating the integral expression and finding and executing the case statement whose tag corresponds to the expression value.[3] A case statement may also be associated with a *default tag*, which matches any expression value.

We will implement our static switch construct as the template metafunction SWITCH<>. This metafunction takes an integral expression and a list of cases, where each case is a pair of an integral tag and a type. The job of this metafunction is to select the first case matching the expression value, that is, the first case whose tag is equal to the expression value or to some designated default tag, and to return the type contained in this case. We can implement the case list using the list techniques discussed in Section 10.10.5. Before we take a look at the implementation details, let us first show you how SWITCH<> is used in client code. Figure 10-28 gives a simple example. Because the first argument to SWITCH<> evaluates to 0, the default case is selected and type D is returned.

The case list from Figure 10-28 is illustrated in Figure 10-29. As you can see, each case is represented by the template CASE<> with three members: tag, Type, and Next. The case list is terminated with NilCase. The implementation of CASE<> and NilCase is given in Figure 10-30. DEFAULT is a tag value used for the default case. Please note that we follow the convention to write elements of static control structures appearing in user code in all capital letters, for example, DEFAULT, CASE<>, SWITCH<>, and IF<>. This helps us to clearly distinguish static control flow structures from other code.

switch.cpp

```
struct A {static void execute() { cout << "A" << endl;} };
struct B {static void execute() { cout << "B" << endl;} };
struct D {static void execute() { cout << "Default" << endl;} };

// ...
SWITCH<(1+1-2),
    CASE<1,A,
    CASE<2,B,
    CASE<DEFAULT,D > > >
>::RET::execute();              //prints "Default"
```

Figure 10-28 *Example of using* SWITCH<>

---

3. To be more precise, this characterization assumes that each case statement is terminated by a *break-statement*.

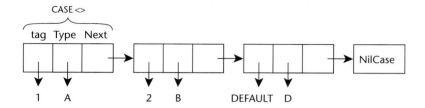

Figure 10-29 *Example of a case list*

The implementation of SWITCH<> is given in Figure 10-31. SWITCH<> takes an integer value and a case list and recursively searches for the first matching case, that is, the first case whose tag is equal to the first SWITCH<> argument or DEFAULT. If such a case is found, its Type member is returned. If no matching case is found, NilCase is returned. This is encoded in the template specialization, which terminates the recursion.

An implementation of SWITCH<> without partial template specialization is given in Section 10.11.1.4.

10.11.1.3 Taking Advantage of Lazy Behavior

As you may recall, template instantiation is the process of creating a concrete function, class, or member of a template class out of a template. Template instantiation is usually done lazily and we can take advantage of this laziness when writing static code. Before

switch.cpp

```
const int DEFAULT = ~(~0u >> 1); //initialize with the smallest
                                 //int

struct NilCase
{};

template <int tag_, class Type_, class Next_ = NilCase>
struct CASE
{ enum { tag = tag_ };
  typedef Type_ Type;
  typedef Next_ Next;
};
```

Figure 10-30 *Implementation of case lists*

```
template<int tag, class Case>
class SWITCH
{ typedef typename Case::Next NextCase;
  enum {
    caseTag = Case::tag,
    found   = (caseTag == tag || caseTag == DEFAULT)
  };
public:
  typedef IF<found,
             typename Case::Type,
             typename SWITCH<tag, NextCase>::RET
          >::RET RET;
};


template<int tag>
class SWITCH<tag, NilCase>
{public:
  typedef NilCase RET;
};
```

switch.cpp

Figure 10-31 *Implementation of* SWITCH<>

explaining how this works, let's take a look at the instantiation process itself.

Partial versus full instantiation

An instantiation may be either *partial* or *full*. A partial instantiation of a class template is like a declaration of an ordinary class when no body is supplied. Similarly, a partial instantiation of a function template is like a declaration of a function. On the other hand, a full instantiation involves generating a class or function definition, that is, it includes the body. However, it is important to note that the full instantiation of a class template implies only that the members of the instance are partially but not necessarily fully instantiated.

The C++ compiler (or the linker) instantiates a template on two occasions. First, you can force the instantiation of a template for a given set of arguments by using the following special syntax:

```
template class vector<int>; //requests the full instantiation
                            //of vector<int>
```

This is referred to as an *explicit instantiation*, and it causes the full instantiation of vector<int> as well as its members. Second, whenever you use a template with a given set of arguments, the compiler (or the linker) will make sure that the template is fully instantiated for these arguments at the point where the instantiated function, class, or member is really needed. This is called *implicit instantiation*. There is an important point to note about implicit instantiation: The use of a template supplied with arguments (e.g., vector<int>) in a program causes a partial instantiation of the template for these arguments, but not all kinds of uses cause a full instantiation. A full instantiation occurs at the point where the use of the type requires it to be a complete type. In other words, it is done as soon as necessary, but no sooner. We say that the implicit instantiation occurs *lazily*.[4] For example, consider the following code:

```
typedef vector<int> IntVector; //vector<int> is partially
                               //instantiated
IntVector *piv; //vector<int> is partially instantiated
IntVector iv; //vector<int> gets fully instantiated
```

The first line causes vector<int> to be partially instantiated (the compiler basically makes an entry for this type in its symbol table). The second line only requires vector<int> to be partially instantiated, so nothing happens. Finally, the last line requires the type vector<int> to be fully defined and therefore, it causes the full instantiation of vector<int>. Please note, however, that this causes the partial instantiation of the members of vector<int>, except for the standard constructor, which is called in this declaration and needs to be fully instantiated, and the members called by the constructor.

As stated previously, partial instantiation does not instantiate the body, so it can be generated based on an incomplete template, for example:

```
template<class T> class A;
A<int> *x;
```

---

4. It is important to note that the ISO/ANSI C++ Standard requires this laziness. This not only has the positive effect of avoiding unnecessary code bloat, it also has semantic consequences. For example, it is perfectly okay for some members of a template to be semantically incorrect for some template arguments (e.g., they could call undefined member functions on the arguments) as long as they are not used! Eager instantiation would make such programs invalid.

Even though no body has been supplied for the class template A, a partial instantiation of A<int> can be produced. If you declared x to be A<int>, you would get an error.

Accessing a member of an instance of a class template causes the full instantiation of the instance, for example:

```
typedef vector<int> IntVector; //vector<int> is partially
                                //instantiated
typedef IntVector::iterator Iter; //vector<int> is fully
                                   //instantiated

IntVector iv;
Iter i;
...
i = iv.begin(); //vector<int>::begin() is fully instantiated
```

You have to take the template instantiation behavior of C++ into account when writing static code. Let us illustrate this point with a simple example. Consider the dynamic implementation of the factorial function in Figure 10-32.

The recursion of factorial() terminates for n==0 (we assume that the function is called for n=>0). This is so because the conditional operator ?: evaluates the selected expression only. In other words, for n==0, the expression (n==0) ? 1 : n*factorial(n-1) evaluates to 1 and factorial(n-1) is not called. We also say that the conditional operator behaves lazily: only the *needed* argument expression is evaluated. A naive translation of the dynamic implementation into static code is given in Figure 10-33.

This code doesn't work. Due to the access to the RET member of Factorial<n-1>, Factorial<n-1> is fully instantiated. Thus, Factorial<n-1>::RET is still computed, even though the result is not selected. As a result, the recursion does not terminate for n==0. The compiler will stop the recursion at some point and report an error. One way to fix this is to terminate the recursion by specializing Factorial<> for n==0 as in Figure 10-5. Another solution is to avoid requesting RET when not needed. This is shown in Figure 10-34.

*dynamic_
factorial.cpp*

```
int factorial(int n)
{ return (n==0) ? 1 : n*factorial(n-1); }
```

Figure 10-32 *Dynamic implementation of a recursive factorial function*

*infinite_*
recursion.cpp

```
template<int n>
struct Factorial
{ enum { RET = (n==0) ? 1 : Factorial<n-1>::RET * n };
};
```

Figure 10-33 *Naive static implementation of the factorial function*

The main idea behind this implementation is the fact that RET is requested from Factorial<n-1> only for n>0 because, for n==0, PreviousFactorial refers to Stop. In other words, Factorial<-1> is never fully instantiated and we avoid infinite recursion that way. As you will see in Section 10.11.3.1, this technique often leads to a more compact implementation of recursive metafunctions.

The unexpected instantiation of arguments may also catch you by surprise when using IF<> or SWITCH<>. These constructs behave lazily; however, their lazy behavior is easily defeated if you use the usual "metafunction calls" as arguments, for example:

```
typedef IF<true, F1<A>::RET, F2::RET>::RET Result;
```

Both the then-argument and the else-argument are instantiated, although only the first one is returned. This is because both arguments involve accessing the RET member. However, the instantiation of both arguments may be undesirable because the unused argument could be invalid, for example, it could cause infinite

*factorial_*
lazy.cpp

```
struct Stop
{ enum { RET = 1 };
};

template<int n>
struct Factorial
{ typedef
    IF<n==0, Stop, Factorial<n-1> >::RET PreviousFactorial;
  enum { RET = (n==0)
              ? PreviousFactorial::RET
              : PreviousFactorial::RET * n };
};
```

Figure 10-34 *Static implementation of the factorial function based on lazy instantiation behavior*

recursion as in the case on `Factorial<>` in Figure 10-33. We can avoid this problem by moving the access to `RET` behind `IF<>`:

```
typedef IF<true, F1<A>, F2 >::RET::RET Result;
```

In this case, only `F1<A>::RET` is instantiated. You should remember this when writing static code.

The way C++ instantiates templates also influences the design of compile-time data structures. In particular, it explains the reason why we defined `head` and `Tail` in `End` (see Figure 10-16 in Section 10.10.5). As you may remember, we defined `head` and `Tail` in `Cons<>` to export its parameters, but it was not necessarily obvious why we also needed them in `End`. In order to understand this decision, consider the list metafunction `Every2nd<>` in Figure 10-35. This metafunction takes a list and copies every second element in the list into the result list. Each recursion step of this metafunction "consumes" two list nodes. It first accesses the second node on line #1. If the second node is not an `End`, it puts the `head` of this node into the result list and calls itself on the `tail` of the second node (line #3). Now consider a call to `Every2nd<>` on a list with one element. The result is `End`, which is returned on line #2. However, this is not all that happens here. Because we explicitly refer to

every2nd.cpp

```
template<class List>
class Every2nd
{ typedef typename List::Tail Tail;                        //#1
public:
  typedef
    IF<
      IsEmpty<Tail>::RET,
      End,                                                 //#2
      Cons<Tail::head,
           typename Every2nd<typename Tail::Tail>::RET>//#3
    >::RET RET;
};

template<>
class Every2nd<End>
{public:
  typedef End RET;
};
```

Figure 10-35 `Every2nd<>` *processes two list nodes at a time*

`Tail::head` and `Tail::Tail` on line #3, both members will be instantiated. This is the reason why `End` needs to have the members `head` and `Tail`. As stated previously, `Every2nd<>` looks at two list nodes at a time. But you can have metafunctions that look at three or more nodes at a time (e.g., `Every3rd<>` would look at three nodes at a time). Therefore, not only does `End::Tail` have to be valid, but also `End::Tail::Tail`, `End::Tail::Tail::Tail`, and so on. This requirement is satisfied by defining `End::Tail` to be `End` (see Figure 10-16).

10.11.1.4 `SWITCH<>` without Partial Template Specialization

The `SWITCH<>` implementation given in Section 10.11.1.2 uses partial template specialization to terminate the recursion on a case list. Because many compilers still do not support this feature, we'll give you an alternative implementation of `SWITCH<>` without partial template specialization.

The code is shown in Figure 10-36. It is similar to the implementation in Figure 10-31 with a few exceptions. `NilCase` also has the member `tag`, which is used to detect the end of a case list. In the original implementation in Figure 10-31, recursion is terminated by the partial specialization for `Case==NilCase`. In the new implementation, the recursion is terminated by the extra `IF<>` on line #1. `NextSwitch` refers to a recursive call only if `NextCase` is not `NilCase`. This usage of `IF<>` corresponds to the one in `Factorial<>` in Figure 10-34.

10.11.2 Template Recursion As a Looping Construct

As you already know, the basic looping mechanism in template metaprogramming is template recursion. As far as looping goes, recursion is not only sufficient for coding any algorithm, it is usually the most appropriate mechanism in many cases. Recursion often leads to a very concise code. However, there are also cases where a simple recursive definition of an algorithm is very inefficient. Such cases contribute to the misguided perception that recursion is inefficient in general. A classic example of a problem having a simple, but inefficient, recursive formulation is computing Fibonacci numbers. Fibonacci numbers are defined as follows:

$$fib_{n+1} = fib_n + fib_{n-1} \quad \text{where } n > 0$$

and $fib_0 = 0$ and $fib_1 = 1$.

A direct recursive implementation is given in Figure 10-37. Please note that a call to `fib()` for *n>1* results in two other calls to

*switch_without_
partial_
specialization.
cpp*

```
// case list
const int DEFAULT  = ~(~0u >> 1); //initialize with the
                                  //smallest int
const int nilValue = DEFAULT+1;

struct NilCase
{ enum {tag = nilValue};
  typedef NilCase RET;
};


template <int tag_,class Type_,class Next_ = NilCase>
struct CASE
{ enum {tag = tag_};
  typedef Type_ Type;
  typedef Next_ Next;
};


// SWITCH<>
template <int tag, class Case>
class SWITCH
{ typedef typename Case::Next NextCase;
  enum { caseTag = Case::tag,
         nextTag = NextCase::tag,
         found   = (caseTag == tag || caseTag == DEFAULT)
       };
  typedef IF<(nextTag == nilValue),      //#1
             NilCase,
             SWITCH<tag,NextCase>
            >::RET NextSwitch;
public:
  typedef IF<(found != 0),
             typename Case::Type,
             typename NextSwitch::RET
            >::RET RET;
};
```

Figure 10-36 SWITCH<> *without partial template specialization*

fib(). Thus, the total number of calls grows exponentially, which makes this implementation impractical. On a closer look, you'll see that the problem with this implementation is multiple computation of the same values, for example, f(5) calls f(2) three times (see Figure 10-38). We can avoid this by storing already computed

*fibonacci_*
*dynamic_*
simple_recursive
.cpp

```
int fib(int n)
{ if (n==0) return 0;
  if (n==1) return 1;
  return fib(n-1) + fib(n-2);
}
```

Figure 10-37 *Recursive implementation of* `fib()`

values in temporary variables. This leads to an iterative implementation with linear time complexity (see Figure 10-39; x and y store two consecutive Fibonacci numbers, f_i and f_{i-1}, respectively).

The iterative implementation from Figure 10-39 can be easily translated into static code using recursion. All you need to do is represent the loop as a recursive metafunction. This helper metafunction has to take all variables used in the loop, that is, n, i, x, and y, as explicit parameters. Furthermore, we add an extra

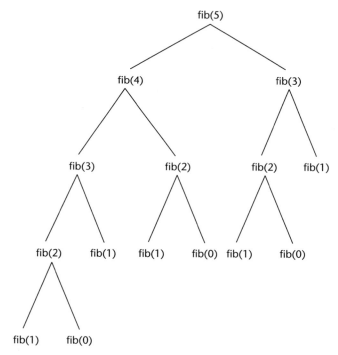

Figure 10-38 *Call tree for* `fib(5)`

*fibonacci_*
*dynamic_*
iterative.cpp

```
int
fib(int n) //where n>0
{ int i=1, x=1, y=0;
  while (i<n)
  { i = i+1;
    x = x+y;
    y = x-y;
  };
  return x;
}
```

Figure 10-39 *Iterative implementation of* `fib()`

Boolean parameter to represent a continuation condition control-ling the recursion: The recursion stops when the condition is `false`. We name the helper metafunction `Fib_<>` and call it from `Fib<>` (see Figure 10-40). This example demonstrates how you can translate any iterative dynamic code into recursive static code: A loop is translated into a recursive helper function with the continu-ation condition and state variables as arguments.

*fibonacci_static_*
*with_recursive_*
helper.cpp

```
template<bool cond, int n, int i, int x, int y>
struct Fib_
{ enum { RET = Fib_<(i+1<n), n, i+1, x+y, x>::RET };
};

template<int n, int i, int x, int y>
struct Fib_<false,n,i,x,y>
{ enum { RET = x };
};

template<int n>
struct Fib
{ enum { RET = Fib_<(n>1),n,1,1,0>::RET };
};

//...
cout << Fib<8>::RET << endl;
```

Figure 10-40 *Static re-implementation of the iterative version from Figure 10-39*

Simple recursive definitions need not be inefficient when implemented statically. Figure 10-41 shows the static translation of the simple recursive definition of Fibonacci numbers from Figure 10-37. Interestingly, this static code does not suffer from the inefficiencies of its dynamic counterpart! As you may remember, a call to fib(n) in Figure 10-37 for n>2 involves calling fib() for the same argument more than once. However, this is not a problem in the static code because Fib<> in Figure 10-41 is instantiated only on the first use with a given argument, and subsequent uses with the same argument do not require new instantiations. In other words, template instantiation takes care of remembering previously computed results automatically.

We have compared the compilation time for the simple recursive implementation from Figure 10-41 and the recursive implementation with the helper metafunction from Figure 10-40. The results are shown in Figure 10-42. The test involved compiling a simple test program using the egcs-1.1 compiler version 2.91.57 on a Pentium 133 MHz machine with 80 MB RAM running Windows 95. Here is the code of the test program:

```
void main()
{ cout << Fib<n>::RET << endl; //compile with different values
                                            //of n
}
```

*fibonacci_static_
simple_
recursive_.cpp*

```
template<int n>
struct Fib
{ enum { RET = Fib<n-1>::RET + Fib<n-2>::RET };
};

template<>
struct Fib<0>
{ enum { RET = 0 };
};

template<>
struct Fib<1>
{ enum { RET = 1 };
};
```

Figure 10-41 Static code for the simple recursive formulation from Figure 10-37

Figure 10-42 shows the compilation times of this program for the two different implementations of Fib<> and different values of *n* (see the two curves in the middle of the diagram). The value of *n* determines the maximum nesting depth of the recursive template instantiations required to compile each of these programs, which has a profound impact on the time and memory needed for the compilation.[5] As you can see, for *n* of up to 7000, both implementations need about the same time to compile. However, we were not able to compile the version with the helper metafunction for *n*>9000 due to virtual memory exhaustion on the test platform. The simple recursive implementation, on the other hand, gets the same problem for *n*>12000. In other words, the simple recursive implementation requires less memory to compile for a given *n*. Interestingly, it turns out that, although the template instantiation nesting depth of the implementation with the helper function is equal to *n*, the nesting depth of the simple recursive implementation is half as large.[6] Furthermore, the helper metafunction Fib_<> takes more parameters than the simple recursive Fib<> and thus needs more memory for each instantiation. Figure 10-42 also shows the execution time of the dynamic implementations from Figure 10-37 and Figure 10-39. As you can see, the dynamic implementation of the simple recursive version (Figure 10-37) is unusable. On our test platform, computing f(30) takes less than a second, but f(41) already takes two minutes. On the other hand, the iterative version (Figure 10-39) needs a fraction of a second for *n*=10000. It is important to note that the iterative version is superior to the simple recursive version not because it is iterative, but

---

5. As you may remember, the nesting depth of recursive template instantiation is defined as the number of templates being instantiated at a given time. The compiler keeps track of the nesting depth as follows: First, the depth is initialized to 0. Whenever a full template instance is being generated and its scope is pushed onto the compiler-internal scope stack, the depth is incremented. Whenever the scope is complete and then popped from the stack, the depth is decremented. We discussed the recursive template instantiation nesting depth in Section 10.6.5.

6. The reason for this is that, when fully instantiating Fib<n>, the egcs compiler pushes the scope of Fib<n-1> onto its internal scope stack only after the full instantiation of Fib<n-2> is completed and its scope popped from the stack, for example, [Fib<4>, Fib<2>, Fib<0>] → [Fib<4>, Fib<2>, Fib<1>] → [Fib<4>, Fib<3>] → [Fib<4>] → []. However, this behavior is compiler implementation dependent, for example, compilers based on the EDG front-end will push Fib<n>, Fib<n-1>, and Fib<n-2> and pop them in the reverse order. As a result, the maximum nesting depth for Fib<n> will be, in this case, n.

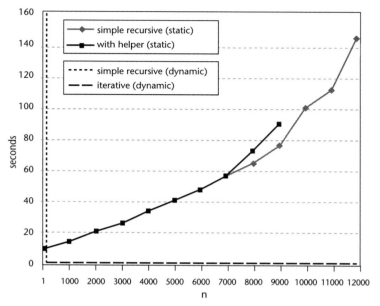

Figure 10-42 Compilation times of two different static implementations computing Fibonacci numbers (the inner two curves) and execution times of the corresponding dynamic implementations (the outer two curves)

rather because of its looping structure. We can also implement a dynamic *recursive* version of `fib()` using a recursive helper `fib_()`. The time complexity of such implementation will be linear—just as in the case of the iterative version. The inefficiency of the simple recursive version lies in its recursive structure with exponential time complexity. Thus, we can draw the somewhat surprising conclusion that, due to template instantiation, the static implementation of a dynamically impractical but simple recursive schema may outperform the static implementation of a dynamically efficient recursive schema.

Let us summarize our observations regarding recursion in static code so far.

♦ Runtime loops can be directly translated into recursive metafunctions taking a condition parameter and the needed state parameters.

♦ Simple recursive formulations, although often impractical for dynamic implementation, may be very appropriate for static implementation.

10.11.3   Explicit Looping Constructs (WHILE<>, DO<>, and FOR<>)

At this point, you may still wonder whether we can implement static equivalents to the runtime looping statements while, do, and for, the way we did for the selection statements if and switch. Yes, this is possible. The resulting static loops are slightly more awkward to use than IF<> or SWITCH<>. Nevertheless, they allow you to easily translate any dynamic code using looping statements into static code. We'll start our discussion by deriving the static while-loop. This will take three iterations. Finally, we will model the do- and for-loop similar to the final while-loop implementation.

10.11.3.1   While-Loop (WHILE<>)

First, let us take a look at how a conventional while-loop works. A while-loop takes a condition and executes a user-defined body in each iteration as long as the condition is true. Each iteration causes some state changes so that the loop can eventually terminate (hopefully!). Thus, a static loop will also take a condition as a parameter. Furthermore, it needs to take some code to execute in each iteration. We can achieve this by passing it a template metafunction as a parameter. The last concern is how to model state changes on each iteration. Because static code does not allow side effects, each iteration will have to receive initial state and return new state explicitly. We'll see that in a moment.

Before showing the implementation of the static loop WHILE<>, we will take a look at how to use it in client code. As an example, we will re-implement the iterative variant for computing Fibonacci numbers from Figure 10-39 in static code. As stated earlier, we have to pass all necessary state to WHILE<> explicitly. In our example, we have the variables n, i, x, and y. In order to be able to pass them all to WHILE<> in a generic way, we have to bundle them in one type. We call such a type an *environment* because it keeps the state of the static computation. The environment for the Fibonacci example is given in Figure 10-43.

Next, we need a metafunction that does the actual work in each iteration. The metafunction takes an environment as a parameter and returns a new one (see Figure 10-44). Its body increments i and computes the new x and y.

Finally, we need a continuation condition. This is implemented as a metafunction taking the current environment as an argument and comparing i and n (see Figure 10-45).

Now, we are ready to implement Fib<> (see Figure 10-46). Fib<> calls WHILE<> with the continuation condition, the iteration statement, and the initial environment as arguments. WHILE<>

```
//environment for Fib<>
template<int n_, int i_, int x_, int y_>
struct FibEnv
{ enum { n = n_,
         i = i_,
         x = x_,
         y = y_
       };
};
```

Figure 10-43 State environment for computing Fibonacci numbers

returns the final environment, and we access its member x to retrieve the result.

Finally, we can take a look at the implementation of WHILE<> (see Figure 10-47). WHILE<> uses the recursive helper metafunction idea from Figure 10-40. The first parameter of the helper metafunction WHILE_<> is the continuation condition. The helper metafunction calls itself recursively until the recursion terminates in the

```
//iteration statement for Fib<>
template<class Env>
struct FibIter
{ enum { new_i = Env::i+1,
         new_x = Env::x+Env::y,
         new_y = Env::x
       };
  typedef FibEnv<Env::n, new_i, new_x, new_y> RET;
};
```

Figure 10-44 Metafunction representing the iteration statement for computing Fibonacci numbers

```
//continue condition for Fib<>
template<class Env>
struct FibCond
{ enum { RET = Env::i < Env::n };
};
```

Figure 10-45 Continuation condition

*static_while_
first_version_
and_fibonacci.
cpp*

```
//Fib<>
template<int n>
struct Fib
{ enum { RET = WHILE<FibCond,
                     FibIter,
                     FibEnv<n,1,1,0> >::RET::x };
};


//...
cout << Fib<8>::RET << endl;
```

Figure 10-46 `Fib<>` *implementation using* `WHILE<>`

template specialization for `continue_==false`. On each iteration, `Statement<>` is used to compute the new environment.

The use of `WHILE<>` is a bit awkward because we have to implement three templates, namely the environment, the statement, and the condition, for each use of `WHILE<>`. This situation can be improved by merging the environment into the statement. In other words, the statement will take the state it manipulates as direct parameters. This is shown in Figure 10-48. Please note that the statement returns itself with new state under the `typedef`-name `Next`.

The original environment in Figure 10-43 also had the parameter n. Because only the condition and not the statement is interested in n, we declare it as a parameter of the condition (see Figure 10-49). In order to do so, we have to move the condition code into a member template whose parameter is the statement.

The metafunction calling `WHILE<>` with the new condition and statement is shown in Figure 10-50.

After getting rid of the environment and modifying the statement and the condition, we have to revise the implementation of `WHILE<>`. The result is shown in Figure 10-51.

The `WHILE<>` implementation can be considerably simplified by using `IF<>` (see Figure 10-52). Depending on the condition, the if-statement returns either a recursive call to `WHILE<>` or `STOP<>`. Please note that `RET` has been moved behind `IF<>` to avoid infinite recursion (we explained this technique in Section 10.11.1.3).

In addition to being simple, the `WHILE<>` implementation in Figure 10-52 does not require advanced template features, such as partial template specialization or templates as template parameters.

```
namespace intimate
{
  template<
    bool continue_,
    template<class>class Condition,
    template<class>class Statement,
    class Env
  >
  struct WHILE_
  { typedef typename Statement<Env>::RET NewEnv; //compute new
                                                 //environment
    typedef typename //make recursive call
      WHILE_<Condition<NewEnv>::RET,
             Condition, Statement, NewEnv>::RET RET;
  };

  //specialize for continue_==false to return the initial Env
  template<
    template<class>class Condition,
    template<class>class Statement,
    class Env
  >
  struct WHILE_<false,Condition,Statement,Env>
  { typedef Env RET;
  };
}; //end of namespace intimate

//WHILE
template<
  template<class>class Condition,
  template<class>class Statement,
  class InitEnv
>
struct WHILE
{ typedef typename //make a call to the helper metafunction
    intimate::WHILE_<Condition<InitEnv>::RET,
                     Condition, Statement, InitEnv>::RET RET;
};
```

static_while_ first_version_ and_fibonacci. cpp

Figure 10-47 *Implementation of* WHILE<>

```
template<int i_, int x_, int y>
struct FibStat
{ enum { i = i_,
         x = x_
       };
  typedef FibStat<i+1, x+y, x> Next;
};
```

Figure 10-48 *New statement for the while-loop computing Fibonacci numbers*

```
template<int n>
struct FibCond
{ template<class Statement>
  struct Code
  { enum { RET = Statement::i < n };
  };
};
```

Figure 10-49 *New condition for the while-loop computing Fibonacci numbers*

```
template<int n>
struct Fib
{ enum { RET = WHILE<FibCond<n>,FibStat<1,1,0> >::RET::x };
};
```

Figure 10-50 *Metafunction calling* WHILE<> *with the new condition and new statement*

10.11.3.2 Do-Loop (DO<>)

Similar to a while-loop, a do-loop executes its body repeatedly as long as the loop condition is true. However, unlike a while-loop, the do-loop condition is checked after executing the body, that is, the body is executed at least once. Do-loops are much more rarely used than other kinds of loops. Nevertheless, they are quite convenient in some cases, particularly when the loop body computes a value needed for the termination condition. As an example, consider a

```
namespace intimate
{
  template<
    bool continue_,
    class Condition,
    class Statement
  >
  struct WHILE_
  { typedef typename Statement::Next NewStatement; //get new
                                                   //statement
    typedef typename Condition::Code<NewStatement> ConditionCode;
    typedef typename //make recursive call
      WHILE_<ConditionCode::RET,
              Condition, NewStatement>::RET RET;
  };

  //specialize for continue_==false to return the initial
  //Statement
  template<
    class Condition,
    class Statement
  >
  struct WHILE_<false,Condition,Statement>
  { typedef Statement RET;
  };
}; //end of namespace intimate

//WHILE
template<
  class Condition,
  class Statement
>
struct WHILE
{ typedef typename Condition::Code<Statement> ConditionCode;
  typedef typename //make call to the helper metafunction
    intimate::WHILE_<ConditionCode::RET,
                     Condition, Statement>::RET RET;
};
```

static_while_ second_version_ and_fibonacci. cpp

Figure 10-51 *Revised* `WHILE<>` *implementation*

simple function for computing the square root of an integer (see Figure 10-53). To be more precise, the algorithm computes the *integral* part of the square root, that is, the result is also an integer.

```
namespace intimate
{ template<class Statement>
  struct STOP
  { typedef Statement RET;
  };
};

template<class Condition, class Statement>
struct WHILE
{ typedef typename IF<Condition::template Code<Statement>::RET,
                      WHILE<Condition,typename Statement::Next>,
                      intimate::STOP<Statement>
                      >::RET::RET RET;
};
```

Figure 10-52 *Final* WHILE<> *implementation*

The first step to translate this dynamic code into static code is to come up with the body statement for the do-loop. A quick look at the dynamic code reveals that the loop body involves two variables, namely n and p. Thus, the static body statement needs two parameters corresponding to these variables (see Figure 10-54). Furthermore, the statement has to publish these parameters, so that the condition can access n, and we also can read out the resulting p. Finally, the statement with the new state is published as Next.

The continuation condition is very simple. We check whether n is greater than or equal to 0 (see Figure 10-55).

```
int sqrt(int n)
{ int p = -1;
  do
  { p += 2;
    n -= p;
  } while (n>=0);
  return p/2;
}
```

Figure 10-53 *Function computing the integral part of the square
root of an integer n>=0*

```
template<int n_, int p_>
struct SqrtStat
{ enum { p = p_,
         n = n_
       };
  typedef SqrtStat<n-p-2, p+2> Next;
};
```

Figure 10-54 *Static loop-body statement*

```
struct SqrtCond
{ template<class Statement>
  struct Code
  { enum { RET = Statement::n >= 0 };
  };
};
```

Figure 10-55 *Continuation condition*

Finally, the complete metafunction for computing square root is given in Figure 10-56. Similar to its dynamic counterpart, the condition is passed as a second argument after the body statement.

The implementation of DO<> is similar to the implementation of WHILE<> in Figure 10-52. The only difference is that both the condition and STOP<> take the new statement as arguments. The implementation of DO<> is given in Figure 10-57 (STOP<> is shown in Figure 10-52).

```
template<int n>
struct Sqrt
{ enum { p = DO<SqrtStat<n,-1>,SqrtCond>::RET::p,
         RET = p/2
       };
};
```

Figure 10-56 *Metafunction computing the integral part of the square root of an integer*

static_do_and_sqrt.cpp

```
template<class Statement, class Condition>
class DO
{ typedef typename Statement::Next NewStatement;
public:
  typedef typename
    IF<Condition::template Code<NewStatement>::RET,
        DO<NewStatement,Condition>,
         intimate::STOP<NewStatement>
      >::RET::RET RET;
};
```

Figure 10-57 *Implementation of* DO<>

10.11.3.3 For-Loop (FOR<>)

A for-loop is the most versatile kind of loop in C++. It combines loop initialization, continuation condition, and incrementing into one construct. Any of these elements can be empty, or you can put a lot of logic into them. However, for our purpose, we will only consider the most common usage of a for-loop as demonstrated in Figure 10-58. The loop initialization involves declaring and initializing i. Then the body of the loop is repeatedly executed until i reaches n.

As in the case of a while- or do-loop, the first step of translating a dynamic for-loop into static code involves writing the body statement. The body of the loop in Figure 10-58 involves two variables x and y. Thus, our static statement will have two parameters (see Figure 10-59). The only difference between this and the other static loop statements is that the statement body has been moved into the member template Code<>. This allows us to

dynamic_for_and_fibronacci.cpp

```
int fib(int n)
{ int x=1, y=0;
  for (int i=1; i<n; ++i)
  { x = x+y;
    y = x-y;
  };
  return x;
}
```

Figure 10-58 *Fibonacci function demonstrating the use of a for-loop* *static_for_and_fibronacci.cpp*

```
template<int x_, int y>
struct FibStat
{ template<int i>
  struct Code
  { enum { x = x_ }; //need to read out the result later
    typedef FibStat<x+y,x> Next;
  };
};
```

Figure 10-59 *Body statement for the for-loop computing Fibonacci numbers*

introduce the new parameter `i`, which corresponds to the variable `i` in Figure 10-58.

The body statement is all we need to implement before using the for-loop `FOR<>`. `FOR<>` takes a few more parameters than the other static loops. The metafunction using `FOR<>` to compute Fibonacci numbers is given in Figure 10-60. The first parameter is the initial value of `i`. The second parameter is a comparator, in our case `Less`. The comparator and the third parameter constitute the continuation condition. The loop continues as long as `i` is less than the third parameter. The forth parameter is the increment stride for `i`. In each iteration, the stride is added to `i`. Finally, the last parameter is the body statement. The loop returns the final statement, and we can read `x` out of it.

Of course, there are other comparators in addition to `Less`, for example, `LessEqual`, `Greater`, and `GreaterEqual` (see Figure 10-61).

The implementation of `FOR<>` is similar to the implementation of `WHILE<>` with the main difference being that `from` is advanced by `by` and passed to `Statement::Code<>` (see Figure 10-62).

static_for_and_fibronacci.cpp

```
template<int n>
struct Fib
{ enum { RET = FOR<1,Less,n,+1,FibStat<1,0> >::RET::x };
};
```

Figure 10-60 *Metafunction for computing Fibonacci numbers using* `FOR<>`

```
struct Greater
{ template<int x, int y>
  struct Code
  { enum { RET = x>y };
  };
};

struct GreaterEqual
{ template<int x, int y>
  struct Code
  { enum { RET = x>=y };
  };
};

struct Less
{ template<int x, int y>
  struct Code
  { enum { RET = x<y };
  };
};

struct LessEqual
{ template<int x, int y>
  struct Code
  { enum { RET = x<=y };
  };
};
```

*static_for_
and_fibronacci.
cpp*

Figure 10-61 *Comparators to be used with* FOR<>

```
template<int from, class Compare, int to, int by,
         class Statement>
struct FOR
{ typedef typename
    IF<Compare::template Code<from,to>::RET,
      FOR<from+by,Compare,to,by,
          typename Statement::Code<from>::Next>,
          intimate::STOP<typename Statement::Code<from> >
    >::RET::RET RET;
};
```

*staticc_for_
and_fibronacci.
cpp*

Figure 10-62 *Implementation of* FOR<>

10.12   Code Generation

We can use template metaprograms to generate code. More specifically, we can compose code fragments, compose templates, and unroll loops at compile time. This is useful for generating highly optimized and compact code for a given deployment context.

10.12.1   Simple Code Selection

We start with a simple example illustrating compile-time code selection. Assume that we have two types implementing two different variants of some algorithm:

*code_selection_*
using_static_if.
cpp

```
struct AlgorithmVariantA
{ static void execute()
   { cout << "AlgorithmVariantA" << endl; }
};

struct AlgorithmVariantB
{ static void execute()
   { cout << "AlgorithmVariantB" << endl; }
};
```

Each of them defines the static inline method `execute()`. Now, consider the following statement:

```
IF<(1<2),
   AlgorithmVariantA,
   AlgorithmVariantB>::RET::execute();
```

Because the condition 1<2 is `true`, `AlgorithmVariantA` ends up in `RET`. Thus, the previous statement compiles into machine code, which is equivalent to the machine code obtained by compiling the following statements:

```
cout << "AlgorithmVariantA" << endl;
```

The reason is that `execute()` is declared as a static inline method and the compiler can optimize away any overhead associated with the method call. This is just a very simple example, but in general you can imagine a metafunction that takes a number of parameters and does some arbitrarily complex computation in order to select the type with the right method:

```
SomeMetafunction</* takes some parameters here */
            >::RET::executeSomeCode();
```

The code in `executeSomeCode()` can also use different metafunctions in order to select other methods it calls. In effect, we are able to compose code fragments at compile time based on the selection algorithms encoded in the metafunctions.

At this point, you may be wondering how this is different from using preprocessor directives, such as `#if`, `#ifdef`, and `#define`. Template metaprogramming allows you much more control in selecting code than preprocessor directives. The major difference is that static metaprogramming can interpret static C++ data embedded in your C++ program (e.g., in configuration repositories) and compute new static data, which is then used in the program. Preprocessor directives, on the other hand, are not integrated into the C++ level. There is only a one-way communication between the preprocessor and the C++ compiler: All you can do is to do some simple computation on data defined by preprocessor macros and contribute the result to a C++ program, but you cannot use static C++ data from the program at the preprocessor level. For example, you can write the following code:

```
#define X 1
#define Y 2
#define TEST(x,y) ((x)<(y))
```

code_selection_ using_if_ directive.cpp

```
#if TEST(X,Y) //#if accepts a constant expression as a
                //condition
  cout << "AlgorithmVariantA" << endl;
#else
  cout << "AlgorithmVariantB" << endl;
#endif
```

However, the condition used in `#if` cannot contain C++ static data, such as constants or enumerators or the operator `sizeof`. Furthermore, preprocessor directives do not support recursion or any other kind of looping. In effect, you cannot express more complex code selection algorithms. If all you want to do is to control the selection of code using the same global flag in several places, use the preprocessor directive `#ifdef`. However, if you need finer control, for example, controlling the selection of code in several places by a more complex algorithm (possibly in a coordinated way), you need template metaprogramming.[7]

---

7. There are cases, however, where conditional compilation using preprocessor directives is necessary, for example, to handle differences in syntax accepted by different compilers.

10.12.2   Composing Templates

Another approach to code generation is to have template metaprograms compose class templates. For example, assume that we have the following two class templates.

♦ List<>: A generic implementation of a singly linked list with methods, such as setHead() and setTail().

♦ ListWithLengthCounter<>: A template that represents a wrapper on List<> implementing a counter for keeping track of the length of the list.

Now, based on a flag, we can decide whether to wrap List<> into ListWithLengthCounter<> or not:

```
typedef IF<flag==listWithCounter,
        ListWithLengthCounter<List<ElementType> >
        List<ElementType> >::RET ResultList;
```

You can use this technique to generate concrete types based on a number of abstract flags at compile time. Actually, you can use it to generate custom class hierarchies because the templates being composed may use parameterized inheritance. We'll use this technique in Chapter 12 in order to implement a simple list generator.

10.12.3   Generators Based on Expression Templates

Expression templates [Vel95b] is a programming technique that allows you to generate custom code for C++ expressions involving function and operator calls. We will discuss this technique in Section 14.4.2, but let us give you a general idea about it here. For example, you can use this technique to generate *optimized* code for adding a number of vectors:

```
v4 = v1+v2+v3;
```

The naive implementation of vector addition by overloading the operator + to compute the vector sum is inefficient because each + will create a temporary vector and use a separate pair of loops to add its operands. A more efficient way to compute the addition of a number of vectors is to use only one pair of loops that computes the entire result elementwise. Expression templates allow you to generate such code for the previous expression.

The idea of expression templates is to have each operator in the expression return an object representing the subexpression the operator constitutes together with its operands rather than the result of adding the operands. As a result, the assignment operator has to assign an *expression object* representing the expression v1+v2+v3 to v4, at which point the expression gets evaluated. The main point here is that by implementing the functions and operators to be used within an expression as function and operator templates, the type of the whole expression will completely encode its structure. Thus, the templates will have the effect of generating parse trees of expressions encoded as types, which we can further process using template metaprograms (including our code generation techniques). We will explain this technique in detail in Section 14.4.2 using an example. Without getting into details at this point, let us just state that expression templates allow you to implement:

♦ Compile-time domain-specific checks on the structure of expressions, which the C++ type system cannot express otherwise. (You can implement any kind of checks, even checks spanning the whole expression at once, e.g., "an expression cannot contain more than five plus operators.")
♦ Compile-time optimization transformations and custom code generation for expressions.

In effect, you can use this technique to implement embedded domain-specific language extensions (including domain-specific error checking and optimizations).

10.12.4 Recursive Code Expansion

Template metaprogramming can be used to expand code recursively. You may use recursive code expansion to optimize code by achieving the effect of loop unrolling or to generate test code for template metafunctions. We'll explain the idea of recursive code expansion using two simple examples of loop unrolling in this section. Generating test code will be the topic of Section 10.13.

Consider a simple function for raising m to the power of n, where n and m are integral numbers and n>=0. This is shown in Figure 10-63.

Now assume that you call this function in your program as follows:

```
int m;
cout << "Enter m = ";
cin >> m;
cout << "power(m,3) = " << power(m,3) << endl;
```

In other words, the value of n is 3, and it is known at compile time, but the value of m is not known until runtime. In this case, the loop in Figure 10-63 can be optimized by unrolling it, which is shown in Figure 10-64 (see discussion in Section 10.3 and Figure 10-2 and Figure 10-3). Many C++ compilers will perform loop unrolling for you (see the optimization options of your compiler). However, unrolling all loops that can be unrolled in a program is usually not desirable. Extensive loop unrolling may lead to code bloat, which will degrade the cache performance and thus make the program run slower. In contrast to compiler options, template metaprogramming gives you exact control over which loop to unroll and how much of it to unroll, which is important for writing high-performance libraries.

As an example, let us take a look at how to achieve the effect of loop unrolling using recursive code expansion for power(), where n is known at compile time. The idea of recursive code expansion is to recursively call an inline function, where the termination of the recursion is controlled by a static parameter, for example, the number n. The corresponding code for raising a number to the power of n, where n is known at compile time, is shown in Figure 10-65. n is passed as a template parameter, and the inline function power() is called recursively n times. When you compile this code with the option enabling inlining, the compiler will recursively inline power() resulting in very efficient code. The result of successive inlining power() is shown in Figure 10-66.

A minor imperfection of this technique is that the user has to use a different calling syntax for the unrolled version. However, we will show, in Section 10.14, how to implement a simple calling interface that automatically decides between power(m,n) and power<n>(m).

Some compilers (e.g., Microsoft Visual C++ 5.0 and 6.0) have problems with properly handling explicit template argument speci-

dynamic_power. cpp

```
inline int power(const int& m, int n)
{ int r = 1;
  for (; n>0; --n) r *= m;
  return r;
}
```

Figure 10-63 *Function for raising* m *to the power of* n, *where* m *and* n *are integral numbers and* n>=0

```
inline int power3(const int& m)
{ int r = 1;
  r *= m;
  r *= m;
  r *= m;
  return r;
}
```

Figure 10-64 *Function from Figure 10-63 after unrolling the loop
for* n=3

fication for function templates as used in Figure 10-65. In this case,
you can alternatively use a class template rather than a function
template. This is shown in Figure 10-67 ("D1" in PowerD1<> indicates that one parameter is dynamic).

Our second example demonstrates how to use recursive code
expansion to optimize vector operations. Consider the simple
function for adding two vectors using a for-loop in Figure 10-68.

In the case that size is known at compile time and is relatively small, we can apply recursive inlining to unroll the loop.
The implementation using recursive inlining is given in Figure
10–69. Figure 10-70 shows how the compiler performs recursive

*unrolled_power.
cpp*

```
template<int n>
inline int power(const int& m)
{ return power<n-1>(m) * m; }

template<>
inline int power<1>(const int& m)
{ return m; }

template<>
inline int power<0>(const int& m)
{ return 1; }

//...
cout << power<3>(2) << endl;
```

Figure 10-65 *Raising a number to the power of* n, *where* n *is known
at compile time*

```
cout << power<3>(m) << endl;
        ⇩
cout << power<2>(m) * m << endl;
        ⇩
cout << power<1>(m) * m * m << endl;
        ⇩
cout << m * m * m << endl;
```

Figure 10-66 *Effect of recursively inlining* power<3>(m)

inlining to generate an efficient implementation code for a call to
add_vectors<size>().

    Because of code bloat, full loop unrolling as in Figure 10-69 is
practical only for small size. Furthermore, the implementation
assumed that size is known at compile time. In the case that size

*unrolled_power
struct.cpp*

```
template<int n>
struct PowerD1
{ static int exec(const int& m)
  { return PowerD1<n-1>::exec(m) * m; }
};

template<>
struct PowerD1<1>
{ static int exec(const int& m)
  { return m; }
};

template<>
struct PowerD1<0>
{ static int exec(const int& m)
  { return 1; }
};

//...
cout << PowerD1<3>::exec(m) << endl;
```

Figure 10-67 *Implementation of loop unrolling using a class
template*

```
inline void add_vectors(int size, const double* a,
                         const double* b, double* c)
{ while(size--) *c++ = *a++ + *b++;
};

//test vectors
double a[3] = { 1.1,  2.2,  3.3};
double b[3] = {-1.0, -2.0, -3.0};
double c[3];

//...
add_vectors(3,a,b,c); //c=a+b
```

dynamic_vector_add.cpp

Figure 10-68 *Simple function for adding two vectors*

```
//recursive template
template<int size>
inline void add_vectors(const double* a, const double* b,
                        double* c)
{ *c = *a + *b;
  add_vectors<size-1>(a+1, b+1, c+1);
}

//specialization for size==1
template<>
inline void add_vectors<0>(const double* a, const double* b,
                           double* c)
{}

//test vectors
double a[3] = { 1.1,  2.2,  3.3};
double b[3] = {-1.0, -2.0, -3.0};
double c[3];

//...
add_vectors<3>(a,b,c);  //c = a+b
```

unrolled_vector_add.cpp

Figure 10-69 *Function for adding two vectors using recursive code expansion*

```
add_vectors<3>(a,b,c);
        ⇩
*c    = *a    + *b;
add_vectors<2>(a+1, b+1, c+1);
        ⇩
*c    = *a    + *b;
*(c+1) = *(a+1) + *(b+1);
add_vectors<1>(a+1+1, b+1+1, c+1+1);
        ⇩
*c    = *a    + *b;
*(c+1) = *(a+1) + *(b+1);
*(c+2) = *(a+2) + *(b+2);
add_vectors<0>(a+1+1+1, b+1+1+1, c+1+1+1);
        ⇩
*c    = *a    + *b;
*(c+1) = *(a+1) + *(b+1);
*(c+2) = *(a+2) + *(b+2);
```

Figure 10-70 *Effect of recursively inlining* add_vectors<3>(a,b,c);

is not known until runtime, we can use *partial loop unrolling*. Partial loop unrolling unrolls several iterations only. For example, partially unrolling the vector addition loop from Figure 10-68 involves replacing this loop by another loop that computes several elements of vector c in one iteration. The implementation of vector addition using partial unrolling is shown in Figure 10-71. It uses add_vectors<size>() from Figure 10-69 to generate the code for computing stride elements of c. Please note that size is a dynamic parameter of add_vectors<stride>() in Figure 10-71. Because size may contain more than a whole multiple of stride, we have to use an extra loop to process the "leftover" fraction of elements. The code resulting from inlining is shown in Figure 10-72.

Partial loop unrolling in vector and matrix operations has a particularly positive effect on processors with a large number of registers (e.g., SPARC RISC processors) because the vector or matrix portions being processed in one iteration can be kept directly in the registers. Thus, the value of stride has to be adjusted for a particular architecture. Please note that code bloat is not a problem here because unrolling is independent of data length and is limited by a small fixed value.

```
template<int stride>
inline void add_vectors(
   const int& size, const double* a, const double* b,
   double* c)
{ int leftover = size%stride;
  int i=0;
  for (; i < leftover; ++i)
   add_vectors<1>(a+i,b+i,c+i); //call to add_vectors()
                                //from Figure 10-69


  for (; i < size; i += stride)
    add_vectors<stride>(a+i,b+i,c+i); //call to
                   //add_vectors<size>() from Figure 10-69
};

//test vectors
const int vs = 10;
double a[vs] = { 1.1,  2.2,  3.3,  4.4,  5.5,  6.6,  7.7,
                 8.8,  9.9,  10.1};
double b[vs] = {-1.0, -2.0, -3.0, -4.0, -5.0, -6.0, -7.0,
                -8.0, -9.0, -10.0};
double c[vs];

//...
add_vectors<4>(vs,a,b,c); //c = a+b
```

*partially_
unrolled_
vector_add.cpp*

Figure 10-71 *Function for adding two vectors using partial loop unrolling*

In general, the decision of which loop to unroll and how much of it to unroll depends on many factors including the loop size, the compiler, the processor architecture, cache sizes, and more. The main advantage of using template metaprogramming to perform loop unrolling is the maximum control over how this is done. On the other hand, such explicit optimizations may prevent the compiler from performing some of its standard optimizations because compilers usually expect "normal" code. Thus, you have to determine the effect of template metaprogramming optimizations and tune their applications experimentally in a given context.

```
add_vectors<4>(size,a,b,c)
        ⇓
int leftover = size%4;
int i=0;
for (; i < leftover; ++i)
  add_vectors<4>(a+i,b+i,c+i);
for (; i < size; i += 4)
  add_vectors<4>(a+i,b+i,c+i);
          ⇓
int leftover = size % 4;
int i=0;
for (; i < leftover; ++i)
  *(c+i) = *(a+i) + *(b+i);
for (; i < size; i += 4)
{ int *tmp1 = a+i;
  int *tmp2 = b+i;
  int *tmp3 = c+i;
  *tmp3     = *tmp1     + *tmp2;
  *(tmp3+1) = *(tmp1+1) + *(tmp2+1);
  *(tmp3+2) = *(tmp1+2) + *(tmp2+2);
  *(tmp3+3) = *(tmp1+3) + *(tmp2+3);
}
```

Figure 10-72 Effect of inlining add_vectors <4> (size, a,b,v)

Loop unrolling is relevant in high-performance domains, such as numeric computing, visualization, image processing, and signal processing. There are several libraries that successfully use full and partial loop unrolling by means of template metaprogramming. For example, the Blitz++ library [Blitz] uses partial loop unrolling to optimize operations on numerical arrays. It also provides full loop unrolling for small vectors and matrices, which are relevant in some domains. For example, small 4-by-4 matrices are used in visualization to perform polygon transformations. In addition to loop unrolling, Blitz++ also performs other optimizations using template metaprogramming, such as rearranging the order of nested loops to take advantage of memory storage order, eliminating temporaries, and fusing loops. The combination of these optimizations and a good optimizing compiler (e.g., KAI++ from Kuck and Associates, Inc.) allowed Blitz++ to achieve and even surpass the speed of vendor-tuned Fortran libraries for the first time [Vel97]. Another C++ library attaining the speed of the fastest vendor-tuned matrix libraries available on the market is the Matrix Template Library (MTL, see [SL98a]). MTL uses techniques similar to loop unrolling discussed earlier to implement register and cache tiling.

10.12.5   Explicit Loops for Generating Code (EWHILE<>, EDO<>, and EFOR<>)

Just as we introduced WHILE<>, DO<>, and FOR<> for explicitly expressing looping in static computations in Section 10.11.3, we will introduce similar looping constructs for explicitly controlling recursive code expansion. They will be called EWHILE<>, EDO<>, and EFOR<>, where "E" stands for "execute".

10.12.5.1   EWHILE<>

The first of our "execute"-loops, or e-loops, is EWHILE<>. As an example, we'll use EWHILE<> to generate the following code:

```
cout << 1 << endl;
cout << 2 << endl;
cout << 3 << endl;
cout << 4 << endl;
cout << 5 << endl;
cout << 6 << endl;
cout << 7 << endl;
cout << 8 << endl;
cout << 9 << endl;
```

First, we need a body statement for EWHILE<> (see Figure 10-73). This is similar to the body statement for WHILE<> (see Figure 10-48). In particular, it also defines the member Next providing the next statement. The only difference is that a statement for an

ewhile.cpp

```
template<int i_=1>
struct PrintStat
{ enum { i=i_ };
  static void exec()
  { cout << i << endl; }
  typedef PrintStat<i+1> Next;
};
```

Figure 10-73 Body statement for EWHILE<>

e–loop additionally defines the static method `exec()` whose body is to be recursively inlined by the e-loop.

A condition for `EWHILE<>` has exactly the same form as a condition for `WHILE<>`. The condition for our example is shown in Figure 10-74.

Finally, the compiler will recursively expand the following statement by means of inlining:

```
EWHILE<PrintCond<10>, PrintStat<> >::exec();
```

into the code shown at the beginning of this section.

The implementation of `EWHILE<>` is shown in Figure 10-75. It is similar to the implementation of `WHILE<>` in Figure 10-52.

Static parameters needed by `exec()`, for example, `i`, can be passed as template parameters of the body statement. However, the body of an e-loop sometimes also needs to use one or several runtime variables. For this purpose, we will define `EWHILE1<>` whose `exec()` method takes one argument of arbitrary type. If we need to pass several values, we can bundle them using a `struct`. Let us demonstrate the use of `EWHILE1<>` by re-implementing `PowerD1<>` from Figure 10-67 to use `EWHILE1<>` rather than recursion. As you may remember, `PowerD1<>` generates efficient code for raising `m` to the power of `n`, where `n` is an integer known at compile time and `m` is an integer not known until runtime. Examining the for-loop in Figure 10-63 reveals that our body statement needs two runtime variables, namely `m` and `r`. Therefore, we need to define a `struct` for passing `m` and `r` as one object to `EWHILE1::exec()`. This is shown in Figure 10-76.

The implementation of the body statement, condition, and `PowerD1<>` is straightforward (see Figure 10-77). Please note that `PowStat::exec(PowEnv&)` receives a `PowEnv` by reference. The same is true of `EWHILE1::exec(Env&)`. At the end, the final result stands in `env.r`.

ewhile.cpp

```
template<int n>
struct PrintCond
{ template<class Statement>
  struct Code
  { enum { RET=(Statement::i<n) };
  };
};
```

Figure 10-74 Condition for `EWHILE<>`

```
namespace intimate
{ struct Stop
  { static void exec() {};
  };
};


template <class Condition, class Statement>
struct EWHILE
{ static void exec()
  { IF<Condition::template Code<Statement>::RET,
      Statement,
      intimate::Stop
    >::RET::exec(); //call Statement if Condition OK
   IF<Condition::template Code<Statement>::RET,
      EWHILE<Condition,typename Statement::Next>,
      intimate::Stop
    >::RET::exec(); //call EWHILE recursively
                    //if Condition OK
  }
};
```

ewhile.cpp

Figure 10-75 *Implementation of* EWHILE<>

The implementation of EWHILE1<> is shown in Figure 10-78.[8]
Depending on the compiler, direct recursion may be somewhat more efficient than an e-loop. However loops are useful for

```
struct PowEnv
{ PowEnv(const int& m_, int r_) : m(m_), r(r_) {}
  int m, r;
};
```

ewhile.cpp

Figure 10-76 *Environment struct for passing* m *and* r *to* EWHILE1<>

8. Theoretically, we could have implemented all the members of EWHILE1<> as members of EWHILE<>, saving us from implementing the separate EWHILE1<>. The reason we did not do this is that some compilers would instantiate **exec()** even if we only call **exec(Env)**, which causes errors if **Statement** only implements **exec(Env)**. Although such compilers do not conform to the ISO/ANSI C++ Standard, we decided to avoid this problem by defining two separate loops.

ewhile.cpp

```
//statement
template<int n_, int i_>
struct PowStat
{ enum { n=n_, i=i_ };
  static void exec (PowEnv& env)
  { env.r *= env.m; }
  typedef PowStat<n, i+1> Next;
};

//condition
struct PowCond
{ template<class Statement>
  struct Code
  { enum { RET=(Statement::i<Statement::n) };
  };
};

//PowerD1<>
template<int n>
struct PowerD1
{ static int exec(const int& m)
  { PowEnv env(m,1);
    EWHILE1<PowCond, PowStat<n,0> >::exec(env);
    return env.r;
  }
};

//...
cout << PowerD1<3>::exec(2) << endl;
```

Figure 10-77 Implementation of PowerD1<> *using* EWHILE1<>

expressing control flow more explicitly, and dynamic code using loops can be more easily re-implemented using e-loops. Finally, if you use e-loops to iterate over types to test metafunctions or template configurations (as in Section 10.13), the minimal performance difference is not an issue.

10.12.5.2 EDO<>

EDO<> is very similar to EWHILE<>. The only difference is that EDO<> checks its continuation condition after inlining Statement::

```
namespace intimate
{ struct Stop
  { static void exec() {}; //this is used by EWHILE<> only
    template<class Env>
    static void exec(Env&) {};
  };
};

template <class Condition, class Statement>
struct EWHILE1
{ template<class Env>
  static void exec(Env& env)
  { IF<Condition::template Code<Statement>::RET,
      Statement,
      intimate::Stop
    >::RET::exec(env);
    IF<Condition::template Code<Statement>::RET,
      EWHILE1<Condition,typename Statement::Next>,
      intimate::Stop
    >::RET::exec(env);
  }
};
```

ewhile.cpp

Figure 10-78 *Implementation of* EWHILE1<>

exec(). Furthermore, the body statement is the first parameter and
condition is the second parameter of EDO<>, for example:

```
//PrintStat<> from Figure 10-73 and PrintCond<> from Figure
//10-74
EDO< PrintStat<1>, PrintCond<10> >::exec();
```

The implementation of EDO<> and EDO1<> is given in Figure
10–79.

We can now re-implement EWHILE<> and EWHILE1<> from Figure 10-75 and Figure 10–78 using EDO<> and EDO1<>, which results
in much shorter code shown in Figure 10–80.

10.12.5.3 EFOR<>

Similar to FOR<>, EFOR<> takes five static parameters: starting index
value, comparator, value for the right side of the comparator,

```
namespace intimate
{ struct Stop
  { static void exec() {};
    template<class Env>
    static void exec(Env& env) {};
  };
};

template <class Statement, class Condition>
class EDO
{ typedef typename Statement::Next NextStatement;
public:
  static void exec()
  { Statement::exec();
    IF<Condition::template Code<NextStatement>::RET,
       EDO<NextStatement,Condition>,
       intimate::Stop
    >::RET::exec();
  }
};

template <class Statement, class Condition>
class EDO1
{ typedef typename Statement::Next NextStatement;
public:
  template<class Env>
  static void exec(Env& env)
  { Statement::exec(env);
    IF<Condition::template Code<NextStatement>::RET,
       EDO1<NextStatement,Condition>,
       intimate::Stop
    >::RET::exec(env);
  }
};
```

edo.cpp

Figure 10-79 Implementation of EDO<> *and* EDO1<>

stride, and body statement. The body statement has to contain the member template Code<>, which is instantiated with the current index value in each iteration. Figure 10-81 demonstrates the use of EFOR<>. The re-implementation of PowerD1<> from Figure 10-67 to use EFOR1<> rather than recursion is given in Figure 10-82.

```
template<class Condition, class Statement >
struct EWHILE
{ static void exec()
  { IF<Condition::template Code<Statement>::RET,
      EDO<Statement,Condition>,
      intimate::Stop
    >::RET::exec();
  }
};


template<class Condition, class Statement >
struct EWHILE1
{ template<class Env>
  static void exec(Env& env)
  { IF<Condition::template Code<Statement>::RET,
      EDO1<Statement,Condition>,
      intimate::Stop
    >::RET::exec(env);
  }
};
```

*simplified_
ewhile.cpp*

Figure 10-80 *Implementation of* EWHILE<> *and* EWHILE1<> *using*
EDO<> *and* ED01<>[9]

The implementation of EFOR<> and EFOR1<> is shown in Figure
10-83.

10.12.5.4 Nesting Static E-Loops

In day-to-day C++ programming, you nest loops routinely. Similarly, you will sometimes need to nest static e-loops. Nesting static e-loops is straightforward—once you've seen how to do it. You usually need nested loops in order to iterate over multidimensional arrays. For example, to iterate over a two-dimensional array, you need two nested loops, where each loop iterates over one dimension. Figure 10-84 shows two such nested for-loops that iterate over a 5-by-5 square. The output of this program is shown in Figure 10-85.

Given that the size of each dimension is known at compile time, we can translate the two nested for-loops into two nested

---

9. Thanks to Johannes Knaupp for suggesting this simplification.

```
//statement
struct PrintStat
{ template<int i>
  struct Code
  { static void exec()
    { cout << i << endl; }
  };
};
//...
EFOR<1,Less,10,+1,PrintStat>::exec();
/* the above statement expands into:
cout << 1 << endl;
cout << 2 << endl;
cout << 3 << endl;
cout << 4 << endl;
cout << 5 << endl;
cout << 6 << endl;
cout << 7 << endl;
cout << 8 << endl;
cout << 9 << endl;
*/
```

efor.cpp

Figure 10-81 Example using EFOR<>

static efor-loops. The result is shown in Figure 10-86. The outer loop (line #2) takes OuterPrintLoopStat as its statement. The inner loop (line #1)—just as in the dynamic version—is part of the outer loop statement. Both the inner loop and the inner loop statement (InnerPrintLoopStat) are members of the template member Code<> of the outer loop statement. This way, they both have access to the index i of the outer loop. The equivalent code to which this implementation is expanded by the compiler is shown in Figure 10-87. The runtime output is the same as in Figure 10-85.

If you have to iterate over a two-dimensional array, that is, a matrix, there is an alternative to nesting loops. You can use just one loop and compute the necessary two-dimensional index from the one-dimensional index. For example, think of a matrix with *height* number of rows and *width* number of columns. We can iterate over each element of this matrix using one loop starting at $i = 0$ and running through as long as $i < height \cdot width$. The row index can now be computed as follows:

efor.cpp

```
//environment
struct PowEnv
{ int m, r;
  PowEnv(const int& m_) : m(m_), r(1) {};
};
//statement
struct PowStat
{ template<int i>
  struct Code
  { static void exec(PowEnv& env)
    { env.r *= env.m; }
  };
};
//PowerD1<>
template<int n>
struct PowerD1
{ static int exec(const int& m)
  { PowEnv env(m);
    EFOR1<0,Less,n,+1,PowStat>::exec(env);
    return env.r;
  }
};
//...
cout << PowerD1<3>::exec(2) << endl;
```

Figure 10-82 *Implementation of* `PowerD1<>` *using* `EFOR1<>`

$$r = i \ / \ width$$

where "/" stands for integral division.

For the column index, on the other hand, use this formula:

$$c = i \bmod width$$

where "mod" computes the remainder of integral division.

The two-dimensional index (r,c) can be mapped back onto i as follows:

$$i = r \cdot width + c$$

These formulas allow us to replace the two nested efor-loops in Figure 10-86 by only one efor-loop. This is shown in Figure 10-88.

```
namespace intimate
{ struct Stop
  { static void exec() {};
    template<class Env>
    static void exec(Env& env) {};
  };
};

template <int from, class Compare, int to, int by,
          class Statement>
struct EFOR
{ static void exec()
  { IF<Compare::template Code<from,to>::RET,
       typename Statement::Code<from>,
       intimate::Stop
     >::RET::exec();
    IF<Compare::template Code<from,to>::RET,
       EFOR<from+by,Compare,to,by,Statement>,
       intimate::Stop
     >::RET::exec();
  }
};

template <int from, class Compare, int to, int by,
          class Statement>
struct EFOR1
{ template<class Env>
  static void exec(Env& env)
  { IF<Compare::template Code<from,to>::RET,
       typename Statement::Code<from>,
       intimate::Stop
     >::RET::exec(env);
    IF<Compare::template Code<from,to>::RET,
       EFOR1<from+by,Compare,to,by,Statement>,
       intimate::Stop
     >::RET::exec(env);
  }
};

//Greater<>, GreaterEqual<>, Less<>, and LessEqual<> are
//implemented as in Figure 10-61
```

efor.cpp

Figure 10-83 Implementation of EFOR<> *and* EFOR1<>

nested_for.cpp

```
for(int i=0; i<5; ++i)
{ for(int j=0; j<5; ++j)
    cout << '(' << i << ',' << j << ")\t";
  cout << endl;
}
```

Figure 10-84 *Two nested for-loops iterating over a 5-by-5 square*

```
Print a 5-by-5 square:
(0,0)   (0,1)   (0,2)   (0,3)   (0,4)
(1,0)   (1,1)   (1,2)   (1,3)   (1,4)
(2,0)   (2,1)   (2,2)   (2,3)   (2,4)
(3,0)   (3,1)   (3,2)   (3,3)   (3,4)
(4,0)   (4,1)   (4,2)   (4,3)   (4,4)
```

Figure 10-85 *Output of Figure 10-84*

nested_efor.cpp

```
//outer loop statement
struct OuterPrintLoopStat
{ template<int i>
  struct Code
  { struct InnerPrintLoopStat
    { template<int j>
      struct Code
      { static void exec()
        { cout << '(' << i << ',' << j << ")\t";
        }
      };
    };
    static void exec()
    { EFOR<0,Less,5,+1,InnerPrintLoopStat>::exec(); //#1
      cout << endl;
    }
  };
};

//...
cout << "Print a 5-by-5 square:" << endl;
EFOR<0,Less,5,+1,OuterPrintLoopStat>::exec(); //#2
```

Figure 10-86 *Two nested static efor-loops iterating over a 5-by-5 square*

```
cout << '(' << 0 << ',' << 0 << ")\t";
cout << '(' << 0 << ',' << 1 << ")\t";
cout << '(' << 0 << ',' << 2 << ")\t";
cout << '(' << 0 << ',' << 3 << ")\t";
cout << '(' << 0 << ',' << 4 << ")\t";
cout << endl;
cout << '(' << 1 << ',' << 0 << ")\t";
cout << '(' << 1 << ',' << 1 << ")\t";
...
cout << '(' << 4 << ',' << 4 << ")\t";
cout << endl;
```

Figure 10-87 Code generated by Figure 10-86

index_mapping. cpp

```
template <int width>
struct Square
{ enum { size = width*width };
};

template <int width, int hight>
struct Rectangle
{ enum { size = width*hight };
};

template <int width, int index>
struct MapToRectangle
{ enum { i = index / width,
         j = index % width
       };
};

//statement
template<int width, template<int,int>class MapToShape>
struct PrintStat
{ template<int n>
  struct Code
  { enum { i = MapToShape<width,n>::i,
           j = MapToShape<width,n>::j
         };
    static void exec()
```

(continued)

Figure 10-88 Iterating over matrices using one efor-loop only

```
    { cout << '(' << i << ',' << j << ")\t";
      if (j==width-1) cout << endl;
    }
  };
};


//...
cout << "Print a 5-by-5 square:" << endl;
EFOR<0,Less,Square<5>::size,+1,PrintStat<5,MapToRectangle>
    >::exec();

cout << "Print a 5-by-4 rectangle:" << endl;
EFOR<0,Less,Rectangle<5,4>::size,+1,PrintStat<5,MapToRectangle>
    >::exec();
```

Figure 10-88 *Iterating over matrices using one efor-loop only (continued)*

Square<> is used to compute the stop index for iterating over a square and Rectangle<> for iterating over a rectangle. MapToRectangle<> maps *i* to *r* and *c*, as in the formulas given previously.

Sometimes we need to iterate over a part of a matrix only, for example, over the upper triangle of the matrix with or without the diagonal (see Figure 10-89). (For example, we will need this functionality in Section 10.13 to test the promotion metafunction Promote<>.) For this purpose, we need new stop-index and index-mapping metafunctions. They are given in Figure 10-90. Triangle<> computes the stop index for iterating over a triangle of a

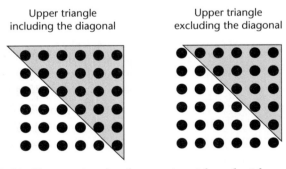

Figure 10-89 *Upper triangle of a matrix with and without the diagonal*

```
template <int width>
struct Triangle
{ enum { size = width*(width + 1)/2 };
};

template <int width>
struct StrictTriangle
{ enum { size = Triangle<width-1>::size };
};

namespace intimate
{
  template <int width,int index>
  struct TriangleCalcI
  { enum { i = TriangleCalcI<(index>=width ? width-1    : 0),
                            (index>=width ? index-width : 0)
                 >::i+1
         };
  };

  template<>
  struct TriangleCalcI<0,0>
  { enum { i = -1 };
  };
}; //end of namespace intimate

template <int width,int index>
struct MapToUpperTriangle
{ enum { i = intimate::TriangleCalcI<width,index>::i,
         j = index + Triangle<i>::size - i*width
       };
};

template <int width,int index>
struct MapToStrictUpperTriangle
{ enum { i = MapToUpperTriangle<width-1,index>::i,
         j = MapToUpperTriangle<width-1,index>::j+1
       };
};
```

index_mapping.
cpp

(continued)

Figure 10-90 *Iterating over the upper triangle of a matrix including the diagonal or excluding the diagonal using one for efor-loop only*

```
//statement PrintStat<> as in Figure 10-88
//...

//...
cout << "Print a 5-by-5 upper triangle:" << endl;
EFOR<0,Less,Triangle<5>::size,+1,PrintStat<5,MapToUpperTriangle>
    >::exec();

cout << "Print a 5-by-5 upper triangle without diagonal:"
     << endl;
EFOR<0,Less,StrictTriangle<5>::size,+1,
     PrintStat<5,MapToStrictUpperTriangle>
     >::exec();
```

Figure 10-90 *Iterating over the upper triangle of a matrix including the diagonal or excluding the diagonal using one for efor-loop only (continued)*

```
Print a 5-by-5 upper triangle:
(0,0)   (0,1)   (0,2)   (0,3)   (0,4)
(1,1)   (1,2)   (1,3)   (1,4)
(2,2)   (2,3)   (2,4)
(3,3)   (3,4)
(4,4)
Print a 5-by-5 upper triangle without diagonal:
(0,1)   (0,2)   (0,3)   (0,4)
(1,2)   (1,3)   (1,4)
(2,3)   (2,4)
(3,4)
```

Figure 10-91 *Runtime output of Figure 10-90*

matrix including the diagonal. StrictTriangle<> computes the stop index for iterating over a triangle of a matrix excluding the diagonal. The corresponding index-mapping metafunctions are MapToUpperTriangle<> and MapToStrictUpperTriangle<>. Figure 10-91 shows the runtime output of this program.

10.13 Example: Using Static Execute Loops to Test Metafunctions

We need to test metafunctions just as any new function we write. We usually test functions by subjecting them to a set of test data and checking the results. This might involve calling them with different argument combinations in a loop. Obviously, when testing metafunctions, we need to generate *static* test data, and normal loops, such as while or for, are not appropriate for this task. For example, you cannot use the loop index of a for-loop as an argument of a metafunction because the index is a runtime variable. So, we have to use one of our static loops. Actually, we need one of our static e-loops because they allow us to generate diagnostic code for printing the test results in each iteration.

Let's take a look at a concrete example. Suppose that we want to test the type promoting metafunction Promote<> from Figure 10-14 in Section 10.10.4. As you may remember, Promote<> takes two numeric types and returns the numerically larger one. For example, when confronted with float and double, it returns double. Obviously, Promote<> should be commutative, that is, Promote<float,double>::RET ought to be the same as Promote<double,float>::RET. To make sure that this is really the case for the implementation in Figure 10-14, we'll write some code to test it.

The testing involves checking whether Promote<A,B>::RET is the same as Promote<B,A>::RET for all possible pairs (*A,B*) of relevant numeric types. Let's assume that our set of relevant numeric types consists of the following fourteen types: wchar_t, bool, char, signed char, unsigned char, short, unsigned short, int, unsigned int, long, unsigned long, float, double, and long double. The testing code needs to enumerate over these types and generate and

test_promote.
cpp

```
template<int no> struct TypeNo {};
template<> struct TypeNo<0>  {typedef wchar_t Type;};
template<> struct TypeNo<1>  {typedef bool Type;};
template<> struct TypeNo<2>  {typedef char Type;};
template<> struct TypeNo<3>  {typedef signed char Type;};
template<> struct TypeNo<4>  {typedef unsigned char Type;};
template<> struct TypeNo<5>  {typedef short Type;};
template<> struct TypeNo<6>  {typedef unsigned short Type;};
template<> struct TypeNo<7>  {typedef int Type;};
template<> struct TypeNo<8>  {typedef unsigned int Type;};
template<> struct TypeNo<9>  {typedef long Type;};
template<> struct TypeNo<10> {typedef unsigned long Type;};
template<> struct TypeNo<11> {typedef float Type;};
template<> struct TypeNo<12> {typedef double Type;};
template<> struct TypeNo<13> {typedef long double Type;};
```

Figure 10-92 Template mapping integers to types

test_promote. cpp

```
template<class A> struct TypeTraits {};
template<> struct TypeTraits<wchar_t>
  {enum {no=  0}; static char* name() {return "wchar_t";}};
template<> struct TypeTraits<bool>
  {enum {no=  1}; static char* name() {return "bool";}};
template<> struct TypeTraits<char>
  {enum {no=  2}; static char* name() {return "char";}};
template<> struct TypeTraits<signed char>
  {enum {no=  3}; static char* name() {return "signed char";}};
template<> struct TypeTraits<unsigned char>
  {enum {no=  4}; static char* name() {return "unsigned char";}};
template<> struct TypeTraits<short>
  {enum {no=  5}; static char* name() {return "short";}};
//in MS VC++ 5.0, unsigned short is the same as wchar_t, so
//the following specialization is not allowed for MS VC++5.0
#ifndef _MSC_VER
template<> struct TypeTraits<unsigned short>
  {enum {no=  6};static char* name() {return "unsigned short";}};
#endif
template<> struct TypeTraits<int>
  {enum {no=  7}; static char* name() {return "int";}};
template<> struct TypeTraits<unsigned int>
  {enum {no=  8}; static char* name() {return "unsigned int";}};
template<> struct TypeTraits<long>
  {enum {no=  9}; static char* name() {return "long";}};
template<> struct TypeTraits<unsigned long>
  {enum {no= 10}; static char* name() {return "unsigned long"";}};
template<> struct TypeTraits<float>
  {enum {no= 11}; static char* name() {return "float";}};
template<> struct TypeTraits<double>
  {enum {no= 12}; static char* name() {return "double";}};
template<> struct TypeTraits<long double>
  {enum {no= 13}; static char* name() {return "long double";}};
```

Figure 10-93 Type traits template providing the ID and the name of each numeric type

check the different type combinations. There are two ways to enumerate over a number of types: We can either enumerate over a list of types as in Section 10.10.5 or map the types to numbers and enumerate over the corresponding numbers. We'll use the latter method for our testing code.

So, we need to give each numeric type an identification number. We do this by defining two templates, one for retrieving a type given its ID (TypeNo<> in Figure 10-92) and one for finding out the ID of a given type (TypeTraits<> in Figure 10-93). The latter also allows us to find out the name of a type at runtime.

Now we can start designing the testing code. We will use a static e-loop to generate the needed type combinations, or more precisely, combinations of type IDs. All combinations of two types out of the set of fourteen numeric types can be organized into a 14-by-14 matrix (see Figure 10-94). Because checking commutativity for the pair of types (*A*,*B*) also checks (*B*,*A*) and the result of promoting (*A*,*A*) given the implementation in Figure 10-14 can only be *A*, we only need to check one triangle of the matrix without the diagonal (i.e., the shaded region in Figure 10-94).

Thus, our testing code needs to iterate over one triangle of the matrix without the diagonal. For this purpose, we'll use one static efor-loop and the index mapping metafunctions described in Section 10.12.5.4. The resulting code is shown in Figure 10-95. To make things more interesting, we use IF<> to detect inconsistent promotions rather than if. But we could also have used if, which would be equivalent to using IF<> in case you enable appropriate optimization options and let the compiler eliminate unreachable if-branches.

The primitive alternative to using the efor-loop is to write out the test for each pair manually. This would be quite tedious and

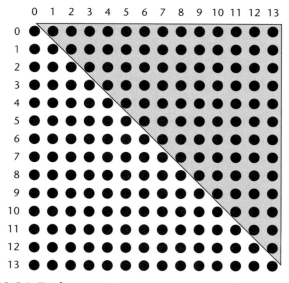

Figure 10-94 *Each point (i,j) represents a pair of types (A,B), where i is the ID of A and j the ID of B*

```
template<int nTypes>
struct CheckPromote
{ template <int n>
  struct Code
  { enum { i = MapToStrictUpperTriangle<nTypes,n>::i,
           j = MapToStrictUpperTriangle<nTypes,n>::j
         };
    typedef typename TypeNo<i>::Type T1;
    typedef typename TypeNo<j>::Type T2;
    typedef typename Promote<T1,T2>::RET R1;
    typedef typename Promote<T2,T1>::RET R2;
    struct Ok
    { static void print()
      {}
    };
    struct Error
    { static void print()
      { cout << "Inconsistent promotion detected:" << endl
             << "\"Promote<" << TypeTraits<T1>::name() << ','
             << TypeTraits<T2>::name() << ">\" yields \""
             << TypeTraits<R1>::name() << "\" whereas" << endl
             << "\"Promote<" << TypeTraits<T2>::name() << ','
             << TypeTraits<T1>::name() << ">\" yields \""
             << TypeTraits<R2>::name() << "\"" << endl << endl;
      }
    };
    static void exec()
    { typedef typename
        IF<TypeTraits<R1>::no != TypeTraits <R2>::no
           Error,Ok>::RET Code1;
      Code1::print();
    }
  };
};
//...
EFOR<0,Less,StrictTriangle<14>::size,+1,CheckPromote<14>
    >::exec();
```

test_promote. cpp

Figure 10-95 Code checking the commutativity of Promote<>

error prone because of the large number of type combinations. Obviously, the number of checked combinations is equal to the number of elements in one triangle of an *n*-by-*n* matrix without the diagonal, that is, $\frac{1}{2}n(n-1)$, where *n* is the number of numeric

types for which Promote<> works. In our case, this amounts to
½·14·(14–1), or 91 combinations. Furthermore, whenever adding
the support for the *n*+1 numeric type (e.g., complex), we would
have to write *n* more tests.

You'd expect that running our testing code wouldn't report
any inconsistencies. However, this will probably not be the case.
Figure 10-96 shows the output of running the testing code after
compiling it with Microsoft Visual C++ 5.0. What is the reason for
these inconsistencies? Printing out the properties of the types for
which these inconsistencies occur reveals that they are equal with
respect to numeric_limits<>::max_exponent10 and numeric_
limits<>::digits. This has the effect that the IF<> in Figure 10-14
always returns the then-branch for these types. This situation fully
conforms to the C++ Standard, nevertheless it is still compiler
dependent. Hence compiling the testing code with different compilers and executing it may result in different outputs. To fix this
problem, we need to provide new specializations of Promote<> for
these pathological cases. We decided that promoting char and
signed char will yield char and that the other promotions should
always return the conceptually larger type. The file promote_
patch.h, whose contents is shown in Figure 10-97, contains the
fixes specific to Microsoft Visual C++ 5.0. After including
promote_patch.h subsequent to promote.h and recompiling and
running the testing code, no inconsistencies are reported.

```
Inconsistent promotion detected:
"Promote<char,signed char>" yields "char" whereas
"Promote<signed char,char>" yields "signed char"
Inconsistent promotion detected:
"Promote<int,long>" yields "int" whereas
"Promote<long,int>" yields "long"
Inconsistent promotion detected:
"Promote<unsigned int,unsigned long>" yields "unsigned int"
whereas
"Promote<unsigned long,unsigned int>" yields "unsigned long"
Inconsistent promotion detected:
"Promote<double,long double>" yields "double" whereas
"Promote<long double,double>" yields "long double"
```

*Figure 10-96 Runtime output of the testing code after compiling it with
MS VC++ 5.0*

*promote_*
patch.h

```
template<>
struct Promote<double,long double>
{ typedef long double RET;
};
template<>
struct Promote<unsigned int,unsigned long>
{ typedef unsigned long RET;
};
template<>
struct Promote<int,long>
{ typedef long RET;
};
template<>
struct Promote<signed char,char>
{ typedef char RET;
};
```

Figure 10-97 `promote_patch.h` *fixes problems of* `promote.h` *from Figure 10-14 (MS VC++ 5.0 specific)*

10.14 Partial Evaluation in C++

If all or some of the parameters of a function are known at compile time, the function can be fully or partially evaluated at compile time. As we discussed in Section 10.3, this can be performed by special systems called *partial evaluators* or *program specializers*. Interestingly, much of the effect of partial evaluation can be attained in C++ using template metaprogramming, that is, without the need of any special system.

We'll explain the idea of partial evaluation in C++ using a power function as an example. Our familiar implementation of a power function is shown again in Figure 10-98.

partialeval.cpp

```
inline int power(const int& m, int n)
{ int r = 1;
  for (; n>0; --n) r *= m;
  return r;
}
```

Figure 10-98 *Function for raising* m *to the power of* n, *where* m *and* n *are integral numbers and* n>=0

There are three interesting cases when calling power(m,n):

1. n and m are known at compile time.
2. n is known at compile time and m is not known until runtime.
3. n and m are not known until runtime.

In the first case, we can compute the result at compile time. In C++, we can do it using a metafunction (see Figure 10-99). In the second case, we can unroll the for-loop. We have already discussed this in Section 10.12.4 (see Figure 10-64). The necessary implementation is given again in Figure 10-100. In the third case, we have to use the original implementation from Figure 10-98.

So we can easily cover all of the three interesting cases in C++. The only inconvenience is that the caller has to use a different syntax for each case:

♦ Power<n,m>::RET
♦ power<n>(m)
♦ power(m,n)

How can we get rid of this inconvenience? The idea is to define one power(m,n) function and use overloading to distinguish between the three implementations. Unfortunately, there are two problems. First, overloading requires that the arguments expected by each of the three implementations differ in type. But the problem is that there is no type difference between runtime int-values and static int-values, for example, literals. The other problem is that you cannot use a function parameter as a static value inside that function, even if you pass a static value as an argument. The

partialeval.cpp

```
template<int m, int n>
struct Power
{ enum { RET = Power<m,n-1>::RET * m };
};
template<int m>
struct Power<m,0>
{ enum { RET = 1 };
};
//...
cout << Power<3>::exec(2) << endl;
```

Figure 10-99 *Metafunction for raising* m *to the power of* n *at compile time*

partialeval.cpp

```
template<int n>
inline int power(const int& m)
{ return power<n-1>(m) * m; }
template<>
inline int power<1>(const int& m)
{ return m; }
template<>
inline int power<0>(const int& m)
{ return 1; }
//...
cout << power<3>(2) << endl
```

Figure 10-100 *Recursive inlining generates optimized code for static* n

solution is to provide a special type representing static int-values. This type has to carry the static int-value as a part of it. The implementation is shown in Figure 10-101. Thanks to the type conversion operator, you can use an instance of StaticInt<> wherever an integer would be appropriate.

Now we can use StaticInt<> to provide a uniform interface to all three implementations. This is demonstrated in Figure 10-102. The dynamic version is overloaded for static n and m and for static n. The static values are accessed at compile time. Please note that power(n,m) for static n and m also returns an instance of StaticInt<>. This way we can use the return value of this function as a static value for another function expecting a static value. For example, the result of power(c2,power(c2,c3)) is computed fully at compile time.

As discussed in Section 10.3, we don't want to execute a computationally intensive numeric program fully using a compiler—this could take a long time. However, by selectively wrapping integer constants in StaticInt<>, we can control which parts of a

partialeval.cpp

```
template<int n>
struct StaticInt
{ enum { RET = n };
  operator const int() const { return n; }
};
```

Figure 10-101 *Type representing static integers*

```
//power(int,int) as in Figure 10-98
//Power<int,int> as in Figure 10-99
//power<int>(int) as in Figure 10-100

//overload power(m,n) for static m and n
template<int m, int n>
inline StaticInt<Power<m,n>::RET>
power(const StaticInt<m>&, const StaticInt<n>&)
{ return StaticInt<Power<m,n>::RET>();
}

//overload power(m,n) for static n
template<int n>
inline int power(const int& m, const StaticInt<n>&)
{ return power<n>(m);
}

//...
//declare two static integers
StaticInt<2> c2;
StaticInt<3> c3;

cout << power(2,3)    << endl;             //uses for-loop
cout << power(c2,3)   << endl;             //uses for-loop
cout << power(2,c3)   << endl;             //cout << 2*2*2 << endl;
cout << power(c2,c3)  << endl;             //cout << 8       << endl;
cout << power(c2,power(c2,c3)) << endl; //cout << 256     << endl;
```

partialeval.cpp

Figure 10-102 *Uniform calling interface to a power function and its versions with full and partial evaluation at compile time*

C++ program will be evaluated at compile time and which will not. This corresponds to the concept of *offline partial evaluation* (see Section 10.3), where an expert annotates the program code to advise the partial evaluator as to which parts to evaluate. The only difference between using a partial evaluator and the techniques from this section is that a partial evaluator can produce specialized versions of a function automatically, that is, the programmer only needs to write the general dynamic case. With template metaprogramming, on the other hand, the library writer has to explicitly implement the general dynamic case and the versions with full and partial evaluation at compile time.

10.15 Workarounds for Partial Template Specialization

As you saw in the previous sections, partial specialization allows you to terminate the recursion of a template in which some parameters remain fixed during all iterations and other parameters vary from iteration to iteration. Unfortunately, as of this writing, many compilers do not support partial specialization. But here is the good news: We've always been able to find a workaround. This section gives you the necessary techniques for doing without partial specialization.

We start with a recursive metafunction with numeric arguments. A classic example of a numeric function requiring partial specialization is raising a number to the power of n, which we've already seen in Figure 10-99. This function takes m and n as arguments and recursively computes the result by calling Power<m,n-1>. Thus, the first argument remains constant, while the second argument is "consumed." The final call is Power<m,0>, which is a classic case for partial specialization: One argument could be anything and the other one is fixed.

If your C++ compiler does not support partial specialization, you need another solution. The required technique is to map the final call to one that has all of its arguments fixed, for example, Power<1,0>. This can be easily done by using extra conditional operators:

```
template<int n1, int n>
struct Power
{  enum { RET = n>0
               ? Power<(n>0)? m:1, (n>0)? n-1:0>::RET * n1
               : 1 };
};


template<>
struct Power<1,0>
{  enum { RET = 1 };
};


// prints "8"
cout << "Power<2,3>::RET = " << Power<2,3>::RET << endl;
```

We can use a similar technique to get rid of partial specialization in the metafunction Append1<> (see Figure 10-20 in Section 10.10.5). All we have to do is map the recursion termination to a case where both arguments are fixed:

```
template<class List, int n>
class Append1
{ enum { new_head = IsEmpty<List>::RET ? endValue : n }; 
public:
  typedef
    IF<IsEmpty<List>::RET,
      Cons<n>,
      Cons<List::head,
          typename Append1<typename List::Tail, new_head>::RET >
    >::RET RET;
};


template<>
struct Append1<End, endValue>
{ typedef End RET;
};
```

Of course, the previous code uses the IF<> version without partial specialization (see Figure 10-27).

The same technique also works with type arguments. Here is a version of the metafunction Append<> (see Figure 10-21) without partial specialization (remember that the second argument in the original implementation was constant during recursion):

```
template<class List1, class List2>
class Append
{ typedef IF<IsEmpty<List1>::RET,
             End,
             List2
           >::RET NewList2;
public:
  typedef IF<IsEmpty<List1>::RET,
             List2,
             Cons<List1::head,
                 typename Append<typename List1::Tail,
                                 NewList2>::RET
           >
         >::RET RET;
};


template<>
struct Append<End, End>
{ typedef End RET;
};
```

10.16   Problems of Template Metaprogramming

Template metaprogramming also has several problems, particularly in the areas of debugging, error reporting, code readability, compilation speed, internal capacity and robustness of compilers, and portability. We discuss these problems in Section 14.4.2.11.

10.17   Historical Notes

The need for representing metainformation at compile time became apparent during the development of the C++ Standard Library. Streams, strings, and containers are all classes parameterized by the type of their elements. However, it turns out that each of these components also requires additional information, which depends on the actual element type parameter. For example, the special value representing "end of file" (EOF) for a stream is different for char and w_char. Of course, you could add an extra parameter to pass this metainformation about the element type to a component. But this would require the user to supply the extra parameter values manually, even though the information can be derived automatically. This problem has been solved by the traits template idiom [BN94, Mye95], which we discussed in Section 10.10.3. For example, the C++ Standard Library provides character traits templates defining, among other properties, EOF and conversion functions for different character types. The idea to use traits classes as "configuration repositories" was first published in [Eis96].

A major milestone was the discovery of the possibility of using a C++ compiler to perform arbitrary computations at compile time. The first known program of this kind was written by Erwin Unruh [Unr94]. It computed prime numbers using templates and printed them as compile-time warnings (see Figure 10-103). Unruh circulated it as a "curiosity" among the participants of a C++ standardization committee meeting in 1994.

The first article on template metaprogramming [Vel95a] was published by Todd Veldhuizen in 1995. This article explicitly identified template specialization as a compile-time selection construct and template recursion as a looping construct. Expression templates were proposed in [Vel96b]. Veldhuizen used both techniques to develop the numerical array package Blitz++ [Vel97], which we mentioned in Section 8.7.4. Blitz++ achieves the performance of hand-crafted C or Fortran code while preserving the high abstraction level of object-oriented programming.

```
P:\HC\D386_O> type primes.cpp
// Prime number computation by Erwin Unruh -- erwin.unruh@mch.sni.de.
template <int i> struct D { D(void*); operator int(); };

template <int p, int i> struct is_prime {
    enum { prim = (p%i) && is_prime<(i > 2 ? p : 0), i -1>::prim };
    };

template <int i> struct Prime_print {
    Prime_print<i-1> a;
    enum { prim = is_prime<i, i-1>::prim };
    void f() { D<i> d = prim; }
    };

struct is_prime<0,0>  { enum { prim = 1 }; };
struct is_prime<0,1>  { enum { prim = 1 }; };
struct Prime_print<2>  { enum { prim = 1 }; void f() { D<2> d = prim; } };
#ifndef LAST
#define LAST 10
#endif
main() {
    Prime_print<LAST> a;
    }

P:\HC\D386_O> hc3 i primes.cpp -DLAST=30
MetaWare High C/C++ Compiler R2.6
(c) Copyright 1987-94, MetaWare Incorporated
E "primes.cpp",L16/C63(#416):    prim
|    Type 'enum{}' can't be converted to type 'D<2>' ("primes.cpp",...
-- Detected during instantiation of Prime_print<30> at "primes.cpp",...
E "primes.cpp",L16/C63(#416):    prim
|    Type 'enum{}' can't be converted to type 'D<3>' ("primes.cpp",...
-- Detected during instantiation of Prime_print<30> at "primes.cpp",...
E "primes.cpp",L16/C63(#416):    prim
|    Type 'enum{}' can't be converted to type 'D<5>' ("primes.cpp",...
-- Detected during instantiation of Prime_print<30> at "primes.cpp",...
E "primes.cpp",L16/C63(#416):    prim
|    Type 'enum{}' can't be converted to type 'D<7>' ("primes.cpp",...
-- Detected during instantiation of Prime_print<30> at "primes.cpp",...
```

Figure 10-103 *The original metaprogram computing prime numbers at compile time by Erwin Unruh*

The IF<> template was the first control structure in a generic form [Cza97]. The remaining control structures were published in [EC99]. In addition to Blitz++, there are several other libraries that use template metaprogramming, for example, Pooma [POOMA], A++/P++ [BDQ97], MTL [SL98a], and the generative matrix package described in Chapter 14.

Chapter 11

Intentional Programming

Language exists to conceal true thought.

—Attributed to
Charles Maurice
de Talleyrand-Périgord

11.1 Why Is This Chapter Worth Reading?

This chapter presents groundbreaking concepts and technologies that have the potential to revolutionize software development as we know it today. We will discuss *Intentional Programming* (IP), which represents a perfect implementation platform for Generative Programming. IP is an extendible programming and metaprogramming environment based on *active source*, that is, a source that may provide its own editing, rendering, compiling, debugging, and versioning behavior. The benefits of the IP technology are exciting, in particular:

- It enables the achievement of natural notations, great flexibility, and excellent performance simultaneously.
- It provides optimal, domain-specific support in all programming tasks (supports effective typing, rich notations, debugging, error reporting, and so on).
- It addresses the code tangling problem by allowing you to implement and easily distribute aspect-oriented language features.
- It allows you to include more design information in the code and to raise its intentionality (or as some like to say, "to raise the level of abstraction").
- It helps with software evolution by supporting automated editing and refactoring of code.
- It makes your domain-specific libraries less vulnerable to changes on the market of general-purpose programming languages.
- It can be introduced into an organization in an evolutionary way with exciting benefits for the minimal cost of initial training.

♦ It supports all of your legacy code and allows you to improve it.
♦ It provides third-party vendors with a common infrastructure and a common internal source representation for implementing and distributing language extensions and language-based tools.
♦ It promotes domain specialization and facilitates more effective sharing of domain-specific knowledge.

The main ideas of Intentional Programming include

♦ Representing both general and domain-specific programming abstractions directly as language features (called *intentions*).
♦ Replacing traditional, fixed programming languages with configurations of intentions that can be loaded into the system as needed.
♦ Representing program source not as a passive, plain text, but as active source allowing the programmer to interact with it at programming time.
♦ Allowing for domain-specific extensions of any part of the programming environment including the compiler, debugger, editor (which displays active source and allows its entry), version control system, and so on. This feature enables you to provide domain-specific optimizations, domain-specific notations (including graphical ones), domain-specific error-handling and debugging support, and so on.

In this chapter, you'll learn about the philosophy and technology behind Intentional Programming.

11.2 What Is Intentional Programming?

Extension libraries

Programming versus metaprogramming environment

Intentional Programming (IP) is a new, groundbreaking extendible programming and metaprogramming environment based on active source, which is being developed at Microsoft.[1] As a programming environment, IP optimally supports application programmers in their programming tasks and allows them to load *extension libraries* to extend it with new general-purpose and domain-specific programming language extensions as needed for a given application. Extension libraries may extend any part of the environment including the compiler, debugger, editor, version control system, and so on. As a metaprogramming environment, IP optimally supports language implementers developing extension libraries. It

---

1. See www.research.microsoft.com/ip and [Sim95, Sim96, Sim97, ADK+98, Röd99].

provides metaprogramming capabilities including a code-transformation framework, protocols for coordinating the compilation of code using independently developed language extensions, special debugging facilities for debugging metacode, and sets of standard APIs for extending the various parts of the environment. Similar to application programmers, language implementers can also take advantage of the extensibility of IP and load extension libraries providing notations and facilities that help to do their job more efficiently.

Active source, methods, intentions

One of the main ideas of IP is to represent program source not as plain ASCII text, but as *active source*, that is, a graph data structure with behavior at programming time. The behavior of program source is implemented using *methods* operating on the source graph. The methods define different aspects of the source including its visualization, entry, browsing, compilation, debugging, and versioning behavior. User programs are written using language abstractions loaded into the system. In the simplest case, you may load a set of C programming abstractions, which will let you write C code. However, any useful combination of general-purpose and domain-specific language abstraction can be loaded and used in a program. In the IP terminology, language abstractions are referred to as *intentions*. IP lets you implement new intentions by declaring them and implementing their methods. The methods are then compiled into extension libraries (which are basically a general kind of active libraries discussed in Section 8.7.4). When you want to use certain intentions, you load the corresponding extension libraries into the development environment. Thanks to the code in the extension libraries, the IP system will know how to display source using these intentions as well as know how to support its entry, browsing, compilation, debugging, versioning, and so on.

Intentions versus object classes

Intentions are not to be confused with object classes: The methods of an intention are called at programming time, and they support all the different aspects of program development that uses this intention. This is also the added value of intentions: By implementing abstractions as intentions rather than classes, your abstractions can actively support editing, compiling, optimizing, profiling, testing, and browsing programs that use these abstractions.[2]

Rendering and optimizing domain-specific abstractions

An exciting aspect of IP is the possibility of implementing and using domain-specific abstractions as intentions. This gives you the opportunity to implement domain-specific notations, for example,

2. Please note that intentions live one level above object classes: An intention implements a language feature, that is, you can implement the class construct as an intention.

mathematical formulas can be displayed using true two-dimensional notation (e.g., variables with subscripts). You can also have graphical notations or embed GUI controls in the source (see Figure 11-14 through Figure 11-20 for IP screen shots demonstrating these capabilities). There are virtually no limitations to the kind of notation you can implement. Also, you can truly interact with an instance of an intention in a program. For example, the program source can contain an instance of a decision table, which is rendered as a table control, and the data you enter in the table is checked for consistency during entry. However, the most exciting point is that domain-specific notations may implement their own domain-specific optimizations. For example, you can have a nicely visualized mathematical formula (just like in a math textbook) and still have the system generate very efficient code for it. In fact, the code could be more efficient than what you would manually write in C or even Assembler. This is so because the system can apply complex optimizations of the application code that would not be practical to perform manually (e.g., a set of matrix intentions could implement various complex cache-based optimizations of matrix code). Because the system allows you to implement different alternative visualizations that you can switch between, you can have different views showing selected aspects of the source code in different textual and/or graphical notations. This is similar to the way CAD systems work, by letting you choose a particular view on a complex structure.

Eliminating the need for parsing

Another feature of IP is the elimination of the need for parsing. This is very useful because parsing limits the extendibility of current programming languages. For example, the grammar of C++ is context sensitive, extremely complex (contains several reduce/reduce ambiguities), and difficult to extend without making it unparsable. Furthermore, standard C++ has a number of artificial syntax rules that had to be added to the language in order to keep it parsable. An example of such a rule is the necessity to separate two closing angle brackets in template expressions by an extra space (e.g., foo<bar<foobaz> >) in order to distinguish them from the right-shift operator (i.e., >>). Another example is the strange way of distinguishing the declaration of the postfix variant of the increment operator from the prefix one (i.e., ++() versus ++(int)). IP does not have such problems because it eliminates the need for parsing altogether. The source graph is built as you type. When you enter a name of an intention, the system will create an instance of it and may activate some of the intention's methods to help enter further nodes. For example, if you type in the name of a procedure declared elsewhere, the system will create a procedure call and insert a placeholder for each argument. Next, you can tab through the placeholders and replace them by the actual arguments. You can think of the editing process as working with a WYSIWYG[3] word processor rather than with a simple text editor. That is, while editing, you are modifying a more complex underlying representation rather than just simple text. Furthermore, each text element may exhibit its own behavior. However, it is important to point out that the IP editor is not a syntax-oriented editor, and this is good. You are in full control over what kind of source graph you are building. There are commands that help you navigate in the graph and make any changes you wish. In other words, you can enter programs that would not compile (the structure of the program is checked when you compile it). This is very useful during coding because the requirement to adhere to some program syntax at any point in time is impractical. All in all, direct editing allows IP to support extendible and feature-rich domain-specific notations.

Intentional encoding

Thanks to the possibility of introducing new language abstractions, you can capture more analysis and design information in the source code. This is so because you can introduce new intentions to represent the analysis and design abstractions for your software and use them right in the source. In many cases, the information that would otherwise make a great comment can actually be represented in a machine-processable form. You can achieve this in IP by introducing new abstractions to represent this information. Furthermore, programmers can introduce intentions to capture common patterns and idioms they would otherwise have to enter manually over and over again. Most importantly, such intentions would not be just simple textual macros, but proper language features. Thus, the main goal of IP is to help to represent source as *intentionally* as possible, that is, without any loss of information or obscure language idioms and clutter.

Refactoring and software evolution

The main reason refactoring is so difficult to do today is that most of the design information is missing from the conventional implementation source. IP changes this situation. Because the source is represented as an extensible abstract syntax tree, and you can provide higher-level representations of your program, it becomes possible to automate refactoring and evolution to a high degree. You don't have to parse textual source and recognize code patterns and higher-level design structures in it before refactoring (which is not possible to do automatically in implementations

---

3. What You See Is What You Get

*Investment
protection*

using conventional general-purpose programming languages) because they are present directly in the source.

A problem faced by library vendors today is that general-purpose languages come and go, and the vendors are often forced to reimplement their domain-specific libraries in a new language. This is different with IP because your domain knowledge is represented using domain-specific abstractions and structures. Thus, the changes you apply to the source are dictated by the development in the domain and by the need to improve your source to better reflect the domain rather than by changes on the market of general-purpose languages. As a result, your investment into domain-specific code is better protected.

*Sustainable and
iterative
improvement*

Given the possibility of concentrating on domain-specific representations and the support for automated refactoring, you can actually constantly improve and evolve your software. As you "grow" your domain-specific libraries, you can improve the domain-specific notations, add more and more sophisticated domain-specific optimizations based on the newest research, provide interoperability with other domain-specific libraries that are likely to be used with yours, and so on. Unlike the integration of runtime components, such as JavaBeans, COM, or CORBA components, there are no runtime performance penalties for the integration of extension libraries. This is so because extension libraries interact at compile time to generate efficient code. All in all, IP allows you to improve the sources of your libraries in an iterative and sustainable way, so that you can become and then grow as a champion of your domains.

*Meta-
programming*

One way of thinking about IP is to view it as a perfect environment for metaprogramming. This is particularly true if you compare it to template metaprogramming in C++ (see Table 14-18 in Section 14.4.3). Template metaprogramming gives you only a limited set of abstractions to express metaprograms. In IP, on the other hand, you can use the same facilities at the metalevel as those available at the base level. That is, you can use the same intentions to write application code and extension libraries. However, if you wish to use special declarative notations to specify language extensions, you may provide them as extension libraries. A further shortcoming of C++ is that you cannot provide your own library-specific compile-time warnings. This is different in IP because extension libraries may attach user-defined error warnings to erroneous locations in the source they help to compile. Another problem with template metaprogramming is that you cannot debug template metaprograms because you cannot debug the compilation process. The IP environment, on the other hand, provides a debugger that you can use to debug the metacode. In particular, it lets you debug code transformations so you can view the different intermediate results of code transformation and also step through the execution of the code at the source level or the different intermediate transformation levels. Additionally, IP lets you debug the execution of the metacode itself. Finally, template metaprograms only extend the compilation process, whereas extension libraries may also contain metacode that implements other aspects of intentions including their visualization, entry, debugging, and so on.

Aspect-oriented programming

You can also think of IP as a perfect implementation platform for aspects (see Chapter 8). You can implement aspect languages and aspectual composition mechanisms as extension libraries. In addition to compile-time weaving, you can also implement different aspectual views as different kinds of visualization of a single source.

Working with legacy code

Finally, it is important to note that existing code written in any language can be imported into the IP system. In order to import legacy code in a given language, you only need to provide a parser and a set of intentions for that language (import parsers for C, C++, and Java are already available in the IP system). Once imported into the IP system, you can start improving the legacy source by introducing higher-level abstractions that were not present in the original language (e.g., introducing templates or preconditions and postconditions, intentions representing common idioms in the source, and domain-specific abstractions) and restructuring the code. All the refactoring capabilities of IP can be used in this process. So, the introduction of IP can be an evolutionary process instead of a revolutionary one. You can keep your legacy code and actually reengineer and improve it using IP. Thus, the introduction of more radical domain-specific notations does not have to be a revolutionary change. IP allows you to perfectly mimic the traditional text-based way of typing in source code (you'll see this in Section 11.4.1).

Short history

IP is the brainchild of Charles Simonyi,[4] who has been leading its development since the early nineties. He refers to IP as an "OS for abstractions" [WTH+99], meaning that IP provides a set of basic APIs and an infrastructure for developing language abstractions. The initial version of IP was implemented in C and after implementing the C intentions, the system was bootstrapped, that is, all IP sources were imported into IP.[5] This way, the system "lib-

---

4. Charles Simonyi hired and lead the teams that originally developed the Microsoft Word and Excel products.
5. C++ would have certainly been a more appropriate choice for implementing such a complex system. According to the IP development team, completing the first bootstrap had the highest priority, however. This was the reason IP was originally implemented in C. Implementing C intentions was by far a simpler job than implementing C++ intentions. The C++ intentions were implemented later.

erated" itself from C, and since then, new intentions have been added and also used in its implementation. Since the first bootstrap in 1995 [Sim95], all IP development has been done in IP itself. This provides the IP development team with an excellent opportunity to refine and improve the system as they use it.

11.3   Technology Behind IP[6]

11.3.1   System Architecture

The IP system is an extendible programming and metaprogramming environment containing all the usual components of a typical integrated development environment (IDE) including an editor and browsing tools, a compilation component (*reduction engine*), a debugger, a version control system, and parsers for importing legacy source. All these components operate on the IP source graph. The architecture of the IP IDE is shown in Figure 11-1.

Compared to the components of a conventional IDE, the components of the IP IDE have special capabilities including

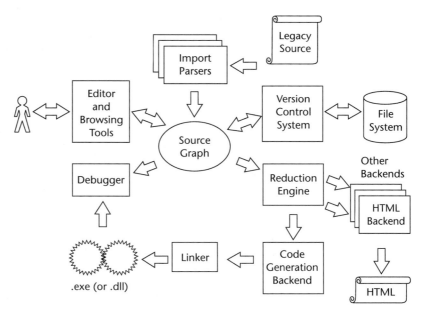

Figure 11-1 *Main components of the IP system*

---

6. As of this writing, the IP system is still under development, and the rest of this chapter describes the status of the system at the end of 1999.

♦ *Editor and browsing tools:* As in any IDE, the editor is used for viewing and entering program source. However, the IP editor is not simply a text editor, but rather a graph data structure because the program source in IP is not text (more precisely: syntax tree with links to declarations). This data structure is built up immediately as the source is being typed in (i.e., we can say that the editor replaces the parser of a traditional IDE). Furthermore, the IP editor supports true two-dimensional textual and graphical source views and allows the programmer to interact with the elements of the program source at programming time. In particular, mouse clicks and keystrokes entered on a given program element may be handled by this element (more precisely: by its methods). The IDE also provides a set of browsing tools and facilities for navigating in the program source. Because the program source has the form of a syntax tree with links to declarations, full and up-to-date browsing information is available all the time. We will discuss the editor and browsing tools in Section 11.4.

♦ *Reduction engine, code generation backends, and linker:* The IP reduction engine is the code-transformation framework of IP, and it plays the role of a compiler. There are several differences between the reduction engine and a compiler, however. First of all, there is no parser because the source is already available as a syntax tree with links to declarations. Furthermore, the reduction engine implements a transformational approach to compilation. After checking the structural correctness of the source, the reduction engine applies a series of transformations in order to generate an implementation consisting of a limited set of primitive abstractions called the *reduced code* or *R-code*. The ordering of the application of transformations is done partly by the reduction engine and partly by the transformation writers. Different R-codes can be defined for different target platforms, and the source can be reduced to different R-codes. Finally, an appropriate backend generates the platform-specific object code from a given R-code. For example, the backend from the Visual Studio product family is used to generate machine code for the Intel processors, and a different backend is used to generate Java bytecodes. The resulting object files are linked by a standard linker into an executable or a library. The reduction engine, together with some appropriate backend, can also be used to generate artifacts other than executable programs. For example, we can use this capability to generate documentation from the program source or implement higher-level language for generating Web pages.

♦ *Debugger:* The debugger allows the programmer to step through the execution of the program at different levels: the source level or any selected intermediate level produced by the transformations. You can also use the debugger to debug the IP system itself and the extension libraries (i.e., the metacode you write).

♦ *Version control system:* IP provides a team-enabled version control system, which works on binary IP source files. In contrast to conventional text-based version control systems, the IP version control system allows you to automatically merge two versions of a source, where one contains renamed and relocated functions and the other incorporates modifications in the bodies of these functions. After merging, the modifications will be incorporated in the renamed and relocated functions.

♦ *Import parsers:* Language parsers, for example, for C++ or Java, are needed for importing legacy code into the IP system. A given legacy code needs to be imported only once. The imported code is then saved in the IP program source format.

In contrast to traditional IDEs, any part of the IP system is extensible. The editor, reduction engine, debugger, and version control system may call system-provided default methods or user-provided methods (which may override the default ones) to handle new language abstractions (i.e., intentions). Methods defining the programming-time behavior of intentions are compiled into extension libraries, which can then be dynamically loaded into the IP system. For example, you can load the extension library for the C++ language, which will enable you to write C++ code. You can also load other sets of general and domain-specific intentions (which can extend the editor to handle a new kind of textual or graphical notation) and use them all at once.

11.3.2   Representing Programs in IP: The Source Graph

Source trees and source graphs

One of the main ideas behind IP is to represent source code directly as abstract syntax trees (ASTs) and let the user enter, modify, and compile them without ever having to work directly on program code stored as plain ASCII text. In IP, each AST node has a link to its declaration (e.g., a variable has a link to its declaration), for this reason IP actually represents programs as *source graphs*, which can be thought of as sets of interlinked *source trees*.[7] In the following four

---

7. In compiler design, ASTs whose elements have links to their declarations are referred to as "resolved ASTs." Conventional compilers usually first build unresolved ASTs using a parser, and then turn them into resolved ASTs by adding links to declarations during the semantic analysis stage. Formally, resolved ASTs are graphs, but not trees.

sections, we'll take a closer look at the structure of source graphs. This knowledge will help us understand how IP works internally. However, please keep in mind that as an application programmer using IP, you will not be permanently confronted with these details.

11.3.2.1 Treelike Structures

Tree elements and operands

Suppose that you want to represent the expression x+x as a source tree, that is, as an AST. To do so, you need a parent node representing the occurrence of the operator + and two child nodes representing the two occurrences of the variable x (see Figure 11-2). In IP, the nodes of a source tree are also referred to as *tree elements* (or *TEs*), and the child nodes are often called *operands*.

11.3.2.2 Graphlike Structures

Declarations and instances

In IP, anything you use has to be declared and defined somewhere. So, although the source tree in Figure 11-2 contains nodes representing just the *occurrences* of the operator + and variable x, the actual operator + and variable x have to be declared somewhere. Furthermore, every tree node in IP maintains a link to its *declaration*. This is illustrated in Figure 11-3. The figure shows our familiar source tree from Figure 11-2 plus the links to the declarations. The parent has a link to a node representing the declaration of the operator +, and the children have links to another node representing the declaration of the variable x. The links to declarations give meaning to the three tree elements on the left: Now, we know that the parent node is an occurrence, that is, an *instance* of the operator +, and the children are two instances of the variable x. It is interesting to note that thanks to the links to declarations we do not have to store any names in the tree elements on the left. If we

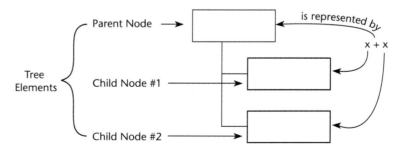

Figure 11-2 *Source tree representing the expression* x+x. *Child nodes are always drawn below their parent node and are counted in the top-down direction.*

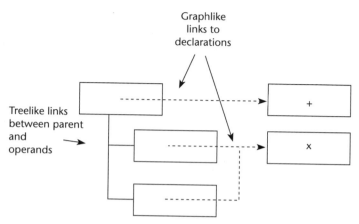

Figure 11-3 *Source tree of* x+x *plus declarations. Graphlike links to declarations are drawn as dashed arrows. Nodes with a name label are declaration nodes.*

need the name of any of the tree elements (e.g., the variable name "x"), we can retrieve it from the corresponding declaration. This representation has an enormous advantage over textual code: If you want to change the name of an abstraction (e.g., the variable name), you only need to change it in the declaration and do not need to update the places *referring* to the declaration. You'll see how this works in practice in Section 11.4.1.

Treelike and graphlike links

Even though the links between parent and child nodes always span a tree, this is not the case with the links to declarations. The

---

NOTE

It is important to note that names are only needed for the communication with the human programmer. The system does not need names because it references nodes using links, which are either pointers (for declarations and operands that are in the same address space) or globally unique identifiers (for declarations that are in a different address space). Furthermore, IP gives us the opportunity to use names that are not stored, but computed on-the-fly based on a given source pattern. For example, the generated name for a function parameter of type char* could be pchar. This is not always satisfactory, but if it is, it may save the programmer some tedious work. Finally, IP also allows you to give more than one name to an intention. For example, you may use short names for easy typing and then display source with long names for easy maintenance.

latter may point to declaration nodes located in the same tree or a different tree, and several nodes may have links to the same declaration (e.g., several occurrences of x point to the same declaration x). That's why we refer to the links between parent and child nodes as *treelike links* and the links to declarations as *graphlike links* (see Figure 11-3).

DCL—the declaration of all declarations

As stated earlier, every node is an instance of some abstraction, and every abstraction is declared somewhere. Therefore, there is also a declaration declaring the very abstraction of "declaring," and every declaration node has a graphlike link to it (see Figure 11-4). This special declaration is called DCL. Because DCL is also a declaration, it has a graphlike link to itself. Furthermore, declaration nodes may also have child nodes—just as any other node. Figure 11-4 illustrates this for the declaration of x. The first child node of this declaration node represents the variable type, which is int. The second child is optional and represents the initializer—in our example the value 1. This node has a graphlike link to the declaration constant (i.e., it is an instance of the abstraction constant). The actual value is stored as binary data attached to the node, which is indicated as "1". It is interesting to note that declaration names are also stored by attaching their binary representation to—in this case—declaration nodes.

Declarations versus references (to declarations)

Graphlike links always point to *declarations*, which are the nodes with graphlike links to DCL. Examples of declarations in Figure 11-4 are +, x, int, constant, and DCL. Nodes that are not declarations (i.e., nodes without a graph-like link to DCL) are called *references to* declarations to which they have graphlike links. For example, the first child of the declaration node x is a "reference to

---

NOTE

In IP, treelike links are bidirectional, that is, you can navigate through these links in both directions. Graphlike links, on the other hand, are unidirectional and point towards a declaration node of an intention; that is, an instance knows its declaration, but a declaration does not know its instances. Furthermore, the point where a link "leaves" a node can be identified through a name tag (i.e., bidirectional links have tags at both ends, and unidirectional links have a tag at their origin). This is similar to annotating associations with role names in UML class diagrams. For example, the link connecting an instance of + with its left operand x could have the tag leftOp at the + end and parent at the x end. IP provides an API for accessing nodes and links based on name tags.

NOTE

It is interesting to note that IP does not introduce an explicit "variable intention" (i.e., an abstraction of variables). The declaration of a variable (e.g., x)
represents its own variable intention.

---

int." According to the terminology introduced at the beginning of
this section, you can also call it an "instance of int."

11.3.2.3 Source Graphs: The Big Picture

Intentions   Any programming abstraction you want to use in your program
has to be declared first. You can then use it by referring to its declaration. For example, if you need to use a variable, you have to
declare it first. As seen earlier, this is also true for language abstractions, that is, *intentions*, such as +, int, constant, if, while, and so
on. Of course, to be really useful, the abstractions not only need to
be declared, but also defined, which can be accomplished by associating appropriate methods with their declarations. These methods define their semantics, appearance, debugging behavior, and so
on. We will discuss methods in Section 11.3.3. Obviously, as a programmer, you don't have to declare and implement basic intentions, such as if or while yourself—they will come with libraries
distributed with the IP system. Furthermore, you will use third-
party libraries for domain-specific intentions or general-purpose
intentions with some interesting behavior. And you will also be
able to implement your own intentions for your area of specialty.

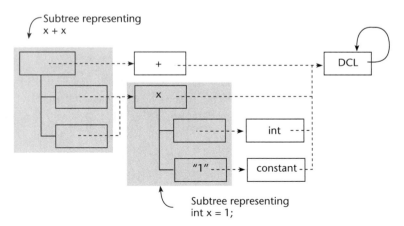

Figure 11-4 Source trees representing int x=1; *and* x+x

To get the big picture of how IP represents programs, let us take a look at a larger example of a source graph (see Figure 11-5). This graph contains the source tree of the following piece of C code:

```
int x;
x = 1;
while (x<5)
    ++x;
```

The source tree of this program is shown in Figure 11-5 on the left. It consists of a list of three statements. Each subtree representing one of the statements is enclosed in a gray box. Please note that the two child nodes of the third statement (i.e., the while-statement) represent the condition expression and the iteration statement, respectively. The nodes on the right-hand side represent the declarations of the intentions used in the user program. These intentions are located in extension libraries loaded into the IP

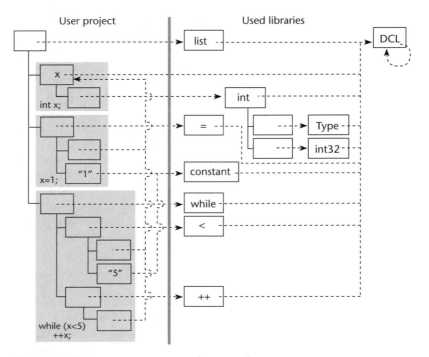

Figure 11-5 Larger source graph example

system. For simplicity, not all children of the declaration nodes on the right-hand side are shown in this figure.

11.3.2.4 The Essence of Source Graphs: Abstraction Sharing and Parameterization

Treelike links represent parameterization

As stated previously, source graphs contain two kinds of links: graphlike and treelike links. Graphlike links represent the concept of referring to a declaration or being an instance of the declared *abstraction*. Treelike links represent the concept of *parameterization*: An instance of an abstraction can be specialized and concretized for a given context by attaching child nodes to it. That is, the child nodes of an instance can be seen as its actual parameters.

Graphlike links represent sharing

The idea of abstractions is central to source graphs. As previously stated, abstractions have to be declared, and then you can use them by referring to them. For example, think of a source tree containing two identical sequences of statements in two different places. Obviously, you would like to eliminate this duplication to have only one, shared sequence of these statements. We can achieve this by introducing an abstraction: We declare a procedure whose body is the statement sequence and replace the original sequences in the original tree by calls to (i.e., instances of or references to) this new procedure. Now, think of this abstraction process in general terms: Any duplicate subtrees can be eliminated by introducing an abstraction, and then referring to it. In other words, the purpose of graphlike links is to enable *sharing* of structures in a source graph.

Of course, the subtrees that we want to abstract need not be identical. If they are not identical, they have some differences, and we can turn these differences into parameters of the abstraction. When we are using an abstraction, we have to be able to supply actual parameters to a particular instance of use. That's what treelike links are for. For example, an instance of a while-intention takes two parameters: the continuation condition and the iteration statement. A procedure call (i.e., an instance of a procedure) takes actual parameters. A template instantiation takes actual template parameters.

11.3.3 Source Graph + Methods = Active Source

Rendering, type-in, and reduction

One of the main ideas behind IP is to represent programs as *active source*, that is, source with behavior at programming time. Active source knows how to display and compile itself and provides convenient and domain-specific ways of editing and debugging it. In IP, this is achieved by defining methods (i.e., pieces of code) operating on the source graph. Different sets of methods implement different aspects of source behavior: There are methods for implementing the visualization of the source graph (i.e., *rendering*), supporting its entry (i.e., *type-in*), implementing its compilation (i.e., *reduction*), debugging, and automatic editing and refactoring.

Abstractly, the idea of methods in IP is similar to the idea of methods in object-oriented languages. Just as the methods attached to a class define the behavior of the class's instances, the methods associated with a declaration of an abstraction in an IP source graph define the behavior of the abstraction's instances.

There is an important difference, however: Methods in object-oriented languages are designed to be executed on class instances at runtime, whereas IP methods are specially designed to operate on source graphs at programming time. Consequently, the method calling, lookup, and inheritance mechanisms in IP are radically different from those found in object-oriented languages. In particular, IP methods are associated with patterns of nodes rather than just single nodes and are specially designed to support efficient source-graph traversals. We will discuss the IP method mechanism in Sections 11.5.1 to 11.5.4.

Default methods   The IP system is organized like an object-oriented framework: The system calls sets of system-defined *default methods* and user-defined methods. The idea is that the default behavior is defined by default methods, but language implementers can define specialized behavior for new intentions by overriding the inherited methods.

Please note that methods are written by developers of extension libraries only, so that application programmers using IP do not have to worry about them. However, just for the purpose of understanding how IP works, let us take a look at the different kinds of methods we can have in IP.

11.3.3.1 Kinds of Methods

We classify extension methods according to their purpose. The main categories are as follows [Sha98].

- ♦ *Rendering methods*: Rendering methods display the source graph on the screen. They use the rendering API to produce display representations of the source graph. This can be simple text or any kind of two-dimensional representation, for example, two-dimensional mathematical formulas, diagrams, tables, bitmaps (see Figure 11-14 through Figure 11-23), and so on. Furthermore, you can define several sets of rendering methods, each one implementing one specific visualization of the source graph (including domain-specific modeling notations, different formatting conventions, call graphs, metrics, rendering names in different natural languages, and so on).

♦ *Type-in methods:* Type-in methods are called when the source tree is entered or manipulated. They assist the programmer in typing in source. For example, you can define a method that inserts the appropriate number of place holders when you type in a reference to an intention (e.g., after typing in the name of a procedure, the appropriate number of place holders for the arguments are inserted) or when you want to do any other kind of special editing (e.g., typing in a type will replace the type by a declaration of a variable of this type). There are methods that define how to select the elements shown on the screen, the tabbing order, and so on.

Reduced code (i.e., R-code)

♦ *Reduction methods:* The process of transforming source trees into lower-level trees is referred to as *reduction*. The final result of this process is a tree containing only the instances of a predefined set of low-level abstractions for which machine code can be directly generated (in the phase called *code generation*). This representation is referred to as *reduced code* or *R-code*. When you tell the system to compile your program, the system will ask the root node of your program for its R-code, which involves activating the reduction method for this node (which in turn activates the reduction methods of its subnodes, and so on). Reduction methods compute the R-code by successively reimplementing higher-level constructs by lower-level ones. An example of a reduction step could be implementing a while-loop using an if- and a goto-statement, for example:

```
while (x<5)            TEST: if (x<5)
    ++x;       ───────▶       {  ++x;
                                  goto TEST;
                               }
```

As you will see in Section 11.5.5, the lower-level representations are actually attached to the original source tree rather than replacing the parts being reduced. Indeed, a reduction method is not allowed to delete any links in a source graph, but only to add new ones. In other words, during reduction, the source graph grows monotonically as more and more lower-level abstractions are attached to the tree. This way, it is easy to make sure that the reduction process is actually progressing and will terminate at some point. Of course, just as in any compilation process, reduction methods also perform structural analysis (e.g., syntax and type checking) and code optimizations. For this purpose, a method operating on a node can ask for information not only about the near context of this node, but also remote parts of the source graph. Finally, there may be several sets of R-code intentions—each set defined for a different target platform, for example, the Intel 86 family of processors or Java bytecodes. In many cases, you can implement methods for the high-level intentions such that they can be reduced towards different target platforms. However, there can be intentions that cannot be reduced towards some specific platform, that is, they cannot be implemented using the platform-specific set of R-code intentions. For example, pointer arithmetic cannot be "reduced" to Java bytecodes in an efficient way.

♦ *Debugging methods:* The standard functionality of a debugger is to allow you to watch the execution of some executable at its source level and inspect the runtime values of its variables. Implementing this functionality requires being able to identify the place in the source that corresponds to the lower-level construct being currently executed. This is not a problem as long as the mapping between the corresponding locations in the source and the executable is a linear one (i.e., continuous blocks of source map to continuous blocks of executable code). (We have discussed the concepts and problems of linear and nonlinear code mapping in Section 8.7.2.) Debugging code with a linear mapping is handled by the debugger automatically. Unfortunately, if we want to support code optimizations and/or aspect-oriented language features, this mapping will be nonlinear. For example, code optimizations may eliminate parts of the source or change the ordering of instructions. Furthermore, code weaving needed for aspect-oriented language features will merge different code pieces into a single one. And because we want to be able to write reduction methods implementing domain-specific optimizations and code weaving in IP, we need to deal with the problem of nonlinear code mapping. The solution to this problem is to provide *debugging methods*, which can compute the desired mapping from lower-level implementation back to the higher-level source for the nonlinear case. For example, a reduction method can optimize away certain variables present in the source. If we want to step through the execution of the optimized code at the source level, we need to provide a debugging method that recreates the values of the variables in the source from the values of some other relevant variables at the execution level. Only in this way will we be able to inspect the source-level variables during debugging. So the idea is that, if an intention provides a reduction method with nonlinear code transformations, it also needs to provide an appropriate debugging method that allows the debugger to do the mapping back. Furthermore, aspect-oriented and domain-specific language features can require some special debugging support, for example, highlighting timing constraints when they are violated. Such extra, domain-specific debugging features can also be provided as debugging methods. Finally, because IP is both a programming and metaprogramming environment, it supports the debugging not only of application code, but also metacode (i.e., extension libraries). For example, in order to debug reduction methods, you can make calls to a special function that takes a snapshot of the intermediate state of the tree being reduced by a given reduction method. This way, you can later inspect the different intermediate representations produced during the reduction process. The debugger will also let you debug the execution of the executable produced by the reduction methods at any of these intermediate levels. Therefore, you may also want to equip your new intentions with debugging methods that support not only debugging at the source level, but also at the intermediate levels.

♦ *Editing and refactoring methods:* Because program source in IP is represented as an AST, it is quite easy to write methods for mechanical source editing and restructuring. You can have simple editing methods, such as applying De Morgan's laws to logical expressions or turning a number of selected instructions into a procedure and replacing them by a call to this procedure (in IP this is done with the *lift* command). Other methods may perform complex design-level restructuring of legacy code (i.e., refactorings), for example, extracting the interface between different parts of the source and modifying the module structure of a software, replacing inheritance through aggregation, finding and eliminating duplicate or similar code, and so on.

♦ *Version control methods:* Version control methods allow us to define specialized protocols for resolving conflicts when two or more developers edit the same piece of code. In general, versioning is subject to intentions-specific handling because you can treat language abstractions (e.g., modules, procedures, classes, and methods) as units to be locked and versioned separately.

There are also other methods that do not fit in any of these categories.

11.4 Working with the IP Programming Environment

IP document

The IP programming environment supports all the usual programming activities: writing and versioning code, compiling, and debugging. Figure 11-6 shows a screenshot of a typical programming session. The editor subwindow contains a simple "Hello World" program using C abstractions. The program can be stored on a disk in a single binary IP source file referred to as a *document*. In general, a program can consist of more than one document. The smaller subwindow located to the right of the document editor subwindow is the *declarations list tool*. This tool allows the developer to do a name-based search for a declaration among the currently loaded declarations. A click on one of the displayed names opens the document containing the corresponding declaration in the current editor window. There are other browsing tools, such as the *references list tool*, which shows all the references to a certain declaration; *libraries list tool*, which enumerates all the currently opened libraries; *to-do list tool*, which displays a list of to-do annotations in the current document; and so on. There is also a tree inspector, which graphically shows the exact tree structure of the selected code. Finally, you can jump to the declaration of a selected node using the go-to-declaration button located on the menu bar.

The "Hello World" program can be compiled by simply pushing the compile button on the menu bar. This initiates the reduction process, which, if successfully completed, is followed by the generation of the executable. If there are syntax or semantic errors in the source, the error notifications are attached to the appropriate

Figure 11-6 *Screenshot of a typical programming session with the IP system*

nodes, so that they appear on the screen in a different color next to the erroneous positions in the code, and you can use a "jump to next error" tool to visit these positions. After a successful compilation, it is possible to step through the intermediate results of the reduction process (these are recorded by a snapshot function, which can be called at various places in the reduction methods). Finally, you can debug the program by stepping through its execution at the source level or any of the intermediate levels.

11.4.1 Editing

Probably the most unusual experience to a beginning IP programmer is editing. This is because you edit the tree directly, which is quite different from text-based editing. To give you an idea of how tree editing works, we will walk through a simple editing example. Figure 11-7 shows you how to type in the following simple program:

```
int x = 1;
int y;
y = x + 1;
```

Each box in Figure 11-7 shows you the editing screen after typing the text shown below the preceding arrow. We start with the empty screen and type in "int". While typing it, the gray selection indicates that we have still not finished typing the token. We finish typing it by pressing <tab> or <space> (the first is preferred because it automatically positions the cursor at the next reasonable type-in position). After pressing <tab>, the system will perform a couple of actions behind the scenes leading to the creation of a variable declaration with type int (see box 2 in Figure 11-7). Let us take a closer look at these actions. After we've pressed <tab>, the system first tries to find a binding for the token we have just typed in. In our case, the system finds that the token "int" matches the name of the declaration of the type int. Next, the system calls the type-in method of int. This method creates a variable declaration with type int, that is, a declaration node with a reference to int as its child. To be more precise, int does not provide its own type-in method, but inherits one from Type, an intention that is the type of all types (see Figure 11-5). The name of the newly created declaration is set to "???". We can see the result in box 2 in Figure 11-7. Because we've pressed <tab> last, the cursor is now positioned at the next reasonable type-in position. In our case, the declaration name (i.e., "???") is now selected, and we can type in the name of the declaration, for example, "x". The result is shown in

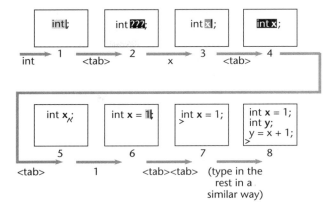

Figure 11-7 Typing in a simple program in IP

box 3. We finish typing this token by pressing <tab> and then press an extra <tab> to position the cursor for typing in the initializer (see box 5), which in our case is "1". The result of entering "1" is in box 6. The source tree corresponding to what we've typed in, that is, int x=1;, is shown in Figure 11-4. Please note that we did not explicitly type in the equal sign. This character is merely a display artifact displayed by the rendering method of the declaration. Next, by pressing an extra <tab>, we position the cursor behind the declaration statement in the current statement list and are ready to type in the next statement (see box 7). We type in the subsequent two statements in an analogous way. Please note that we actually have to explicitly enter an equal sign in the third statement because here it denotes an assignment.

Earlier, we said that changing a name (of a variable, function, class, and so on) in IP is very easy because we only need to change it in the declaration and do not need to search for all the places where it is used in order to replace it. Let us take a look at this in practice. For example, we might want to rename x in the sample code we've just typed in, let's say, to z. All we have to do in IP is

---

NOTE

IP also lets you to finish typing the name of a variable declaration by typing "=" instead of pressing <tab>, in which case you'll be expected to enter the initializer as next. In other words, IP not only supports alternative renderings, but also alternative ways of type in—to suit your most natural way of typing code.

select the name of the first declaration (box 1 in Figure 11-8) and change it to z (see box 3). Because all references to the declaration x do not store its name (but the display method retrieves it from the declaration for display), the third statement displays the correct name immediately (see box 3). This simple example illustrates the power of the IP source representation compared to text-based representations. Also, if we select z and then push the go-to-declaration button, the cursor will jump to the z declaration. So, you can always verify which abstraction is meant by a given token on the screen. In fact, we could have changed the name of the declaration y to z as well. In this case, the last statement would contain two references to z, that is, it would read z=z+1, but both references would still correctly point to the two different previous declarations (we could verify this using the jump-to-declaration button).

As a second example, let us take a look at how to enter the "Hello World" example from Figure 11-6. First you need to open a new document named "Hello World" using the "new" button from the menu bar. This will give you the window shown in Figure 11-9. The document now contains a new module named Hello World.

Next, we need to import the system library, which provides the declaration of the function main() and the declaration (and imple-

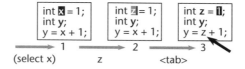

Figure 11-8 *Changing the name of a declaration*

NOTE

It is interesting to note that if there is more than one declaration with the same name in a given scope, typing in the name will actually not bind it to any of them. The name (i.e., the token we've typed) would turn yellow instead, indicating a dangling reference. We could still bind it using a list tool listing the candidate declarations and select the one we would like to bind it to. Another interesting observation is that scoping rules are implemented by the editing methods.

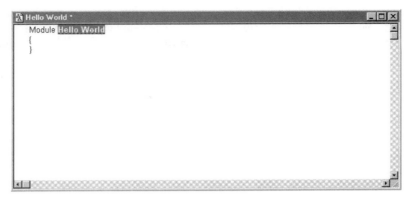

Figure 11-9 *New document named "Hello World"*

mentation) of the function `printf()`. This can be achieved by using a command or typing it in directly. The result is shown in Figure 11-10.

Now, we are ready to define an implementation of the `main()` function. The idea is that the function `main()` is declared in the system library, but we want to define its body here. This can be done using a so-called "define procedure body" declaration, which is an example of a special intention provided by IP. Starting with the situation in Figure 11-10, we type "DefineProcBody" between the braces and press <tab>. This creates a declaration with the type `DefineProcBody`. The result is shown in Figure 11-11. The first "???" should be replaced by a reference to a procedure declaration that we want to define the body for. The second "???" should be replaced by the name we want to give to our "define procedure body" declaration.

Next, we replace the first "???" by "main", which will create a reference to the declaration of the function `main()`. At this point, the rendering method for the declaration `DefineProcBody` will display the argument list of `main()` as declared in the system library. This is shown in Figure 11-12. In other words, the argument list you see in this figure is not part of the source tree you just typed in, but is merely a display artifact (which is indicated by its gray color). The idea is that the argument list is defined only in one (remote) place (which is the declaration of `main()` located somewhere in the system library), and you can still see the argument list while implementing the procedure body.

Now you can start typing the body of the procedure. For example, when you type in "printf" and press <tab>, this will be

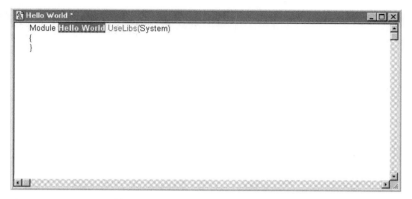

Figure 11-10 *"Hello World" module importing the system library*

expanded to a call to `printf()`. Because the declaration of `printf()` located in the standard library indicates that the function takes one argument, the system will provide a placeholder for that argument in the call (see Figure 11-13).

By replacing the argument placeholder with the string "Hello World", entering the final return statement, and replacing the remaining "???" with the name "dpbHelloWorldMain", you get the desired result shown in Figure 11-6.

11.4.2 Further Capabilities of the IP Editor

Different types of selections

Clicking on a token on the screen does not select its letters (as it would in the case of a traditional text editor), but instead selects

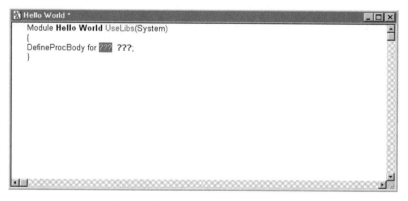

Figure 11-11 *"Hello World" module with an empty* `DefineProc-Body` *declaration*

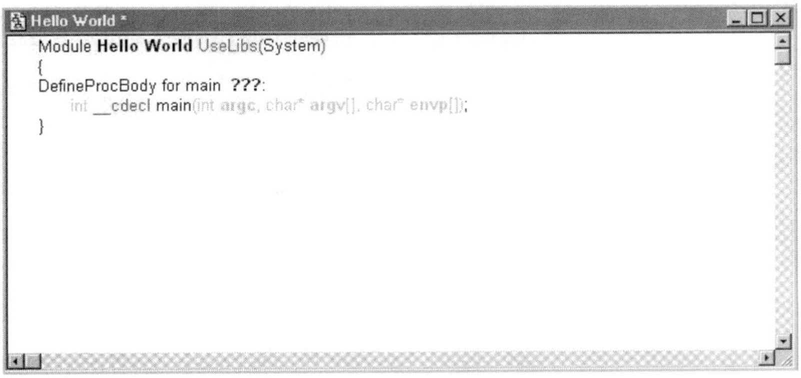

Figure 11-12 *"Hello World" module with an empty* `DefineProc-Body` *declaration for* `main()`

the corresponding tree node or subtree. In fact, there are a number of different selection types. You can select one node (*crown selection*), or a node including all its subnodes (*tree selection*), or you can select a place between two nodes (*place selection*). It is also possible to select the token as such and change its name (*contents selection*). If the token is a reference, then the reference will be rebound based on the new name. If the token is a name of a declaration, the name will simply be changed (as in Figure 11-8). There are also other types of selections (which will not be discussed). You can achieve the desired selection type by holding down an appropriate modifier key while clicking on a given token.

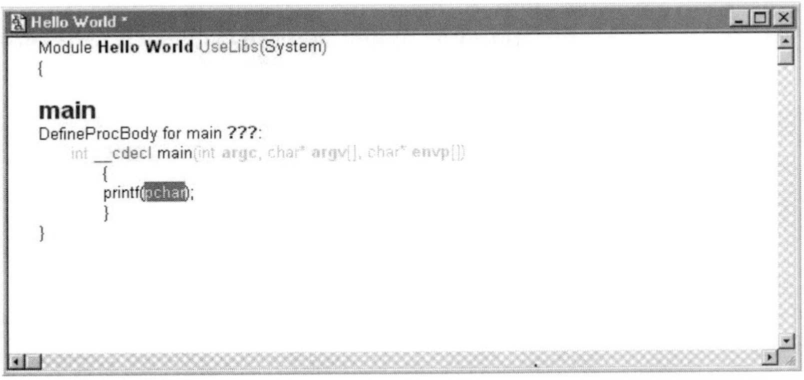

Figure 11-13 *"Hello World" module with a* `DefineProcBody` *declaration for* `main()` *with a body containing an incomplete call to* `printf(0)`

As already stated, the IP editor is not a syntax-oriented editor, that is, it is perfectly acceptable for the edited tree to be in a state that would not compile. For example, if you type a name that cannot be bound to any declaration (because there is not one with this name), the token will turn yellow, and you'll know that you need to fix this before attempting to compile the source. Also, as you type, the structure of the tree can be syntactically incorrect. On the other hand, through type-in methods, intentions may provide the programmer with type-in templates and suggest what to type in next (as we saw in the previous section). In effect, syntax errors are quite rare, and you still have the freedom to type in the source as you wish without being forced into the straightjacket of some syntax at every moment.

The major advantage of editing active source is that we are not dealing with passive text, but instead, the source has an interactive behavior. The intentions can even exhibit different type-in behaviors based on their tree context or the currently active view. Furthermore, they can interact with the developer through menus, dialogs, and so on.

Achieving clean encoding and high performance at the same time

The IP source rendering provides unique opportunities. First, intentions can be rendered in a true two-dimensional way allowing you to provide pretty mathematical notation. For example, Figure 11-14 shows an implementation of the Bessel function using C and some special mathematical intentions. This example is attractive in two ways. First, it is expressed in an easy to understand and pretty mathematical notation, which is close to what you find in math books. Second, there is a somewhat more complicated but reusable optimization transformation attached to the helping function t(). The display of this transformation is suppressed in Figure 11-14. The transformation transforms the costly, recursive function t() into a linear-cost function (basically by remembering previously computed values in a temporary). Thanks to it, the Bessel function compiles into a very efficient implementation—one that we otherwise could only get by writing hand-optimized, but messy code. But thanks to IP rendering and the possibility of contributing domain-specific optimizations, we get an easy to understand and nice looking formulation of the Bessel function plus one messy, but reusable optimization transformation instead of one efficient, but messy Bessel function.

Avoiding the parsing problem

Figure 11-15 demonstrates a few mathematical notations for handling matrices. An interesting point about these naturally looking notations is that they would be extremely difficult to parse if we wanted to provide them using traditional input technology utilizing text and parsing. In general, mathematical notations found

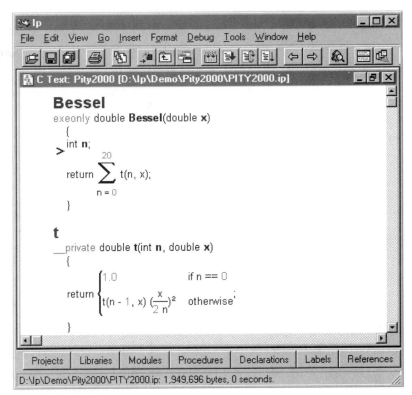

Figure 11-14 *Example of a domain-specific notation for mathematical formulas (from [Sha98])*

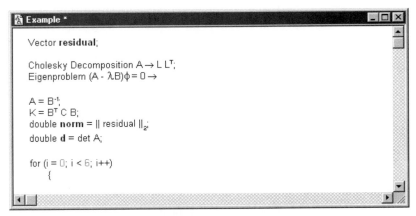

Figure 11-15 *Example of specialized notations for handling matrices[8]*

---

8. Courtesy of Lutz Röder.

in math books are too ambiguous to be parsable. This is not a problem in IP because the rendering of some code can be ambiguous, but the underlying source is not (the rendering shows less information than what's in the source). And you can use commands to enter unambiguous source that is rendered ambiguously.

The IP source rendering also allows you to embed graphics and graphical notations in your programs. A view containing graphics can also be provided as an alternative view to a textual view. For example, Figure 11-16 and Figure 11-17 show two alternative renderings of the same C function implementing some logical formula. One rendering uses the usual C notation, and the other one uses a graphical notation based on a circuit with logical gates. As Figure 11-18 shows, textual and graphical notations can also be easily mixed. You can readily imagine that you can use these capabilities to provide general-purpose and domain-specific graphical modeling notations.

Another interesting capability of the IP editor is shown in Figure 11-19, where a bitmap (in this example, one representing an icon) is passed as an argument and its actual contents is rendered in the source (see the little bitmap passed to `__BitmapName()` in Figure 11-19). This is much more expressive than passing a literal

---

NOTE

You may wonder why a syntactically ambiguous representation may still be useful. This is so because syntactic ambiguities can often be disambiguated based on additional semantic information. This idea is frequently used in math books to make math formulas easier to understand. In all but the simplest cases, such ambiguities cannot be resolved in the parser because parsers do not have access to higher-level semantic information. In IP, however, the disambiguation is done by the programmer while typing.

As Eric van Wyk pointed out, there are two issues resulting from the separation of display and type-in from the actual source structure that IP novices may find somewhat confusing. First, most programmers are accustomed to the idea that the code they see is actually the source with all the details it contains, but as stated previously this is often not the case in IP. The IP programmer may have to navigate in the code or use the detailed source tree view described at the end of this section to discover the actual structure of the source. Second, just viewing some code in IP will not tell you how to type it in. This problem may be easily solved in the future by having intentions provide "show me your type-in" commands, which would explain to the programmer how to use a given intention.

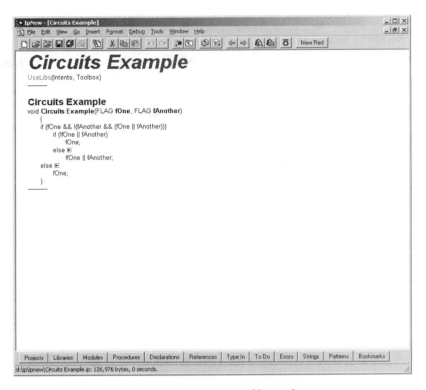

Figure 11-16 C-like, textual rendering of logical expressions

array containing the numbers that represent pixels. Furthermore, you can simply capture the bitmap somewhere from the screen and paste in the source.

IP rendering also allows you to enrich programming notations with any kind of GUI controls. A very common kind of controls used in programming are tables (e.g., decision tables). An example of a special table control used in program source is shown in Figure 11-20. This table is used to manage the specifications of menus for the GUI of the Microsoft Outlook product.

The IP editor lets you embed references to declarations in a comment. For example, a comment about some function may contain references to other similar functions. References basically amount to hyperlinks because you can use the go-to-declaration button to jump to the declaration being referenced. References embedded in comments are rendered underlined. This is shown in Figure 11-21. For example, one of the comments starts with gregsh:, where gregsh is a reference to the declaration declaring the developer Greg, who is the author of this comment. The

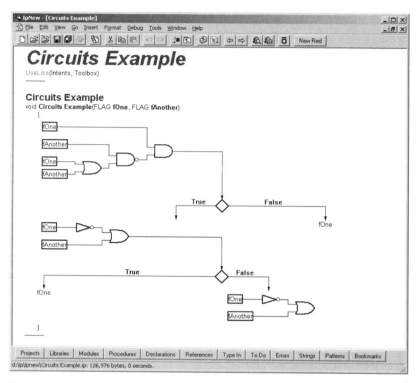

***Figure 11-17** Graphical rendering of the logical expressions from Figure 11-16*

reference <u>FotTypeface</u> is a reference to the declaration of the function FotTypeface(). The important point about references embedded in comments is that—just as in the case of references embedded elsewhere—you don't need to update their names after changing names of the declarations being referenced (e.g., after changing the name of the function FotTypeface()).

Aspectual views

The ability to provide alternative renderings for a single source is in the spirit of aspect-orientation and is a useful addition for implementing aspects by separate modules. You can use alternative renderings to show certain aspects and suppress other aspects of the source. For example, you can use alternative renderings to suppress the display of exception specifications in function signatures, when needed. It is important to note that not only can we compute aspectual views on the underlying source graph, but also support their editing. In general, renderings can provide radically different views of the source including program visualization and metrics.

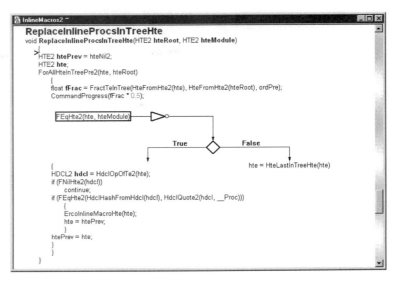

Figure 11-18 Example of mixing textual and graphical notations

Renderings in different languages

Another exciting use of alternative renderings is the possibility of rendering intention names in different languages, such as English or Chinese. This is illustrated in Figure 11-22 and Figure 11-23. This feature is very useful in the age of globalization because many organizations already engage in program development that involves teams from different countries (e.g., outsourcing the development of system components to different countries).

```
 MatrixImpl\UI *                                              _ □ X

        HteAppendOpnd2(hannotMatrixConfig, hexprRows);
        HteAppendOpnd2(hannotMatrixConfig, hexprCols);
        }
    }

CmdShapeAndFormatOfExprMatrix
    __BitmapName(    ) __MenuName("Matrix shape and format.....") ERCO PROCWRAP
    CmdShapeAndFormatOfExprMatrix(HTE2_CUR hte, __WrapWith(twMs) __MenuName("Shape:") _MS_MF ms)
    {
    if (!FEqHdclQOfTe2(hte, MATRIX))
        return ercoNotAMatrixType;

    HANNOT2 hannotMatrixConfig = HannotQOfTe2(hte, matrixConfig __Noop);

    if (FNilHte2(hannotMatrixConfig))
        {
```

Figure 11-19 Example of passing a bitmap constant as an argument

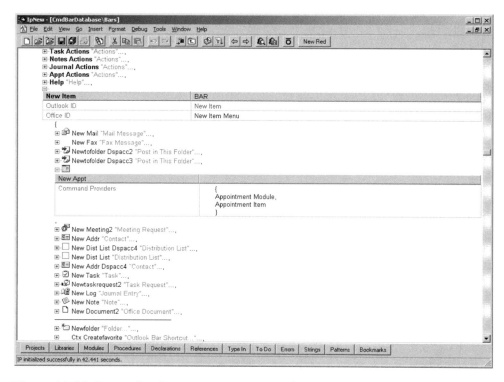

Figure 11-20 Example of source containing a table control

NOTE

We said earlier that important information that would otherwise make a great comment can often be captured in a machine processable way by introducing appropriate intentions. So you may ask why we still need comments. There are several reasons why comments are still useful. First, you often want to communicate something informal to other humans (e.g., "this line of code makes me feel so proud . . ."). Second, you may not have the time to state something formally (i.e., in a machine-processable way). Third, the intentions needed to state the information formally may be unavailable and defining them may not be an option. Why? *(1)* Maybe you don't have the time or skills. Remember: Intentions have to be well designed, and its not everyone that should introduce new intentions, but only intention designers, that is, language and library designers. *(2)* Or the intention could be so unique (i.e., of low reusability) that it would not be worth investing the effort. There is one important point about comments in IP, though: You can always come back and rewrite them in a machine-processable form when the necessary intentions become available.

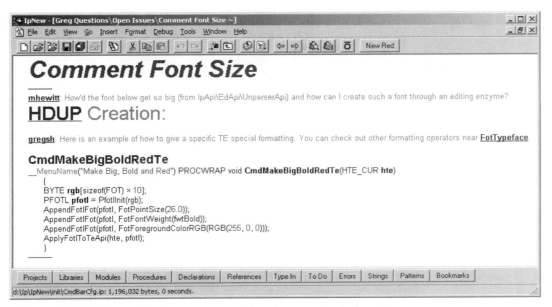

Figure 11-21 *Example of comments with references to declarations*

Core view

Most renderings display only a select part of the information contained in the source. For example, even the "Hello World" program shown in Figure 11-6 does not show all the detail contained in the underlying source graph. However, IP provides a special rendering called the *core view*, which shows more details of the underlying source graph. Intention programmers can use this rendering to debug the underlying program representations, but the intention users need not worry about it. The "Hello World" program in the core view is shown in Figure 11-24.

11.4.3 Extending the IP System with New Intentions

When you write an application, you simply use the general-purpose and domain-specific intentions provided by the extension libraries you've loaded into the IP system. Developing extension libraries is a different activity than application programming, however. This activity involves utilizing extension APIs and adhering to special IP protocols (e.g., the reduction protocol discussed in Section 11.5.5) and requires language design and implementation skills.

Library interfaces and extension DLLs

When implementing new intentions, you usually declare them in a separate file called the *library interface*. Next, you implement the reduction, rendering, type-in, debugging, and other methods in one or more other files. In most cases, you'll need at least the

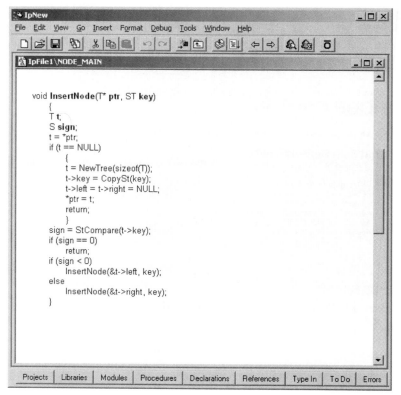

Figure 11-22 A C function rendered in English

reduction, rendering, and type-in methods. The methods use the extension APIs, that is, the reduction API, rendering API, type-in API, and so on. The files containing the methods are compiled into an *extension DLL*. You would usually package related intentions, for example, intentions implementing a domain-specific notation, in a single DLL. The interface file and the extension DLL get handed out to the application programmers. When the application programmers import the interface module of an extension library into their application project, the corresponding extension DLL gets loaded automatically into their IP system. The DLL contains the code needed to type in, render, and reduce the application program using the new intentions. The DLL can also contain special commands for working with the new notation (e.g., typing aids, analysis tools, and so on), which can automatically be made available on the IP menu bar after loading the DLL.

Let us take a look at the steps performed by a typical reduction method. A reduction method first analyzes the context of the tree

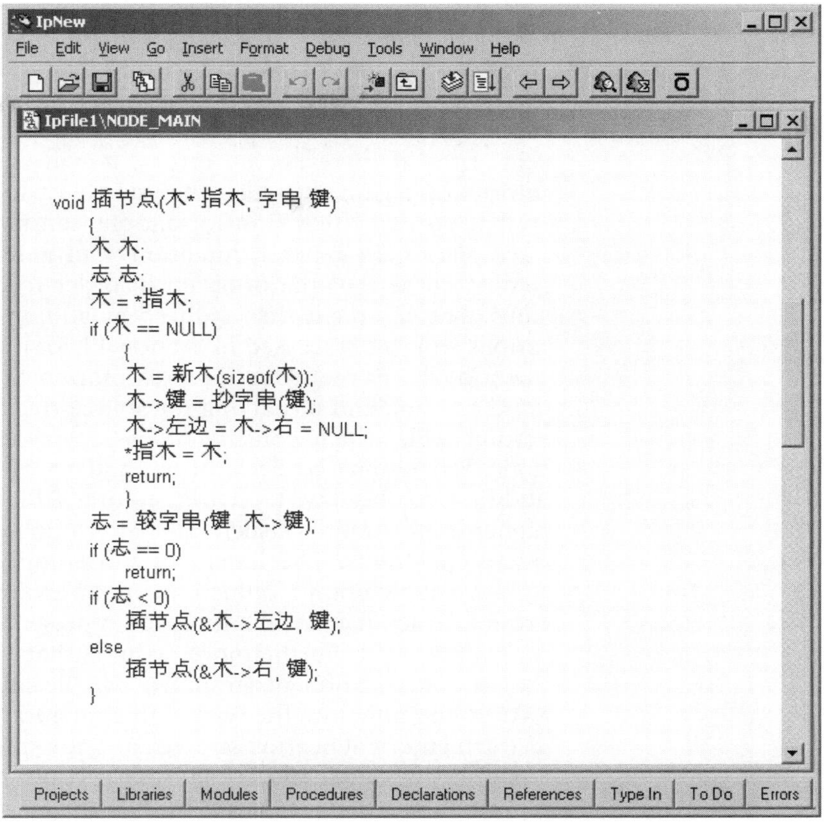

Figure 11-23 *The C function from Figure 11-22 rendered in Chinese*

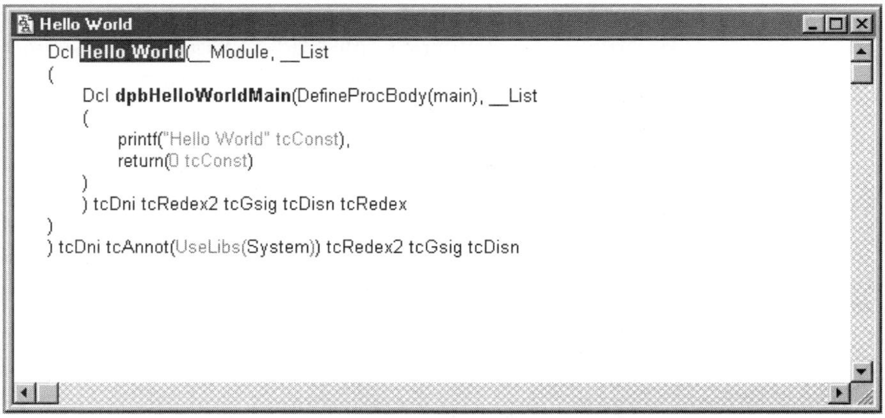

Figure 11-24 *The "Hello World" program from Figure 11-6 rendered in the core view*

element it was called on. It checks to see if the structure of the subtree is correct, so that it can then reduce it. It basically looks for syntax and semantic errors. If it discovers any errors, it attaches error annotations to the locations in the source where they are present. Even if there are no errors, it will still attach some other information gained in the analysis to various tree nodes in the source, so that other transformations can take advantage of it in later phases. In general, intentions can gather information from remote corners of the program in order to do various optimizations. The subtree is then reduced by adding lower-level representations to it (as discussed in Section 11.5.5). Finally, the reduction method returns the reduced representation of the source.

Accessing and modifying the source tree is done using the tree editing API, which consists of basic operations, such as create node, set the link to declaration, add an operand, and so on. In addition to this low-level tree editing API, there are also some higher-level facilities, such as pattern matching functions and quote constructs. The latter allow a compact definition of trees used for matching or reduction. As an example, assume that we are implementing an intention for representing matrices, that is, the type MATRIX. Furthermore, assume that we design the type so that the application programmer can declare a variable of type MATRIX and annotate the type with configuration parameters, such as the memory allocation strategy and the shape of the matrix. For example, the application programmer could declare a dynamically allocated, rectangular matrix as follows:

```
configuration(dynamic, rectangular) MATRIX m;
```

The implementation of MATRIX would, among other methods, require a reduction method for declarations with type MATRIX. Depending on the configuration parameters, this method would reduce a variable declaration with type MATRIX to a variable declaration whose type is a C array (for statically allocated matrices), or a C struct containing the number of rows and columns and a pointer to the matrix elements (for dynamically allocated matrices), or some other C data structure. The core of this reduction method could look like this:

```
HTYPE htype;
if (matrix_description.allocation == dynamic &&
    matrix_description.Shape == rectangular)
{
    htype = `struct
        {
```

```
          int rows;
          int cols;
          $htypeElement* elements;
          };
} else { ... }; //other cases
```

Quote and unquote operators

htype is a handle to a tree element that represents the type to which MATRIX gets reduced. matrix_description is a struct that was created during the analysis of the configuration parameters of the matrix declaration shown earlier. The statement inside the if-then branch assigns htype a tree representing a C struct. The struct contains the number of rows and columns and a pointer to the matrix elements. Instead of constructing this tree using the low-level tree editing API (i.e., calling the operations to create a node, setting the reference to declaration, adding the operands, and so on), we simply write the C code to be created preceded by the quote operator `.[9] Once we have the tree representing the C data structure, we would attach it to the original source. Next, we would reduce the C intentions by calling their reduction methods.

Using the tree editing API and the simple metaprogramming constructs, such as quote and unquote, are still quite low level and tedious. However, you can implement more sophisticated, declarative notations for defining language extensions and provide them to intention programmers as extension libraries.

11.5   Advanced Topics

In the following five sections, we'll describe some more advanced concepts including questions, methods, and reduction. These topics are relevant to implementers of extension libraries, not to application programmers.

NOTE

Please note that htypeElement is a variable computed elsewhere and is used in the quoted code. In order to use its value, the variable is preceded by the unquote operator $.

---

9. The quote construct suppresses the standard reduction of the quoted code. Instead, the quoted code is reduced to code, which, when executed, actually creates the quoted source tree. The IP quote facility is analogous to the quote found in Lisp.

11.5.1   Questions, Methods, and a Frameworklike Organization

Questions

In IP, methods are invoked by asking *questions* of nodes. Questions are polymorphic operations on tree elements. Similar to polymorphic operations in object-oriented languages, you can have several different methods (i.e., implementation codes) associated with a single question (i.e., polymorphic operation). If you ask a node a question, there is a built-in lookup mechanism that will find the appropriate method to answer the question.

You can implement new intentions by declaring them and implementing the methods that define their semantics, appearance, and so on. As already discussed, the declarations and the methods go into separate modules. The module containing the declarations is called the library interface. The module with the methods gets compiled into a dynamic-link library (DLL), called an extension DLL, which can be dynamically linked to the IP system to extend it. If you want to use the new intentions in a program, you import the interface module, which will trigger the IP system to automatically link the corresponding extension library to itself. The system will now use this library to render, compile, and debug the instances located in your program that refer to the intentions in the declaration module.

When implementing extension libraries, you use a set of standard APIs defined by the IP system for rendering, type-in, reduction, versioning, and so on. These APIs consist of (1) declarations of procedures that you can call and (2) questions that the system calls and you provide methods (i.e., implementations) for. The questions are the entry points where user-defined code for rendering, type-in, reduction, and so on gets called. The system provides default implementations of these questions (i.e., default methods), which you can override. For example, the default implementation of the rendering question (i.e., the question returning the display representation of a source tree) is to display source trees in a functional notation. So, the tree in Figure 11-2 would be rendered by the default rendering method as follows: +(x,x). If you want it to be rendered as x+x, you need to override the default rendering method for references to +.

Rcode question

An example of a question for which you usually need to provide your own methods when implementing new intentions is the reduction question, that is, the Rcode question. The system asks this question of the root node of a user program in order to initiate its reduction. The result of this question is the reduced version of the program, that is, a graph containing only instances of the R-code intentions for a given target platform.

As you can see, the IP system is structured like a framework making calls to default and user-defined methods, where the latter

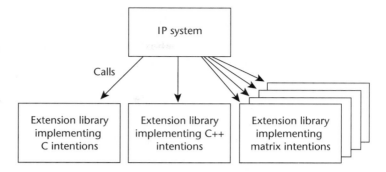

Figure 11-25 *The IP system calls extensions libraries*

are located in extensions libraries. This is illustrated in Figure 11–25.

In addition to standard, system-defined questions, extension libraries may also define their own new questions. For example, the implementation of the C intentions defines the question Type, which returns the type of an expression. Methods implementing the Rcode question ask the Type question during the static analysis of the C code being reduced.

11.5.2   Source-Pattern-Based Polymorphism

As stated earlier, if you ask a node a question, there is a built-in lookup mechanism that will find the appropriate method to answer this question. Which method gets selected depends on the structure of the source graph the node lives in. This is so because you can register different methods to answer a given question for different node patterns in the source graph. We say that questions are polymorphic on source patterns.

When a node is asked a question, the system first checks to see if there is an appropriate method registered for the node pattern the node lives in. If not, the question is resubmitted to the declaration of the node. This is a kind of a method inheritance mechanism specially designed for source graphs.

It is important to be able to register methods for different source patterns because we want to define different behaviors for different constellations of instances of intentions. For example, we need different code to display and compile:

♦ A reference to a declaration of a type
♦ A declaration with that type
♦ A reference to a declaration with that type

Suppose that you want to implement the type int. First, you need to declare int, and then implement and register the Rcode methods (i.e., the methods answering the Rcode question) for the following tree patterns: references to int, declarations with type int (i.e., declarations of variables of type int), and references to declarations with type int. You don't need to implement any rendering and type-in methods because the default ones are good enough for int.

The system defines the question Rcode as follows:[10]

```
Rcode(linkAsking, phteRcodeRoot)
```

This question returns the reduced version of the subtree it is called on. The first argument, that is, linkAsking, is the link that is asking this question. (When a node asks its neighbor the Rcode question, you can think of the question as traveling along the graphlike or treelike link connecting both nodes. This is the "link asking a question".) The second argument, that is, phteRcodeRoot,[11] is a pointer to where the method activated by the question will store the result, that is, a handle to the root of the reduced tree. A method implementing the question can refer to the node it operates on using hteThis, which is similar to the pseudovariable this in C++.

As stated previously, you need to implement and register methods handling this question for different source patterns. For example, you need a method handling the question Rcode for references to declarations with type int:

```
<ref_to.dcl_with_type_that_is.int>::Rcode(linkAsking,
                                           phteRcodeRoot)
{
   ... //implementation of the method
}
```

Let us take a look at the whole picture (Figure 11-26). The user program (on the left) contains a declaration with type int, a reference to the declaration of int, and a reference to the declara-

---

10. The code samples shown here are slightly simplified.
11. The naming conventions used in the IP system are called Hungarian notation [SM91]. For example, "phte" stands for "pointer to a handle to a tree element." (A handle is a machine-independent implementation of a pointer.) Hungarian notation was invented by Charles Simonyi and propagated through the Microsoft Windows API.

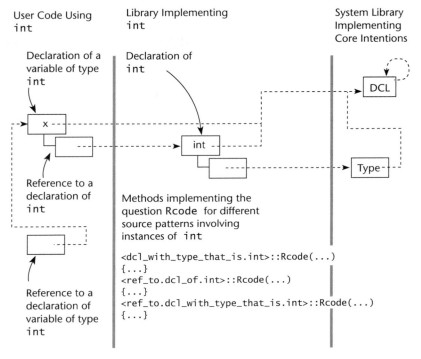

Figure 11-26 *An implementation of an intention consists of a declaration and methods registered for different source patterns involving instances of this intention*

tion with type int. The library in the middle implements int. First, there is the declaration of int, which would be located in the interface part of the library. This interface part would be imported by the user program (like a header file in C). Then you have the three methods implementing the Rcode question for the three different patterns involving instances of int. These methods would be compiled into an extension DLL and dynamically linked into the IP system. When you compile the user program, the system will call the corresponding reduction methods from the extension DLL.

11.5.3 Methods as Visitors

In IP, a method is not simply a piece of code called on one node, but rather it has the form of a visitor traversing the nodes of the pattern the method is registered for. The visitor may execute some user-defined code on each node being traversed. The accumulated data is passed along the traversed path. The implementation of methods as visitors is not surprising because a large portion of code of any compiler deals with traversing ASTs.

There are cases where you only need to collect data from one node. For example, consider the question Type, which returns the type of an expression. When implementing the addition operator +, you need to implement a method handling this question for references to +. The method will be a visitor visiting only the reference node. During this visit, it will ask the question Type of the children of this node and then compute the return type. However, there are also cases where a visitor needs to traverse several nodes and execute different code on each of them.

11.5.4 Asking Questions Synchronously and Asynchronously

Questions can be asked synchronously or asynchronously. When you ask a question synchronously, you give the control to the system, and when the call returns, you have the answer. For example, a node can ask its neighbor the Rcode question as follows:

```
AskQuestion("Rcode", linkAsked, phteRcodeRoot);
```

In this call, linkAsked is the link connecting the node asking the question to the neighbor being asked, and phteRcodeRoot is the return parameter.

Alternatively, you can ask questions asynchronously. In this case, you first submit a question, continue with your work, and later ask for the result, which may cause blocking until the system has answered the question. The idea of asynchronously asking questions is that you can first submit several questions and then, when you block waiting for the first answer, the system may compute the answers to all the submitted questions in any order it chooses. Thus, you should call questions asynchronously whenever the order of answering the questions is not relevant to your code. For example, the method answering the question Type for a reference to + will ask its children the question Type, and then compute the resulting type. Because it does not matter whether we first ask the left child or the right child, both questions are asked asynchronously:

```
//submit the first question and return a handle to it
hsq1 = SubmitQuestion("Type", hteLeftOperand);
```

NOTE

As of this writing, the IP visitor mechanism is implemented using closures.

```
//submit the second question and return a handle to it
hsq2 = SubmitQuestion("Type", hteRightOperand);
//get the results
WaitForQuestion(hsq1, phteLeftType); //at this point the
                                     //system may compute
                                     //the answer to hsq1 and
                                     //then hsq2 or
                                     //the other way round
WaitForQuestion(hsq2, phteRightType);
```

The ability to delegate the order of answering questions to the system is very important because it promotes the composability of extension libraries. We'll explain this in the following section. It also creates the opportunities for parallel execution on multi-processor machines.

11.5.5   Reduction[12]

As stated earlier, reduction is the process of transforming source trees into lower-level trees. It corresponds to compilation in conventional programming environments. Reduction is initiated by the system when it asks the question Rcode of the root node of a user program. This question computes and returns the R-code representation of the program for a given platform. This computation involves asking the Rcode and many other questions of other nodes in the source. In particular, these questions check the structure of the program source for correctness, perform optimizations, and generate the R-code representation. It is important to note that optimizations in IP can be and often are domain-specific because domain-specific abstractions provide their own reduction and optimization methods. Furthermore, optimizations in IP may inspect remote parts of the source tree, that is, we can have optimizations of wide scope. Of course, the process of reducing a higher-level abstraction can take advantage of the existence of lower-level abstractions. For example, the reduction method of a new high-level abstraction may first generate its implementation in C-abstractions, and then ask this implementation for its R-code.

The reduction process is governed by a few general principles. First of all, reduction methods are not allowed to delete links and nodes in the source, but only to add new links and nodes. The idea is that any new information computed by the reduction methods

---

12. This section describes the IP reduction protocol as of this writing. In particular, the version described here supersedes the one described in [ADK+98].

(e.g., typing information, intermediate representations, R-code representations, and so on) has to be attached to the source. If you ask a node a question for some representation, the question will first check to see if the representation has already been computed and is present in the source, and then it would return the existing answer or compute it if no answer was available. In other words, you can think of reduction as a process of growing the source graph until it incorporates its low-level R-code implementation. At that point, the source graph contains the original source, all the intermediate representations, and the R-code implementation. By not deleting any information during reduction, the process is monotonic, and you can control its progress. If the reduction methods were allowed to delete information, you basically could not always guarantee that reduction would terminate. An example of attaching lower-level representations to the original source is shown in Figure 11-27. This figure shows the reduction of `while` to an implementation using `if` and `goto`. The new implementation (shown in gray) is simply attached to the original tree. Because the condition of `if` is the original condition of `while` and the original body statement of `while` is also part of the body statement list of `if`, both trees share these statements. This is achieved through special docking points provided by treelike links.

The second principle is that nodes are only allowed to directly access their local neighborhood. More precisely, a method executing on a node is allowed to add links only to this node and access only the nodes to which the original node has direct links to or the nodes that were passed as parameters to the method. If a method needs any information from any remote nodes or needs to add links to remote nodes, it has to ask questions of their own direct neighbors, which may need to ask questions of their neighbors, and so on until the target nodes are reached. The idea behind this principle is that, because the question mechanism crosses the system, the system can automatically monitor which nodes acquire information from or add links to which other nodes. This way, as the reduction proceeds, the system builds a map of dependencies in the source (which is basically the record of who asked which question of whom). You'll see in the following paragraphs what this is good for.

The third principle is that the answer to a question may never change during the reduction. Even if a node asks a particular question of some other node only once, it has to be guaranteed that if the node asked that question again, it would get the same answer. This is not simple to guarantee at all because methods can add new links, that is, they can have side effects. For example, if a node asked some other node about its number of children and got the

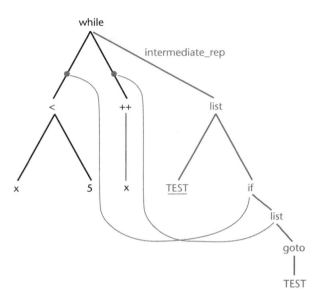

Figure 11-27 Reduction of while *by attaching a lower-level representation using* if *and* goto. *Please note that only treelike links are shown and each node except for* TEST *(which is a declaration) and* 5 *is represented by the name of its declaration.*

answer 3, this answer is not allowed to change and effectively no other method is allowed to add any children to that node once this question has been asked. The system checks this principle automatically. Whenever new links are added to a node, all questions that were run on this node are automatically reevaluated by the system to check to see if the answer is still the same. If the answers are different, the previous answers to these and all other questions calling these questions are invalidated. As a result of this invalidation, the system rolls back the reduction to the point where no answers are invalid and then tries asking the questions in a different order. Please remember that you can ask several questions asynchronously (see Section 11.5.4)—that's why the system has the opportunity to answer some questions in an order selected by the system. In other words, reduction involves a search for an order of answering questions that does not lead to the invalidation of any previous answer. In our example, if the question trying to add an extra child and the question about the number of children were asked asynchronously, the system would make sure that the question adding a child would run before the question about the number of children.

The basic idea behind this whole reduction protocol is that a method can acquire anything it needs to perform its job through asking questions, and it is guaranteed that the answers to the questions it asks remain valid and won't be silently invalidated by some other method. Because nodes can acquire information from or modify remote nodes *only* through asking questions, and the answer to a question cannot change, the nodes actually acquire a view on the source that is static throughout the whole reduction process. In other words, the local changes performed by a method occur based on a view of the source that is still valid at the end of the reduction. Thus, when a method starts its execution, it can basically assume that the source already has its final form except for the additions to be made by this method.

The reduction protocol is designed to support combining extension libraries from different vendors. By asking questions asynchronously, you avoid overspecifying the order of invoking transformations. This is very useful whenever you want to extend or modify the compilation of certain instances of intentions, for example, by plugging in an extension library that optimizes certain patterns in the intermediate representations generated by other libraries. The new extension library could require a specific order of transformations, so that it can view all these patterns at one point and transform them. In other words, some extension libraries may constrain the set of possible transformation orders of other libraries. Because libraries support sets of alternative transformation orders rather than enforcing just one particular order, there is a higher probability that there is a transformation order that works for a composition of several libraries.

Of course, it is possible that the sets of transformation orders supported by several libraries are disjoint, meaning that no order can be found and the reduction process fails. However, this can only happen whenever the libraries want to transform instances of the same intentions and do it in incompatible ways. Such incompatibilities have to be resolved by the vendors of these libraries. The system at least guarantees that no garbage code will be generated due to such library interaction.

In order to minimize the search for valid transformation orders during reduction, future releases of the IP system will allow libraries to specify preferred orderings of transformations that are more likely to yield success.

11.6   The Philosophy behind IP

11.6.1   Why Do We Need Extendible Programming Environments? or What Is the Problem with Fixed Programming Languages?

Most real-world applications require many domain-specific abstractions. There are at least two obvious alternative ways to deal with this requirement. One solution is to use a general-purpose programming language with abstraction mechanisms, such as procedures or objects, which you can use to implement your own libraries of domain-specific abstractions. This is the conventional and widely-practiced solution. The second solution is to provide one comprehensive application-specific language for each kind of application you need to build. By saying a *comprehensive* application-specific language, we mean that the language contains dedicated language features for representing all the domain-specific abstractions needed for the given kind of application. It turns out that both solutions have severe problems, which we describe in the following two sections.

11.6.1.1   Problems with General-Purpose Languages and Conventional Libraries

There are four main problems with the "general-purpose programming language and conventional library" approach: loss of design information, code tangling, performance penalties, and no domain-specific programming support. Let us take a look at each of them.

♦ *Loss of design information:* When you use a general-purpose programming language, you have to map domain-specific abstractions onto the features and idioms of the programming language. The resulting code usually includes extra clutter and fails to represent the abstractions intentionally because some of the domain information is lost during this transformation. For example, there are many ways to implement the *singleton* pattern [GHJV95].[13] And given a particular implementation code only, it is not 100 percent certain that the intention of the code is to implement the singleton pattern. This information could be included in a comment, but such information is lost to the compiler. On the other hand, with the domain-specific (or application-specific) language approach, we would provide the special class annotation *singleton*, which would allow us to unambiguously express the singleton intention. The loss of design information makes software evolution

---

13. Singleton is an idiom of OO languages for implementing classes that can have only one instance.

extremely difficult because change requests from the customers are usually expressed at a higher level of abstraction. Using the general-purpose programming language and conventional library approach, program evolution requires code analysis to recover the intended abstractions, which, as we illustrated with the singleton concept, is impossible to automatically perform fully.

◆ *Code tangling:* Programming problems are usually analyzed from different perspectives and an adequate, intentional encoding should preserve the separation of perspectives (e.g., separating synchronization code from functional code). As we saw in Section 8.7, in most cases, achieving this separation requires domain-specific transformations, but such transformations cannot be encapsulated in conventional libraries unless the language supports static metaprogramming.[14] In other words, we need to put some code extending the compiler into the library, but this is usually not supported by current library technologies. Thus, when using conventional procedural or class libraries, we are forced to apply these transformations manually. In effect, we produce tangled code, which is difficult to understand and maintain. We investigated these issues in Chapter 8 in great detail.

◆ *Performance penalties:* The structure of the domain-level specification does not necessarily correspond to the structure of its efficient implementation. Unfortunately, the main property of procedures and objects is that they preserve the static structure of a program into runtime. A compiler for a general-purpose programming language can only apply simple optimizations because it only knows the level of that language, but not the domain level. For example, as we discussed in Section 9.8.1, no compiler could possibly optimize the call EXP(x,2) to the exponentiation function EXP() (which is implemented using the Taylor expansion formula) into x*x or optimize EXP(0.5,x*x) into x. In general, a considerable amount of domain-specific computation at compile time might be required in order to map a domain-level representation into an efficient implementation. With the general-purpose programming language and library approach, no such computation takes place (again, this would require static metaprogramming).

◆ *No domain-specific programming support:* Domain-specific abstractions usually require some special debugging support (e.g., debugging synchronization constraints), special display and

---

14. We saw in Chapter 10 that compile-time metaprogramming is possible in C++ in the form of template metaprogramming. However, template metaprogramming, although Turing complete, has only very limited program structuring constructs.

editing support (e.g., displaying and editing pretty mathematical formulas), and so on. Such support requires that libraries, in addition to the procedures and classes to be used in client programs, also contain extensions of the various components of the programming environment. However, current programming technologies do not support such extensions.

11.6.1.2 Problems with Comprehensive Application-Specific Languages

Given a comprehensive application-specific language containing all language features we need for a given application, we could implement a programming environment with all the necessary optimizations and debugging, displaying, and editing facilities. The language itself would allow us to write intentional, well-separated application code. In other words, we would solve all the problems mentioned in the previous section. Unfortunately, there are four major problems with this approach: the parsing problem, high cost of specialized compilers and programming environments, problems of distributing new language extensions, and problems of evolving domain- and application-specific languages.

♦ *Parsing problem:* Conventional compiler technology uses parsing in order to transform program text into the internal program representation used in a compiler. Parsing poses two problems to feature-rich and domain-specific text-based languages. First, it is difficult or impossible to add more and more new language features to a language without eventually making it unparsable. As already discussed, C++ is a good example of a language reaching this limit (see Section 11.2). Second, the requirement of parsability represents quite a restriction on domain-specific notations. This is so because natural domain-specific notations often do not reveal all the detail of the underlying model and allow for views that contain too many ambiguities to be parsable. Mathematical books are full of notations that are impossible to be directly represented as conventional, text-based computer languages. As already discussed in Section 11.4.2, this is caused by the fact that they do not have to show all the details of the underlying representation (which is unambiguous). For example, when editing text in a WYSIWYG text editor, such as Microsoft Word, one does not see whether two paragraphs were assigned the same style (e.g., *body text*) because they could have the same text properties (e.g., font size, font type, and so on). An example of an unambiguous textual representation is the T_EX file format [Knu86], where all the formatting information is included inline as special commands. However, viewing a T_EX file in an ASCII editor is not WYSIWYG. Other limitations of textual representation include being confined to one-dimensional representations, no pictures, no graphics, no hyperlinks, and so on.

♦ *High cost of specialized compilers and programming environments:* The cost of developing compilers and programming environments is extremely high. For example, in [Vel98a], Veldhuizen cites Arch Robinson, lead developer of Kuck and Associates, Inc. (which is the maker of the high-performance KAI C++ compiler), estimating the cost of compiler development at $80 and more per line of code (as of 1998). Given such a high cost, vendors of compilers for general-purpose languages usually do not have the resources to extend their products with domain- or application-specific features (e.g., domain-specific optimizations for scientific computing), which are only useful to a relatively small group of users. Developing dedicated programming environments for whole domain-specific languages is even more costly and definitely should not be undertaken by application developers. The only solution to this economic problem is to provide a common (meta-) programming infrastructure that can be reused across different languages and build a third-party market for specialized language extensions on top of it.

♦ *Problems of distributing new language extensions:* Even if we extend a language with new features, dissemination of the new features is extremely difficult because languages are traditionally defined in terms of fixed grammars and compilers, and programming environments do not support an easy and incremental language extensibility. That is why, as Simonyi notes in [Sim97], new useful features have the chance to reach a large audience only if they are lucky enough to be part of a new, widely disseminated language. A good example of such feature are interfaces in Java. The only problem is that such opportunities are quite rare. Furthermore, Java is also a good example of a language that is extremely difficult to extend because of its wide use and the legacy problem that comes with it. This is also the reason why, as of this writing, genericity is still not in the language. Another problem is that just as new features are difficult to add to a widely used language, bad features that are already in the language are difficult or impossible to get rid of.

♦ *Problem of evolving domain- and application-specific languages:* As Eric Van Wyk pointed out, domains evolve and "may evolve out of the coverage of any domain-specific language." As discussed in the previous point, fixed grammars, compilers, and language infrastructures make it difficult to evolve domain-specific languages to adequately support evolving domains.

11.6.1.3 The IP Solution: An Extendible Programming Environment

Fortunately, there is a third way to provide adequate support for domain-specific abstractions without running into the problems discussed in the previous two sections. The solution is to use an extendible programming environment, such as IP, which replaces the fixed-programming-language view with the idea of configuring your programming notation by composing active libraries implementing single or sets of language features (i.e., intentions). IP addresses the aforementioned problems as follows.

- Loss of design information and code tangling are avoided by providing domain-specific language extensions, that is, specialized language constructs that capture your domain-specific abstractions intentionally. In IP, language extensions are packaged into active libraries called extension libraries, which you can load into the programming environment in order to extend it.
- Performance penalties are avoided by applying domain-specific optimizations, which are distributed as a part of the extension libraries.
- Domain-specific programming support (e.g., domain-specific debugging, editing, displaying, and so on) can also be provided as a part of the extension libraries.
- The parsing problem is solved in IP by abandoning the textual representation altogether and allowing direct and unambiguous entry of AST nodes using commands. Furthermore, thanks to rendering, any kind of notation can be supported.
- Some of the high development cost of specialized compilers and programming environments is reduced by providing a common reusable (meta-) programming platform (i.e., the IP system), so that only the language extensions themselves need to be programmed. Furthermore, you can usually reuse a given language feature with different configurations of other language features. The interoperability between the language features has to be provided by the vendors of the language features or frameworks of language features, which may require special extension libraries with glue code.
- Extension libraries represent a convenient and economical means for distributing language extensions. New features can be added to the programming environment as the application scales. For new development, you can easily exclude deprecated features by simply not loading them (although you can still load them for legacy code).
- IP provides a platform for language evolution driven by the evolution of domains and by market needs. Charles Simonyi

compares this evolution to the processes found in biological systems by referring to the future intention market as an "ecology of intentions" [Sim95].

11.6.2 Moving Focus from Fixed Languages to Language Features and the Emergence of an Intention Market

As Simonyi notes in [Sim97], with IP we have a major shift of focus from languages to language features, that is, intentions. Currently, new language constructs have to look for a host language and this is quite difficult because the most popular languages are difficult to extend (this requires updating all the compilers, standards, manuals, and so on, which are not designed to be extendible). As we mentioned previously, new features can only spread through new and successful languages, such as Java. Unfortunately, not only good features reach large audiences this way. If a bad feature makes it into one of the widely used languages, it is difficult, or impossible, to get rid of it. The situation is very different in IP: Programming abstractions become true entities with their own "life." They have to survive based on their own merits. They encapsulate the knowledge they need to be displayed, compiled, and debugged in different contexts and can be easily distributed as extension libraries.

The research on design patterns and idioms gives a further motivation for the need of change of focus from languages to programming abstractions (see e.g., [GL98]). The pattern work attempts to classify new useful domain-specific and general programming abstractions and mechanisms. There is the conviction that programs are essentially assembled from these fundamental building blocks. On the other hand, as more of such patterns are identified and documented, it becomes increasingly difficult for any language to express them adequately. Few of these abstractions make it into languages. For example, dynamic polymorphism or inheritance require implementation idioms in C, but they are part of OO languages. However, hardly any existing language could keep up with the explosion of new abstractions.

The vision of IP is the emergence of an intention market. In such a market, there will be intention vendors, who will develop new intentions and will have to make sure that these intentions cooperate whenever there is a need for it. Obviously, there will be different categories of vendors, for example:

♦ Vendors providing frameworks of intentions implementing general purpose programming and modeling notations.

◆ Vendors providing frameworks of intentions implementing domain-specific programming and modeling notations.
◆ Smaller vendors providing nifty, innovative extensions to the existing notations.

Given such a market, language abstractions are no longer "looking for" host languages, but rather for customers [Sim97]. With all the critique of current programming languages, they are still very important from the IP viewpoint: They are sources of useful language features and notations. As Simonyi predicts in [WTH+99], the development of the intention market will probably start with vendors providing extension libraries implementing existing programming languages (such as Java, C++, COBOL, and so on), and then supplying useful additions to them (e.g., genericity, preconditions and postconditions, procedure specialization, and so on). The next step will be the development of domain-specific intentions.

It is important to note that IP creates an enormous development potential in several areas including novel debugging mechanisms, specialized rendering and editing support, domain-specific optimizations, language-specific refactoring support and so on, which goes much beyond the mere evolution of programming languages we have today. This is so because it gives third-party vendors a common infrastructure and a common internal source representation for implementing and distributing language extensions and language-based tools, which they didn't have before.

11.6.3 Intentional Programming and Component-Based Development

Intentional Programming provides advanced support for Component-Based Development (CBD). As a particular focus, in addition to promoting building applications from reusable, replaceable parts, IP enables automating their assembly in unique ways.

Now, you may wonder: What is the relationship between IP and component standards, such as CORBA, COM, or JavaBeans? First, let us take a look at the similarities (for brevity, in the rest of this section, we refer to CORBA, COM, or JavaBeans components as just "components").

◆ Both intentions and components are building blocks used by application programmers to build applications.
◆ Just like intentions, components may also have design-mode methods used to enter, visualize, and manipulate them at programming time.
◆ Both intentions and components support visual programming.

♦ They both have globally unique identifiers allowing their global distribution.

However, there are also several important differences. In contrast to IP, most CBD environments based on the CORBA, COM, or JavaBeans standards have the following deficiencies.

♦ They only allow you to create assemblies of components whose structure will be preserved into runtime. In other words, transformations implementing domain-specific optimizations and weaving and distributed as part of the components are not supported. This usually leads to poor separation of concerns and/or poor runtime performance.
♦ They do not support domain-specific debugging capabilities distributed as part of the components.
♦ They are not capable of mimicking the traditional, textual way of programming using tree editing like IP does, that is, they only provide visual programming as a direct way to manipulate components. (Alternatively, you can use traditional textual, scripting languages to glue components, but such code has all the problems of traditional programming, for example, it has no adequate support for refactoring, extendibility, and so on).
♦ They still need conventional, textual languages to code the components. In contrast, IP does not have this conceptual discontinuity: Everything (including intentions) is coded using intentions and all the source can enjoy all the advantages of intentional encoding.

Put another way: If you implement a component-based programming environment that:

♦ Contains a code-transformation framework for generating efficient code from design-time assemblies of components and that supports the integration of independently developed transformations
♦ Provides a special support for metaprogramming including debugging of transformations
♦ Provides a set of standard APIs for extending any part of the environment (including the debugger)
♦ Supports not only visual programming, but it also views traditional, textual language features as components and perfectly mimics the traditional type-in of such features and
♦ Is completely implemented in itself, that is, it does not need any traditional programming technology to implement any of its components

then you've got another IP.

11.6.4 Frequently Asked Questions

IP represents quite a radical paradigm change departing from many current programming traditions. Therefore, it isn't surprising that there are a number of questions frequently brought up in discussions about IP.

Q1: General-purpose programming languages are commonly understood. On the other hand, each new domain-specific notation needs to be learned first. Isn't the cost of learning new domain-specific notations prohibitive?

If you code a library of domain-specific abstractions in a general-purpose programming language, the library user will need to learn the domain concepts behind the library in order to be able to use it. The understanding of the general-purpose programming language will be of little help in understanding the domain concepts. Thus, learning a conventional library of domain-specific abstractions is much the same as learning a new domain-specific language. By using a domain-specific language instead of the conventional library approach, you get many advantages, however. Problems expressed in a domain-specific language are often more concise and contain less clutter. An encoding in a domain-specific language is more intentional because you don't have to take the detour of coding idioms and patterns to express key domain concepts, that is, domain knowledge doesn't get lost. Finally, you get all the advantages of domain-specific support including domain-specific optimizations, natural notations, domain-specific error reporting and debugging (see Table 8-2 in Section 8.7.1). For example, the STL [MS96] is famous for causing long and cryptic error reports (due to the long and complicated identifiers generated during template instantiation) when you have an error in your application code using STL. With domain-specific error support, the library would actually be able to issue clear-text, domain-specific compile-time error reports telling you what is wrong with the way you used a given container in your program.

It is often said that a common general-purpose language promotes communication between developers. Yes, this is true for the general-purpose programming mechanisms it provides. But, this advantage can be easily carried over to domain-specific, extensible languages: If necessary, a domain specific notation can be based on widely known general-purpose programming mechanisms. Furthermore, just as standard libraries help to foster a common communication basis beyond the syntax of their implementation language, standard domain-specific notations will emerge and serve the same purpose.

Q2: Using simpler languages is easier and makes clearer programs. IP propagates feature-rich languages. Isn't programming in feature-rich languages more complicated and doesn't it result in more complicated programs?

First, we need to be clear about our goal: Do we want to have a simpler language or one that simplifies the task of writing a given program? Probably the latter. Assembler is a simple language with few language features, but writing and maintaining complex assembler programs can be a nightmare. We definitely want to use an optimal set of language features for a given problem, that is, we don't want to use more features or more complicated features than necessary. (As Albert Einstein once said: "Make it as simple as possible, but no simpler than that.") Unfortunately, simplicity is often confused with primitiveness.

An intense discussion about simplifying languages has been sparked by Java, whose simplicity compared to C++ is considered its main advantage. Java definitely makes programming certain kinds of applications simpler (e.g., due to its automatic memory management). However, because certain useful general-purpose features are missing, some classes of problems are not as easy to code in Java. For example, due to missing genericity, programming with containers is quite a tedious task. Furthermore, the intentionality of the code suffers. For example, you cannot express enumerations in Java intentionally—you have to simulate them using constants, and therefore, you don't get specialized type-checking as in C++ (this and other painful omissions from Java are discussed in [Gil99]). This is not a critique of Java as a language. First, Java can be seen as a useful language redesign based on other object-oriented languages. Language redesign and evolution is very important and extendible programming environments like IP just make it simpler. Second, Java is a fine, well-selected set of features including some new useful features (e.g., interfaces). And it should be seen as that. That is, you can use it for a given problem if it fits it well, but you should be able to extend it if you need to. Extendible programming environments do not prevent you from using a well-selected set of features for your problem. In fact, they make it simpler because you can also add problem-specific features, which are generally missing in general-purpose languages, but can greatly simplify the programming task. Furthermore, as your application scales and evolves, the "set of optimal languages features" also changes. If you are using an extendible programming environment, you can evolve this set more easily.

Another argument on language simplicity brought up by Guy Steele in his excellent and entertaining OOPSLA'98 keynote

[Ste98] is that simple[15] languages enforce clarity and promote understandability by using fewer special terms and being more verbose (i.e., by showing more of the definition of terms). In other words, he supports the standpoint that domain-specific languages are cryptic. (As Mason Cooley once said: "Jargon is any technical language we do not understand.") Yes, domain-specific languages are cryptic to those that do not know a given domain. But then, they should either learn it or should not be programming in that domain. We feel that only beginners can be helped with somewhat more verbose encoding. However, if this is the goal, then you can provide a verbose rendering of the code in IP (i.e., the intentions can be rendered in a more verbose fashion, showing more of their definitions). By using verbose encoding (rather than just verbose rendering), however, you loose design information because you don't get unique handles on the important domain concepts in the code, but rather code patterns representing them. Finally, to experts, verbose renderings are awkward and annoying.[16]

At last, what can be more simple to use than a domain-specific representation, which was specially designed to make the task at hand simpler?

Q3: Won't letting any programmer extend a language create a notational havoc?

The problem of opportunistic language extensions is pertinent to languages with an extensive, built-in support for metaprogramming, such as CLOS or Smalltalk. Such languages make it easier for an application programmer to include metacode implementing some ad hoc language extensions directly in the application code. The problem is that, although metacode makes the base code simpler, it is usually itself inherently more complex, harder to debug, and errors in the metacode often have a more severe impact on a system than errors in the base code. On the other hand, well-designed and reusable metacode can greatly simplify application development.

The situation in IP is quite different than in languages with built-in metaprogramming capabilities. This is because IP makes a

---

15. In the sense of "primitive."
16. In fact, Steele's OOPSLA99 keynote transcript [Ste98] demonstrates just that. The keynote itself is written using a primitive subset of English, which is also defined in the paper. The intention was to show how far one can go with a primitive language. Despite an impressive demonstration of this point, to a fluent English speaker, the keynote text appears awkward. Thank God we don't have to communicate using a primitive English in everyday life!

clear separation between programming and metaprogramming. Application programmers use IP together with general-purpose and domain-specific extension libraries that optimally support their job. Writing language extensions (i.e., extension libraries) is a separate and completely different activity than application programming. It involves utilizing extension APIs and adhering to special IP protocols and requires language design and implementation skills. Developing extension libraries will be the business of library vendors, not application developers.

Just as standard, conventional libraries emerge in different domains today, standard domain-specific notations will emerge. (Many fields already have their domain-specific notations, IP will just help to implement them as sharable and embeddable sets of programming abstractions.) In the presence of an intention market, developers will have access to high-quality and sophisticated domain-specific intentions, so that the temptation to invent their own ad hoc solutions will diminish. An intention market will promote strong specialization, which will allow us to build systems of greater quality and complexity.

Finally, having a common platform for language extensions will help us to eliminate "islands of insulated domain- and application-specific languages," which are common today.

Q4: How about the interoperability of extension libraries? Doesn't the problem of feature interactions (i.e., adding a new feature may easily break the language) render extending programming languages impractical?

Kinds of language extensions

Before answering how IP addresses the problem of feature interactions and what the challenges are, let us first take a look at the two possible kinds of language extensions.

♦ *Encapsulated language extensions:* Encapsulated language extensions do not affect the semantics of the language features of the language being extended. Technically, this means that an encapsulated language extension does not contribute transformations that would participate in the compilation of the language features in the language being extended. An example of such an extension is embedded SQL, where the compilation of the host code (e.g., written in Java) and the embedded SQL code are two different activities. The only requirement is that the embedded SQL code returns values of types understood by the host language. Composing encapsulated language extensions is analogous to composing well-encapsulated components (such as JavaBeans, COM, or CORBA components).

◆ *Language extensions with external influence:* Language extensions with external influence affect the semantics of the language features of the language being extended. For example, a language extension with external influence could contribute wide-scope, domain-specific optimizations, which also transform instances of the language features of the language being extended. Other examples of features with wide influence are evaluation mode (eager versus lazy evaluation), exception handling, and memory management. In other words, language extensions with external influence have an aspect-oriented character.

Kinds of language feature interactions

In the context of language extensions, we can have three kinds of feature interactions.

◆ *Syntactic feature interactions:* A language extension could introduce parsing ambiguities and make the resulting language unparsable.
◆ *Semantic feature interactions between encapsulated language extensions:* This kind of feature interactions is the same as feature interactions between conventional, encapsulated components (e.g., JavaBeans, COM, or CORBA components).
◆ *Semantic feature interactions involving language extensions with external influence:* These are the hardest kind of interactions to deal with. It involves coordinating transformations across several components (possibly from different vendors).

Now, we can take a look at how IP helps to resolve each of these three kinds of feature interactions.

NOTE

It is important to realize that "components with metaprogramming capabilities = language features." Indeed, you could build a source tree out of a set of JavaBeans or COM instances and association relationships. The links to declarations would be the instantiation relationships between the components and the instances. You could construct this tree in a COM or JavaBeans component builder. If the component hierarchy is deployed as is (i.e., the structure of the components is preserved into runtime), you've got the typical functionality of a component-based development environment. However, if the components are asked to generate code and perform transformations, you can think of each of the components as a language feature! Put another way, the requirement to support traditional components and metaprogramming (i.e., aspectual components, automatic configuration, and so on) blurs the borderline between components and language features!

♦ *Syntactic feature interactions:* This problem is completely solved in IP by abandoning parsing altogether.

♦ *Semantic feature interactions between encapsulated language extensions:* As stated previously, these kind of feature interactions are the same as feature interactions between conventional, encapsulated components. The usual way of resolving such interactions is to provide glue code taking care of the incompatibilities. The same strategy can be applied in IP. But, in IP, we can do even better than that. Conventional glue code introduces additional levels of indirections incurring runtime penalties. With IP, we can apply domain-specific transformations to eliminate this overhead, that is, we get zero-overhead glue code. However, it is important to note that this approach often involves turning encapsulated extensions into ones with external influence. On the other hand, the latter are the specialty of IP. Finally, IP gives us another great advantage when it comes to embedding domain-specific language extensions. For example, when using a conventional database technology, such as JDBC (Java Database Connectivity), syntax errors in embedded SQL queries are not detected at compile time, but at runtime (when the query is sent to and evaluated by the server). However, if you implement embedded SQL as a true language extension of the host language (which is how you do it in IP), syntax errors in a query will be detected during the compilation of the client.

♦ *Semantic feature interactions involving language extensions with external influence:* As, stated earlier, these are the hardest kind of interactions to deal with. This problem involves coordinating transformations across several extension libraries (possibly from different vendors). IP addresses this problem with its sophisticated reduction protocol. As we discussed in Section 11.5.5, extension libraries may provide partial orderings of transformations and let the IP system find a valid total ordering for a set of extension libraries. Expressing language extension in terms of partial orderings of transformations rather than total ones increases the chance that a given set of extension libraries will cooperate. Practically, this means that an extension library may request a particular transformation order and will look at some transformation results of other libraries. Of course, this kind of library interaction (i.e., where transformations from different vendors try to reduce the same instances of intentions) will require some kind of cooperation between the library vendors, for example, they will need to agree on some common interfaces and protocols.

As you can see, IP improves the situation in all three cases. However, there is still a great need for new research on language extensibility. The idea of modularly extendible languages is only beginning to gain popularity in the research community (e.g., see [Hud98, DNW+99, KFD99]). In particular, we need to work on domain models of general-purpose language abstractions and mechanisms (i.e., studying which combinations of features are possible, which are useful, which are preferred, and so on). Furthermore, we need more work on language features for encapsulating aspects in the context of other features (such as the work on aspect-oriented features in object-orientation as discussed in Chapter 8). We need to study interfaces between features and work towards standard protocols for metaprogramming. Work on typing components that implement language features is an active research area (see e.g., [MPW99]). Such type systems will allow an extendible programming environment to determine whether a given configuration of language features is compatible or not.

Q5: With program source expressed as text, I see all the information contained in the source at once. By introducing internal representations and rendering, I usually don't. Isn't it confusing?

In our mind, seeing all the detail of a complex system at once is confusing. In IP, you can, but usually don't want to view the core rendering of the source (see Figure 11-24). Just as in the case of a CAD system, the separation of internal representation and rendering gives us the opportunity to build even more complex systems because we are not forced to work in the most-detailed view all the time.

Q6: Some people still haven't made the transition to OO. IP seems to be a completely new paradigm. Isn't IP too big a paradigm change to digest for the average programmer?

A very exciting property of IP is that you can introduce it in an evolutionary way. The only necessary initial investment in terms of training is teaching your developers to work with the IP editor, which is not much. At this basic level, your developers can continue working with the same language(s) and paradigm(s) as they did previously. You basically import all the legacy code into IP and use IP as a development environment. Even at this basic level, you already get several of the following benefits.

♦ You get the benefits of tree editing including more efficient typing and the ease of changing names.
♦ You get browsing information that is present and up-to-date all the time.
♦ You get all the refactoring functionality that comes with IP.

In other words, the basic level is to use IP as an efficient forward and reverse engineering environment. At the next level, as new and useful general-purpose and domain-specific language extensions, refactoring, and other tool extensions for your language appear on the market, you can use them to improve your code. Finally, as you collect more and more expertise in a given domain, you may consider developing and marketing your own extension libraries.

It is important to note that IP is not displacing any existing language paradigms (such as the object-oriented paradigm), but only helps to better harvest their benefits by promoting multiparadigm programming and the evolution of language paradigms.

11.7 Summary

The main advantages of IP stem from the way IP represents domain concepts, which is summarized in Figure 11-28. The structure of a domain concept is given by the structure of its source graph. Its external representation is defined by the rendering and type-in methods and its semantics is given by the reduction methods.

This separation has profound consequences. If you represent a specific concept using a source graph, the structure of the graph represents the most invariant part of the concept. But, the concept's external view and semantics may depend on the context: The concept may be displayed differently at different times (e.g., editing or debugging time) or it may be displayed differently depending on its source context (i.e., on the way it is used in a program). The generated code may depend on the tree context, on the platform, and so on. Given this separation, it is usually enough to modify or extend the reduction methods to implement new optimizations and adapt the client code to a new context, new platform, and so on without having to modify the client code at all.

If we need to change the source representation itself, it is easier to do this than to change a textual representation. Tree editing has many advantages over text editing, such as fewer syntax errors,

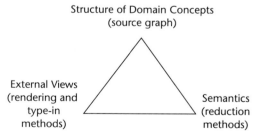

Figure 11-28 *Separation of structure, external representation, and semantics in IP [Sim98]*

active interaction with the intentions during editing, and often less typing (e.g., using additional, short intention names for efficient typing; using "display-only artifacts" to avoid retyping signatures of remotely declared procedures and methods; using automatic type-in templates; and so on). Also, automatic refactoring and reengineering of code is easier if the source is already in the form of a resolved AST.

Rendering allows different views, formatting conventions, special notations, graphical representations, the translation of names into different national languages (e.g., English or Chinese), and so on, and together with the binary source graph representation, it gives an opportunity for realizing a true document-based programming (as in Knuth's literate programming [Knu92]). You can embed animations and hyperlinks in the comments, use pretty notations for the code, embed bitmaps and controls, and so on. At the same time, the reduction methods may perform complex computations in order to generate highly-optimized code for these programs.

At last, after learning so much about the IP technology, let's go over the benefits of IP again.

- ◆ It enables the achievement of natural notations, great flexibility, and excellent performance simultaneously.
- ◆ It provides optimal, domain-specific support in all programming tasks (supports effective typing, rich notations, debugging, error reporting, and so on).
- ◆ It addresses the code tangling problem by allowing you to implement and easily distribute aspect-oriented language features.
- ◆ It allows you to include more design information in the code and to raise its intentionality.
- ◆ It helps with software evolution by supporting automated editing and refactoring of code.
- ◆ It makes your domain-specific libraries less vulnerable to changes on the market of general-purpose programming languages.
- ◆ It can be introduced into an organization in an evolutionary way with exciting benefits for the minimal cost of initial training.
- ◆ It supports all of your legacy code and allows you to improve it.
- ◆ It provides third-party vendors with a common infrastructure and a common internal source representation for implementing and distributing language extensions and language-based tools.
- ◆ It promotes domain specialization and facilitates more effective sharing of domain-specific knowledge.

Part III

APPLICATION EXAMPLES

Chapter 12

List Container[1]

12.1 Why Is This Chapter Worth Reading?

Finally, we have all the bits and pieces to work through our first complete example, which will be a list container generator. The generator will be capable of taking an abstract description of a list container and synthesizing a concrete list container type implementing this description. We will demonstrate all the necessary development steps starting with Domain Analysis and ending with C++ code. You will learn how to design an appropriate set of implementation components and how to implement a generator using template metaprogramming.

12.2 Overview

The development of a family of list containers will start by analyzing the common and variable features of list containers and the dependencies between the variable features. We will then come up with a target architecture and identify the implementation components. We'll implement the components using C++ templates, and then show that their manual composition is not a good idea. As a consequence, we'll use template metaprogramming to implement a configuration generator capable of translating specifications into concrete configurations of the implementation components.

---

1. An earlier version of the material contained in this chapter was published in K. Czarnecki and U. W. Eisenecker, Synthesizing Objects; in Proceedings of ECOOP'99—Object-Oriented Programming; R. Guerraoui, (Ed.), LNCS 1628, Springer-Verlag, Berlin and Heidelberg, Germany, 1999, p. 18–42. © 1999 by Springer-Verlag, Berlin and Heidelberg, Germany. Reprinted by permission.

12.3 Domain Analysis

Data containers represent a typical example of reusable components containing large amounts of variability. Areas of variability in containers include type of elements, element traversal, storage layout, ownership, memory allocation and management, error detection, synchronization of concurrent access, and so on. If we were going to develop a container library, we would analyze our target markets and the different requirements the target applications could have in these variability areas. For the purpose of our simple example, we will just consider one kind of container, namely singly linked lists, with a selection of variable features shown in Figure 12-1. As you may remember from our discussion in Chapter 4, this figure is an example of a feature diagram consisting of three kinds of features.

- *Mandatory features:* Pointed to by simple edges ending with a filled circle, for example, ElementType (i.e., every list has ElementType)
- *Alternative features:* Pointed to by edges connected by an arc, for example, monomorphic and polymorphic (i.e., a list can be either monomorphic or polymorphic)

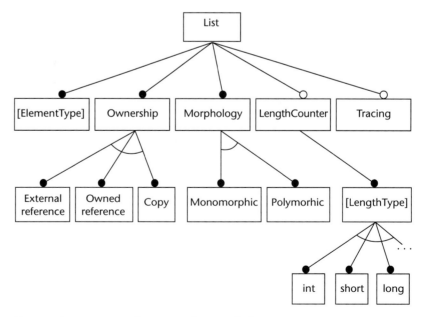

Figure 12-1 Feature diagram of a simple list container

♦ *Optional features:* Pointed to by simple edges ending with an empty circle, for example, LengthCounter (i.e., a list may or may not have a LengthCounter)

Let us take a look at each of these features. ElementType is the type of the elements stored in the list and is a free parameter (i.e., any type can be substituted for ElementType)[2] as indicated by the square brackets. Ownership specifies whether the list keeps references to the original elements and is not responsible for element deallocation (i.e., external reference), or keeps references and is responsible for element deallocation (i.e., owned reference), or keeps copies of the original elements and is responsible for their allocation and deallocation (i.e., copy). Morphology describes whether the list is monomorphic (i.e., all elements have the same type) or polymorphic (i.e., can contain elements of different types). Each list element may also contain a length counter allowing for an efficient implementation of the length operation (i.e., one of constant time complexity). This is specified by the optional feature LengthCounter. LengthType is the type of the counter, which should be an integral type. Finally, the list may trace its operation, for example, by logging operation calls to the console. This is indicated by the optional feature Tracing. Of course, this diagram could be extended with further features.

Without counting ElementType and LengthType, the diagram in Figure 12-1 describes 24 list variants (three different ownership kinds, two morphology kinds, an optional length counter, and an optional tracing, i.e., $3 \cdot 2 \cdot 2 \cdot 2 = 24$). In our example, all of these different feature configurations are valid, but this is not always the case in practice. Constraints that you cannot express in a feature diagram have to be recorded separately. We'll see examples of such constraints in Chapters 13 and 14.

The important property of a feature diagram is that it allows you to model variability without having to commit to a particular implementation mechanism, such as inheritance, aggregation, templates, or #ifdef-directives.

12.4 Domain Design

Now we need to come up with the architecture for our family of list containers. In general, developing an architecture involves

---

2. To be more precise, in some list configurations, the ElementType will be required to provide a copy constructor or a special polymorphic clone method. You'll see this in Section 12.5.

answering questions, such as what kinds of components are needed, how will they be connected, what kind of middleware or component model will be used, what interfaces the component categories will have, how will they accommodate the requirements, and so on. Designing an architecture is an iterative process, and it usually requires prototyping. Studying existing architecture styles and patterns will greatly help you in this process (e.g., see [BMR+96]).

For our list example, we'll use a particular kind of layered architecture, called a GenVoca architecture, which we discussed in Section 9.8.2 in great detail. It is basically an object-oriented architecture consisting of a set of configurable layers containing one or more classes. The layers can be thought of as abstraction layers found in object-oriented frameworks. This kind of architecture proves to be useful for a wide variety of systems (see Section 9.8.2).

Designing a GenVoca architecture requires the following steps.

1. Identify the main responsibilities in the feature diagrams from the Domain Analysis.
2. Enumerate component categories and components per category.
3. Identify "uses" dependencies between component categories.
4. Sort the categories into a layered architecture.
5. Write down the GenVoca grammar.

Let's perform these steps for our family of list containers.

- *Identify the main responsibilities in the feature diagrams from the Domain Analysis:* Obviously, the main responsibility of a list container is to store elements. Furthermore, Ownership suggests that we might need to be able to copy and destroy elements. Morphology suggests that, in some cases, we should be able to check the type of the elements being inserted at runtime. LengthCounter implies an efficient implementation of the length operation, and finally, Tracing implies some tracing capability.
- *Enumerate component categories and components per category:* Now, we'll introduce a component category for each responsibility identified in the previous step. If a responsibility has more than one alternative implementation, the corresponding component category will contain a component for each alternative. The component categories for our list con-

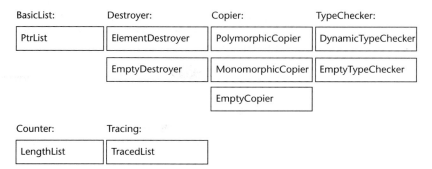

Figure 12-2 Component categories for the list container family

tainer family and the components per category are shown in Figure 12-2. The component category BasicList provides the basic functionality and is responsible for storing elements. In our simple example, we have only one implementation of BasicList, which is the singly linked pointer list PtrList. Destroyers are responsible for destroying elements. Element-Destroyer is used in owned-reference or copying lists, where the list is responsible for deallocating its elements. Otherwise, we use EmptyDestroyer, which does nothing. Copiers are responsible for copying elements. A polymorphic copying list uses PolymorphicCopier and a monomorphic copying list uses MonomorphicCopier. Otherwise, EmptyCopier is used, which does nothing. TypeCheckers are responsible for checking the type of the element being inserted at runtime. DynamicTypeChecker is used by monomorphic lists. Polymorphic lists use EmptyTypeChecker. Counter is responsible for providing a length counter and a length operation. We have only one implementation called LengthList. Tracing is responsible for tracing and the only implementation component is TracedList.

- *Identify "uses" dependencies between component categories:* Tracing and Counter use BasicList (see Figure 12-3 a). Furthermore, Tracing can also print the value of the counter, so we also add a dependency from Tracing to Counter. BasicList uses Destroyer, Copier, and TypeChecker.
- *Sort the categories into a layered architecture:* We arrange the component categories into a hierarchy of layers, where each layer represents a category and the categories that most

other categories depend on are moved towards the bottom of the hierarchy (see Figure 12-3 b). Finally, we add a `ConfigurationRepository` at the bottom, which encapsulates several smaller components and types, namely `Destroyer`, `Copier`, `TypeChecker`, `ElementType`, and `LengthType` (see Figure 12-3 c). `ConfigurationRepository` is used to communicate configuration information to all layers. This is possible because a layer may retrieve information from any layer located directly or indirectly below it. You'll see how this works in Section 12.5. The dashed box around `Tracing` and `Counter` indicates that these layers are optional. Alternative components in `ConfigurationRepository` are separated by vertical bars.

- *Write down the GenVoca grammar:* The main idea of the layered architecture in Figure 12-3 c is that a component from a given layer takes another component from the layer just below it as its parameter, for example, `TracedList` takes `LengthList` as its parameter. Because the `Counter` layer is

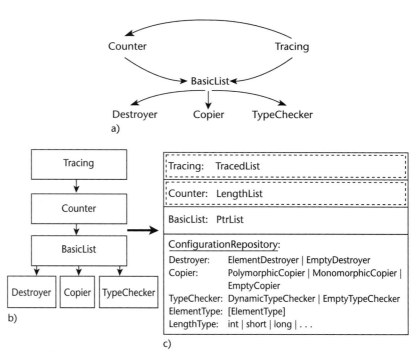

Figure 12-3 Derivation of a layered architecture

```
List            : TracedList[OptCounterList] | OptCounterList
OptCounterList  : LengthList[BasicList] | BasicList
BasicList       : PtrList[Config]
Config          :
   ElementType  : [ElementType]
   Destroyer    : ElementDestroyer | EmptyDestroyer
   Copier       : PolymorphicCopier | MonomorphicCopier |
                  EmptyCopier
   TypeChecker  : DynamicTypeChecker | EmptyTypeChecker
   LengthType   : int | short | long | ...
   ReturnType   //the final list type
```

Figure 12-4 *GenVoca grammar for the list container family*

optional, `Tracing` may also take `PtrList` as its parameter, that is, we may have `TracedList[LengthList[...]]` or `TracedList[PtrList[...]]`. Using this idea, we can represent this layered architecture as a set of grammar rules shown in Figure 12-4). Please note that vertical bars separate alternative components, and we have abbreviated `Configura-tionRepository` to `Config`. Furthermore, `Config` also contains `ReturnType`, which is the type of a fully configured list. You can view this GenVoca grammar as a language describing the configuration space for our implementation components. We call such a language *Implementation Components Configuration Language* (ICCL).

At this point, the architecture for our list container family is finished. Of course, the previous steps require an iterative process and prototyping to design the final set of components. The latter is also needed to find a stable interface for each of the component categories (each component in a category is required to implement the category interface).

Before designing a means for specifying lists and the generator, we'll first implement the implementation components and play with manual configuration.

12.5 Implementation Components

Once we have the architecture, we can implement the components. As stated previously, a component from a given layer takes a component from the layer below it as its parameter, that is, we need to implement the components as parameterized components. In C++, we can use class templates for this purpose. We start with the implementation of the pointer list:[3]

```
template<class Config_>
class PtrList
{
public:
  //make Config available as a member type
  typedef Config_ Config;

private:
  //retrieve needed types from the configuration repository
  typedef typename Config::ElementType ElementType;
  typedef typename
    Config::SetHeadElementType SetHeadElementType;
  typedef typename Config::ReturnType ReturnType;

  typedef typename Config::Destroyer Destroyer;
  typedef typename Config::TypeChecker TypeChecker;
  typedef typename Config::Copier Copier;

public:
  PtrList(SetHeadElementType& h, ReturnType *t = 0) :
    head_(0), tail_(t)
  { setHead(h); }

  ~PtrList()
  { Destroyer::destroy(head_); }

  void setHead(SetHeadElementType& h)
  { TypeChecker::check(h);
    head_ = Copier::copy(h);
  }

  ElementType& head()
  { return *head_; }

  void setTail(ReturnType *t)
  { tail_ = t; }
```

---

3. The keyword **typename** is required by ANSI C++ to tell the compiler that a member of a template parameter is expected to be a type.

```
    ReturnType *tail() const
    { return tail_; }

private:
  ElementType* head_;
  ReturnType* tail_;
};
```

PtrList takes Config_ as its parameter and publishes it under the new name Config. Any other component that takes PtrList as its parameter can retrieve Config from it using the C++ scope operator ::, that is, PtrList::Config. PtrList has two instance variables: head_ and tail_. head_ points to the head element, and tail_ points to the rest of the list. Please note that the type of tail_ is ReturnType, which is the final type of the list. We cannot use PtrList as the type of tail_ because we will derive a list with counter and a list with tracing from PtrList. Whenever we derive classes from PtrList and want to create instances of the *most refined type*, tail_ has to be of the most refined type. Because this type is unknown in PtrList, PtrList retrieves it from the configuration repository Config.[4]

Another interesting point about PtrList is that methods setting the head (i.e., the constructor and setHead()) use the type SetHeadElementType&. This type should be either ElementType& or const ElementType&, depending whether the list stores references to elements or copies of elements. Because this is unknown in PtrList, PtrList retrieves the appropriate SetHeadElementType from the configuration repository.

Finally, PtrList delegates some of its work to other components: The destructor delegates its job to the member type Destroyer, which is retrieved from the configuration repository. Similarly, setHead() delegates type checking and copying to TypeChecker and Copier, respectively. The member types Destroyer, TypeChecker, and Copier may point to different components as specified in Figure 12-4.

We have two destroyer components: ElementDestroyer and EmptyDestroyer. ElementDestroyer deletes an element and is used if a list keeps element copies or owned references. We've implemented

---

4. Our example demonstrates how configuration repositories can help in typing recursive classes, that is, classes that are used directly or indirectly in their own definition (e.g., a list).

it as a struct rather than a class because it defines only one public operation and struct members are public by default:

```
template<class ElementType>
struct ElementDestroyer
{ static void destroy(ElementType *e)
  { delete e; }
};
```

EmptyDestroyer does nothing and is used in lists that keep external references to the original elements. Because its destroy() method is implemented inline, an optimizing compiler will remove any calls to this method:

```
template<class ElementType>
struct EmptyDestroyer
{ static void destroy(ElementType *e)
  {} //do nothing
};
```

DynamicTypeChecker is used to assure that a monomorphic list contains elements of one type only:

```
template<class ElementType>
struct DynamicTypeChecker
{ static void check(const ElementType& e)
  { assert(typeid(e)==typeid(ElementType)); }
};
```

EmptyTypeChecker does nothing and is used in a polymorphic list:

```
template<class ElementType>
struct EmptyTypeChecker
{ static void check(const ElementType& e)
  {}
};
```

PolymorphicCopier copies an element by calling the virtual function clone():

```
template<class ElementType>
struct PolymorphicCopier
{ static ElementType* copy(const ElementType& e)
```

```
  { return e.clone(); } //call a virtual clone()
};
```

`MonomorphicCopier` copies an element by calling its copy constructor:

```
template<class ElementType>
struct MonomorphicCopier
{ static ElementType* copy(const ElementType& e)
  { return new ElementType(e); } //call copy constructor
};
```

Finally, `EmptyCopier` simply returns the original element:

```
template<class ElementType>
struct EmptyCopier
{ static ElementType* copy(ElementType& e) //pass by non-const
                                           //reference!
  { return &e; } //simply return the original
};
```

Next, we need the two wrappers `LengthList` and `TracedList` to implement length counter and tracing. `LengthList` is implemented as an *inheritance-based wrapper*, that is, a template class derived from its parameter.[5] It overrides the method `setTail()` to keep track of the list length and adds the method `length()`. Please note that the component retrieves the configuration repository from its parameter:

```
template<class BaseList>
class LengthList : public BaseList
{
public:
  //retrieve the configuration repository
  typedef typename BaseList::Config Config;

private:
  //retrieve the necessary types from the repository
  typedef typename Config::ElementType ElementType;
```

---

5. Inheritance-based wrappers are useful whenever we only want to override a few methods and inherit the remaining ones. Otherwise, we can use *aggregation-based wrappers* (i.e., forwarding-based wrapper; see Section 9.8.2.4).

```
      typedef typename
        Config::SetHeadElementType SetHeadElementType;
      typedef typename Config::ReturnType ReturnType;
      typedef typename Config::LengthType LengthType;

  public:
    LengthList(SetHeadElementType& h, ReturnType *t = 0) :
      BaseList(h,t), length_(computedLength())
    {}

    void setTail(ReturnType *t)
    { BaseList::setTail(t);
      length_ = computedLength();
    }

    const LengthType& length() const
    { return length_; }

  private:
    LengthType computedLength() const
    { return tail() ? tail()->length()+1
                    : 1;
    }

    LengthType length_;
};
```

TracedList is also implemented as an inheritance-based wrapper:

```
template<class BaseList>
class TracedList : public BaseList
{
public:
  typedef typename BaseList::Config Config;

private:
  typedef typename Config::ElementType ElementType;
  typedef typename
    Config::SetHeadElementType SetHeadElementType;
  typedef typename Config::ReturnType ReturnType;

public:
  TracedList(SetHeadElementType& h, ReturnType *t = 0) :
```

```
        BaseList(h,t)
    {}

    void setHead(SetHeadElementType& h)
    { cout << "setHead(" << h << ")"<< endl;
      BaseList::setHead(h);
    }

    ElementType& head()
    { cout << "head()"<< endl;
      return BaseList::head();
    }

    void setTail(ReturnType *t)
    { cout << "setTail(t)"<< endl;
      BaseList::setTail(t);
    }
};
```

And this completes the set of implementation components.

12.6 Manual Assembly

Now that we have the implementation components, we can build different lists by documenting different configuration repositories in which the appropriate components are assembled together. For example, the configuration repository in Figure 12-5 defines a monomorphic list that keeps copies of elements of type Person and provides a length counter and tracing.

TracedCopyMonoPersonLenListConfig is implemented as a so-called *traits class* (see Section 10.10.2), that is, a class that aggregates a number of types and constants to be passed to a template as a parameter. MyList contains the type we want to produce. The gray boxes and arrows visualize the flow of types from the configuration repository to PtrList to LengthList and finally, to TracedList. Among these types is ReturnType, which represents the final list type. The list components can retrieve it from the repository. It is interesting to note the circularity involving the configuration repository: The components are composed in the configuration repository and the repository is passed to the components. This circularity allows us to model circular dependency graphs, and the complete dependency graph for our list example is circular! This is so because BasicList uses ReturnType, which may contain LengthList or TracedList, depending on the final

```
struct TracedCopyMonoPersonLenlistConfig
{
    //provide the different type names required by the components
    typedef Person                                  ElementType;
    typedef const ElementType                       SetHeadElementType;
    typedef int                                     LengthType;
    typedef ElementDestroyer<ElementType>           Destroyer;
    typedef DynamicTypeChecker<ElementType>         TypeChecker;
    typedef MomomorphicCopier<ElementType>          Copier;

    //wrap PtrList into LenList and TracedList
    typedef
      TracedList<
        LengthList<
          PtrList<TracedCopyMonoPersonLenListConfig> > > ReturnType;
};
//define a short name for our list
typedef TracedCopyMonoPersonLenListConfig::ReturnType Mylist;
```

Figure 12-5 *Configuration repository defining a monomorphic list that keeps copies of elements of type* Person *and provides a length counter and tracing*

configuration. The arrows back to Counter and Tracing create cycles (see Figure 12-6).

It is also worth noting that because all variation points in our example are static, we use static parameterization and inlining to avoid the unnecessary cost of virtual function calls and the cost of function calls for small functions. Templates and inlining allow composing code fragments without any runtime cost. As a result, the composed types are as efficient as manually coded concrete variants. If we need dynamically reconfigurable variation points, we can use virtual functions. If the decision between dynamic and static binding should be parameterized, we can use the idiom shown in Section 7.9.

Without counting ElementType and LengthType, the feature diagram in Figure 12-1 defines 24 different list configurations. We can define a configuration repository for each of them, for example, a polymorphic list that keeps external references to original elements of type Person or derived types:

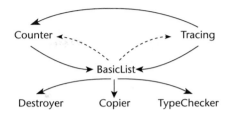

Figure 12-6 Full dependency graph for our list container family

```
struct RefPolyPersonListConfig
{
  typedef Person                          ElementType;
  typedef ElementType                     SetHeadElementType;
  typedef EmptyDestroyer<ElementType>     Destroyer;
  typedef EmptyTypeChecker<ElementType>   TypeChecker;
  typedef EmptyCopier<ElementType>        Copier;

  typedef PtrList<RefPolyPersonListConfig>    ReturnType;
};
typedef RefPolyPersonListConfig::ReturnType RefPolyPersonList;
```

Writing configuration repositories is a tedious exercise. The person writing them needs to know what implementation components are available, what the valid configurations are, and which configurations are more optimal or satisfy some other requirement. Thus, requiring the application programmers to write a configuration repository places quite a burden on them. Even worse, it makes client code too strongly coupled with the architecture and the implementation components because changes to the architecture (e.g., adding a new layer) may require modifying all configuration repositories.

An alternative would be to include all possible configuration repositories in the library. However, this is usually not practicable because there is normally a large number of configurations (e.g., the matrix computation library described in Chapter 14 would require 1840 configuration repositories) and each of them is usually longer than those in the list example. The solution is to generate the configuration repositories out of more abstract descriptions. But before taking a look at how this works, we need to figure out what an "abstract description" means in our context, that is, how to conveniently "order" a list container.

12.7   Specifying Lists

Now we need to define the vocabulary for specifying lists. For our simple example, we'll take the features defined in Figure 12-1 and represent them using enumeration types:

```
enum Ownership    {ext_ref, own_ref, cp};
enum Morphology   {mono, poly};
enum CounterFlag  {with_counter, no_counter};
enum TracingFlag  {with_tracing, no_tracing};
```

Application programmers will use this vocabulary to specify a list. If they do not specify some feature, an appropriate default value should be selected. In general, we can have direct default settings, which are independent from other features, and computed default settings, which depend on the selection of other features. For our simple list example, we'll assume the following direct default settings:

```
Ownership   = cp
Morphology  = mono
CounterFlag = no_counter
TracingFlag = no_tracing
LengthType  = int
```

You'll see an example of computed defaults in Chapter 14.

The vocabulary for specifying members of a family is called a *configuration DSL.*[6] The previous configuration DSL is a very simple one. In general, there are several other design issues and trade-offs we have to consider while developing a configuration DSL. We'll discuss them in Chapters 13 and 14.

12.8   The Generator

A generator takes a specification of a system or component and returns the finished system or component. In general, a *configuration generator* [CE99b] performs the following steps (see Figure 12-7): It completes the specification (by computing defaults), checks to see if the specified system can be built, and assembles the implementation components. In our list example, however, there is no buildability checking (because the domain-specific language doesn't give us an opportunity to specify illegal feature combina-

---

6. DSL stands for Domain-Specific Language.

Generator

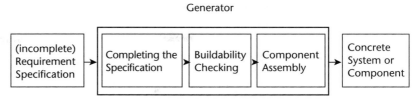

Figure 12-7 Stages of a configuration generator

tions) and there are no computed defaults (as you'll see in a moment, the few direct default settings are specified in the parameter list of the generator).

Of course, we could implement the generator as a preprocessor that generates configuration repositories in C++ source code. A better alternative, however, is to use the built-in metaprogramming capabilities of C++, that is, *template metaprogramming*. We discussed template metaprogramming in Chapter 10 in great detail. As you may remember, the idea behind it was that C++ templates constitute a compile-time, Turing-complete sublanguage of C++, and you can use this capability to write configuration code to be executed at compile time. We will implement the generator as a template that takes the description of a list as its parameter and returns the finished list type in a specially designated member, which is by convention called RET (which stands for RETURN). To make this discussion more concrete, let's take a look at how you would create an instance of a polymorphic list that keeps copies of elements of type Person and provides a length counter and tracing:

```
LIST_GENERATOR<Person, cp, poly, with_counter,
            with_tracing>::RET list1;
```

A polymorphic list that keeps external references to original elements of type Person or derived types can be declared as follows:

```
LIST_GENERATOR<Person, ext_ref, poly>::RET list2;
```

The implementation of LIST_GENERATOR is given in the following code. It uses the template IF, which corresponds to the familiar selection statement if. We described its implementation in Chapter 10. More complex generators may use other control structures including SWITCH, decision tables, and loops. You'll see examples in Chapters 13 and 14.

```
template<
  class       ElementType_,
  Ownership   ownership   = cp,
  Morphology  morphology  = mono,
  CounterFlag counterFlag = no_counter,
  TracingFlag tracingFlag = no_tracing,
  class       LengthType_ = int
>
class LIST_GENERATOR
{
public:
  typedef LIST_GENERATOR<
    ElementType_,
    ownership,
    morphology,
    counterFlag,
    tracingFlag,
    LengthType_> Generator;

private:
  enum {
    isCopy      = ownership==cp,
    isOwnRef    = ownership==own_ref,
    isMono      = morphology==mono,
    hasCounter  = counterFlag==with_counter,
    doesTracing = tracingFlag==with_tracing };

  typedef
    IF<isCopy || isOwnRef,
      ElementDestroyer<ElementType_>,
      EmptyDestroyer<ElementType_>
    >::RET Destroyer_;

  typedef
    IF<isMono,
      DynamicTypeChecker<ElementType_>,
      EmptyTypeChecker<ElementType_>
    >::RET TypeChecker_;

  typedef
    IF<isCopy,
      IF<isMono,
        MonomorphicCopier<ElementType_>,
        PolymorphicCopier<ElementType_> >::RET,
```

```
          EmptyCopier<ElementType_>
        >::RET Copier_;

    typedef
      IF<isCopy,
        const ElementType_,
        ElementType_
      >::RET SetHeadElementType_;

    typedef PtrList<Generator> List;

    typedef
      IF<hasCounter,
        LengthList<List>,
        List
      >::RET List_with_counter_or_not;

    typedef
      IF<doesTracing,
        TracedList<List_with_counter_or_not>,
        List_with_counter_or_not
      >::RET List_with_tracing_or_not;
public:
    typedef List_with_tracing_or_not RET;

    struct Config
    {
      typedef ElementType_          ElementType;
      typedef SetHeadElementType_   SetHeadElementType;
      typedef Destroyer_            Destroyer;
      typedef TypeChecker_          TypeChecker;
      typedef Copier_               Copier;
      typedef LengthType_           LengthType;
      typedef RET                   ReturnType;
    };
};
```

LIST_GENERATOR<> evaluates the input parameters, computes the types for the configuration repository, wraps PtrList (if necessary) in LengthList and/or TracedList, and returns the final list type in RET. The last part of LIST_GENERATOR<> is the configuration repository, which we no longer have to manually implement for each list configuration. Please note that PtrList takes Generator as its parameter rather than Config. Because Config is a member of

Generator, PtrList can retrieve Config from Generator. For this reason, we need to slightly modify the following two lines in PtrList (the modifications are highlighted):

```
template<class Generator>
class PtrList
{
public:
  typedef typename Generator::Config Config;
//the rest as previously
//...
```

The advantage of the implementation using template metaprogramming is that the generator can be used simply as any other template, and we don't need any extra preprocessors.

Generators introduce a separation between the featural descriptions in the problem space and the implementation components in the solution space, which allows you to make useful extensions to the implementation components (e.g., modify the component structure or add new components) without having to change existing client code. This is possible as long as the abstract feature space can still be mapped on the new components. Moreover, we can even make certain extensions to the feature space without the need to change existing client code. For example, we could append new parameters, for example, memory allocation, to the parameter list expected by the generator. By choosing appropriate defaults for the new parameters, existing calls to the generator will still work properly.

12.9 Extensions

The previous section demonstrated the basic techniques using a very simple example. Applying these techniques to larger problems requires several extensions.

♦ *Nested features:* Our sample generator expects a flat list of features, although feature diagrams are trees. This was acceptable for this small example, but in general configuration generators accept treelike structures. We can represent treelike feature structures in C++ using types and templates. For example, we could model counterFlag as a type parameter with the values no_counter and with_counter<>. no_counter would be a struct and with_counter<> a template struct expecting LengthType as its parameter. You'll see an example of nested features in Chapters 13 and 14.

♦ *Multistage configuration generators:* Large feature models may contain many constraints and default dependency rules. In this case, a configuration generator consists of several stages (see Figure 12-7): specification completion stage (computes defaults for the unspecified features based on default dependency rules and constraints), feature combination checking stage (checks whether the feature combinations satisfy the constraints), and component assembly stage (assembles components into the final type). You'll see a multistage generator in Chapter 14. Dependency rules and constraints are specified using *decision tables* (see Section 14.4.1.3.2), which you can implement using a table evaluation metafunction (see Section 14.4.1.3.3).

♦ *Nested configuration repositories:* Name clashes in the configuration repository may require introducing separate name scopes within the repository. For example, two different components retrieve the member type `ElementType`, but each of them should be supplied a different type. This can be resolved by providing a separate name scope for each of these components in the repository. We can model such nested name scopes in C++ as nested classes (see Section 7.11.3).

♦ *Generators reading configuration repositories of other generated types:* Each generated type has a configuration repository as its part under the name `Config`, for example, `MyList::Config`. This feature can be used by other generators, such as generators that produce customized algorithms that operate on generated data types. For example, we will use the configuration repository of a matrix type in order to generate optimized matrix operation code using expression templates in Chapter 14. A matrix algorithm generator can retrieve the properties of a matrix type from its `Config` (e.g., `ElementType`, `Ownership`, and so on) and use this information to generate optimized algorithms.

♦ *Traits templates for encoding metainformation:* Metainformation about types can be encoded as *traits templates* [Mye95], which basically correspond to metafunctions that take types as parameters and return their properties. For example, our polymorphic copier in Section 12.5 assumes that the element type provides the virtual `clone()` method. If a particular element type does not provide this method, we can use an adapter. In this case, we could use a traits template on element type to retrieve the appropriate (user-provided) adapter. Furthermore, we could use a traits template to make sure that `DynamicTypeChecker` is used only for types having a virtual function table.

♦ *Metafunctions as part of configuration repositories:* Sometimes one component is used more than once in a configuration and each instance needs different configuration parameters. In this case, the component does not retrieve the required type from the configuration repository directly, but it retrieves a metafunction. Each instance can then supply a different parameter to the metafunction to compute the needed type. In C++, class templates can be defined as members of other classes. This way it is possible to pass around a metafunction as a type, which corresponds to the idea of higher-order metafunctions (see Section 10.9).

We used the previously listed extensions in the implementation of two applications described in the following chapters.

The generator approach described here can also be used to synthesize frameworks. Frameworks can be modeled as compositions of collaborations and the latter can be implemented as *mixin layers* [SB98]. In C++, a mixin layer may be implemented as a class containing a number of nested classes. Each of the nested classes implements a particular role. The nested classes can inherit from their parameters, so that they can be used to extend other classes. A mixin layer takes another layer as its parameter, accesses the classes nested in the parameter, and uses them as superclasses of some of its own nested classes (see Section 9.8.2.4 for details). Just as we used our configuration generator to compose parameterized classes, we can also use it to compose mixin layers.

Chapter 13

Bank Account[1]

13.1 Why Is This Chapter Worth Reading?

The previous chapter demonstrated the basic steps necessary to design and implement a generative domain model in the context of data structures. This chapter will show you how to apply these steps in a commercial domain. We will also shed some light on additional issues not discussed in the previous chapter. We will start by demonstrating the shortcomings of object technology in the context of software reuse, and then move to develop a generative domain model. This time, we will pay more attention to the process, for example, what issues to consider during Domain Analysis, and how much analysis is enough. Our example will require a more complex language for ordering concrete systems, which will give us the opportunity to discuss the related design issues and tradeoffs, for example, safe versus unsafe configuration DSLs, and how to take advantage of the vocabulary used in the target business domain. The generator we develop in the end will include buildability checking as an additional step. We will conclude with some ideas for testing generators and their products.

13.2 The Successful Programming Shop

Suppose that you're visiting your new customer, a small local bank. The bank wants to replace its old cashless payment system

---

1. An earlier version of the material contained in this chapter was published in U. Eisenecker and K. Czarnecki; Vom Einzelsystem zur Systemfamilie: Generative Programmierung—Teil 1; in *Microsoft System Journal* (German Edition), Nr. 4, 1999, pp. 68–75; and U. Eisenecker and K. Czarnecki; Generatoren bauen leicht gemacht: Generative Programmierung—Teil 2; in *Microsoft System Journal* (German Edition), Nr. 5, 1999, pp. 80–85. © 1999 by Microsoft System Journal, Unterschleißheim, Germany. Reprinted by permission.

with a new one, which should be developed using object-oriented technology. One of the important concepts in the system is an account. During the analysis, you quickly realize that an account has an owner, a balance, and a number, and that you can use it to deposit, withdraw, or transfer money. Possibly, this might even correspond directly to the implementation of a class account shown in Figure 13-1.

You successfully build the system within the agreed time and budget. Your success story gets around and you get the next contract from another bank. This time, however, the system needs to distinguish between *accounts for cashless payments* (as in the original system) and *savings accounts*. A savings account does not support money transfer. Furthermore, there should be two kinds of accounts for cashless payments: a *checking account*, which doesn't provide an overdraft credit, and an *open account*, which does. Thus, you cannot directly reuse the original account class in the new system. You can't even reuse it as a base class because it implements money transfer, which savings accounts do not provide. Therefore, you design an appropriate class hierarchy (see Figure 13-2).

In a later project at yet another bank, you need to allow for different balancing periods depending on the account type and possibly an individual arrangement with the customer (balancing involves, among other functions, calculating the interest and charging the account-carrying fees). Therefore, in order to avoid increasing the number of accounts (k) by a factor that is the number of different balancing periods (p), you use the "strategy" pattern [GHJV95]. This reduces the total number of classes from $k \cdot p$ to $k + p$ (see Figure 13-3). `Balancing` is the common abstract class of all balancing strategies. It declares the abstract method `close()` for balancing an account. The concrete subclasses provide concrete implementations of `close()`. We call points at which variation occurs, as in the case of balancing, *variation points*.

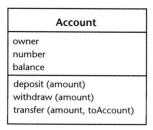

Figure 13-1 Simple account class

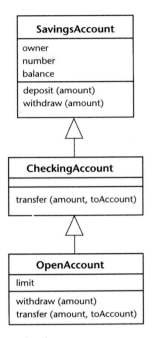

Figure 13-2 Class hierarchy for accounts

While working in the banking sector, you realize that the currency an account is kept in and the numeric type of the balance may vary, therefore you add the necessary parameterization to the previous model. Later, you realize that the types of owner, opening date, number of transactions, and account number may also vary. For example, account numbers can be generated using different strategies. Sometimes they contain information about the owner or the account, and sometimes they need to be added together to create checksums for summary transfers. At this point, the corresponding UML diagram would already be quite complex. Furthermore, you know that a UML class diagram doesn't let you model variation points without deciding which mechanisms to use for their implementation. For example, we used inheritance to model different account types and association combined with inheritance to model different balancing strategies (see Figure 13-3). And we possibly modeled the remaining variation points using parameterized classes. So why shouldn't it be okay to use class parameterization to model different balancing strategies or to implement the owner using the "bridge" pattern?

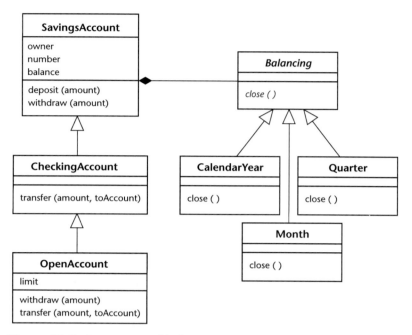

Figure 13-3 Accounts and balancing strategies

13.3 Design Patterns, Frameworks, and Components

Design patterns live at a higher level than programming languages. They document common solutions to recurring design problems using natural language, diagrams, and programming examples.

The previous section discussed the development of an application framework—a process that normally takes several iterations. An application framework contains the common boilerplate for a family of applications and all the necessary variation points. Furthermore, it will usually also provide a couple of typical variants for each variation point, for example, savings and checking accounts and yearly and quarterly balancing periods in our example. The idea is that an application programmer can complete a framework to get a specific application by selecting some of the existing variants and by adding application-specific classes.

Several aspects of framework development and use are problematic. The implementation of many variation points and the composite use of design patterns in an OO language lead to a disproportionately high complexity of the design. At the same time, it is often the case that some of the implemented variation points are not needed (i.e., we have the problem of "speculative generality"

[FBB+99]). And other, important ones could be missing. In general, understanding and documenting frameworks is extremely difficult and costly. A well-known problem is that the numerous inter-dependencies within a framework prevent the understanding and use of any of its parts in separation. For instance, you choose one class, discover that the chosen class is dependent on other classes, and before you know it you're struggling to comprehend the entire framework. Furthermore, you often get performance problems due to the indirection levels introduced by the intensive use of design patterns based on dynamic polymorphism.

Components represent only a partial remedy. On the positive side, they usually provide you with a larger variety of prefabricated variants per variation point. As a result, you can use components as "black boxes." They allow you to adjust their properties through a graphical or programmatic interface in order to customize them for the target context. In other words, you can use them without having to understand their internal design as in the case of frameworks. This reduces the overall programming effort. However, components often have a high consumption of resources, poor runtime performance, and no or only effort-intensive means of adaptation.

13.4 Domain Engineering and Generative Programming

Design patterns, frameworks, and components are attempts to get something out of an approach for developing single applications that you can use for developing further, similar applications. This stands in quite a contrast to Domain Engineering, which is designed to model application families. The results of Domain Engineering provide a completely different basis for developing concrete applications within the family, that is, Application Engineering. Generative Programming combines Domain Engineering with appropriate technologies for implementing the elementary components of an application family and for their automatic assembly.

As you already know, Domain Engineering methods cover three steps. The first step is Domain Analysis, which involves domain scoping, analyzing the commonalities, variabilities, and dependencies within a family of systems, and the development of reusable, configurable requirements. The second step is Domain Design, which covers the design of a common architecture consisting of sets of elementary components and also, in the case of Generative Programming, means for specifying system family members and their automatic assembly from the components. Finally, during Domain Implementation, you implement the components, the specification means, and the generators.

An important activity of Domain Analysis is domain scoping, which involves deciding what's in a domain and what is not. This is an extremely strategic activity. It requires a careful market and economic analysis. It requires identifying and involving the domain stakeholders and finding the right sources of information and financing.

Defining well-scoped concepts at the appropriate level of generality is extremely important. If you choose too general a scope, there will hardly be any commonalities, and you'll get complicated models of which only a small part can be reused. Timothy Korson reports on his experience related to this issue, which he gained as a consultant in the area of reuse and OO technology as follows [Kor96].

> Cost/benefit tradeoffs must also be considered. [. . .] A colleague of mine shared a story with me of one of his clients that spent a half a million dollars on developing and populating a corporate class library only to find that a year later no more than 30% of the classes had been reused. I have a large bank as a client. During my last consulting visit to the bank, the subject of an "account" class came up. It seems that the various departments had been arguing about the attributes and behavior of a generalized account class to go into the corporate reuse repository. Once all perspectives were factored out, the only attributes that could be agreed on were name and account number, and they were still arguing about account number. The benefits of maintaining such a watered-down class in the corporate repository do not justify the cost. However, there is enough functionality that can be put in a "money-market account" class to justify the costs of maintaining it in a department repository.

However, it is important to note that generative implementation technologies allow you to effectively handle much larger levels of variation than you can handle with OO frameworks. In Generative Programming, the variation is covered by a set of elementary components that implement the different aspects of a domain concept and which you can combine in a vast number of ways. Other than in the case of frameworks or conventional component-based technologies, the application programmer does not have to handle these elementary components manually, which would be very tedious, ineffective, and error prone. Instead, application programmers can specify the needed concept in abstract terms and have generators assemble it from the elementary components. Two different generated artifacts need not even share one elementary component, although they often will share several. The important point is that you can still reuse the construction knowledge and the generators for the different supporting domains (e.g., for an account, you'll need to provide support domains, such as currency, date and time, numeric values, auditing, and so on).

When you analyze a domain, you certainly don't want to analyze it to "death." You always have to keep in mind that any domain can be infinitely refined with more and more details and variants. Domain Analysis techniques will help you to guide the process and organize the analysis results, but you always want to get usable, concrete results within a reasonable time and budget. For your first project in a given domain, you will do some Domain Analysis, take a look at one or two existing systems, read a book or two on the subject, and talk to a couple of domain experts. You don't need and don't want to know every possible variation in the domain. You need to make sure that there is some stakeholder for every feature you are going to implement. When you do subsequent projects in the same domain, you will have the opportunity to revise and improve your domain models and widen their scope.

13.5 Feature Modeling

Let's return to our bank account example and model it using a feature diagram (see Figure 13-4). In contrast to a UML class diagram, a feature diagram allows you to represent variability in an implementation-independent way.

The root of the diagram represents the concept "personal account" (there are many other account types, e.g., trust accounts, impersonal accounts, business accounts, custodianship accounts, securities portfolios, money market accounts, and so on, but we won't discuss them here). The diagram shows you several variation points: owner, account number, balance, overdraft, payment, balancing period, currency, opening date, and number of transactions. All but payment are dimensions with several alternative subfeatures. The subfeatures of payment are or-features, that is, you can select any nonempty subset of them.

A banking expert will quickly recognize that this feature diagram is quite incomplete. In order to simplify our example, we've left out several important variation points, such as calculation of interest, minimum balance, contract period, conditions of termination, power to operate an account, and so on. Furthermore, in the real world, we would have to analyze several support domains including currency (symbols, formats, conversions, and so on), date and time (natural and fiscal calendars, periods, conversions, and so on), payment methods (payment vehicle, formats, and so on), and auditing (recording and accessing tracking information).

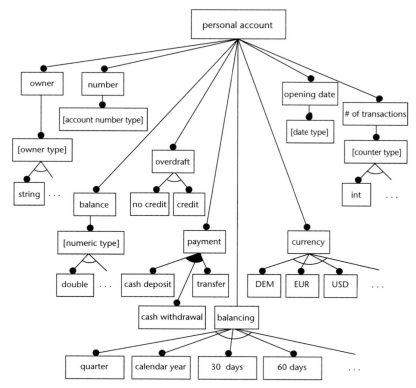

Figure 13-4 *Feature model of the concept "personal account"*

Each feature diagram you develop should be accompanied by additional information including the source where you got each feature from, its stakeholder, rationale for its use, constraints and dependencies between features, standard settings, binding time and mode (e.g., static or dynamic), and so on. (see Section 4.4.2). You can keep this information separately in text form or store it together with the diagrams in a d atabase of a tool. We won't include all this information in our example for space reasons, but we'll give you the necessary explanations whenever appropriate.

13.6 Architecture Design

The previously identified features provide us with hints about the needed implementation components. For example, we'll need the currencies deutschmark (DEM), euro (EUR), and U.S. dollar (USD), and the payment methods cash deposit, cash withdrawal, and transfer. First, we need to get some order by classifying the needed implementation components into component categories (see Figure 13-5).

In our simple example, each variation point has a corresponding component category, and there is an implementation component for each subfeature. In the case of account number type, we've provided two implementations: StaticNo, whose creation involves incrementing a class variable, and PersistentNo, whose creation involves incrementing a number stored in a file.

Let's analyze the dependencies between the component categories (see Figure 13-6). According to the feature diagram, every account has an owner, an opening date, a number, and a balance. Furthermore, it keeps track of the number of transactions and its currency. There are no dependencies between these basic categories. But all other categories depend on them. Therefore, we collect the basic categories into a configuration repository. Overdraft, payment, and balancing all need an account to do anything useful. Thus, they all depend on Account. Whether you can perform a payment or not, depends on overdraft, which results in an arrow from Payment to Overdraft. Payment keeps track of each transaction, and Balancing needs this information. Therefore, Balancing has access to Payment.

Now we can sort the component categories into a GenVoca layered architecture (see Figure 13-7). Each layer corresponds to a component category, and the categories with the most incoming dependency arrows go towards the bottom. The layer at the very bottom is the configuration repository.

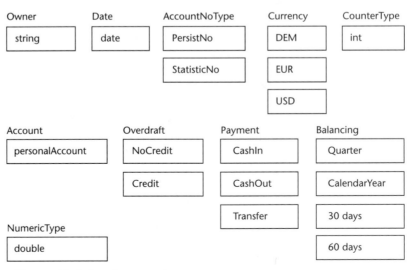

Figure 13-5 Implementation components

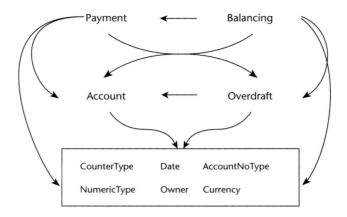

Figure 13-6 *Dependencies between component categories*

Each layer contains one or more parameterized components. Alternative components are separated by vertical bars, for example, `Quarter | CalendarYear`. Components separated by commas have "or" semantics: You can select one or any other nonempty subset. The corresponding GenVoca grammar is shown in Figure 13-8. Given this grammar, you can define a savings account as follows:

`CalendarYear[CashIn[CashOut[NoCredit[PersonalAccount[C1]]]]]`

And here is an open account:

`Quarter[Transfer[CashIn[CashOut[Credit[PersonalAccount[C2]]]]]]`

`C1` and `C2` are two different configuration repositories.

Balancing	: Quarter | Calendar Year | 30 days | 60 days			
Payment	: CashIn, CashOut, Transfer			
Overdraft	: NoCredit | Credit			
Account	: PersonalAccount			
Config	Owner : string | ... Currency : DEM | EUR | USD | ... AccountNoType : StaticNo | PersistentNo | ... Date : date | ... NumericType : double | ... CounterType : int | ...			

Figure 13-7 *GenVoca layered architecture*

```
AccountWithBalancing          : Quarter[Payment] |
                                CalendarYear[Payment] |
                                30 days[Payment] | 60 days
                                [Payment] ...
Payment                       : CashIn[Overdraft | Payment] |
                                CashOut[Overdraft | Payment] |
                                Transfer[Overdraft | Payment]
Overdraft                     : NoCredit[Account] |
                                Credit[Account]
Account                       : PersonalAccount[Config]
Config                        :
    Owner           : string | ...
    Currency        : DEM | EUR | USD | ...
    AccountNoType   : StaticNo | PersistentNo | ...
    Date            : date | ...
    NumericType     : double | ...
    CounterType     : int | ...
```

Figure 13-8 *GenVoca grammar for the implementation components*

13.7 Implementation Components

As in the previous chapter, we'll implement the parameterized components as class templates. In that sense, you can think of the whole GenVoca architecture as a configurable class hierarchy, where each layer represents a horizontal slice of the hierarchy. We'll present the implementation of the components in a bottom-up order.

The types for Owner, NumericType, and CounterType are provided by C++. We use string from the standard library to represent Owner. NumericType is the type used for representing the balance and booking amounts. We usually use double for this purpose. CounterType is used for counting, and it has to be an integral type, such as int. date is not in the standard library, so we have to provide it ourselves (the implementation is not shown here). It has to implement at least the following operators: equality and inequality operators, stream output operator, computing the difference between two dates in days, and adding a number of days to a date.

Our currency components are very simple. They only provide the currency symbol (a real implementation would need to provide conversions, formats, and so on):

```
struct DEM
{   static const char * const symbol()
```

```
                    {   return "DEM"; }
        };

        struct EUR
        {   static const char * const symbol()
            {   return "EUR"; }
        };

        struct USD
        {   static const char * const symbol()
            {   return "USD"; }
        };
```

We provide two kinds of account numbers: `StaticNo`, whose creation involves incrementing a class variable, and `PersistentNo`, which increments a value stored in a file. Because account numbers have to be unique, the assignment operator and copy constructor are declared as private. Thus, they cannot be called from outside of the classes. Furthermore, we need stream output operators for both classes. In the following code, we only take a look at the implementation of `StaticNo`:

```
class StaticNo
{   public:
        StaticNo():number_(counter_++)
        {}
        void print(ostream& os) const
        {   os << number_; }
    private:
        long int number_;
        static long int counter_;
        // prohibit the following operations:
        StaticNo(const StaticNo&)
        {}
        StaticNo& operator=(const StaticNo&)
        {   return *this; }
};

long int StaticNo::counter_ = 0;

ostream& operator<<(ostream& os,const StaticNo& accNo)
{   accNo.print(os);
    return os;
}
```

Now we need to implement `PersonalAccount`. According to our GenVoca grammar (see Figure 13-7), this component takes `Config` as its parameter, so we'll take a look at the latter first. As you may remember, `Config` is the configuration repository. It provides a number of components and types under standard names. Also the complete account type gets assembled in a configuration repository. Thus, you can create a concrete account type by writing an appropriate configuration repository for it. For example, the following configuration repository defines a savings account:

```
struct C1
{   typedef string      Owner;
    typedef DEM         Currency;
    typedef date        Date;
    typedef double      NumericType;
    typedef int         CounterType;
    typedef StaticNo    AccountNoType;
    typedef CalendarYear<CashOut<CashIn<NoCredit
            <PersonalAccount<C1> > > > > Account;
};
```

As you'll see in a moment, the names defined in a configuration repository will be accessed by the account implementation components. The last `typedef` in `C1` corresponds to a statement of our GenVoca grammar, namely:

```
CalendarYear[CashOut[CashIn[NoCredit[PersonalAccount[C1]]]]]
```

The most inner parameter, that is, `C1`, is the repository itself. `PersonalAccount[C1]` is then the parameter of `NoCredit[]` and so on, until we get the complete component, which is assigned the name `Account`. You can create an instance of our savings account as follows:

```
C1::Account a;
```

The only parameter of `PersonalAccount`, whose implementation is given in the following code, is `Config_`. The first action in this implementation is to export `Config_` using `typedef` under the name `Config`. This way, other components can access it. The next step is then to retrieve all the needed types from `Config`, for example, `Config::Owner`. The implementation code is

```
template <class Config_>
class PersonalAccount
{   public:
        typedef Config_ Config;
        typedef typename Config::Owner Owner;
        typedef typename Config::Currency Currency;
        typedef typename Config::Date Date;
        typedef typename Config::NumericType NumericType;
        typedef typename Config::CounterType CounterType;
        typedef typename Config::AccountNoType AccountNoType;

        PersonalAccount(const Owner& own):   owner_(own),
                                             balance_(0),
                                             transactions_(0)
        {}
        const Owner& owner() const
        {   return owner_; }
        const AccountNoType& number() const
        {   return accountNo_; }
        const NumericType& balance() const
        {   return balance_; }
        const CounterType& transactions() const
        {   return transactions_; }
        const Date& openedOn() const
        {   return openedOn_; }
        const char * const currency() const
        {   return Currency::symbol(); }
        void credit(const NumericType& amount)
        {   assert(amount > 0);
            book(amount);
        }
        void debit(const NumericType& amount)
        {   assert(amount > 0);
            book(- amount);
        }
    protected:
        NumericType balance_;
        CounterType transactions_;
    private:
        void book(const NumericType& amount)
        {   balance_ += amount;
            ++ transactions_;
        }
        Owner owner_;
```

```
        const AccountNoType accountNo_;
        const Date openedOn_;
        // prohibit the following operations:
        PersonalAccount(const PersonalAccount& )
        {}
        PersonalAccount& operator=(const PersonalAccount&)
        {   return *this; }
};
```

Now let's take a look at the overdraft components NoCredit and Credit. They implement the overdraft strategy and therefore need to redefine the method debit() of Account. NoCredit prevents a successful debit(amount) if not enough money is available on the account. Credit allows for a credit up to a certain limit, and thus it needs to add the attribute limit_ and the member function limit(). Because the overdraft components only need to redefine one member function of Account (i.e., debit()) and leave other account operations unchanged, we'll implement them as inheritance-based wrappers, that is, templates derived from their parameter, which in this case is the base account to be refined:

```
template <class Base>
class NoCredit: public Base
{   public:
        typedef typename Base::Config Config;
        typedef typename Config::Owner Owner;
        typedef typename Base::NumericType NumericType;
        NoCredit(const Owner& own):Base(own)
        {}
        void debit(const NumericType& amount)
        {   assert(amount > 0);
            if (Base::balance() - amount < 0)
            throw "No credit available";
            else Base::debit(amount);
        }
};


template <class Base>
class Credit: public Base
{   public:
        typedef typename Base::Config Config;
        typedef typename Config::Owner Owner;
        typedef typename Base::NumericType NumericType;
```

```
        Credit(const Owner& own):Base(own),limit_(0)
        {}
        const NumericType& limit() const
        {    return limit_; }
        void limit(const NumericType& newLimit)
        {    assert(newLimit >= 0);
             limit_ = newLimit;
        }
        void debit(const NumericType& amount)
        {    assert(amount > 0);
             if (Base::balance() - amount < - limit())
             throw "Account overdrawn";
             else Base::debit(amount);
        }
    private:
        NumericType limit_;
};
```

Payment components are also implemented as inheritance-based wrappers. CashIn adds deposit(), CashOut adds debit(), and Transfer adds transfer(). Let's just take a look at CashIn (CashOut and Transfer are implemented in a similar way):

```
template <class Base>
class CashIn: public Base
{    public:
        typedef typename Base::Config Config;
        typedef typename Config::NumericType NumericType;
        typedef typename Config::Owner Owner;
        CashIn(const Owner& own):Base(own)
        {}
        void deposit(const NumericType& amount)
        {    Base::credit(amount); }
};
```

The balancing components, which we turn to next, provide the operation close() for printing out the account statement (a real close() would also compute the interest and charge the account-carrying fees if applicable). CalendarYear and Quarter have the standard form of inheritance-based wrappers as in the other components we've seen so far. However, ThirtyDays and SixtyDays illustrate that deviations from the standard implementation form are possible and sometimes desirable. If we implemented the components in the standard way, the resulting code would be the same except for the number of days. Therefore, we'll first implement a generic AfterNoOfDays component, which we then use to define the other two components:

```
template <class Base,int numberOfDays>
class AfterNoOfDays: public Base
{   public:
        typedef typename Base::Config Config;
        typedef typename Config::Date Date;
        typedef typename Config::Owner Owner;
        AfterNoOfDays(const Owner& own):Base(own),
            lastBalancing_(Base::openedOn())
        {}
        void close(ostream& os = cout)
        {   Date d(lastBalancing_ + numberOfDays);
            os  << "Statement on " << d << endl
                << "For account no. "
                << Base::number() << endl
                << "Owner " << Base::owner() << endl
                << "Transactions " << Base::transactions()
                << endl
                << "Balance " << Base::balance()
                << ' ' << Base::currency() << endl;
            Base::transactions_ = 0;
            lastBalancing_ = d;
        }
    private:
        Date lastBalancing_;
};

//now define ThirtyDays and SixtyDays using AfterNoOfDays
template <class Base>    // 1 banking month has 30 days
class ThirtyDays: public AfterNoOfDays<Base,30>
{   public:
        typedef typename Base::Config Config;
        typedef typename Config::Owner Owner;
        ThirtyDays(const Owner& own):
            AfterNoOfDays<Base,30>(own)
        {}
};

template <class Base>   // 2 banking months, each 30 days
class SixtyDays: public AfterNoOfDays<Base,60>
{   public:
        typedef typename Base::Config Config;
```

```
        typedef typename Config::Owner Owner;
        SixtyDays(const Owner& own):
                AfterNoOfDays<Base,60>(own)
        {}
};
```

The components ThirtyDays and SixtyDays can be used in the standard way, just as CalendarYear and Quarter.

13.8 Configurable Class Hierarchies

Most of the components in the previous section were inheritance-based wrappers. Composing such components amounts to composing a particular class hierarchy. Depending on the number of payment components used in a configuration, the depth of the resulting class hierarchy for an account varies between four and six. In our simple example, each component was a single class. However, as shown in Section 9.8.2.4, you can also use nested classes to build configurable class hierarchies that horizontally span more than one class. As already mentioned, this feature is useful to configure frameworks.

Given the inheritance depths of six and more, you may wonder if this design does not incur performance penalties at runtime. If you take a closer look at the components, you'll realize that all member functions are implemented inline. If you activate the appropriate compiler options, all calls to such functions will be replaced by their implementations. This eliminates any runtime penalties for having "many little classes and methods."

Let's illustrate the effect of inlining using the method CashOut::withdraw(). The implementation in CashOut looks like this:

```
void withdraw(const NumericType& amount)
{   Base::debit(amount); }
```

Let's assume that we have an open account, that is, the configuration uses Credit, and CashOut will be calling Credit::debit():

```
void debit(const NumericType& amount)
{   assert(amount > 0);
    if (Base::balance() - amount < - limit())
    throw "Account overdrawn";
    else Base::debit(amount);
}
```

In this code, Base points to `PersonalAccount`, whose `debit()` is implemented as follows:

```
void debit(const NumericType& amount)
{   assert(amount > 0);
    book(- amount);
}
```

If we perform the inlining manually, we get the following implementation of `debit()`:

```
void withdraw(const NumericType& amount)
{   assert(amount > 0);
    if (Base::balance() - amount < - limit())
    throw "Account overdrawn";
    else {
        assert(amount > 0);
        book(- amount);
    }
}
```

As you can see, the assert `amount > 0` is checked twice. This tells us that it might sometimes be worthwhile to analyze the implementation components whether they contain such unnecessary, overhead-incurring redundancies or not. In this example, the problem is caused by the fact that we did not introduce a separate component category for representing amounts. Furthermore, in practice, you would parameterize and control error checking and reaction to errors through the configuration repository.

There are still two functions, namely `limit()` and `book()`, that we need to inline:

```
void withdraw(const NumericType& amount)
{   assert(amount > 0);
    if (Base::balance() - amount < - limit_)
    throw "Account overdrawn";
    else {
        assert(amount > 0);
        balance_ += - amount;
        ++ transactions_;
    }
}
```

As you can see, inlining produces very compact code, which doesn't contain any function calls. Because the resulting function is also inline, calls to it will be replaced by this compact code.

Let us mention a couple of effects resulting from inlining. First, if you call an empty inline function, the call will be completely eliminated. In contrast to empty virtual functions, empty inline functions do not incur any penalties, and you can use them without hesitation.

Instead of parameter passing by value, we generally use const-references. As a result, we get the following effects: In the case of large objects, we save time because they get passed using a pointer rather than a copy. On the other hand, in the case of small objects, such as char, we can possibly get extra overhead because the pointer could be larger than the object itself. However, in combination with inlining, this negative effect is avoided: If the argument is a variable passed as a const-reference, the variable will neither be copied nor will any pointer be created. Rather, the variable will be used in the function body directly! You've seen this in the manually inlined code shown earlier. If a call involves passing a constant, the constant will be used directly. If the use of the constant requires calling a type-conversion constructor, the compiler can safely create a temporary object.

13.9 Designing a Domain-Specific Language

Now that we have all the implementation components, we can use them to create concrete accounts. As already shown, you define an account by documenting a configuration repository. For example, an open account in USD can be constructed as follows:

```
struct C2
{   typedef string       Owner;
    typedef USD          Currency;
    typedef date         Date;
    typedef double       NumericType;
    typedef int          CounterType;
    typedef PersistentNo AccountNoType;
    typedef Quartal<Transfer<CashOut<CashIn<Credit
            <PersonalAccount<C2> > > > > > Account;
};
```

According to the feature diagram in Figure 13-4, we can have 2 (account number type) times 2 (overdraft) times (3+2+1) (payment) times 4 (balancing) times 3 (currency) = 288 different possible configurations. For simplicity, we counted owner, date, and so on with only one variant. Several of these 288 configurations are not very useful. For example, we don't want accounts whose only operation is cash deposit or cash withdrawal. Furthermore, a savings account is always balanced at the end of a calendar year, and the balancing period for open and checking accounts is always quarterly (at least in Germany). But even after subtracting the invalid configurations, there are still at least 15 different useful configurations left, and their number will grow exponentially as you add new variation points and strategies.

Writing configuration repositories is tedious and error prone, and we don't want to place this burden on the application programmer. Programmers know their high-level requirements, but do not necessarily know all the implementation components, how to correctly configure them, and how to achieve certain requirements. As discussed in the previous chapter, including all possible configurations in a library is not an option. First, you would have to manage an immense amount of code (you may need thousands of long configurations for a real domain). Second, how would you find the right configuration?

So, how do the domain experts handle this great amount of variation in the bank account domain? A closer look at the banking domain reveals that banks will not let the customer select every possible variation at his or her pleasure. This would result in high operating costs and kill their profit margins. Instead, they offer a portfolio of banking products consisting of a set of main products plus various options. For example, if you need an account, a bank would let you choose between a deposit at short notice, a fixed-term deposit, a checking account, an open account, and a savings account. If you select a fixed-term deposit, you may still choose between a number of different terms and other options. In other words, the business world creates new vocabulary in order to handle the variation in a given business domain. This is the vocabulary that you, as a customer, will find in a company's product brochure.

The purpose of Generative Programming is to develop and implement a generative model for a domain (see Figure 13-9). In our example, we already have the solution space, which is constituted by the implementation components. Now we need to capture the aforementioned vocabulary from the problem space in the form of a domain-specific language (DSL). In our example, we want to design a high-level banking language for defining accounts. Given such a language, we can then implement a generator that takes a high-level account specification in this language and produces the desired account by automatically assembling the appropriate implementation components.

The separation between the problem and the solution space offers the fundamental benefit of allowing a somewhat independent evolution of the product space and the technology space. You don't have to offer products that would utilize the full variation covered by the solution space. But you can provide innovative products if the market situation requires it, and the implementation components in the solution space should easily cover the required functionality (or you can easily integrate any new, additionally needed implementation components). On the other hand, you'll be able to extend, renew, and optimize the technology in the solution space without breaking the existing product specifications.

An important issue in designing a DSL is whether the language should allow for the specification of valid systems only or not. You can compare a DSL that produces only valid systems to direct-manipulation graphical interfaces that don't allow any incorrect input. You often have to pay for this luxury with expensive and unwieldy handling. In the case where the DSL allows the specification of incorrect systems, you'll need an extra phase in the generator for checking the buildability of the specified system. Another issue to consider when deciding for or against a safe DSL is the proportion between the number of specifications of correct and incorrect systems. If the portion of incorrect specifications is high, you should redesign the language to make it more safe. This way, you'll save less proficient users from the frustrating experience of producing large amounts of invalid specifications. On the other hand, if allowing for a few incorrect specifications greatly simplifies the DSL, it might be worth paying this price. In general, we can also provide several DSLs for different target users. This requires that we design our generators with respect to DSL analysis and

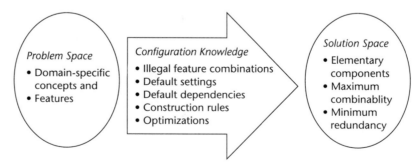

Figure 13-9 Elements of a generative domain model

> **NOTE**
>
> For simplicity, we did not model contract period and termination in our implementation components, but we included these aspects in Table 13-1 for explanatory purposes.

buildability checking in a modular way (you'll see how to do this in Chapter 14).

Let's start designing the domain-specific language for bank accounts. First, we need to take a look at the properties of the main banking products we'd like to offer (see Table 13-1).

As you can see in Table 13-1, deposit at short notice and fixed-term deposit allow for different balancing periods. Our implementation components cover balancing after one or two months, but we could easily implement additional components for three, six and twelve months using `AfterNumberOfDays`. For checking and open accounts, we'll generally use quarterly balancing (i.e., `Quarter`). Finally, savings accounts will be balanced at the end of a calendar year (i.e., `CalendarYear`).

An account specification consists of the account type, currency type, account number type, numeric type, counter type, and date type (see Figure 13-10). In the case of deposits, we also have to specify the balancing strategy. The possible values are thirty days, sixty days, quarter, and calendar year. Quarter and calendar year are not appropriate for deposits, but we included them in the DSL in order to show you the implementation of buildability checking in the generator. That is, if you use quarter or calendar year for deposits, the generator will report the error "wrong balancing period". The DSL does not let you explicitly specify overdraft credit because this feature is automatically implied by the account type (i.e., only an open account provides an overdraft credit). The definition of the DSL has the familiar form of a GenVoca grammar.

> **NOTE**
>
> Please note that `TwelveMonths` is not the same as `CalendarYear`: `CalendarYear` implements balancing at the end of a calendar year, whereas `TwelveMonths` implements balancing after twelve banking months, that is, 360 days, starting from the account opening date. There is a similar difference between `ThreeMonths` and `Quarter`.

Table 13-1 Types of Accounts Typically Offered by Banks in Germany

Type of Account	Purpose	Contract Period	Termination	Balancing	Overdraft Credit
Deposit at short notice	Short-term investment	No fixed term, but a fixed withdrawal period of at least 30 days and a maximum of 12 months	Termination at the end of the withdrawal period starting from the withdrawal notice; no right to terminate before the end of the withdrawal period	At the end of the withdrawal period	No
Fixed-term deposit	Short-term investment	At least 30 days and a maximum of 12 months	No right to terminate before the end of the term; termination sometimes possible at lower interest	At the end of the fixed term	No
Checking account	Participation in cashless payment transactions	Perpetual	Termination without notice period possible	At least once a year, but mostly quarterly	No
Open account	Participation in cashless payment transactions and the use of overdraft credit	Perpetual	Termination without notice period possible	At least once a year, but mostly quarterly	Yes
Savings account	Long-term savings	Perpetual	Termination possible only at the end of an agreed withdrawal period of at least 30 days and mostly 6, 12, or 24 months up to 6 years	At the end of a calendar year	No

The DSL user does not always have to specify an account completely because there will be reasonable default settings for the unspecified parameters. For our account DSL, we can assume the direct default settings shown in Figure 13-11. However, other

```
AccountSpecification  :   Account, CurrencyType, AccNoType, NumType,
                          CountType, OwnerType, DateType
Account               :   fixedTermDeposit[Balancing] |
                          shortNoticeDeposit[Balancing] |
                          checking | openAccount | savings
Balancing             :   thirtyDays | sixtyDays | quarter | calendarYear
CurrencyType          :   DEM | EUR | USD | ...
AccNoType             :   StaticNo | PersistentNo | ...
NumType               :   double | ...
CountType             :   int | ...
OwnerType             :   string | ...
DateType              :   date | ...
```

Figure 13-10   GenVoca grammar of the DSL for specifying accounts

DSLs may require some default settings to be computed based on the value of other parameters. This would require an extra step in the generator.

We can easily implement the account DSL grammar using enumeration constants and class templates. First, we define the vocabulary for the different account types, balancing strategies, and credit strategies as enumeration constants:

```
enum AccountTypes
{   fixedTermDeposit,
    shortNoticeDeposit,
    checking,
    openAccount,
    savings
};
```

```
Account       :   openAccount
CurrencyType  :   DEM
AccNoType     :   PersistentNo
NumType       :   double
CountType     :   int
OwnerType     :   string
DateType      :   date
```

Figure 13-11   Default settings

```
enum BalancingStrategies
{   thirtyDays,
    sixtyDays,
    quarter,
    calendarYear
};


enum CreditStrategies
{   noCredit,
    credit
};
```

The enumeration constants of `AccountType` and `CreditStrategies` will be needed internally only (they are basically type identifications as described in Section 10.10.1), that is, they will not be used by the DSL user directly.

Fixed term deposit and deposit at short notice are implemented as templates taking a balancing strategy as a parameter:

```
template <BalancingStrategies Balancing = thirtyDays>
struct FixedTermDeposit
{   enum
    {   accountType     = fixedTermDeposit,
        balancing       = Balancing,
        creditStrategy  = noCredit
    };
};


template <BalancingStrategies Balancing = thirtyDays>
struct ShortNoticeDeposit
{   enum
    {   accountType     = shortNoticeDeposit,
        balancing       = Balancing,
        creditStrategy  = noCredit
    };
};
```

Please note that the account type, balancing strategy, and credit strategy are defined as member constants of both templates.

The remaining account types are implemented in a similar way. The only difference is that they are not templates because each of them has only one possible balancing strategy, which is directly specified as a member constant (see Section 10.10.1):

```
struct Checking
{   enum
    {   accountType    = checking,
        balancing      = quarter,
        creditStrategy = noCredit
    };
};

struct OpenAccount
{   enum
    {   accountType    = openAccount,
        balancing      = quarter,
        creditStrategy = credit
    };
};

struct Savings
{   enum
    {   accountType    = savings,
        balancing      = calendarYear,
        creditStrategy = noCredit
    };
};
```

The last part of the DSL corresponds to the parameter list of the generator:

```
template<   class Account = OpenAccount,class CurrencyType = DEM,
            class AccNoType = PersistentNo, class NumType = double,
            class CountType = int,class OwnerType = string,
            class DateType = date
        >
struct ACCOUNT_GENERATOR
{   //...
```

13.10 Bank Account Generator

We'll implement the generator as a template metafunction using the techniques presented in the previous chapter. The first action in the generator is to introduce a short name for the fully parameterized generator template. The next step is to retrieve all the needed parameters from the account specification. We then check the buildability, which amounts to making sure that a deposit is not combined with a quarterly or yearly balancing. If this is the case, the compiler will report an error. (You'll see in a moment how this works.) If the parameters specify a buildable account, the implementation components get assembled into a complete account type. The assembly part uses the metacontrol structures IF<> and SWITCH<> to select the appropriate implementation components based on the specification parameters. Finally, we create the configuration repository in the form of a member struct. Here is the complete generator code:

```
template<    class Account = OpenAccount,class CurrencyType = DEM,
             class AccNoType = PersistentNo, class NumType = double,
             class CountType = int,class OwnerType = string,
             class DateType = date
        >
struct ACCOUNT_GENERATOR
{    // define a short name for the complete generator
     typedef ACCOUNT_GENERATOR<   Account,CurrencyType,AccNoType,
                                  NumType,CountType,OwnerType,
                                  DateType> Generator;
     // parse DSL
     enum {
         accountType   = Account::accountType,
         withCredit    = (CreditStrategies)Account::creditStrategy ==
                           credit,
         withCashOut   = true, // Cash withdrawal always possible
         withCashIn    = true, // Cash deposit always possible
         withTransfer  = (AccountTypes)accountType == checking ||
                           (AccountTypes)accountType == openAccount,
         withBalancing = Account::balancing
     };

     // check buildability
     enum {errorCode =
         (((BalancingStrategies)withBalancing ==
           quarter ||
           (BalancingStrategies)withBalancing ==
           calendarYear) &&
          ((AccountTypes)accountType ==
           fixedTermDeposit ||
           (AccountTypes)accountType ==
           shortNoticeDeposit)) ?
         wrongBalancingStrategy : noError
     };
```

```
typedef SWITCH<errorCode,
          CASE<noError,              Error<NoError>,
          CASE<wrongBalancingStrategy,
                                  Error<WrongBalancingStrategy>
       > > >::RET ErrorChecking;
enum    {   everythingOK = ErrorChecking::everythingOK
       };


// assemble components
typedef PersonalAccount<Generator> BaseAccount;
typedef IF<withCredit,
          Credit<BaseAccount>,
          NoCredit<BaseAccount> >::RET
       OptionalOverdraft;
typedef IF<withCashOut,
          CashOut<OptionalOverdraft>,
          OptionalOverdraft>::RET
       OptionalCashOut;
typedef IF<withCashIn,
          CashIn<OptionalCashOut>,
          OptionalCashOut>::RET
       OptionalCashIn;
typedef IF<withTransfer,
          Transfer<OptionalCashIn>,
          OptionalCashIn>::RET
       OptionalTransfer;
typedef SWITCH<withBalancing,
          CASE<thirtyDays,ThirtyDays<OptionalTransfer>,
          CASE<sixtyDays,SixtyDays<OptionalTransfer>,
          CASE<quarter,Quarter<OptionalTransfer>,
          CASE<calendarYear,CalendarYear<OptionalTransfer>
       > > > > >::RET RET;
// create config
struct Config
{   typedef OwnerType    Owner;
    typedef CurrencyType Currency;
    typedef DateType     Date;
    typedef NumType      NumericType;
    typedef CountType    CounterType;
    typedef AccNoType    AccountNoType;
    enum    {   AccountType    = Account::accountType,
                Balancing      = withBalancing,
                Credit         = Account::creditStrategy,
                CashDeposit    = withCashIn,
                CashWithdrawal = withCashOut,
```

```
                    Transfer          = withTransfer
            };
      };
};
```

Buildability checking works as follows. In the generator, you check for erroneous parameter combinations and return different error conditions depending on the kind of illegal combination. In our simple example, we have only one possible error code, which is wrongBalancingStrategy. If the parameter combinations are okay, you return noError. wrongBalancingStrategy and noError are enumeration constants:

```
enum ErrorCodes
{ noError,
  wrongBalancingStrategy
};
```

You can extend ErrorCodes to cover more error conditions, of course. The next step in the generator is to check the resulting error code and report an error if appropriate. This is done using the template Error, which is specialized for the different error conditions, as shown in the following code. The generator accesses the member everythingOK of Error, but the member is only present in the base template, which is selected for the instantiation Error<NoError>. If Error gets instantiated with one of the error types, the compiler will complain that it cannot find the member, for example, "no member everythingOK in Error<WrongBalancingStrategy>". Here is the code for the auxiliary error checking types:

```
struct NoError {};
struct WrongBalancingStrategy {};

template <class ErrorType>
struct Error
{    enum { everythingOK };
};

template<>
struct Error<WrongBalancingStrategy>
{};
```

Because the generator passes Generator to PersonalAccount instead of Config, we need a final adjustment to the previously shown implementation of `PersonalAccount`. The necessary changes are highlighted:

```
template <class Generator>
class PersonalAccount
{   public:
        typedef typename Generator::Config Config;
        //...
```

The use of a configuration generator is as always simple. For example, you can create an account for a fixed-term deposit in euro like this:

```
ACCOUNT_GENERATOR<FixedTermDeposit<sixtyDays>, EUR>::RET a1;
```

The following line demonstrates an invalid specification. It will result in a compile-time error because you cannot use quarterly balancing for a deposit:

```
ACCOUNT_GENERATOR<FixedTermDeposit<quarter>, EUR>::RET a1;
```

13.11   Testing Generators and Their Products

At this point, you may be wondering how to test generators and their products. Despite the potentially huge number of produced variants, you can quite easily provide different kinds of testing facilities. First, you can write testing scripts using metaloops to automatically run a generator on different generated specifications (we demonstrated this in Section 10.13). Furthermore, the code testing the generated systems can access the configuration repository of each generated system and use it to decide which tests are appropriate for the given system. Finally, you can also extend the generator with testing components and have it produce instrumented versions of systems. The testing scope and strategy can also be controlled by an appropriate DSL.

Chapter 14

Generative Matrix Computation Library (GMCL)

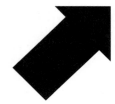

14.1 Why Is This Chapter Worth Reading?

We conclude this book with an example of a more realistic size. We will develop a scaled-down version of a generative matrix computation library. The library will contain two interacting generators, one that produces different types of matrices (i.e., with different combinations of element and index type, shape, density, storage format, and error checking strategies) and one that generates optimized implementations of matrix expressions involving matrix addition and multiplication.

We will cover several new aspects of generative development in this chapter. First, we will describe the development process including domain scoping and definition resulting in a domain feature model, and the specification of configuration knowledge using dependency tables in a more refined way than in previous chapters. Furthermore, you will see that feature modeling and other familiar development steps can be applied with equal success to both abstract data types and algorithms.

We will also present some new implementation techniques and technologies. In addition to a full C++ implementation, we will briefly discuss our experience with a prototype library implementation in the Intentional Programming system and compare both technologies. We will introduce the technique of expression templates and use it to implement a matrix expression generator performing domain-specific optimizations. The matrix expression generator will interact with a multistage configuration generator for matrix types. The latter, compared to the configuration generators discussed in the previous chapters, will accept a more complex DSL and not only check buildability, but also compute dependent defaults. Each generation step will be implemented as a separate metafunction. We will also present a template metafunction for directly encoding configuration knowledge using dependency tables.

14.2 Why Matrix Computations?

This chapter applies the DEMRAL method described in Chapter 5. The example presented is a scaled-down version of GMCL, a full-size matrix computation library described in [Neu98, Cza98].

Matrix computations is a domain with plenty of documented domain knowledge and thus a perfect candidate for Domain Engineering. Given some 30 years of development, it is a complex domain with a lot of variability. It is also a very useful domain with many application areas including structural engineering, flow analysis, economic modeling, power system networks, circuit simulations, nuclear physics, quantum chemistry, surveying, air traffic control, stealth airplane technology, noise reduction, oceanic modeling, and more.

There are many sophisticated matrix computation libraries written in Fortran and C. They've been tuned and improved for decades. Therefore, you may wonder why one would want to implement another one. The success of object-oriented and generic programming in other areas sparked the interest of the scientific computing community to implement new libraries using these new technologies. The expected benefits included providing a higher-level interface to the library users and increasing the flexibility and adaptability of library code. It turned out that representing domain concepts as objects definitely helped to raise the abstraction level, but at the cost of performance, which in this area was unacceptable.

So, the challenge was to raise the level of abstraction while preserving high performance at the same time. As discussed in Chapter 9, achieving this required domain-specific optimizations, and including them in libraries became possible only after developing template metaprogramming. Indeed, the Blitz++ project [Blitz] by Todd Veldhuizen and the POOMA project [POOMA] at Los Alamos are both efforts in the area of scientific computing that have immensely contributed to the development of template metaprogramming. Armed with generic programming and template metaprogramming, the implementation of new matrix computation libraries became attractive. In fact, the Matrix Template Library (MTL) [SL98a, SL98b] is a generic and generative C++ matrix library, which topples the performance of vendor-tuned Fortran codes. The main goal of our work was to develop a library using a systematic, Domain Engineering approach. Furthermore, we came up with a new design that combined configuration generators with expression templates, which gave the library user a very abstract interface while preserving maximum performance. This design was recently adopted by the MTL. The following sections describe this design and the development process in detail.

14.3 Domain Analysis

14.3.1 Domain Definition

We start Domain Analysis by defining the target domain, which requires a number of activities. First, we need to identify the project goals and stakeholders. Next, we need to find appropriate sources of domain knowledge, for example, books, existing systems, and domain experts. Then, we have to identify and organize the different classes of target users and their requirements. We complement this activity by analyzing the main capabilities and characteristics of the existing systems and solutions in the domain. The results of both analyses are high-level requirements and capabilities, which we document in a domain feature diagram. Finally, we annotate the requirements and capabilities with priorities based on the project goals. The resulting domain-feature model represents the domain definition. An additional activity is to identify support domains that will help us to implement aspects of our target domain.

Let's start defining the target domain for our example, which is the *domain of matrix computation libraries*. The most important group of stakeholders are users solving linear algebra problems. For simplicity, we'll ignore any other stakeholders and organizational issues. The library we want to develop should be highly reusable, adaptable, and very efficient. It should also provide a highly intentional, easy to use interface to application programmers.

Matrix computations is a synonym for doing linear algebra on the computer. It is a mature domain, which has been around for over 30 years (e.g., see [Wil61]). There are two classes of software for doing matrix computations. First, you have complete problem solving environments, such as Matlab [Pra95], which include an interactive GUI, an interpretative kernel, and visualization capabilities. The other class includes matrix computation libraries, which are intended to be used by other applications. A matrix computation library contains ADTs, such as vectors and matrices and algorithm families for matrix computations, for example, solving a system of linear equations or computing eigenvalues.

NOTE

Matrix computation libraries are an example of a horizontal domain, whereas problem solving environments represent a vertical domain (see Section 2.7.2).

As stated previously, matrix computations is a mature domain and there is plenty of published material on both the theory of linear algebra and the efficient implementations of algorithms and data structures for solving linear algebra problems (e.g., [GL96, JK93]). There are many existing libraries with widely available source code and documentation (e.g., [LHKK79, DDHH88, DDDH90, CHL+96, OONP]; see [Cza98] for more references) and even a repository of sample matrices from different application areas, such as quantum chemistry, civil engineering, astrophysics, and so on [MM]. You can use this information to analyze both the potential application areas and existing solutions.

From the aforementioned and other sources, we were able to identify 29 areas that use matrix computations. Next, we listed the types of matrices and algorithms needed in each of these areas in a table format demonstrated in Table 14-1. We used a similar table to analyze the types of matrices and algorithms provided by existing matrix libraries (see Table 14-2). Our analysis covered 15 libraries written in Fortran and C++, which we found on the Internet.

The analysis of application areas and existing libraries gives us an idea about the types of matrices and computations found in matrix computations. The next step is to summarize our findings in a domain feature diagram, which represents the domain definition. The diagram is shown in Figure 14-1. It states that a complete matrix computation library has to provide a number of matrix types and matrix computations. As you can see, some matrix properties are represented as or-features and some are optional. For example, we have to at least provide dense or sparse matrices, but we can also implement both, and we may or may not provide symmetric matrices. The diagram defines comprehensive matrix computation libraries, but we can also split it in two parts: one defining libraries of matrices and the other defining libraries of matrix computations.

Each of the variable domain features in the diagram is annotated with a priority. We assigned the priorities based on the frequency that a given feature occurred in the analyzed application

Table 14-1 Application Areas for Dense and Sparse Matrix Computations*

Application Area	Dense Matrix Types	Computational Problems
Electromagnetics (Helmholtz equation), for example, radar technology, stealth (i.e., "radar-invisible") airplane technology	Complex, Hermitian (rarely also non-Hermitian), for example, 55296 by 55296	Boundary integral solution (specifically the method of moments)
Flow analysis (Laplace or Poisson equation), for example, airflow past an airplane wing, flow around ships	Symmetric, for example, 12088 by 12088	Boundary integral solution (specifically the panel method)
...	...	...

Application Area	Sparse Matrix Types	Computational Problems
Static analyses in structural engineering,[1] for example, static analysis of buildings, roofs, bridges, airplanes, and so on	Real symmetric positive definite, pattern symmetric indefinite, for example, 3948 by 3948 with 60882 entries	Generalized symmetric eigenvalue problem, finite-element modeling, linear systems
Dynamic analysis in structural engineering, for example, dynamic analysis of fluids, suspension bridges, transmission towers, robotic control	Real symmetric and positive definite or positive semi-definite or indefinite	Symmetric eigenvalue problems, linear systems
...	...	...

*For the complete table with 9 application areas for dense matrices and 20 for sparse matrices see [Cza98].

areas and existing libraries. Of course, you should adjust these priorities based on your project goals and target users.

Any domain you analyze will have its own special vocabulary. Therefore, you should establish a glossary of domain terms at the beginning of Domain Analysis and update it as you go. A glossary of matrix computation terms is given in Appendix D.

14.3.2 Domain Modeling

Now that we have defined our target domain, we can move to the second and last activity of Domain Analysis, which is Domain

---

1. Structural engineering is concerned with the planning, analysis, design, and construction of buildings, bridges, industrial facilities, aerospace structures, and other structures.

Table 14-2 Existing Matrix Computation Libraries and Their Features*

Matrix Computations Library	Features
LAPACK	*Language*: Fortran
A matrix computation library for dense linear problems; supersedes both LINPACK and EISPACK	*Matrix types*: Dense, real, complex, rectangular, band, symmetric, triangular, and tridiagonal
See [ABB+94] and www.netlib.org/lapack	*Computations*: Systems of linear equations, linear least squares problems, eigenvalue problems, and singular value problems
ARPACK	*Language*: Fortran
A comprehensive library for solving real or complex and symmetric or unsymmetric eigenvalue problems; uses LAPACK and BLAS	*Matrix types:* Uses matrices provided by BLAS and LAPACK
See [LSY98] and www.caam.rice.edu/software/ARPACK	*Computations*: Implicitly Restarted Arnoldi Method (IRAM), Implicitly Restarted Lanczos Method (IRLM), and supporting methods for solving real or complex and symmetric or unsymmetric eigenvalue problems
MTL (Matrix Template Library)	*Language*: C++, extensive use of templates
A C++ matrix library with an STL-like template-based design; it implements register blocking using template metaprogramming and exhibits an excellent performance comparable to tuned Fortran 90 code	*Matrix types*: Dense, sparse, real, complex, rectangular, symmetric, band
See [SL98a, SL98b] and www.lsc.nd.edu/	
...	...

*For the complete table with 15 entries see [Cza98].

Modeling. The purpose of this activity is to develop a domain model, which involves identifying the key domain concepts, their common and variable features, and the dependencies between the variable features.

We have already identified the key concepts of matrix computations during domain definition to be vectors and matrices and families of matrix computation algorithms. For the purpose of our example, we will mainly concentrate on matrices and provide you

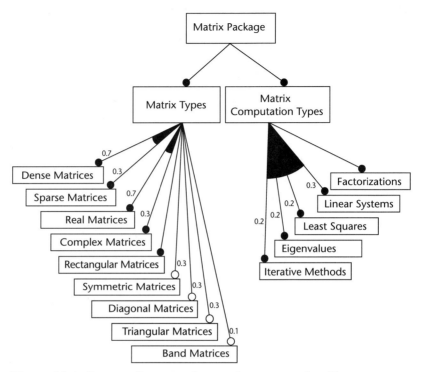

Figure 14-1 *Feature diagram of a matrix computation library*

with only a small example of a feature diagram for matrix factorization algorithms.

The main activity of Domain Modeling is to develop feature models of the key concepts. As you may remember, a feature model consists of a feature diagram and additional information, such as the source of each feature, its rationale, binding time, stakeholders, and so on. The feature diagram for the concept "matrix" is shown in Figure 14-2.

The feature diagram covers the following main features: element type, subscripts, density, shape, format, memory management, error checking, and operations. The following list contains their short descriptions.

♦ *Element type:* Matrix elements can be either real or complex numbers. The number types can be of single (e.g., *float*) or double precision (e.g., *double*).

- ◆ *Subscripts:* Subscripts can be represented using different integral types, such as `short` or `int`. The start index can be `0` (as in C) or `1` (as in Fortran).
- ◆ *Density:* Density describes the percentage of nonzero elements in a matrix. A matrix with a high density is called dense and one with low density is called sparse (usually less than 10 percent). Sparse matrices are stored by storing their nonzero elements only, which saves memory.

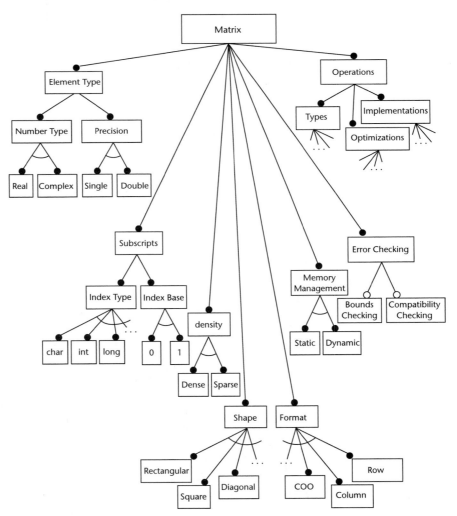

Figure 14-2 *Feature diagram of the concept "matrix"*

◆ *Shape:* Shape describes the arrangement of nonzero elements in a matrix, for example, a diagonal matrix may have nonzero elements only on its diagonal, and a lower-triangular matrix may have nonzero elements only on the diagonal and below it. Knowing the shape of a matrix allows you to use more efficient storage formats and processing algorithms. There is a large number of different shapes used in practice, for example, symmetric, skew-symmetric, band, Hessenberg, Toeplitz, and so on (you'll find a description of different shapes in [Cza98]). Some applications may also use special shapes requiring custom formats and algorithms.

◆ *Format:* Different formats may be used to store the elements of a matrix. Which format is the most efficient depends on the density and shape of the matrix. For example, dense rectangular matrices can be stored row-wise (C style) or column-wise (Fortran style) in a two-dimensional array, and a dense, diagonal matrix is best stored in a vector. Examples of storage formats for sparse matrices include the coordinate format (COO), which stores the nonzero elements together with their coordinates; the compressed sparse row or column format, which stores rows or columns in sparse vectors; or the skyline format, which is particularly useful for storing band triangular matrices.

◆ *Memory management:* Memory needed for storing matrix elements can be allocated statically or dynamically. If you know the size of a matrix at compile time, you can allocate the necessary amount of memory statically. If you don't, you have to allocate it dynamically.

◆ *Error checking:* Error checking can be done in several places. We can optionally check to see if the indices used to access a matrix are within its bounds (i.e., bounds checking). Another kind of check is to make sure that the numbers of rows and columns of matrices involved in an operation (e.g., addition or multiplication) are compatible (i.e., compatibility checking). The checks should be optional because some programs can guarantee that nothing bad can happen, in which case we can improve performance by not performing the checks.

◆ *Operations:* Operations are necessary to perform computations on matrices. There are unary matrix operations (e.g., transposition, various matrix norms) and binary vector-vector, matrix-vector, and matrix-matrix operations (e.g., matrix addition and multiplication). Each operation may be implemented in different ways, and the most optimal one depends on different factors, such as the shape and density of the operands. Furthermore, we can optimize not only single operations, but whole matrix expressions.

As indicated in the previous descriptions, there are many dependencies between features. For example, the choice of the storage format for a matrix depends on its density and shape. Also the choice of an algorithm for computing an operation depends on the density and shapes of the operands. We won't go into any more detail about the matrix features here, but if you are interested in a complete description, you'll find it in [Cza98].

We'll implement a subset of the matrix feature model in the remaining sections. But before we do, let us briefly demonstrate how to do feature modeling for an algorithm family. We take the family of matrix factorization algorithms as an example. In general, matrix factorizations decompose matrices into factor matrices with some desired properties. For example, the LU factorization of a matrix A computes the lower-triangular matrix L and the upper-triangular matrix U, such that A=L*U. The LU factorization can be used to solve a linear system of the form A*x=b, where A is the coefficient matrix, b is the right-hand side vector, and x is the sought-after solution vector. After factoring A into L and U, we can find x by solving the two triangular systems: L*y=b and U*x=y, which is very simple to do using forward or back substitution. There are also other kinds of factorizations, but let us focus on LU only (you'll find more details on this topic in [GL96]).

There are different variants of LU factorization. Its general form, that is, *general LU*, corresponds to the Gaussian elimination method of solving linear systems. The general LU can be specialized in order to more efficiently handle systems whose coefficient matrix A has some special properties. For example, if A is square and positive definite, we should use the special form of LU called Cholesky. Furthermore, there are specialized versions of LU for different matrix shapes, for example, band matrices or Hessenberg matrices. Another variable aspect of factorization algorithms is *pivoting*, which involves data movements, such as the interchange of two matrix rows (and columns, in some approaches). LU without pivoting fails for a certain class of linear systems, in which case we have to use pivoting. However, if pivoting is not necessary, it should be avoided because it degrades performance. Not only is there the question of whether or not to use pivoting, but if you do need pivoting, you have to choose the right pivoting strategy, for example, partial, complete, symmetric, or diagonal pivoting.

You can model all the different algorithm variants and dimensions using a feature diagram. The feature diagram for the LU family is shown in Figure 14-3. Each algorithm variant is annotated with the properties a matrix should have to be successfully factored using this algorithm.

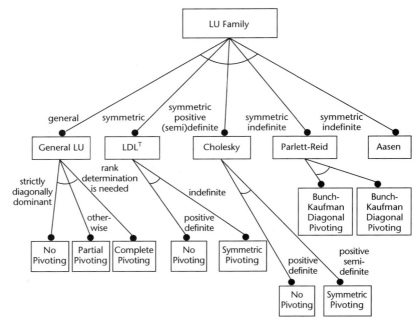

Figure 14-3 *Feature diagram of the LU family*

You can implement this diagram using the techniques demonstrated in the previous chapters, that is, you can model the various alternative and optional parts of the algorithms as class templates, define a GenVoca grammar for the components, define an algorithm description DSL, and finally implement a generator mapping algorithm specifications into concrete configurations of the class templates. In fact, such a generative library of LU factorization has been implemented by Johannes Knaupp [Kna98]. This example shows that you can use feature modeling and the generative programming techniques not only for ADTs but also for algorithms.

14.4 Domain Design and Implementation

In the remainder of this chapter, we'll show you how to implement a subset of the matrix feature model from the previous section. This will require developing two cooperating generators: one generating matrix types and the other generating implementations of matrix expressions. We will first show you an implementation in C++, and then give you a brief overview of an implementation in the Intentional Programming system. Compared to the generators presented in the previous sections, this chapter's generators demonstrate a number of new aspects including the cooperation between generators, modular multistage generators, explicit encoding of configuration knowledge using dependency tables, computing default values, implementing abstract features and more complex DSLs, and expression generators based on expression templates.

The feature model we are going to implement is shown in Figure 14-4. It covers `ElementType` and `IndexType` parameters, a subscript base of `0`, dense matrices only, four shapes, two formats, a dynamic allocation, optional bounds checking, and mandatory compatibility checking. In the case of the array format, you can choose between row-wise (`cLike`) or column-wise (`fortranLike`) storage. Furthermore, we will implement matrix addition, subtraction, and multiplication. We will also support two types of matrix expression optimizations (shape-based optimization and loop fusing).

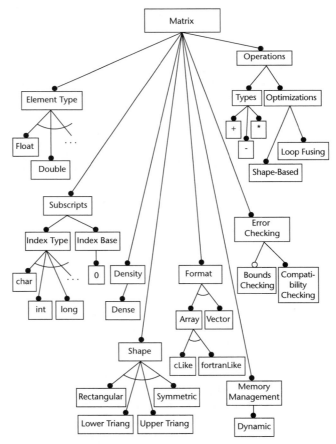

Figure 14-4 *Matrix features to be implemented*

The C++ implementation will have the form of a generative C++ template library, that is, it will contain generic template components and metatemplate programs. In order to get a better idea of where we are heading, let's take a look at a sample C++ client code using the generative matrix library:

```cpp
#include "GenerativeMatrix.h"
void main()
{
    //define a general rectangular matrix with element type double.
    typedef MATRIX_GENERATOR<
            matrix< double,    //this here is a
                    rect<>     //matrix configuration
            >                  //specification
        >::RET RectMatrixType;

    //define a symmetric matrix with element type double.
    typedef MATRIX_GENERATOR<
            matrix< double,
                    symm<>
            >
        >::RET SymmMatrixType;

    //declare four 3x3 matrices
    RectMatrixType  RectMatrix1(3, 3),
                    RectMatrix2(3, 3);
    SymmMatrixType  SymmMatrix1(3, 3),
                    SymmMatrix2(3, 3);

    //initialize the matrices
    RectMatrix2=    1, 0, 3,    //initialization using
                    0, 1, 4,    //a comma-separated
                    2, 0, 1;    //list

    SymmMatrix1=    4, 4, 5,
                    4, 2, 6,
                    5, 6, 1;

    SymmMatrix2=    1, 4, 5,
                    4, 1, 6,
                    5, 6, 1;

    //evaluate a matrix expression
    RectMatrix1= (SymmMatrix1 + RectMatrix2)*
                 (SymmMatrix2 + RectMatrix2);
```

```
                  //print the result
                  cout << "RectMatrix1 = " << endl << RectMatrix1 << endl;
}
```

The library allows us to specify different kinds of matrix types and generate them using `MATRIX_GENERATOR`, initialize matrix instances using a nice comma-separated list notation, and write matrix expressions involving matrix addition, subtraction, and multiplication. We have highlighted an example of each of these capabilities in the previous code.

How will our library support these capabilities? As already indicated in the code, matrix types will be generated using the configuration generator `MATRIX_GENERATOR`, which is similar to those presented in the previous chapters. The generator takes a matrix specification as its parameter and returns a finished matrix type, which is composed from a number of class templates. Matrix initialization using comma-separated lists will be implemented by a special component, which we call `CommaInitializer`. It uses the possibility of overloading the comma operator in C++. Finally, matrix expressions simply use overloaded addition, subtraction, and multiplication operators. However, these operators do not directly implement matrix addition, subtraction, or multiplication. Rather, they are constructors of expression objects representing the structure of the expression they are used in. The evaluation of the tree of expression objects constructed this way is carried out by the assignment operator. Without going into details at this point, this kind of implementation allows us to actually generate custom implementation code based on the expression structure and the types of the operands. This way we can implement shape-based optimizations and loop fusing.

Consequently, the generative matrix library contains two generators, one for generating matrix types and the other for generating optimized implementations of matrix expressions (see Figure 14-5). The evaluation of some matrix expressions requires computing intermediate results. The matrix types needed for representing the intermediate results are also generated using the matrix generator. Thus, the expression generator sometimes has to call the matrix generator. Furthermore, the expression generator has to access the configuration repositories of the generated matrix types in order to generate code that is optimized for the shapes and densities of the operands.

We will now describe the design and implementation of the library. We will start with the part responsible for generating matrix types, and then move to the part implementing matrix

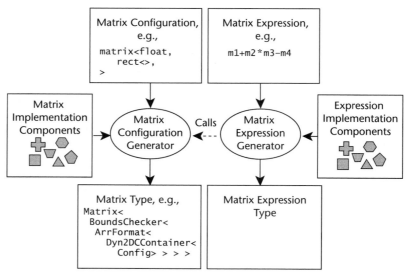

Figure 14-5 *Generators of the generative matrix library*

expressions. In contrast to the previous chapters, we will first show the specification of a small part and then its implementation, rather than giving you the full specification first. This way you'll see right away how to implement different parts of the library.

14.4.1 Matrix Type Generation

The part responsible for generating matrix types will have all the usual elements of a generative domain model: a problem space consisting of a domain-specific language for specifying matrices, a solution space consisting of a GenVoca architecture with components implemented as class templates, and a generator implementing the configuration knowledge consisting of illegal feature combinations, direct and computed default settings, and construction rules (see Figure 5-1 in Section 5.2). We will start by specifying the target GenVoca architecture with its implementation components and GenVoca grammar. Then we'll take a look at the implementation of the components. The next step will be to design a DSL for specifying matrices and implement it using templates and enumeration constants. Finally, we'll take a look at a multi-stage generator, which performs parsing the input specification, checking for illegal feature combinations, computing default settings for unspecified features, and assembling the implementation components. The generator will be implemented using template metaprogramming techniques.

14.4.1.1 Target Architecture and Matrix Implementation Components

The GenVoca model for the matrix implementation components is shown in Figure 14-6. The bottom layer is the configuration repository, which will contain all the features from the matrix specification given to the matrix generator (i.e., DSL features) and the components needed by other layers, such as `CommaInitializer` and `MatrixType` (i.e., the finished matrix type). The next layer contains three alternative element containers. `Dyn1DContainer` is a one-dimensional container (i.e., vector) with dynamic allocation. `Dyn2DCContainer` is a two-dimensional container stored row-wise, that is, each row is stored in one consecutive piece of memory (which is the C style of storing multidimensional arrays). `Dyn2DFContainer` is a two-dimensional column-wise container, that is, each column is stored in one consecutive piece of memory (which is the Fortran style of storing multidimensional arrays).

Containers are used as parameters in one of the three alternative storage formats `ArrFormat`, `LoTriangVecFormat`, and `UpTriangVecFormat`. `ArrFormat` is used for storing rectangular and triangular matrices in a two-dimensional array, that is, this format takes one of the two-dimensional containers as its parameter. `LoTriangVecFormat` implements storing a lower-triangular matrix in a vector, that is, a one-dimensional container. Similarly, `UpTriangVecFormat` implements storing an upper-triangular matrix in a vector. Storing triangular matrices in a vector rather than in a two-dimensional array saves memory because only the nonzero half of the matrix needs to be stored in the vector. On the other hand, accessing elements of a triangular matrix stored in a vector has the overhead of mapping two-dimensional matrix element indices onto the one-dimensional vector indices. You can avoid this overhead if you store it in a two-dimensional array directly, but at the cost of memory space. In other words, storing triangular matrices in a vector saves memory, whereas storing them in a two-dimensional array saves execution time.

The next two layers are optional. You use `Symm` for symmetric matrices only. It maps the lower and upper half of a symmetric matrix onto the lower half of the underlying format, that is, it allows you to store symmetric matrices in a lower-triangular format. `BoundsChecker` implements bounds checking and is used only if you request it in the specification.

Finally, the top layer contains the component `Matrix`, which wraps all matrix types and provides some basic operations, such as

Top Layer	Matrix
Bounds Checking	BoundsChecker
Symmetry	Symm
Formats Layer	ArrFormat | LoTriangVecFormat | UpTriangVecFormat
Basic Containers Layer	Dyn1DContainer | Dyn2DCContainer | Dyn2DFContainer
Config	MatrixType, CommaInitializer, ElementType, IndexType, DSLFeatures (i.e., DSLFeatures contains all the DSL features of a configuration)

Figure 14-6 *Layers of the matrix implementation components*

assignment operators and initialization using `CommaInitializer`, and so on.

The corresponding GenVoca grammar is shown in Figure 14-7. This grammar is our implementation components configuration language (ICCL), that is, the language of the solution space.

Each of the matrix implementation components will be implemented by a class template. The first implementation step is to col-

```
MatrixType:              Matrix[OptBoundsCheckedMatrix]
OptBoundsCheckedMatrix:  OptSymmetricMatrix |
                         BoundsChecker[OptSymmetricMatrix]
OptSymmetricMatrix:      Format | Symm[Format]
Format:                  ArrFormat[Array] | LoTriangVecFormat[Vector] |
                         UpTriangVecFormat[Vector]
Array:                   Dyn2DCContainer[Config] | Dyn2DFContainer[Config]
Vector:                  Dyn1DContainer[Config]
Config:                  MatrixType, CommaInitializer, ElementType, IndexType,
                         DSLFeatures
```

Figure 14-7 *GenVoca grammar for the matrix implementation components*

lect all the declarations of the implementation components in a separate header called ICCL.h. This header specifies our ICCL from Figure 14-7. Here is its contents:

ICCL.h

```
namespace MatrixICCL {

//Matrix :  Matrix [OptBoundsCheckedMatrix]
template<class OptBoundsCheckedMatrix>class Matrix;

//OptBoundsCheckedMatrix:   OptSymmetricMatrix |
//                          BoundsChecker[OptSymmetricMatrix]
template<class OptSymmetricMatrix>class BoundsChecker;

//OptSymmetricMatrix: MatrixContainer | Symm[MatrixContainer]
template<class MatrixContainer>class Symm;

//Format: ArrFormat[Array] | LoTriangVecFormat[Vector] |
//        UpTriangVecFormat[Vector]
template<class Array>class ArrFormat;
template<class Vector>class LoTriangVecFormat;
template<class Vector>class UpTriangVecFormat;

//Array: Dyn2DCContainer[Config] | Dyn2DFContainer[Config]
template<class Generator>class Dyn2DCContainer;
template<class Generator>class Dyn2DFContainer;

//Vector: Dyn1DContainer[Config]
template<class Generator> class Dyn1DContainer;

//CommaInitializer: DenseCCommaInitializer |
//                  DenseFCommaInitializer
template<class MatrixType>class DenseCCommaInitializer;
template<class MatrixType>class DenseFCommaInitializer;

} //namespace MatrixICCL
```

We use CommaInitializer to provide matrix initialization by comma-separated lists of numbers. Please note that the containers take Generator as their parameter rather than Config, but the latter is part of Generator and can be retrieved from it.

Each category of implementation components is implemented in a separate file. We start with the containers:

Containers.h

```
namespace MatrixICCL{
template<class Generator>
class Dyn1DContainer
{public:
    typedef typename Generator::Config Config;
    typedef typename Config::ElementType ElementType;
    typedef typename Config::IndexType IndexType;
```

As already stated, Generator is expected to provide Config as its member type. Config, in turn, contains element and index type. All matrix components can access these types in this fashion. Dyn1DContainer allocates the memory for storing its elements from the heap:

```
protected:
    IndexType size_;
    ElementType* pContainer;

public:
    Dyn1DContainer(const IndexType& l)
        : size_(l)
    {   assert(size()>0);
        pContainer = new ElementType [size()];
        assert( pContainer != 0 );
    }

    ~Dyn1DContainer() {delete [] pContainer;}

    void setElement(const IndexType& i, const ElementType& v)
    {   checkBounds( i );
        pContainer[ i ] = v;
    }

    const ElementType& getElement(const IndexType& i) const
    {   checkBounds( i );
        return pContainer[ i ];
    }

    const IndexType& size() const {return size_;}

    void initElements(const ElementType& v)
    {   for( IndexType i = size(); --i; )
            setElement( i, v );
    }
```

```
protected:
    void checkBounds(const IndexType& i) const
    {   assert(i>=0 && i<size());   }
};
```

Dyn2DCContainer is a two-dimensional container storing its elements row-wise:

```
template<class Generator>
class Dyn2DCContainer
{public:
    typedef typename Generator::Config Config;
    typedef typename Config::ElementType ElementType;
    typedef typename Config::IndexType IndexType;

protected:
    IndexType r_, c_;
    ElementType* elements_;
    ElementType** rows_;

public:
    Dyn2DCContainer(const IndexType& r, const IndexType& c)
        : r_(r), c_(c)
    {   assert(r_>0); assert(c_>0);

        elements_ = new ElementType[r*c];
        rows_ = new ElementType*[r];
        assert(elements_ != 0);
        assert(rows_ != 0);

        ElementType* p= elements_;
        for (IndexType i= 0; i<r; i++, p+= c) rows_[i]= p;
    }

    ~Dyn2DCContainer()
    {   delete [] elements_;
        delete [] rows_;
    }

    void setElement(
        const IndexType& i, const IndexType& j, const ElementType& v)
    {   checkBounds(i, j);
        rows_[i][j] = v;
    }
```

```
        const ElementType& getElement(const IndexType& i,
                                       const IndexType& j) const
    {   checkBounds(i, j);
        return rows_[i][j];
    }

    const IndexType& rows() const { return r_; }
    const IndexType& cols() const { return c_; }

    void initElements(const ElementType& v)
    {   for(IndexType i = rows(); --i;)
            for(IndexType j = cols(); --j;)
                setElement(i, j, v);
    }

protected:
    void checkBounds(const IndexType& i, const IndexType& j) const
    {   assert(i>=0 && i<rows());
        assert(j>=0 && j<cols());
    }
};
```

Dyn2DFContainer is a two-dimensional container storing its elements column-wise. We can easily derive its implementation from Dyn2DCContainer by inheritance. All we have to do is to override setElement() and getElement() to swap the argument indices and also override rows() and cols() to call the base cols() and rows(), respectively:

```
template<class Generator>
class Dyn2DFContainer : public Dyn2DCContainer<Generator>
{   typedef Dyn2DCContainer<Generator> BaseClass;

public:
    Dyn2DFContainer(const IndexType& r, const IndexType& c)
        : BaseClass(c, r)
    {}

    void setElement(const IndexType& i,
                    const IndexType& j,
                    const ElementType& v)
    {   BaseClass::setElement(j, i, v);    }
```

```
    const ElementType& getElement(
        const IndexType& i, const IndexType& j) const
    {   return BaseClass::getElement(j, i);   }

    const IndexType& rows() const {   return BaseClass::cols();   }
    const IndexType& cols() const {   return BaseClass::rows();   }
};
} //namespace MatrixICCL
```

Next, we take a look at the formats. We start with ArrFormat. Because ArrFormat stores matrix elements in a two-dimensional container directly, there is hardly any difference between storing the elements of rectangular and triangular matrices. The only detail we have to do differently for triangular matrices is to directly return zero for their zero element halves rather than accessing the corresponding container elements. We will encapsulate this detail in the function nonZeroRegion(), which will take the indices i and j and return true if they address an element within the nonzero region of a matrix and false otherwise. We will have three different implementations of this function: one for rectangular matrices, one for lower-triangular matrices, and one for upper-triangular matrices. We will implement each variant of this function as a static function contained in a struct and use a metafunction to select the appropriate struct based on the shape stored in Config. Here is the implementation of nonZeroRegion() for rectangular matrices:

Formats.h

```
namespace MatrixICCL{

struct RectNonZeroRegion
{   template<class M>
    static bool nonZeroRegion(
        const M* m,
        const typename M::Config::IndexType& i,
        const typename M::Config::IndexType& j)
    {   return true;   }
};
```

nonZeroRegion() takes a number of parameters that are not relevant for this variant because we always return true. This is so because any element of a rectangular matrix can be a nonzero element. This is different for a lower-triangular matrix:

```
struct LowerTriangNonZeroRegion
{   template<class M>
```

```
    static bool nonZeroRegion(
        const M* m,
        const typename M::Config::IndexType& i,
        const typename M::Config::IndexType& j)
    {   return i>=j;    }
};
```

The first parameter of nonZeroRegion() is a pointer to the matrix format calling this function. The only purpose of this parameter is to provide type information: We retrieve the index type from its Config. The code for the nonzero region of an upper-triangular matrix is the same as the previous code except for the return expression, which is negated:

```
struct UpperTriangNonZeroRegion
{   template<class M>
    static bool nonZeroRegion(
        const M* m,
        const typename M::Config::IndexType& i,
        const typename M::Config::IndexType& j)
    {   return i<=j;    }
};
```

And here is the metafunction for selecting the appropriate implementation of nonZeroRegion() based on the matrix shape:

```
template<class MatrixType>
struct FORMAT_NON_ZERO_REGION
{   typedef typename MatrixType::Config Config;
    typedef typename Config::DSLFeatures DSLFeatures;
    typedef typename DSLFeatures::Shape Shape;

    typedef IF< EQUAL<Shape::id, Shape::lower_triang_id>::RET ||
                EQUAL<Shape::id, Shape::symm_id>::RET,
                    LowerTriangNonZeroRegion,

            IF< EQUAL<Shape::id, Shape::upper_triang_id>::RET,
                    UpperTriangNonZeroRegion,

            RectNonZeroRegion>::RET>::RET RET;
};
```

The metafunction uses nested IFs (see Section 12.8) to select the appropriate implementation. Now, we can implement ArrFormat as follows:

```
template<class Array>
class ArrFormat
{public:
    typename typedef Array::Config Config;
    typename typedef Config::ElementType ElementType;
    typename typedef Config::IndexType IndexType;
    typename typedef Config::MatrixType MatrixType;

private:
    Array elements_;

public:
    ArrFormat(const IndexType& r, const IndexType& c)
        : elements_(r, c)
    {}

    const IndexType& rows() const { return elements_.rows(); }
    const IndexType& cols() const { return elements_.cols(); }

    void setElement(
    const IndexType& i, const IndexType& j,const ElementType& v)
    {   checkBounds( i, j );
        if (nonZeroRegion(i, j)) elements_.setElement(i, j, v);
        else assert(v == ElementType( 0 ));
    }

    ElementType getElement(const IndexType& i, const IndexType& j) const
    {   checkBounds(i, j);
        return nonZeroRegion(i, j) ?
            elements_.getElement(i, j) : ElementType(0);
    }

    void initElements(const ElementType& v)
    {   elements_.initElements(v);    }

protected:
    void checkBounds(const IndexType& i, const IndexType& j) const
    {   assert(i < rows());  assert(j < cols());    }

    bool nonZeroRegion(const IndexType& i, const IndexType& j) const
    {   return
        FORMAT_NON_ZERO_REGION<MatrixType>::RET::nonZeroRegion(this,i,j);
    }
};
```

The last return demonstrates the call to nonZeroRegion(). The struct containing the appropriate function implementation is returned by the metafunction FORMAT_NON_ZERO_REGION<>. Because we declared all implementations of nonZeroRegion() as static inline functions of the structs, the C++ compiler should be able to inline the appropriate function to eliminate any overhead. This technique represents a static alternative to virtual functions.

LoTriangVecFormat stores the elements of a lower-triangular matrix row-wise in a vector:

```
template<class Vector>
class LoTriangVecFormat
{public:
    typedef typename Vector::Config Config;
    typedef typename Config::ElementType ElementType;
    typedef typename Config::IndexType IndexType;

private:
    const IndexType order_;
    Vector elements_;

public:
    LoTriangVecFormat(const IndexType& r,const IndexType& c)
        : order_(r), elements_(rows() * (rows() + 1) * 0.5)
    {   assert(rows()==cols());   }

    const IndexType& rows() const { return order_; }
    const IndexType& cols() const { return order_; }

    void setElement(
        const IndexType& i,
        const IndexType& j,
        const ElementType& v)
    {   checkBounds(i, j);
        if (i >= j) elements_.setElement(getIndex(i, j), v);
        else assert(v == ElementType( 0 ));
    }

    ElementType getElement(const IndexType& i,
                           const IndexType& j) const
    {   checkBounds(i, j);
        return i >= j ?
            elements_.getElement(getIndex(i, j)):
            ElementType(0);
    }
```

```
    void initElements(const ElementType& v)
    {   elements_.initElements(v);    }

protected:
    void checkBounds(const IndexType& i,
                     const IndexType& j) const
    {   assert( i < rows() );
        assert( j < cols() );
    }

    IndexType getIndex(const IndexType& i, const IndexType& j) const
    {   return (i + 1) * i * 0.5 + j;    }
};
```

UpTriangVecFormat can be easily derived from LoTriangVecFormat. We only need to override setElement() and getElement() in order to swap the row and column index (we don't need to swap row() and cols() because triangular matrices are always square):

```
template<class Vector>
class UpTriangVecFormat : public LoTriangVecFormat<Vector>
{public:
    UpTriangVecFormat(const IndexType& r,const IndexType& c)
        : LoTriangVecFormat(r, c)
    {}

    void setElement(
        const IndexType& i,
        const IndexType& j,
        const ElementType& v)
    {   LoTriangVecFormat::setElement(j, i, v);    }

    ElementType getElement(const IndexType& i,
                           const IndexType& j) const
    {   return LoTriangVecFormat::getElement( j, i );    }
};
```

Finally, we need to implement Symm. Symm takes a lower-triangular format as its parameter and turns it into a symmetric one. Symm is derived from its parameter and overrides setElement() and getElement() (in this example, we only have one lower-triangular format, but a larger library will have several alternative lower-triangular formats, and Symm would work with all of them):

```
template<class Format>
class Symm : public Format
{public:
    typedef Format::Config Config;
    typedef Config::ElementType ElementType;
    typedef Config::IndexType IndexType;

    Symm(const IndexType& rows,const IndexType& cols)
        : Format(rows, cols)
    {}

    void setElement(
        const IndexType& i,
        const IndexType& j,
        const ElementType& v )
    {   if( i >= j ) Format::setElement( i, j, v );
        else Format::setElement( j, i, v );
    }

    ElementType getElement( const IndexType& i,
                                 const IndexType& j ) const
    {   return ( i >= j ) ?
             Format::getElement( i, j ) :
             Format::getElement( j, i );
    }
};
} //namespace MatrixICCL
```

Bounds checking is implemented by a wrapper similar to `Symm` shown previously. Here is the implementation:

Bounds Checker.h

```
namespace MatrixICCL{

template<class OptSymmMatrix>
class BoundsChecker : public OptSymmMatrix
{public:
    typedef typename OptSymmMatrix::Config Config;
    typedef typename Config::ElementType ElementType;
    typedef typename Config::IndexType IndexType;

    BoundsChecker(const IndexType& r, const IndexType& c)
        : OptSymmMatrix(r, c)
    {}
```

```
     void setElement(const IndexType& i,
                     const IndexType& j,
                     const ElementType& v)
     {   checkBounds(i, j);
         OptSymmMatrix::setElement(i, j, v);
     }

     ElementType getElement(const IndexType& i,
             const IndexType& j) const
     {           checkBounds(i, j);
         return OptSymmMatrix::getElement(i, j);
     }

protected:
     void checkBounds(const IndexType& i,
                      const IndexType& j) const
     {   if (i < 0 || i >= rows() ||
             j < 0 || j >= cols())
             throw "subscript(s) out of bounds";
     }
};
} //namespace MatrixICCL
```

The top-level wrapper `Matrix` defines a number of useful functions for all matrices: an assignment operator for initializing a matrix using a comma-separated list of numbers, an assignment operator for assigning binary expressions, an assignment operator for assigning matrices to matrices, and a function for printing the contents of a matrix:

TopWrapper.h

```
template<class ExpressionType> class BinaryExpression;

namespace MatrixICCL{

template<class OptBoundsCheckedMatrix>
class Matrix : public OptBoundsCheckedMatrix
{public:
     typedef typename OptBoundsCheckedMatrix::Config Config;
     typedef typename Config::IndexType IndexType;
     typedef typename Config::ElementType ElementType;
     typedef typename Config::CommaInitializer CommaInitializer;

     Matrix(IndexType rows= 0,
            IndexType cols= 0,
```

```
            ElementType InitElem = ElementType(0) )
        : OptBoundsCheckedMatrix(rows, cols)
{   initElements(InitElem);
}


//initialization by a comma-separated list of numbers
CommaInitializer operator=(const ElementType& v)
{   return CommaInitializer(*this, v);
}
```

The following assignment operator allows us to assign binary expressions to a matrix (we'll discuss the class template BinaryExpression in Section 14.4.2.5):

```
//assignment operator for binary expressions
template <class Expr>
Matrix& operator=(const BinaryExpression<Expr>& expr)
{   expr.assign(this);
    return *this;
}
```

Finally, we need an assignment for assigning matrices to matrices. The implementation code depends on the shape of the source matrix. Thus, we use a technique similar to the one used in the case of nonZeroRegion(): We select the appropriate implementation using a metafunction (we give you the code for the metafunction and the different assignment variants in Section 14.4.2.9):

```
//matrix assignment
template<class A>
Matrix& operator=(const Matrix<A>& m)
{   MATRIX_ASSIGNMENT<A>::RET::assign(this, &m);
    return *this;
}

//assignment operators for other kinds of expressions
//...

//print matrix to ostream
ostream& display(ostream& out) const
{   for( IndexType i = 0; i < rows(); ++i )
    {   for( IndexType j = 0; j < cols(); ++j )
            out << getElement( i, j ) << "   ";
        out << endl;
    }
```

```
        return out;
    }
};
} //namespace MatrixICCL

//output operator for printing a matrix to a stream
template <class A>
ostream& operator<<(ostream& out, const Matrix<A>& m)
{   return m.display(out);
}
```

The last component we take a look at is the comma initializer, which allows the library user to initialize matrices using a comma-separated list of numbers, for example:

```
aMatrix =    7, 1, 0,    //this assignment operator takes
                         //a number and returns
             0, 2, 1,    //an instance of comma initializer;
                         //the latter
             4, 0, 3;    //overrides the comma
                         //operator to take a number and
                         //return a comma initializer, etc.
```

There are two comma initializers: `DenseCCommaInitializer` for matrices stored row-wise and `DenseFCommaInitializer` for matrices stored column-wise. We only take a look at `DenseCCommaInitializer` (the other comma initializer is implemented similarly):[2]

Comma Initializer.h

```
template <class Generator>
class DenseCCommaInitializer
{public:
    typedef typename Generator::Config Config;
    typedef typename Config::MatrixType MatrixType;
    typedef typename Config::IndexType IndexType;
    typedef typename Config::ElementType ElementType;

private:
    MatrixType& matrix_;
    IndexType i_, j_;
```

---

2. The idea behind the comma initializer comes from the Blitz++ library [Blitz] by Todd Veldhuizen.

```
public:
    DenseCCommaInitializer(MatrixType& m,
                           const ElementType& first_val)
        : matrix_(m), i_(0), j_(0)
    {   insert(first_val);
    }

    DenseCCommaInitializer& operator,(const ElementType& val)
    {   insert(val);
        return *this;
    }

protected:
    void insert(const ElementType& v)
    {   assert(i_<matrix_.rows());
        assert(j_<matrix_.cols());
        _matrix.setElement(i_, j_, v);
        ++j_;
        if (j_==matrix_.cols()) {j_= 0; ++i_;}
    }
};
```

14.4.1.2   Matrix Configuration DSL

The matrix configuration DSL that we are going to implement is shown in Figure 14-8 as a feature diagram. The DSL allows us to specify matrix element type, matrix shape, whether to optimize for speed or space, whether or not to do bounds checking, storage format, and index type. We derived the DSL from the diagram in Figure 14-4 by dropping features that need not be specified (e.g., density or base index), by representing the optional BoundsChecking using a dimension with the alternative values checkBounds and noBoundsChecking, and by reordering the dimensions, so that the ones that need to be specified explicitly in most cases are listed first (the unspecified dimensions are always assigned default values). Furthermore, we added the dimension OptFlag to represent an optimization flag. This is an example of an abstract feature that lets you specify your preference to optimize for speed or space.

The grammar specification of the configuration DSL is given in Figure 14-9.

We implement the DSL using nested class templates. The first thing we do is copy the grammar definition from Figure 14-9 and paste it into the file DSL.h as a comment. Next, under each grammar production, we directly type in the corresponding template declarations:

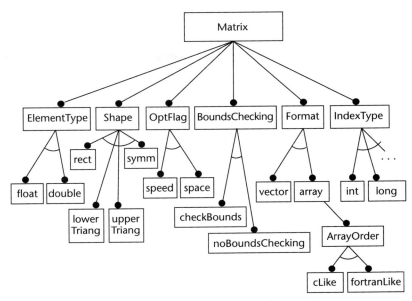

Figure 14-8 Matrix configuration DSL as a feature diagram

DSL.*h*

```
namespace MatrixDSL {

//Matrix:   matrix[ElementType, Shape, OptFlag,
//                 BoundsChecking, Format, IndexType ]
template<class ElementType, class Shape, class OptFlag,
         class BoundsChecking, class Format,
         class IndexType>struct matrix;
```

```
Matrix:         matrix[ElementType, Shape, OptFlag, BoundsChecking, Format,
                    IndexType]
ElementType:    float | double | long double | ...
Shape:          rect | lowerTriang | upperTriang | symm
OptFlag:        speed | space
BoundsChecking: checkBounds | noBoundsChecking
Format:         vector | array[ArrayOrder]
ArrayOrder:     cLike | fortranLike
IndexType:      char | short | int | long | unsigned int | ...
```

Figure 14-9 Grammar specification of the demo matrix configuration DSL

```
//ElementType : float | double | long double | ...
//built-in types - nothing to declare

//Shape:    rect | upperTriang | lowerTriang | symm
template<class dummy>struct rect;
template<class dummy>struct lower_triang;
template<class dummy>struct upper_riang;
template<class dummy>struct symm;
```

You may wonder what the parameter dummy is good for. We don't use it for anything. But we want to define the shape values as templates rather than structs, and thus we need a parameter. The purpose of defining the values as templates is that we can later add subfeatures to them (e.g., a subfeature of lower_triangular<> could specify whether the diagonal should only contain zero elements or not) without having to change existing client code. All we have to do is make sure that each template parameter has a default. In the case where a client writes

```
rect<>
```

we do not know how many parameters the template rect has, so changing their number won't affect this code. Here are the remaining declarations:

```
//OptFlag :    speed | space
template<class dummy>struct speed;
template<class dummy>struct space;

//BoundsChecking : checkBounds | noBoundsChecking
template<class dummy>struct check_bounds;
template<class dummy>struct no_bounds_checking;

//Format:    vector | array[ArrayOrder]
template<class dummy>struct vector;
template<class ArrOrder>struct array;

//ArrOrder:    cLike | fortranLike
template<class dummy>struct c_like;
template<class dummy>struct fortran_like;

//IndexType :    char | short | int | long | unsigned char |
//               unsigned short |
//               unsigned int | unsigned long | signed char
```

```
//type denoting "value unspecified"
struct whatever;
```

The last struct whatever denotes "value unspecified". We can use this feature in matrix configuration expressions if we don't want to specify some feature in the middle of a parameter list, for example:

```
matrix<float,lower_triang<>,speed<>,noBoundsChecking<>,
    whatever,char>
```

Now, let's take a look at the implementation of the DSL features. We start with the implementation of whatever, which also defines the identification numbers for all DSL features. Identification numbers, or IDs, are used to test types for equality (see Section 10.10.1).

```
struct whatever
{   enum {
        whatever_id = -1,
        // IDs of Shape values
        rect_id, lower_triang_id, upper_triang_id, symm_id,
        //IDs of OptFlag values
        speed_id, space_id,
        //IDs of BoundsChecking values
        check_bounds_id, no_bounds_checking_id,
        //IDs of Format values
        array_id, vector_id,
        //IDs of ArrOrder values
        c_like_id, fortran_like_id,
        //my own ID
        id=whatever_id };
};
```

Here is the implementation of the first DSL production:

```
//Matrix:   matrix[ElementType, Shape, Format, OptFlag,
//          BoundsChecking, IndexType ]
template<
    class ElementType    = whatever,
    class Shape          = whatever,
    class OptFlag        = whatever,
    class BoundsChecking = whatever,
    class Format         = whatever,
```

```
        class IndexType       = whatever >
struct matrix
{    typedef ElementType      elementType;
     typedef Shape            shape;
     typedef OptFlag          optFlag;
     typedef BoundsChecking boundsChecking;
     typedef Format           format;
     typedef IndexType        indexType;
};
```

Let us make some comments here. We use whatever as the
default value for each parameter. The generator will assign more
useful default values later. The reason for not assigning the
defaults here is that we want to assign all (i.e., both direct and
computed) defaults in one place, that is, in the generator. The next
interesting point is that matrix<> defines each parameter type as its
member type, so that we can access them like this:

```
matrix<float,rect<> >::shape //this is equivalent to rect<>
```

The next production consists of a number of alternative values:

```
//Shape :        rect | lowerTriang | upperTriang | symm
template<class dummy = whatever>
struct rect : whatever
{   enum { id=rect_id };
};

template<class dummy = whatever>
struct lower_triang : whatever
{   enum { id = lower_triang_id };
};

template<class dummy = whatever>
struct upper_triang : whatever
{   enum { id = upper_triang_id };
};

template<class dummy = whatever>
struct symm : whatever
{   enum { id = symm_id };
};
```

Each "dummy" parameter has whatever as its default. As you may remember, the purpose of this parameter is to make values without subfeatures templates, so that new subfeatures can be added later without having to modify existing client code. Each value "publishes" its ID using an enum declaration. The initialization values for the IDs are defined in whatever, which is used as the superclass of all feature values. The following example demonstrates the use of IDs:

```
typedef rect<> Shape1;
typedef upper_triang<> Shape2;
typedef upper_triang<> Shape3;

cout << (Shape1::id == Shape2::id);    //prints: 0
cout << (Shape2::id == Shape3::id);    //prints: 1
```

IDs allow for an even finer testing than just type equality: We can test to see if two types are instantiated from the same class template even if the types are not equal (i.e., different parameters were used):

```
typedef array<c_like<> > Format1; //array<> and c_like are
                                  //defined below
typedef array<fortran_like<> > Format2; //fortran_like<> is
                                        //defined below

cout << (Format1::id == Format2::id);    //prints: 1
```

NOTE

If you just want to test whether two typenames point to the same type, you can use the following metafunction (this solution was suggested by Dietmar Kühl and Johannes Knaupp):

```
template<class A, class B>
struct AreTypesIdentical
{ enum { RET = false };
};

template<class A>
struct AreTypesIdentical<A, A>
{ enum { RET = true };
};
```

The remaining DSL features are specified in a similar way:

```
//OptFlag :     speed | space
template<class dummy = whatever>
struct speed : whatever
{   enum { id = speed_id };
};

template<class dummy = whatever>
struct space : whatever
{   enum { id = space_id };
};

//BoundsChecking :   checkBounds | noBoundsChecking
template<class dummy = whatever>
struct check_bounds : whatever
{   enum { id = check_bounds_id };
};

template<class dummy = whatever>
struct no_bounds_checking : whatever
{   enum { id = no_bounds_checking_id };
};

//Format :    vector | array[ArrOrder]
template<class dummy = whatever>
struct vector : whatever
{   enum {id = vector_id};
};

template<class ArrOrder = whatever>
struct array : whatever
{   enum {id = array_id};
    typedef ArrOrder arr_order;
};

//ArrOrder:     cLike | fortranLike
template<class dummy = whatever>
struct c_like : whatever
{   enum { id = c_like_id };
};

template<class dummy = whatever>
struct fortran_like : whatever
```

```
{    enum {id = fortran_like_id};
};
} //namespace MatrixDSL
```

This concludes the implementation of the matrix configuration DSL.

14.4.1.3 Matrix Configuration Generator

The matrix configuration generator takes a matrix configuration description, for example, `matrix<double,rect<> >`, and returns a matrix type with the properties specified in the configuration description. Given the previous configuration description, it generates the following matrix type:

```
Matrix<BoundsChecker<ArrFormat<Dyn2DCContainer<
    MATRIX_ASSEMBLE_COMPONENTS<...> > > > >
```

The generator performs three steps.

1. Parsing the configuration description by reading out the nested DSL features
2. Assigning defaults to the unspecified DSL features and checking for invalid features and feature combinations
3. Assembling the matrix implementation components according to the DSL features

These steps are shown in Figure 14-10. Each step is performed by a template metafunction. The result of the parsing metafunction `MATRIX_DSL_PARSER<>` is a set of DSL parameters (see Figure 14-9) containing the values specified in the matrix specification. The unspecified parameters have the value `whatever`. The next metafunction, that is, `MATRIX_DSL_ASSIGN_DEFAULTS<>`, computes the default values for the unspecified parameters, so that every parameter has a concrete value. The parameters passed between the metafunctions are encoded as member types of the traits class `DSLFeatures`. We refer to the `DSLFeatures` as the "flat" configuration of a matrix because it completely describes a matrix type.

NOTE

`MATRIX_ASSEMBLE_COMPONENTS` is the Generator parameter of `Dyn2DCContainer`. It contains `Config` as its member type.

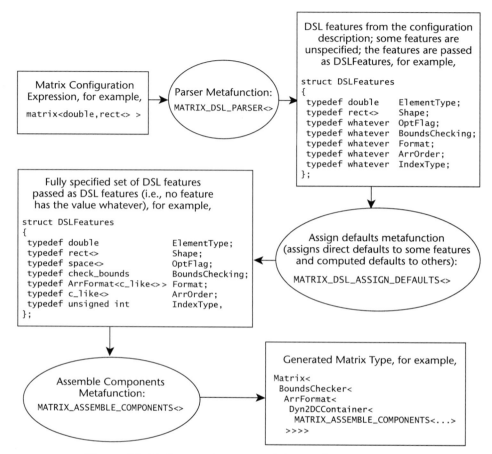

Figure 14-10 Processing steps of the configuration generator

The generator itself is a metafunction that takes two parameters: the matrix configuration description and a flag specifying what to do. The latter has the following purpose: It allows us to be able to pass not only a configuration DSL expression to the generator, but also DSLFeatures containing some unspecified features and DSLFeatures with all features specified. In other words, if you take a look at Figure 14-10, we want to be able to enter the generation process just before any of the three processing steps. The reason for this is that we will sometimes already have DSLFeatures and just need to generate the corresponding matrix type, which will be the case in the matrix expression generator shown in Section 14.4.2.

Therefore, we first need to define the flags: `do_all`, `defaults_and_assemble`, and `assemble_components`. They have the following meanings.

- ◆ `do_all`: Do parsing, assigning defaults, and component assembly; the generator expects a configuration DSL expression.
- ◆ `defaults_and_assemble`: Do assigning defaults and component assembly; the generator expects `DSLFeatures` whose features do not have to be fully specified.
- ◆ `assemble_components`: Do component assembly; the generator expects `DSLFeatures` whose features have to be fully specified.

We implement the flags as integer constants:

Matrix Generator.h

```
enum {
    do_all,
    defaults_and_assemble,
    assemble_components
};
```

Now we can implement our configuration generator. As indicated in Figure 14-10, the generator delegates all the work to three other metafunctions, each of which defines one processing step:

```
MATRIX_DSL_PARSER<>
MATRIX_DSL_ASSIGN_DEFAULTS<>
MATRIX_ASSEMBLE_COMPONENTS<>
```

The generator returns (in its public section) the generated matrix type (as `RET`). The computation in the generator involves reading the "what-to-do" flag and calling the appropriate metafunctions:[3]

```
template< class InputDSL = matrix<>, int WhatToDo =  do_all >
class MATRIX_GENERATOR
{
    // parse InputDSL (or dummy)
    typedef SWITCH< WhatToDo                      //dummy spec
          , CASE< assemble_components,    matrix<>
                                          // dummy spec
          , CASE< defaults_and_assemble,  matrix<>
```

---

3. This solution using a metaswitch was suggested by Johannes Knaupp.

```
                  , DEFAULT<                          InputDSL
                  > > > >::RET DSL_Description;
          typedef MATRIX_DSL_PARSER< DSL_Description >::RET ParsedDSL__;
```

Please note that we have to use the two dummy matrix specifications because `MATRIX_DSL_ASSIGN_DEFAULTS<>` will be "executed" in all cases, and we need to pass it a matrix specification even if the result for the two first cases won't be used. We code the two remaining steps in a similar way:

```
// assign defaults to DSL (or to dummy)
typedef SWITCH< WhatToDo                          // dummy
          , CASE< assemble_components,    ParsedDSL__
          , CASE< defaults_and_assemble,  InputDSL
          , DEFAULT<                       ParsedDSL__
          > > > >::RET ParsedDSL_;
typedef MATRIX_DSL_ASSIGN_DEFAULTS< ParsedDSL_ >::RET
                                                CompleteDSL__;


// convert DSL to ICCL
typedef SWITCH< WhatToDo
          , CASE< assemble_components,    InputDSL
          , CASE< defaults_and_assemble,  CompleteDSL__
          , DEFAULT<                       CompleteDSL__
          > > > >::RET CompleteDSL_;
typedef MATRIX_ASSEMBLE_COMPONENTS< CompleteDSL_ > Result;
```

Finally, we have our public return:

```
public:
    typedef Result::RET     RET;
};
```

The following three sections describe the metafunctions that implement the three generation steps.

14.4.1.3.1   Configuration DSL Parser

The configuration DSL parser `MATRIX_DSL_PARSER<>` takes a matrix specification and produces `DSLFeatures` containing the values of the features explicitly specified in the configuration expression (the unspecified features have the value `whatever`; see Figure 14-10).

Before we show you the parser code, we need a small helper metafunction for testing whether a DSL feature is unspecified or not:

DSLParser.h

```
using namespace MatrixDSL;

template<class TYPE> struct IsUnspecifiedDSLFeature
{ enum { RET=0 }; };
template<> struct IsUnspecifiedDSLFeature<whatever>
{ enum { RET=1 }; };
```

The parser retrieves all the DSLFeatures features from the matrix configuration (i.e., its parameter DSLDescription) one at a time and returns the computed DSLFeatures:

```
template<class DSLDescription>
class MATRIX_DSL_PARSER
{private
    //ElementType
    typedef typename DSLDescription::elementType ElementType_;

    //Shape
    typedef typename DSLDescription::shape Shape_;

    //OptFlag
    typedef typename DSLDescription::optFlag OptFlag_;

    //BoundsChecking
    typedef typename DSLDescription::boundsChecking
                     BoundsChecking_;

    //Format
    typedef typename DSLDescription::format Format_;
```

The retrieval code for ArrOrder_ looks slightly different because this feature is only nested in one value of Format_, namely array<>. Thus, we first have to check to see if the value of Format_ is array<...>, in which case we return the actual value of Format_, and otherwise we simply return array<>. Then we retrieve arr_order from the previous result (of course, the value ArrOrder_ is only significant if Feature_ points to array<...>):

```
    //ArrOrder
    typedef IF<EQUAL<Format_::id, Format_::array_id>::RET,
               Format_,
```

```
                              array<> >::RET ArrayFormat_;
             typedef typename ArrayFormat_::arr_order ArrOrder_;


             //IndexType
             typedef typename DSLDescription::indexType IndexType_;
```

Finally, we define DSLFeatures with all the DSL parameters as its member types and return it:

```
public:
    struct DSLFeatures
    {   typedef ElementType_     ElementType;
        typedef Shape_           Shape;
        typedef OptFlag_         OptFlag;
        typedef BoundsChecking_  BoundsChecking;
        typedef Format_          Format;
        typedef ArrOrder_        ArrOrder;
        typedef IndexType_       IndexType;
    };


    typedef DSLFeatures RET;
};
```

14.4.1.3.2 Assigning Defaults to DSL Features

The second step of matrix generation is to assign default values to the unspecified features in DSLFeatures returned by the parser (see Figure 14-10) and to check for illegal features and feature combinations. Some unspecified features are assigned direct default values, and some default values need to be computed. We first need to specify the direct and the computed defaults for our matrix configuration DSL.

Dependency tables

The direct defaults are listed in Table 14-3. The only computed default is Format and the computation formula is given in Table 14-4, which is a *dependency table*. We use such tables to specify dependencies between parameters. Each table column, as indicated in the head row, corresponds to a parameter, and the cells below contain parameter values. The columns to the left of the double dividing line correspond to input parameters and those to the right represent output parameters. Dependency tables are interpreted in a top-down fashion: You go into the table with the actual values of the input parameters and match them with one row after another starting with the top one until you get a match. If you get a match, you stop and read the corresponding values of the output parameters. If you don't get a match, the result is undefined. An "*" matches any value. Table 14-4 has two input parameters, namely Shape and Opt-Flag, and one output parameter, which is Format, that is, the default value of Format depends on the values of Shape and OptFlag. As you can see, we only use vector for triangular and symmetric matrices if the optimization flag is set to space. As you may remember, storing such matrices in a vector saves memory, but storing them directly in an array results in faster element access.

There is one more detail we have to specify: It is illegal to set Shape to rect and Format to vector simultaneously. This combination does not seem to be useful, and we choose to forbid it explicitly. This is specified in Table 14-5.

Given the previous specifications, we can move to the C++ implementation. First, we implement the table with the direct feature defaults (i.e., Table 14-3) in a struct. This way we have all the direct defaults in one place, which is good for maintenance reasons:

Table 14-3 Direct Feature Defaults for the Matrix DSL

ElementType	:	double
Shape	:	rect
BoundsChecking	:	checkBounds
OptFlag	:	space
ArrayOrder	:	cLike
IndexType	:	unsigned int

Table 14-4 Computing Default Value for Format

Shape	OptFlag	Format
rect	*	array
lowerTriang upperTriang symm	speed	array
	space	vector

Table 14-5 Illegal Feature Combination

Shape	Format
rect	vector

```
using namespace MatrixDSL;

//DSLFeatureDefaults implements Table 14-3 (i.e. direct feature
//defaults)
struct DSLFeatureDefaults
{    typedef double                ElementType;
     typedef rect<>                Shape;
     typedef space<>               OptFlag;
     typedef check_bounds<>        BoundsChecking;
     typedef c_like<>              ArrOrder;
     typedef unsigned int          IndexType;
};
```

The metafunction for assigning feature defaults does more than just assign defaults: It also checks to make sure that the specified feature values are correct and that the feature combinations are correct. Thus, for example, if we specified the shape of a matrix as speed<>, this would be the place to catch this error.

The implementation of error checking is a bit tricky. A major deficiency of template metaprogramming is that we do not have any means to report a string to the programmer during compilation. In our code, we use the following partial solution to this problem (which you already saw in the previous chapter): If we want to report an error, we access the nonexistent member SOME_MEMBER of some type SOME_TYPE, which, of course, causes the compiler to issue a compilation error that says something like: "'SOME_MEMBER' is not a member of 'SOME_TYPE'". Now, the idea is to give the name of the kind of error we want to report to SOME_TYPE and to encode the error text in the name of SOME_MEMBER. Here is the implementation of "SOME_TYPE", which, in our case, we call DSL_FEATURE_ERROR:

```
struct DSL_FEATURE_ERROR {};
```

DSL_FEATURE_ERROR is usually returned by an IF checking for an error condition. Thus, we also need some type to return if there is no error:

```
struct DSL_FEATURE_OK
{    typedef DSL_FEATURE_OK WRONG_SHAPE;
     typedef DSL_FEATURE_OK WRONG_FORMAT_OR_FORMAT_SHAPE_COMBINATION;
     typedef DSL_FEATURE_OK WRONG_ARR_ORDER;
     typedef DSL_FEATURE_OK WRONG_OPT_FLAG;
```

```
        typedef DSL_FEATURE_OK WRONG_BOUNDS_CHECKING;
};
```

DSL_FEATURE_OK encodes error strings as member type names. Only the member type names are relevant, but not the type they point to (we just let them point to DSL_FEATURE_OK itself).

Now, for each DSL parameter, we implement a checking metafunction that checks to see if the value of the parameter is one of the valid values according to the DSL grammar (see Figure 14-9):

```
template<class Shape>
struct CheckShape
{   typedef typename
            IF< EQUAL<Shape::id, Shape::rect_id>::RET ||
                EQUAL<Shape::id, Shape::lower_triang_id>::RET ||
                EQUAL<Shape::id, Shape::upper_triang_id>::RET ||
                EQUAL<Shape::id, Shape::symm_id>::RET,
                    DSL_FEATURE_OK,
                    DSL_FEATURE_ERROR>::RET::WRONG_SHAPE RET;
};
```

Thus, if Shape is not rect<>, lower_triang<>, upper_triang<>, or symm<>, IF will return DSL_FEATURE_ERROR and the subsequent access to WRONG_SHAPE of DSL_FEATURE_ERROR will result in a compile-time error. Otherwise, IF will return DSL_FEATURE_OK, which defines WRONG_SHAPE as its member, and this will compile successfully.

In practice, our error reporting approach has this effect: If we try to compile the following line with VC++ 6.0:

```
typedef MATRIX_GENERATOR<matrix<double, speed<> > >::RET MyMatrixType;
```

the compiler will issue this error report:

```
error C2039: 'WRONG_SHAPE' : is not a member of 'DSL_FEATURE_ERROR'
```

This error indicates that the second parameter passed to matrix<> is not a valid shape value. Unfortunately, the compiler will not tell us the source line where we used the wrong parameter value but rather the line where the erroneous member access occurred, which is somewhere within the library implementation.

Checking Format is a bit more complex because we need to implement Table 14-5. This table states that we don't want to allow a rectangular matrix to be stored in a vector. Thus, the checking metafunction takes Format and Shape as parameters:

```
template<class Format, class Shape>
struct CheckFormatAndFormatShapeCombination
{    typedef typename
            IF<(EQUAL<Shape::id, Shape::rect_id>::RET &&
                    EQUAL<Format::id, Format::array_id>::RET) ||

                ((EQUAL<Shape::id, Shape::lower_triang_id>::RET ||
                  EQUAL<Shape::id, Shape::upper_triang_id>::RET ||
                  EQUAL<Shape::id, Shape::symm_id>::RET) &&
                      (EQUAL<Format::id, Format::vector_id>::RET ||
                       EQUAL<Format::id, Format::array_id>::RET)),

                DSL_FEATURE_OK,
                DSL_FEATURE_ERROR
            >::RET::WRONG_FORMAT_OR_FORMAT_SHAPE_COMBINATION RET;
};
```

The metafunctions for checking the remaining three DSL parameters ArrOrder, OptFlag, and BoundsChecking are similar to CheckShape shown previously.

We do not implement checking for element type and index type. The reason is that we do not want to unnecessarily limit the number of types that can be used in their place. This is particularly true of element type because we also would like to be able to create matrices of user-defined types. If you want to use such matrices in expressions, the element types will have to provide numeric operators, such as +, *, -, +=, and so on.

Finally, we are ready to implement our metafunction for assigning defaults:

```
template<class ParsedDSLDescription>
class MATRIX_DSL_ASSIGN_DEFAULTS
{    typedef ParsedDSLDescription ParsedDSL;

    //ElementType
    typedef IF<IsUnspecifiedDSLFeature<typename
                ParsedDSL::ElementType>::RET,
            DSLFeatureDefaults::ElementType,
            typename ParsedDSL::ElementType>::RET ElementType_;
```

If ElementType is unspecified, the previous code assigns it a direct default from Table 14-3. We do the same for Shape, OptFlag, and BoundsChecking:

```
    //Shape
    typedef IF<IsUnspecifiedDSLFeature<typename
```

```
                    ParsedDSL::Shape>::RET,
                DSLFeatureDefaults::Shape,
                    typename ParsedDSL::Shape>::RET Shape_;
typedef CheckShape<Shape_>::RET check_shape_;
```

The last typedef calls the checking metafunction for Shape. We call a checking metafunction after assigning a default value.

```
//OptFlag
typedef IF<IsUnspecifiedDSLFeature<typename
                ParsedDSL::OptFlag>::RET,
            DSLFeatureDefaults::OptFlag,
                typename ParsedDSL::OptFlag>::RET OptFlag_;
typedef CheckOptFlag<OptFlag_>::RET check_opt_flag_;

//BoundsChecking
typedef IF<IsUnspecifiedDSLFeature<typename
                ParsedDSL::BoundsChecking>::RET,
            DSLFeatureDefaults::BoundsChecking,
                typename ParsedDSL::BoundsChecking>::RET
        BoundsChecking_;
typedef CheckBoundsChecking<BoundsChecking_>::RET
        check_bounds_checking_;
```

Format is a special case because it does not have a direct default value. Its default value is determined based on Shape and OptFlag as specified in Table 14-4:

```
//Format
typedef
    IF< (EQUAL<Shape_::id, Shape_::lower_triang_id>::RET ||
        EQUAL<Shape_::id, Shape_::upper_triang_id>::RET ||
        EQUAL<Shape_::id, Shape_::symm_id>::RET) &&
            EQUAL<OptFlag_::id, OptFlag_::space_id>::RET,

            vector<>,
            array<> >::RET ComputedFormat_;

typedef IF<IsUnspecifiedDSLFeature<typename
                ParsedDSL::Format>::RET,
            ComputedFormat_,
                typename ParsedDSL::Format>::RET Format_;
```

Next, we need to check the format-shape combination (see Table 14-5) and process `ArrayOrder` and `IndexType`:

```
typedef CheckFormatAndFormatShapeCombination<Format_,
            Shape_>::RET
        check_format_and_format_shape_combination_;


//ArrOrder
typedef IF<IsUnspecifiedDSLFeature<typename
            ParsedDSL::ArrOrder>::RET,
        DSLFeatureDefaults::ArrOrder,
        typename ParsedDSL::ArrOrder>::RET ArrOrder_;
            typedef CheckArrOrder<ArrOrder_>::RET
            check_arr_order_;


//IndexType
typedef IF<IsUnspecifiedDSLFeature<typename
            ParsedDSL::IndexType>::RET,
        DSLFeatureDefaults::IndexType,
        typename ParsedDSL::IndexType>::RET IndexType_;
```

Finally, we return the `DSLFeatures` containing all the DSL parameters:

```
public:
    struct DSLFeatures
    {   typedef ElementType_      ElementType;
        typedef Shape_            Shape;
        typedef Format_           Format;
        typedef BoundsChecking_   BoundsChecking;
        typedef ArrOrder_         ArrOrder;
        typedef OptFlag_          OptFlag;
        typedef IndexType_        IndexType;
    };

    typedef DSLFeatures RET;
};
```

14.4.1.3.3 Matrix Component Assembler

The final step of matrix type generation is to assemble the matrix implementation components according to the fully specified DSL features (i.e., `DSLFeatures`) produced in the earlier stages (see Figure 14-10).

First, we need to specify how to compute the ICCL parameters from the DSL parameters. According to the ICCL grammar in Figure 14-7, we have the following ICCL parameters with more than one alternative value:

```
Array
Format
OptSymmetricMatrix
OptBoundsCheckedMatrix
```

Table 14-6 through Table 14-9 specify how to compute these parameters based on the DSL features. Because some ICCL and DSL parameters have the same name, we will explicitly indicate which one we mean, for example, Format (DSL) or Format (ICCL). Furthermore, an equal sign in a table indicates that we specify a value using another parameter.

Table 14-6 Table for Computing the ICCL Parameter Array

ArrOrder	Array
cLike	Dyn2DCContainer
fortranLike	Dyn2DFContainer

Table 14-7 Table for Computing the ICCL Parameter Format

Shape	Format (DSL)	Format (ICCL)
lowerTriangular symmetric	vector	LoTriangVecFormat
upperTriangular	vector	UpTriangVecFormat
*	*	ArrFormat

Table 14-8 Table for Computing the ICCL Parameter OptSymmetricMatrix

Shape	OptSymmetricMatrix
symm	Symm
*	= Format (ICCL)

Table 14-9 Table for Computing the ICCL Parameter
OptBoundsCheckedMatrix

BoundsChecking	OptBoundsCheckedMatrix
checkBounds	BoundsChecker
noBoundsChecking	= OptSymmetricMatrix

According to the ICCL grammar, the value of Vector is Dyn1DContainer[Config]. Finally, the types provided by the configuration repository (i.e., Config, see Figure 14-7) are determined using Table 14-10 and Table 14-11.

Here is the metafunction for assembling components:

Assemble Components.h

```
using namespace MatrixDSL;
using namespace MatrixICCL;

template<class CompleteDSLDescription>
class MATRIX_ASSEMBLE_COMPONENTS
{   //short names
    typedef MATRIX_ASSEMBLE_COMPONENTS<CompleteDSLDescription>
            Generator;
    typedef CompleteDSLDescription DSLFeatures;
```

Each of the following typedefs implements one ICCL parameter (we cite the corresponding specification tables in the comments):

Table 14-10 Table for Computing the ICCL Parameters
ElementType **and** IndexType

ElementType (ICCL)	=	ElementType (DSL)
IndexType (ICCL)	=	IndexType (DSL)

Table 14-11 Table for Computing the ICCL Parameter
CommaInitializer

ArrOrder	CommaInitializer
cLike	DenseCCommaInitializer
fortranLike	DenseFCommaInitializer

```
//ElementType (see Table 14-10)
typedef typename DSLFeatures::ElementType ElementType_;

//IndexType (see Table 14-10)
typedef typename DSLFeatures::IndexType IndexType_;

//Vector (see Figure 14-7)
typedef Dyn1DContainer<Generator> Vector;

//Array (see Table 14-6)
typedef IF<EQUAL<DSLFeatures::ArrOrder::id,
                 DSLFeatures::ArrOrder::c_like_id>::RET,
           Dyn2DCContainer<Generator>,
           Dyn2DFContainer<Generator> >::RET Array;
```

Please note that we passed `Generator` to the basic containers in the previous `typedefs` for `Vector` and `Array`.

The dependency table for computing `Format` (see Table 14-7) is a bit more complex. This gives us the opportunity to demonstrate a more intentional encoding of dependency tables than just nested `IF`s. We will encode the `Format` table using the new metafunction `EVAL_DEPENDENCY_TABLE<>`, which is specially designed for encoding dependency tables. This metafunction takes two parameters: a list of input parameters representing the table head row and a list of rows representing the table body. Each body row is a list of input and output parameter values, as in a dependency table. Lists are represented as nested templates.

The metafunction implements the semantics of a dependency table, that is, it searches for a matching row in a top-down direction. If a matching row is found, the corresponding output parameter value is returned; otherwise, you get a compile-time error. Let's take a look at a simple example. Here is a dependency table we would like to encode:

p1	p2	result
4	3	Foo1
1	5	Foo2
1	2	Foo3
2	3	Foo4

And here is the encoding using `EVAL_DEPENDENCY_TABLE<>`:

```
enum { p1 = 1, p2 = 2 };

typedef EVAL_DEPENDENCY_TABLE
        // head row *********************************
        <       CELL< p1,  CELL< p2                  > >
        //***********************************************
        , ROW< CELL< 4,     CELL< 3,    RET< Foo1  > > >
        , ROW< CELL< 1,     CELL< 5,    RET< Foo2  > > >
        , ROW< CELL< 1,     CELL< 2,    RET< Foo3  > > >
        , ROW< CELL< 2,     CELL< 3,    RET< Foo4  > > >
        //***********************************************
        > > > >  >::RET result;       // result is Foo3
```

The head row has two input parameters, p1 and p2. Then there are four body rows with one output value per row (enclosed in RET<>). Because the head row matches the third body row, the result of evaluating the table is Foo3. The implementation of EVAL_DEPENDENCY_TABLE<> is given in Appendix E.

Before we can conveniently encode the Format table, we need to define short names for all the needed parameters and values:

```
enum
{   shapeID       = DSLFeatures::Shape::id,
    lowerTriang   = DSLFeatures::Shape::lower_triang_id,
    symmetric     = DSLFeatures::Shape::symm_id,
    upperTriang   = DSLFeatures::Shape::upper_triang_id,

    formatID      = DSLFeatures::Format::id,
    vector        = DSLFeatures::Format::vector_id
};
```

And here is the encoding of Table 14-7 using EVAL_DEPENDENCY_TABLE<> ("*" is represented using anyValue):

```
//**********************************************************************************
  typedef EVAL_DEPENDENCY_TABLE              //Format (see Table 14-7)
//**********************************************************************************
<       CELL< shapeID,   CELL< formatID                                  > >
//**********************************************************************************
, ROW< CELL< lowerTriang, CELL< vector,  RET< LoTriangVecFormat<Vector> > > >
, ROW< CELL< symmetric,   CELL< vector,  RET< LoTriangVecFormat<Vector> > > >
, ROW< CELL< upperTriang, CELL< vector,  RET< UpTriangVecFormat<Vector> > > >
, ROW< CELL< anyValue,    CELL< anyValue,RET< ArrFormat<Array>          > > >
//**********************************************************************************
> > > > >::RET Format;
```

Here are the remaining ICCL parameters:

```
//OptSymmetricMatrix (see Table 14-8)
typedef IF<EQUAL<DSLFeatures::Shape::id,
                 DSLFeatures::Shape::symm_id>::RET,
           Symm<Format>,
           Format>::RET OptSymmetricMatrix;

//OptBoundsCheckedMatrix (see Table 14-9)
typedef IF<EQUAL<DSLFeatures::BoundsChecking::id,
                 DSLFeatures::BoundsChecking::check_bounds_id>::RET,
           BoundsChecker<OptSymmetricMatrix>,
           OptSymmetricMatrix>::RET OptBoundsCheckedMatrix;

//MatrixType;
typedef Matrix<OptBoundsCheckedMatrix> MatrixType_;

//CommaInitializer (see Table 14-11)
typedef IF<EQUAL<DSLFeatures::ArrOrder::id,
                 DSLFeatures::ArrOrder::c_like_id>::RET,
           DenseCCommaInitializer<Generator>,
           DenseFCommaInitializer<Generator>
          >::RET CommaInitializer_;
```

Finally, we need to create Config and return the generated matrix type:

```
public:
    struct Config
    {   //DSL features
        typedef CompleteDSLDescription DSLFeatures;

        //ICCL features
        typedef ElementType_ ElementType;
        typedef IndexType_ IndexType;

        //MatrixType
        typedef MatrixType_ MatrixType;
        typedef CommaInitializer_ CommaInitializer;
    };

    typedef MatrixType_ RET; //here is our generated matrix type!!!
};
```

14.4.2 Generating Code for Matrix Expressions

In this section, we will develop a generator for matrix expressions. Its purpose is to allow the library user to write matrix expressions in a natural way, for example, A+B+C*D, and have the compiler generate efficient code for it. Before we take a look at how to implement the generator, we need to figure out what it means to evaluate matrix expressions in an efficient way, that is, what kinds of domain-specific optimizations our generator should perform.

14.4.2.1 Evaluating Matrix Expressions

Let's assume that A, B, C, D, and E are matrices, and that they have compatible sizes and types to be used in the following assignment statement:

```
E = (A + B) * (C + D);
```

There are two principal ways to compute this assignment [Neu98].

1. Expression evaluation with temporaries:

```
temp1 = A + B;
temp2 = C + D;
temp3 = temp1 * temp2;
E     = temp3;
```

2. Elementwise expression evaluation (i.e., without temporaries):

$$e_{11} = (a_{11} + b_{11}) * (c_{11} + d_{11}) +$$
$$(a_{12} + b_{12}) * (c_{21} + d_{21}) +$$
$$\vdots$$
$$\vdots$$
$$e_{21} = \ldots$$
$$\vdots$$
$$\vdots$$
$$e_{mn} = \ldots$$

Each of these approaches has its advantages and disadvantages. The first approach is simple to implement using overloaded binary operators. Unfortunately, the initialization of temporaries, the separate loops needed for each binary operation, and the final assignment cause a significant overhead. This kind of naive implementation using binary operator overloading has already prompted some people to say that "object-oriented programming" would be inappropriate for high-performance scientific computing.

The second (i.e., elementwise) approach is particularly useful if we want to compute only some elements of a matrix expression (remember that the first approach computes all elements of each subexpression). Furthermore, it is also superior if the elements of the argument matrices or subexpressions are accessed only once during the whole computation. This is the case for expressions or subexpressions consisting of matrix additions only. In this case, the elementwise approach is very efficient: We use two nested loops to iterate over the nonzero region of the resulting matrix, and in each iteration the current element of the resulting matrix is assigned the sum of the corresponding elements from all the argument matrices. Thus, we don't need any temporaries or extra loops as in the first approach.[4] For example, the expression A+B+C can be computed as follows:

```
for(i=0; i< m; ++i)
    for(j=0; j<n; ++j)
        E(i,j) = A(i,j) + B(i,j) +C(i,j);
```

Unfortunately, the elementwise approach is inefficient for matrix multiplication because matrix multiplication accesses the elements of the argument matrices more than once, which is illustrated in Figure 14-11.

In our example, the elementwise computation of multiplication requires that each element of the argument matrices be accessed three times. If the argument matrices are actually matrix expressions, their elements will be computed three times, which is very inefficient. We can address this problem in two ways.

◆ *Elementwise evaluation for addition, evaluation with temporaries for multiplication:* Whenever one of the arguments to a

$$\begin{bmatrix} a_{11} & a_{12} \\ a_{21} & a_{22} \\ a_{31} & a_{32} \end{bmatrix} \bullet \begin{bmatrix} b_{11} & b_{12} & b_{13} \\ b_{21} & b_{22} & b_{23} \end{bmatrix} = \begin{bmatrix} a_{11}b_{11} + a_{12}b_{21} & a_{11}b_{12} + a_{12}b_{22} & a_{11}b_{13} + a_{12}b_{23} \\ a_{21}b_{11} + a_{22}b_{21} & a_{21}b_{12} + a_{22}b_{22} & a_{21}b_{13} + a_{22}b_{23} \\ a_{31}b_{11} + a_{32}b_{21} & a_{31}b_{12} + a_{32}b_{22} & a_{31}b_{13} + a_{32}b_{23} \end{bmatrix}$$

Figure 14-11 *Elementwise computation of the multiplication of two sample matrices*

---

4. That's why we say that this approach involves elimination of temporaries and loop fusing.

NOTE

There are also significant differences between the two approaches. Compared to the first one, the second approach has the caching overhead (i.e., it stores the computed element on the first access and does the extra check whether the element has been already computed or not on each access). The effect of this overhead depends on many factors, such as element type (i.e., precision, real or complex), number of operations per access, and access time for the storage formats used. On the other hand, the element-wise with cache approach is superior if we only want to compute some but not all of the expression elements. For example, if we are only interested in elements (1,1), (1,2), and (1,3) of the result matrix in Figure 14-11 and the argument matrices are actually expressions, the elementwise with cache approach is likely to be faster than using temporaries for multiplication.

---

matrix multiplication is an expression, we create a temporary matrix and assign the expression to it. We use the elementwise approach for matrix addition only.

◆ *Elementwise expression evaluation with cache:* Instead of creating temporaries for the argument expressions to matrix multiplication, we create cache matrices. This way the argument expression elements will be computed on first access only. In effect, we use an elementwise approach for both addition and multiplication and avoid recomputing elements of subexpressions by storing them in a cache.

Both approaches avoid the creation of temporaries for assignment (e.g., temp3 in our original example) and for expression arguments to matrix addition.

Because our generator will use the elementwise with cache approach, let's take a look at how to model it with objects.

14.4.2.2 Modeling the Elementwise Expression Evaluation Using Objects

We can represent a matrix expression as a syntax tree with nodes being matrix or expression objects. For example, the object tree representing the expression A+B+C, which is equivalent to (A+B)+C, is shown in Figure 14-12. A, B, and C are instances of Matrix, and the two addition subexpressions are instances of AdditionExpression.

We can implement the elementwise expression evaluation by not only having Matrix provide the method getElement(i,j), but

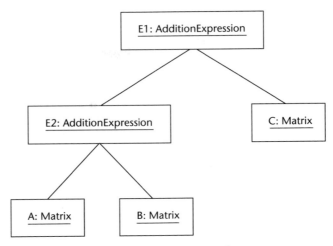

Figure 14-12 *UML object diagram representing the expression* (A+B)+C

also the expression objects. The UML collaboration diagram in Figure 14-13 shows how AdditionExpression::getElement() works.

If the calls to getElement() are statically bound and we use inlining, the code generated for (A+B+C).getElement(i,j) looks like this:

```
A.getElement(i,j) + B.getElement(i,j) + C.getElement(i,j)
```

Now, assume that we want to assign our expression A+B+C to matrix D:

```
D=A+B+C
```

This scenario is illustrated in Figure 14-14. We send the message "=" to D with E1 (which represents A+B+C) as its parameter. The assignment code (shown in the note) iterates through all elements of D and assigns each of them the value computed by sending getElement() to E1.

If we use inlining, the code generated for D=A+B+C will look like this:

```
for i=0...m-1
   for j=0...n-1
      D.setElement(A.getElement(i,j) +
                   B.getElement(i,j) +
                   C.getElement(i,j));
```

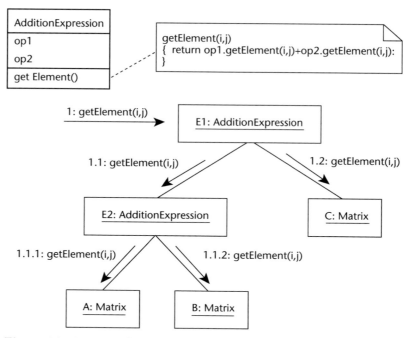

Figure 14-13 *UML diagrams illustrating the execution of*
`((A+B)+C).getElement(i,j)`

This is as efficient as we can get for general matrices.

Figure 14-15 shows us how `getElement(i,j)` works in an expression containing matrix multiplication. The second operand of the multiplication expression is an addition expression. Because the elements of a multiplication operand are accessed several times, we need a `MatrixCache` between the multiplication expression and the operand expression. `getElement(i,j)` of `MatrixCache` checks to see if the element has already been computed. If yes (i.e., we have a cache hit), the value stored in the cache matrix is returned. If not, the value is requested from the cached expression, then stored in the cache matrix, and finally returned.

The sample codes for `getElement()` and the assignment operation shown previously do not assume any special shape of the argument matrices. However, if the arguments have some special shape, we can usually design a faster implementation for both methods. For example, if the left operand of a matrix multiplication expression has a diagonal shape, `MultiplicationExpression` can use the following implementation of `getElement()`:

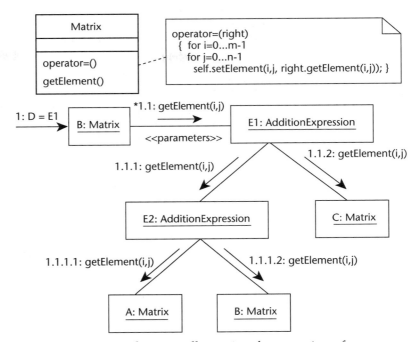

Figure 14-14 UML *diagrams illustrating the execution of* D=A+B+C

```
getElement(i,j)
{    result = op1.getElement(i,i) * op2.getElement(i,j;)
     return result;   }
```

This code is much simpler than the one in Figure 14-15. First, we don't need a loop. Second, because computing all elements of such a multiplication expression requires accessing the elements of the operands only once, we don't need a MatrixCache for operand expressions.

Similarly, if the resulting shape of an expression is smaller than rectangular (e.g., triangular or diagonal), we only need to iterate over the nonzero region of the expression when assigning it to another matrix. In general, we can implement assignment by initializing the target matrix and iterating over the nonzero part of the expression and assigning the computed elements to the corresponding elements of the matrix.

Expression templates

Now, let's summarize the steps a generator for matrix expressions will have to perform. The generator gets an expression as an input and first needs to create an expression tree of the form

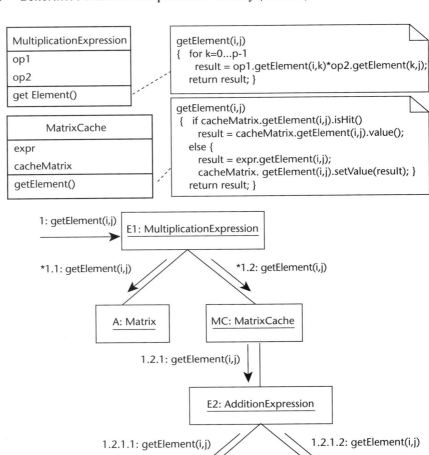

Figure 14-15 *UML diagrams illustrating the execution of* A*(B+C)

described previously. The tree will contain the matrix objects, expression objects for each operator, and, whenever necessary, matrix caches. The expression tree will be constructed using so-called *expression templates* [Vel95b]. The idea is that when you write A+B+C, the resulting object is not a matrix, but the expression tree. You can get this effect by appropriately implementing the operators +, −, and * to return expression objects. The evaluation of the expression will take place when you assign the expression tree to a matrix, for example, D=A+B+C. We illustrated this idea in

Figure 14-14. The second step is to select an appropriate implementation of `getElement()` for `AdditionExpression` and `MultiplicationExpression` based on the shape (and density) of the operands. This is done using template metafunctions. Finally, another template metafunction will select an appropriate implementation of the assignment operator depending on the shape (and density) of the source expression.

14.4.2.3 Overview of the Implementation

The C++ implementation of the generator for matrix expressions consists of six parts.

1. *Matrix operator templates:* These are the operator templates that implement +, –, and * for matrices. They are responsible for creating the expression tree.
2. *Matrix expression templates:* These class templates represent addition, subtraction, and multiplication expressions. Their instances are used as nodes in the expression tree.
3. *Matrix cache:* Matrix cache is used to wrap operand expressions for matrix multiplication.
4. *Generating* `getElement()` *for expressions:* `getElement()` returns one element of a matrix expression. There will be different implementations for different shape combinations of the expression's operands. The appropriate implementation will automatically be selected by a template metafunction.
5. *Metafunctions for computing result types of expressions:* Metafunctions give us the ability to compute the resulting matrix type of an expression, that is, the matrix properties of an expression, such as element type, shape, format, and so on. These properties are computed from the properties of the expression's operands. Different kinds of expressions will use different computation formulas. (We need the matrix type of an expression in order to select an appropriate implementation of `getElement()` in the parent expression or an appropriate implementation of the assignment operator. Furthermore, we also need it to generate a `MatrixCache` of the appropriate type.)
6. *Generating assignment functions for assigning expressions and matrices to matrices:* There will be different implementations of the assignment functions for different shapes of the source matrix or expression, and the appropriate implementation will be selected using a template metafunction.

We describe each of these parts in the following sections. We only consider matrix addition and multiplication because matrix subtraction is similar to matrix addition.

14.4.2.4 Matrix Operator Templates

The main idea behind expression templates is the following: If you add two matrices, such as A+B, you do not return the result matrix, but instead, an object representing the addition expression. If you have a more complicated expression, such as A*(B+C), you return a nested expression object (see Figure 14-15). This is done as follows: The plus operator is executed first, which returns a matrix addition expression. Then, the multiplication operator is executed, which returns a multiplication expression pointing to A and the addition expression (possibly wrapped into a matrix cache) as its operands.

Because we implement the operators + and * using overloaded operator templates, we will know the complete type of a complex expression at compile time. The expression type describes the structure of the expression, and we can pass it to metafunctions to analyze its structure and generate optimized code for its methods. Furthermore, we can even transform the structure of the expression before evaluating it. For example, the assignment operator for assigning an expression to a matrix can look like this:

```
Matrix& Matrix::operator=(const Expression<Expr>& expr)
{
    TRANSFORM_EXPRESSION< Expression<Expr> >::RET
                                    transformed_expr(expr);
    transformed_expr.assign(this);
    return *this;
}
```

In this example, TRANSFORM_EXPRESSION<> represents a template metafunction that takes a concrete expression type and returns a transformed one. This metafunction can analyze the structure of the expression and the properties of the operand matrices and produce a more optimal structure plus optimized methods to evaluate it. The transformed type would be computed at compile time, and the only runtime overhead is to create an instance of the new structure and initialize it with data from the original expression object. The next step is to call assign(), which can actually be generated inline by TRANSFORM_EXPRESSION<> for this particular expression structure. Using these techniques, you can implement arbitrary expression optimizations and structure checking (i.e., you can detect ill-structured expressions at compile time).

Fortunately, we don't need to make things as complicated for our matrix expressions. As explained in Section 14.4.2.2, we don't need to transform the structure of matrix expressions, we only have to generate appropriate `getElement()` and assignment operations based on the shape of operands.

Let's move to the operator templates. We need the following operator implementations.

♦ + for two matrices, for example, A+B
♦ + for a matrix and an addition expression, for example, A+(B+C)
♦ + for an addition expression and a matrix, for example, (A+B)+C
♦ + for two addition expressions, for example, (A+B)+(C+D)

Furthermore, we would need a similar set of four implementations of * and implementations for all the combinations of addition and multiplication expressions, for example, (A+B)*C, (A+B)*(C+D), and so on. The latter leads to a combinatorial explosion. But we can avoid it by wrapping multiplication and addition expressions into binary expressions. In this case, we only need four implementations of + and four implementations of *. Here is the C++ code:

MatrixOper Templates.h

```
/*** Addition **/

//Matrix + Matrix
template <class M1, class M2>
inline BinaryExpression<AdditionExpression<
                         Matrix<M1>,
                         Matrix<M2> > >
operator+(const Matrix<M1>& m1, const Matrix<M2>& m2)
{return BinaryExpression<AdditionExpression<
                         Matrix<M1>,
                         Matrix<M2> > >(m1, m2);
}


//Expression + Matrix
template <class Expr, class M>
inline  BinaryExpression<AdditionExpression<
                         BinaryExpression<Expr>,
                         Matrix<M> > >
operator+(const BinaryExpression<Expr>& expr, const Matrix<M>& m)
{return BinaryExpression<AdditionExpression<
                         BinaryExpression<Expr>,
```

```
                                      Matrix<M> > >(expr, m);
        }


//Matrix + Expression
template <class M, class Expr>
inline  BinaryExpression<AdditionExpression<
                           Matrix<M>,
                           BinaryExpression<Expr> > >
operator+(const Matrix<M>& m, const BinaryExpression<Expr>& expr)
{return BinaryExpression<AdditionExpression<
                           Matrix<M>,
                           BinaryExpression<Expr> > >(m, expr);
}


//Expression + Expression
template <class Expr1, class Expr2>
inline  BinaryExpression<AdditionExpression<
                           BinaryExpression<Expr1>,
                           BinaryExpression<Expr2> > >
operator+(const BinaryExpression<Expr1>& expr1,
          const BinaryExpression<Expr2>& expr2)
{return BinaryExpression<AdditionExpression<
                           BinaryExpression<Expr1>,
                           BinaryExpression<Expr2> > >(expr1,
                                                       expr2);
}


/*** Multiplication **/

//Matrix * Matrix
template <class M1, class M2>
inline BinaryExpression<MultiplicationExpression<
                           Matrix<M1>,
                           Matrix<M2> > >
operator*(const Matrix<M1>& m1, const Matrix<M2>& m2)
{return BinaryExpression<MultiplicationExpression<
                           Matrix<M1>,
                           Matrix<M2> > >(m1, m2);
}


//Expression * Matrix
template <class Expr, class M>
inline  BinaryExpression<MultiplicationExpression<
                           BinaryExpression<Expr>,
                           Matrix<M> > >
```

```
operator*(const BinaryExpression<Expr>& expr, const Matrix<M>& m)
{return BinaryExpression<MultiplicationExpression<
                            BinaryExpression<Expr>,
                            Matrix<M> > >(expr, m);
}

//Matrix * Expression
template <class M, class Expr>
inline  BinaryExpression<MultiplicationExpression<
                            Matrix<M>,
                            BinaryExpression<Expr> > >
operator*(const Matrix<M>& m, const BinaryExpression<Expr>& expr)
{return BinaryExpression<MultiplicationExpression<
                            Matrix<M>,
                            BinaryExpression<Expr> > >(m, expr);
}

//Expression * Expression
template <class Expr1, class Expr2>
inline  BinaryExpression<MultiplicationExpression<
                            BinaryExpression<Expr1>,
                            BinaryExpression<Expr2> > >
operator*(const BinaryExpression<Expr1>& expr1,
          const BinaryExpression<Expr2>& expr2)
{return BinaryExpression<MultiplicationExpression<
                            BinaryExpression<Expr1>,
                            BinaryExpression<Expr2> > >(expr1,
                                                        expr2);
}
```

You can think of the operator templates as a parsing facility. For example, given the matrix expression:

```
(RectMatrix1 + RectMatrix2)*(RectMatrix1 + RectMatrix2)
```

where `RectMatrix1` and `RectMatrix2` are instances of the matrix type

```
Matrix<BoundsChecker<ArrFormat<Dyn2DCContainer<
  MATRIX_ASSEMBLE_COMPONENTS<...> > > > >
```

the C++ compiler will derive the following expression type:

```
BinaryExpression<
  MultiplicationExpression<
    BinaryExpression<
      AdditionExpression<
```

```
        Matrix<BoundsChecker<ArrFormat<Dyn2DCContainer<
          MATRIX_ASSEMBLE_COMPONENTS<...> > > > >,
        Matrix<BoundsChecker<ArrFormat<Dyn2DCContainer<
          MATRIX_ASSEMBLE_COMPONENTS<...> > > > >
      >
    >,
    BinaryExpression<
      AdditionExpression<
        Matrix<BoundsChecker<ArrFormat<Dyn2DCContainer<
          MATRIX_ASSEMBLE_COMPONENTS<...> > > > >,
        Matrix<BoundsChecker<ArrFormat<Dyn2DCContainer<
          MATRIX_ASSEMBLE_COMPONENTS<...> > > > >
      >
    >
  >
>
```

Please note that `MATRIX_ASSEMBLE_COMPONENTS<...>` contains `Config` as its member, that is, the previous expression type encodes not only the expression structure, but also the properties of the operand matrices.

14.4.2.5 Matrix Expression Templates

Matrix expression templates are used to represent the nodes of an expression tree. The class template `AdditionExpression<>` represents the addition of two operands, `MultiplicationExpression<>` represents the multiplication of two operands, and `BinaryExpression<>` is used to wrap the previous two to make them look alike.

We start with the implementation of `AdditionExpression<>`:

MatrixExpr
Templates.h

```
template<class A, class B>
class AdditionExpression
{public:
    typedef A LeftType;
    typedef B RightType;
```

`LeftType` and `RightType` can be either a matrix type or a binary expression type. Next, we need to compute the result matrix type of the expression, that is, the matrix type that would be appropriate for storing the result of evaluating the expression. This is done using the metafunction `ADD_RESULT_TYPE<>`, which we'll discuss in Section 14.4.2.8. We publish the configuration repository of the result type as `Config`. Thus, an addition expression has a `Config` describing its matrix type—just as any matrix type does. Indeed, `ADD_RESULT_TYPE<>` uses the `Config`s of the operands in order to compute the resulting `Config`:

```
typedef typename
  ADD_RESULT_TYPE<LeftType, RightType>::RET::Config
  Config;
```

Next, we retrieve the element and index type for this expression from the `Config`:

```
typedef typename Config::ElementType ElementType;
typedef typename Config::IndexType IndexType;
```

The addition expression needs two variables pointing to its operands:

```
private:
    const LeftType& left_;
    const RightType& right_;
protected:
    const IndexType rows_, cols_;
```

The constructor initializes the instance variables and checks to see if the dimensions of the operands are compatible:

```
public:
    AdditionExpression(const LeftType& m1, const RightType& m2)
        : left_(m1), right_(m2), rows_(m1.rows()), cols_(m1.cols())
    {   if (m1.cols() != m2.cols() || m1.rows() != m2.rows())
            throw "argument matrices are incompatible";
    }
```

The addition expression defines a `getElement()` method for accessing its elements. An element is computed using the expression operands. The code implementing this computation depends on the shape of the operands, and we use the template metafunction `MATRIX_ADD_GET_ELEMENT<>` to select the appropriate implementation (we'll give you the code of the metafunction in Section 14.4.2.7):

```
ElementType getElement( const IndexType& i,
                        const IndexType& j )const
```

```
{   return MATRIX_ADD_GET_ELEMENT<
            LeftType,
            RightType>::RET::getElement(i, j, this,
                                        left_, right_);
}

IndexType rows() const {return rows_;}
IndexType cols() const {return cols_;}
};
```

The beginning of MultiplicationExpression looks similar to AdditionExpression except that we additionally retrieve the left and the right matrix type, which we need to compute operand caches later:

```
template<class A, class B>
class MultiplicationExpression
{public:
    typedef A LeftType;
    typedef B RightType;
    typedef typename LeftType::Config::MatrixType LeftMatrixType;
    typedef typename RightType::Config::MatrixType RightMatrixType;

    typedef MULTIPLY_RESULT_TYPE<LeftType, RightType>::RET::Config
            Config;

    typedef typename Config::ElementType ElementType;
    typedef typename Config::IndexType IndexType;
```

As explained earlier, in the case of matrix multiplication, we need caches for those operands that are expressions. Again, the reason is that matrix multiplication accesses each element of its operands more than once, and by using a cache, we avoid the recalculation of the elements on each access. We compute the type of the caches from the corresponding operand types with a metafunction, which we show in Section 14.4.2.6. Finally, we provide variables for keeping track of the operands and the caches (if any):

```
private:
    typedef CACHE_MATRIX_TYPE<LeftMatrixType>::RET
            LeftCacheMatrixType;
    typedef CACHE_MATRIX_TYPE<RightMatrixType>::RET
            RightCacheMatrixType;
```

```
        const LeftType& left_;
        const RightType& right_;

        LeftCacheMatrixType* left_cache_matrix_;
        RightCacheMatrixType* right_cache_matrix_;

protected:
        const IndexType rows_, cols_;
```

The multiplication expression needs four constructors, each of them for one of the following operand combinations.

- ◆ Both operands are simple matrices.
- ◆ Left operand is a matrix and right operand is an expression.
- ◆ Right operand is an expression and left operand is a matrix.
- ◆ Both operands are expressions.

We start with two matrices. In this case, we don't need any caches:

```
public:
        template<class M1, class M2>
        MultiplicationExpression(const Matrix<M1>& m1,
                                     const Matrix<M2>& m2)
            : left_(m1), right_(m2),
            left_cache_matrix_(0), right_cache_matrix_(0),
            rows_(m1.rows()), cols_(m2.cols())
        {   ParameterCheck(m1, m2);
        }
```

The following two constructors have to create a cache for the one operand that is an expression:

```
template<class Expr, class M2>
MultiplicationExpression(
        const BinaryExpression<Expr>& expr,
        const Matrix<M2>& m)
        : left_(expr),  right_(m),
        right_cache_matrix_(0),
        rows_(expr.rows()), cols_(m.cols())
{   ParameterCheck(expr, m);
        left_cache_matrix_ = new LeftCacheMatrixType(expr.rows(),
                                                       expr.cols());
}
```

```
template<class M, class Expr>
MultiplicationExpression(
    const Matrix<M>& m,
    const BinaryExpression<Expr>& expr)
    :left_(m),  right_(expr),
    left_cache_matrix_(0),
    rows_(m.rows()), cols_(expr.cols())
{   ParameterCheck(m, expr);
    right_cache_matrix_ =
        new RightCacheMatrixType(expr.rows(), expr.cols());
}
```

Finally, the fourth constructor creates two caches, each one for one of its operands:

```
template<class Expr1, class Expr2>
MultiplicationExpression(
    const BinaryExpression<Expr1>& expr1,
    const BinaryExpression<Expr2>& expr2)
    :left_(expr1),  right_(expr2),
    rows_(expr1.rows()), cols_(expr2.cols())
{   ParameterCheck(expr1, expr2);
    left_cache_matrix_ =
        new LeftCacheMatrixType(expr1.rows(), expr1.cols());
    right_cache_matrix_ =
        new RightCacheMatrixType(expr2.rows(), expr2.cols());
}
```

Because expressions are returned by the operator templates by copy, our multiplication expression needs a copy constructor. When the expression is copied, the cache variables of the new copy will point to the caches of the old expression. Thus, we need to reset the cache variables in the old expression to 0, so that its destructor won't destroy the caches:

```
MultiplicationExpression(MultiplicationExpression& old)
    : left_(old.left_), right_(old.right_),
    left_cache_matrix_(old.left_cache_matrix_),
    right_cache_matrix_(old.right_cache_matrix_),
    rows_(old.rows()), cols_(old.cols())
{   old.left_cache_matrix_= 0;
    old.right_cache_matrix_= 0;
}
```

The destructor deletes the caches, if any:

```
~MultiplicationExpression()
{   delete left_cache_matrix_;
    delete right_cache_matrix_;
}
```

Finally, we need the getElement() function, which also uses a metafunction to select the most appropriate implementation based on the shape of the operands:

```
ElementType getElement(const IndexType& i,
                       const IndexType& j) const
{   return
      MATRIX_MULTIPLY_GET_ELEMENT<
        LeftType,
        RightType>::RET::getElement(
          i,j,this,left_,right_,
          left_cache_matrix_,right_cache_matrix_);
}

IndexType rows() const {return rows_;}
IndexType cols() const {return cols_;}

private:
    void ParameterCheck(const A& m1, const B& m2)
    {   if (m1.cols() != m2.rows())
            throw "argument matrices are incompatible";
    }
};
```

The last expression template is BinaryExpression<>. It is derived from its parameter, that is, ExpressionTemplate, which could be AdditionExpression or MultiplicationExpression. Thus, it inherits Config and getElement() from the expression it wraps.

```
template<class ExpressionType>
class BinaryExpression : public ExpressionType
{public:
    typedef typename ExpressionType::LeftType LeftType;
    typedef typename ExpressionType::RightType RightType;
    typedef typename ExpressionType::Config::MatrixType MatrixType;
```

```
typedef typename ExpressionType::IndexType IndexType;

BinaryExpression(const LeftType& __op1, const RightType& __op2)
    : ExpressionType(__op1, __op2)
{}
```

The following method implements assignment and is called from the assignment operator in `Matrix` (see Section 14.4.1.1):

```
template<class Res>
Matrix<Res>* assign(Matrix<Res>* const result) const
{   MATRIX_ASSIGNMENT<MatrixType>::RET::assign(result, this);
    return result;
}

ostream& display(ostream& out) const
{   IndexType r= rows(), c= cols();
    for( IndexType i = 0; i < r; ++i )
    {   for( IndexType j = 0; j < c; ++j )
            out << getElement( i, j ) << "   ";
        out << endl;
    }
    return out;
}
};
```

14.4.2.6 Matrix Cache

As stated previously, matrix multiplication uses a cache to avoid recomputing elements of an operand expression. We implement the cache as a matrix whose elements are cache elements rather than numbers. A cache element has a variable for storing the cached element value and a flag indicating if the value is in cache or not:

MatrixCache.h

```
template<class ElementType>
class CacheElementType
{public:
    CacheElementType() : element(ElementType(0)), valid(false) {}

    CacheElementType(const ElementType& elem)
        : element(elem), valid(false) {}
```

```
    const bool& isHit() const
    { return valid; }

    const ElementType& getValue() const
    { return element; }

    void setValue(const ElementType& elem)
    {   valid = true;
        element = elem;
    }

    ostream& display(ostream& out) const
    {
        out << "(" << element << "; " << valid << ")";
        return out;
    }

private:
    bool valid; //if true the value is already cached (cache-hit),
                //if false it isn't
    ElementType element;
};

template <class A>
ostream& operator<<(ostream& out, const CacheElementType<A>& elem)
{   return elem.display(out);
}
```

Next, we implement a metafunction that takes a matrix type and returns the corresponding matrix cache type. The only difference between these two types is the element type: The element type of the cache is CacheElementType<> parameterized with the element type of the original matrix type. The cache type derivation involves retrieving the description of the matrix type, that is, DSLFeatures, constructing a derived DSLFeatures whose inherited element type gets overridden by the new cache element type, and finally passing the new DSLFeatures to the matrix generator, which generates the cache matrix. The derived DSLFeatures is called CachedMatrixDSL. Here is the metafunction:

```
template<class MatrixType>
class CACHE_MATRIX_TYPE
{   typedef typename MatrixType::Config Config;
```

```
        typedef typename Config::DSLFeatures DSLFeatures;

        struct CachedMatrixDSL : public DSLFeatures
        { typedef CacheElementType<typename DSLFeatures::ElementType>
                ElementType;
        };
    public:
        typedef MATRIX_GENERATOR<CachedMatrixDSL,
                                assemble_components>::RET RET;
    };
```

14.4.2.7 Generating `getElement()`

The implementations of `getElement()` for the addition expression
and the multiplication expression depend on the shape of their
operands. Therefore, we will use a template metafunction to select
the appropriate implementation. More precisely, we will put each
method variant into a separate `struct` and select the needed
`struct` using a metafunction.

In the case of addition, we provide three algorithms: a general
one for adding rectangular matrices (which also works in all other
cases), one for adding lower-triangular matrices, and one for
adding upper-triangular matrices:

GetElement.h
```
struct RectAddGetElement
{   template<class IndexType, class ResultType,
            class LeftType, class RightType>
    static typename ResultType::ElementType
    getElement(const IndexType& i, const IndexType& j,
            const ResultType* res, const LeftType& left,
            const RightType& right)
    {   return left.getElement(i, j) + right.getElement(i, j);
    }
};

struct LowerTriangAddGetElement
{   template<class IndexType, class ResultType,
            class LeftType, class RightType>
    static typename ResultType::ElementType
    getElement(const IndexType& i, const IndexType& j,
            const ResultType* res, const LeftType& left,
            const RightType& right)
    {   typedef typename ResultType::ElementType ElementType;
```

```
            return i >= j ? left.getElement(i, j) +
                            right.getElement(i, j)
                          : ElementType(0);
    }
};


struct UpperTriangAddGetElement
{   template<class IndexType, class ResultType,
             class LeftType, class RightType>
    static typename ResultType::ElementType
    getElement(const IndexType& i, const IndexType& j,
        const ResultType* res, const LeftType& left,
const RightType& right)
    {   typedef typename ResultType::ElementType ElementType;
        return i <= j ? left.getElement(i, j) +
                        right.getElement(i, j)
                      : ElementType(0);
    }
};
```

The following metafunction selects the appropriate `getElement()` algorithm for an addition expression: It returns `LowerTriangAddGetElement` for two lower-triangular matrices, `UpperTriangAddGetElement` for two upper-triangular matrices, and `RectAddGetElement` for all the other shape combinations:

```
template<class Matrix1, class Matrix2>
struct MATRIX_ADD_GET_ELEMENT
{   typedef Matrix1::Config::DSLFeatures::Shape Shape1;
    typedef Matrix2::Config::DSLFeatures::Shape Shape2;

    typedef IF< EQUAL<Shape1::id,
                      Shape1::lower_triang_id>::RET &&
                EQUAL<Shape2::id,
                      Shape2::lower_triang_id>::RET,
                  LowerTriangAddGetElement,
             IF< EQUAL<Shape1::id,
                       Shape1::upper_triang_id>::RET &&
                 EQUAL<Shape2::id,
                       Shape2::upper_triang_id>::RET,
                   UpperTriangAddGetElement,
             RectAddGetElement>::RET>::RET RET;
};
```

The following is the implementation of getElement() for the multiplication of two rectangular matrices:

```
struct RectMultiplyGetElement
{   template<class _IndexType,
        class ResultType, class LeftType, class RightType,
        class LeftCacheType, class RightCacheType>
    static typename ResultType::ElementType
    getElement(const _IndexType& i, const _IndexType& j,
        const ResultType* res, const LeftType& left,
const RightType& right,
        LeftCacheType* left_cache= 0,
        RightCacheType* right_cache= 0)
    {   typedef typename ResultType::Config Config;
        typedef typename Config::ElementType ElementType;
        typedef typename Config::IndexType IndexType;

        ElementType result= ElementType(0);

        for(IndexType k= left.cols(); --k;)
            result+= getCachedElement(i, k, left, left_cache) *
                    getCachedElement(k, j, right, right_cache);
        return result;
    }

private:
    template<class IndexType, class MatrixType, class CacheType>
    static typename MatrixType::ElementType
    getCachedElement(const IndexType& i, const IndexType& j,
        const MatrixType& matrix, CacheType* cache)
    {   if (cache == 0) return matrix.getElement(i, j);
        else
        {   CacheType::ElementType& tmpCacheElem =
                cache->getElement(i, j);
            if (!tmpCacheElem.isHit())
                tmpCacheElem.setValue(matrix.getElement(i, j));
            return tmpCacheElem.getValue();
        }
    }
};
```

The variants of getElement() for multiplying two lower-triangular matrices and two upper-triangular matrices are analogous and not shown here.

Here is the metafunction for selecting the implementation of getElement() for multiplication expressions:

```
template<class Matrix1, class Matrix2>
struct MATRIX_MULTIPLY_GET_ELEMENT
{   typedef Matrix1::Config::DSLFeatures::Shape Shape1;
    typedef Matrix2::Config::DSLFeatures::Shape Shape2;

    typedef IF< EQUAL<Shape1::id,
                      Shape1::lower_triang_id>::RET &&
                EQUAL<Shape2::id,
                      Shape2::lower_triang_id>::RET,
                LowerTriangMultiplyGetElement,
            IF< EQUAL<Shape1::id,
                      Shape1::upper_triang_id>::RET &&
                EQUAL<Shape2::id,
                      Shape2::upper_triang_id>::RET,
                UpperTriangMultiplyGetElement,
            RectMultiplyGetElement>::RET>::RET RET;
};
```

14.4.2.8 Metafunctions for Computing Result Types of Expressions

As you may remember, the addition expression and multiplication expression class templates call the metafunctions to compute the matrix result type for addition and multiplication:

```
ADD_RESULT_TYPE<MatrixType1, MatrixType2>::RET
MULTIPLY_RESULT_TYPE<MatrixType1, MatrixType2>::RET
```

These metafunctions work as follows: They retrieve the DSLFeatures from each of the operands, compute the resulting DSLFeatures, and call the matrix generator with the resulting DSLFeatures to generate the result matrix type.

We first need to specify how to compute the resulting DSLFeatures from the argument DSLFeatures. As you may remember, DSLFeatures contains the following features:

```
ElementType
Shape
OptFlag
BoundsChecking
Format
ArrayOrder
IndexType
```

We need to compute these features for the result matrix from the features of the argument matrices. The following features are computed in the same way for both addition and multiplication:

```
ElementType
OptFlag
BoundsChecking
ArrayOrder
IndexType
```

`ElementType` and `IndexType` are computed using the numeric promote metafunction shown in Figure 10-14 in Section 10.10.4. The table for computing `Format` is given later in this section. The other features are computed as follows: If the value of a given feature in one argument matrix is equal to the value of the same feature in the other argument matrix, the resulting feature value is equal to the other two values. If this is not the case, the resulting feature value is `whatever` (see Table 14-12). This makes sense because the matrix generator will assign appropriate default values for the unspecified features.

The resulting shape is computed differently for addition and for multiplication. This is shown in Table 14-13 and Table 14-14.

Table 14-12 General Formula for Computing Result Values of Nonmathematical DSL Features

Feature1	Feature2	Result
(value)	(value)	=(value)
*	*	whatever

Table 14-13 Computing the Resulting Shape for Matrix Addition

Shape1	Shape2	Shape Result
symm	symm	symm
lowerTriang	lowerTriang	lowerTriang
upperTriang	upperTriang	upperTriang
*	*	rect

Table 14-14 Computing the Resulting Shape for Matrix Multiplication		
Shape1	**Shape2**	**Shape Result**
lowerTriang	lowerTriang	lowerTriang
upperTriang	upperTriang	upperTriang
*	*	rect

The resulting `Format` not only depends on the `Format` of the operands, but also on the shape of the result. In particular, adding a lower-triangular matrix to an upper-triangular yields a rectangular matrix. If the format of both operands is vector, we cannot simply assume vector for the result because a rectangular matrix should be stored in an array. This is specified in Table 14-15.

We start with a metafunction that encodes the general formula from Table 14-12:

ComputeResult Type.h

```
template<class Feature1, class Feature2>
struct DEFAULT_RESULT
{   typedef IF<EQUAL<Feature1::id, Feature2::id>::RET,
            Feature1,
            whatever>::RET RET;
};
```

`RESULT_FORMAT<>` implements Table 14-15, which is the same for addition and multiplication:

```
template<class Shape, class Format1, class Format2>
struct RESULT_FORMAT
{   typedef
```

Table 14-15 Computing the Resulting Format			
Shape Result	**Format1**	**Format2**	**Format Result**
rect	vector	vector	whatever
*	(value)	(value)	=(value)
*	*	*	whatever

```
            IF< EQUAL<Shape::id, Shape::rect_id>::RET &&
                EQUAL<Format1::id, Format1::vector_id>::RET &&
                EQUAL<Format2::id, Format2::vector_id>::RET,
                whatever,

            IF< EQUAL<Format1::id, Format2::id>::RET,
                Format1,
            whatever>::RET>::RET RET;
};
```

The following metafunction computes the result shape for matrix addition (see Table 14-13):

```
template<class Shape1, class Shape2>
struct ADD_RESULT_SHAPE
{   typedef
        IF< EQUAL<Shape1::id, Shape1::symm_id>::RET &&
            EQUAL<Shape2::id, Shape2::symm_id>::RET,
            symm<>,

        IF< EQUAL<Shape1::id, Shape1::lower_triang_id>::RET &&
            EQUAL<Shape2::id, Shape2::lower_triang_id>::RET,
            lower_triang<>,

        IF< EQUAL<Shape1::id, Shape1::upper_triang_id>::RET &&
            EQUAL<Shape2::id, Shape2::upper_triang_id>::RET,
            upper_triang<>,

        rect<> >::RET>::RET>::RET RET;
};
```

ADD_RESULT_DSL_FEATURES<> computes the resulting DSLFeatures from two argument DSLFeatures. We refer to the resulting DSLFeatures as ParsedDSL because it may contain some unspecified features (thus, it has the same form as the DSLFeatures returned by the MATRIX_DSL_PARSER).

```
template<class DSLFeatures1, class DSLFeatures2>
class ADD_RESULT_DSL_FEATURES
{   //ElementType
    //PROMOTE_NUMERIC_TYPE<> is given in Figure 10-14 (as Promote<>)
    typedef PROMOTE_NUMERIC_TYPE<
        typename DSLFeatures1::ElementType,
        typename DSLFeatures2::ElementType>::RET ElementType_;
```

```
    //Shape
    typedef ADD_RESULT_SHAPE<
        typename DSLFeatures1::Shape,
        typename DSLFeatures2::Shape>::RET Shape_;

    //OptFlag
    typedef DEFAULT_RESULT<
        typename DSLFeatures1::OptFlag,
        typename DSLFeatures2::OptFlag>::RET OptFlag_;

    //BoundsChecking
    typedef DEFAULT_RESULT<
        typename DSLFeatures1::BoundsChecking,
        typename DSLFeatures2::BoundsChecking>::RET
    BoundsChecking_;

    //Format
    typedef RESULT_FORMAT<
        Shape_,
        typename DSLFeatures1::Format,
        typename DSLFeatures2::Format>::RET Format_;

    //ArrOrder
    typedef DEFAULT_RESULT<
        typename DSLFeatures1::ArrOrder,
        typename DSLFeatures2::ArrOrder>::RET ArrOrder_;

    //IndexType
    typedef PROMOTE_NUMERIC_TYPE<
        typename DSLFeatures1::IndexType,
        typename DSLFeatures2::IndexType>::RET IndexType_;

public:
    struct ParsedDSL
    {   typedef ElementType_     ElementType;
        typedef Shape_           Shape;
        typedef OptFlag_         OptFlag;
        typedef BoundsChecking_  BoundsChecking;
        typedef Format_          Format;
        typedef ArrOrder_        ArrOrder;
        typedef IndexType_       IndexType;
    };

    typedef ParsedDSL RET;
};
```

ADD_RESULT_TYPE<> returns the result matrix type for addition. It calls the previous metafunction in order to compute the resulting DSL features and the matrix generator to generate the matrix type:

```
template<class MatrixType1, class MatrixType2>
struct ADD_RESULT_TYPE
{   typedef ADD_RESULT_DSL_FEATURES<
        typename MatrixType1::Config::DSLFeatures,
        typename MatrixType2::Config::DSLFeatures> BaseClass;
    typedef MATRIX_GENERATOR<
            BaseClass::ParsedDSL,
            defaults_and_assemble>::RET RET;
};
```

The remaining metafunctions to compute the result type of multiplication, that is:

```
MULTIPLY_RESULT_SHAPE<>
MULTIPLY_RESULT_DSL_FEATURES<>
MULTIPLY_RESULT_TYPE<>
```

are implemented in a similar way.

14.4.2.9 Generating Matrix Assignment

The implementation of matrix assignment depends on the shape of the source matrix (or source expression). Our assignment implementations perform two steps: initializing the target matrix with zero elements and assigning the nonzero elements from the source matrix. Thus, we only have to iterate over the nonzero region of the source matrix.

We provide implementations for assigning rectangular, lower-triangular, and upper-triangular matrices (see Table 14-16). The symmetric case is handled by the implementation for rectangular matrices.

Table 14-16 Selecting the Assignment Algorithm

Shape (source matrix)	Assignment
lower_triang	LowerTriangAssignment
upper_triang	UpperTriangAssignment
*	RectAssignment

Here is the C++ code for the three assignment variants:

Assignment.h

```
struct RectAssignment
{   template<class Res, class M>
    static void assign(Res* res, M* m)
    {   typedef typename Res::Config::IndexType IndexType;
        for (IndexType i= m->rows(); --i;)
            for (IndexType j= m->cols(); --j;)
                res->setElement(i, j, m->getElement(i, j));
    }
};

struct LowerTriangAssignment
{   template<class Res, class M>
    static void assign(Res* res, M* m)
    {   typedef typename Res::Config::IndexType IndexType;
        for(IndexType i= 0; i< res->rows(); ++i)
            for(IndexType j= 0; j<=i; ++j)
                res->setElement(i, j, m->getElement(i, j));
    }
};

struct UpperTriangAssignment
{   template<class Res, class M>
    static void assign(Res* res, M* m)
    {   typedef typename Res::Config::IndexType IndexType;

        for(IndexType i= 0; i< res->rows(); ++i)
            for(IndexType j= i; j< res->rows(); ++j)
                res->setElement(i, j, m->getElement(i, j));
    }
};
```

The following metafunction implements Table 14-16:

```
template<class RightMatrixType>
struct MATRIX_ASSIGNMENT
{   typedef typename RightMatrixType::Config::DSLFeatures::Shape
                    Shape;

    typedef IF<EQUAL<Shape::id, Shape::lower_triang_id>::RET,
                LowerTriangAssignment,
            IF< EQUAL<Shape::id, Shape::upper_triang_id>::RET,
                UpperTriangAssignment,
```

```
                      RectAssignment>::RET>::RET RET;
};
```

This concludes the implementation of the matrix library.

14.4.2.10 Lessons Learned

The library described previously covers only a few matrix variants, but a full implementation of the feature model from Section 14.3.2 using the techniques presented earlier was done by Tobias Neubert (see [Neu98, Cza98]). The full implementation includes several matrix shapes (rectangular, square, identity, scalar, diagonal, triangular, and band), dense and sparse matrices, static and dynamic memory allocation, and several sparse and dense storage formats. Without counting element and index type, the matrix generator can generate over 1800 different matrix variants. The implementation comprises 7500 lines of C++ code (6000 lines for the configuration generator and the matrix components, and 1500 lines for the operations). The full implementation of the library illustrates a number of important points.

- ◆ *Separation between problem and solution space:* The use of a configuration DSL implemented by a separate set of templates hides the internal library architecture (i.e., the ICCL) from the application programmer. It is possible to change the ICCL (e.g., add new components or even component categories) without having to modify the existing client code. All we have to do is map the existing DSL onto the new ICCL structure, which requires changes in the configuration generator. To a certain extent, we can even extend the configuration DSL without invalidating the existing client code. For example, you can enlarge the value scope of existing DSL parameters (e.g., you can add new matrix shapes) or append new parameters to existing parameter lists (e.g., you can add new parameters at the end of the matrix parameter list; furthermore, you can also add new subfeatures to any of the leave nodes of the DSL feature diagram because all DSL features are implemented as templates). Thus, the separation between DSL and ICCL gives you more flexibility compared to libraries, such as the STL, where the application programmer has to use the ICCL directly (and basically hardwire ICCL expressions in the client code, making it dependent on the library implementation).
- ◆ *More declarative specification:* The client code can request a matrix using a configuration DSL expression that specifies exactly as much detail as the client wishes to specify. Because the

generator tries to derive reasonable feature defaults from the explicitly specified features, the client code does not have to specify details that do not concern it directly. Consider the following analogy: When you buy a car, you do not have to specify all the bolts and wires. There is complex machinery between you and the car factory to figure out how to satisfy your abstract needs. On the other hand, if you need the car for racing, you may actually want to request some specially customized parts (provided you have the technical knowledge to do so). The same applies to a configuration DSL: You should be able to specify any detail in the DSL expression you want, but you should not be forced to specify details if you don't want to (this would make you unnecessarily dependent on the library's implementation, as in the case of libraries that provide an ICCL only). However, you should be able to specify more detail if this can help the library provide you with better performance. For example, if you know the shape of the matrices in your application, you can specify it and have the library generate optimized code.

♦ *Minimal redundancy within the library:* Parameterizing differences allows you to avoid situations where two components contain largely the same code except for a few details that are different. Furthermore, there is a good chance that the "little" components implementing these details can be reused as parameters of more than one parameterized component. Thanks to an aggressive parameterization, the generative matrix library provides over 1800 matrix variants with only 7500 lines of C++ code. The use of a configuration DSL allows us to hide the code fragmentation caused by this aggressive parameterization from the library user.

♦ *Coverage of a large number of variants:* The matrix configuration DSL covers some 1840 different kinds of matrices. This number does not take element type, index type, and all the number-valued parameters, such as number of rows or the static scalar value, into account. Given the library code size of 7500 lines, the average number of lines per matrix variant is about four. If you count the 12 different element types and the 8 different index types, the number of matrix variants increases to 176,640. The different possible values for extension, diagonal range, scalar value, and so on (they can all be specified statically or dynamically) increase this number even more.

♦ *Very good performance:* Despite the large number of provided matrix variants, the performance of the generated code is comparable with the performance of manually coded variants. This is achieved by the exclusive use of static binding, which is often combined with inlining. We did not implement any special matrix optimizations, such as register blocking or cache blocking. However, the work in [SL98b] demonstrates that by implementing blocking optimizations using template metaprogramming, it is possible to parallel the performance of highly tuned Fortran 90 matrix libraries.

14.4.2.11 Problems with Template Metaprogramming

Unfortunately, the presented C++ techniques also have a number of problems.

♦ *Debugging:* Debugging template metaprograms is very difficult. There is no such thing as a debugger for the C++ compilation process. Over time, we had to develop a number of tricks and strategies for getting the information we needed (e.g., requesting a nonexistent type member in order to force the compiler to print out the contents of a typename in an error report, which corresponds to inspecting the value of a variable in a regular program). Unfortunately, they are not always effective. For example, many compilers will not show the entire type in an error report if the name exceeds a certain number of characters (e.g., 255). And the length of typenames in template metaprogramming can easily reach thousands of characters due to deep template nesting (see Figure 14-16).

♦ *Error reporting:* There is no way for a template metaprogram to output a string during compilation. On the other hand, template metaprograms are used for structure checking (e.g., parsing the configuration DSL) and other compilation tasks, and we need to be able to report problems about the data the metaprogram works on. The solution you saw in Section 14.4.1.3.2 is just a partial one because there is no way to specify the place where the logical error occurred. In order to do this properly, we would need access to the internal parse tree of the compiler.

♦ *Readability of the code:* The readability of template metacode is not very high. We were able to improve on this point by providing explicit control structures (see Section 10.11) and using specialized metafunctions, such as the table evaluation metafunction in Section 14.4.1.3.3. Despite all of this, the code still remains quite peculiar and obscure. Template metaprogramming is not a result of a careful language design but an accident.

♦ *Compilation times:* Template metaprograms may extend compilation times by orders of magnitude. There are at least two reasons for this situation: Template metacode is interpreted rather than compiled, and C++ compilers are not tuned for this kind of

```
MultiplicationExpression<class LazyBinaryExpression<class
AdditionExpression<class MatrixICCL::Matrix<class
MatrixICCL::BoundsChecker<class MatrixICCL::ArrFormat<class MatrixICCL::StatExt<
struct MatrixDSL::int_number<int,7>,struct MatrixDSL::int_number<int,7>>,class
MatrixICCL::Rect<class MatrixICCL::StatExt<struct
MatrixDSL::int_number<int,7>,struct MatrixDSL::int_number<int,7>>>,class
MatrixICCL::Dyn2DCContainer<class MATRIX_ASSEMBLE_COMPONENTS<class
MATRIX_DSL_ASSIGN_DEFAULTS<class MATRIX_DSL_PARSER<struct
MatrixDSL::matrix<int,struct MatrixDSL::structure<struct MatrixDSL::rect<struct
MatrixDSL::stat_val<struct MatrixDSL::int_number<int,7>>,struct
MatrixDSL::stat_val<struct MatrixDSL::int_number<int,7>>,struct
MatrixDSL::whatever>,struct MatrixDSL::dense<struct MatrixDSL::whatever>,struct
MatrixDSL::dyn<struct MatrixDSL::whatever>>,struct MatrixDSL::speed<struct
MatrixDSL::whatever>,struct MatrixDSL::whatever,struct
MatrixDSL::whatever,struct MatrixDSL::whatever,struct
MatrixDSL::whatever>>::DSLConfig>::DSLConfig>>>>,class
MatrixICCL::Matrix<class MatrixICCL::BoundsChecker<class MatrixICCL::ArrFormat<
class MatrixICCL::StatExt<struct MatrixDSL::int_number<int,7>,struct
MatrixDSL::int_number<int,7>>,class MatrixICCL::Rect<class MatrixICCL::StatExt<
struct MatrixDSL::int_number<int,7>,struct MatrixDSL::int_number<int,7>>>,class
MatrixICCL::Dyn2DCContainer<class MATRIX_ASSEMBLE_COMPONENTS<class
MATRIX_DSL_ASSIGN_DEFAULTS<class MATRIX_DSL_PARSER<struct
MatrixDSL::matrix<int,struct MatrixDSL::structure<struct MatrixDSL::rect<struct
MatrixDSL::stat_val<struct MatrixDSL::int_number<int,7>>,struct
MatrixDSL::stat_val<struct MatrixDSL::int_number<int,7>>,struct
MatrixDSL::whatever>,struct MatrixDSL::dense<struct MatrixDSL::whatever>,struct
Ma...
```

Figure 14-16 *Fragment of the type generated by the C++ compiler for the matrix expression (A+B)*C*

use (or abuse). The compilation time of a particular metacode depends on its complexity and the programming style (which may have a different effect on different compilers).

♦ *Compiler limits:* Because computation is done quasi "as a byproduct" of type construction and inference in template metaprogramming, complex computations quickly lead to very complex types. The complexity and size limits of different compilers vary, but, in general, the limits may be quickly reached. Thus, the complexity of the computations is also limited (e.g., certain loops cannot iterate more than some limited number of times).

♦ *Limitations of expression templates:* Expression templates allow you to implement domain-specific optimizations for expressions, but they won't help if you need an optimization that spans several statements (there are no "global type variables" through which you can secretly pass information between expressions at compile time in C++). A further problem is the lack of a "type of initializer" and "typeof" features in C++. For example, if you want to declare a matrix variable and initialize it with a matrix expression, you have to know the resulting type of the expression in order to choose the right type for the variable. Now, if the expression is complicated and the participating matrices have different properties (e.g., shapes and densities), you have to manually compute the result type, even though the expression computes it automatically and stores it in its configuration repository. An alternative would be to explicitly use the metafunctions that compute the result type, for example:

```
//Matrix1, Matrix2, and Matrix3 are matrix
//types with different properties;
//m1, m2, and m3 are of type Matrix1,
//Matrix2, and Matrix3, respectively
MULTIPLY_RESULT_TYPE<
   ADD_RESULT_TYPE<Matrix1,Matrix2>::RET,
   Matrix3
>::RET r = (m1+m2)*m3;
```

The problem with this solution is that you have to duplicate the structure of the expression in the type computation. If C++ supported "type of initializer" and "typeof", we could rewrite this code as follows:

```
typeofinitializer e = (m1+m2)*m3;
typeof(e)::Config::MatrixType r = e;
```

If we were using Intentional Programming (IP), adding both features would not be a problem. In fact, [ADK+98] describes how to extend C with "type of initializer" in IP. (Interestingly, gcc 2.91 already supports typeof as a nonstandard feature.)

♦ *Portability:* Template metaprogramming is based on many advanced C++ language features, which are not (yet) widely supported by compilers. There may even be differences in the way different compilers support the same feature. Thus, currently, template metaprograms have quite a limited portability. This situation will hopefully improve over the next few years when more and more compiler vendors start to support the newly completed ISO C++ standard.

We can conclude that the complexity of template metaprograms is limited mainly by compiler limits, compilation times, and debugging problems. Intentional Programming, which we discuss next, does not suffer from these problems.

14.4.3 Implementing the Matrix Component in IP

This section gives you a short overview of a prototype implementation of the matrix library in the Intentional Programming System described in Chapter 11.[5] The prototype covers only a small selection of matrix features, namely element type, shape (rectangular, diagonal, lower triangular, upper triangular, symmetric, and identity), format (array and vector), and dynamic or static memory allocation.

The implementation consists of two IP files.

♦ *Interface file:* Contains the declaration of the matrix intentions (e.g., matrix type, matrix operations, configuration DSL parameters and values)

♦ *Implementation file:* Contains implementation modules with rendering, editing, and transformation methods.

You can compile the implementation file into an extension DLL and give it, together with the interface file, to application programmers. They can include the interface file in their project, which will automatically load the DLL into their IP programming environment. This way they'll be able to write and compile matrix code as part of their application program.

Figure 14-17 shows some matrix application code written using the intentions defined in our prototype matrix library. The code displayed in the editor is rendered by the rendering methods contained in the extension DLL. The DLL also provides editing methods, which, for example, allow us to tab through the elements of the matrix literal used to initialize the matrix variable mFoo (i.e., the matrix literal behaves like a spreadsheet).

In order to demonstrate the effect of the rendering methods, Figure 14-18 shows how the same matrix code looks when the extension library is not loaded. In this case, the source tree is

---

5. The prototype was developed with the kind supervision and help of Greg Shaw during Krzysztof Czarnecki's visit to the Intentional Programming Group at Microsoft Research in Redmond, Washington, in January 1998.

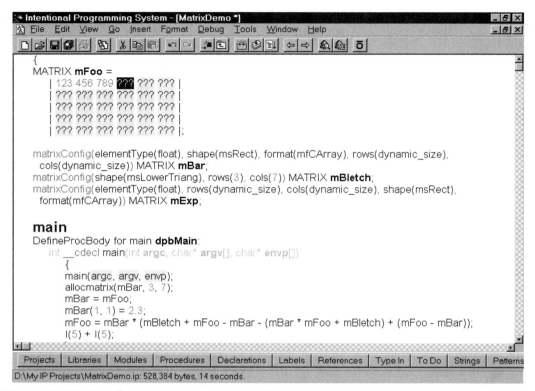

Figure 14-17 Sample matrix program using the matrix implementation in IP

displayed using the default rendering methods provided by the system. These methods render the source tree in a functional style.

The prototype allows you to declare a matrix as follows:

```
matrixConfig(elementType(float), shape(msRect), format(mfCArray),
rows(dynamic_size), cols(dynamic_size)) MATRIX aRectangularMatrix;
```

MATRIX denotes the matrix type. It is annotated by matrixConfig, which specifies matrix parameters. This declaration is quite similar to what we had in the C++ implementation. However, in contrast to the latter, the IP implementation lets you specify the parameter values by name in any order.

A matrix expression in IP looks exactly like one in C++, for example:

```
mFoo = mBar * (mBletch + mFoo - mBar - (mBar * mFoo + mBletch) +
    (mFoo - mBar));
```

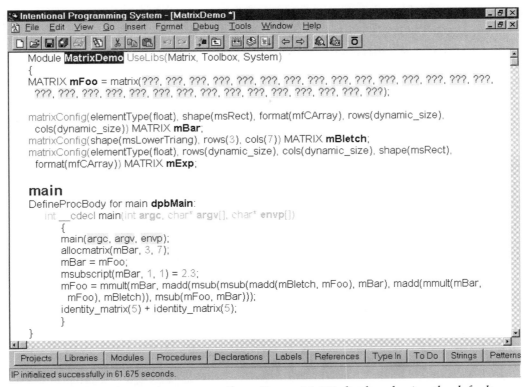

Figure 14-18 Sample matrix program (from Figure 14-17) displayed using the default rendering (`mmult`* is the name of the intention representing matrix multiplication; similarly,* `madd` *is the name of the intention representing matrix addition)*

Of course, in a full implementation, you could easily provide all the special matrix notations found in math books.

Table 14-17 gives an overview of the different implementation parts of the library.

The functionality covered by the module `MatrixTypeTransforms` corresponds to the configuration generator and the matrix configuration components. However, there are two main differences.

♦ The generating part in `MatrixTypeTransforms` is implemented using regular C code (mainly `if` and `case` statements) rather than template metaprogramming.

♦ `MatrixTypeTransforms` has to reduce matrix application code to C, which is much more complex to implement than composing class templates as in our C++ implementation (at the time of

**Table 14-17 Overview of the IP Implementation
of the Matrix Library**

IP Document (i.e., IP File)	Module	Contents
Matrix interface (`Matrix.ip`)	ADTs	Declares intentions representing matrix type, matrix literal, and all the matrix operations (multiplication, addition, subtraction, number of rows, number of columns, subscripts, initialization, and so on)
	Config	Declares intentions representing the configuration DSL parameters and parameter values (e.g., Elementtype, shape, format, rect, lowertriang, and so on)
Matrix implementation (`MatrixImpl.ip`)	RenderingAnd-Editing	Implements the rendering and editing methods for matrix type, matrix literal, matrix operations, and matrix configuration DSL specifications
	MatrixType-Transforms	Implements processing matrix configurations (structure check, computing defaults, assembling a flat configuration) and generating the data structures for a matrix (e.g., C structs) according to the flat configuration
	Operation-Transforms	Implements checking and transforming matrix expressions, computing the result type of expressions, and generating operation implementations in C
	UI	Implements a number of dialog boxes, for example, for entering matrix configuration descriptions using radio buttons (optional) and for setting the number of rows and columns of a matrix literal

developing the prototype, the implementation of C++ in IP was not complete).

The module OperationTransforms implements the functionality covered in the operations section of the C++ implementation (i.e., Section 14.4.2). There are functions for computing result types of expressions, checking their structure, optimizing, and generating C code.

RenderingAndEditing is the only implementation module that does not have its counterpart in the C++ implementation. This is so because C++ matrix programs are represented by ASCII text and no special support is needed to display them. On the other hand, IP rendering allows you to provide a more natural notation for matrices. The spreadsheetlike initializer of mFoo is just one example (although the C++ comma initializer came pretty close to it), and Figure 11-15 in Section 11.4.2 shows you more examples. But the main point is that with IP there is no limitation on the kind of visualization you can provide.

Implementing the matrix library in IP has the following advantages over the template metaprogramming approach.

♦ Metacode is easier to write because you can write it as usual C code.
♦ Debugging is easier because you can debug metacode using a debugger. You can also debug the generated code at different levels of reduction.
♦ You can easily issue error reports and warnings. They can be attached to the source tree nodes next to where the error occurred.
♦ You can provide domain-specific visualizations for abstractions (e.g., the matrix literal).

On the negative side, the basic IP APIs for rendering, editing, and transforming are still quite low level and require writing relatively low-level code. Also, the fact that we had to reduce to C rather than C++ added a lot of complexity. This situation will improve as more and more higher-level abstractions become available in IP.

A more detailed comparison between the template metaprogramming and the IP approach is given in Table 14-18. Please note that the comparison applies to the C++ compilers and the IP system as of this writing and may look quite different in future. Also, this comparison was done in the context of our programming experiment. There are other exciting features of IP, such as code refactoring and code reengineering, which are not considered here.

Table 14-18 Comparison between Template Metaprogramming and IP

Criterion	Template Metaprogramming	Intentional Programming
Complexity limits	The complexity of metaprograms is limited by the C++ compiler limits (e.g., maximal nesting depth for template instantiations).	There are no such limits.
Debugging support	There is no debugging support.	Metacode can be debugged using a debugger. The generated code can be debugged at different levels of reduction.
Error reporting	Inadequate.	Error reports and warnings can be attached directly to source tree nodes close to the locations where a problem occurred.
Programming effort	Template metaprograms may require significant programming effort due to the lack of debugging support, error-prone syntax (e.g., lots of angle brackets), and current compiler limits. On the other hand, the code to be generated can be represented using easy to configure class templates.	The current IP system also requires significant programming effort. This is due to the low-level APIs, for example, tree editing, rendering, and so on. The system provides only a few declarative mechanisms (e.g., tree quote and simple pattern matching). Also the unavailability of the C++ mechanisms (classes, templates, and so on) adds programming complexity. On the other hand, the system can be extended with declarative mechanisms at any time. This is more scalable than the template metaprogramming approach.
Readability of the metacode	Low.	Due to the (currently) low-level APIs, the readability is also low, but can be easily improved in the future.
Compilation speed	Larger metaprograms (especially with recursion) may have unacceptable compilation times. Template metaprograms are interpreted.	Because IP has been designed for supporting metaprogramming, it does not have the same problems as those in template metaprogramming (e.g., IP metaprograms are compiled). Nevertheless, compiling a C program using a commercial C compiler is much faster than compiling it using the current version of IP. This situation is expected to improve in future versions of IP.
Portability/ availability	Potentially wide availability, but better support for the C++ standard is required. The same applies to portability.	The IP system is not yet commercially available.
Performance of the generated code	Comparable to manually written code. The complexity of optimizations is limited by the complexity limits of template metaprograms.	Comparable to manually written code or even better because very complex optimizations can be implemented.
Displaying and editing	ASCII.	Supports two-dimensional rendering, bit-maps, special symbols, graphics, and so on.

APPENDICES

Appendix A

Conceptual Modeling

A.1 What Are Concepts?

Propositional representation

One fundamental question has occupied psychologists, philosophers, cognitive and other scientists for long time: What is the language of the mind? Do we think using a natural language, such as English, German, or Polish? Although we have the ability to process natural language, it seems that there must be some internal mental representation other than natural language. We clearly sense the distinction between having a thought and putting it into words. Defining even the most simple concept, such as *house* or *dog*, seems to be increasingly difficult the more precise we try to be. We find ourselves retrieving more and more facts about the concepts to be defined and realizing how complex they are. This phenomenon also supports the view that there must be some mental representation other than natural language. Cognitive psychologists refer to this representation as *propositional representation*.

Concepts, categories, and classes

One of the most important properties of the human mind is the fact that people do not store all information about the objects they encounter. In [SM81], Smith and Medin note that "If we perceived each entity as unique, we would be overwhelmed by the sheer diversity of what we experience and unable to remember more than a minute fraction of what we encounter. And if each individual entity needed a distinct name, our language would be staggeringly complex and communication virtually impossible." Fortunately, we have the ability to recognize new objects as instances of *concepts* we already know—whereby a concept stands for the knowledge about objects having certain properties. The task of recognizing an object as an instance of a concept is referred to as *categorization* or *classification*. For this reason, in the context of categorization, concepts are often called *categories* or *classes*. This chapter focuses on categorization, but it is important to note that categorization is not the only process involving concepts: The processes of acquiring and evolving concepts are equally important.

NOTE

There have been numerous experiments providing evidence to support the theory of a separate propositional representation. A classic example is the experiment by Sachs [Sac67]. In the experiment, subjects listened to paragraphs on various topics. The reading of the paragraphs was interrupted, and subjects were given a number of sentences. Their task was to choose the sentence that had occurred in the previous paragraph. In addition to the correct sentence, the candidate sentences included other sentences that sounded similar to the correct one, but had a different meaning as well as sentences that had the same meaning, but used different wording. The finding of the experiment was that subjects rarely selected a sentence with the wrong meaning, but often thought that they had heard one of the sentences using different wording. A reasonable explanation of this finding is that subjects translated the text they had listened to into their propositional representation, and then translated it back into natural language in the second part of the experiment. The fact that the propositional representation can be translated into a number of equivalent sentences accounts for a subject's confusion.

Concepts are central to the nature of the propositional representation. By studying concepts we can certainly learn more about how knowledge is not only represented but also processed in the mind.

You may question what all of this has to do with programming. Well, programming is about conceptual modeling. We build conceptual models in our heads to solve problems in our everyday life. In programming, we build models that we can run on a machine. By learning about how concepts are represented in the mind, we should be able to improve our means to represent concepts externally, that is, in software. In this appendix, you will see that the current object-oriented paradigm is based on a very simplistic view of the world, namely the classical view. In the end, you will realize that adequate implementations of concepts have to cover enormous amounts of variability. This observation provides the motivation for Part I of this book.

A.2 Theories of Concepts

The origins of the study of categorization and concepts date back to Aristotle, the great Greek philosopher, who is also seen as the father of the so-called *classical view* of categorization. According to [SM81], Hull's 1920 monograph on concept attainment [Hul20] initiates a period of modern and intensive research on a theory of concepts. Contemporary work on concepts includes philosophically oriented studies of language (e.g., [Fod75]), linguistic studies (e.g., [Bol75]), psycholinguistics (e.g., [CC77]), and studies in the area of cognitive psychology (e.g., [And90]). Thus, concepts have been studied in multiple disciplines: philosophy, linguistics, psychology, cognitive science, and more recently, computer science (especially artificial intelligence).

In the course of this research, three major views about the nature of concepts emerged.

♦ The *classical* view
♦ The *probabilistic* view (also referred to as the *prototype* view)
♦ The *exemplar* view

Before discussing these three views, we first introduce some basic terminology.

A.2.1 Basic Terminology

In our discussion, we will distinguish between two concepts: *mathematical* concepts and *natural* concepts.

Examples of mathematical concepts are numbers, geometric figures, matrices, and so on. The most important property of a mathematical concept is that it has a precise definition. By natural concepts, we mean concepts used in our everyday communication with natural language, for example, *dog, table, furniture, customer, bank account,* and so on. In Section A.2.2, we will see that in most cases the definition of natural concepts is problematic.[1]

We describe concepts by listing their properties. Smith and Medin distinguish between two major types of concept properties [SM81].

♦ *Features*
♦ *Dimensions*

Features

We use features to represent qualitative properties of concepts. Table A-1 gives some examples of features. For example, the features of a chicken are *animate, feathered,* and *pecks.* Thus, each concept is described by a list of features.

---

1. Of course, there are also other ways to categorize concepts, for example, object concepts (e.g., *dog, table*), abstract concepts (e.g., *love, brilliance*), scientific concepts (e.g., *gravity, electromagnetic waves*), and so on.

Table A-1 Examples of Features (adapted from [SM81])				
Concept:	**Robin**	**Chicken**	**Collie**	**Daisy**
Features:	Animate	Animate	Animate	Inanimate
	Feathered	Feathered	Furry	Stem
	Flies	Pecks	Brown-Gray	White
	Red Breast			

Dimensions   *Dimensions* are usually used to express quantitative properties, such as *size* or *weight*. The value range of a dimension can be continuous (e.g., a real number) or discrete (e.g., *small*, *midsize*, and *large* for the dimension *size*). Typically, there is the requirement that the values of a dimension are ordered. If we drop this requirement, we get a "weak notion of dimensions," which is referred to as *attributes*. In contrast to featural descriptions, we use just one set of dimensions to represent a number of concepts: Each concept is represented by a tuple of values (one value for each dimension). Examples of a dimensional description are given in Table A-2.

We will discuss a number of important issues regarding features in Section A.3. But first, we focus our attention on the three views of concepts.

Table A-2 Examples of Dimensions (S and F stand for some appropriate value; adapted from [SM81])			
Concept:	**Robin**	**Chicken**	**Collie**
Dimensions:	Animacy: *animate*	Animacy: *animate*	Animacy: *animate*
	Size: S_R	Size: C_{Ch}	Size: S_C
	Ferocity: F_R	Ferocity: F_{Ch}	Ferocity: F_C

A.2.2 The Classical View

Necessary and sufficient properties   According to the *classical view*, any concept (or category) can be defined by listing a number of *necessary* and *sufficient* properties that an object must possess in order to be an instance of the concept. For example, the concept of a square can be defined using the following four features.

♦ Closed figure
♦ Four sides
♦ Sides equal in length
♦ Right angles

*Summary
description*

All four features are jointly sufficient and each of them is singly necessary in order to define a square. Thus, the essence of the classical view is that a concept can be precisely defined using a single *summary description* (e.g., the four features in our example). This summary description is the result of an abstraction and generalization process that takes a number of concrete concept instances as its input (see Section A.3.6). This summary description is the *essence* of a concept and corresponds to what software developers often refer to as "the right abstraction." A precise summary description can be given for mathematical concepts because they are defined precisely. Unfortunately, this is usually not the case for natural concepts. For example, how would you define the concept of a *game*? This classic example by Wittgenstein [Wit53] illustrates the problems of defining natural concepts ([SM81]).

*Criticism of the
classical view*

What is a necessary feature of the concept of games? It cannot be competition between teams, or even the stipulation that there must be at least two individuals involved, for solitaire is a game that has neither feature. Similarly, a game cannot be defined as something that must have a winner, for the child's game of ring-around-a-rosy has no such feature. Or let us try a more abstract feature—say that anything is a game if it provides amusement or diversion. Football is clearly a game, but it is doubtful that professional football players consider their Sunday endeavors as amusing or diverting. And even if they do, and if amusement is a necessary feature of a game, that alone cannot be sufficient, for whistling can also be an amusement and no one would consider it a game.[2]

During the 1970s and the 1980s, the criticism of the classical view intensified. Some of the then-identified problems of this view included [SM81]

♦ *Failure to specify defining features:* Natural concepts for which—as in the case of a *game*—no defining (i.e., necessary and sufficient) features have been found are abundant.

---

2. As an exercise, try to define the concept "table." You will quickly realize that this is as hopeless as trying to define "game."

Totally and partially disjunctive concepts

♦ *Existence of disjunctive concepts:* If the feature sets of any two instances of a concept are disjunctive, the concept is referred to as a *totally disjunctive concept*. If a concept is not totally disjunctive and if the feature sets of any two of its instances are only partially overlapping, the concept is called *partially disjunctive* (see Figure A-1). Both partially and totally disjunctive concepts violate the requirement of the classical view that a concept is defined by a *single* set of sufficient and necessary features. According to Rosch et al. [RMG+76], very general concepts, such as *furniture*, are often disjunctive.

♦ *Simple typicality effects:* Smith and Medin note that [SM81]: "People find it a natural task to rate the various subsets or members of a concept with respect to how typical or representative each one is of a concept." This finding cannot be reconciled with the classical view.

Non-necessary features

♦ *Use of nonnecessary features in categorization:* As documented by Hampton [Ham79], people often use *non-necessary features* (i.e., features that only some instances of a concept have) in the categorization of objects. An example of a nonnecessary feature of birds is "able to fly" because some birds don't fly. This suggests that nonnecessary features play an important role in defining concepts.

Nesting of concept's defining features in subsets

In addition to the single summary description consisting of sufficient and necessary properties, the classical view has one more assumption [SM81]:

"If concept X is a subset of a concept Y, the defining features of Y are nested in those of X."

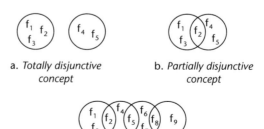

a. *Totally disjunctive concept*

b. *Partially disjunctive concept*

c. *Another example of a totally disjunctive concept*

Figure A-1 *Disjunctive concepts (f stands for a feature; each circle represents a set of features describing an instance of a concept)*

For example, consider the concepts *rectangles* and *squares*. All instances of the concept *square* are clearly instances of the concept *rectangle*. Also, the defining features of *rectangle* (i.e., closed figure, four sides, and right angles) are nested in those of *square* (i.e., closed figure, four sides, right angles, and sides equal in length).

This assumption also turns out to be problematic. It is—in many cases—too strong, and it has to be weakened in order to reflect reality more adequately. As Smith and Medin note [SM81], many people, when asked: "Is tomato a fruit?", are unsure of whether this particular subset relation holds. People often even change their mind over time about whether a particular subset relation holds or not and there always seem to be exceptions violating assumed subset relations. The classical view is unable to account for these effects.

The criticism of the classical view discussed in this section eventually leads to the development of the probabilistic and exemplar views. Some of the most influential work supporting this criticism is that by Rosch and Mervis (e.g., [Ros73, Ros75, Ros77, RM75, RMG+76]).

A.2.3 The Probabilistic View

In the probabilistic view, each concept is described—just as in the classical view—by a list of properties, that is, we also have a single summary description of a concept. The main difference between them is that in the probabilistic view each feature has a likelihood associated with it. For example, one could associate the likelihood of 0.9 with the feature *flies* of the concept *bird* in order to indicate that most (but not all) birds fly.

At odds with the term "probabilistic view," the number associated with each feature is usually not a probability value. Rather, it is a weight whose value could be calculated depending on many factors, for example, the probability that the feature is true of an instance of a concept, the degree to which the feature distinguishes the concept from other concepts, and the past usefulness or frequency of the feature in perception and reasoning [SM81].

Semantic networks

Spreading activation

An example of a probabilistic representation of the concepts *vegetable* and *green bean* is shown in Figure A-2. This kind of network representation is also referred to as a *propositional* or *semantic network* (please note that, in general, a semantic network need not be probabilistic). A possible classification procedure based on this representation is *spreading activation* [CL75]. For example, in order to check to see if green bean is a vegetable, the corresponding nodes in Figure A-2 are activated (imagine that the

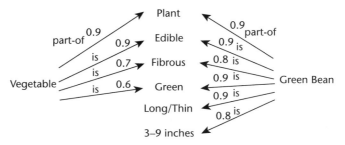

Figure A-2 *A small part of a probabilistic semantic network (adapted from [SWC+95], © 1995 by The MIT Press)*

net in Figure A-2 is just part of a larger network). The activation spreads along all the paths starting from each of the two nodes. The amount of activation depends on the weights. Some of the activated paths will intersect forming a pathway connecting the two nodes. The amount of activation in the pathways will be used to decide if *green bean* is a *vegetable*.

A.2.4 The Exemplar View

In the exemplar view, a concept is defined by its exemplars (i.e., representative instances) rather than by an abstract summary. Exemplars can be specific concept instances as well as subsets. For example, the representation of the concept *bird* could include the subset concept *robin* and the specific instance *"Fluffy"* (see Figure A-3). The exemplar representation is especially well suited for representing disjunctive concepts (see Section A.2.2).

Connectionist approaches

In the case of an exemplar representation, new objects are categorized based on their similarity to the stored exemplars. One problem in this context is how to efficiently store and process a large number of exemplars. A possible approach is to deploy a *connectionist architecture*, that is, a massively parallel architecture consisting of a large number of simple, networked processing units, such as a *neural network* (see [Kru92]). In a neural network, for example, a new exemplar is stored by adjusting the weights associated with the connections between neurons. This adjustment can be accomplished using the *back-propagation algorithm* (see e.g., [HN90]).

A.2.5 Summary of the Three Views

All three views have been summarized in Figure A-4. Both the probabilistic and the exemplar view do not suffer from the specific

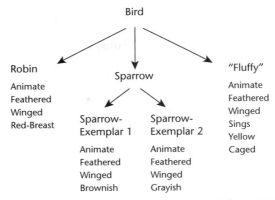

Figure A-3 An exemplar representation (adapted from [SM81])

problems of the classical view listed in Section A.2.2. This state of affairs does not invalidate the classical view, however. Certain problems can be adequately represented and solved using the classical view. Because concepts capture some relevant properties of objects in a given context, a classical representation might be feasible in some specific context at hand. In such cases, there is no need to use the more complicated probabilistic or exemplar views. As Winston notes [Win92]: "Once a problem is described using appropriate representation, the problem is almost solved." There is also evidence that the human mind deploys both abstract and exemplar representations, and that all three views will have to be reflected in a comprehensive theory of concepts.

One important lesson follows from this presentation, however: Natural concepts, which we deal with on a daily basis and try to model in software, are inherently complex. The classical view works best for mathematical concepts. It might also be adequate

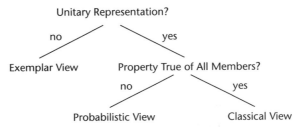

Figure A-4 Three views of concepts (from [SM81])

for creating simplified models of natural concepts. However, it usually breaks if we try to cover the diversity of natural concepts more adequately. This finding is particularly relevant to software reuse, whose goal is to provide generic solutions that work in many contexts.

A.3 Important Issues Concerning Concepts

So far we have covered some basic terminology as well as the three major views of concepts. In the following six sections we will focus on some important issues concerning concepts. These issues are concept stability, concept core, information contents of features, relationships between features, quality of features, and the relationship between abstraction and generalization.

A.3.1 Stability of Concepts

Any natural concept, even the simplest, involves an enormous amount of knowledge. Stillings et al. expressed this fact in this excellent example [SWC+95]:

> Your knowledge about cucumbers, for example, might include tactile information ('those tiny bumps with little spines growing out of them'), the picking size for several varieties, when and how to plant, type of machinery and labor needed for farm harvest, how to test for bitterness, smell when rotting, use in several of the world's cuisines, next-door neighbors hate them, waxy grocery store surface an unnatural phenomenon, and so on.

The knowledge that different persons associate with a concept varies from person to person, and it also evolves over time. Furthermore, it also depends on the context. Before explaining this idea, we first need to consider the basic architecture of the human mind.

Long-term and working memory

Roughly speaking, the human mind has two kinds of storage: the *long-term memory* and the *working memory* (also called *short-term memory*). The long-term memory is where all the knowledge that we maintain over long periods of time (minutes to years) is stored. The knowledge in the long-term memory is not directly accessible to thought processes. The working memory, on the other hand, contains the knowledge that is directly accessible. However, the working memory is limited both in terms of time and space. Knowledge in the working memory needs to be "refreshed" every few seconds in order to stay there. The space limitation is

NOTE

In [New90], Newell notes that the current understanding of these two kinds of storage is that the working memory is a part of the long-term memory rather than a separate memory requiring transfer. This view aligns well with the idea of spreading activation discussed in Section A.2.3.

described by the famous "rule of seven, plus or minus two" by Miller [Mil56], which states that a person can only remember about seven, plus or minus two, items at a time.

Because of this limitation of the working memory, only these aspects of a concept will be brought into the working memory, which are considered relevant to solving the problem at hand. In a sense, you can think of concepts as actually being assembled "on-the-fly" as they are needed. This effect tells us that the content of a concept depends on the context in which the concept is currently used.

A.3.2 Concept Core

Essential properties

For a graphical figure to be an instance of a square, it must have the following four defining properties: *closed figure, four sides, sides equal in length,* and *equal angles.* These properties are common to all instances of the concept *square.* They are not only common to all squares—they are *essential* for a square to be a square. Squares have other properties, for example, a certain *size,* which is nonessential. The essential properties of a concept constitute its *core.*

Concepts are used in the inference process during problem solving. Once we assume, for example, that a certain object is a square, we can infer the four essential properties of squareness from this assumption.

Concepts are used to solve different problems in different contexts. Not all properties are relevant in all contexts, but the more contexts a property is relevant in, the more essential the property is. Necessary properties that, by definition, hold for all instances of an object are very likely to be essential because one can rely on the fact that they hold, and they are usually used in many contexts. Therefore, we assert that defining properties are essential. But this statement describes essentiality only in the context of the classical view, which assumes that concepts have their defining properties. In general, as you may remember, this view is too restrictive.

Nonnecessary but essential properties

If we subscribe to the probabilistic view, from the fact that an object is an instance of a concept, we can infer that it has some property only with a certain probability. Such inference is still useful and used by humans. And the more situations the nonnecessary property can be used in, the more essential it is. Thus, an essential property does not need to be common to all instances of a concept. For example, the property *flies* is an essential property of *birds*, but it does not hold for all instances of this concept.

A.3.3 Informational Contents of Features

The simplest and most natural way of describing a concept is by listing its properties. For example, for the concept *daisy* we listed *inanimate*, *stem*, and *white* (see Table A-1). By listing *stem* as its feature, we mean more specifically that a *daisy* has a *stem* as its part. We can represent this fact by drawing an arrow from *daisy* to *stem* and annotating this arrow with *part-of*. This is exactly how we produced the semantic net in Figure A-2. Thus, a feature can be represented as another concept plus its relationship to the concept that is being described. But a feature can also be represented using more than one concept (and more than one relationship) as in the case of *red breast* (see Table A-1), that is, *robin* $\xleftarrow{\text{part of}}$ *breast* $\xrightarrow{\text{is}}$ *red*. If we would like to reveal more semantics of *red* and *breast*, we would have to grow this graph bigger and bigger by adding new concepts and relationships. Relationships may be themselves concepts. For example, the properties of *part-of* can be modeled by another semantic network.

Concepts versus features

We can view concepts as chunks of knowledge. Features are also chunks of knowledge used to build a larger chunk of knowledge, that is, the concept they describe. It becomes immediately clear that the distinction between a concept and a feature is a relative one and determined by the focus of the description. If we would like to know the contents of a feature, we would move our focus to that feature and break it down piece by piece, as we did it with the initial concept.

A.3.4 Feature Composition and Relationships between Features

Relationships between features are particularly interesting in the context of feature composition. Feature composition can be regarded as a means of creating concepts or concept instances. In this context, relationships between features are manifested through *constraints on feature combinations* and *translations between features*.

◆ *Constraints on feature combinations:* In general, features cannot be freely combined because certain feature combinations may lead to a contradiction. For example, a matrix cannot be non-

WHY DO FEATURES SEEM SO NATURAL FOR DESCRIBING CONCEPTS?

Features allow us to describe concepts by using few items or chunks. As you may remember, the working memory of the human mind can store only a limited number of chunks at a time— seven or so (see Section A.3.1). There-fore, it is convenient to list *inanimate*, *stem*, and *white* for a daisy and not to instantly think of all the detail that these features imply. These details can be retrieved from the long-term memory as needed. Chunking, that is, orga-nizing information in units and doing this in a recursive way, is believed to be the basic property of human memory (see [New90]). It tells us that the human mind internally employs modularity and that any models we build have to be modular in order to be understandable.

square and diagonal at the same time because diagonal implies square.

♦ *Translations between features:* Certain features (or feature com-binations) may imply some other features. In our matrix exam-ple, if a matrix is diagonal, then it is also square.

A.3.5   Quality of Features

The quality of features has to be judged in the context of the tasks they are used for. However, three general feature qualities are

♦ *Primitiveness:* Features express differences and similarities between concepts. A feature is primitive if it does not have to be decomposed in order to show some relevant differences among concept instances.

♦ *Generality:* A feature is more general if it applies to a large num-ber of concepts. A set of features is general if it describes a large number of concepts with a minimal number of features.

♦ *Independency:* The fewer constraints on feature combinations that apply to a set of features, the larger number of concepts that can be described by combining the features.

These are structural qualities that tell us how "economical" a set of features is in describing relevant concepts.

A.3.6   Abstraction and Generalization

Both in the classical and the probabilistic view, a concept is defined through an abstract summary description. This abstract descrip-tion is usually the result of an abstraction and generalization

Abstraction

process, which takes a number of sample objects (i.e., exemplars) as its input.

Abstraction involves the extraction of properties of an object according to some focus: properties that are selected are only those relevant with respect to the focus (e.g., a certain class of problems). Thus, abstraction is an information filtering process that reduces the initial amount of information to be used in problem solving.

Generalization

Generalization is an inductive process of collecting information about a number of objects and presenting this information in a single description. Generalization usually results in the increase of information. The construction of a generalized description of a number of instances can also lead to a larger description than each individual object description. For example, in the first step, a number of object descriptions could be lumped together (which corresponds to the exemplar view). In the second step, the compound description could be restated in a more declarative form and, as a result, becomes more concise (no information is lost in this process, i.e., all original objects could be reproduced from this description). However, in most cases, generalization and abstractions are combined when describing a set of objects. This combination produces an abstract and generalized description that is even more concise because the information not relevant to the abstraction focus is removed.

Abstraction, concretization, generalization, and specialization are operations on concepts.

♦ *Generalization:* An existing description of a set of objects can be further *generalized* by adding new objects to the set and modifying the description to take these new objects into account.

Specialization

♦ *Specialization:* The inverse operation to generalization is *specialization*. Specializing the description of a set of objects involves the reduction of the set to a subset.

♦ *Abstraction:* An existing description of a set of objects can be further *abstracted* using a new focus and filtering away all parts of the description that are not relevant with respect to the new focus.

Concretization (refinement)

♦ *Concretization:* The inverse operation to abstraction is *concretization* (also called *refinement*). Concretization results in the increase of detail per object.

These operations give rise to relationships between concepts. For example, the input and the output of the abstraction operation are related by the abstraction relationship. We get generalization, concretization, and specialization relationships in an analogous

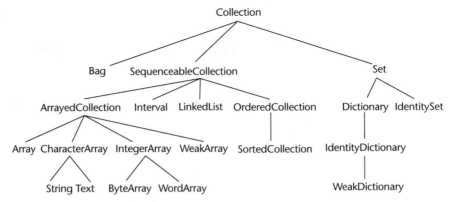

Figure A-5 *Part of the collection inheritance hierarchy in Smalltalk\Visual-Works 3.0*

way. Of course, the inverse of an abstraction relationship is a concretization relationship, and the inverse of a generalization relationship is a specialization relationship.

Abstraction and generalization usually occur together. For example, a typical hierarchy of data structure concepts, such as the one in Figure A-5, can be interpreted both as an abstraction and generalization hierarchy. Indeed, the relationships in Figure A-5 represent both abstraction and generalization relationships. For example, *Collection* is a generalization of *OrderedCollection* because the set of all ordered collections is a subset of the set of all collections in Smalltalk. At the same time, *Collection* is an abstraction of *OrderedCollection* because *Collection* abstracts away the property *ordered* of *OrderedCollection*. Furthermore, the abstraction relationships in Figure A-5 use multiple abstraction criteria (e.g., indexed or not, ordered or not, sorted or not, weak or not, different element types, and so on).[3] You'll find a thorough treatment of the topic of generalization and abstraction in the context of computer science in [Nav96].

---

3. As we discussed in Section 4.5, feature diagrams allow us to represent multidimensional classification in a more effective and complete way than single inheritance hierarchies. For example, the properties weak or identity appear multiple times in different places of the hierarchy in Figure A-5.

A.4 Conceptual Modeling, Object-Orientation, and Software Reuse

Concepts can be regarded as natural modeling elements because they represent a theory about knowledge organization in the human mind. The relationship between concepts and object-orientation (specifically the classical object model) is apparent: Concepts correspond to classes. The major difference is that object-orientation makes more specific assumptions about objects: They have *state*, *behavior*, and *identity* and collaborate through *interactions*.

Based on the presentation of the three views of concepts we can draw the following conclusions.

♦ The classical view of concepts is well-suited for representing well-defined concepts that are defined by a set of necessary and sufficient properties. In the classical object model, this view is adequately modeled by classes. A class represents a unitary and exact description of all its instances.

♦ Natural concepts are modeled more adequately using probabilistic and exemplar representations. In software engineering, concepts, such as customer and bank account, are examples of natural concepts. The probabilistic and the exemplar views allow us to represent the great structural variety of instances of natural concepts. This structural variety is related to the fact that natural concepts are used in a large number of different contexts—each requiring different structures. In the classical object model, the structural variety of a concept can only be expressed in indirect ways, for example, encoded in the state space of an object or as an often large and complicated inheritance hierarchy. It would clearly be desirable to have a means of explicitly and concisely representing concepts including a convenient mechanism for expressing their variants. This critique aligns well with the famous "critique of pure objects" by Harrison and Ossher [HO93], which points out the inadequate handling of subjectivity and context dependency of objects by the classical object model. The need for an adequate support for modeling concept variations is particularly important in the context of reusable software.

♦ Featural and dimensional descriptions represent a convenient model for representing the variability of concepts. In this context, the issues concerning concepts, features, and dimensions discussed in Section A.3 (e.g., essentiality of features, relationships between features, and qualities of features) become relevant.

♦ The probabilistic and the exemplar representation models are well suited for implementing component retrieval mechanisms because they allow us to capture the relationships between natural language terms (i.e., words used to index reusable components).

BIBLIOGRAPHIC NOTES

The book by Stillings et al. [SWC+95] represents a modern and comprehensive treatment of cognitive science. For an excellent treatment of the three views and a comprehensive survey of theories of concepts see [SM81]. The book by Newell [New90]—one of the AI classics—provides a survey of theories of cognition. The topic of abstraction and generalization in the context of computer science is discussed in [Nav96].

Appendix B

Instance-Specific Extension Protocol for Smalltalk

This appendix contains the implementation of the instance-specific extension protocol described in Section 8.5.7.3 for Smalltalk\Visual Works.[1] The protocol allows us to define methods in instances and add instance variables to instances. This code has been tested with VisualWorks versions 2.0, 2.5, and 3.0.[2] It is also available at [DCOOL].[3]

Object **methods in protocol** `'instance specialization'`:

specialize: aString
  "Compile aString as a method for this instance only."

```
self specialize.
self basicClass compile: aString notifying: nil.
```

---

1. VisualWorks is a product of Cincom, Inc. A free noncommercial version can be downloaded at www.cincom.com/visualworks/downloads.html. As of this writing, you can also obtain it from ObjectShare, Inc. at www.objectshare.com/VWNC/.

2. Before installing the implementation shown in this appendix in Visual-Works 3.0, we have to patch a bug in the VisualWorks 3.0 base image by defining the method nonMetaClass in Behavior. The contents of the method should be ^self.

3. This site also features an implementation of the extension protocol that does not require the use of the compiler in the deliverable. The implementation allows you to install precompiled methods, which you store in some helper class.

addInstanceVariable: aString
"Add an instance variable and accessing
methods based on the name aString"

self specialize.
self incrementNumberOfInstVarsInMyClassFormat.
self mutateSelfToReflectNewClassFormat.
self addAccessingMethodsForLastInstVarUsing: aString.

unspecialize
"Get rid of my private aBehavior, if any."

self isSpecialized ifFalse: [^self].
self changeClassToThatOf: self class basicNew.

isSpecialized
"Check if I am specialized by checking if my class is aBehavior."

^self basicClass shouldBeRegistered not

basicClass
"Answer the object that is the receiver's class."

<primitive: 111>
self primitiveFailed

Object methods in protocol
'private - instance specialization':

specialize
"Insert a private instance of Behavior between me and my class."

| class |
self isSpecialized ifTrue: [^self].
class := Behavior new
  superclass: self class;
  setInstanceFormat: self class format;
  methodDictionary: MethodDictionary new.
self changeClassToThatOf: class basicNew.
self basicClass compile:
  'class
    ^super class superclass'
  notifying: nil.

incrementNumberOfInstVarsInMyClassFormat
   "Set the format of my class so that it defines the number
   of instance variables to be higher by one than previously"

   | format newInstVarListSize |
   newInstVarListSize := self basicClass instSize - self class instSize + 1.
   format := ClassBuilder new
     genFormat: newInstVarListSize
     under: self class
     format: self basicClass format.
   self basicClass setInstanceFormat: format.

mutateSelfToReflectNewClassFormat
   "Mutate self to get in sync with the new format of my class"

   | newIVSize mappingArray newInst |
   newIVSize := self basicClass instSize.
   mappingArray := Array new: newIVSize.
   1 to: newIVSize - 1 do: [:i | mappingArray at: i put: i].
   mappingArray at: newIVSize put: 0.
   newInst := ClassBuilder new
     createCopy: self
     under: self basicClass
     using: mappingArray.
   self become: newInst.

addAccessingMethodsForLastInstVarUsing: aString
   "Add getters and setters for the last instance
   variable using aString for naming"

   | lastIVIndex getMeth putMeth |
   lastIVIndex := self basicClass instSize.
   getMeth := aString, ' ^self instVarAt: ',
     lastIVIndex printString.
   self basicClass compile: getMeth notifying: nil.
   putMeth := aString, ': aValue self instVarAt: ',
     lastIVIndex printString, ' put: aValue'.
   self basicClass compile: putMeth notifying: nil.

Appendix C

Protocol for Attaching Listener Objects in Smalltalk

This appendix contains the implementation of the noninvasive, dynamic composition mechanism described in Section 8.5.7 for Smalltalk\VisualWorks.[1] This code has been tested with Visual-Works versions 2.0, 2.5, and 3.0.[2] It is also available at [DCOOL].

`Object` **methods in protocol** `'attaching objects'`:

attach: anObject at: selector
  "Attach anObject at selector. All messages selector
  sent to self are redirected to anObject."

  self makeObjectAttachable.
  self redirectMessage: selector.

  self listenersDictionary at: selector put: anObject.

attach: anObject at: selector1 and: selector2
  "Attach anObject at selector1 and selector2. All messages
  selector1 and selector2 sent to self are redirected to
  anObject."

---

1. VisualWorks is a product of Cincom, Inc. A free noncommercial version can be downloaded at www.cincom.com/visualworks/downloads.html. As of this writing, you can also obtain it from ObjectShare, Inc. at www.objectshare.com/VWNC/.
2. This implementation also requires installing the code from Appendix B.

```
self makeObjectAttachable.
self redirectMessage: selector1.
self redirectMessage: selector2.

self listenersDictionary at: selector1 put: anObject.
self listenersDictionary at: selector2 put: anObject.
```

attach: anObject atSelectors: aCollection
"Attach anObject at selectors contained in aCollection."

```
self makeObjectAttachable.
aCollection do: [ :selector |
  self redirectMessage: selector.
  self listenersDictionary at: selector put: anObject ].
```

attach: anObject at: selector1 sending: selector2
"Attach anObject at selector1. All messages selector1
sent to self are converted to selector2 and redirected to anObject.
selector2 has to be an unary message selector, i.e. expects no arguments."

```
self makeObjectAttachable.
self redirectMessage: selector1 as: selector2.

self listenersDictionary at: selector1 put: anObject.
```

detachAt: selector
"Stop redirecting messages of the form 'selector'."

```
self basicClass removeSelector: selector.
self listenersDictionary removeKey: selector.
```

baseCall
"This method is intended to be invoked directly or indirectly by
a redirected message. baseCall calls the base method, i.e. the
method that would be called if it the message was not
redirected."

```
| baseContext selector baseMethod na args |
baseContext := self baseContext.

"find out the selector of the originally dispatched method"
selector := baseContext receiver basicClass
  selectorAtMethod: baseContext
  method ifAbsent: [ self error: 'method not found - should not happen' ].
```

```
"retrieve the arguments of the originally dispatched method"
na := selector numArgs.
args := Array new: na.
1 to: na do: [ :i | args at: i put: (baseContext localAt: i) ].

"look up the base method; if not found, report an error"
baseMethod := baseContext receiver class findSelector: selector.
baseMethod isNil ifTrue: [
  Object messageNotUnderstoodSignal
    raiseRequestWith: (Message selector: selector arguments: args)
    errorString: 'superCall: Message not understood by the base object: '
                 , selector. ].
baseMethod := baseMethod at: 2.

"execute the base method"
^baseContext receiver performMethod: baseMethod arguments: args
```

baseContext
```
  "Return the initial method context of the redirected message.
  Override this method if you have a direct reference to baseObject
  in a sublass. In that case, test if receiver == baseObject
  instead of isObjectAttachable."

  | ctx |
  ctx := thisContext.
  [ ctx == nil or: [
    ctx receiver isObjectAttachable and: [ ctx receiver ~~ self]]] whileFalse: [
      ctx := ctx sender ].
  ctx == nil ifTrue: [ self error: 'base context not found' ].
  ^ctx
```

baseObject
```
  "Return the original receiver of the redirected message."

  ^self baseContext receiver
```

Object **methods in protocol** `'private - attaching objects'`:

makeObjectAttachable
```
  "Prepare this object for redirecting messages."

  self isObjectAttachable ifTrue: [ ^self ].
  self
```

```
        addInstanceVariable: 'listenersDictionary';
        listenersDictionary: IdentityDictionary new.
```

isObjectAttachable
  "Is this object prepared to redirect messages?"

```
  ^self basicClass includesSelector: #listenersDictionary
```

redirectMessage: selector
  "Redirect messages of the form 'selector' to self to the appropriate listener
  object."

```
  self redirectMessage: selector as: nil
```

redirectMessage: selector1 as: selector2OrNil
  "Redirect messages of the form 'selector1' to self to the appropriate listener
  object. If selector2OrNil is not nil, convert the message to selector2OrNil."

```
  | dispatchMeth aStream selectorWithArguments newSelector |

  (self messageIsRedirected: selector1) ifTrue: [ ^self ].
  selectorWithArguments := self insertArgumentsInto: selector1.
  newSelector := selector2OrNil isNil
    ifTrue: [ selectorWithArguments ]
    ifFalse: [ selector2OrNil ].

  aStream := WriteStream on: (String new: 100).
  aStream
    nextPutAll: selectorWithArguments;
    nextPutAll: ' ^(self listenersDictionary at: #';
    nextPutAll: selector1;
    nextPutAll: ') ';
    nextPutAll: newSelector.

  dispatchMeth := aStream contents.
  self basicClass compile: dispatchMeth notifying: nil.
```

messageIsRedirected: selector

```
  ^self basicClass includesSelector: selector
```

insertArgumentsInto: selector
  "self
    insertArgumentsInto: 'messageArg1:with:' returns 'messageArg1: t1 with: t2' "

```
| aStream numArgs |
aStream := WriteStream on: (String new: 60).
(numArgs := selector numArgs) = 0
  ifTrue: [ aStream nextPutAll: selector ]
  ifFalse: [
    selector keywords with: (1 to: numArgs) do: [ :word :i |
      aStream nextPutAll: word; nextPutAll: ' t'; print: i; space ]].
^aStream contents
```

Appendix D

Glossary of Matrix Computation Terms

Banded: "A banded matrix has its nonzero elements within a 'band' about the diagonal. The bandwidth of a matrix A is defined as the maximum of $|i\text{-}j|$ for which a_{ij} is nonzero. The upper bandwidth is the maximum $j\text{-}i$ for which a_{ij} is nonzero and $j>i$. See diagonal, tridiagonal, and triangular matrices as particular cases." [MM]

Cache-Based Optimizations: Code optimizations aiming at the optimal utilization of different caching levels of a computer.

Cache Tiling: A cache-based optimization, where operations on large matrices are computed in terms of their submatrices fitting into the cache.

C-Like Storage: A storage format for arrays, where each of two neighboring elements of one row are stored adjacently in memory. This is how arrays are stored in C.

Compressed Sparse Row/Column: Storage formats for sparse matrices, where each row/column is stored in a sparse vector (i.e., only the nonzero elements are stored).

Coordinate Format: Storage format for sparse matrices, where only the nonzero elements are stored together with their coordinates.

Definiteness: "A matrix A is positive definite if $x^T A\, x > 0$ for all nonzero x. Positive definite matrices have other interesting properties, such as being nonsingular, having its largest element on the diagonal, and having all positive diagonal elements. Like diagonal dominance, positive definiteness obviates the need for pivoting in Gaussian elimination. A positive semidefinite matrix has $x^T A\, x >= 0$ for all nonzero x. Negative definite and negative semidefinite matrices have the inequality signs reversed above." [MM]

Dense: A dense matrix or vector contains a relatively large number of nonzero elements.

Density: Density describes the percentage of nonzero elements in a matrix or vector.

Diagonal: A diagonal matrix has its only nonzero elements on the main diagonal.

Diagonal Dominance: "A matrix is diagonally dominant if the absolute value of each diagonal element is greater than the sum of the absolute values of the other elements in its row (or column). Pivoting in Gaussian elimination is not necessary for a diagonally dominant matrix." [MM]

Elementwise with Cache: An approach for evaluating matrix expressions, where both addition and multiplication are computed elementwise, and operand expressions are wrapped into cache wrappers. This approach effectively achieves loop fusing and temporaries elimination for matrix addition.

Factorizations: Matrix factorizations decompose matrices into factor matrices with some desired properties. For example, the LU factorization of a matrix A computes the lower-triangular matrix L and the upper-triangular matrix U, such that $A=L*U$.

Fortran-Like Storage: A storage format for arrays, where each of two neighboring elements of one column are stored adjacently in memory. This is how arrays are stored in Fortran.

Hermitian: "A Hermitian matrix A is self adjoint, that is $A^H = A$, where A^H, the adjoint, is the complex conjugate of the transpose of A." [MM]

Hessenberg: "A Hessenberg matrix is 'almost' triangular, that is, it is (upper or lower) triangular with one additional off-diagonal band (immediately adjacent to the main diagonal). A unsymmetric matrix can always be reduced to Hessenberg form by a finite sequence of similarity transformations." [MM]

Linear System Solving: Solving a linear system $A*x=b$—where A is the given coefficient matrix and b is the given right-hand side vector—involves finding the unknown solution vector x.

Rank: "The rank of a matrix is the maximum number of independent rows or columns. A matrix of order n is rank deficient if it has *rank < n*." [MM]

Register Tiling: A cache-based optimization, where operations on large matrices are computed in terms of their submatrices fitting into the registers.

Result Type Computation: Determining the properties (e.g., element type, shape, density) of a matrix expression based on the properties of its operands.

Shape: The arrangement of the nonzero elements of a matrix (e.g., diagonal or triangular).

Shape-Based Optimizations: Optimizing storage format of matrices based on their shape, and optimizing matrix algorithms based on the shape of their arguments.

Singular: "A singular matrix has no inverse. Singular matrices have zero determinants." [MM]

Skew-symmetric: "A skew-symmetric matrix has $a_{ij} = -a_{ji}$, or $A = -A^T$; consequently, its diagonal elements are zero." [MM]

Sparse: A sparse matrix or vector contains only a relatively small number of nonzero elements (often less than 1 percent).

Storage Format: The data structures used to store the elements of a matrix.

Symmetric: "A symmetric matrix has the same elements above the diagonal as below it, that is, $a_{ij} = a_{ji}$, or $A = A^T$." [MM]

Toeplitz: "A matrix A is a Toeplitz if its diagonals are constant; that is, $a_{ij} = f_{j-i}$ for some vector f." [MM]

Triangular: "An upper-triangular matrix has its only nonzero elements on or above the main diagonal, that is $a_{ij}=0$ if $i>j$. Similarly, a lower-triangular matrix has its nonzero elements on or below the diagonal, that is $a_{ij}=0$ if $i<j$." [MM]

Tridiagonal: A tridiagonal matrix has its only nonzero elements on the main diagonal or the off-diagonal immediately to either side of the diagonal.

Appendix E

Metafunction for Evaluating Dependency Tables

This appendix contains the implementation of the template meta-function EVAL_DEPENDENCY_TABLE<> for representing and evaluating dependency tables discussed in Section 14.4.1.3.3. We start with a program demonstrating the use of this metafunction:

```
#include <iostream>
using namespace std;
//include the table file shown later
#include "table.h"

//this just for testing
template< int val_ >
struct Num
{  enum { val = val_ };
};

//a couple of types for testing
typedef Num< 1 > One;
typedef Num< 2 > Two;
typedef Num< 3 > Three;
typedef Num< 4 > Four;

void main ()
{  // test table with a single return type column
   typedef EVAL_DEPENDENCY_TABLE
      //**********************************************
      <         CELL< 1,  CELL< 2                   > >
      , ROW< CELL< 1,  CELL< 3,  RET< One    > > >
      , ROW< CELL< 1,  CELL< 3,  RET< Two    > > >
      , ROW< CELL< 1,  CELL< 2,  RET< Three  > > >
      , ROW< CELL< 1,  CELL< 3,  RET< Four   > > >
      //**********************************************
```

```
                    > > > > >::RET Table_1_Return;

                cout << Table_1_Return::val << endl; //prints "3"

            // test table with two return type columns
            typedef EVAL_DEPENDENCY_TABLE
                //************************************************************
                <         CELL<        4, CELL<   7                                > >
                , ROW< CELL<        3, CELL<   7,        RET< Three, RET< Four  > > > >
                , ROW< CELL<        4, CELL<   5,        RET< Four,  RET< Three > > > >
                , ROW< CELL< anyValue, CELL<   7,        RET< One,   RET< Two   > > > >
                , ROW< CELL< anyValue, CELL< anyValue, RET< Two,   RET< One   > > > >
                //************************************************************
                > > > > >::RET_List ResultRow;

            typedef ResultRow::        ResultType ReturnType_1;
            typedef ResultRow::Tail::ResultType ReturnType_2;

            cout << ReturnType_1::val << '\t'
                 << ReturnType_2::val << endl; //prints "1   2"
}
```

And here is the contents of table.h:[1]

```
#ifndef TABLE_H
#define TABLE_H

#pragma warning( disable : 4786 )        // disable warning: identifier shortened
                                         // to 255 chars in debug information

#include "IF.H"
//*********************** helper structs *********************************

struct Nil {};

enum { endValue = ~(~0u >> 1),        // smallest signed integer value
       anyValue = endValue + 1        // second smallest int
     };

struct End
{ enum   { value = endValue };
```

-----

1. Thanks to Johannes Knaupp, who contributed to this implementation.

```
    typedef End Head;
    typedef End Tail;
};

template< int found_, class ResultList_ >
struct ResultOfRowEval
{   enum    { found = found_ };
    typedef ResultList_ ResultList;
};

struct ERROR__NoMatchingTableRow
{   typedef ERROR__NoMatchingTableRow ResultType;
};

//************ syntax elements for expressing case lists ********************

template< class ThisRow, class FollowingRows = End >
struct ROW
{   typedef ThisRow        Head;
    typedef FollowingRows  Tail;
};

template< int value_, class FurtherCells = End >
struct CELL
{   enum    { value = value_ };
    typedef FurtherCells  Tail;
};


template< class ThisResultType, class FurtherResultTypes = End >
struct RET
{   typedef ThisResultType      ResultType;
    typedef FurtherResultTypes  Tail;
    enum    { value = endValue };
};

//** metafunction EVAL_ROW for matching the head row against one body row **

template< class HeadRow, class TestRow >
class EVAL_ROW
{   //replace later by a case statement
    typedef typename HeadRow::Tail HeadTail;
    typedef typename TestRow::Tail RowTail;
```

```
      enum { headValue = HeadRow::value,
             testValue = TestRow::value,
             isLast    = (HeadTail::value == endValue),
             isMatch   = (testValue == anyValue) || (testValue == headValue)
           };

      typedef IF< isLast,
                  ResultOfRowEval< true, RowTail >,
                  typename EVAL_ROW< HeadTail, RowTail >::RET
              >::RET ResultOfFollowingCols;

public:
      typedef IF< isMatch,
                  ResultOfFollowingCols,
                  ResultOfRowEval< false, ERROR__NoMatchingTableRow >
              >::RET RET;
};



template<>
class EVAL_ROW< End, End >
{public:
      typedef Nil RET;
};

//****************** metafunction EVAL_DEPENDENCY_TABLE *********************

template< class HeadRow, class TableBody >
class EVAL_DEPENDENCY_TABLE
{   typedef EVAL_ROW< HeadRow, typename TableBody::Head >::RET RowResult;
    typedef typename RowResult::ResultList ResultList;
    typedef typename TableBody::Tail FurtherRows;
    typedef typename FurtherRows::Head FurtherRowsHead;

    enum { found      = RowResult::found,
           isLastRow  = (FurtherRowsHead::value == endValue)
         };

    typedef IF< isLastRow, End, HeadRow >::RET HeadRow_;
    typedef IF< isLastRow,
                ERROR__NoMatchingTableRow,
                typename EVAL_DEPENDENCY_TABLE<HeadRow_, FurtherRows>::RET_List
            >::RET NextTry;
```

```
public:
    typedef IF< found, ResultList, NextTry >::RET RET_List;
    typedef typename RET_List::ResultType RET;
};

template<>
class EVAL_DEPENDENCY_TABLE< End, End >
{public:
    typedef Nil RET_List;
};

#endif   // #ifndef TABLE_H
//**************************** END OF FILE ********************************
```

Glossary of Generative Programming Terms

Active Library: A library, which, in addition to the base procedures and classes to be executed at runtime, also contains metacode for configuration, generation, optimization, error checking and reporting, debugging and profiling, editing and visualization of code, code refactoring, versioning, and so on [CEG+98] (also see extendible programming environment)

Application Engineering: The process of producing concrete members of a system family using the reusable assets developed during Domain Engineering.

Configuration Knowledge: The knowledge necessary to automate the assembly of system family members out of implementation components. It specifies illegal combinations of system features, default settings, default dependencies, optimizations, and construction rules stating which configurations of components satisfy which configurations of features. Configuration knowledge can be implemented using generators.

Domain: An area of knowledge that *(1)* is scoped to maximize the satisfaction of the requirements of its stakeholders, *(2)* includes a set of concepts and terminology understood by practitioners in that area, and *(3)* includes the knowledge of how to build software systems (or parts of software systems) in that area.

Domain Engineering: The activity of collecting, organizing, and storing past experience in building systems or parts of systems in a particular domain in the form of reusable assets (i.e., reusable work products), as well as providing an adequate means for reusing these assets (i.e., retrieval, qualification, dissemination, adaptation, assembly, and so on) when building new systems.

Economies of scale: "The condition where fewer inputs, such as effort and time, are needed to produce greater quantities of a single output." [Wit96]

Economies of scope: "The condition where fewer inputs, such as effort and time, are needed to produce a greater variety of outputs. Greater business value is achieved by jointly producing different outputs. Producing each output independently fails to leverage commonalities that affect costs. Economies of scope occur when it is less costly to combine two or more products in one production system than to produce them separately." [Wit96]

Extendible Programming Environment: A programming environment that supports the idea of active libraries, that is, libraries of reusable programming abstractions, which also contain abstraction-specific metacode extending the environment in different areas including program visualization, debugging, profiling, error diagnosis and reporting, optimization, code generation, refactoring, and versioning.

Feature: A property of a domain concept, which is relevant to some domain stakeholder and is used to discriminate between concept instances.

Generative Domain Model: A model of a system family that allows the automatic generation of family members from abstract specifications. It consists of a means of specifying family members, the implementation components from which each member can be assembled, and the configuration knowledge.

Generative Programming (GP): A software development paradigm based on modeling software system families such that, given a particular requirements specification, a highly customized and optimized intermediate or end-product can be automatically manufactured on demand from elementary, reusable implementation components by means of configuration knowledge. The generated products may also contain nonsoftware artifacts, such as test plans, manuals, tutorials, maintenance and troubleshooting guidelines, and so on.

Generator: A program that takes a higher-level specification of a piece of software and produces its implementation. Generators may also be used to generate nonsoftware artifacts, such as test plans, manuals, tutorials, maintenance and troubleshooting guidelines, and so on.

Implementation Components: The elementary components from which the members of a system family can be assembled. They are designed to minimize code duplication and to be combinable in as many ways as possible, and thus to maximize reuse.

Metaprogramming: The discipline of writing programs that represent and manipulate other programs or themselves.

Problem Space: The terminology used to specify the members of a system family.

Product Family: "A product family is a group of products that can be built from a common set of assets." [Wit96]

Product Line: "A product line is a group of products sharing a common, managed set of features that satisfy the specific needs of a selected market." [Wit96]

Solution Space: The implementation components of a system family together with their possible configurations.

System Family: See "Product Family"

References

[ABB+94] E. Anderson, Z. Bai, C. Bischof, J. W. Demmel, J. Dongarra, J. Du Croz, A. Greenbaum, S. Hammarling, A. McKenney, S. Ostrouchov, and D. Sorensen. *LAPACK User's Guide*. Society for Industrial and Applied Mathematics (SIAM), Philadelphia, PA, 1994, see www.netlib.org/lapack/lug/lapack_lug.html

[ABE+97] S. V. Adve, D. Berger, R. Eigenmann, A. Rawsthorne, M. D. Smith, C. H. Gebotys, M. T. Kandemir, D. J. Lilja, A. N. Choudhary, J. Z. Fang, and P.-C. Yew. Changing Interaction of Compiler and Architecture. In *IEEE Computer*, December 1997, pp. 50–58, © IEEE 1997

[ABSB94] M. Aksit, J. Bosch, W. v. d. Sterren, and L. Bergmans. Real-Time Specification Inheritance Anomalies and Real-Time Filters. In *Proceedings of the ECOOP'94 Conference*, LNCS 821, Springer-Verlag, Berlin and Heidelberg, Germany, July 1994, pp. 386–407, see [CF]

[ABV92] M. Aksit, L. Bergmans, and S. Vural. An Object-Oriented Language-Database Integration Model: The Composition-Filters Approach. In *Proceedings of the ECOOP'92 Conference*, LNCS 615, Springer-Verlag, Berlin and Heidelberg, Germany, 1992

[AC96] M. Abadi and L. Cardelli. *A Theory of Objects*. Springer-Verlag, New York, NY, 1996

[ADAGE] World Wide Web home page of the DSSA/ADAGE project at www.lmowego.com/owegofs/dssa/

NOTE

Updates of online references will be published at www.generative-programming.org.

[ADK+98] W. Aitken, B. Dickens, P. Kwiatkowski, O. de Moor, D. Richter, and C. Simonyi. Transformation in Intentional Programming. In [DP98], pp. 114–123, also [IPH]

[AFM97] O. Agsen, S. Freund, and J. C. Mitchell. Adding parameterized types to Java. In Proceedings of *the Conference on Object-Oriented Programming, Systems, Languages, and Applications (OOPSLA'97)*, SIGPLAN Notices, Vol. 32, No. 10, October 1997, pp. 49–65

[AJ] Homepage of AspectJ, Xerox Palo Alto Research Center (Xerox PARC), Palo Alto, CA, see http://aspectj.org

[AKR+97] R. Akers, E. Kant, C. Randall, S. Steinberg, and R. Young. SciNapse: A Problem-Solving Environment for Partial Differential Equations. In *IEEE Computational Science and Engineering*, vol. 4, no. 3, July-September 1997, pp. 32–42, © IEEE 1997, also [SC]

[Aks89] M. Aksit. On the Design of the Object-Oriented Language Sina. Ph. D. Thesis, Department of Computer Science, University of Twente, The Netherlands, 1989

[Ame85] *The American Heritage Dictionary*. Houghton Mifflin, Boston, MA, 1985

[Ams72] B. K. Amsterdam. Mirror self-image reactions before age two. In *Developmental Psychology*, No. 5, 1972, pp. 297–305

[And90] J. R. Anderson. *The architecture of cognition*. Harward University Press, Cambridge, MA, 1990

[And93] P. H. Andersen. Partial Evaluation Applied to Ray Tracing. DIKU Technical Report, University of Copenhagen, 1993, www.diku.dk/research-groups/topps/bibliography/1993.html#D-178

[And94] L. O. Andersen. Program Analysis and Specialization for the C Programming Language. Ph. D. Thesis, DIKU, University of Copenhagen, May 1994, also see the C-Mix home page at www.diku.dk/research-groups/topps/activities/cmix/

[ANSI83] ANSI and AJPO. Military Standard: Ada Programming Language (American National Standards Institute and US Government Department of Defense, Ada Joint Program Office). ANSI/MIL-STD-1815A-1983, February 17, 1983

[AOP] Homepage of the Aspect-Oriented Programming Project, Xerox Palo Alto Research Center (Xerox PARC), Palo Alto, CA, www.parc.xerox.com/aop/

[AOP97] K. Mens, C. Lopes, B. Tekinerdogan, and G. Kiczales, (Organizers). *Proceedings of the ECOOP'98 Workshop on Aspect-*

Oriented Programming, Jyväskylä, Finland, June, 1997, see http://wwwtrese.cs.utwente.nl/aop-ecoop97/

[AOP98]   C. Lopes, G. Kiczales, G. Murphy, and A. Lee (Organizers). *Proceedings of the ICSE'98 Workshop on Aspect-Oriented Programming,* Kyoto, Japan, April 20, 1998, see [AOP]

[Ara88]   G. Arango. Domain Engineering for Software Reuse. Ph. D. Thesis, Department of Information and Computer Science, University of California, Irvine, CA, 1988

[Ara89]   G. Arango. Domain Analysis: From Art Form to Engineering Discipline. In *ACM SIGSOFT Software Engineering Notes,* vol. 14, no. 3, May 1989, pp. 152–159

[Ara94]   G. Arango. Domain Analysis Methods. In *Software Reusability,* W. Schäfer, R. Prieto-Díaz, and M. Matsumoto (Eds.), Ellis Horwood, New York, NY, 1994, pp. 17–49

[Arch]   World Wide Web home page of the Architecture Resources Guide at http://www-ast.tds-gn.lmco.com/arch/guide.html

[ASU86]   A. V. Aho, R. Sethi, and J. D. Ullman. *Compilers: Principles, Techniques, and Tools.* Addison-Wesley, Reading, MA, 1986

[AT88]   M. Aksit and A. Tripathi, Data Abstraction Mechanisms in Sina/ST. In *Proceedings of the Conference on Object-Oriented Programming, Systems, Languages, and Applications (OOPSLA'88),* ACM SIGPLAN Notices, vol. 23, no. 11, 1988, pp. 265–275

[AT96]   G. Attardi and T. Flagella, Memory Management in the PoSSo Solver. In *Journal of Symbolic Computing,* 21, 1996, pp. 1–20, see www.di.unipi.it/~attardi/papers.html

[ATB96]   M. Aksit, B. Tekinerdogan, and L. Bergmans. Achieving adaptability through separation and composition of concerns. In *Proceedings of the ECOOP Workshop on Adaptability in Object-Oriented Software Development,* Linz, Austria, July 1996, published in [Müh97], pp. 12–23

[AWB+93]   M. Aksit, K. Wakita, J. Bosch, L. Bergmans and A. Yonezawa. Abstracting Object Interactions Using Composition Filters. In *Proceedings of the ECOOP'93 Workshop on Object-Based Distributed Programming,* LNCS 791, Springr-Verlag, New York, NY, 1993, pp. 152–184

[Aus98]   M. H. Austern. *Generic Programming and the STL: Using and Extending the C++ Standard Template Library.* Addison-Wesley, Reading, MA, 1998

[Bai92]   S. Bailin. KAPTUR: A Tool for the Preservation and Use of Engineering Legacy. CTA Inc., Rockville, MD, 1992, http://www-ast.tds-gn.lmco.com/arch/kaptur.html

[Bai93]   S. Bailin. Domain Analysis with KAPTUR. In *Tutorials of TRI-Ada'93*, Vol. I, ACM, New York, NY, September 1993

[Bai97]   S. Bailin. Applying Multi-Media to the Reuse of Design Knowledge. In the *Proceedings of the Eighth Annual Workshop on Software Reuse*, 1997, www.umcs.maine.edu/~ftp/wisr/wisr8/papers.html

[Bal85]   R. Balzer. A 15 Year Perspective on Automatic Programming. In *IEEE Transactions on Software Engineering*, vol. SE-11, no. 11, November 1985, pp. 1257–1268, © IEEE 1985

[Bat96]   D. Batory. Software System Generators, Architectures, and Reuse. Tutorial Notes, Fourth International Conference on Software Reuse, April 23–26, 1996, Orlando, FL, also see [SSGRG]

[Bax90]   I. Baxter. Transformational Maintenance by Reuse of Design Histories. Ph.D. Thesis, Technical Report TR 90–36, Department of Information and Computer Science, University of California at Irvine, November 1990

[Bax92]   I. Baxter. Design Maintenance System. In *Communications ACM*, vol. 35, no. 4, April 1992, pp. 73–89

[Bax96]   I. Baxter. Transformation Systems: Theory, Implementation, and Survey. Tutorial Notes, Fourth International Conference on Software Reuse, April 23–26, 1996, Orlando, FL

[Bax99]   I. Baxter. Transformation Systems: Theory, Implementation, and Survey. Tutorial Notes, First International Symposium on Generative and Component-Based Software Engineering (GCSE'99), September 28–30, 1999, Erfurt, Germany

[BBG+88]   D. Batory, J. R. Barnett, J. F. Garza, K. P. Smith, K. Tuskuda, B. C. Twichell, and T. E. Wise. GENESIS: An Extensible Database Management System. In *IEEE Transactions on Software Engineering*, vol. 14, no. 11, November 1988, 1711–1730, © IEEE 1988

[BC90]   G. Bracha and W. Cook. Mixin-Based Inheritance. In *Proceedings of the 8th Conference on Object-Oriented Programming, Systems, Languages, and Applications / European Conference on Object-Oriented Programming (OOPSLA/ECOOP), ACM SIGPLAN Notices*, vol. 25, no. 10, 1990, pp. 303–311

[BC96]   L. Brownsword and P. Clements. A Case Study in Successful Product Line Development. Technical Report, SEI-96-TR-016, Software Engineering Institute, Carnegie Mellon University, Pittsburgh, PA, October, 1996 , www.sei.cmu.edu

[BCD+89]   P. Borras, D. Clément, T. Despeyroux, J. Incerpi, G. Kahn, B. Lang, and V. Pascual. CENTAUR: the system. In *Proceedings of the ACM SIGSOFT/SIGPLAN Symposium on Practical Software Development Environments*, 1989, pp. 14–24, also www.inria.fr/croap/centaur/centaur.html

[BCGS95] D. Batory, L. Coglianese, M. Goodwin, and S. Shafer. Creating Reference Architectures: An Example from Avionics. In *Proceedings of the ACM SIGSOFT Symposium on Software Reusability*, April 28–30, 1995, Seattle, WA, pp. 27–37, also as Technical Report ADAGE-UT-93-06C, also www.lmowego.com/owegofs/dssa/ut-docs/ut-docs.html

[BCK98] L. Bass, P. Clements, and R. Kazman. *Software Architecture in Practice*. Addison-Wesley, Reading, MA, 1998

[BCR94] V. Basili, G. Caldiera, and D. Rombach, The Experience Factory. In *Encyclopedia of Software Engineering*, J. J. Marciniak, (Ed.), John Wiley & Sons, Inc., New York, NY 1994, ftp://ftp.cs.umd.edu/pub/sel/papers/fact.ps.Z

[BCRW98] D. Batory, G. Chen, E. Robertson, and T. Wang. Design Wizards and Visual Programming Environments for Generators. In [DP98], pp. 255–267, also [SSGRG]

[BD98] B. Bokowski and M. Dahm. Poor Man's Genericity for Java. In *Proceedings of JIT'98*, Springer-Verlag, Berlin and Heidelberg, Germany, 1998, see www.inf.fu-berlin.de/~bokowski/pmgjava/

[BDF98] L. Berger, A. M. Dery, M. Fornarino. Interactions between objects: an aspect of object-oriented languages. In [AOP98], pp. 13–18

[BDQ97] F. Bassetti, K. Davis, and D. Quinlan. A Comparison of Performance-Enhancing Strategies for Parallel Numerical Object-Oriented Frameworks. In *Proceedings of the first International Scientific Computing in Object-Oriented Parallel Environments Conference (ISCOPE'97), Marina del Rey, California, Dec 1997*, LNCS Vol. 1343, Springer-Verlag, Berlin and Heidelberg, Germany, 1997, www.c3.lanl.gov/~kei/publications.html

[Bec93a] K. Beck. Smalltalk Idioms: Instance specific behavior, Part 1. In *Smalltalk Report*, no. 2, vol. 6, March/April 1993, pp. 13–15

[Bec93b] K. Beck. Smalltalk Idioms: Instance specific behavior, Part 2. In *Smalltalk Report*, no. 2, vol. 7, May/June 1993

[Bec95] K. Beck. Smalltalk Idioms: What? What happened to garbage collection? In *Smalltalk Report*, no. 4, vol. 4, March/April 1995, pp. 27–32

[Bec97] K. Beck. *Smalltalk Best Practices Patterns*. Prentice Hall, Englewood Cliffs, NJ, 1997

[BEH+87]   F. L. Bauer, H Ehler, A. Horsch, B. Möller, H. Partsch, O. Paukner, and P. Pepper. *The Munich project CIP: Volume II, the Transformation System CIP-S*. LNCS 292, Springer-Verlag, Berlin and Heidelberg, Germany, 1987

[BEJV96]   P. Binns, M. Englehart, M. Jackson, and S. Vestal. Domain-Specific Software Architectures for Guidance, Navigation and Control. In *International Journal of Software Engineering and Knowledge Engineering*, Vol. 6, No. 2, 1996, also see http://www-ast.tds-gn.lmco.com/arch/dssa.html

[Ber94]   L. M. J. Bergmans. Composing Concurrent Objects — Applying Composition Filters for the Development and Reuse of Concurrent Object-Oriented Programs. Ph. D. Thesis, Department of Computer Science, University of Twente, The Netherlands, 1994, see ftp://ftp.cs.utwente.nl/pub/doc/TRESE/bergmans.phd.tar

[BF96]   S. Blazy and P. Facon. Interprocedural Analysis for Program Comprehension by Specialization. In *Proceedings of the 4th Workshop on Program Comprehension (March 29–31, Berlin, Germany, 1996), WPC'96*, A. Cimitile and H. A. Müller (Eds.), IEEE Computer Society Press, Los Alamitos, CA, 1996, pp. 133–141, © IEEE 1996

[BFJR98]   J. Brant, B. Foote, R. Johnson, and D. Roberts. Wrappers to Rescue. In *Proceedings of the 12th European Conference on Object-Oriented Programming (ECOOP'98)*, E. Jul (Ed.), LNCS 1445, Springer-Verlag, Berlin and Heidelberg, Germany, 1998, pp. 396–417

[BFK+99]   J. Bayer, O. Flege, P. Knauber, R. Laqua, D. Muthig, K. Schmid, T. Widen, and J.-M. DeBaud. PuLSE: A methodology to develop software product lines. In *Proceedings of the Symposium on Software Reuse*, May 1999, pp. 122–131

[BG77]   B. R. Burstall and J. A. Goguen. Putting theories togethor to make specifications. In *Proceedings of the Fifth International Joint Conference on Artificial Intelligence (Cambridge, MA, 22–25, 1977), IJCAI*, 1977, pp. 1045–1058

[BG96]   D. Batory and B. J. Geraci. Validating Component Compositions in Software System Generators. In [Sit96], pp. 72–81, also extended version as Technical Report TR-95-03, Department of Computer Sciences, University of Texas at Austin, June 1995, also [SSGRG]

[BG97]   D. Batory and B. J. Geraci. Composition Validation and Subjectivity in GenVoca Generators. In *IEEE Transactions on*

Software Engineering, special issue on Software Reuse, February 1997, pp. 67–82, © IEEE 1997, also [SSGRG]

[BG98]   C. Becker and K. Gheis. Quality of Service—Aspect of Distributed Programs. In [AOP98], pp. 7–12

[BGT94]   D. Batory, B. Geraci, and J. Thomas. Introductory P2 System Manual. Technical Report TR-94-26, Department of Computer Sciences, University of Texas at Austin, November 1994, see [SSGRT]

[BHW97]   J. Boyle, T. Harmer, and V. Winter. The TAMPR Program Transformation System: Simplifying the Development of Numerical Software. In *Modern Software Tools for Scientific Computing Age*, Erland et al. (Eds.), Birkhäuser Boston, 1997, pp. 353–372

[Big94]   T. Biggerstaff. The Library Scaling Problem and the Limits of Concrete Component Reuse. In *Proceedings of the 3rd International Conference on Software Reuse*, W. B. Frakes (Ed.), IEEE Computer Society Press, 1994, pp. 102–109, © IEEE 1994

[Big97]   T. Biggerstaff. A Perspective of Generative Reuse. Technical Report MSR-TR-97-26, Microsoft Corporation, Redmond, WA, 1997

[Big98a]   T. Biggerstaff. Anticipatory Optimization in Domain Specific Translation. In *Proceedings of the Fifth International Conference on Software Reuse (ICSR'98)*, P. Devanbu and J. Paulin, (Eds.), IEEE Computer Society Press, 1998, pp. 124–133, © IEEE 1998

[Big98b]   T. Biggerstaff. Composite Folding and Optimization in Domain Specific Translation. Technical Report, MSR-TR-98-22, Microsoft Research, June 1998

[BJ66]   C. Böhm and G. Jacopini. Flow diagrams, Turing machines and languages with only two formations rules. In *Communications of the ACM*, Nr. 9, 1966

[BLAS97]   Basic Linear Algebra Subprograms: A Quick Reference Guide. University of Tennessee, Oak Ridge National Laboratory, and Numerical Algorithms Group Ltd., May 11, 1997, see www.netlib.org/blas/blasqr.ps

[Blitz]   Homepage of the Blitz++ Project, http://oonumerics.org/blitz/

[BLS98]   D. Batory, B. Lofaso, and Y. Smaragdakis. JTS: Tools for Implementing Domain-Specific Languages. In [DP98], pp. 143–153, also [SSGRG]

[BM76]   J. A. Bondy and U. S. R. Murty. *Graph Theory with Applications*. North-Holland, NY, 1976

[BM84]   J. M. Boyle and M. N. Muralidharan. Program Reusability through Program Transformation. In *IEEE Transactions on Software Engineering*, vol. SE-10, no. 5, September 1984, pp. 574–588, © IEEE 1984

[BM97]   I. D. Baxter and M. Mehlich. Reverse Engineering is Reverse Forward Engineering. In *Proceedings of the Working Conference on Reverse Engineering (October 6–8, Amsterdam, The Netherlands)*, 1997, also [SD]

[BMR+96]   F. Buschmann, R. Meunier, H. Rohnert, P. Sommerlad, and M. Stal. *Pattern-Oriented Software Architecture. A System of Patterns*. John Wiley & Sons Ltd., Chichester, UK, 1996

[BN94]   J. Barton and L. R. Nackman. *Scientific and Engineering C++: An Introduction with Advanced Techniques and Applications*. Addison-Wesley, Reading, MA, 1994

[BO92]   D. Batory and S. O'Malley. The Design and Implementation of Hierarchical Software Systems with Reusable Components. In *ACM Transactions on Software Engineering and Methodology*, vol. 1, no. 4, October 1992, pp. 355–398, also [SSGRG]

[Boh98]   K. A. Bohrer. Architecture of the San Francisco Frameworks. In *IBM Systems Journal*, vol. 37, no. 2, 1998, p. 156–169

[Bol75]   D. L. Bolinger. *Aspects of language*. Second edition, Harcourt Brace Jovanovich, New York, NY, 1975

[Böl99]   K. Böllert. On Weaving Aspects. In *Proceedings of the ECOOP'98 Workshop on Aspect-Oriented Programming*, 1999, www.parc.xerox.com/aop

[Boo87]   G. Booch. *Software Components with Ada*. Benjamin/Cummings, Redwood City, CA, 1987

[Boo94]   G. Booch. *Object-Oriented Analysis and Design with Applications*. Second edition, Benjamin/Cummings, Redwood City, CA, 1994

[Bos98]   J. Bosch. Design Patterns as Language Constructs. In *Journal of Object-Oriented Programming (JOOP)*, May 1998, pp. 18–32

[BOSW98]   G. Bracha, M. Odersky, D. Stoutamire, and P. Wadler. Making the future safe for the past: Adding Genericity to the Java Programming Language. In *Proceedings of the Conference on Object-Oriented Programming, Systems, Languages, and Applications (OOPSLA'98)*, 1988, see http://cm.bell-labs.com/cm/cs/who/wadler/topics/gj.html

[BP89]   T. Biggerstaff and A. Perlis. *Software Reusability. Volume I: Concepts and Models.* ACM Press, Frontier Series, Addison-Wesley, Reading, MA, 1989

[BP97]   I. D. Baxter and C. W. Pidgeon. Software Change Through Design Maintenance. In *Proceedings of International Conference on Software Maintenance (ICSM'97),* IEEE Press, 1997, © IEEE 1997, also [SD]

[Bre98]   U. Breymann. *Designing Components with the C++ STL: A new approach to programming.* Addison-Wesley, Reading, MA, 1998

[BRJ99]   G. Booch, J. Rumbaugh, and I. Jacobson. *The Unified Modeling Language User Guide.* Addison-Wesley, Reading, MA, 1999

[Bro83]   M. Broy. Program constructuin by transformation: A family tree of sorting programs. In *Computer Program Synthesis Methodologies,* A. W. Biermann and G. Guiho (Eds.), D. Reidel Publishing Company, Dordrecht, Holland, 1983, pp. 1–49

[BSS92]   D. Batory, V. Singhal, and M. Sirkin. Implementing a Domain Model for Data Structures. In *International Journal of Software Engineering and Knowledge Engineering,* vol. 2, no. 3, September 1992, pp. 375–402, also [SSGRG]

[BT]   Homepage of Bayfront Technologies, Inc., at www.bayfront-technologies.com, 1998

[Buc97]   S. Buckingham Shum. Negotiating the Construction and Reconstruction of Organisational Memories. In *Journal of Universal Computer Science,* Special Issue on IT for Knowledge Management, vol. 3, no. 8, 1997, pp. 899–928, www.iicm.edu/jucs_3_8/negotiating_the_construction_and/, also see http://kmi.open.ac.uk/~simonb/DR.html

[Bud94]   T. Budd. *Multiparadigm Programming in Leda.* Addison-Wesley, Reading, MA, 1994

[BW85]   M. Barr and C. Wells. *Toposes, triples and theories. Grundlagen der mathematischen Wissenschaften,* vol. 278, Springer-Verlag, New York, NY, 1985

[BW90]   A. Berlin and D. Weise. Compiling Scientific Code Using Partial Evaluation. In *IEEE Computer,* December 1990, pp. 25–37, © IEEE 1990

[CAB+94]   D. Coleman, P. Arnold, S. Bodoff, C. Dollin, H. Gilchrist, F. Hayes, and P. Jeremaes. *Object-Oriented Development: The Fusion Method.* Prentice Hall, Englewood Cliffs, NJ, 1994

[CARDS94]   Software Technology For Adaptable, Reliable Systems (STARS). Domain Engineering Methods and Tools Handbook:

Volume I — Methods: Comprehensive Approach to Reusable Defense Software (CARDS). STARS Informal Technical Report, STARS-VC-K017R1/001/00, December 31, 1994

[CC77]   H. H. Clark and E. V. Clark. *Psychology and language*. Harcourt Brace Jovanovich, New York, NY, 1977

[CCH+89]   P. Canning, W. Cook, W. Hill, W. Olthoff, and J.C. Mitchell. F-bounded polymorphism for object-oriented programming. In *Proceedings of the Conference on Functional Programming Languages and Computer Architecture*, ACM, 1989, pp. 273–280

[CE00]   K. Czarnecki and U. W. Eisenecker (Eds.). *Proceedings of the First International Symposium on Generative and Component-Based Software Engineering (GCSE'99)*. To be published as LNCS 1799 by Springer-Verlag, Berlin and Heidelberg, Germany, 2000

[CE99a]   K. Czarnecki and U. W. Eisenecker. Components and Generative Programming. Invited talk, in *Proceedings of the 7th European Software Engineering Conference, held jointly with the 7th ACM SIGSOFT Symposium on the Foundations of Software Engineering (ESEC/FSE '99), Toulouse, France, September 1999*, O. Nierstrasz and M. Lemoine (Eds.), LNCS 1687, Springer-Verlag, Berlin and Heidelberg, Germany, 1999, pp. 2–19, www.prakinf.tu-ilmenau.de/~czarn/esec99

[CE99b]   K. Czarnecki and U. W. Eisenecker. Synthesizing Objects. In *Proceedings of ECOOP'99—Object-Oriented Programming*, R. Guerraoui, (Ed.), LNCS 1628, Springer-Verlag, Berlin and Heidelberg, Germany, 1999, p. 18–42, see www.prakinf.tu-ilmenau.de/~czarn/ecoop99/

[CE98]   K. Czarnecki and U. W. Eisenecker. Template-Metaprogramming, http://home.t-online.de/home/Ulrich.Eisenecker/meta.htm

[CEG+98]   K. Czarnecki, U. W. Eisenecker, R. Glück, D. Vandevoorde, and T. Veldhuizen. Generative Programming and Active Libraries. To appear in *Proceedings of the Dagstuhl Seminar 98171 on Generic Programming, Schloß Dagstuhl, Germany, April 26-May 5, 1998*, LNCS, Springer-Verlag, Berlin and Heidelberg, Germany, 1999, see www.prakinf.tu-ilmenau.de/~czarn/dagstuhl99/

[CF]   Homepage of the TRESE Project, University of Twente, The Netherlands, http://wwwtrese.cs.utwente.nl/; also see the online tutorial on Composition Filters at http://wwwtrese.cs.utwente.nl/sina/cfom/index.html

[Cha97]   C. Chambers. The Cecil Language: Specification & Rationale. Technical Report, University of Washington, Version 2.1, March 7, 1997, www.cs.washington.edu/research/projects/cecil/www/Papers/cecil-spec.html

[Chi95]   S. Chiba. A Metaobject Protocol for C++. In *Proceedings of the 10th Annual Conference on Object-Oriented Programming, Systems, Languages and Applications (OOPSLA'95)*, ACM SIGPLAN Notices, vol. 30, no. 10, 1995, pp. 285–299, the Open C++ system is available at www.softlab.is.tsukuba.ac.jp/~chiba/openc++.html

[CHL+96]   S. Carney, M. Heroux, G. Li, R. Pozo, K. Remington, and K. Wu. A Revised Proposal for a Sparse BLAS Tookit. SPARKER Working Note #3, January 1996

[CHW98]   J. Coplien, D. Hoffman, and D. Weiss. Commonality and Variability in Software Engineering. In *IEEE Software*, November/December 1998, pp. 37–45, © IEEE 1998

[CIOO96]   L. Bergans and P. Cointe (Organizers). *Proceedings of the ECOOP'96 Workshop on Composability Issues in Object Orientation (CIOO'96)*, Linz, Austria, July 8–9, 1996. In [Müh97], pp. 53–123

[CK95]   P. Clements and P. Kogut. Features of Architecture Description Languages. In *Proceedings of the 7th Annual Software Technology Conference*, Salt Lake City, UT, April 1995

[CL75]   A. Collins and E. F. Loftus. A spreading activation theory of semantic processing. In *Psychological Review*, no. 82, 1997, pp. 407–428

[Cle96]   P. Clements. A Survey of Architecture Description Languages. In *Proceedings of Eighth International Workshop on Software Specification and Design*, Paderborn, Germany, March 1996

[Cle00]   J. C. Cleaveland. *Program Generators Using XML and Java*. Prentice-Hall, XML Book Series, to be published in 2000

[CN98]   S. Cohen and L. M. Northrop. Object-Oriented Technology and Domain Analysis. In [DP98], pp. 86–93

[CN99]   P. Clements, L. M. Northrop, et al. A Framework for Software Product Line Practice, Version 2.0, Report from the Product Line System Program, Software Engineering Institute, Pittsburgh, PA, July 1999, www.sei.cmu.edu/plp/

[Coh99]   S. Cohen. From Product Line Architectures to Products. Position paper for the ECOOP'99 Workshop on Object-Technology for Product-Line Architectures, Lisbon, Portugal, June 1999

[Con97]   E. Conklin. Designing Organizational Memory: Preserving Intellectual Assets in a Knowledge Economy. Technical Note, Group Decision Support Systems, www.gdss.com/DOM.htm, 1997

[Cop92]   J. O. Coplien. *Advanced C++: Programming Styles and Idioms.* Addison-Wesley, Reading, MA, 1992

[Cop95]   J. O. Coplien. A Generative Development-Process Pattern Language. In *Pattern Languages of Program Design*, J. O. Coplien and D. C. Schmidt, (Eds.), Addison-Wesley, Reading, MA, 1995, pp. 183–239

[Cop98]   J. O. Coplien. *Multi-Paradigm Design for C++.* Addison-Wesley, Reading, MA, 1998

[Cox90]   B. J. Cox. Planning the Software Industrial Revolution. In *IEEE Software*, November 1990, © IEEE 1990, see www.virtualschool.edu

[CS92]   J. Cordy and M. Shukla. Practical Metaprogramming. In *Proceedings of CASCON '92*, IBM Centre for Advances Studies Conference, Toronto, November 1992, also www.qucis.queensu.ca/home/cordy/TXL-Info/index.html

[CSJ+92]   S. Cohen, J. Stanley, S. Peterson, and R. Krut. Application of Feature-Oriented Domain Analysis to the Army Movement Control Domain. Technical Report, CMU/SEI-91-TR-28, Software Engineering Institute, Carnegie Mellon University, Pittsburgh, PA, 1992, www.sei.cmu.edu

[CT93]   L. Coglianese and W. Tracz. Architecture-Based Development Guidelines for Avionics Software. Version 2.1, Technical Report, ADAGE-IBM-92-03, 1993

[CW]   ControlWORKS, a machine and process control software package for semiconductor process equipment by Texas Instruments, Inc.; see product data sheets at www.ti.com/control/

[CW85]   L. Cardelli and P. Wegner. On Understanding Types, Data Abstraction and Polymorphism. In *ACM Computing Surveys*, Vol. 17, No. 4, December 1985, pp. 471–522

[CY90]   P. Coad and E. Yourdon. *Object-Oriented Analysis.* Prentice-Hall, Englewood Cliffs, NJ, 1990

[Cza96]   K. Czarnecki. Metaprogrammierung für jedermann: Ein Mustersystem für leichtgewichtige Framework-Erweiterungen in Smalltalk, Teil II. In *OBJEKTspektrum*, July/August 1996, pp. 96–99, www.prakinf.tu-ilmenau.de/~czarn/

[Cza97]   K. Czarnecki. Statische Konfiguration in C++. In *OBJEKTspektrum* 4/1997, pp. 86–91, see www.prakinf.tu-ilmenau.de/~czarn

[Cza98]   K. Czarnecki. Generative Programming: Principles and Techniques of Software Engineering Based on Automated Configuration and Fragment-Based Component Models. Ph. D. Thesis, Department of Computer Science and Automation, Technical University of Ilmenau, Germany, October 1998, see www.prakinf.tu-ilmenau.de/~czarn/

[DB95]   D. Das and D. Batory. Prairie: A Rule Specification Framework for Query Optimizers. In *Proceedings 11th International Conference on Data Engineering*, Taipei, March 1995, also [SSGRG]

[DBMS79]   J. Dongarra, J. Bunch, C. Moler, and G. Stewart. *LINPACK Users' Guide*. Society for Industrial and Applied Mathematics (SIAM), Philadelphia, PA, 1979

[DCOOL]   K. Czarnecki. Dynamic Cool, a prototype implementation of a dynamic version of Cool in Smalltalk, available at www.prakinf.tu-ilmenau.de/~czarn/aop

[DD87]   H. Dreyfus and S. Dreyfus. *Künstliche Intelligenz: von den Grenzen der Denkmaschine und dem Wert der Intuition*. Rowohlt, rororo Computer 8144, Reinbek, 1987

[DDDH90]   J. Dongarra, I. Duff, J. DuCroz, and S. Hammarling. A Set of Level 3 Basic Linear Algebra Subprograms. In *ACM Transactions on Mathematical Software*, vol. 16, 1990, pp. 1–17, see www.netlib.org/blas/blas2-paper.ps

[DDHH88]   J. Dongarra, J. DuCroz, S. Hammarling, and R. Hanson. An Extended Set of Fortran Basic Linear Algebra Subprograms. In *ACM Transactions on Mathematical Software*, vol. 14, no. 1, 1988, pp. 1–32, see www.netlib.org/blas/blas3-paper.ps

[Dem]   Homepage of the Demeter Project, Northeastern University, Boston, MA, www.ccs.neu.edu/research/demeter/

[DG87]   L. Demighiel and R. Gabriel. The Common Lisp Object System: An overview. In *Proceedings of the European Conference on Object-Oriented Programming (ECOOP87)*, 1987, pp. 151–170

[DH96]   K. Driesen and U. Hölzle. The Direct Cost of Virtual Function Calls in C++. In *Proceedings OOPSLA'96, SIGPLAN Notices*, vol. 31, no. 10, October 1996, see www.cs.ucsb.edu/oocsb/papers/oopsla96.shtml

[DHK96]   A. van Deursen, J. Heering, P. Klint (Eds.). *Language Prototyping: An Algebraic Specification Approach*. World Scientific Publishing, 1996, also see www.cwi.nl/~gipe/

[Dij70]   E. Dijkstra. Structured Programming. In *Software Engineering Techniques,* J. Buxton and B. Randell, (Eds.), NATO Scientific Affairs Division, Brussels, Belgium, 1979, pp. 84–87

[Dij76]   E. W. Dijkstra. *A Discipline of Programming*. Prentice Hall, Englewood Cliffs, NJ, 1976

[DISA93]   DISA/CIM Software Reuse Program. Domain Analysis and Design Process, Version 1. Technical Report 1222-04-210/30.1, DISA Center for Information Management, Arlington, VA, March 1993

[DK98]   A. van Deursen and P. Klint. Little Languages: Little Maintenance? In *Journal of Software Maintenance*, no. 10, 1998, pp. 75–92, see www.cwi.nl/~arie

[DLPR96]   J. Dongarra, A. Lumsdaine, R. Pozo, and K. Remington. IML++ v. 1.2 Iterative Method Library Reference Guide, 1996, see ftp://gams.nist.gov/pub/pozo/docs/iml.ps.gz

[DLPRJ94] J. Dongarra, A. Lumsdaine, R. Pozo, and K. Remington. A Sparse Matrix Library in C++ for High Performance Architectures. In *Proceedings of the Second Object Oriented Numerics Conference*, 1994, pp. 214–218, see ftp://gams.nist.gov/pub/pozo/papers/sparse.ps.Z

[DNW+99]   S. Dobson, P. Nixon, V. Wade, S. Terzis, and J. Fuller. Vanilla: an open language framework. In [CE00]

[DP98]   P. Devanbu and J. Poulin, (Eds.). *Proceedings of the Fifth International Conference on Software Reuse (Victoria, Canada, June 1998)*. IEEE Computer Society Press, 1998, © IEEE 1998

[DPW93]   J. Dongarra, R. Pozo, and D. Walker. LAPACK++: A Design Overview of Object-Oriented Extensions for High Performance Linear Algebra. In *Proceedings of Supercomputing '93*, IEEE Computer Society Press, 1993, pp. 162–171, © IEEE 1993, see http://math.nist.gov/lapack++/

[DW97]   D. F. D'Souza and A. C. Wills. *Objects, Components and Frameworks with UML*. Addison-Wesley, Reading, MA, 1997, see www.iconcomp.com/catalysis/

[EC99]   U. Eisenecker and K. Czarnecki. Template-Metaprogrammierung: Kontrollstrukturen. In *OBJEKTspektrum*, No. 4, July/August 1999, pp. 81–86, see http://home.t-online.de/home/Ulrich.Eisenecker/cpp.htm

[Ede91]   A. Edelman. The first annual large dense linear system survey. In *SIGNUM Newsletter*, no. 26, October 1991, pp. 6–12, see ftp://theory.lcs.mit.edu/pub/people/edelman/parallel/survey1991.ps

[Ede93]   A. Edelman. Large Dense Numerical Linear Algebra in 1993: The Parallel Computing Influence by A. Edelman. In *Journal of Supercomputing Applications*, vol. 7, 1993, pp. 113–128, see ftp:// theory.lcs.mit.edu/pub/people/edelman/parallel/1993.ps

[Ede94]   A. Edelman. Large Numerical Linear Algebra in 1994: The
          Continuing Influence of Parallel Computing. In *Proceedings of
          the 1994 Scalable High Performance Computing Conference*,
          IEEE Computer Society Press, Los Alamitos, CA, 1994,
          pp. 781–787, © IEEE 1994, see ftp://theory.lcs.mit.edu/pub/-
          people/ edelman/parallel/large94.ps

[Efr94]   S. Efremides. On Program Transformations. Ph.D. Thesis, Cor-
          nell University, May 1994, available from http://cs-tr.cs.
          cornell.edu/

[EGK97]   Z. Erel, A. Gur, and S. Kariv. Object Oriented Testing, Lecture
          notes, 1997

[Eis95]   U. W. Eisenecker. Recht auf Fehler. In *iX*, no. 6, 1996, pp. 184–
          189

[Eis96]   U. W. Eisenecker. Generatives Programmieren mit C++. In
          OBJEKTspektrum, No. 6, November/December 1996, pp. 79–
          84, see http://home.t-online.de/home/Ulrich.Eisenecker/cpp.htm

[Eis99]   U. W. Eisenecker. Polymorphism in Object-Oriented Languages.
          An Overview. In *Overload*, vol. 32, June 1999, pp. 15–19,
          http://home.t-online.de/home/Ulrich.Eisenecker/pm.htm

[Enc98]   *Encarta® 98 Desk Encyclopedia* © &℗ 1996–97 Microsoft
          Corporation

[Eng97]   D. R. Engler. Incorporating application semantics and control
          into compilation. In *Proceedings USENIX Conference on
          Domain-Specific Languages (DSL'97)*, 1997

[EP98]   H.-E. Eriksson and M. Penker. UML Toolkit. John Wiley &
          Sons, Inc., New York, NY, 1998

[FBB+99] M. Fowler, with K. Beck, J. Brant, W. Opdyke, and D. Roberts.
          Refactoring: Improving the Design of Existing Code. Addison-
          Wesley, Reading, MA, 1999

[FD98]   I. R. Forman and S. H. Danforth. *Putting Metaclasses to Work:
          A New Dimension in Object-Oriented Programming*. Addi-
          son-Wesley, Reading, MA, 1998

[Fea86]   M. Feather. A Survey and Classification of Some Program
          Transformation Approaches and Techniques. IFIP WG21
          Working Conference on Program Specification and Transfor-
          mation, Bad Toelz, Germany, April 1986

[Fin96]   R. A. Finkel. *Advanced Programming Language Design*. Addi-
          son-Wesley, Reading, MA, 1996

[Fod75]   J. A. Fodor. *The language of thought*. Crowell, New York, NY,
          1975

[Fow96]   M. Fowler. A Survey of Object-Oriented Analysis and Design
            Methods. Tutorial notes, presented at OOPSLA'96, 1996

[Fow97]   M. Fowler. *Analysis Patterns: Reusable Object Models.* Addi-
            son-Wesley, Reading, MA, 1997

[FP96]   B. Frakes and R. Prieto-Díaz. Introduction to Domain Analysis
            and Domain Engineering. Tutorial Notes, The Fourth Interna-
            tional Conference on Software Reuse, Orlando, FL, April
            23–26, 1996

[FPF96]   W. Frakes, R. Prieto-Díaz, and Christopher Fox. DARE:
            Domain Analysis and Reuse Environment. Draft submitted for
            publication, April 7, 1996

[FS97]   F. Gomes and D. Sorensen. C++: A C++ implementation of
            ARPACK eigenvalue package. User's Manual, draft version,
            August 7, 1997, see www.caam.rice.edu/software/ARPACK/
            arpackpp.ps.gz

[FY95]   B. Foote and J. Yoder. Evolution. Architecture, and Metamor-
            phosis. In *Pattern Languages of Program Design 2.* J. M. Vlis-
            sides, J. O. Coplien, and N. L. Kerth, (Eds.), Addison-Wesley,
            Reading, MA, 1995, pp. 272–314

[GB80]   J. Goguen and R. Burstall. CAT, a system for the structured
            elaboration of correct programs from structured specifications.
            Technical Report CSL-118, SRI Computer Science Lab, Octo-
            ber 1980

[GB92]   J. Goguen and R. Burstall. Institutions: Abstract Model Theory
            for Specification and Programming. In *Journal of the ACM,*
            vol. 39, no. 1, 1992, pp. 95–146

[GBW93]   R. G. Gabriel and D. G. Bobrow, and J. L. White. CLOS in
            Context—The Shape of the Design Space. In *Object Oriented
            Programming—The CLOS perspective.* The MIT Press, Cam-
            bridge, MA, 1993, pp. 29–61

[GFA98]   M. L. Griss, J. Favaro, and M. d'Alessandro. Integrating Fea-
            ture Modeling with the RSEB. In [DP98], pp. 76–85, see
            www.intecs.it

[GHJV95]   E. Gamma, R. Helm, R. Johnson, and J. Vlissides. *Design Pat-
            terns: Elements of Reusable Object-Oriented Software.* Addi-
            son-Wesley, Reading, MA, 1995

[GHJV95]   E. Gamma, R. Helm, R. Johnson, and J. Vlissides. *Design Pat-
            terns: Elements of Reusable Object-Oriented Software.* Addi-
            son-Wesley, Reading, MA, 1995

[GI]   GJ—A Generic Java Language Extension, see http://cm.
            bell-labs.com/cm/cs/who/wadler/pizza/gj/

[Gil99]   R. Gillam. Some Holes, and How to Fill Them. "Java Liaison" Column in C++ *Report*, no. 3, vol. 11, March 1999, pp. 7–13

[GJ97]   R. Glück and J. Jørgensen. An automatic program generator for multi-level specialization. In *Lisp and Symbolic Computation*, vol. 10, no. 2, 1997, pp. 113–158

[GK97]   M. Golm and J. Kleinöder. MetaJava. In *STJA'97 Conference Proceedings*, Technische Universität Ilmenau, September 10, 1997, Erfurt, Germany 1997, pp. 73–79. Also available at http://www4.informatik.uni-erlangen.de/metajava/ publications.html

[GKS+94]   H. Gomaa, L. Kerschberg, V. Sugumaran, C. Bosch, and I. Tavakoli. A Prototype Domain Modeling Environment for Reusable Software Architectures. In *Proceedings of the Third International Conference on Software Reuse*, Rio de Janeiro, Brazil, W. Frakes (Ed.), IEEE Computer Society Press, Los Alamitos, CA, 1994, pp. 74–83, © IEEE 1994

[GL96]   G. Golub and C. van Loan. *Matrix Computations*. Third edition. The John Hopkins University Press, Baltimore and London, 1996

[GL98]   J. Gil and D. H. Lorenz. Design Patterns and Language Design. In *IEEE Computer*, vol. 31, no. 3, March 1998, pp. 118–120, © IEEE 1998

[Gla95]   M. Glandrup. Extending C++ Using the Concepts of Composition Filters. Master's Thesis, Department of Computer Science, University of Twente, The Netherlands, November 1995, see [CF]

[GNZ95]   R. Glück, R. Nakashige, and R. Zöchling. Binding-Time Analysis Applied to Mathematical Algorithms. In *System Modeling and Optimization*, J. Dolevzal and J. Fidler, (Eds.), Volume of Chapman & Hall, 1995, pp. 137–146, www.diku.dk/research-groups/topps/bibliography/1995.html#D-244

[GO93]   G. H. Golub and J. M. Ortega. *Scientific Computing: An Introduction with Parallel Computing*. Academic Press, Boston, MA, 1993

[Gog79]   J. A. Goguen. Abstract errors for abstract data types. In *IFIP Working Conference on Formal Description Programming Concepts*, P. Neuhold, (Ed.), MIT Press, Cambridge, MA, 1979, pp. 370–376

[Gog83]   J. A. Goguen. LIL—A Library Interconnection Language. In *Report on Program Libraries Workshop*, SRI International, Menlo Park, CA, October 1983, pp. 12–51

[Gog84]   J. A. Goguen. Parameterized Programming. In *IEEE Transactions on Software Engineering*, Vol. SE-10, No. 5, September 1984, pp. 528–543, © IEEE 1984

[Gog85]   J. A. Goguen. Suggestions for using and organizing libraries in software development. In *Proceedings of the First International Conference on Supercomputing Systems*, Kartashev and Kartashev, (Eds.), IEEE, 1985, pp. 349–360, © IEEE 1985

[Gog86]   J. A. Goguen. Reusing and Interconnecting Software Components. In *IEEE Computer*, February 1986, pp. 16–28, also in [PA91], pp. 125–147, © IEEE 1986

[Gog96]   J. A. Goguen. Parameterized Programming and Software Architecture. In [Sit96], pp. 2–10

[Gol79]   R. Goldblatt. *TOPOI: the Categorial Analysis of Logic*. Studies and Logic and the Foundations of Mathematics, vol. 98, J. Barwise et al. (Eds.), North-Holland Publishing Company, 1979

[Gom92]   H. Gomaa. An Object-Oriented Domain Analysis and Modeling Method for Software Reuse. In *Proceedings of the Hawaii International Conference on System Sciences*, Hawaii, January 1992

[Gon81]   L. Gonzales. A domain language for processing standardized tests. Master's Thesis, Department of Information and Computer Science, University of California, 1981

[GR83]   A. Goldberg and D. Robson. *Smalltalk 80: The Language and its Implementation*. Addison-Wesley, Reading, MA, 1983

[GR95]   A. Goldberg and K. Rubin. *Succeeding with Objects. Decision Frameworks for Project Management*. Addison-Wesley, Reading, MA, 1995

[GT96]   J. Goguen and W. Tracz. An Implementation-Oriented Semantics for Module Composition. Draft available from [ADAGE], 1996

[Ham79]   J. A. Hampton. Polymorphous concepts in semantic memory. In *Journal of Verbal Learning and Verbal Behavior*, no. 18, 1979, pp. 441–461

[Hay94]   F. Hayes-Roth. Architecture-Based Acquisition and Development of Software: Guidelines and Recommendations from the ARPA Domain-Specific Software Architecture (DSSA) Program. Version 1.01, Informal Technical Report, Teknowledge Federal Systems, February 4, 1994, available from [ADAGE]

[HC91]   J. Hooper and R. Chester. *Software reuse: guidelines and methods*. Plenum Press, New York, NY, 1991

[Hig96]   N. Higham. Recent Developments in Dense Numerical Linear Algebra. Numerical Analysis Report No. 288, Manchester Centre for Computational Mathematics, University of Manchester, August 1996; to appear in *The State of the Art in Numerical Analysis*, I. Duff and G. Watson, (Eds.), Oxford University Press, 1997, see ftp://ftp.ma.man.ac.uk/pub/narep/narep288.ps.gz

[HJ96]   B. Hinkle and R. E. Johnson. Deep in the Heart of Smalltalk: The active life is the life for me! In *Smalltalk Report*, May, 1996

[HK93]   B. Hoffmann and B. Krieg-Brückner (Eds.). *PROgram development by SPECification and TRAnsformation: Methodology—Language Family—System*. Springer-Verlag, Berlin and Heidelberg, Germany, LNCS 680, 1993

[HN90]   R. Hecht-Nielsen. *Neurocomputing*. Addison-Wesley, Reading, MA, 1990

[HNC+90]   J. Hess, W. Novak, P. Carroll, S. Cohen, R. Holibaugh, K. Kang, and A. Peterson. A Domain Analysis Bibliography. Technical Report, CMU/SEI-90-SR-3, Software Engineering Institute, Carnegie Mellon University, Pittsburgh, Pennsylvania, 1990. Reprinted in [PA91], pp. 258–259. Also available from www.sei.cmu.edu

[HO93]   W. Harrison and H. Ossher. Subject-oriented programming (A critique of pure objects). In *Proceedings of the 8th Conference on Object-Oriented Programming, Systems, Languages, and Applications (OOPSLA '93), ACM SIGPLAN Notices,* vol. 28, no. 10, 1993, pp. 411–428

[Hol93]   R. Holibaugh. Joint Integrated Avionics Working Group (JIAWG) Object-Oriented Domain Analysis Method (JODA). Version 1.3, Technical Report, CMU/SEI-92-SR-3, Software Engineering Institute, Carnegie Mellon University, Pittsburgh, PA, November 1993, www.sei.cmu.edu

[Höl94]   U. Hölzle. Adaptive Optimization in SELF: Reconciling High Performance with Exploratory Programming. Ph. D. Thesis, Department of Computer Science, Stanford University, 1994, see www.cs.ucsb.edu/oocsb/papers/urs-thesis.html

[HP94]   J. S. Heidemann and G. J. Popek. File-system development with stackable layers. In *ACM Transactions on Computer Systems*, vol. 12, no. 1, 1994, pp. 58–89, also as UCLA Technical Report CSD-930019, also http://fmg-www.cs.ucla.edu/fmg/summary.html

[HPOA89]   N. Hutchinson, L. Peterson, S. O'Malley, and M. Abbott. RPC in the x-Kernel: Evaluating New Design Technique. In

Proceedings of the Symposium on Operating System Principles, December 1989, pp. 91–101

[HT94]   F. Hayes-Roth and W. Tracz. DSSA Tool Requirements For Key Process Functions. Version 2.0, Technical Report, ADAGE-IBM-93-13B, October 24, 1994, available from [ADAGE]

[HU79]   J. E. Hopcroft and J. D. Ullman. *Introduction to Automata Theory, Languages, and Computation*. Addison-Wesley, Reading, MA, 1979

[Hud98]   P. Hudak. Modular Domain Specific Languages and Tools. In [DP98], pp. 134–142

[Hul20]   C. L. Hull. Quantitative aspects of the evolution of concepts. In *Psychological monographs*, Whole no. 123, 1920

[IHS+96]   Y. Ishikawa, A. Hori, M. Sato, M. Matsuda, J. Nolte, H. Tezuka, H. Konaka, M. Maeda, and K. Kubota. Design and Implementation of Metalevel Architecture in C++—MPC++ approach. In *Proceedings of Reflection'96*, 1996

[ILG+97]   J. Irwin, J.-M. Loingtier, J. Gilbert, G. Kiczales, J. Lamping, A. Mendhekar, and T. Shpeisman. Aspect-Oriented Programming of Sparse Matrix Code. Xerox PARC Technical Report SPL97-007 P9710045, February 1997, see [AOP]

[IPD]   Intentional Programming Development Team, Personal Communication, see also [IPH]

[IPH]   Homepage of the Intentional Programming Project, Microsoft Research, Redmond, WA, www.research.microsoft.com/research/ip/

[Jar90]   R. Jarrett. Cybernetics in Industry. Online article available at www.morph.demon.co.uk/Electronics/robots.htm, 1990

[JBR99]   I. Jacobson, G. Booch, and J. Rumbaugh. *The Unified Software Development Process*. Addison-Wesley, Reading, MA, 1999

[JCJO92]   I. Jacobson, M. Christerson, P. Jonsson, and G. Overgaard. *Object-Oriented Software Engineering*. Addison-Wesley, Workingham, England, 1992

[JEJ94]   I. Jacobson, M. Ericsson, and A. Jacobson. *The Object Advantage—Business Process Reengineering with Object Technology*. Addison-Wesley, Menlo Park, CA, 1994

[JGJ98]   I. Jacobson, M. Griss, and P. Jonsson. *Software Reuse: Architecture, Process and Organization for Business Success*. Addison-Wesley, Reading, MA, May 1997

[JGS93]   N. D. Jones, C. K. Gomard, and P. Sestoft. *Partial Evaluation and Automatic Program Generation*. Prentice Hall International, 1993, also www.dina.kvl.dk/~sestoft/pebook/pebook.html

[JK93]   A. Jennings and J. McKeown. *Matrix Computation*. Second edition, John Wiley & Sons Ltd., Chichester, UK, 1993

[JLMS98] M. Jazayeri, R. Loos, D. Musser, and A. Stepanov. Report of the Dagstuhl Seminar 9817 "Generic Programming", Schloß Dagstuhl, April 27–30, 1998, see http://www-ca.informatik.uni-tuebingen.de/dagstuhl/gpdag_2.html

[Joh92]   R. E. Johnson. Documenting Frameworks using Patterns. In *Proceedings of the Annual Conference on Object-Oriented Programming, Systems, Languages, and Applications (OOPSLA'92)*, ACM SIGPLAN Notices, vol. 27, no. 10, October 1992, pp. 63–76

[Kan93]   E. Kant. Synthesis of Mathematical Modeling Software. In *IEEE Software*, vol. 10, no. 3, May 1993, pp. 30–41, © IEEE 1993, also [SC]

[KCH+90] K. Kang, S. Cohen, J. Hess, W. Nowak, and S. Peterson. Feature-Oriented Domain Analysis (FODA) Feasibility Study. Technical Report, CMU/SEI-90-TR-21, Software Engineering Institute, Carnegie Mellon University, Pittsburgh, PA, November 1990

[Kee89]   S. Keene. *Object-oriented programming in Common Lisp: a Programmer's Guide to CLOS*. Addison-Wesley, Reading, MA, 1989

[KFD99]   S. Krishnamurthi, M. Felleisen, and B. F. Duba. From Macros to Reusable Generative Programming. In [CE00]

[KI]   Publications of the Kestrel Institute, Palo Alto, CA, www.kestrel.edu/HTML/ publications.html

[Kic98]   G. Kiczales. Aspect-Oriented Programming. Transparencies for the invited talk at the OOP'98 in Munich, see www.parc.xerox.com/aop

[KL98]   K. Kreft and A. Langer. Allocator Types. In *C++ Report*, vol. 10, no. 6, 1998, pp. 54–61 and p. 68

[KLL+97] G. Kiczales, J. Lamping, C. V. Lopes, C. Maeda, A. Mendhekar, and G. Murphy. Open Implementation Design Guidelines. In *Proceedings of the 19th International Conference on Software Engineering (ICSE'97)*, 1997, pp. 481–490

[KLM+97] G. Kiczales, J. Lamping, A. Mendhekar, C. Maeda, C. V. Lopes, J.-M. Loingtier, and J. Irwin. Aspect-Oriented Programming. In *Proceedings ECOOP'97 — Object-Oriented Programming, 11th European Conference, Jyväskylä, Finland,*

June 1997, M. Aksit and S. Matsuoka (Eds.), LNCS 1241, Springer-Verlag, Berlin and Heidelberg, Germany, 1997, also see [AOP]

[KM90]   G. B. Kotik and L. Z. Markosian. Program Transformation: the Key to Automating Software Maintenance and Reengineering. In *IEEE Transactions on Software Engineering*, vol. 16, no. 9, 1990, 1024–1043, © IEEE 1990

[Kna98]   J. Knaupp. Algorithm Generators: A First Experience. Presented at the STJA'98 Conference, Erfurt, 1998, see www.prakinf.tu-ilmenau.de/~czarn/generate/stja98/knaupp.zip

[Knu86]   D. E. Knuth. *The $T_EX$book*. Addison-Wesley, Reading, MA, 1986

[Knu92]   D. E. Knuth. *Literate Programming (Center for the Study of Language and Information—Lecture Notes, No 27)*. Stanford University Center for the Study, May 1992

[KO96]   B. B. Kristensen and K. Østerbye. Roles: Conceptual Abstraction Theory & Practical Language Issues. In *Theory and Practice of Object Systems* (TAPOS), vol. 2, no. 3, 1996, pp. 143–160, also www.mip.ou.dk/~bbk/research/publications.html

[Kor96]   T. Korson. Managing Reuse (Applying the law of gravity). In *Object Magazine*, SIGS Publications, April 1996, p. 34–36, www.software-architects.com/publications/korson/Korson9604om.html

[Köt98]   U. Köthe. Reusable Software in Computer Vision. To appear in *Handbook of Computer Vision and Applications: Volume 3: Systems and Applications*, B. Jähne, H. Haussecker, and P. Geissler, (Eds.), Academic Press, Boston, MA, 1998, see www.egd.igd.fhg.de/~ulli/papers/

[KRB91]   G. Kiczales, J. des Rivières, and D.-G. Bobrow. *The Art of the Metaobject Protocol*. The MIT Press, Cambridge, MA, 1991

[Kru92]   J.K. Kruschke. ALCOVE: An exemplar-based connectionist model of category learning. In *Psychological Review*, no. 99, 1992, pp. 22–44

[Kru93]   R. Krut. Integrating 001 Tool Support into the Feature-Oriented Domain Analysis Methodology. Technical Report, CMU/SEI-93-TR-11, ESC-TR-93-188, Software Engineering Institute, Carnegie Mellon University, Pittsburgh, PA, 1993, www.sei.cmu.edu

[Kru95]   P. Kruchten. The 4+1 View Model of Architecture. In *IEEE Software*, vol. 12, no. 6, November 1995, pp. 42–50, © IEEE 1995

[KW97]   D. Kühl and K. Weihe. Data access templates. In *C++ Report*, July/August, 1997

[LAB+81] B. H. Liskov, R. Atkinson, T. Bloom, E. Moss, J. C. Schaffert, R. Scheifler, and A. Snyder. *CLU Reference Manual, Springer-Verlag*, Berlin-New York, 1981

[LB79]   M. Lewis and J. Brooks-Gunn. *Social cognition and the acquisition of self*. Plenum, New York, NY, 1979

[Lea88]   D. Lea. libg++, the GUN C++ library. In *Proceedings of the USENIX C++ Conference*, 1988

[Lea97]   D. Lea. *Concurrent Programming in Java™: Design Principles and Patterns*. Addison-Wesley, Reading, MA, 1997

[LEW96]   J. Loeckx, H. D. Ehrich, and M. Wolf. *Specification of Abstract Data Types*. John Wiley & Sons Ltd, Chichester, UK, and B. G. Teubner, Stuttgart, Germany, 1996

[LHK87]   D. Luckham, F. von Henke, B. Krieg-Brückner, and O. Owe. *Anna: A Language For Annotating Ada Programs. Language Reference Manual*. Lecture Notes in Computer Science, no. 260, Springer-Verlag, Berlin and Heidelberg, Germany, 1987

[LHKK79] C. Lawson, R. Hanson, D. Kincaid, and F. Krogh. Basic Linear Algebra Subprograms for Fortran Usage. In *ACM Transactions on Mathematical Software*, vol. 5, 1979, pp. 308–325

[LHR88]   K. J. Lieberherr, I. Holland, and A. J. Riel. Object-oriented programming: an objective sense of style. In *Proceedings of the Conference on Object-Oriented Programming Systems, Languages and Applications (OOPSLA'88), ACM SIGPLAN Notices*, vol. 23, no.11, 1988, pp. 323–334

[Lie86a] H. Lieberman. Using Prototypical Objects to Implement Shared Behavior. In *Proceedings of the Conference on Object-Oriented Programming Systems, Languages and Applications (OOPSLA'86)*, ACM SIGPLAN Notices, vol. 21, no. 11, 1986, pp. 214–223

[Lie86b] H. Lieberman. Delegation and Inheritance: Two Mechanisms for Sharing Knowledge in Object Oriented Systems. In *3eme Journees d'Etudes Langages Orientes Objets*, J. Bezivin, P. Cointe, (Eds.), AFCET, Paris, France, 1986

[Lie92]   K. Lieberherr. Component Enhancement: An Adaptive Reusability Mechanism for Groups of Collaborating Classes. In *Information Processing'92, 12th World Computer Congress, Madrid, Spain*, J. van Leeuwen, (Ed.), Elsevier, 1992, pp. 179–185

[Lie96]   K. Lieberherr. *Adaptive Object-Oriented Software: The Demeter Method with Propagation Patterns*. PWS Publishing Company, Boston, MA, 1996

[Lie97]   K. Lieberherr. Demeter and Aspect-Oriented Programming. In *Proceedings of the STJA'97 Conference,* Erfurt, Germany, September 10–11, 1997, pp. 40–43, see [DM]

[Lie98]   K. Lieberherr. Connections between Demeter/Adaptive Programming and Aspect-Oriented Programming. Informal note at www.ccs.neu.edu/home/lieber/connection-to-aop.html

[LK97]   C. V. Lopes and G. Kiczales. D: A Language Framework for Distributed Programming. Xerox PARC Technical Report SPL97-010 P9710047, February 1997, see [AOP]

[LKA+95]   D. Luckham, J. Kenney, L. Augustin, J. Vera, D. Bryan, and W. Mann. Specification and Analysis of System Architecture Using Rapide. In *IEEE Transaction on Software Engineering*, vol. 21, no. 4, April 1995, pp. 336–355, © IEEE 1995

[LKRR92]   J. Lamping, G. Kiczales, L. H. Rodriguez Jr., and E. Ruf. An Architecture for an Open Compiler. In *Proceedings of the IMSA'92 Workshop on Reflection and Meta-level Architectures,* 1992, see www.parc.xerox.com/spl/groups/eca/pubs/complete.html

[LL94]   C. V. Lopes and K. Lieberherr. *Abstracting Process-to-Function Relations in Concurrent Object-Oriented Applications.* In Proceedings of the European Conference on Object-Oriented Programming (ECOOP'94), Bologna, Italy, 1994, pp. 81–99

[LMB95]   J. R. Levine, T. Mason, and D. Brown. *lex & yacc.* O'Reilly & Associates, Sebastopol, CA, 1995 (first printed in 1990)

[LO97]   K. Lieberherr and D. Orleans. Preventive Program Maintenance in Demeter/Java. In *Proceedings of International Conference on Software Engineering (ICSE 1997),* Boston, MA, pp. 604–605, see [Dem]

[Lop95]   C. V. Lopes. Graph-based optimizations for parameter passing in remote invocations. In *Proceeding of the 4th International Workshop on Object Orientation in Operating Systems (I-WOOOS'95),* Lund, Sweden, IEEE Computer Society Press, August 1995, © IEEE 1995

[Lop97]   C. V. Lopes. D: A Language Framework for Distributed Programming. Ph.D. Thesis, Graduate School of College of Computer Science, Northeastern University, Boston, MA, 1997, see [Dem]

[LP97]   K. Lieberherr and B. Patt-Shamir. Traversals of Object Structures: Specification and Efficient Implementation. Technical Report NU-CCS-97-15, Northeastern University, Boston, MA, September 1997, see [Dem]

[LS86]   S. Letovsky and E. Soloway. Delocalized Plans and Program Comprehension. In *IEEE Software*, vol. 3, no. 3, 1986, pp. 41–49, © IEEE 1986

[LSY98]   R. Lehoucq, D. Sorensen, and C. Yang. *ARPACK Users' Guide: Solution of Large Scale Eigenvalue Problems with Implicitly Restarted Arnoldi Methods.* Society for Industrial and Applied Mathematics (SIAM), 1998, see www.caam.rice.edu/software/ARPACK/usergd.html

[Lub91]   M. Lubars. Domain Analysis and Domain Engineering in IDeA. In [PA91], pp. 163–178

[MB85]   S. L. Messick and K. L. Beck. Active Variables in Smalltalk-80. Technical Report CR-85-09, Computer Research Lab, Tektronix, Inc., 1985

[MB97]   M. Mehlich and I. D. Baxter. Mechanical Tool Support for High Integrity Software Development. In *Proceedings of Conference on High Integrity Systems '97 (October 15–14, Albuquerque, New Mexico)*, IEEE Press, 1997, © IEEE 1997, also [SD]

[MBL97]   A. C. Myers, J. A. Bank, and B. Liskov. Parameterized Types for Java. In *Proceedings of the 24th ACM Symposium on Principles of Programming Languages (Paris, France, January 1997)*, pp. 132–145, see www.pmg.lcs.mit.edu/papers/popl97/popl97.html

[MBSE97]   Software Engineering Institute. Model-Based Software Engineering. World Wide Web pages, www.sei.cmu.edu/mbse/, 1997

[MC96]   T. Moran and J. Carroll, (Eds.). *Design Rationale: Concepts, techniques, and use.* Lawrence Erlbaum Associates, Hillsdale, NJ, 1996

[McC88]   R. McCartney. Synthesizing Algorithms with Performance Constraints. Ph.D. Thesis, Technical Report CS-87-28, Department of Computer Science, Brown University, 1988

[MCK97]   M. Meusel, K. Czarnecki, and W. Köpf. A Model for Structuring User Documentation of Object-Oriented Frameworks Using Patterns and Hypertext. In *Proceedings of the European Conference on Object-Oriented Programming (ECOOP'97)*, M. Aksit and S. Matsuoka (Eds.), LNCS 1241, Springer-Verlag, Berlin and Heidelberg, Germany, 1997, pp. 496–510

[MD95]   J. Mordhorst and W. van Dijk. Composition Filters in Smalltalk. Master's Thesis, Department of Computer Science, University of Twente, The Netherlands, July 1995, see [CF]

[Mey88]   B. Meyer. *Object-oriented Software Construction*. Prentice-Hall, London, 1988

[Mey90]   B. Meyer. *Introduction to the Theory of Programming Languages*. Prentice-Hall, Englewood Cliffs, NJ, 1990

[Mez97a]   M. Mezini. Variation-Oriented Programming: Beyond Classes and Inheritance. Ph. D. Thesis, Fachbereich Elektrotechnik und Informatik, Universität-Gesamthochschule Siegen, Germany, 1997, see www.informatik.uni-siegen.de/~mira/thesis.html

[Mez97b]   M. Mezini. Dynamic Object Evolution without Name Collisions. In *Proceedings of 11th European Conference on Object-Oriented Programming (ECOOP '97)*, M. Aksit and S. Matsuoka, (Eds.), LNCS 1241, Springer-Verlag, Berlin and Heidelberg, Germany, 1997, pp. 190–219, www.informatik.uni-siegen.de/~mira/public.html

[Mil56]   G. A. Miller. The magic number seven, plus or minus two: Some limits of our capacity for processing information. In *Psychological Review*, no. 63, 1956, pp. 81–97

[Mil84]   R. Milner. A Proposal for Standard ML. In *Proceedings of the Symposium on Lisp and Functional Programming*, ACM, 1984, pp. 184–197

[MKL97]   A. Mendhekar, G. Kiczales, and J. Lamping. RG: A Case-Study for Aspect-Oriented Programming. Xerox PARC Technical Report SPL97-009 P9710044, February 1997, see [AOP]

[ML98]   M. Mezini and K. Lieberherr. Adaptive Plug-and-Play Components for Evolutionary Software Development. In *Proceedings of the Conference on Object-Oriented Programming Languages and Applications (OOPSLA '98)*, 1998 and Technical Report NU-CCS-98-3, Northeastern University, Boston, MA, 1998, see [Dem]

[MLMK97]   C. Maeda, A. Lee, G. Murphy, and G. Kiczales. Open Implementation Analysis and Design. In *Proceedings of the 1997 Symposium on Software Reusability (SSR'97)*, M. Harandi, (Ed.), ACM Software Engineering Notes, vol 22, no. 3, May 1997, pp. 44–52

[MM]   Matrix Market at http://math.nist.gov/MatrixMarket/, an on-line repository of matrices and matrix generation tools, Mathematical and Computational Science Division within the Information Technology Laboratory of the National Institute of Standards and Technology (NIST), Gaithersburg, MD

[Mon99]   R. Monson-Haefel. *Enterprise Java Beans*. O'Reilly & Associates Inc., Sebastopol, CA, 1999

[Moo86] D. A. Moon. Object-Oriented Programming with Flavors. In *Proceedings of the 1st ACM Conference on Object-Oriented Programming Languages and Applications (OOPSLA '86), ACM SIGPLAN Notices*, vol. 21, no. 11, 1986, pp. 1–8

[Mor73] J. H. Morris. Types are not sets. In *Proceedings of the First ACM Symposium on the Principles of Programming Languages*, ACM Press, New York, NY, 1973

[MPW99] O. de Moor, S. Peyton-Jones, and E. Van Wyk. Aspect_Oriented Compilers. In [CE00]

[MS89a] D. R. Musser and A. A. Stepanov. Generic Programming. In *Proceedings of the First International Joint Conference of ISSAC'88 and AAECC-6*, LNCS 358, Springer-Verlag, Berlin and Heidelberg, Germany, 1989, pp. 13–25

[MS89b] D. R. Musser and A. A Stepanov. *The Ada Generic Library: Linear List Processing Packages.* Springer-Verlag, New York, NY, 1989

[MS93] D. R. Musser and A. A. Stepanov. Algorithm-Oriented Generic Libraries. In *Software Practice and Experience*, Vol. 24, No. 7, July 1994

[MS96] D. R. Musser and A. Saini. *STL Tutorial and Reference Guide.* Addison-Wesley, Reading, MA, 1996

[MS97] T. Margaria and B. Steffen. Coarse-grain Component-Based Software Development: The METAFrame Approach. In *Proceedings of Smalltalk and Java in Industry and Academia (STJA'97)*, Erfurt, Germany, 1997, pp. 29–34

[MTH90] R. Milner, M. Tofte, and R. Harper. *The Definition of Standard ML.* The MIT Press, Cambridge, MA, 1990

[Müh97] Mühlhäuser (Ed.). *Special Issues in Object-Oriented Programming: Workshop Reader of ECOOP'96*, dpunkt.verlag, 1997

[Mur99] M. Murawa. The Streamlined Wings of Progress: Transportation Trends in the 1930s. Online article available at www.cala.umn.edu/chicagofair/indtemp/michal.htm, 1999

[MWY90] S. Matsuoka, K. Wakita, and A. Yonezawa. Synchronization constraints with inheritance: What is not possible—so what is? Technical Report 10, Department of Information Science, The University of Tokyo, 1990

[MY93] S. Matsuoka and A. Yonezawa. Inheritance Anomaly in Object-Oriented Concurrent Programming Languages. In *Research Directions in Concurrent Object-Oriented Programming*, G. Agha, P. Wegner, and A. Yonezawa, (Eds.), The MIT Press, Cambridge, MA, April 1993, pp. 107–150

[Mye95]   N. C. Myers. Traits: a new and useful template technique. In *C++ Report*, June 1995, see www.cantrip.org/traits.html

[Nav96]   P. Návrat. A closer look at programming expertise: critical survey of some methodological issues. In *Information and Software Technology*, no. 38, 1996, Elsevier, pp. 37–46

[Nei80]   J. Neighbors. Software construction using components. Ph. D. Thesis, (Technical Repeport TR-160), Department Information and Computer Science, University of California, Irvine, 1980, also [BT]

[Nei84]   J. Neighbors. The Draco Approach to Construction Software from Reusable Components. In *IEEE Transactions on Software Engineering*, vol. SE-10, no. 5, September 1984, pp. 564–573, © IEEE 1984

[Nei89]   J. Neighbors. Draco: A Method for Engineering Reusable Software Systems. In [BP89], pp. 295–319

[Neu98]   T. Neubert. Anwendung von generativen Programmiertechniken am Beispiel der Matrixalgebra. Diplomarbeit, Technical University of Chemnitz, Germany, 1998

[New90]   A. Newell. *Unified Theories of Cognition.* Harvard University Press, Cambridge, MA, 1990

[NHCL96]   F. Noël, L. Hornof, C. Consel, and J. L. Lawall. Automatic, Template-Based Run-Time Specialization: Implementation and Experimental Study. Technical Report, IRISA, Campus de Beaulieu, Rennes Cedex, France, 1996

[NT95]   O. Nierstrasz and D. Tsichritzis. *Object-Oriented Software Composition.* Prentice Hall, Englewood Cliffs, NJ, 1995

[Obd92]   W. F. Obdyke. Refactoring Object-Oriented Frameworks. Ph. D. Thesis, University of Illinois at Urbana-Champaign, 1992, see ftp://st.cs.uiuc.edu/pub/papers/refactoring/opdyke-thesis.ps.Z

[OKH+95]   H. Ossher, M. Kaplan, W. Harrison, A. Katz and V. Kruskal. Subject-Oriented Composition Rules. In *Proceedings of the 10th Conference on Object-Oriented Programming, Systems, Languages, and Applications (OOPSLA '95), ACM SIGPLAN Notices,* vol. 30, no. 10, 1995, pp. 235–250

[OKK+96]   H. Ossher, M. Kaplan, A. Katz, W. Harrison, and V. Kruskal. Specifying Subject-Oriented Composition. In *Theory and Practice of Object Systems*, vol. 2, no. 3, 1996

[OONP]   The Object-Oriented Numerics Page at http://oonumerics.org/

[OP92]   S. W. O'Malley and L. L. Peterson. A dynamic network architecture. In *ACM Transactions on Computer Systems*, vol. 10, no. 2, May 1992, pp. 110–143, also www.cs.arizona.edu/xkernel/bibliography.html

[OPB92]   E. Ostertag, R. Prieto-Díaz, and C. Braun. Computing Similarity in a Reuse Library System: An AI-Based Approach. In *ACM Transactions on Software Engineering and Methodology*, vol. 1, no. 3, July 1992, pp. 205–228

[OS]   ObjectSpace, Inc. Generic Collection Library for Java, see www.objectspace.com/jgl

[OSVA99]   Objektorientierte Softwarewiederverwendung in verteilten Architekturen. Final report of the OSVA project. Sponsored by the German Federal Ministry of Education, Science, Research and Technology (BMBF), grant no. 01IS605A4, Mai 1999

[OT98]   H. Ossher and P. Tarr. Operation-Level Composition: A Case in (Join) Point. In [AOP98], pp. 28–31

[OW97]   M. Odersky and P. Wadler. Pizza into Java: Translating theory into practice. In *Proceedings of the 24th ACM Symposium on Principles of Programming Languages (Paris, France, January 1997)*, pp. 146–159, see http://cm.bell-labs.com/cm/cs/who/wadler/topics/gj.html

[PA91]   R. Prieto-Diaz and G. Arango (Eds.). *Domain Analysis and Software Systems Modeling*. IEEE Computer Society Press, Los Alamitos, CA, 1991, © IEEE 1991

[PAB+95]   C. Pu, T. Autrey, A. Black, C. Consel, C. Cowan, J. Inouye, L. Kethana, J. Walpole, and K. Zhang. Optimistic incremental specialization: Streamlining a commercial operating system. In *Proceedings of the 1995 ACM Symposium on Operating Systems Principles. ACM Operating Systems Reviews*, vol. 29, no. 5, ACM Press, New York, NY, 1995

[Pai94]   R. Paige. Viewing a program transformation system at work. In *Proceedings of PLILP'94*, LNCS 844, M. Hermenegildo, and J. Penjam (Eds.), Springer-Verlag, Berlin and Heidelberg, Germany, Sep. 1994, pp. 5–24, also http://cs.nyu.edu/cs/faculty/paige/research.html

[Pak96]   I. Pak. Social History Page. Online article available at www.math.harvard.edu/~pak/sh.html, 1996

[Par76]   D. Parnas. On the design and development of program families. In *IEEE Transactions on Software Engineering*, vol. SE-2, no. 1, 1976, pp. 1–9, © IEEE 1976

[Par90]   H. A. Partsch. *Specification and Transformation of Programs: A Formal Approach to Software Development*. Texts and Monographs in Computer Science, Springer-Verlag, Berlin and Heidelberg, Germany, 1990

[PC86]   D. L. Parnas and P. C. Clemens. A Rational Design Process: How and Why to Fake It. In *IEEE Transactions to Software Engineering*, vol. SE-12, no. 2, February 1986, pp. 251–257, © IEEE 1986

[PC91]   S. Peterson and S. Cohen. A Context Analysis of the Movement Control Domain for the Army Tactical Command and Control System. Technical Report, CMU/SEI-91-SR-3, Software Engineering Institute, Carnegie Mellon University, Pittsburgh, PA, 1991

[Pes98]   C. Pescio. Multiple Dispatch: A New Approach Using Templates and RTTI. In *C++ Report,* vol. 10, no. 6, June 1998

[PF87]   R. Prieto-Díaz and P. Freeman. Classifying Software for Reusability. In *IEEE Software*, January 1987, pp. 6–16, © IEEE 1987

[PK82]   R. Paige and S. Koenig. Finite differencing of computable expressions. In *ACM Transactions on Programming Languages and Systems*, vol. 4, no. 3, 1982, pp. 401–454

[POOMA]   POOMA: Parallel Object-Oriented Methods and Applications. A framework for scientific computing applications on parallel computers. Available at www.acl.lanl.gov/pooma

[Poz96]   R. Pozo. Template Numerical Toolkit for Linear Algebra: high performance programming with C++ and the Standard Template Library. Presented at the Workshop on Environments and Tools For Parallel Scientific Computing III, held on August 21–23, 1996 at Domaine de Faverges-de-la-Tour near Lyon, France, 1996, see http://math.nist.gov/tnt/

[Pra95]   R. Pratap. *Getting Started with Matlab.* Sounders College Publishing, Fort Worth, TX, 1995

[Pre95]   W. Pree. *Design Patterns for Object-Oriented Software Development.* Addison-Wesley, Reading, MA, 1995

[Pri85]   R. Prieto-Díaz. A Software Classification Scheme. Ph. D. Thesis, Department of Information and Computer Science, University of California, Irvine, 1985

[Pri87]   R. Prieto-Díaz. Domain Analysis For Reusability. In *Proceedings of COMPSAC'87,* 1987, pp. 23–29 and reprinted in [PA91], pp. 63–69

[Pri91a] R. Prieto-Díaz. Implementing Faceted Classification for Software Reuse. In *Communications of the ACM*, vol. 34, no. 5, May 1991, pp. 88–97

[Pri91b] R. Prieto-Díaz. Reuse Library Process Model. Technical Report, IBM STARS 03041-002, Electronic Systems Division,

Air Force Systems Command, USAF, Hanscom Air Force Base, Hanscom, MA, July, 1991

[Rat98a] Rational Software Corporation. Rational Objectory Process 4.1—Your UML Process. White paper, 1998, see www.rational.com

[Rat98b] Rational Software Corporation. Rational Objectory Process 4.1. Commercially available process description, see www.rational.com

[Rat98c] Rational Software Corporation. Unified Modeling Language (UML), version 1.1. Documentation set available from www.rational.com/uml/

[Rat98d] Rational Software Corporation. Object Constraint Language Specification. Documentation available from www.rational.com/uml/

[RBJ98] D. Roberts, J. Brand, and R. Johnson. A Refactoring Tool for Smalltalk. Submitted to *Theory and Practice of Object Systems*, 1998, see http://st-www.cs.uiuc.edu/users/droberts/homePage.html and http://st-www.cs.uiuc.edu/~brant/Refactory/RefactoringBrowser.html

[RBP+91] J. Rumbaugh, M. Blaha, W. Premerlani, F. Eddy, W. Lorensen. *Object-Oriented Modeling and Design*. Prentice Hall, Englewood Cliffs, NJ, 1991

[Ree96] T. Reenskaug with P. Wold and O. A. Lehne. *Working with Objects: The OOram Software Engineering Method*. Manning Publications Co., Greenwich, CT, 1996

[RF92] C. Rich and Y. A. Feldman. Seven Layers of Knowledge Representation and Reasoning in Support of Software Development. In *IEEE Transactions on Software Engineering*, vol. 18, no. 6. June 1992, pp. 451–469, © IEEE 1992

[Rie97] D. Riehle. Composite Design Patterns. In *Proceedings of the 12th Annual Conference on Object-Oriented Programming, Systems, Languages, and Applications (OOPSLA'97), ACM SIGPLAN Notices*, vol. 32, no. 10, October 1997, pp. 218–228

[RK97] C. Randall and E. Kant. Numerical Options Models Without Programming. In *Proceedings of the IEEE/IAFE Conference on Computational Intelligence for Financial Engineering*, New York, NY, March 23–25, 1997, pp. 15–21, also [SC]

[RM75] E. Rosch and C. B. Mervis. Family resemblances: Studies in the internal structure of categories. In *Cognitive Psychology*, no. 7, 1975, 573–605

[RMG+76]　E. Rosch, C. B. Mervis, W. Gray, D. Johnson, and P. Boyes-Braem. Basic objects in natural categories. In *Cognitive Psychology*, no. 3, 1976, pp. 382–439

[RMI97]　Java Remote Method Invocation. Specification, Sun Microsystems, December 1997, see http://java.sun.com/products/jdk/rmi/index.html

[Röd99]　L. Röder. Transformation and Visualization of Abstractions Using the Intentional Programming System. Invited talk at the GCSE'99 Young Researchers Workshop held at the First International Symposium on Generative and Component-Based Software Engineering (GCSE'99), Erfurt, Germany, 1999, see www.uni-weimar.de/~roeder/paper/gcse99.doc

[Ros73]　E. Rosch. On the internal structure of perceptual and semantic categories. In *Cognitive development and the acquisition of language*, T.E. Moore (Ed.), Academic Press, NY, 1973, pp. 111–144

[Ros75]　E. Rosch. Cognitive representations of semantic categories. In *Journal of Experimental Psychology: General,* 104, 1975, pp. 192–233

[Ros77]　E. Rosch. Human categorization. In *Studies in cross-cultural psychology*, Vol. 1, N. Warren (Ed.), Academic Press, NY, 1977, pp. 1–49

[Ros95]　L. Rosenstein. MacApp: First Commercially Successful Framework. In *Object-Oriented Application Frameworks*, T. Lewis et al., Manning Publications Co., Greenwich, CT, 1995, pp. 111–136

[RT89]　T. Reps and T. Teitelbaum. *The Synthesizer Generator: A System for Constructing Language-Based Editors.* Springer-Verlag, New York, NY, 1989, also see www.grammatech.com

[Rus97]　G. Lo Russo. An interview with Stepanov. In *Computer Programming*, no. 60, Gruppo Editoriale Infomedia, July/August 1997, pp. 51–57, see www.stlport.org/resources/StepanovUSA.html

[RW90]　C. Rich and R. C. Waters. *The Programmer's Apprentice.* ACM Press and Addison-Wesley, Reading, MA, 1990

[RW96]　G. X. Ritter and Joseph N. Wilson. *Handbook of Computer Vision Algorithms in Image Algebra.* CRC Press, Boca Raton, FL, 1996

[Sac67]　J. S. Sachs. Recognition memory for syntactic and semantic aspects of connected discourse. In *Perception and Psychophysics*, no. 2, 1967, pp. 437–442

[SB93]   V. Singhal and D. Batory. P++: A Language for Large-Scale Reusable Software Components. *In Proceedings of the 6th Annual Workshop on Software Reuse*, Owego, NY, November 1993, also [SSGRG]

[SB97]   Y. Smaragdakis and D. Batory. DiSTiL: A Transformation Library for Data Structures. In *Proceedings of USENIX Conference on Domain-Specific Languages*, October 1997, also [SSGRG]

[SB98]   Y. Smaragdakis and D. Batory. Implementing Layered Designs with Mixin Layers. In *Proceeding of the 12th European Conference on Object-Oriented Programming (ECOOP'98)*, E. Jul, (Ed.), 1998, pp. 550–570

[SB98a]   Y. Smaragdakis and D. Batory. Implementing Layered Designs with Mixin Layers. In *Proceedings of the 12th European Conference Object-Oriented Programming (ECOOP'98)*, E. Jul, (Ed.), LNCS 1445, Springer-Verlag, Berlin and Heidelberg, Germany, 1998, pp. 550–570, see [SSGR]

[SB98b]   Y. Smaragdakis and D. Batory. Implementing Reusable Object-Oriented Components. In [DP98], pp. 36–45, also [SSGRG]

[SBD+76]   B. Smith, J. Boyle, J. Dongarra, B. Garbow, Y. Ikebe, V. Klema, and C. Moler. *Matrix Eigensystem Routines—EISPACK Guide*. Second edition, vol. 6 of Lecture Notes in Computer Science, Springer-Verlag, Berlin, Germany, 1976

[SBS93]   M. Sirkin, D. Batory, and V. Singhal. Software Components in a Data Structure Precompiler. In *Proceedings of the 15th International Conference on Software Engineering*, Baltimore, MD, May 1993, pp. 437–446, also [SSGRG]

[SC]   Homepage of SciComp, Inc., Austin, TX, www.scicomp.com/

[SC93]   M. Simos and R. E. Creps. Organization Domain Modeling (ODM), Vol. I—Conceptual Foundations, Process and Workproduct Descriptions. Version 0.5, Unisys STARS Technical Report No. STARS-UC-05156/024/00, STARS Technology Center, Arlington, VA, 1993

[Sch94]   D. C. Schmidt. The ADAPTIVE Communication Environment: Object-Oriented Network Programming Components for Developing Client/Server Applications. In *Proceedings of the 12th Annual Sun Users Group Conference (SUG)*, San Francisco, CA, June 1994, pp. 214–225; the ACE toolkit is available at www.cs.wustl.edu/~schmidt/ACE-obtain.html

[Sch95]   D. C. Schmidt. An OO Encapsulation of Lightweight OS Concurrency Mechanisms in the ACE Toolkit. Technical Report

WUCS-95-31, Washington University, 1995, see www.cs. wustl.edu/~schmidt/ACE-concurrency.ps.gz

[SGI]   Silicon Graphics, Inc. STL Documentation available at www.sgi.com/Technology/STL

[SCK+96] M. Simos, D. Creps, C. Klinger, L. Levine, and D. Allemang. Organization Domain Modeling (ODM) Guidebook, Version 2.0. Informal Technical Report for STARS, STARS-VC-A025/001/00, June 14, 1996, available from http://domain-modeling.com

[SD]   Homepage of Semantic Designs, Inc., Austin, TX, www. semdesigns.com/

[Ses97] R. Sessions. *Com and Dcom: Microsoft's Vision for Distributed Objects.* John Wiley & Sons, Inc., New York, NY, 1997

[SG96] D. R. Smith and C. Green Toward Practical Applications of Software Synthesis. In *Proceedings of FMSP'96, The First Workshop on Formal Methods in Software Practice,* San Diego, CA, January 1996, pp. 31–39, also [KI]

[SG96] M. Shaw and D. Garlan. *Software Architecture: Perspectives on a Emerging Discipline.* Prentice Hall, Englewood Cliffs, NJ, 1996

[SG97] J. Stichnoth and T. Gross. Code composition as an implementation language for compilers. In *Proceedings USENIX Conference on Domain-Specific Languages (DSL'97),* 1997

[Sha77] D. Shapere. Scientific Theories and Their Domains. In *The Structure of Scientific Theories*, F. Suppe (Ed.), University of Illinois Press, Champaign, IL,1977, pp. 519–565

[Sha98] G. Shaw. Intentional Programming. An internal online tutorial, Microsoft Corporation, Redmond, WA, 1998

[SHS94] I. Silva-Lepe, W. Hürsch, and G. Sullivan. A Report on Demeter C++. In *C++ Report,* vol. 6, no. 2, November 1994, pp. 24–30, see [Dem]

[Shu91] S. Shum, Cognitive Dimensions of Design Rationale. In *People and Computers VI: Proceedings of HCI'91,* D. Diaper and N. Hammond, (Eds.), Cambridge University Press, Cambridge, MA, 1991, pp. 331–344, http://kmi.open.ac.uk/~simonb/DR.html

[Sim91] M. Simos. The Growing of an Organon: A Hybrid Knowledge-Based Technology for Software Reuse. In [PA91], pp. 204–221

[Sim95] C. Simonyi. The Death of Computer Languages, The Birth of Intentional Program-ming. Technical Report MSR-TR-95-52, Microsoft Research, 1995, ftp://ftp.research.microsoft.com/pub/tech-reports/Summer95/TR-95-52.doc

[Sim96]   C. Simonyi. Intentional Programming—Innovation in the Legacy Age. Position paper presented at IFIP WG 2.1 meeting, June 4, 1996, also [IPH]

[Sim97]   C. Simonyi. Intentional Programming. Talk given at the Usenix Conference on Domain Specific Languages, Santa Barbara, CA, October 16, 1997, transparencies available from [IPH]

[Sim97]   M. Simos. Organization Domain Modeling and OO Analysis and Design: Distinctions, Integration, New Directions. In *Proceedings 3rd STJA Conference (Smalltalk and Java in Industry and Education, Erfurt, September 1997),* Technical University of Ilmenau, 1997, pp. 126–132, see www.prakinf.tu-ilmenau.de/~czarn/generate/stja97/

[Sim98]   C. Simonyi, private communication, January 1998

[Sin96]   V. P. Singhal. A Programming Language for Writing Domain-Specific Software System Generators. Ph. D. Thesis, Department of Computer Sciences, University of Texas at Austin, September 1996, also [SSGRG]

[Sit96]   M. Sitaraman (Ed.). *Proceedings of the Fourth International Conference on Software Reuse, April 23–26, Orlando, Florida.* IEEE Computer Society Press, Los Alamitos, CA, 1996, © IEEE 1996

[SJ95]   Y. Srinivas and R. Jüllig. Specware™: Formal Support for Composing Software. In *Proceedings of the Conference on Mathematics of Program Construction*, B. Moeller, (Ed.), Lecture Notes in Computer Science, vol. 947, Springer-Verlag, Berlin, Germany, 1995, also see [KI]

[SKW85]   D. R. Smith, G. B. Kotik, and S. J. Westfold. Research on Knowledge-Based Software Environments at Kestrel Institute. In *IEEE Transactions on Software Engineering*, vol. SE-11, no. 11, November 1985, pp. 1278–1295, © IEEE 1985, also see [KI]

[SL95]   A. A. Stepanov and Meng Lee. The Standard Template Library. Hewlett-Packard, Palo Alto, CA, 1995

[SL98a]   J. G. Siek and A. Lumsdaine. The Matrix Template Library: A Unifying Framework for Numerical Linear Algebra. In *Proceedings of the ECOOP'98 Workshop on Parallel Object-Oriented Computing (POOSC'98),* 1998, see www.lsc.nd.edu/

[SL98b]   J. G. Siek and A. Lumsdaine. A Rational Approach to Portable High Performance: The Basic Linear Algebra Instruction Set (BLAIS) and the Fixed Algorithm Size Template (FAST) Library. In *Proceedings of the ECOOP'98 Workshop on Parallel Object-Oriented Computing (POOSC'98),* 1998, see www.lsc.nd.edu/

[SM81]   E. E. Smith and D. L. Medin. *Categories and concepts*. Harvard University Press, Cambridge, MA, 1981

[SM91]   C. Simonyi and M. Heller. The Hungarian Revolution. In *Byte*, August, 1991, pp. 131–138, see also www.freenet.tlh.fl.us/ ~joeo/hungarian.html

[SM96]   Y. V. Srinivas and J. L. McDonald. The Architecture of Specware, a Formal Software Development System. Technical Report KES.U.96.7, Kestrel Institute, August 1996, also [KI]

[SMCB96] B. Steffen, T. Margaria, A. Claßen, and V. Braun. The METAFrame'95 Environment. In *Proceedings CAV'96 (July-August 1996, Brunswick, New Jersey, USA)*, LNCS 1102, Springer-Verlag, Berlin and Heidelberg, Germany, 1996, pp. 450–453

[Smi90a]   D. R. Smith. KIDS: A Semi-Automatic Program Development System. *In IEEE Transactions on Software Engineering*, Vol. 16, No. 9, September 1990, pp. 1024–1043, © IEEE 1990, also [KI]

[Smi90b]   B. Smith's definition of "reflection" published in the Report on the OOPSLA'90 Workshop on Reflection and Metalevel Architectures in Object-Oriented Programming, *Addendum to the OOPSLA'90 Proceedings*, 1990

[Smi96]   D.R. Smith. Toward a Classification Approach to Design. In *Proceedings of Algebraic Methodology & Software Technology, AMAST'96, Munich, Germany, July 1996*, M. Wirsing and M. Nivat (Eds.), LNCS 1101, Springer-Verlag, Berlin and Heidelberg, Germany, 1996, pp. 62–84, also [KI]

[Son97]   X. Song. Systematic Integration of Design Methods. In *IEEE Software*, March/April 1997, pp. 107–117, © IEEE 1997

[SOP]   Homepage of the Subject-Oriented Programming Project, IBM Thomas J. Watson Research Center, Yorktown Heights, NY, www.research.ibm.com/sop/; also see www.research.ibm.com/ hyperspace

[SOPD]   Subject-oriented programming and design patterns. Draft, IBM Thomas J. Watson Research Center, Yorktown Heights, NY, see www.research.ibm.com/sop/sopcpats.htm

[Sou95]   J. Soukup. Implementing Patterns. In *Pattern Languages of Programm Design*, J. O. Coplien and D. C. Schmidt, (Eds.), Addison-Wesley, Reading, MA, 1995, pp. 395–412

[SPC92]   Software Productivity Consortium. Reuse Adoption Guidebook. Technical Report, SPC-92051-CMC, Software Productivity Consortium, Herndon, VA, 1992, www.asset.com

[SPC93]   Software Productivity Consortium. Reuse-Driven Software Processes Guidebook. Version 02.00.03, Technical Report, SPC-92019-CMC, Software Productivity Consortium, Herndon, VA, November 1993, www.asset.com

[SPL 96]   L. M. Seiter, J. Palsberg, K. Lieberherr. Evolution of Object Behavior Using Context Relations. In *Proceedings of the 4th ACM SIGSOFT Symposium on Foundations of Software Engineering*, Garlan D., (Ed.), Software Engineering Notes, vol. 21, no. 6, ACM Press, New York, NY, 1996, pp. 46–56, see [Dem]

[SPW95]   D. Smith, E. Parra, and S. Westfold. Synthesis of High-Performance Transportation Schedulers. Technical Report, KES.U.1, Kestrel Institute, February 1995, also [KI]

[Sri91]   Y. Srinivas. Algebraic specification for domains. In [PA91], pp. 90–124

[SSGRG]   Homepage of the Software Systems Generator Research Group at the University of Texas at Austin www.cs.utexas.edu/users/schwartz

[ST88a]   D. Sannella and A. Tarlecki. Specifications in an arbitrary institution. In *Information and Computation*, no. 76, 1988, pp. 165–210

[ST88b]   D. Sannella and A. Tarlecki. Toward formal development of programs from algebraic specifications: Implementations revisited. In *Acta Informatica*, vol. 25, no. 3, 1988, pp. 233–281

[STARS94]   Software Technology For Adaptable, Reliable Systems (STARS). Army STARS Demonstration Project Experience Report. STARS Informal Technical Report, STARS-VC-A011R/002/01, November 30, 1994

[Ste87]   L. A. Stein. Delegation Is Inheritance. In *Proceedings of the Conference on Object-Oriented Programming, Systems, Languages, and Applications (OOPSLA '87), ACM SIGPLAN Notices*, vol. 22, no. 12, 1987, pp. 138–146

[Ste98]   G. L. Steele. Growing a Language. Keynote address at the OOPSLA98. Transcript available at http://cm.bell-labs.com/cm/cs/who/wadler

[Str67]   C. Strachey. Fundamental concepts in programming languages. Lecture notes for the International Summer School in Computer Programming, Copenhagen, August 1967

[Str94]   B. Stroustrup. *The Design and Evolution of* C++. Addison-Wesley, Reading, MA, 1994

[Str97]   B. Stroustrup. *The C++ Programming Language, Third Edition*. Addison-Wesley, Reading, MA, 1997

[Sun]   Sun Microsystems, Inc. JDK 1.2:-The Java Collections Frame-
            work, see http://java.sun.com/products/jdk/1.2/docs/guide/
            collections/index.html

[Sun83]   S. Sundfor. Draco domain analysis for real time application:
            The analysis. Technical Report, RTP 015, Department of Infor-
            mation and Computer Science, University of California,
            Irvine, 1983

[Sun97a]   Sun Microsystems, Inc. JavaBeans 1.01. Specification docu-
            ment, Mountain View, CA, 1997, see http://java.sun.com/
            beans/docs/spec.html

[Sun97b]   Sun Microsystems, Inc. The Java Core Reflection Specification.
            Available at http://java.sun.com/products/jdk/1.1/docs/guide/
            reflection/index.html

[SWC+95]   N. A. Stillings, S. E. Weisler, C. H. Chase, M. H. Feinstein, J. L.
            Garfield and E. L. Rissland. *Cognitive Science: An Introduc-
            tion.* Second Edition, The MIT Press, Cambridge, MA, 1995

[TC92]   W. Tracz and L. Coglianese. DSSA Engineering Process Guide-
            lines. Technical Report, ADAGE-IBM-9202, IBM Federal Sys-
            tems Company, December 1992

[TH93]   D. Tansley and C. Hayball. *Knowledge-Based Systems Analy-
            sis and Design: A KADS Developer's Handbook.* Prentice Hall,
            Englewood Cliffs, NJ, 1993

[THE+94]   A. Terry, F. Hayes-Roth, L. Erman, N. Coleman, M. Devito, G.
            Papanagopoulos, and B. Hayes-Roth. Overview of Teknowl-
            edge's Domain-Specific Software Architecture Program. In
            ACM SIGSOFT Software Engineering Notes, vol. 19, no. 4,
            October 1994, pp. 68–76, see www.teknowledge.com/DSSA/

[Tho97]   K. K. Thorup. Genericity in Java with Virtual Types. In *Pro-
            ceedings of 11th European Conference on Object-Oriented
            Programming (ECOOP '97),* M. Aksit and S. Matsuoka,
            (Eds.), LNCS 1241, Springer-Verlag, Berlin and Heidelberg,
            Germany, 1997, pp. 444–471

[Tra93]   W. Tracz. Parameterized programming in LILEANA. In *Pro-
            ceedings of ACM Symposium on Applied Computing, SAC'93,*
            February 1993, pp. 77–86

[Tra95]   W. Tracz. Domain-Specific Software Architecture Pedagogical
            Example. In *ACM SIGSOFT Software Engineering Notes*, vol.
            20, no. 4, July 1995, pp. 49–62, also available from [ADAGE]]

[TTC95]   R. Taylor, W. Tracz, and L. Coglianese. Software Development
            Using Domain-Specific Software Architectures: CDRL A011—
            A Curriculum Module in the SEI Style. In *ACM SIGSOFT*

Software Engineering Notes, vol. 20, no. 5, December 1995, pp. 27–37, also available from [ADAGE]

[Tur85]   D. A. Turner. Miranda: A non-strict functional language with polymorphic types. In *Proceedings of Functional Programming Languages and Computer Architecture (Nancy, France, September 1985)*, LNCS Vol. 201, Springer-Verlag, Berlin and Heidelberg, Germany, 1985, pp. 1–16

[Uni88]   Unisys. Reusability Library Framework AdaKNET and AdaTAU Design Report. Technical Report, PAO D4705-CV-880601-1, Unisys Defense Systems, System Development Group, Paoli, PA, 1988

[Unr94]   E. Unruh. Prime number computation. ANSI X3J16-94-0075/SO WG21-462

[VAM+98]   A. D. Vici, N. Argentieri, A. Mansour, M. d'Alessandro, and J. Favaro. FODAcom: An Experience with Domain Analysis in the Italian Telecom Industry. In [DP98], pp. 166–175, see www.intecs.it

[Van98]   D. Vandevoorde, Hewlett-Packard, California Language Lab, Cupertino, CA. Personal communication, 1998

[Vel95a]   T. Veldhuizen. Using C++ template metaprograms. In *C++ Report*, vol. 7, no. 4, May 1995, pp. 36–43, see http://oonumerics.org/blitz/papers/

[Vel95b]   T. Veldhuizen. Expression Templates. In *C++ Report*, vol. 7 no. 5, June 1995, pp. 26–31, see http://oonumerics.org/blitz/papers/

[Vel96]   T. Veldhuizen. Rapid Linear Algebra in C++. In *Dr. Dobb's Journal*, August 1996, see [Blitz]

[Vel97]   T. Veldhuizen. Scientific Computing: C++ versus Fortran. In *Dr. Dobb's Journal*, November 1997, pp. 34–41, see http://extreme.indiana.edu/~tveldhui/ and [Blitz]

[Vel98a]   T. Veldhuizen. Scientific computing using the Blitz++ class library. Talk presented at the Dagstuhl Seminar 9817 "Generic Programming", Schloß Dagstuhl, April 27–30, 1998, see [Blitz]

[Vel98b]   T. Veldhuizen. Arrays in Blitz++. *In Proceedings of the Second International Symposium on Computing in Object-oriented Parallel Environments (ISCOPE'98), Santa Fe, New Mexico, December 8–11,* D. Caromel, R. R. Oldehoeft, M. Tholburn, (Eds.), LNCS 1505, Springer-Verlag, Berlin and Heidelberg, Germany, 1998, pp. 223–230, see [Blitz]

[Vel98c]   T. Veldhuizen. Techniques for Scientific C++. Course notes available from http://oonumerics.org/blitz/papers/, April 1998

[Vel99]   T. Veldhuizen. C++ Templates as Partial Evaluation. In *Proceedings of 1999 ACM SIGPLAN Workshop on Partial Evaluation and Semantics-Based Program Manipulation (PEPM'99)*, 1999, see http://extreme.indiana.edu/~tveldhui/ and [Blitz]

[VG90]   W. Vitaletti and E. Guerrieri. Domain Analysis within the ISEC Rapid Center. In *Proceedings of Eighth Annual National Conference on Ada Technology*, March 1990

[VH97]   M. VanHilst. Role-Oriented Programming for Software Evolution. Ph. D. Thesis, University of Washington, Computer Science and Engineering, 1997

[VHN96]   M. VanHilst and D. Notkin. Using Role Components to Implement Collaboration-Based Designs. In *Proceedings of the 1996 ACM Conference on Object-Oriented Programming Systems, Languages and Applications* (OOPSLA'96), 1996, pp. 359–369

[VIGRA]   Homepage of the VIGRA (Vision with Generic Algorithms) library, see www.egd.igd.fhg.de/~ulli/vigra/

[VJ97]   T. Veldhuizen and M. Ed Jernigan. Will C++ be faster than Fortran? In *Proceedings of the Second International Symposium on Computing in Object-oriented Parallel Environments (ISCOPE'97)*, 1997, see [Blitz]

[Wal97]   R. van der Wal. Algorithmic Object. In C++ *Report*, vol. 9, no. 6, June 1997, pp. 23–27

[WBM98]   R. W. Walker, E.L.A. Baniassad, and G. Murphy. Assessing Aspect-Oriented Programming and Design. In *Proceedings of Workshop on Aspect-Oriented Programming at the International Conference of Software Engineering*, 1998, www.parc.xerox.com/aop/

[Weg97]   P. Wegner. Why Interaction Is More Powerful Than Algorithms. In *Communications of the ACM*, May 1997, see www.cs.brown.edu/people/pw/

[Weg98]   P. Wegner. Interactive Foundations of Computing. Final draft, February 1998, to appear in *Theoretical Computer Science,* see www.cs.brown.edu/people/pw/

[Wei96]   D. Weiss. Creating Domain-Specific Languages: The FAST Process. Transparencies presented at the First ACM-SIGPLAN Workshop on Domain-Specific Languages, Paris, France, January 18, 1997, http://www-sal.cs.uiuc.edu/~kamin/dsl/index.html

[WHB00]   K. E. Williamson, M. J. Healy, and R. A. Baker. Reuse of Knowledge at the Appropriate Level of Abstraction. In *Proceedings of the Sixth International Conference on Software Reuse (ICSR6)*, 2000

[Wil61]   J. Wilkinson. Error Analysis of Direct Methods of Matrix Inversion. In *Journal of the ACM*, vol. 8, 1961, pp. 281–330

[Wil83]   D. Wile. Program Developments: Formal Explanations of Implementations. In *Communications of the ACM*, vol. 26, no. 11, November 1983

[Wil91]   D. Wile. Popart Manual. Technical Report, Information Science Institute, University of Southern Calofornia, 1991, see www.isi.edu/software-sciences/wile/Popart/popart.html

[Wil92]   P. R. Wilson. Uniprocessor garbage collection techniques. In *Memory Management*, Y. Bekkers and J. Cohen, (Eds.), LNCS 637, Springer-Verlag, Berlin and Heidelberg, Germany, 1992, pp. 1–42

[Wil97]   A. Willey. Technology Transition: An Historical Perspective. Online article available at www.virtualschool.edu, June 6, 1997

[Win92]   P. H. Winston. *Artificial Intelligence*. Third edition, Addison-Wesley, Reading, MA, 1992

[Wir83]   M. Wirsing. Structured algebraic specifications: A kernel language. In *Theoretical Computer Science* 42, 1986, pp. 123–249. A slight revision of his Habilitationsschrift, Technical University of Munich, Germany, 1983

[Wit53]   L. Wittgenstein. *Philosophical investigations*. G. E. M. Anscombe. Blackwell, Oxford, 1953

[Wit94]   J. Withey. Implementing Model Based Software Engineering in your Organization: An Approach to Domain Engineering. Draft, Technical Report, CMU/SEI-94-TR-01, Software Engineering Institute, Carnegie Mellon University, Pittsburgh, PA, 1994

[Wit96]   J. Withey. Investment Analysis of Software Assets for Product Lines. Technical Report, CMU/SEI-96-TR-010, Software Engineering Institute, Carnegie Mellon University, Pittsburgh, PA, November 1996, www.sei.cmu.edu

[WL99]   D. M. Weiss and C. T. R. Lai. *Software Product-Line Engineering: A Family-Based Software Development Process*. Addison-Wesley, Reading, MA, 1999

[WM95]   R. Wilhelm and D. Maurer. *Compiler Design*. Addison-Wesley, Reading, MA, 1995

[Wol91]   S. Wolfram. *Mathematica, A System for Doing Mathematics by Computer*. Addison-Wesley, Reading, MA, 1991. Mathematica is sold by Wolfram Research, ftp://www.wri.com/

[WP92]   S. Wartik and R. Prieto-Díaz. Criteria for Comparing Domain Analysis Approaches. In *International Journal of Software*

Engineering and Knowledge Engineering, vol. 2, no. 3, September 1992, pp. 403–431

[WTH+99] L. Wall, D. A. Taylor, C. Horn, P. Bassett, J.K. Ousterhout, M. L. Griss, R. M. Soley, J. Waldo, and C. Simonyi. Software [R]evolution: A Roundtable. In *IEEE Computer*, May 1999, pp. 48–57, © IEEE 1999

[X3M] X^3M Solutions: Container and Algorithm Library for the Java Platform, see www.x3m.com/

[XER97] AspectJ: Primer. Xerox Palo Alto Research Center (Xerox PARC), Palo Alto, CA, October 1997

[XER98a] AspectJ: User's Guide and Primer. Xerox Palo Alto Research Center (Xerox PARC), Palo Alto, CA, March 1998, see [AJ]

[XER98b] AspectJ Specification. Xerox Palo Alto Research Center (Xerox PARC), Palo Alto, CA, March 1998, see [AJ]

[Zal96] N. Zalman. Making The Method Fit: An Industrial Experience in Adopting Feature-Oriented Domain Analysis (FODA). In *Proceedings of the Fourth International Conference on Software Reuse*, M. Sitaraman, (Ed.), IEEE Computer Society Press, Los Alamitos, CA, 1996, pp. 233–235, © IEEE 1996

Index

Addison-Wesley Professional

How to
Register
Your Book

Register this Book

Visit: **http://www.aw.com/cseng/register**

Enter the ISBN*

Then you will receive:

- Notices and reminders about upcoming author appearances, tradeshows, and online chats with special guests
- Advanced notice of forthcoming editions of your book
- Book recommendations
- Notification about special contests and promotions throughout the year

*The ISBN can be found on the copyright page of the book

Visit our Web site

http://www.aw.com/cseng

When you think you've read enough, there's always more content for you at Addison-Wesley's web site. Our web site contains a directory of complete product information including:

- Chapters
- Exclusive author interviews
- Links to authors' pages
- Tables of contents
- Source code

You can also discover what tradeshows and conferences Addison-Wesley will be attending, read what others are saying about our titles, and find out where and when you can meet our authors and have them sign your book.

We encourage you to patronize the many fine retailers who stock Addison-Wesley titles. Visit our online directory to find stores near you.

Contact Us via Email

cepubprof@awl.com

Ask general questions about our books.
Sign up for our electronic mailing lists.
Submit corrections for our web site.

cepubeditors@awl.com

Submit a book proposal.
Send errata for a book.

cepubpublicity@awl.com

Request a review copy for a member of the media interested in reviewing new titles.

registration@awl.com

Request information about book registration.

Addison-Wesley Professional
One Jacob Way, Reading, Massachusetts 01867 USA
TEL 781-944-3700 • FAX 781-942-3076